THE 48 LAWS OF POWER

ROBERT GREENE has a degree in classical studies
and has been an editor at *Esquire* and other magazines.
He is also a playwright and lives in Los Angeles.

JOOST ELFERS is the producer of *The 48 Laws of Power*
and also of

The Secret Language of Birthdays
with Gary Goldschneider

The Secret Language of Relationships
with Gary Goldschneider

Play with Your Food
with Saxton Freymann

THE 48 LAWS OF

POWER

ROBERT GREENE

A JOOST ELFFERS PRODUCTION

P

PROFILE BOOKS

This paperback edition published in 2000

Reprinted 2001, 2002, 2003, 2006, 2010, 2013, 2015

First published in Great Britain in 1998 by
PROFILE BOOKS LTD
3 Holford Yard,
Bevin Way,
London WC1X 9HD
www.profilebooks.com

First published in the United States in 1998 by
Viking, a division of Penguin Putnam Inc.

12

A portion of this work first appeared in *The Utne Reader*

Typeset in BE Baskerville
Printed in China

A CIP catalogue record for this book is available from the British Library.

ISBN 978 1 86197 278 1

A Treasury of Jewish Folklore by Nathan Ausubel. Copyright © 1948, 1976 by Crown Publishers, Inc. Reprinted by permission of Crown Publishers, Inc.

The Chinese Looking Glass by Dennis Bloodworth. Copyright © 1966, 1967 by Dennis Bloodworth. By permission of Ferrar, Straus and Giroux.

The Book of the Courtier by Baldesar Castiglione, translated by George Bull; Penguin Books (London). Copyright © George Bull, 1967.

The Golden Dream: Seekers of El Dorado by Walker Chapman; Bobbs-Merrill. Copyright © 1967 by Walker Chapman.

The Borgias by Ivan Cloulas, translated by Gilda Roberts; Franklin Watts, Inc. Copyright © 1987 by Librairie Artheme Fayard. Translation copyright © 1989 by Franklin Watts, Inc.

Various Fables from Various Places, edited by Diane Di Prima; Capricorn Books / G. P. Putnam's Sons. © 1960 G. P. Putnam's Sons.

Armenian Folk-tales and Fables, translated by Charles Downing; Oxford University Press. © Charles Downing 1972.

The Little Brown Book of Anecdotes, edited by Clifton Fadiman; Little, Brown and Company. Copyright © 1985 by Little, Brown and Company (Inc.)

The Power of the Charlatan by Grete de Francesco, translated by Miriam Beard. Copyright, 1939, by Yale University Press. By permission of Yale University Press.

The Oracle: A Manual of the Art of Discretion by Baltasar Gracián, translated by L. B. Walton; Orion Press.

Behind the Scenes of Royal Palaces in Korea (Yi Dynasty) by Ha Tae-hung. Copyright © 1983 by Ha Tae-hung. By permission of Yonsei University Press, Seoul.

The Histories by Herodotus, translated by Aubrey de Sélincourt, revised by A. R. Burn; Penguin Books (London). Copyright © the Estate of Aubrey de Sélincourt, 1954. Copyright © A. R. Burn, 1972.

Hollywood by Garson Kanin (Viking). Copyright © 1967, 1974 by T. F. T. Corporation.

Fables from Africa, collected by Jan Knappert; Evan Brothers Limited (London). Collection © 1980 Jan Knappert.

The Great Fables of All Nations, selected by Manuel Komroff; Tudor Publishing Company. Copyright, 1928, by Dial Press, Inc.

Selected Fables by Jean de La Fontaine, translated by James Michie; Penguin Books (London). Translation copyright © James Michie, 1979.

The Romance of the Rose by Guillaume de Lorris, translated by Charles Dahlberg; Princeton University Press.

The Complete Essays by Michel de Montaigne, translated by M. A. Screech; Penguin Books (London). Translation copyright © M. A. Screech, 1987, 1991.

A Book of Five Rings by Miyamoto Musashi, translated by Victor Harris; Overlook Press. Copyright © 1974 by Victor Harris.

The New Oxford Annotated Bible with the Apocrypha, revised standard version, edited by Herbert G. May and Bruce M. Metzger; Oxford University Press. Copyright © 1973 by Oxford University Press, Inc.

Makers of Rome: Nine Lives by Plutarch, translated by Ian Scott-Kilvert; Penguin Books (London). Copyright © Ian Scott-Kilvert, 1965.

The Rise and Fall of Athens: Nine Greek Lives by Plutarch, translated by Ian Scott-Kilvert; Penguin Books (London). Copyright © Ian Scott-Kilvert, 1960.

Cha-no-yu: The Japanese Tea Ceremony by A. L. Sadler; Charles E. Tuttle Company. © 1962 by Charles E. Tuttle Co.

Amoral Politics: The Persistent Truth of Machiavellism by Ben-Ami Scharfstein; State University of New York Press. © 1995 State University of New York.

Caravan of Dreams by Idries Shah; Octagon Press (London). Copyright © 1970, 1980 by Idries Shah.

Tales of the Dervishes by Idries Shah. Copyright © Idries Shah, 1967. Used by permission of Penguin Putnam Inc. and Octagon Press (London).

The Craft of Power by R. G. H. Siu; John Wiley & Sons. Copyright © 1979 by John Wiley & Sons, Inc.

The Subtle Ruse: The Book of Arabic Wisdom and Guile, translated by Rene R. Khawam; East-West Publications. Copyright © 1980 English translation East-West Publications (U.K.) Ltd.

The Art of War by Sun-tzu, translated by Thomas Cleary; Shambhala Publications. © 1988 by Thomas Cleary.

The Art of War by Sun-tzu, translated by Yuan Shibing. © 1987 by General Tao Hanshang. Used by permission of Sterling Publishing Co., Inc., 387 Park Avenue South, New York, NY 10016.

The History of the Peloponnesian War by Thucydides, translated by Rex Warner; Penguin Books (London). Translation copyright Rex Warner, 1954.

The Thurber Carnival by James Thurber; HarperCollins. Copyright 1945 by James Thurber.

The Court Artist: On the Ancestry of the Modern Artist by Martin Warnke, translated by David McLintock. Translation © Maison des Sciences de l'Homme and Cambridge University Press 1993. By permission of Cambridge University Press.

The Con Game and "Yellow Kid" Weil: The Autobiography of the Famous Con Artist as told to W. T. Brannon; Dover Publications. Copyright © 1948 by W. T. Brannon.

To Anna Biller, and to my parents
R. G.

ACKNOWLEDGMENTS

First I would like to thank Anna Biller, who helped edit and research this book, and whose invaluable insights played a critical role in the shape and content of *The 48 Laws*. Without her, none of this would have been possible.

I must also thank my dear friend Michiel Schwarz who was responsible for involving me in the art school Fabrika in Italy and introducing me there to Joost Elffers, my partner and producer of *The 48 Laws of Power*. It was in the scheming world of Fabrika that Joost and I saw the timelessness of Machiavelli and from our discussions in Venice, Italy, this book was born.

I would like to thank Henri Le Goubin, who supplied me with many Machiavellian anecdotes over the years, particularly concerning the numerous French characters who play such a large role in this book.

I would also like to thank Les and Sumiko Biller, who lent me their library on Japanese history and helped me with the Japanese Tea Ceremony part of the book. Similarly, I must thank my good friend Elizabeth Yang who advised me on Chinese history.

A book like this depended greatly on the research material available and I am particularly grateful to the UCLA Research Library; I spent many pleasant days wandering through its incomparable collections.

My parents, Laurette and Stanley Green, deserve endless thanks for their patience and support.

And I must not forget to pay tribute to my cat, Boris, who kept me company throughout the never-ending days of writing.

Finally, to those people in my life who have so skillfully used the game of power to manipulate, torture, and cause me pain over the years, I bear you no grudges and I thank you for supplying me with inspiration for *The 48 Laws of Power*.

Robert Greene

CONTENTS

PREFACE

The feeling of having no power over people and events is generally unbearable to us—when we feel helpless we feel miserable. No one wants less power; everyone wants more. In the world today, however, it is dangerous to seem too power hungry, to be overt with your power moves. We have to seem fair and decent. So we need to be subtle—congenial yet cunning, democratic yet devious.

This game of constant duplicity most resembles the power dynamic that existed in the scheming world of the old aristocratic court. Throughout history, a court has always formed itself around the person in power—king, queen, emperor, leader. The courtiers who filled this court were in an especially delicate position: They had to serve their masters, but if they seemed to fawn, if they curried favor too obviously, the other courtiers around them would notice and would act against them. Attempts to win the master's favor, then, had to be subtle. And even skilled courtiers capable of such subtlety still had to protect themselves from their fellow courtiers, who at all moments were scheming to push them aside.

Meanwhile the court was supposed to represent the height of civilization and refinement. Violent or overt power moves were frowned upon; courtiers would work silently and secretly against any among them who used force. This was the courtier's dilemma: While appearing the very paragon of elegance, they had to outwit and thwart their own opponents in the subtlest of ways. The successful courtier learned over time to make all of his moves indirect; if he stabbed an opponent in the back, it was with a velvet glove on his hand and the sweetest of smiles on his face. Instead of using coercion or outright treachery, the perfect courtier got his way through seduction, charm, deception, and subtle strategy, always planning several moves ahead. Life in the court was a never-ending game that required constant vigilance and tactical thinking. It was civilized war.

Today we face a peculiarly similar paradox to that of the courtier: Everything must appear civilized, decent, democratic, and fair. But if we play by those rules too strictly, if we take them too literally, we are crushed by those around us who are not so foolish. As the great Renaissance diplomat and courtier Niccolò Machiavelli wrote, "Any man who tries to be good all the time is bound to come to ruin among the great number who are not good." The court imagined itself the pinnacle of refinement, but underneath its glittering surface a cauldron of dark emotions—greed, envy, lust, hatred—boiled and simmered. Our world today similarly imagines itself the pinnacle of fairness, yet the same ugly emotions still stir within us, as they have forever. The game is the same. Outwardly, you must seem to respect the niceties, but inwardly, unless you are a fool, you learn quickly to be prudent, and to do as Napoleon advised: Place your iron hand inside a velvet glove. If, like the courtier of times gone by, you can master the arts of indirection, learning to seduce, charm, deceive, and subtly outmaneuver your opponents, you will attain the heights of power. You will be able to make people bend to your will without their realizing what you have done. And if they do not realize what you have done, they will neither resent nor resist you.

To some people the notion of consciously playing power games—no matter how indirect—seems evil, asocial, a relic of the past. They believe they can opt out of the game by behaving in ways that have nothing to do with power. You must beware of such people, for while they express such opinions outwardly, they are often among the most adept players at power. They utilize strategies that cleverly disguise the nature of the manipulation involved. These types, for example, will often display their weakness and lack of power as a kind of moral virtue. But true powerlessness, without any motive of self-interest, would not publicize its weakness to gain sympathy or respect. Making a show of one's weakness is actually a very effective strategy, subtle and deceptive, in the game of power (see Law 22, the Surrender Tactic).

Another strategy of the supposed nonplayer is to demand equality in every area of life. Everyone must be treated alike, whatever their status and strength. But if, to avoid the taint of power, you attempt to treat everyone equally and fairly, you will confront the problem that some people do certain things better than others. Treating everyone equally means ignoring their differences, elevating the less skillful and suppressing those who excel. Again, many of those who behave this way are actually deploying another power strategy, redistributing people's rewards in a way that they determine.

Yet another way of avoiding the game would be perfect honesty and straightforwardness, since one of the main techniques of those who seek power is deceit and secrecy. But being perfectly honest will inevitably hurt and insult a great many people, some of whom will choose to injure you in return. No one will see your honest statement as completely objective and free of some personal motivation. And they will be right: In truth, the use of honesty is indeed a power strategy, intended to convince people of one's noble, good-hearted, selfless character. It is a form of persuasion, even a subtle form of coercion.

Finally, those who claim to be nonplayers may affect an air of naïveté, to protect them from the accusation that they are after power. Beware again, however, for the appearance of naiveté can be an effective means of

Courts are, unquestionably, the seats of politeness and good breeding; were they not so, they would be the seats of slaughter and desolation. Those who now smile upon and embrace, would affront and stab, each other, if manners did not interpose. . . .

LORD CHESTERFIELD,
1694–1773

There is nothing very odd about lambs disliking birds of prey, but this is no reason for holding it against large birds of prey that they carry off lambs. And when the lambs whisper among themselves, "These birds of prey are evil, and does this not give us a right to say that whatever is the opposite of a bird of prey must be good?" there is nothing intrinsically wrong with such an argument—though the birds of prey will look somewhat quizzically and say, "We have nothing against these good lambs; in fact, we love them; nothing tastes better than a tender lamb."

FRIEDRICH NIETZSCHE,
1844–1900

deceit (see Law 21, Seem Dumber Than Your Mark). And even genuine naiveté is not free of the snares of power. Children may be naive in many ways, but they often act from an elemental need to gain control over those around them. Children suffer greatly from feeling powerless in the adult world, and they use any means available to get their way. Genuinely innocent people may still be playing for power, and are often horribly effective at the game, since they are not hindered by reflection. Once again, those who make a show or display of innocence are the least innocent of all.

You can recognize these supposed nonplayers by the way they flaunt their moral qualities, their piety, their exquisite sense of justice. But since all of us hunger for power, and almost all of our actions are aimed at gaining it, the nonplayers are merely throwing dust in our eyes, distracting us from their power plays with their air of moral superiority. If you observe them closely, you will see in fact that they are often the ones most skillful at indirect manipulation, even if some of them practice it unconsciously. And they greatly resent any publicizing of the tactics they use every day.

If the world is like a giant scheming court and we are trapped inside it, there is no use in trying to opt out of the game. That will only render you powerless, and powerlessness will make you miserable. Instead of struggling against the inevitable, instead of arguing and whining and feeling guilty, it is far better to excel at power. In fact, the better you are at dealing with power, the better friend, lover, husband, wife, and person you become. By following the route of the perfect courtier (see Law 24) you learn to make others feel better about themselves, becoming a source of pleasure to them. They will grow dependent on your abilities and desirous of your presence. By mastering the 48 laws in this book, you spare others the pain that comes from bungling with power—by playing with fire without knowing its properties. If the game of power is inescapable, better to be an artist than a denier or a bungler.

Learning the game of power requires a certain way of looking at the world, a shifting of perspective. It takes effort and years of practice, for much of the game may not come naturally. Certain basic skills are required, and once you master these skills you will be able to apply the laws of power more easily.

The most important of these skills, and power's crucial foundation, is the ability to master your emotions. An emotional response to a situation is the single greatest barrier to power, a mistake that will cost you a lot more than any temporary satisfaction you might gain by expressing your feelings. Emotions cloud reason, and if you cannot see the situation clearly, you cannot prepare for and respond to it with any degree of control.

Anger is the most destructive of emotional responses, for it clouds your vision the most. It also has a ripple effect that invariably makes situations less controllable and heightens your enemy's resolve. If you are trying to destroy an enemy who has hurt you, far better to keep him off-guard by feigning friendliness than showing your anger.

The only means to gain one's ends with people are force and cunning. Love also, they say; but that is to wait for sunshine, and life needs every moment.
JOHANN VON GOETHE, 1749–1832

The arrow shot by the archer may or may not kill a single person. But stratagems devised by a wise man can kill even babes in the womb.
KAUTILYA, INDIAN PHILOSOPHER, THIRD CENTURY B.C.

Love and affection are also potentially destructive, in that they blind you to the often self-serving interests of those whom you least suspect of playing a power game. You cannot repress anger or love, or avoid feeling them, and you should not try. But you should be careful about how you express them, and most important, they should never influence your plans and strategies in any way.

Related to mastering your emotions is the ability to distance yourself from the present moment and think objectively about the past and future. Like Janus, the double-faced Roman deity and guardian of all gates and doorways, you must be able to look in both directions at once, the better to handle danger from wherever it comes. Such is the face you must create for yourself—one face looking continuously to the future and the other to the past.

For the future, the motto is, "No days unalert." Nothing should catch you by surprise because you are constantly imagining problems before they arise. Instead of spending your time dreaming of your plan's happy ending, you must work on calculating every possible permutation and pitfall that might emerge in it. The further you see, the more steps ahead you plan, the more powerful you become.

The other face of Janus looks constantly to the past—though not to remember past hurts or bear grudges. That would only curb your power. Half of the game is learning how to forget those events in the past that eat away at you and cloud your reason. The real purpose of the backward-glancing eye is to educate yourself constantly—you look at the past to learn from those who came before you. (The many historical examples in this book will greatly help that process.) Then, having looked to the past, you look closer at hand, to your own actions and those of your friends. This is the most vital school you can learn from, because it comes from personal experience.

You begin by examining the mistakes you have made in the past, the ones that have most grievously held you back. You analyze them in terms of the 48 laws of power, and you extract from them a lesson and an oath: "I shall never repeat such a mistake; I shall never fall into such a trap again." If you can evaluate and observe yourself in this way, you can learn to break the patterns of the past—an immensely valuable skill.

Power requires the ability to play with appearances. To this end you must learn to wear many masks and keep a bag full of deceptive tricks. Deception and masquerade should not be seen as ugly or immoral. All human interaction requires deception on many levels, and in some ways what separates humans from animals is our ability to lie and deceive. In Greek myths, in India's Mahabharata cycle, in the Middle Eastern epic of Gilgamesh, it is the privilege of the gods to use deceptive arts; a great man, Odysseus for instance, was judged by his ability to rival the craftiness of the gods, stealing some of their divine power by matching them in wits and deception. Deception is a developed art of civilization and the most potent weapon in the game of power.

You cannot succeed at deception unless you take a somewhat distanced approach to yourself—unless you can be many different people, wearing the mask that the day and the moment require. With such a flexible approach to all appearances, including your own, you lose a lot of the inward heaviness that holds people down. Make your face as malleable as the actor's, work to conceal your intentions from others, practice luring people into traps. Playing with appearances and mastering arts of deception are among the aesthetic pleasures of life. They are also key components in the acquisition of power.

If deception is the most potent weapon in your arsenal, then patience in all things is your crucial shield. Patience will protect you from making moronic blunders. Like mastering your emotions, patience is a skill—it does not come naturally. But nothing about power is natural; power is more godlike than anything in the natural world. And patience is the supreme virtue of the gods, who have nothing but time. Everything good will happen—the grass will grow again, if you give it time and see several steps into the future. Impatience, on the other hand, only makes you look weak. It is a principal impediment to power.

Power is essentially amoral and one of the most important skills to acquire is the ability to see circumstances rather than good or evil. Power is a game—this cannot be repeated too often—and in games you do not judge your opponents by their intentions but by the effect of their actions. You measure their strategy and their power by what you can see and feel. How often are someone's intentions made the issue only to cloud and deceive! What does it matter if another player, your friend or rival, intended good things and had only your interests at heart, if the effects of his action lead to so much ruin and confusion? It is only natural for people to cover up their actions with all kinds of justifications, always assuming that they have acted out of goodness. You must learn to inwardly laugh each time you hear this and never get caught up in gauging someone's intentions and actions through a set of moral judgments that are really an excuse for the accumulation of power.

It is a game. Your opponent sits opposite you. Both of you behave as gentlemen or ladies, observing the rules of the game and taking nothing personally. You play with a strategy and you observe your opponent's moves with as much calmness as you can muster. In the end, you will appreciate the politeness of those you are playing with more than their good and sweet intentions. Train your eye to follow the results of their moves, the outward circumstances, and do not be distracted by anything else.

Half of your mastery of power comes from what you do *not* do, what you do *not* allow yourself to get dragged into. For this skill you must learn to judge all things by what they cost you. As Nietzsche wrote, "The value of a thing sometimes lies not in what one attains with it, but in what one pays for it—what it *costs* us." Perhaps you will attain your goal, and a worthy goal at that, but at what price? Apply this standard to everything, including whether to collaborate with other people or come to their aid. In the end, life is short, opportunities are few, and you have only so much energy to draw on. And in this sense time is as important a consideration as any other. Never waste valuable time, or mental peace of mind, on the affairs of others—that is too high a price to pay.

Power is a social game. To learn and master it, you must develop the ability to study and understand people. As the great seventeenth-century thinker and courtier Baltasar Gracián wrote: "Many people spend time studying the properties of animals or herbs; how much more important it would be to study those of people, with whom we must live or die!" To be a master player you must also be a master psychologist. You must recognize motivations and see through the cloud of dust with which people surround their actions. An understanding of people's hidden motives is the single greatest piece of knowledge you can have in acquiring power. It opens up endless possibilities of deception, seduction, and manipulation.

People are of infinite complexity and you can spend a lifetime watching them without ever fully understanding them. So it is all the more important, then, to begin your education now. In doing so you must also keep one principle in mind: Never discriminate as to whom you study and whom you trust. Never trust anyone completely and study everyone, including friends and loved ones.

Finally, you must learn always to take the indirect route to power. Disguise your cunning. Like a billiard ball that caroms several times before it hits its target, your moves must be planned and developed in the least obvious way. By training yourself to be indirect, you can thrive in the modern court, appearing the paragon of decency while being the consummate manipulator.

Consider *The 48 Laws of Power* a kind of handbook on the arts of indirection. The laws are based on the writings of men and women who have studied and mastered the game of power. These writings span a period of more than three thousand years and were created in civilizations as disparate as ancient China and Renaissance Italy; yet they share common threads and themes, together hinting at an essence of power that has yet to be fully articulated. The 48 laws of power are the distillation of this accumulated wisdom, gathered from the writings of the most illustrious strategists (Sun-tzu, Clausewitz), statesmen (Bismarck, Talleyrand), courtiers (Castiglione, Gracián), seducers (Ninon de Lenclos, Casanova), and con artists ("Yellow Kid" Weil) in history.

The laws have a simple premise: Certain actions almost always increase one's power (the observance of the law), while others decrease it and even ruin us (the transgression of the law). These transgressions and observances are illustrated by historical examples. The laws are timeless and definitive.

The 48 Laws of Power can be used in several ways. By reading the book straight through you can learn about power in general. Although several of the laws may seem not to pertain directly to your life, in time you will probably find that all of them have some application, and that in fact they are interrelated. By getting an overview of the entire subject you will best be able to evaluate your own past actions and gain a greater degree of control over your immediate affairs. A thorough reading of the book will inspire thinking and reevaluation long after you finish it.

The book has also been designed for browsing and for examining the law that seems at that particular moment most pertinent to you. Say you are experiencing problems with a superior and cannot understand why your efforts have not lead to more gratitude or a promotion. Several laws specifically address the master-underling relationship, and you are almost certainly transgressing one of them. By browsing the initial paragraphs for the 48 laws in the table of contents, you can identify the pertinent law.

Finally, the book can be browsed through and picked apart for entertainment, for an enjoyable ride through the foibles and great deeds of our predecessors in power. A warning, however, to those who use the book for this purpose: It might be better to turn back. Power is endlessly seductive and deceptive in its own way. It is a labyrinth—your mind becomes consumed with solving its infinite problems, and you soon realize how pleasantly lost you have become. In other words, it becomes most amusing by taking it seriously. Do not be frivolous with such a critical matter. The gods of power frown on the frivolous; they give ultimate satisfaction only to those who study and reflect, and punish those who skim the surfaces looking for a good time.

> *Any man who tries to be good all the time is bound to come to ruin among the great number who are not good. Hence a prince who wants to keep his authority must learn how not to be good, and use that knowledge, or refrain from using it, as necessity requires.*
>
> THE PRINCE, *Niccolò Machiavelli, 1469–1527*

1

NEVER OUTSHINE

THE MASTER

JUDGMENT

Always make those above you feel comfortably superior. In your desire to please and impress them, do not go too far in displaying your talents or you might accomplish the opposite—inspire fear and insecurity. Make your masters appear more brilliant than they are and you will attain the heights of power.

TRANSGRESSION OF THE LAW

Nicolas Fouquet, Louis XIV's finance minister in the first years of his reign, was a generous man who loved lavish parties, pretty women, and poetry. He also loved money, for he led an extravagant lifestyle. Fouquet was clever and very much indispensable to the king, so when the prime minister, Jules Mazarin, died, in 1661, the finance minister expected to be named the successor. Instead, the king decided to abolish the position. This and other signs made Fouquet suspect that he was falling out of favor, and so he decided to ingratiate himself with the king by staging the most spectacular party the world had ever seen. The party's ostensible purpose would be to commemorate the completion of Fouquet's château, Vaux-le-Vicomte, but its real function was to pay tribute to the king, the guest of honor.

The most brilliant nobility of Europe and some of the greatest minds of the time—La Fontaine, La Rochefoucauld, Madame de Sévigné—attended the party. Molière wrote a play for the occasion, in which he himself was to perform at the evening's conclusion. The party began with a lavish seven-course dinner, featuring foods from the Orient never before tasted in France, as well as new dishes created especially for the night. The meal was accompanied with music commissioned by Fouquet to honor the king.

After dinner there was a promenade through the château's gardens. The grounds and fountains of Vaux-le-Vicomte were to be the inspiration for Versailles.

Fouquet personally accompanied the young king through the geometrically aligned arrangements of shrubbery and flower beds. Arriving at the gardens' canals, they witnessed a fireworks display, which was followed by the performance of Molière's play. The party ran well into the night and everyone agreed it was the most amazing affair they had ever attended.

The next day, Fouquet was arrested by the king's head musketeer, D'Artagnan. Three months later he went on trial for stealing from the country's treasury. (Actually, most of the stealing he was accused of he had done on the king's behalf and with the king's permission.) Fouquet was found guilty and sent to the most isolated prison in France, high in the Pyrenees Mountains, where he spent the last twenty years of his life in solitary confinement.

Interpretation

Louis XIV, the Sun King, was a proud and arrogant man who wanted to be the center of attention at all times; he could not countenance being outdone in lavishness by anyone, and certainly not his finance minister. To succeed Fouquet, Louis chose Jean-Baptiste Colbert, a man famous for his parsimony and for giving the dullest parties in Paris. Colbert made sure that any money liberated from the treasury went straight into Louis's hands. With the money, Louis built a palace even more magnificent than Fouquet's—the glorious palace of Versailles. He used the same architects, decorators, and garden designer. And at Versailles, Louis hosted parties even more extravagant than the one that cost Fouquet his freedom.

Let us examine the situation. The evening of the party, as Fouquet presented spectacle on spectacle to Louis, each more magnificent than the one before, he imagined the affair as demonstrating his loyalty and devotion to the king. Not only did he think the party would put him back in the king's favor, he thought it would show his good taste, his connections, and his popularity, making him indispensable to the king and demonstrating that he would make an excellent prime minister. Instead, however, each new spectacle, each appreciative smile bestowed by the guests on Fouquet, made it seem to Louis that his own friends and subjects were more charmed by the finance minister than by the king himself, and that Fouquet was actually flaunting his wealth and power. Rather than flattering Louis XIV, Fouquet's elaborate party offended the king's vanity. Louis would not admit this to anyone, of course—instead, he found a convenient excuse to rid himself of a man who had inadvertently made him feel insecure.

Such is the fate, in some form or other, of all those who unbalance the master's sense of self, poke holes in his vanity, or make him doubt his preeminence.

When the evening began, Fouquet was at the top of the world.
By the time it had ended, he was at the bottom.
Voltaire, 1694–1778

OBSERVANCE OF THE LAW

In the early 1600s, the Italian astronomer and mathematician Galileo found himself in a precarious position. He depended on the generosity of great rulers to support his research, and so, like all Renaissance scientists, he would sometimes make gifts of his inventions and discoveries to the leading patrons of the time. Once, for instance, he presented a military compass he had invented to the Duke of Gonzaga. Then he dedicated a book explaining the use of the compass to the Medicis. Both rulers were grateful, and through them Galileo was able to find more students to teach. No matter how great the discovery, however, his patrons usually paid him with gifts, not cash. This made for a life of constant insecurity and dependence. There must be an easier way, he thought.

Galileo hit on a new strategy in 1610, when he discovered the moons of Jupiter. Instead of dividing the discovery among his patrons—giving one the telescope he had used, dedicating a book to another, and so on—as he had done in the past, he decided to focus exclusively on the Medicis. He chose the Medicis for one reason: Shortly after Cosimo I had established the Medici dynasty, in 1540, he had made Jupiter, the mightiest of the gods, the Medici symbol—a symbol of a power that went beyond politics and banking, one linked to ancient Rome and its divinities.

Galileo turned his discovery of Jupiter's moons into a cosmic event honoring the Medicis' greatness. Shortly after the discovery, he announced that "the bright stars [the moons of Jupiter] offered themselves in the heavens" to his telescope at the same time as Cosimo II's enthronement. He said that the number of the moons—four—harmonized with the number of the Medicis (Cosimo II had three brothers) and that the moons orbited Jupiter as these four sons revolved around Cosimo I, the dynasty's founder. More than coincidence, this showed that the heavens themselves reflected the ascendancy of the Medici family. After he dedicated the discovery to the Medicis, Galileo commissioned an emblem representing Jupiter sitting on a cloud with the four stars circling about him, and presented this to Cosimo II as a symbol of his link to the stars.

In 1610 Cosimo II made Galileo his official court philosopher and mathematician, with a full salary. For a scientist this was the coup of a lifetime. The days of begging for patronage were over.

Interpretation

In one stroke, Galileo gained more with his new strategy than he had in years of begging. The reason is simple: All masters want to appear more brilliant than other people.

They do not care about science or empirical truth or the latest invention; they care about their name and their glory. Galileo gave the Medicis infinitely more glory by linking their name with cosmic forces than he had by making them the patrons of some new scientific gadget or discovery.

Scientists are not spared the vagaries of court life and patronage. They too must serve masters who hold the purse strings. And their great intellectual powers can make the master feel insecure, as if he were only there to supply the funds—an ugly, ignoble job. The producer of a great work wants to feel he is more than just the provider of the financing. He wants to appear creative and powerful, and also more important than the work produced in his name. Instead of insecurity you must give him glory. Galileo did not challenge the intellectual authority of the Medicis with his discovery, or make them feel inferior in any way; by literally aligning them with the stars, he made them shine brilliantly among the courts of Italy. He did not outshine the master, he made the master outshine all others.

KEYS TO POWER

Everyone has insecurities. When you show yourself in the world and display your talents, you naturally stir up all kinds of resentment, envy, and other manifestations of insecurity. This is to be expected. You cannot spend your life worrying about the petty feelings of others. With those above you, however, you must take a different approach: When it comes to power, outshining the master is perhaps the worst mistake of all.

Do not fool yourself into thinking that life has changed much since the days of Louis XIV and the Medicis. Those who attain high standing in life are like kings and queens: They want to feel secure in their positions, and superior to those around them in intelligence, wit, and charm. It is a deadly but common misperception to believe that by displaying and vaunting your gifts and talents, you are winning the master's affection. He may feign appreciation, but at his first opportunity he will replace you with someone less intelligent, less attractive, less threatening, just as Louis XIV replaced the sparkling Fouquet with the bland Colbert. And as with Louis, he will not admit the truth, but will find an excuse to rid himself of your presence.

This Law involves two rules that you must realize. First, you can inadvertently outshine a master simply by being yourself. There are masters who are more insecure than others, monstrously insecure; you may naturally outshine them by your charm and grace.

No one had more natural talents than Astorre Manfredi, prince of Faenza. The most handsome of all the young princes of Italy, he captivated his subjects with his generosity and open spirit.

In the year 1500, Cesare Borgia laid siege to Faenza. When the city surrendered, the citizens expected the worst from the cruel Borgia, who, however, decided to spare the town: He simply occupied its fortress, executed none of its citizens, and allowed Prince Manfredi, eighteen at the time, to remain with his court, in complete freedom.

A few weeks later, though, soldiers hauled Astorre Manfredi away to a Roman prison. A year after that, his body was fished out of the River Tiber, a stone tied around his neck. Borgia justified the horrible deed with some sort of trumped-up charge of treason and conspiracy, but the real problem was that he was notoriously vain and insecure. The young man was outshining him without even trying. Given Manfredi's natural talents, the prince's mere presence made Borgia seem less attractive and charismatic. The lesson is simple: If you cannot help being charming and superior, you must learn to avoid such monsters of vanity. Either that, or find a way to mute your good qualities when in the company of a Cesare Borgia.

Second, never imagine that because the master loves you, you can do anything you want. Entire books could be written about favorites who fell out of favor by taking their status for granted, for daring to outshine. In late-sixteenth-century Japan, the favorite of Emperor Hideyoshi was a man called Sen no Rikyu. The premier artist of the tea ceremony, which had become an obsession with the nobility, he was one of Hideyoshi's most trusted advisers, had his own apartment in the palace, and was honored throughout Japan. Yet in 1591, Hideyoshi had him arrested and sentenced to death. Rikyu took his own life, instead. The cause for his sudden change of fortune was discovered later: It seems that Rikyu, former peasant and later court favorite, had had a wooden statue made of himself wearing sandals (a sign of nobility) and posing loftily. He had had this statue placed in the most important temple inside the palace gates, in clear sight of the royalty who often would pass by. To Hideyoshi this signified that Rikyu had no sense of limits. Presuming that he had the same rights as those of the highest nobility, he had forgotten that his position depended on the emperor, and had come to believe that he had earned it on his own. This was an unforgivable miscalculation of his own importance and he paid for it with his life. Remember the following: Never take your position for granted and never let any favors you receive go to your head.

Knowing the dangers of outshining your master, you can turn this Law to your advantage. First you must flatter and puff up your master. Overt flattery can be effective but has its limits; it is too direct and obvious, and looks bad to other courtiers. Discreet flattery is much more powerful. If you are more intelligent than your master, for example, seem the opposite: Make him appear more intelligent than you. Act naive. Make it seem that you need his expertise. Commit harmless mistakes that will not hurt you in the long run but will give you the chance to ask for his help. Masters adore such requests. A master who cannot bestow on you the gifts of his experience may direct rancor and ill will at you instead.

If your ideas are more creative than your master's, ascribe them to him, in as public a manner as possible. Make it clear that *your* advice is merely an echo of *his* advice.

If you surpass your master in wit, it is okay to play the role of the court jester, but do not make him appear cold and surly by comparison. Tone down your humor if necessary, and find ways to make him seem the dispenser of amusement and good cheer. If you are naturally more sociable and generous than your master, be careful not to be the cloud that blocks his radiance from others. He must appear as the sun around which everyone revolves, radiating power and brilliance, the center of attention. If you are thrust into the position of entertaining him, a display of your limited means may win you his sympathy. Any attempt to impress him with your grace and generosity can prove fatal: Learn from Fouquet or pay the price.

In all of these cases it is not a weakness to disguise your strengths if in the end they lead to power. By letting others outshine you, you remain in control, instead of being a victim of their insecurity. This will all come in handy the day you decide to rise above your inferior status. If, like Galileo, you can make your master shine even more in the eyes of others, then you are a godsend and you will be instantly promoted.

Image:
The Stars in the
Sky. There can be only
one sun at a time. Never
obscure the sunlight, or
rival the sun's brilliance;
rather, fade into the sky and
find ways to heighten
the master star's
intensity.

Authority: Avoid outshining the master. All superiority is odious, but the superiority of a subject over his prince is not only stupid, it is fatal. This is a lesson that the stars in the sky teach us—they may be related to the sun, and just as brilliant, but they never appear in her company. (Baltasar Gracián, 1601–1658)

REVERSAL

You cannot worry about upsetting every person you come across, but you must be selectively cruel. If your superior is a falling star, there is nothing to fear from outshining him. Do not be merciful—your master had no such scruples in his own cold-blooded climb to the top. Gauge his strength. If he is weak, discreetly hasten his downfall: Outdo, outcharm, outsmart him at key moments. If he is *very* weak and ready to fall, let nature take its course. Do not risk outshining a feeble superior—it might appear cruel or spiteful. But if your master is firm in his position, yet you know yourself to be the more capable, bide your time and be patient. It is the natural course of things that power eventually fades and weakens. Your master will fall someday, and if you play it right, you will outlive and someday outshine him.

NEVER PUT TOO MUCH

TRUST IN FRIENDS, LEARN

HOW TO USE ENEMIES

JUDGMENT

Be wary of friends—they will betray you more quickly, for they are easily aroused to envy. They also become spoiled and tyrannical. But hire a former enemy and he will be more loyal than a friend, because he has more to prove. In fact, you have more to fear from friends than from enemies. If you have no enemies, find a way to make them.

TRANSGRESSION OF THE LAW

In the mid–ninth century A.D., a young man named Michael III assumed the throne of the Byzantine Empire. His mother, the Empress Theodora, had been banished to a nunnery, and her lover, Theoctistus, had been murdered; at the head of the conspiracy to depose Theodora and enthrone Michael had been Michael's uncle, Bardas, a man of intelligence and ambition. Michael was now a young, inexperienced ruler, surrounded by intriguers, murderers, and profligates. In this time of peril he needed someone he could trust as his councillor, and his thoughts turned to Basilius, his best friend. Basilius had no experience whatsoever in government and politics—in fact, he was the head of the royal stables—but he had proven his love and gratitude time and again.

They had met a few years before, when Michael had been visiting the stables just as a wild horse got loose. Basilius, a young groom from peasant Macedonian stock, had saved Michael's life. The groom's strength and courage had impressed Michael, who immediately raised Basilius from the obscurity of being a horse trainer to the position of head of the stables. He loaded his friend with gifts and favors and they became inseparable. Basilius was sent to the finest school in Byzantium, and the crude peasant became a cultured and sophisticated courtier.

Now Michael was emperor, and in need of someone loyal. Who could he better trust with the post of chamberlain and chief councillor than a young man who owed him everything?

Basilius could be trained for the job and Michael loved him like a brother. Ignoring the advice of those who recommended the much more qualified Bardas, Michael chose his friend.

Basilius learned well and was soon advising the emperor on all matters of state. The only problem seemed to be money—Basilius never had enough. Exposure to the splendor of Byzantine court life made him avaricious for the perks of power. Michael doubled, then tripled his salary, ennobled him, and married him off to his own mistress, Eudoxia Ingerina. Keeping such a trusted friend and adviser satisfied was worth any price. But more trouble was to come. Bardas was now head of the army, and Basilius convinced Michael that the man was hopelessly ambitious. Under the illusion that he could control his nephew, Bardas had conspired to put him on the throne, and he could conspire again, this time to get rid of Michael and assume the crown himself. Basilius poured poison into Michael's ear until the emperor agreed to have his uncle murdered. During a great horse race, Basilius closed in on Bardas in the crowd and stabbed him to death. Soon after, Basilius asked that he replace Bardas as head of the army, where he could keep control of the realm and quell rebellion. This was granted.

Now Basilius's power and wealth only grew, and a few years later Michael, in financial straits from his own extravagance, asked him to pay back some of the money he had borrowed over the years. To Michael's shock and astonishment, Basilius refused, with a look of such impudence

A snake chased by hunters asked a farmer to save its life. To hide it from its pursuers, the farmer squatted and let the snake crawl into his belly. But when the danger had passed and the farmer asked the snake to come out, the snake refused. It was warm and safe inside. On his way home, the man saw a heron and went up to him and whispered what had happened. The heron told him to squat and strain to eject the snake. When the snake snuck its head out, the heron caught it, pulled it out, and killed it. The farmer was worried that the snake's poison might still be inside him, and the heron told him that the cure for snake poison was to cook and eat six white fowl. "You're a white fowl," said the farmer. "You'll do for a start." He grabbed the heron, put it in a bag, and carried it home, where he hung it up while he told his wife what had happened. "I'm surprised at you," said the wife. "The bird does you a kindness, rids you of the evil in your belly, saves your life in fact, yet you catch it and talk of killing it." She immediately released the heron, and it flew away. But on its way, it gouged out her eyes.

Moral: When you see water flowing uphill, it means that someone is repaying a kindness.

AFRICAN FOLK TALE

that the emperor suddenly realized his predicament: The former stable boy had more money, more allies in the army and senate, and in the end more power than the emperor himself. A few weeks later, after a night of heavy drinking, Michael awoke to find himself surrounded by soldiers. Basilius watched as they stabbed the emperor to death. Then, after proclaiming himself emperor, he rode his horse through the streets of Byzantium, brandishing the head of his former benefactor and best friend at the end of a long pike.

Interpretation

Michael III staked his future on the sense of gratitude he thought Basilius must feel for him. Surely Basilius would serve him best; he owed the emperor his wealth, his education, and his position. Then, once Basilius was in power, anything he needed it was best to give to him, strengthening the bonds between the two men. It was only on the fateful day when the emperor saw that impudent smile on Basilius's face that he realized his deadly mistake.

He had created a monster. He had allowed a man to see power up close—a man who then wanted more, who asked for anything and got it, who felt encumbered by the charity he had received and simply did what many people do in such a situation: They forget the favors they have received and imagine they have earned their success by their own merits.

At Michael's moment of realization, he could still have saved his own life, but friendship and love blind every man to their interests. Nobody believes a friend can betray. And Michael went on disbelieving until the day his head ended up on a pike.

Lord, protect me from my friends; I can take care of my enemies.
Voltaire, 1694–1778

OBSERVANCE OF THE LAW

For several centuries after the fall of the Han Dynasty (A.D. 222), Chinese history followed the same pattern of violent and bloody coups, one after the other. Army men would plot to kill a weak emperor, then would replace him on the Dragon Throne with a strong general. The general would start a new dynasty and crown himself emperor; to ensure his own survival he would kill off his fellow generals. A few years later, however, the pattern would resume: New generals would rise up and assassinate him or his sons in their turn. To be emperor of China was to be alone, surrounded by a pack of enemies—it was the least powerful, least secure position in the realm.

In A.D. 959, General Chao K'uang-yin became Emperor Sung. He knew the odds, the probability that within a year or two he would be murdered; how could he break the pattern? Soon after becoming emperor, Sung ordered a banquet to celebrate the new dynasty, and invited the most powerful commanders in the army. After they had drunk much wine, he dismissed the guards and everybody else except the generals, who now feared he would murder them in one fell swoop. Instead, he addressed them: "The whole day is spent in fear, and I am unhappy both at the table and in my bed. For which one of you does not dream of ascending the throne? I do not doubt your allegiance, but if by some chance your subordinates, seeking wealth and position, were to force the emperor's yellow robe upon you in turn, how could you refuse it?" Drunk and fearing for their lives, the generals proclaimed their innocence and their loyalty. But Sung had other ideas: "The best way to pass one's days is in peaceful enjoyment of riches and honor. If you are willing to give up your commands, I am ready to provide you with fine estates and beautiful dwellings where you may take your pleasure with singers and girls as your companions."

The astonished generals realized that instead of a life of anxiety and struggle Sung was offering them riches and security. The next day, all of the generals tendered their resignations, and they retired as nobles to the estates that Sung bestowed on them.

In one stroke, Sung turned a pack of "friendly" wolves, who would likely have betrayed him, into a group of docile lambs, far from all power.

Over the next few years Sung continued his campaign to secure his rule. In A.D. 971, King Liu of the Southern Han finally surrendered to him after years of rebellion. To Liu's astonishment, Sung gave him a rank in the imperial court and invited him to the palace to seal their newfound friendship with wine. As King Liu took the glass that Sung offered him, he hesitated, fearing it contained poison. "Your subject's crimes certainly merit death," he cried out, "but I beg Your Majesty to spare your subject's life. Indeed I dare not drink this wine." Emperor Sung laughed, took the glass from Liu, and swallowed it himself. There was no poison. From then on Liu became his most trusted and loyal friend.

At the time, China had splintered into many smaller kingdoms. When Ch'ien Shu, the king of one of these, was defeated, Sung's ministers advised the emperor to lock this rebel up. They presented documents proving that he was still conspiring to kill Sung. When Ch'ien Shu came to visit the emperor, however, instead of locking him up, Sung honored him. He also gave him a package, which he told the former king to open when he was halfway home. Ch'ien Shu opened the bundle on his return journey and saw that it contained all the papers documenting his conspiracy. He realized that Sung knew of his murderous plans, yet had spared him nonetheless. This generosity won him over, and he too became one of Sung's most loyal vassals.

Interpretation

A Chinese proverb compares friends to the jaws and teeth of a dangerous animal: If you are not careful, you will find them chewing you up. Emperor Sung knew the jaws he was passing between when he assumed the throne: His "friends" in the army would chew him up like meat, and if he somehow survived, his "friends" in the government would have him for supper.

There are many who think therefore that a wise prince ought, when he has the chance, to foment astutely some enmity, so that by suppressing it he will augment his greatness. Princes, and especially new ones, have found more faith and more usefulness in those men, whom at the beginning of their power they regarded with suspicion, than in those they at first confided in. Pandolfo Petrucci, prince of Siena, governed his state more by those whom he suspected than by others.
NICCOLÒ MACHIAVELLI, 1469–1527

A brahman, a great expert in Veda who has become a great archer as well, offers his services to his good friend, who is now the king. The brahman cries out when he sees the king, "Recognize me, your friend!" The king answers him with contempt and then explains: "Yes, we were friends before, but our friendship was based on what power we had. . . . I was friends with you, good brahman, because it served my purpose. No pauper is friend to the rich, no fool to the wise, no coward to the

brave. An old friend—
who needs him? It is
two men of equal
wealth and equal birth
who contract friend-
ship and marriage, not
a rich man and a
pauper.... An old
friend—who needs
him?

THE MAHABHARATA,
c. THIRD CENTURY B.C.

Emperor Sung would have no truck with "friends"—he bribed his fellow generals with splendid estates and kept them far away. This was a much better way to emasculate them than killing them, which would only have led other generals to seek vengeance. And Sung would have nothing to do with "friendly" ministers. More often than not, they would end up drinking his famous cup of poisoned wine.

Instead of relying on friends, Sung used his enemies, one after the other, transforming them into far more reliable subjects. While a friend expects more and more favors, and seethes with jealousy, these former enemies expected nothing and got everything. A man suddenly spared the guillotine is a grateful man indeed, and will go to the ends of the earth for the man who has pardoned him. In time, these former enemies became Sung's most trusted friends.

And Sung was finally able to break the pattern of coups, violence, and civil war—the Sung Dynasty ruled China for more than three hundred years.

Pick up a bee from
kindness, and learn the
limitations of kindness.

SUFI PROVERB

In a speech Abraham Lincoln delivered at the height of the Civil War, he referred to the Southerners as fellow human beings who were in error. An elderly lady chastised him for not calling them irreconcilable enemies who must be destroyed. "Why, madam," Lincoln replied, "do I not destroy my enemies when I make them my friends?"

Men are more ready to
repay an injury than a
benefit, because grati-
tude is a burden and
revenge a pleasure.

TACITUS, c. A.D. 55–120

KEYS TO POWER

It is natural to want to employ your friends when you find yourself in times of need. The world is a harsh place, and your friends soften the harshness. Besides, you know them. Why depend on a stranger when you have a friend at hand?

The problem is that you often do not know your friends as well as you imagine. Friends often agree on things in order to avoid an argument. They cover up their unpleasant qualities so as to not offend each other. They laugh extra hard at each other's jokes. Since honesty rarely strengthens friendship, you may never know how a friend truly feels. Friends will say that they love your poetry, adore your music, envy your taste in clothes—maybe they mean it, often they do not.

When you decide to hire a friend, you gradually discover the qualities he or she has kept hidden. Strangely enough, it is your act of kindness that unbalances everything. People want to feel they deserve their good fortune. The receipt of a favor can become oppressive: It means you have been chosen because you are a friend, not necessarily because you are deserving. There is almost a touch of condescension in the act of hiring friends that secretly afflicts them. The injury will come out slowly: A little more honesty, flashes of resentment and envy here and there, and before you know it your friendship fades. The more favors and gifts you supply to revive the friendship, the less gratitude you receive.

Ingratitude has a long and deep history. It has demonstrated its powers for so many centuries, that it is truly amazing that people continue to underestimate them. Better to be wary. If you never expect gratitude from a friend, you will be pleasantly surprised when they do prove grateful.

The problem with using or hiring friends is that it will inevitably limit your power. The friend is rarely the one who is most able to help you; and in the end, skill and competence are far more important than friendly feelings. (Michael III had a man right under his nose who would have steered him right and kept him alive: That man was Bardas.)

All working situations require a kind of distance between people. You are trying to work, not make friends; friendliness (real or false) only obscures that fact. The key to power, then, is the ability to judge who is best able to further your interests in all situations. Keep friends for friendship, but work with the skilled and competent.

Your enemies, on the other hand, are an untapped gold mine that you must learn to exploit. When Talleyrand, Napoleon's foreign minister, decided in 1807 that his boss was leading France to ruin, and the time had come to turn against him, he understood the dangers of conspiring against the emperor; he needed a partner, a confederate—what friend could he trust in such a project? He chose Joseph Fouché, head of the secret police, his most hated enemy, a man who had even tried to have him assassinated. He knew that their former hatred would create an opportunity for an emotional reconciliation. He knew that Fouché would expect nothing from him, and in fact would work to prove that he was worthy of Talleyrand's choice; a person who has something to prove will move mountains for you. Finally, he knew that his relationship with Fouché would be based on mutual self-interest, and would not be contaminated by personal feeling. The selection proved perfect; although the conspirators did not succeed in toppling Napoleon, the union of such powerful but unlikely partners generated much interest in the cause; opposition to the emperor slowly began to spread. And from then on, Talleyrand and Fouché had a fruitful working relationship. Whenever you can, bury the hatchet with an enemy, and make a point of putting him in your service.

As Lincoln said, you destroy an enemy when you make a friend of him. In 1971, during the Vietnam War, Henry Kissinger was the target of an unsuccessful kidnapping attempt, a conspiracy involving, among others, the renowned antiwar activist priests the Berrigan brothers, four more Catholic priests, and four nuns. In private, without informing the Secret Service or the Justice Department, Kissinger arranged a Saturday-morning meeting with three of the alleged kidnappers. Explaining to his guests that he would have most American soldiers out of Vietnam by mid-1972, he completely charmed them. They gave him some "Kidnap Kissinger" buttons and one of them remained a friend of his for years, visiting him on several occasions. This was not just a onetime ploy: Kissinger made a policy of working with those who disagreed with him. Colleagues commented that he seemed to get along better with his enemies than with his friends.

Without enemies around us, we grow lazy. An enemy at our heels sharpens our wits, keeping us focused and alert. It is sometimes better,

PROFITING BY OUR
ENEMIES

King Hiero chanced upon a time, speaking with one of his enemies, to be told in a reproachful manner that he had stinking breath. Whereupon the good king, being somewhat dismayed in himself, as soon as he returned home chided his wife, "How does it happen that you never told me of this problem?" The woman, being a simple, chaste, and harmless dame, said, "Sir, I had thought all men's breath had smelled so." Thus it is plain that faults that are evident to the senses, gross and corporal, or otherwise notorious to the world, we know by our enemies sooner than by our friends and familiars.

PLUTARCH,
c. A.D. 46–120

then, to use enemies as enemies rather than transforming them into friends or allies.

Mao Tse-tung saw conflict as key in his approach to power. In 1937 the Japanese invaded China, interrupting the civil war between Mao's Communists and their enemy, the Nationalists.

Fearing that the Japanese would wipe them out, some Communist leaders advocated leaving the Nationalists to fight the Japanese, and using the time to recuperate. Mao disagreed: The Japanese could not possibly defeat and occupy a vast country like China for long. Once they left, the Communists would have grown rusty if they had been out of combat for several years, and would be ill prepared to reopen their struggle with the Nationalists. To fight a formidable foe like the Japanese, in fact, would be the perfect training for the Communists' ragtag army. Mao's plan was adopted, and it worked: By the time the Japanese finally retreated, the Communists had gained the fighting experience that helped them defeat the Nationalists.

Years later, a Japanese visitor tried to apologize to Mao for his country's invasion of China. Mao interrupted, "Should I not thank you instead?" Without a worthy opponent, he explained, a man or group cannot grow stronger.

Mao's strategy of constant conflict has several key components. First, be certain that in the long run you will emerge victorious. Never pick a fight with someone you are not sure you can defeat, as Mao knew the Japanese would be defeated in time. Second, if you have no apparent enemies, you must sometimes set up a convenient target, even turning a friend into an enemy. Mao used this tactic time and again in politics. Third, use such enemies to define your cause more clearly to the public, even framing it as a struggle of good against evil. Mao actually encouraged China's disagreements with the Soviet Union and the United States; without clear-cut enemies, he believed, his people would lose any sense of what Chinese Communism meant. A sharply defined enemy is a far stronger argument for your side than all the words you could possibly put together.

Never let the presence of enemies upset or distress you—you are far better off with a declared opponent or two than not knowing where your real enemies lie. The man of power welcomes conflict, using enemies to enhance his reputation as a surefooted fighter who can be relied upon in times of uncertainty.

Image: The Jaws of Ingratitude.
Knowing what would happen
if you put a finger in
the mouth of a lion,
you would stay
clear of it.
With friends
you will have
no such caution, and
if you hire them, they will
eat you alive with ingratitude.

Authority: Know how to use enemies for your own profit. You must learn to grab a sword not by its blade, which would cut you, but by the handle, which allows you to defend yourself. The wise man profits more from his enemies, than a fool from his friends. (Baltasar Gracián, 1601–1658)

REVERSAL

Although it is generally best not to mix work with friendship, there are times when a friend can be used to greater effect than an enemy. A man of power, for example, often has dirty work that has to be done, but for the sake of appearances it is generally preferable to have other people do it for him; friends often do this the best, since their affection for him makes them willing to take chances. Also, if your plans go awry for some reason, you can use a friend as a convenient scapegoat. This "fall of the favorite" was a trick often used by kings and sovereigns: They would let their closest friend at court take the fall for a mistake, since the public would not believe that they would deliberately sacrifice a friend for such a purpose. Of course, after you play that card, you have lost your friend forever. It is best, then, to reserve the scapegoat role for someone who is close to you but not too close.

Finally, the problem about working with friends is that it confuses the boundaries and distances that working requires. But if both partners in the arrangement understand the dangers involved, a friend often can be employed to great effect. You must never let your guard down in such a venture, however; always be on the lookout for any signs of emotional disturbance such as envy and ingratitude. Nothing is stable in the realm of power, and even the closest of friends can be transformed into the worst of enemies.

CONCEAL YOUR

INTENTIONS

JUDGMENT

*Keep people off-balance and in the dark by never reveal-
ing the purpose behind your actions. If they have no clue
what you are up to, they cannot prepare a defense. Guide
them far enough down the wrong path, envelop them in
enough smoke, and by the time they realize your intentions, it will be too late.*

PART I: USE DECOYED OBJECTS OF DESIRE AND RED HERRINGS TO THROW PEOPLE OFF THE SCENT

If at any point in the deception you practice people have the slightest suspicion as to your intentions, all is lost. Do not give them the chance to sense what you are up to: Throw them off the scent by dragging red herrings across the path. Use false sincerity, send ambiguous signals, set up misleading objects of desire. Unable to distinguish the genuine from the false, they cannot pick out your real goal.

TRANSGRESSION OF THE LAW

Over several weeks, Ninon de Lenclos, the most infamous courtesan of seventeenth-century France, listened patiently as the Marquis de Sevigné explained his struggles in pursuing a beautiful but difficult young countess. Ninon was sixty-two at the time, and more than experienced in matters of love; the marquis was a lad of twenty-two, handsome, dashing, but hopelessly inexperienced in romance. At first Ninon was amused to hear the marquis talk about his mistakes, but finally she had had enough. Unable to bear ineptitude in any realm, least of all in seducing a woman, she decided to take the young man under her wing. First, he had to understand that this was war, and that the beautiful countess was a citadel to which he had to lay siege as carefully as any general. Every step had to be planned and executed with the utmost attention to detail and nuance.

Instructing the marquis to start over, Ninon told him to approach the countess with a bit of distance, an air of nonchalance. The next time the two were alone together, she said, he would confide in the countess as would a friend but not a potential lover. This was to throw her off the scent. The countess was no longer to take his interest in her for granted—perhaps he was only interested in friendship.

Ninon planned ahead. Once the countess was confused, it would be time to make her jealous. At the next encounter, at a major fête in Paris, the marquis would show up with a beautiful young woman at his side. This beautiful young woman had equally beautiful friends, so that wherever the countess would now see the marquis, he would be surrounded by the most stunning young women in Paris. Not only would the countess be seething with jealousy, she would come to see the marquis as someone who was desired by others. It was hard for Ninon to make the marquis understand, but she patiently explained that a woman who is interested in a man wants to see that other women are interested in him, too. Not only does that give him instant value, it makes it all the more satisfying to snatch him from their clutches.

Once the countess was jealous but intrigued, it would be time to beguile her. On Ninon's instructions, the marquis would fail to show up at affairs where the countess expected to see him. Then, suddenly, he would appear at salons he had never frequented before, but that the countess attended often. She would be unable to predict his moves. All of this would push her into the state of emotional confusion that is a prerequisite for successful seduction.

These moves were executed, and took several weeks. Ninon monitored the marquis's progress: Through her network of spies, she heard how the countess would laugh a little harder at his witticisms, listen more closely to his stories. She heard that the countess was suddenly asking questions about him. Her friends told her that at social affairs the countess would often look up at the marquis, following his steps. Ninon felt certain that the young woman was falling under his spell. It was a matter of weeks now, maybe a month or two, but if all went smoothly, the citadel would fall.

A few days later the marquis was at the countess's home. They were alone. Suddenly he was a different man: This time acting on his own impulse, rather than following Ninon's instructions, he took the countess's hands and told her he was in love with her. The young woman seemed confused, a reaction he did not expect. She became polite, then excused herself. For the rest of the evening she avoided his eyes, was not there to say good-night to him. The next few times he visited he was told she was not at home. When she finally admitted him again, the two felt awkward and uncomfortable with each other. The spell was broken.

Interpretation

Ninon de Lenclos knew everything about the art of love. The greatest writers, thinkers, and politicians of the time had been her lovers—men like La Rochefoucauld, Molière, and Richelieu. Seduction was a game to her, to be practiced with skill. As she got older, and her reputation grew, the most important families in France would send their sons to her to be instructed in matters of love.

Ninon knew that men and women are very different, but when it comes to seduction they feel the same: Deep down inside, they often sense when they are being seduced, but they give in because they enjoy the feeling of being led along. It is a pleasure to let go, and to allow the other person to detour you into a strange country. Everything in seduction, however, depends on suggestion. You cannot announce your intentions or reveal them directly in words. Instead you must throw your targets off the scent. To surrender to your guidance they must be appropriately confused. You have to scramble your signals—appear interested in another man or woman (the decoy), then hint at being interested in the target, then feign indifference, on and on. Such patterns not only confuse, they excite.

Imagine this story from the countess's perspective: After a few of the marquis's moves, she sensed the marquis was playing some sort of game, but the game delighted her. She did not know where he was leading her, but so much the better. His moves intrigued her, each of them keeping her waiting for the next one—she even enjoyed her jealousy and confusion, for sometimes any emotion is better than the boredom of security. Perhaps the marquis had ulterior motives; most men do. But she was willing to wait and see, and probably if she had been made to wait long enough, what he was up to would not have mattered.

The moment the marquis uttered that fatal word "love," however, all was changed. This was no longer a game with moves, it was an artless show of passion. His intention was revealed: He *was* seducing her. This put everything he had done in a new light. All that before had been charming now seemed ugly and conniving; the countess felt embarrassed and used. A door closed that would never open again.

Do not be held a cheat, even though it is impossible to live today without being one.
Let your greatest cunning lie in covering up what looks like cunning.
Baltasar Gracián, 1601–1658

OBSERVANCE OF THE LAW

In 1850 the young Otto von Bismarck, then a thirty-five-year-old deputy in the Prussian parliament, was at a turning point in his career. The issues of the day were the unification of the many states (including Prussia) into which Germany was then divided, and a war against Austria, the powerful neighbor to the south that hoped to keep the Germans weak and at odds, even threatening to intervene if they tried to unite. Prince William, next in line to be Prussia's king, was in favor of going to war, and the parliament rallied to the cause, prepared to back any mobilization of troops. The only ones to oppose war were the present king, Frederick William IV, and his ministers, who preferred to appease the powerful Austrians.

Throughout his career, Bismarck had been a loyal, even passionate supporter of Prussian might and power. He dreamed of German unification, of going to war against Austria and humiliating the country that for so long had kept Germany divided. A former soldier, he saw warfare as a glorious business.

This, after all, was the man who years later would say, "The great questions of the time will be decided, not by speeches and resolutions, but by iron and blood."

Passionate patriot and lover of military glory, Bismarck nevertheless gave a speech in parliament at the height of the war fever that astonished all who heard it. "Woe unto the statesman," he said, "who makes war without a reason that will still be valid when the war is over! After the war, you will all look differently at these questions. Will you then have the courage to turn to the peasant contemplating the ashes of his farm, to the man who has been crippled, to the father who has lost his children?" Not only did Bismarck go on to talk of the madness of this war, but, strangest of all, he praised Austria and defended her actions. This went against everything he had stood for. The consequences were immediate. Bismarck was against the war—what could this possibly mean? Other deputies were confused, and several of them changed their votes. Eventually the king and his ministers won out, and war was averted.

A few weeks after Bismarck's infamous speech, the king, grateful that he had spoken for peace, made him a cabinet minister. A few years later he became the Prussian premier. In this role he eventually led his country and a peace-loving king into a war against Austria, crushing the former empire and establishing a mighty German state, with Prussia at its head.

Interpretation

At the time of his speech in 1850, Bismarck made several calculations. First, he sensed that the Prussian military, which had not kept pace with other European armies, was unready for war—that Austria, in fact, might very well win, a disastrous result for the future. Second, if the war were lost and Bismarck had supported it, his career would be gravely jeopardized. The king and his conservative ministers wanted peace; Bismarck wanted power. The answer was to throw people off the scent by supporting a cause he detested, saying things he would laugh at if said by another. A whole country was fooled. It was because of Bismarck's speech that the king made him a minister, a position from which he quickly rose to be prime minister, attaining the power to strengthen the Prussian military and accomplish what he had wanted all along: the humiliation of Austria and the unification of Germany under Prussia's leadership.

Bismarck was certainly one of the cleverest statesman who ever lived, a master of strategy and deception. No one suspected what he was up to in this case. Had he announced his real intentions, arguing that it was better to wait now and fight later, he would not have won the argument, since most Prussians wanted war at that moment and mistakenly believed that their army was superior to the Austrians. Had he played up to the king, asking to be made a minister in exchange for supporting peace, he would not have succeeded either: The king would have distrusted his ambition and doubted his sincerity.

By being completely insincere and sending misleading signals, however, he deceived everyone, concealed his purpose, and attained everything he wanted. Such is the power of hiding your intentions.

KEYS TO POWER

Most people are open books. They say what they feel, blurt out their opinions at every opportunity, and constantly reveal their plans and intentions. They do this for several reasons. First, it is easy and natural to always want to talk about one's feelings and plans for the future. It takes effort to control your tongue and monitor what you reveal. Second, many believe that by being honest and open they are winning people's hearts and showing their good nature.They are greatly deluded. Honesty is actually a blunt instrument, which bloodies more than it cuts. Your honesty is likely to offend people; it is much more prudent to tailor your words, telling people what they want to hear rather than the coarse and ugly truth of what you feel or think. More important, by being unabashedly open you make yourself so predictable and familiar that it is almost impossible to respect or fear you, and power will not accrue to a person who cannot inspire such emotions.

If you yearn for power, quickly lay honesty aside, and train yourself in the art of concealing your intentions. Master the art and you will always have the upper hand. Basic to an ability to conceal one's intentions is a simple truth about human nature: Our first instinct is to always trust appearances. We cannot go around doubting the reality of what we see and hear—constantly imagining that appearances concealed something else would exhaust and terrify us. This fact makes it relatively easy to conceal one's intentions. Simply dangle an object you seem to desire, a goal you seem to aim for, in front of people's eyes and they will take the appearance for reality. Once their eyes focus on the decoy, they will fail to notice what you are really up to. In seduction, set up conflicting signals, such as desire and indifference, and you not only throw them off the scent, you inflame their desire to possess you.

A tactic that is often effective in setting up a red herring is to appear to support an idea or cause that is actually contrary to your own sentiments. (Bismarck used this to great effect in his speech in 1850.) Most people will believe you have experienced a change of heart, since it is so unusual to play so lightly with something as emotional as one's opinions and values. The same applies for any decoyed object of desire: Seem to want something in which you are actually not at all interested and your enemies will be thrown off the scent, making all kinds of errors in their calculations.

During the War of the Spanish Succession in 1711, the Duke of Marlborough, head of the English army, wanted to destroy a key French fort, because it protected a vital thoroughfare into France. Yet he knew that if he destroyed it, the French would realize what he wanted—to advance down that road. Instead, then, he merely captured the fort, and garrisoned it with some of his troops, making it appear as if he wanted it for some purpose of his own. The French attacked the fort and the duke let them recapture it. Once they had it back, though, *they* destroyed it, figuring that the duke had wanted it for some important reason. Now that the fort was gone, the road was unprotected, and Marlborough could easily march into France.

Use this tactic in the following manner: Hide your intentions not by closing up (with the risk of appearing secretive, and making people suspicious) but by talking endlessly about your desires and goals—just not your real ones. You will kill three birds with one stone: You appear friendly, open, and trusting; you conceal your intentions; and you send your rivals on time-consuming wild-goose chases.

Another powerful tool in throwing people off the scent is false sincerity. People easily mistake sincerity for honesty. Remember—their first instinct is to trust appearances, and since they value honesty and *want* to believe in the honesty of those around them, they will rarely doubt you or see through your act. Seeming to believe what you say gives your words great weight. This is how Iago deceived and destroyed Othello: Given the depth of his emotions, the apparent sincerity of his concerns about Desdemona's supposed infidelity, how could Othello distrust him? This is also how the great con artist Yellow Kid Weil pulled the wool over suckers' eyes: Seeming to believe so deeply in the decoyed object he was dangling in front of them (a phony stock, a touted racehorse), he made its reality hard to doubt. It is important, of course, not to go too far in this area. Sincerity is a tricky tool: Appear overpassionate and you raise suspicions. Be measured and believable or your ruse will seem the put-on that it is.

To make your false sincerity an effective weapon in concealing your intentions, espouse a belief in honesty and forthrightness as important social values. Do this as publicly as possible. Emphasize your position on this subject by occasionally divulging some heartfelt thought—though only one that is actually meaningless or irrelevant, of course. Napoleon's minister Talleyrand was a master at taking people into his confidence by revealing some apparent secret. This feigned confidence—a decoy—would then elicit a real confidence on the other person's part.

Remember: The best deceivers do everything they can to cloak their roguish qualities. They cultivate an air of honesty in one area to disguise their dishonesty in others. Honesty is merely another decoy in their arsenal of weapons.

PART II: USE SMOKE SCREENS TO DISGUISE YOUR ACTIONS

Deception is always the best strategy, but the best deceptions require a screen of smoke to distract people's attention from your real purpose. The bland exterior—like the unreadable poker face—is often the perfect smoke screen, hiding your intentions behind the comfortable and familiar. If you lead the sucker down a familiar path, he won't catch on when you lead him into a trap.

OBSERVANCE OF THE LAW 1

In 1910, a Mr. Sam Geezil of Chicago sold his warehouse business for close to $1 million. He settled down to semiretirement and the managing of his many properties, but deep inside he itched for the old days of deal-making. One day a young man named Joseph Weil visited his office, wanting to buy an apartment he had up for sale. Geezil explained the terms: The price was $8,000, but he only required a down payment of $2,000. Weil said he would sleep on it, but he came back the following day and offered to pay the full $8,000 in cash, if Geezil could wait a couple of days, until a deal Weil was working on came through. Even in semiretirement, a clever businessman like Geezil was curious as to how Weil would be able to come up with so much cash (roughly $150,000 today) so quickly. Weil seemed reluctant to say, and quickly changed the subject, but Geezil was persistent. Finally, after assurances of confidentiality, Weil told Geezil the following story.

Weil's uncle was the secretary to a coterie of multimillionaire financiers. These wealthy gentlemen had purchased a hunting lodge in Michigan ten years ago, at a cheap price. They had not used the lodge for a few years, so they had decided to sell it and had asked Weil's uncle to get whatever he could for it. For reasons—good reasons—of his own, the uncle had been nursing a grudge against the millionaires for years; this was his chance to get back at them. He would sell the property for $35,000 to a set-up man (whom it was Weil's job to find). The financiers were too wealthy to worry about this low price. The set-up man would then turn around and sell the property again for its real price, around $155,000. The uncle, Weil, and the third man would split the profits from this second sale. It was all legal and for a good cause—the uncle's just retribution.

Geezil had heard enough: He wanted to be the set-up buyer. Weil was reluctant to involve him, but Geezil would not back down: The idea of a large profit, plus a little adventure, had him champing at the bit. Weil explained that Geezil would have to put up the $35,000 in cash to bring the deal off. Geezil, a millionaire, said he could get the money with a snap of his fingers. Weil finally relented and agreed to arrange a meeting between the uncle, Geezil, and the financiers, in the town of Galesburg, Illinois.

On the train ride to Galesburg, Geezil met the uncle—an impressive

among you, but only
the worshippers of
Ba'al." Then he went in
to offer sacrifices and
burnt offerings.
Now Jehu had
stationed eighty men
outside, and said, "The
man who allows any of
those whom I give into
your hands to escape
shall forfeit his life." So
as soon as he had made
an end of offering the
burnt offering, Jehu
said to the guard and to
the officers, "Go in and
slay them; let not a man
escape."
So when they put them
to the sword, the guard
and the officers cast
them out and went into
the inner room of the
house of Ba'al and they
brought out the pillar
that was in the house of
Ba'al and burned it.
And they demolished
the pillar of Ba'al and
demolished the house
of Ba'al, and made it a
latrine to this day.
Thus Jehu wiped out
Ba'al from Israel.

OLD TESTAMENT,
2 KINGS 10:18–28

man, with whom he avidly discussed business. Weil also brought along a companion, a somewhat paunchy man named George Gross. Weil explained to Geezil that he himself was a boxing trainer, that Gross was one of the promising prizefighters he trained, and that he had asked Gross to come along to make sure the fighter stayed in shape. For a promising fighter, Gross was unimpressive looking—he had gray hair and a beer belly—but Geezil was so excited about the deal that he didn't really think about the man's flabby appearance.

Once in Galesburg, Weil and his uncle went to fetch the financiers while Geezil waited in a hotel room with Gross, who promptly put on his boxing trunks. As Geezil half watched, Gross began to shadowbox. Distracted as he was, Geezil ignored how badly the boxer wheezed after a few minutes of exercise, although his style seemed real enough. An hour later, Weil and his uncle reappeared with the financiers, an impressive, intimidating group of men, all wearing fancy suits. The meeting went well and the financiers agreed to sell the lodge to Geezil, who had already had the $35,000 wired to a local bank.

This minor business now settled, the financiers sat back in their chairs and began to banter about high finance, throwing out the name "J. P. Morgan" as if they knew the man. Finally one of them noticed the boxer in the corner of the room. Weil explained what he was doing there. The financier countered that he too had a boxer in his entourage, whom he named. Weil laughed brazenly and exclaimed that his man could easily knock out their man. Conversation escalated into argument. In the heat of passion, Weil challenged the men to a bet. The financiers eagerly agreed and left to get their man ready for a fight the next day.

As soon as they had left, the uncle yelled at Weil, right in front of Geezil: They did not have enough money to bet with, and once the financiers discovered this, the uncle would be fired. Weil apologized for getting him in this mess, but he had a plan: He knew the other boxer well, and with a little bribe, they could fix the fight. But where would the money come from for the bet? the uncle replied. Without it they were as good as dead. Finally Geezil had heard enough. Unwilling to jeopardize *his* deal with any ill will, he offered his own $35,000 cash for part of the bet. Even if he lost that, he would wire for more money and still make a profit on the sale of the lodge. The uncle and nephew thanked him. With their own $15,000 and Geezil's $35,000 they would manage to have enough for the bet. That evening, as Geezil watched the two boxers rehearse the fix in the hotel room, his mind reeled at the killing he was going to make from both the boxing match and the sale of the lodge.

The fight took place in a gym the next day. Weil handled the cash, which was placed for security in a locked box. Everything was proceeding as planned in the hotel room. The financiers were looking glum at how badly their fighter was doing, and Geezil was dreaming about the easy money he was about to make. Then, suddenly, a wild swing by the financier's fighter hit Gross hard in the face, knocking him down. When he hit the canvas, blood spurted from his mouth. He coughed, then lay still.

One of the financiers, a former doctor, checked his pulse; he was dead. The millionaires panicked: Everyone had to get out before the police arrived—they could all be charged with murder.

Terrified, Geezil hightailed it out of the gym and back to Chicago, leaving behind his $35,000 which he was only too glad to forget, for it seemed a small price to pay to avoid being implicated in a crime. He never wanted to see Weil or any of the others again.

After Geezil scurried out, Gross stood up, under his own steam. The blood that had spurted from his mouth came from a ball filled with chicken blood and hot water that he had hidden in his cheek. The whole affair had been masterminded by Weil, better known as "the Yellow Kid," one of the most creative con artists in history. Weil split the $35,000 with the financiers and the boxers (all fellow con artists)—a nice little profit for a few days' work.

SNEAK ACROSS THE OCEAN IN BROAD DAYLIGHT

This means to create a front that eventually becomes imbued with an atmosphere or impression of familiarity, within which the strategist may maneuver unseen while all eyes are trained to see obvious familiarities.

"THE THIRTY-SIX STRATEGIES," QUOTED IN THE JAPANESE ART OF WAR, THOMAS CLEARY, 1991

Interpretation

The Yellow Kid had staked out Geezil as the perfect sucker long before he set up the con. He knew the boxing-match scam would be the perfect ruse to separate Geezil from his money quickly and definitively. But he also knew that if he had begun by trying to interest Geezil in the boxing match, he would have failed miserably. He had to conceal his intentions and switch attention, create a smoke screen—in this case the sale of the lodge.

On the train ride and in the hotel room Geezil's mind had been completely occupied with the pending deal, the easy money, the chance to hobnob with wealthy men. He had failed to notice that Gross was out of shape and middle-aged at best. Such is the distracting power of a smoke screen. Engrossed in the business deal, Geezil's attention was easily diverted to the boxing match, but only at a point when it was already too late for him to notice the details that would have given Gross away. The match, after all, now depended on a bribe rather than on the boxer's physical condition. And Geezil was so distracted at the end by the illusion of the boxer's death that he completely forgot about his money.

Learn from the Yellow Kid: The familiar, inconspicuous front is the perfect smoke screen. Approach your mark with an idea that seems ordinary enough—a business deal, financial intrigue. The sucker's mind is distracted, his suspicions allayed. That is when you gently guide him onto the second path, the slippery slope down which he slides helplessly into your trap.

OBSERVANCE OF THE LAW II

In the mid-1920s, the powerful warlords of Ethiopia were coming to the realization that a young man of the nobility named Haile Selassie, also known as Ras Tafari, was outcompeting them all and nearing the point where he could proclaim himself their leader, unifying the country for the first time in decades. Most of his rivals could not understand how this wispy, quiet, mild-mannered man had been able to take control. Yet in

1927, Selassie was able to summon the warlords, one at a time, to come to Addis Ababa to declare their loyalty and recognize him as leader.

Some hurried, some hesitated, but only one, Dejazmach Balcha of Sidamo, dared defy Selassie totally. A blustery man, Balcha was a great warrior, and he considered the new leader weak and unworthy. He pointedly stayed away from the capital. Finally Selassie, in his gentle but stern way, commanded Balcha to come. The warlord decided to obey, but in doing so he would turn the tables on this pretender to the Ethiopian throne: He would come to Addis Ababa at his own speed, and with an army of 10,000 men, a force large enough to defend himself, perhaps even start a civil war. Stationing this formidable force in a valley three miles from the capital, he waited, as a king would. Selassie would have to come to him.

Selassie did indeed send emissaries, asking Balcha to attend an afternoon banquet in his honor. But Balcha, no fool, knew history—he knew that previous kings and lords of Ethiopia had used banquets as a trap. Once he was there and full of drink, Selassie would have him arrested or murdered. To signal his understanding of the situation, he agreed to come to the banquet, but only if he could bring his personal bodyguard—600 of his best soldiers, all armed and ready to defend him and themselves. To Balcha's surprise, Selassie answered with the utmost politeness that he would be honored to play host to such warriors.

On the way to the banquet, Balcha warned his soldiers not to get drunk and to be on their guard. When they arrived at the palace, Selassie was his charming best. He deferred to Balcha, treated him as if he desperately needed his approval and cooperation. But Balcha refused to be charmed, and he warned Selassie that if he did not return to his camp by nightfall, his army had orders to attack the capital. Selassie reacted as if hurt by his mistrust. Over the meal, when it came time for the traditional singing of songs in honor of Ethiopia's leaders, he made a point of allowing only songs honoring the warlord of Sidamo. It seemed to Balcha that Selassie was scared, intimidated by this great warrior who could not be outwitted. Sensing the change, Balcha believed that he would be the one to call the shots in the days to come.

At the end of the afternoon, Balcha and his soldiers began their march back to camp amidst cheers and gun salutes. Looking back to the capital over his shoulder, he planned his strategy—how his own soldiers would march through the capital in triumph within weeks, and Selassie would be put in his place, his place being either prison or death. When Balcha came in sight of his camp, however, he saw that something was terribly wrong. Where before there had been colorful tents stretching as far as the eye could see, now there was nothing, only smoke from doused fires. What devil's magic was this?

A witness told Balcha what had happened. During the banquet, a large army, commanded by an ally of Selassie's, had stolen up on Balcha's encampment by a side route he had not seen. This army had not come to fight, however: Knowing that Balcha would have heard a noisy battle and hurried back with his 600-man bodyguard, Selassie had armed his own troops with baskets of gold and cash. They had surrounded Balcha's army and proceeded to purchase every last one of their weapons. Those who refused were easily intimidated. Within a few hours, Balcha's entire force had been disarmed and scattered in all directions.

Realizing his danger, Balcha decided to march south with his 600 soldiers to regroup, but the same army that had disarmed his soldiers blocked his way. The other way out was to march on the capital, but Selassie had set a large army to defend it. Like a chess player, he had predicted Balcha's moves, and had checkmated him. For the first time in his life, Balcha surrendered. To repent his sins of pride and ambition, he agreed to enter a monastery.

Interpretation

Throughout Selassie's long reign, no one could quite figure him out. Ethiopians like their leaders fierce, but Selassie, who wore the front of a gentle, peace-loving man, lasted longer than any of them. Never angry or impatient, he lured his victims with sweet smiles, lulling them with charm and obsequiousness before he attacked. In the case of Balcha, Selassie played on the man's wariness, his suspicion that the banquet was a trap—which in fact it was, but not the one he expected. Selassie's way of allaying Balcha's fears—letting him bring his bodyguard to the banquet, giving him top billing there, making him feel in control—created a thick smoke screen, concealing the real action three miles away.

Remember: The paranoid and wary are often the easiest to deceive. Win their trust in one area and you have a smoke screen that blinds their view in another, letting you creep up and level them with a devastating blow. A helpful or apparently honest gesture, or one that implies the other person's superiority—these are perfect diversionary devices.

Properly set up, the smoke screen is a weapon of great power. It enabled the gentle Selassie to totally destroy his enemy, without firing a single bullet.

> *Do not underestimate the power of Tafari. He creeps*
> *like a mouse but he has jaws like a lion.*
> *Balcha of Sidamo's last words before entering the monastery*

KEYS TO POWER

If you believe that deceivers are colorful folk who mislead with elaborate lies and tall tales, you are greatly mistaken. The best deceivers utilize a bland and inconspicuous front that calls no attention to themselves. They know that extravagant words and gestures immediately raise suspicion. Instead, they envelop their mark in the familiar, the banal, the harmless. In Yellow Kid Weil's dealings with Sam Geezil, the familiar was a business deal. In the Ethiopian case, it was Selassie's misleading obsequiousness—exactly what Balcha would have expected from a weaker warlord.

Once you have lulled your suckers' attention with the familiar, they will not notice the deception being perpetrated behind their backs. This derives from a simple truth: people can only focus on one thing at a time. It is really too difficult for them to imagine that the bland and harmless person they are dealing with is simultaneously setting up something else. The grayer and more uniform the smoke in your smoke screen, the better it conceals your intentions. In the decoy and red herring devices discussed in Part I, you actively distract people; in the smoke screen, you lull your victims, drawing them into your web. Because it is so hypnotic, this is often the best way of concealing your intentions.

The simplest form of smoke screen is facial expression. Behind a bland, unreadable exterior, all sorts of mayhem can be planned, without detection. This is a weapon that the most powerful men in history have learned to perfect. It was said that no one could read Franklin D. Roosevelt's face. Baron James Rothschild made a lifelong practice of disguising his real thoughts behind bland smiles and nondescript looks. Stendhal wrote of Talleyrand, "Never was a face less of a barometer." Henry Kissinger would bore his opponents around the negotiating table to tears with his monotonous voice, his blank look, his endless recitations of details; then, as their eyes glazed over, he would suddenly hit them with a list of bold terms. Caught off-guard, they would be easily intimidated. As one poker manual explains it, "While playing his hand, the good player is seldom an actor. Instead he practices a bland behavior that minimizes readable patterns, frustrates and confuses opponents, permits greater concentration."

An adaptable concept, the smoke screen can be practiced on a number of levels, all playing on the psychological principles of distraction and misdirection. One of the most effective smoke screens is the *noble gesture*. People want to believe apparently noble gestures are genuine, for the belief is pleasant. They rarely notice how deceptive these gestures can be.

The art dealer Joseph Duveen was once confronted with a terrible problem. The millionaires who had paid so dearly for Duveen's paintings were running out of wall space, and with inheritance taxes getting ever higher, it seemed unlikely that they would keep buying. The solution was the National Gallery of Art in Washington, D.C., which Duveen helped create in 1937 by getting Andrew Mellon to donate his collection to it. The National Gallery was the perfect front for Duveen. In one gesture, his clients avoided taxes, cleared wall space for new purchases, and reduced the number of paintings on the market, maintaining the upward pressure on their prices. All this while the donors created the appearance of being public benefactors.

Another effective smoke screen is the *pattern*, the establishment of a series of actions that seduce the victim into believing you will continue in the same way. The pattern plays on the psychology of anticipation: Our behavior conforms to patterns, or so we like to think.

In 1878 the American robber baron Jay Gould created a company that began to threaten the monopoly of the telegraph company Western Union. The directors of Western Union decided to buy Gould's company up—

they had to spend a hefty sum, but they figured they had managed to rid themselves of an irritating competitor. A few months later, though, Gould was it at again, complaining he had been treated unfairly. He started up a second company to compete with Western Union and its new acquisition. The same thing happened again: Western Union bought him out to shut him up. Soon the pattern began for the third time, but now Gould went for the jugular: He suddenly staged a bloody takeover struggle and managed to gain complete control of Western Union. He had established a pattern that had tricked the company's directors into thinking his goal was to be bought out at a handsome rate. Once they paid him off, they relaxed and failed to notice that he was actually playing for higher stakes. The pattern is powerful in that it deceives the other person into expecting the opposite of what you are really doing.

Another psychological weakness on which to construct a smoke screen is the tendency to mistake appearances for reality—the feeling that if someone seems to belong to your group, their belonging must be real. This habit makes the *seamless blend* a very effective front. The trick is simple: You simply blend in with those around you. The better you blend, the less suspicious you become. During the Cold War of the 1950s and '60s, as is now notorious, a slew of British civil servants passed secrets to the Soviets. They went undetected for years because they were apparently decent chaps, had gone to all the right schools, and fit the old-boy network perfectly. Blending in is the perfect smoke screen for spying. The better you do it, the better you can conceal your intentions.

Remember: It takes patience and humility to dull your brilliant colors, to put on the mask of the inconspicuous. Do not despair at having to wear such a bland mask—it is often your unreadability that draws people to you and makes you appear a person of power.

Image: A Sheep's Skin.
A sheep never marauds,
a sheep never deceives,
a sheep is magnificently
dumb and docile. With a
sheepskin on his back,
a fox can pass right
into the chicken coop.

Authority: Have you ever heard of a skillful general, who intends to surprise a citadel, announcing his plan to his enemy? Conceal your purpose and hide your progress; do not disclose the extent of your designs until they cannot be opposed, until the combat is over. Win the victory before you declare the war. In a word, imitate those warlike people whose designs are not known except by the ravaged country through which they have passed. (Ninon de Lenclos, 1623–1706)

REVERSAL

No smoke screen, red herring, false sincerity, or any other diversionary device will succeed in concealing your intentions if you already have an established reputation for deception. And as you get older and achieve success, it often becomes increasingly difficult to disguise your cunning. Everyone knows you practice deception; persist in playing naive and you run the risk of seeming the rankest hypocrite, which will severely limit your room to maneuver. In such cases it is better to own up, to appear the honest rogue, or, better, the repentant rogue. Not only will you be admired for your frankness, but, most wonderful and strange of all, you will be able to continue your stratagems.

As P. T. Barnum, the nineteenth-century king of humbuggery, grew older, he learned to embrace his reputation as a grand deceiver. At one point he organized a buffalo hunt in New Jersey, complete with Indians and a few imported buffalo. He publicized the hunt as genuine, but it came off as so completely fake that the crowd, instead of getting angry and asking for their money back, was greatly amused. They knew Barnum pulled tricks all the time; that was the secret of his success, and they loved him for it. Learning a lesson from this affair, Barnum stopped concealing all of his devices, even revealing his deceptions in a tell-all autobiography. As Kierkegaard wrote, "The world wants to be deceived."

Finally, although it is wiser to divert attention from your purposes by presenting a bland, familiar exterior, there are times when the colorful, conspicuous gesture is the right diversionary tactic. The great charlatan mountebanks of seventeenth- and eighteenth-century Europe used humor and entertainment to deceive their audiences. Dazzled by a great show, the public would not notice the charlatans' real intentions. Thus the star charlatan himself would appear in town in a night-black coach drawn by black horses. Clowns, tightrope walkers, and star entertainers would accompany him, pulling people in to his demonstrations of elixirs and quack potions. The charlatan made entertainment seem like the business of the day; the business of the day was actually the sale of the elixirs and quack potions.

Spectacle and entertainment, clearly, are excellent devices to conceal your intentions, but they cannot be used indefinitely. The public grows tired and suspicious, and eventually catches on to the trick. And indeed the charlatans had to move quickly from town to town, before word spread that the potions were useless and the entertainment a trick. Powerful people with bland exteriors, on the other hand—the Talleyrands, the Rothschilds, the Selassies—can practice their deceptions in the same place throughout their lifetimes. Their act never wears thin, and rarely causes suspicion. The colorful smoke screen should be used cautiously, then, and only when the occasion is right.

LAW
4

ALWAYS SAY LESS

THAN NECESSARY

JUDGMENT

When you are trying to impress people with words, the more you say, the more common you appear, and the less in control. Even if you are saying something banal, it will seem original if you make it vague, open-ended, and sphinxlike. Powerful people impress and intimidate by saying less. The more you say, the more likely you are to say something foolish.

Gnaeus Marcius, also known as Coriolanus, was a great military hero of ancient Rome. In the first half of the fifth century B.C. he won many important battles, saving the city from calamity time and time again. Because he spent most of his time on the battlefield, few Romans knew him personally, making him something of a legendary figure.

In 454 B.C., Coriolanus decided it was time to exploit his reputation and enter politics. He stood for election to the high rank of consul. Candidates for this position traditionally made a public address early in the race, and when Coriolanus came before the people, he began by displaying the dozens of scars he had accumulated over seventeen years of fighting for Rome. Few in the crowd really heard the lengthy speech that followed; those scars, proof of his valor and patriotism, moved the people to tears. Coriolanus's election seemed certain.

When the polling day arrived, however, Coriolanus made an entry into the forum escorted by the entire senate and by the city's patricians, the aristocracy. The common people who saw this were disturbed by such a blustering show of confidence on election day.

And then Coriolanus spoke again, mostly addressing the wealthy citizens who had accompanied him. His words were arrogant and insolent. Claiming certain victory in the vote, he boasted of his battlefield exploits, made sour jokes that appealed only to the patricians, voiced angry accusations against his opponents, and speculated on the riches he would bring to Rome. This time the people listened: They had not realized that this legendary soldier was also a common braggart.

News of Coriolanus's second speech spread quickly through Rome, and the people turned out in great numbers to make sure he was not elected. Defeated, Coriolanus returned to the battlefield, bitter and vowing revenge on the common folk who had voted against him. Some weeks later a large shipment of grain arrived in Rome. The senate was ready to distribute this food to the people, for free, but just as they were preparing to vote on the question Coriolanus appeared on the scene and took the senate floor. The distribution, he argued, would have a harmful effect on the city as a whole. Several senators appeared won over, and the vote on the distribution fell into doubt. Coriolanus did not stop there: He went on to condemn the concept of democracy itself. He advocated getting rid of the people's representatives—the tribunes—and turning over the governing of the city to the patricians.

When word of Coriolanus's latest speech reached the people, their anger knew no bounds. The tribunes were sent to the senate to demand that Coriolanus appear before them. He refused. Riots broke out all over the city. The senate, fearing the people's wrath, finally voted in favor of the grain distribution. The tribunes were appeased, but the people still demanded that Coriolanus speak to them and apologize. If he repented, and agreed to keep his opinions to himself, he would be allowed to return to the battlefield.

Coriolanus did appear one last time before the people, who listened to him in rapt silence. He started slowly and softly, but as the speech went on, he became more and more blunt. Yet again he hurled insults! His tone was arrogant, his expression disdainful. The more he spoke, the angrier the people became. Finally they shouted him down and silenced him.

The tribunes conferred, condemned Coriolanus to death, and ordered the magistrates to take him at once to the top of the Tarpeian rock and throw him over. The delighted crowd seconded the decision. The patricians, however, managed to intervene, and the sentence was commuted to a lifelong banishment. When the people found out that Rome's great military hero would never return to the city, they celebrated in the streets. In fact no one had ever seen such a celebration, not even after the defeat of a foreign enemy.

Interpretation

Before his entrance into politics, the name of Coriolanus evoked awe.

His battlefield accomplishments showed him as a man of great bravery. Since the citizens knew little about him, all kinds of legends became attached to his name. The moment he appeared before the Roman citizens, however, and spoke his mind, all that grandeur and mystery vanished. He bragged and blustered like a common soldier. He insulted and slandered people, as if he felt threatened and insecure. Suddenly he was not at all what the people had imagined. The discrepancy between the legend and the reality proved immensely disappointing to those who wanted to believe in their hero. The more Coriolanus said, the less powerful he appeared—a person who cannot control his words shows that he cannot control himself, and is unworthy of respect.

Had Coriolanus said less, the people would never have had cause to be offended by him, would never have known his true feelings. He would have maintained his powerful aura, would certainly have been elected consul, and would have been able to accomplish his antidemocratic goals. But the human tongue is a beast that few can master. It strains constantly to break out of its cage, and if it is not tamed, it will run wild and cause you grief. Power cannot accrue to those who squander their treasure of words.

> *Oysters open completely when the moon is full; and when the crab sees one it throws a piece of stone or seaweed into it and the oyster cannot close again so that it serves the crab for meat. Such is the fate of him who opens his mouth too much and thereby puts himself at the mercy of the listener.*
> *Leonardo da Vinci, 1452–1519*

OBSERVANCE OF THE LAW

In the court of Louis XIV, nobles and ministers would spend days and nights debating issues of state. They would confer, argue, make and break alliances, and argue again, until finally the critical moment arrived: Two of them would be chosen to represent the different sides to Louis himself, who would decide what should be done. After these persons were chosen,

question from Kissinger—Lord snapped, "Damn it, yes, it's the best I can do." To which Kissinger replied: "Fine, then I guess I'll read it this time."
KISSINGER,
WALTER ISAACSON,
1992

The King [Louis XIV] maintains the most impenetrable secrecy about affairs of State. The ministers attend council meetings, but he confides his plans to them only when he has reflected at length upon them and has come to a definite decision. I wish you might see the King. His expression is inscrutable; his eyes like those of a fox. He never discusses State affairs except with his ministers in Council. When he speaks to courtiers he refers only to their respective prerogatives or duties. Even the most frivolous of his utterances has the air of being the pronouncement of an oracle.
PRIMI VISCONTI,
QUOTED IN
LOUIS XIV,
LOUIS BERTRAND,
1928

everyone would argue some more: How should the issues be phrased? What would appeal to Louis, what would annoy him? At what time of day should the representatives approach him, and in what part of the Versailles palace? What expression should they have on their faces?

Finally, after all this was settled, the fateful moment would finally arrive. The two men would approach Louis—always a delicate matter—and when they finally had his ear, they would talk about the issue at hand, spelling out the options in detail.

Louis would listen in silence, a most enigmatic look on his face. Finally, when each had finished his presentation and had asked for the king's opinion, he would look at them both and say, "I shall see." Then he would walk away.

The ministers and courtiers would never hear another word on this subject from the king—they would simply see the result, weeks later, when he would come to a decision and act. He would never bother to consult them on the matter again.

Interpretation

Louis XIV was a man of very few words. His most famous remark is *"L'état, c'est moi"* ("I am the state"); nothing could be more pithy yet more eloquent. His infamous "I shall see" was one of several extremely short phrases that he would apply to all manner of requests.

Louis was not always this way; as a young man he was known for talking at length, delighting in his own eloquence. His later taciturnity was self-imposed, an act, a mask he used to keep everybody below him off-balance. No one knew exactly where he stood, or could predict his reactions. No one could try to deceive him by saying what they thought he wanted to hear, because no one *knew* what he wanted to hear. As they talked on and on to the silent Louis, they revealed more and more about themselves, information he would later use against them to great effect.

In the end, Louis's silence kept those around him terrified and under his thumb. It was one of the foundations of his power. As Saint-Simon wrote, "No one knew as well as he how to sell his words, his smile, even his glances. Everything in him was valuable because he created differences, and his majesty was enhanced by the sparseness of his words."

It is even more damaging for a minister to say foolish things than to do them.
Cardinal de Retz, 1613–1679

KEYS TO POWER

Power is in many ways a game of appearances, and when you say less than necessary, you inevitably appear greater and more powerful than you are. Your silence will make other people uncomfortable. Humans are machines of interpretation and explanation; they have to know what you are thinking. When you carefully control what you reveal, they cannot pierce your intentions or your meaning.

Your short answers and silences will put them on the defensive, and they will jump in, nervously filling the silence with all kinds of comments that will reveal valuable information about them and their weaknesses. They will leave a meeting with you feeling as if they had been robbed, and they will go home and ponder your every word. This extra attention to your brief comments will only add to your power.

Saying less than necessary is not for kings and statesmen only. In most areas of life, the less you say, the more profound and mysterious you appear. As a young man, the artist Andy Warhol had the revelation that it was generally impossible to get people to do what you wanted them to do by talking to them. They would turn against you, subvert your wishes, disobey you out of sheer perversity. He once told a friend, "I learned that you actually have more power when you shut up."

In his later life Warhol employed this strategy with great success. His interviews were exercises in oracular speech: He would say something vague and ambiguous, and the interviewer would twist in circles trying to figure it out, imagining there was something profound behind his often meaningless phrases. Warhol rarely talked about his work; he let others do the interpreting. He claimed to have learned this technique from that master of enigma Marcel Duchamp, another twentieth-century artist who realized early on that the less he said about his work, the more people talked about it. And the more they talked, the more valuable his work became.

By saying less than necessary you create the appearance of meaning and power. Also, the less you say, the less risk you run of saying something foolish, even dangerous. In 1825 a new czar, Nicholas I, ascended the throne of Russia. A rebellion immediately broke out, led by liberals demanding that the country modernize—that its industries and civil structures catch up with the rest of Europe. Brutally crushing this rebellion (the Decembrist Uprising), Nicholas I sentenced one of its leaders, Kondraty Ryleyev, to death. On the day of the execution Ryleyev stood on the gallows, the noose around his neck. The trapdoor opened—but as Ryleyev dangled, the rope broke, dashing him to the ground. At the time, events like this were considered signs of providence or heavenly will, and a man saved from execution this way was usually pardoned. As Ryleyev got to his feet, bruised and dirtied but believing his neck had been saved, he called out to the crowd, "You see, in Russia they don't know how to do anything properly, not even how to make rope!"

A messenger immediately went to the Winter Palace with news of the failed hanging. Vexed by this disappointing turnabout, Nicholas I nevertheless began to sign the pardon. But then: "Did Ryleyev say anything after this miracle?" the czar asked the messenger. "Sire," the messenger replied, "he said that in Russia they don't even know how to make rope."

"In that case," said the Czar, "let us prove the contrary," and he tore up the pardon. The next day Ryleyev was hanged again. This time the rope did not break.

Learn the lesson: Once the words are out, you cannot take them back. Keep them under control. Be particularly careful with sarcasm: The momentary satisfaction you gain with your biting words will be outweighed by the price you pay.

Image:
The Oracle at Delphi.
When visitors consulted the
Oracle, the priestess would utter
a few enigmatic words that seemed
full of meaning and import. No one
disobeyed the words of the Oracle—
they held power over life and death.

Authority: Never start moving your own lips and teeth before the subordinates do. The longer I keep quiet, the sooner others move their lips and teeth. As they move their lips and teeth, I can thereby understand their real intentions. . . . If the sovereign is not mysterious, the ministers will find opportunity to take and take. (Han-fei-tzu, Chinese philosopher, third century B.C.)

REVERSAL

There are times when it is unwise to be silent. Silence can arouse suspicion and even insecurity, especially in your superiors; a vague or ambiguous comment can open you up to interpretations you had not bargained for. Silence and saying less than necessary must be practiced with caution, then, and in the right situations. It is occasionally wiser to imitate the court jester, who plays the fool but knows he is smarter than the king. He talks and talks and entertains, and no one suspects that he is more than just a fool.

Also, words can sometimes act as a kind of smoke screen for any deception you might practice. By bending your listener's ear with talk, you can distract and mesmerize them; the more you talk, in fact, the less suspicious of you they become. The verbose are not perceived as sly and manipulative but as helpless and unsophisticated. This is the reverse of the silent policy employed by the powerful: By talking more, and making yourself appear weaker and less intelligent than your mark, you can practice deception with greater ease.

5

SO MUCH DEPENDS ON
REPUTATION—GUARD IT
WITH YOUR LIFE

JUDGMENT

Reputation is the cornerstone of power. Through reputa-
tion alone you can intimidate and win; once it slips,
however, you are vulnerable, and will be attacked on all
sides. Make your reputation unassailable. Always be
alert to potential attacks and thwart them before they
happen. Meanwhile, learn to destroy your enemies by
opening holes in their own reputations. Then stand
aside and let public opinion hang them.

OBSERVANCE OF THE LAW I

During China's War of the Three Kingdoms (A.D. 207–265), the great general Chuko Liang, leading the forces of the Shu Kingdom, dispatched his vast army to a distant camp while he rested in a small town with a handful of soldiers. Suddenly sentinels hurried in with the alarming news that an enemy force of over 150,000 troops under Sima Yi was approaching. With only a hundred men to defend him, Chuko Liang's situation was hopeless. The enemy would finally capture this renowned leader.

Without lamenting his fate, or wasting time trying to figure out how he had been caught, Liang ordered his troops to take down their flags, throw open the city gates, and hide. He himself then took a seat on the most visible part of the city's wall, wearing a Taoist robe. He lit some incense, strummed his lute, and began to chant. Minutes later he could see the vast enemy army approaching, an endless phalanx of soldiers. Pretending not to notice them, he continued to sing and play the lute.

Soon the army stood at the town gates. At its head was Sima Yi, who instantly recognized the man on the wall.

Even so, as his soldiers itched to enter the unguarded town through its open gates, Sima Yi hesitated, held them back, and studied Liang on the wall. Then, he ordered an immediate and speedy retreat.

Interpretation

Chuko Liang was commonly known as the "Sleeping Dragon." His exploits in the War of the Three Kingdoms were legendary. Once a man claiming to be a disaffected enemy lieutenant came to his camp, offering help and information. Liang instantly recognized the situation as a setup; this man was a false deserter, and should be beheaded. At the last minute, though, as the ax was about to fall, Liang stopped the execution and offered to spare the man's life if he agreed to become a double agent. Grateful and terrified, the man agreed, and began supplying false information to the enemy. Liang won battle after battle.

On another occasion Liang stole a military seal and created false documents dispatching his enemy's troops to distant locations. Once the troops had dispersed, he was able to capture three cities, so that he controlled an entire corridor of the enemy's kingdom. He also once tricked the enemy into believing one of its best generals was a traitor, forcing the man to escape and join forces with Liang. The Sleeping Dragon carefully cultivated his reputation of being the cleverest man in China, one who always had a trick up his sleeve. As powerful as any weapon, this reputation struck fear into his enemy.

Sima Yi had fought against Chuko Liang dozens of times and knew him well. When he came on the empty city, with Liang praying on the wall, he was stunned. The Taoist robes, the chanting, the incense—this had to be a game of intimidation. The man was obviously taunting him, daring him to walk into a trap. The game was so obvious that for one moment it crossed Yi's mind that Liang actually *was* alone, and desperate. But so great was his fear of Liang that he dared not risk finding out. Such is the power of reputation. It can put a vast army on the defensive, even force them into retreat, without a single arrow being fired.

> *For, as Cicero says, even those who argue against fame still want the books they write against it to bear their name in the title and hope to become famous for despising it. Everything else is subject to barter: we will let our friends have our goods and our lives if need be; but a case of sharing our fame and making someone else the gift of our reputation is hardly to be found.*
>
> *Montaigne 1533–1592*

OBSERVANCE OF THE LAW II

In 1841 the young P. T. Barnum, trying to establish his reputation as America's premier showman, decided to purchase the American Museum in Manhattan and turn it into a collection of curiosities that would secure his fame. The problem was that he had no money. The museum's asking price was $15,000, but Barnum was able to put together a proposal that appealed to the institution's owners even though it replaced cash up front with dozens of guarantees and references. The owners came to a verbal agreement with Barnum, but at the last minute, the principal partner changed his mind, and the museum and its collection were sold to the directors of Peale's Museum. Barnum was infuriated, but the partner explained that business was business—the museum had been sold to Peale's because Peale's had a reputation and Barnum had none.

Barnum immediately decided that if he had no reputation to bank on, his only recourse was to ruin the reputation of Peale's. Accordingly he launched a letter-writing campaign in the newspapers, calling the owners a bunch of "broken-down bank directors" who had no idea how to run a museum or entertain people. He warned the public against buying Peale's stock, since the business's purchase of another museum would invariably spread its resources thin. The campaign was effective, the stock plummeted, and with no more confidence in Peale's track record and reputation, the owners of the American Museum reneged on their deal and sold the whole thing to Barnum.

It took years for Peale's to recover, and they never forgot what Barnum had done. Mr. Peale himself decided to attack Barnum by building a reputation for "high-brow entertainment," promoting his museum's programs as more scientific than those of his vulgar competitor. Mesmerism (hypnotism) was one of Peale's "scientific" attractions, and for a while it drew big crowds and was quite successful. To fight back, Barnum decided to attack Peale's reputation yet again.

Barnum organized a rival mesmeric performance in which he himself apparently put a little girl into a trance. Once she seemed to have fallen deeply under, he tried to hypnotize members of the audience—but no matter how hard he tried, none of the spectators fell under his spell, and many of them began to laugh. A frustrated Barnum finally announced that to prove the little girl's trance was real, he would cut off one of her fingers

*many a sheep
Who'd injured me in
no respect,
And even in my time
been known to try
Shepherd pie.
If need be, then, I'll die.
Yet I suspect
That others also ought
to own their sins.
It's only fair that all
should do their best
To single out the
guiltiest."
"Sire, you're too good
a king," the Fox begins;
"Such scruples are too
delicate. My word,
To eat sheep, that
profane and vulgar
herd,
That's sin? Nay, Sire,
enough for such a crew
To be devoured by
such as you;
While of the shepherds
we may say
That they deserved the
worst they got,
Theirs being the lot
that over us beasts plot
A flimsy dream-
begotten sway."
Thus spake the Fox,
and toady cheers rose
high,
While none dared cast
too cold an eye
On Tiger's, Bear's, and
other eminences'
Most unpardonable
offences.
Each, of never mind
what currish breed,
Was really a saint, they
all agreed.
Then came the Ass, to
say: "I do recall
How once I crossed an
abbey-mead
Where hunger, grass in
plenty, and withal,
I have no doubt, some
imp of greed,
Assailed me, and I
shaved a tongue's-
breadth wide
Where frankly I'd no
right to any grass."*

All forthwith fell full
cry upon the Ass:
A Wolf of some book-
learning testified
That that curst beast
must suffer their
despite,
That gallskinned
author of their piteous
plight.
They judged him fit
for hought but
gallows-bait:
How vile, another's
grass to sequestrate!
His death alone could
expiate
A crime so heinous, as
full well he learns.
The court, as you're of
great or poor estate,
Will paint you either
white or black by turns.

THE BEST FABLES
OF LA FONTAINE,
JEAN DE LA FONTAINE,
1621–1695

without her noticing. But as he sharpened the knife, the little girl's eyes popped open and she ran away, to the audience's delight. He repeated this and other parodies for several weeks. Soon no one could take Peale's show seriously, and attendance went way down. Within a few weeks, the show closed. Over the next few years Barnum established a reputation for audacity and consummate showmanship that lasted his whole life. Peale's reputation, on the other hand, never recovered.

Interpretation

Barnum used two different tactics to ruin Peale's reputation. The first was simple: He sowed doubts about the museum's stability and solvency. Doubt is a powerful weapon: Once you let it out of the bag with insidious rumors, your opponents are in a horrible dilemma. On the one hand they can deny the rumors, even prove that you have slandered them. But a layer of suspicion will remain: Why are they defending themselves so desperately? Maybe the rumor has some truth to it? If, on the other hand, they take the high road and ignore you, the doubts, unrefuted, will be even stronger. If done correctly, the sowing of rumors can so infuriate and unsettle your rivals that in defending themselves they will make numerous mistakes. This is the perfect weapon for those who have no reputation of their own to work from.

Once Barnum did have a reputation of his own, he used the second, gentler tactic, the fake hypnotism demonstration: He ridiculed his rivals' reputation. This too was extremely successful. Once you have a solid base of respect, ridiculing your opponent both puts him on the defensive and draws more attention to you, enhancing your own reputation. Outright slander and insult are too strong at this point; they are ugly, and may hurt you more than help you. But gentle barbs and mockery suggest that you have a strong enough sense of your own worth to enjoy a good laugh at your rival's expense. A humorous front can make you out as a harmless entertainer while poking holes in the reputation of your rival.

It is easier to cope with a bad conscience than with a bad reputation.
Friedrich Nietzsche, 1844–1900

KEYS TO POWER

The people around us, even our closest friends, will always to some extent remain mysterious and unfathomable. Their characters have secret recesses that they never reveal. The unknowableness of other people could prove disturbing if we thought about it long enough, since it would make it impossible for us really to judge other people. So we prefer to ignore this fact, and to judge people on their appearances, on what is most visible to our eyes—clothes, gestures, words, actions. In the social realm, appearances are the barometer of almost all of our judgments, and you must never be misled into believing otherwise. One false slip, one awkward or sudden change in your appearance, can prove disastrous.

This is the reason for the supreme importance of making and maintaining a reputation that is of your own creation.

That reputation will protect you in the dangerous game of appearances, distracting the probing eyes of others from knowing what you are really like, and giving you a degree of control over how the world judges you—a powerful position to be in. Reputation has a power like magic: With one stroke of its wand, it can double your strength. It can also send people scurrying away from you. Whether the exact same deeds appear brilliant or dreadful can depend entirely on the reputation of the doer.

In the ancient Chinese court of the Wei kingdom there was a man named Mi Tzu-hsia who had a reputation for supreme civility and graciousness. He became the ruler's favorite. It was a law in Wei that "whoever rides secretly in the ruler's coach shall have his feet cut off," but when Mi Tzu-hsia's mother fell ill, he used the royal coach to visit her, pretending that the ruler had given him permission. When the ruler found out, he said, "How dutiful is Mi Tzu-hsia! For his mother's sake he even forgot that he was committing a crime making him liable to lose his feet!"

Another time the two of them took a stroll in an orchard. Mi Tzu-hsia began eating a peach that he could not finish, and he gave the ruler the other half to eat. The ruler remarked, "You love me so much that you would even forget your own saliva taste and let me eat the rest of the peach!"

Later, however, envious fellow courtiers, spreading word that Mi Tzu-hsia was actually devious and arrogant, succeeded in damaging his reputation; the ruler came to see his actions in a new light. "This fellow once rode in my coach under pretense of my order," he told the courtiers angrily, "and another time he gave me a half-eaten peach." For the same actions that had charmed the ruler when he was the favorite, Mi Tzu-hsia now had to suffer the penalties. The fate of his feet depended solely on the strength of his reputation.

In the beginning, you must work to establish a reputation for one outstanding quality, whether generosity or honesty or cunning. This quality sets you apart and gets other people to talk about you. You then make your reputation known to as many people as possible (subtly, though; take care to build slowly, and with a firm foundation), and watch as it spreads like wildfire.

A solid reputation increases your presence and exaggerates your strengths without your having to spend much energy. It can also create an aura around you that will instill respect, even fear. In the fighting in the North African desert during World War II, the German general Erwin Rommel had a reputation for cunning and for deceptive maneuvering that struck terror into everyone who faced him. Even when his forces were depleted, and when British tanks outnumbered his by five to one, entire cities would be evacuated at the news of his approach.

As they say, your reputation inevitably precedes you, and if it inspires respect, a lot of your work is done for you before you arrive on the scene, or utter a single word.

Your success seems destined by your past triumphs. Much of the success of Henry Kissinger's shuttle diplomacy rested on his reputation for ironing out differences; no one wanted to be seen as so unreasonable that Kissinger could not sway him. A peace treaty seemed a fait accompli as soon as Kissinger's name became involved in the negotiations.

Make your reputation simple and base it on one sterling quality. This single quality—efficiency, say, or seductiveness—becomes a kind of calling card that announces your presence and places others under a spell. A reputation for honesty will allow you to practice all manner of deception. Casanova used his reputation as a great seducer to pave the way for his future conquests; women who had heard of his powers became immensely curious, and wanted to discover for themselves what had made him so romantically successful.

Perhaps you have already stained your reputation, so that you are prevented from establishing a new one. In such cases it is wise to associate with someone whose image counteracts your own, using their good name to whitewash and elevate yours. It is hard, for example, to erase a reputation for dishonesty by yourself; but a paragon of honesty can help. When P. T. Barnum wanted to clean up a reputation for promoting vulgar entertainment, he brought the singer Jenny Lind over from Europe. She had a stellar, high-class reputation, and the American tour Barnum sponsored for her greatly enhanced his own image. Similarly the great robber barons of nineteenth-century America were long unable to rid themselves of a reputation for cruelty and mean-spiritedness. Only when they began collecting art, so that the names of Morgan and Frick became permanently associated with those of da Vinci and Rembrandt, were they able to soften their unpleasant image.

Reputation is a treasure to be carefully collected and hoarded. Especially when you are first establishing it, you must protect it strictly, anticipating all attacks on it. Once it is solid, do not let yourself get angry or defensive at the slanderous comments of your enemies—that reveals insecurity, not confidence in your reputation. Take the high road instead, and never appear desperate in your self-defense. On the other hand, an attack on another man's reputation is a potent weapon, particularly when you have less power than he does. He has much more to lose in such a battle, and your own thus-far-small reputation gives him a small target when he tries to return your fire. Barnum used such campaigns to great effect in his early career. But this tactic must be practiced with skill; you must not seem to engage in petty vengeance. If you do not break your enemy's reputation cleverly, you will inadvertently ruin your own.

Thomas Edison, considered the inventor who harnessed electricity, believed that a workable system would have to be based on direct current (DC). When the Serbian scientist Nikola Tesla appeared to have succeeded in creating a system based on alternating current (AC), Edison was furious. He determined to ruin Tesla's reputation, by making the public believe that the AC system was inherently unsafe, and Tesla irresponsible in promoting it.

To this end he captured all kinds of household pets and electrocuted them to death with an AC current. When this wasn't enough, in 1890 he got New York State prison authorities to organize the world's first execution by electrocution, using an AC current. But Edison's electrocution experiments had all been with small creatures; the charge was too weak, and the man was only half killed. In perhaps the country's cruelest state-authorized execution, the procedure had to be repeated. It was an awful spectacle.

Although, in the long run, it is Edison's name that has survived, at the time his campaign damaged his own reputation more than Tesla's. He backed off. The lesson is simple—never go too far in attacks like these, for that will draw more attention to your own vengefulness than to the person you are slandering. When your own reputation is solid, use subtler tactics, such as satire and ridicule, to weaken your opponent while making you out as a charming rogue. The mighty lion toys with the mouse that crosses his path—any other reaction would mar his fearsome reputation.

Image:
A Mine Full of
Diamonds and Rubies.
You dug for it, you found it,
and your wealth is now assured.
Guard it with your life. Robbers and thieves
will appear from all sides. Never take your wealth
for granted, and constantly renew it—time
will diminish the jewels' luster,
and bury them from sight.

Authority: Therefore I should wish our courtier to bolster up his inherent worth with skill and cunning, and ensure that whenever he has to go where he is a stranger, he is preceded by a good reputation. . . . For the fame which appears to rest on the opinions of many fosters a certain unshakable belief in a man's worth which is then easily strengthened in minds already thus disposed and prepared. (Baldassare Castiglione, 1478–1529)

REVERSAL
There is no possible Reversal. Reputation is critical; there are no exceptions to this law. Perhaps, not caring what others think of you, you gain a reputation for insolence and arrogance, but that can be a valuable image in itself—Oscar Wilde used it to great advantage. Since we must live in society and must depend on the opinions of others, there is nothing to be gained by neglecting your reputation. By not caring how you are perceived, you let others decide this for you. Be the master of your fate, and also of your reputation.

COURT ATTENTION

AT ALL COST

JUDGMENT

Everything is judged by its appearance; what is unseen counts for nothing. Never let yourself get lost in the crowd, then, or buried in oblivion. Stand out. Be conspicuous, at all cost. Make yourself a magnet of attention by appearing larger, more colorful, more mysterious than the bland and timid masses.

PART I: SURROUND YOUR NAME WITH THE SENSATIONAL AND SCANDALOUS

Draw attention to yourself by creating an unforgettable, even controversial image. Court scandal. Do anything to make yourself seem larger than life and shine more brightly than those around you. Make no distinction between kinds of attention—notoriety of any sort will bring you power. Better to be slandered and attacked than ignored.

OBSERVANCE OF THE LAW

P. T. Barnum, America's premier nineteenth-century showman, started his career as an assistant to the owner of a circus, Aaron Turner. In 1836 the circus stopped in Annapolis, Maryland, for a series of performances. On the morning of opening day, Barnum took a stroll through town, wearing a new black suit. People started to follow him. Someone in the gathering crowd shouted out that he was the Reverend Ephraim K. Avery, infamous as a man acquitted of the charge of murder but still believed guilty by most Americans. The angry mob tore off Barnum's suit and was ready to lynch him. After desperate appeals, Barnum finally convinced them to follow him to the circus, where he could verify his identity.

Once there, old Turner confirmed that this was all a practical joke—he himself had spread the rumor that Barnum was Avery. The crowd dispersed, but Barnum, who had nearly been killed, was not amused. He wanted to know what could have induced his boss to play such a trick. "My dear Mr. Barnum," Turner replied, "it was all for our good. Remember, all we need to ensure success is notoriety." And indeed everyone in town was talking about the joke, and the circus was packed that night and every night it stayed in Annapolis. Barnum had learned a lesson he would never forget.

Barnum's first big venture of his own was the American Museum—a collection of curiosities, located in New York. One day a beggar approached Barnum in the street. Instead of giving him money, Barnum decided to employ him. Taking him back to the museum, he gave the man five bricks and told him to make a slow circuit of several blocks. At certain points he was to lay down a brick on the sidewalk, always keeping one brick in hand. On the return journey he was to replace each brick on the street with the one he held. Meanwhile he was to remain serious of countenance and to answer no questions. Once back at the museum, he was to enter, walk around inside, then leave through the back door and make the same bricklaying circuit again.

On the man's first walk through the streets, several hundred people watched his mysterious movements. By his fourth circuit, onlookers swarmed around him, debating what he was doing. Every time he entered the museum he was followed by people who bought tickets to keep watching him. Many of them were distracted by the museum's collections, and stayed inside. By the end of the first day, the brick man had drawn over a

THE WASP AND THE PRINCE

A wasp named Pin Tail was long in quest of some deed that would make him forever famous. So one day he entered the king's palace and stung the little prince, who was in bed. The prince awoke with loud cries. The king and his courtiers rushed in to see what had happened. The prince was yelling as the wasp stung him again and again. The courtiers tried to catch the wasp, and each in turn was stung. The whole royal household rushed in, the news soon spread, and people flocked to the palace. The city was in an uproar, all business suspended. Said the wasp to itself, before it expired from its efforts, "A name without fame is like fire without flame. There is nothing like attracting notice at any cost."

INDIAN FABLE

thousand people into the museum. A few days later the police ordered him to cease and desist from his walks—the crowds were blocking traffic. The bricklaying stopped but thousands of New Yorkers had entered the museum, and many of those had become P. T. Barnum converts.

Barnum would put a band of musicians on a balcony overlooking the street, beneath a huge banner proclaiming FREE MUSIC FOR THE MILLIONS. What generosity, New Yorkers thought, and they flocked to hear the free concerts. But Barnum took pains to hire the worst musicians he could find, and soon after the band struck up, people would hurry to buy tickets to the museum, where they would be out of earshot of the band's noise, and of the booing of the crowd.

One of the first oddities Barnum toured around the country was Joice Heth, a woman he claimed was 161 years old, and whom he advertised as a slave who had once been George Washington's nurse. After several months the crowds began to dwindle, so Barnum sent an anonymous letter to the papers, claiming that Heth was a clever fraud. "Joice Heth," he wrote, "is not a human being but an automaton, made up of whalebone, india-rubber, and numberless springs." Those who had not bothered to see her before were immediately curious, and those who had already seen her paid to see her again, to find out whether the rumor that she was a robot was true.

In 1842, Barnum purchased the carcass of what was purported to be a mermaid. This creature resembled a monkey with the body of a fish, but the head and body were perfectly joined—it was truly a wonder. After some research Barnum discovered that the creature had been expertly put together in Japan, where the hoax had caused quite a stir.

He nevertheless planted articles in newspapers around the country claiming the capture of a mermaid in the Fiji Islands. He also sent the papers woodcut prints of paintings showing mermaids. By the time he showed the specimen in his museum, a national debate had been sparked over the existence of these mythical creatures. A few months before Barnum's campaign, no one had cared or even known about mermaids; now everyone was talking about them as if they were real. Crowds flocked in record numbers to see the Fiji Mermaid, and to hear debates on the subject.

A few years later, Barnum toured Europe with General Tom Thumb, a five-year-old dwarf from Connecticut whom Barnum claimed was an eleven-year-old English boy, and whom he had trained to do many remarkable acts. During this tour Barnum's name attracted such attention that Queen Victoria, that paragon of sobriety, requested a private audience with him and his talented dwarf at Buckingham Palace. The English press may have ridiculed Barnum, but Victoria was royally entertained by him, and respected him ever after.

Interpretation

Barnum understood the fundamental truth about attracting attention: Once people's eyes are on you, you have a special legitimacy. For Barnum, creating interest meant creating a crowd; as he later wrote, "Every crowd has a silver lining." And crowds tend to act in conjunction. If one person stops to see your beggarman laying bricks in the street, more will do the same. They will gather like dust bunnies. Then, given a gentle push, they will enter your museum or watch your show. To create a crowd you have to do something different and odd. Any kind of curiosity will serve the purpose, for crowds are magnetically attracted by the unusual and inexplicable. And once you have their attention, never let it go. If it veers toward other people, it does so at your expense. Barnum would ruthlessly suck attention from his competitors, knowing what a valuable commodity it is.

At the beginning of your rise to the top, then, spend all your energy on attracting attention. Most important: The *quality* of the attention is irrelevant. No matter how badly his shows were reviewed, or how slanderously personal were the attacks on his hoaxes, Barnum would never complain. If a newspaper critic reviled him particularly badly, in fact, he made sure to invite the man to an opening and to give him the best seat in the house. He would even write anonymous attacks on his own work, just to keep his name in the papers. From Barnum's vantage, attention—whether negative or positive—was the main ingredient of his success. The worst fate in the world for a man who yearns fame, glory, and, of course, power is to be ignored.

> *If the courtier happens to engage in arms in some public spectacle*
> *such as jousting . . . he will ensure that the horse he has is beautifully*
> *caparisoned, that he himself is suitably attired, with appropriate*
> *mottoes and ingenious devices to attract the eyes of the onlookers*
> *in his direction as surely as the lodestone attracts iron.*
> Baldassare Castiglione, 1478–1529

KEYS TO POWER

Burning more brightly than those around you is a skill that no one is born with. You have to *learn* to attract attention, "as surely as the lodestone attracts iron." At the start of your career, you must attach your name and reputation to a quality, an image, that sets you apart from other people. This image can be something like a characteristic style of dress, or a personality quirk that amuses people and gets talked about. Once the image is established, you have an appearance, a place in the sky for your star.

It is a common mistake to imagine that this peculiar appearance of yours should not be controversial, that to be attacked is somehow bad. Nothing could be further from the truth. To avoid being a flash in the pan, and having your notoriety eclipsed by another, you must not discriminate between different types of attention; in the end, every kind will work in your favor. Barnum, we have seen, welcomed personal attacks and felt no need to defend himself. He deliberately courted the image of being a humbug.

reports that Gossaert attracted the attention of Emperor Charles V by wearing a fantastic paper costume. In doing so he was adopting the tactics used by Dinocrates, who, in order to gain access to Alexander the Great, is said to have appeared disguised as the naked Hercules when the monarch was sitting in judgment.

THE COURT ARTIST, MARTIN WARNKE, 1993

The court of Louis XIV contained many talented writers, artists, great beauties, and men and women of impeccable virtue, but no one was more talked about than the singular Duc de Lauzun. The duke was short, almost dwarfish, and he was prone to the most insolent kinds of behavior—he slept with the king's mistress, and openly insulted not only other courtiers but the king himself. Louis, however, was so beguiled by the duke's eccentricities that he could not bear his absences from the court. It was simple: The strangeness of the duke's character attracted attention. Once people were enthralled by him, they wanted him around at any cost.

Society craves larger-than-life figures, people who stand above the general mediocrity. Never be afraid, then, of the qualities that set you apart and draw attention to you. Court controversy, even scandal. It is better to be attacked, even slandered, than ignored. All professions are ruled by this law, and all professionals must have a bit of the showman about them.

The great scientist Thomas Edison knew that to raise money he had to remain in the public eye at any cost. Almost as important as the inventions themselves was how he presented them to the public and courted attention.

Edison would design visually dazzling experiments to display his discoveries with electricity. He would talk of future inventions that seemed fantastic at the time—robots, and machines that could photograph thought—and that he had no intention of wasting his energy on, but that made the public talk about him. He did everything he could to make sure that he received more attention than his great rival Nikola Tesla, who may actually have been more brilliant than he was but whose name was far less known. In 1915, it was rumored that Edison and Tesla would be joint recipients of that year's Nobel Prize in physics. The prize was eventually given to a pair of English physicists; only later was it discovered that the prize committee had actually approached Edison, but he had turned them down, refusing to share the prize with Tesla. By that time his fame was more secure than Tesla's, and he thought it better to refuse the honor than to allow his rival the attention that would have come even from sharing the prize.

If you find yourself in a lowly position that offers little opportunity for you to draw attention, an effective trick is to attack the most visible, most famous, most powerful person you can find. When Pietro Aretino, a young Roman servant boy of the early sixteenth century, wanted to get attention as a writer of verses, he decided to publish a series of satirical poems ridiculing the pope and his affection for a pet elephant. The attack put Aretino in the public eye immediately. A slanderous attack on a person in a position of power would have a similar effect. Remember, however, to use such tactics sparingly after you have the public's attention, when the act can wear thin.

Once in the limelight you must constantly renew it by adapting and varying your method of courting attention. If you don't, the public will grow tired, will take you for granted, and will move on to a newer star. The game requires constant vigilance and creativity. Pablo Picasso never allowed himself to fade into the background; if his name became too attached to a particular style, he would deliberately upset the public with a new series of paintings that went against all expectations. Better to create something ugly and disturbing, he believed, than to let viewers grow too familiar with his work. Understand: People feel superior to the person whose actions they can predict. If you show them who is in control by playing *against* their expectations, you both gain their respect and tighten your hold on their fleeting attention.

I m a g e :
The Limelight. The
actor who steps into this brilliant light attains a heightened
presence. All eyes are on him. There
is room for only one actor at a time in
the limelight's narrow beam; do whatever it takes to make yourself its focus.
Make your gestures so large, amusing, and scandalous that the
light stays on you while the.
other actors are left in
the shadows.

Authority: Be ostentatious and
be seen. . . . What is not seen is
as though it did not exist. . . . It
was light that first caused all creation to shine forth. Display fills
up many blanks, covers up deficiencies, and gives everything
a second life, especially when it
is backed by genuine merit.
(Baltasar Gracián, 1601–1658)

PART II: CREATE AN AIR OF MYSTERY

In a world growing increasingly banal and familiar, what seems enigmatic instantly draws attention. Never make it too clear what you are doing or about to do. Do not show all your cards. An air of mystery heightens your presence; it also creates anticipation—everyone will be watching you to see what happens next. Use mystery to beguile, seduce, even frighten.

OBSERVANCE OF THE LAW

Beginning in 1905, rumors started to spread throughout Paris of a young Oriental girl who danced in a private home, wrapped in veils that she gradually discarded. A local journalist who had seen her dancing reported that "a woman from the Far East had come to Europe laden with perfume and jewels, to introduce some of the richness of the Oriental colour and life into the satiated society of European cities." Soon everyone knew the dancer's name: Mata Hari.

Early that year, in the winter, small and select audiences would gather in a salon filled with Indian statues and other relics while an orchestra played music inspired by Hindu and Javanese melodies. After keeping the audience waiting and wondering, Mata Hari would suddenly appear, in a startling costume: a white cotton brassiere covered with Indian-type jewels; jeweled bands at the waist supporting a sarong that revealed as much as it concealed; bracelets up the arms. Then Mata Hari would dance, in a style no one in France had seen before, her whole body swaying as if she were in a trance. She told her excited and curious audience that her dances told stories from Indian mythology and Javanese folktales. Soon the cream of Paris, and ambassadors from far-off lands, were competing for invitations to the salon, where it was rumored that Mata Hari was actually performing sacred dances in the nude.

The public wanted to know more about her. She told journalists that she was actually Dutch in origin, but had grown up on the island of Java. She would also talk about time spent in India, how she had learned sacred Hindu dances there, and how Indian women "can shoot straight, ride horseback, and are capable of doing logarithms and talk philosophy." By the summer of 1905, although few Parisians had actually seen Mata Hari dance, her name was on everyone's lips.

As Mata Hari gave more interviews, the story of her origins kept changing: She had grown up in India, her grandmother was the daughter of a Javanese princess, she had lived on the island of Sumatra where she had spent her time "horseback riding, gun in hand, and risking her life." No one knew anything certain about her, but journalists did not mind these changes in her biography. They compared her to an Indian goddess, a creature from the pages of Baudelaire—whatever their imagination wanted to see in this mysterious woman from the East.

In August of 1905, Mata Hari performed for the first time in public.

Crowds thronging to see her on opening night caused a riot. She had now become a cult figure, spawning many imitations. One reviewer wrote, "Mata Hari personifies all the poetry of India, its mysticism, its voluptuousness, its hypnotizing charm." Another noted, "If India possesses such unexpected treasures, then all Frenchmen will emigrate to the shores of the Ganges."

Soon the fame of Mata Hari and her sacred Indian dances spread beyond Paris. She was invited to Berlin, Vienna, Milan. Over the next few years she performed throughout Europe, mixed with the highest social circles, and earned an income that gave her an independence rarely enjoyed by a woman of the period. Then, near the end of World War I, she was arrested in France, tried, convicted, and finally executed as a German spy. Only during the trial did the truth come out: Mata Hari was not from Java or India, had not grown up in the Orient, did not have a drop of Eastern blood in her body. Her real name was Margaretha Zelle, and she came from the stolid northern province of Friesland, Holland.

Interpretation

When Margaretha Zelle arrived in Paris, in 1904, she had half a franc in her pocket. She was one of the thousands of beautiful young girls who flocked to Paris every year, taking work as artists' models, nightclub dancers, or vaudeville performers at the Folies Bergère. After a few years they would inevitably be replaced by younger girls, and would often end up on the streets, turning to prostitution, or else returning to the town they came from, older and chastened.

Zelle had higher ambitions. She had no dance experience and had never performed in the theater, but as a young girl she had traveled with her family and had witnessed local dances in Java and Sumatra. Zelle clearly understood that what was important in her act was not the dance itself, or even her face or figure, but her ability to create an air of mystery about herself. The mystery she created lay not just in her dancing, or her costumes, or the stories she would tell, or her endless lies about her origins; it lay in an atmosphere enveloping everything she did. There was nothing you could say for sure about her—she was always changing, always surprising her audience with new costumes, new dances, new stories. This air of mystery left the public always wanting to know more, always wondering about her next move. Mata Hari was no more beautiful than many of the other young girls who came to Paris, and she was not a particularly good dancer. What separated her from the mass, what attracted and held the public's attention and made her famous and wealthy, was her mystery. People are enthralled by mystery; because it invites constant interpretation, they never tire of it. The mysterious cannot be grasped. And what cannot be seized and consumed creates power.

KEYS TO POWER

In the past, the world was filled with the terrifying and unknowable—diseases, disasters, capricious despots, the mystery of death itself. What we could not understand we reimagined as myths and spirits. Over the centuries, though, we have managed, through science and reason, to illuminate the darkness; what was mysterious and forbidding has grown familiar and comfortable. Yet this light has a price: in a world that is ever more banal, that has had its mystery and myth squeezed out of it, we secretly crave enigmas, people or things that cannot be instantly interpreted, seized, and consumed.

That is the power of the mysterious: It invites layers of interpretation, excites our imagination, seduces us into believing that it conceals something marvelous. The world has become so familiar and its inhabitants so predictable that what wraps itself in mystery will almost always draw the limelight to it and make us watch it.

Do not imagine that to create an air of mystery you have to be grand and awe-inspiring. Mystery that is woven into your day-to-day demeanor, and is subtle, has that much more power to fascinate and attract attention. Remember: Most people are upfront, can be read like an open book, take little care to control their words or image, and are hopelessly predictable. By simply holding back, keeping silent, occasionally uttering ambiguous phrases, deliberately appearing inconsistent, and acting odd in the subtlest of ways, you will emanate an aura of mystery. The people around you will then magnify that aura by constantly trying to interpret you.

Both artists and con artists understand the vital link between being mysterious and attracting interest. Count Victor Lustig, the aristocrat of swindlers, played the game to perfection. He was always doing things that were different, or seemed to make no sense. He would show up at the best hotels in a limo driven by a Japanese chauffeur; no one had ever seen a Japanese chauffeur before, so this seemed exotic and strange. Lustig would dress in the most expensive clothing, but always with something—a medal, a flower, an armband—out of place, at least in conventional terms. This was seen not as tasteless but as odd and intriguing. In hotels he would be seen receiving telegrams at all hours, one after the other, brought to him by his Japanese chauffeur—telegrams he would tear up with utter nonchalance. (In fact they were fakes, completely blank.) He would sit alone in the dining room, reading a large and impressive-looking book, smiling at people yet remaining aloof. Within a few days, of course, the entire hotel would be abuzz with interest in this strange man.

All this attention allowed Lustig to lure suckers in with ease. They would beg for his confidence and his company. Everyone wanted to be seen with this mysterious aristocrat. And in the presence of this distracting enigma, they wouldn't even notice that they were being robbed blind.

An air of mystery can make the mediocre appear intelligent and profound. It made Mata Hari, a woman of average appearance and intelligence, seem like a goddess, and her dancing divinely inspired. An air of mystery about an artist makes his or her artwork immediately more intriguing, a trick Marcel Duchamp played to great effect. It is all very easy to do—say little about your work, tease and titillate with alluring, even contradictory comments, then stand back and let others try to make sense of it all.

Mysterious people put others in a kind of inferior position—that of trying to figure them out. To degrees that they can control, they also elicit the fear surrounding anything uncertain or unknown. All great leaders know that an aura of mystery draws attention to them and creates an intimidating presence. Mao Tse-tung, for example, cleverly cultivated an enigmatic image; he had no worries about seeming inconsistent or contradicting himself—the very contradictoriness of his actions and words meant that he always had the upper hand. No one, not even his own wife, ever felt they understood him, and he therefore seemed larger than life. This also meant that the public paid constant attention to him, ever anxious to witness his next move.

If your social position prevents you from completely wrapping your actions in mystery, you must at least learn to make yourself less obvious. Every now and then, act in a way that does not mesh with other people's perception of you. This way you keep those around you on the defensive, eliciting the kind of attention that makes you powerful. Done right, the creation of enigma can also draw the kind of attention that strikes terror into your enemy.

During the Second Punic War (219–202 B.C.), the great Carthaginian general Hannibal was wreaking havoc in his march on Rome. Hannibal was known for his cleverness and duplicity.

Under his leadership Carthage's army, though smaller than those of the Romans, had constantly outmaneuvered them. On one occasion, though, Hannibal's scouts made a horrible blunder, leading his troops into a marshy terrain with the sea at their back. The Roman army blocked the mountain passes that led inland, and its general, Fabius, was ecstatic—at last he had Hannibal trapped. Posting his best sentries on the passes, he worked on a plan to destroy Hannibal's forces. But in the middle of the night, the sentries looked down to see a mysterious sight: A huge procession of lights was heading up the mountain. Thousands and thousands of lights. If this was Hannibal's army, it had suddenly grown a hundredfold.

The sentries argued heatedly about what this could mean: Reinforcements from the sea? Troops that had been hidden in the area? Ghosts? No explanation made sense.

As they watched, fires broke out all over the mountain, and a horrible noise drifted up to them from below, like the blowing of a million horns. Demons, they thought. The sentries, the bravest and most sensible in the Roman army, fled their posts in a panic.

By the next day, Hannibal had escaped from the marshland. What was his trick? Had he really conjured up demons? Actually what he had done was order bundles of twigs to be fastened to the horns of the thousands of oxen that traveled with his troops as beasts of burden. The twigs were then lit, giving the impression of the torches of a vast army heading up the mountain. When the flames burned down to the oxen's skin, they stampeded in all directions, bellowing like mad and setting fires all over the mountainside. The key to this device's success was not the torches, the fires, or the noises in themselves, however, but the fact that Hannibal had created a puzzle that captivated the sentries' attention and gradually terrified them. From the mountaintop there was no way to explain this bizarre sight. If the sentries could have explained it they would have stayed at their posts.

If you find yourself trapped, cornered, and on the defensive in some situation, try a simple experiment: Do something that cannot be easily explained or interpreted. Choose a simple action, but carry it out in a way that unsettles your opponent, a way with many possible interpretations, making your intentions obscure. Don't just be unpredictable (although this tactic too can be successful—see Law 17); like Hannibal, create a scene that cannot be read. There will seem to be no method to your madness, no rhyme or reason, no single explanation. If you do this right, you will inspire fear and trembling and the sentries will abandon their posts. Call it the "feigned madness of Hamlet" tactic, for Hamlet uses it to great effect in Shakespeare's play, frightening his stepfather Claudius through the mystery of his behavior. The mysterious makes your forces seem larger, your power more terrifying.

Image: The Dance of
the Veils—the veils
envelop the dancer.
What they reveal
causes excitement.
What they conceal
heightens interest. The
essence of mystery.

Authority: If you do not declare yourself immediately, you arouse expectation. . . . Mix a little mystery with everything, and the very mystery stirs up veneration. And when you explain, be not too explicit. . . . In this manner you imitate the Divine way when you cause men to wonder and watch. (Baltasar Gracián, 1601–1658)

REVERSAL

In the beginning of your rise to the top, you must attract attention at all cost, but as you rise higher you must constantly adapt. Never wear the public out with the same tactic. An air of mystery works wonders for those who need to develop an aura of power and get themselves noticed, but it must seem measured and under control. Mata Hari went too far with her fabrications; although the accusation that she was a spy was false, at the time it was a reasonable presumption because all her lies made her seem suspicious and nefarious. Do not let your air of mystery be slowly transformed into a reputation for deceit. The mystery you create must seem a game, playful and unthreatening. Recognize when it goes too far, and pull back.

There are times when the need for attention must be deferred, and when scandal and notoriety are the last things you want to create. The attention you attract must never offend or challenge the reputation of those above you—not, at any rate, if they are secure. You will seem not only paltry but desperate by comparison. There is an art to knowing when to draw notice and when to withdraw.

Lola Montez was one of the great practitioners of the art of attracting attention. She managed to rise from a middle-class Irish background to being the lover of Franz Liszt and then the mistress and political adviser of King Ludwig of Bavaria. In her later years, though, she lost her sense of proportion.

In London in 1850 there was to be a performance of Shakespeare's *Macbeth* featuring the greatest actor of the time, Charles John Kean. Everyone of consequence in English society was to be there; it was rumored that even Queen Victoria and Prince Albert were to make a public appearance. The custom of the period demanded that everyone be seated before the queen arrived. So the audience got there a little early, and when the queen entered her royal box, they observed the convention of standing up and applauding her. The royal couple waited, then bowed. Everyone sat down and the lights were dimmed. Then, suddenly, all eyes turned to a box opposite Queen Victoria's: A woman appeared from the shadows, taking her seat later than the queen. It was Lola Montez. She wore a diamond tiara on her dark hair and a long fur coat over her shoulders. People whispered in amazement as the ermine cloak was dropped to reveal a low-necked gown of crimson velvet. By turning their heads, the audience could see that the royal couple deliberately avoided looking at Lola's box. They followed Victoria's example, and for the rest of the evening Lola Montez was ignored. After that evening no one in fashionable society dared to be seen with her. All her magnetic powers were reversed. People would flee her sight. Her future in England was finished.

Never appear overly greedy for attention, then, for it signals insecurity, and insecurity drives power away. Understand that there are times when it is not in your interest to be the center of attention. When in the presence of a king or queen, for instance, or the equivalent thereof, bow and retreat to the shadows; never compete.

GET OTHERS TO DO THE

WORK FOR YOU, BUT

ALWAYS TAKE THE CREDIT

JUDGMENT

Use the wisdom, knowledge, and legwork of other people to further your own cause. Not only will such assistance save you valuable time and energy, it will give you a godlike aura of efficiency and speed. In the end your helpers will be forgotten and you will be remembered. Never do yourself what others can do for you.

TRANSGRESSION AND OBSERVANCE OF THE LAW

In 1883 a young Serbian scientist named Nikola Tesla was working for the European division of the Continental Edison Company. He was a brilliant inventor, and Charles Batchelor, a plant manager and a personal friend of Thomas Edison, persuaded him he should seek his fortune in America, giving him a letter of introduction to Edison himself. So began a life of woe and tribulation that lasted until Tesla's death.

When Tesla met Edison in New York, the famous inventor hired him on the spot. Tesla worked eighteen-hour days, finding ways to improve the primitive Edison dynamos. Finally he offered to redesign them completely. To Edison this seemed a monumental task that could last years without paying off, but he told Tesla, "There's fifty thousand dollars in it for you—*if* you can do it." Tesla labored day and night on the project and after only a year he produced a greatly improved version of the dynamo, complete with automatic controls. He went to Edison to break the good news and receive his $50,000. Edison was pleased with the improvement, for which he and his company would take credit, but when it came to the issue of the money he told the young Serb, "Tesla, you don't understand our American humor!," and offered a small raise instead.

Tesla's obsession was to create an alternating-current system (AC) of electricity. Edison believed in the direct-current system (DC), and not only refused to support Tesla's research but later did all he could to sabotage him. Tesla turned to the great Pittsburgh magnate George Westinghouse, who had started his own electricity company. Westinghouse completely funded Tesla's research and offered him a generous royalty agreement on future profits. The AC system Tesla developed is still the standard today— but after patents were filed in his name, other scientists came forward to take credit for the invention, claiming that they had laid the groundwork for him. His name was lost in the shuffle, and the public came to associate the invention with Westinghouse himself.

A year later, Westinghouse was caught in a takeover bid from J. Pierpont Morgan, who made him rescind the generous royalty contract he had signed with Tesla. Westinghouse explained to the scientist that his company would not survive if it had to pay him his full royalties; he persuaded Tesla to accept a buyout of his patents for $216,000—a large sum, no doubt, but far less than the $12 million they were worth at the time. The financiers had divested Tesla of the riches, the patents, and essentially the credit for the greatest invention of his career.

The name of Guglielmo Marconi is forever linked with the invention of radio. But few know that in producing his invention—he broadcast a signal across the English Channel in 1899—Marconi made use of a patent Tesla had filed in 1897, and that his work depended on Tesla's research. Once again Tesla received no money and no credit. Tesla invented an induction motor as well as the AC power system, and he is the real "father of radio." Yet none of these discoveries bear his name. As an old man, he lived in poverty.

THE TORTOISE, THE ELEPHANT, AND THE HIPPOPOTAMUS

One day the tortoise met the elephant, who trumpeted, "Out of my way, you weakling— I might step on you!" The tortoise was not afraid and stayed where he was, so the elephant stepped on him, but could not crush him. "Do not boast, Mr. Elephant, I am as strong as you are!" said the tortoise, but the elephant just laughed. So the tortoise asked him to come to his hill the next morning.
The next day, before sunrise, the tortoise ran down the hill to the river, where he met the hippopotamus, who was just on his way back into the water after his nocturnal feeding. "Mr Hippo! Shall we have a tug-of-war? I bet I'm as strong as you are!" said the tortoise. The hippopotamus laughed at this ridiculous idea, but agreed. The tortoise produced a long rope and told the hippo to hold it in his mouth until the tortoise shouted "Hey!"
Then the tortoise ran back up the hill where he found the elephant, who was getting impatient. He gave the elephant the other end of the rope and said, "When I say 'Hey!' pull, and you'll see which of us is the strongest." Then he ran halfway back down the

In 1917, during his later impoverished years, Tesla was told he was to receive the Edison Medal of the American Institute of Electrical Engineers. He turned the medal down. "You propose," he said, "to honor me with a medal which I could pin upon my coat and strut for a vain hour before the members of your Institute. You would decorate my body and continue to let starve, for failure to supply recognition, my mind and its creative products, which have supplied the foundation upon which the major portion of your Institute exists."

Interpretation

Many harbor the illusion that science, dealing with facts as it does, is beyond the petty rivalries that trouble the rest of the world. Nikola Tesla was one of those. He believed science had nothing to do with politics, and claimed not to care for fame and riches. As he grew older, though, this ruined his scientific work. Not associated with any particular discovery, he could attract no investors to his many ideas. While he pondered great inventions for the future, others stole the patents he had already developed and got the glory for themselves.

He wanted to do everything on his own, but merely exhausted and impoverished himself in the process.

Edison was Tesla's polar opposite. He wasn't actually much of a scientific thinker or inventor; he once said that he had no need to be a mathematician because he could always hire one. That was Edison's main method. He was really a businessman and publicist, spotting the trends and the opportunities that were out there, then hiring the best in the field to do the work for him. If he had to he would steal from his competitors. Yet his name is much better known than Tesla's, and is associated with more inventions.

The lesson is twofold: First, the credit for an invention or creation is as important, if not more important, than the invention itself. You must secure the credit for yourself and keep others from stealing it away, or from piggybacking on your hard work. To accomplish this you must always be vigilant and ruthless, keeping your creation quiet until you can be sure there are no vultures circling overhead. Second, learn to take advantage of other people's work to further your own cause. Time is precious and life is short. If you try to do it all on your own, you run yourself ragged, waste energy, and burn yourself out. It is far better to conserve your forces, pounce on the work others have done, and find a way to make it your own.

> *Everybody steals in commerce and industry.*
> *I've stolen a lot myself.*
> *But I know how to steal.*
> *Thomas Edison, 1847–1931*

KEYS TO POWER

The world of power has the dynamics of the jungle: There are those who live by hunting and killing, and there are also vast numbers of creatures (hyenas, vultures) who live off the hunting of others. These latter, less imaginative types are often incapable of doing the work that is essential for the creation of power. They understand early on, though, that if they wait long enough, they can always find another animal to do the work for them. Do not be naive: At this very moment, while you are slaving away on some project, there are vultures circling above trying to figure out a way to survive and even thrive off your creativity. It is useless to complain about this, or to wear yourself ragged with bitterness, as Tesla did. Better to protect yourself and join the game. Once you have established a power base, become a vulture yourself, and save yourself a lot of time and energy.

Of the two poles of this game, one can be illustrated by the example of the explorer Vasco Núñez de Balboa. Balboa had an obsession—the discovery of El Dorado, a legendary city of vast riches.

Early in the sixteenth century, after countless hardships and brushes with death, he found evidence of a great and wealthy empire to the south of Mexico, in present-day Peru. By conquering this empire, the Incan, and seizing its gold, he would make himself the next Cortés. The problem was that even as he made this discovery, word of it spread among hundreds of other conquistadors. He did not understand that half the game was keeping it quiet, and carefully watching those around him. A few years after he discovered the location of the Incan empire, a soldier in his own army, Francisco Pizarro, helped to get him beheaded for treason. Pizarro went on to take what Balboa had spent so many years trying to find.

The other pole is that of the artist Peter Paul Rubens, who, late in his career, found himself deluged with requests for paintings. He created a system: In his large studio he employed dozens of outstanding painters, one specializing in robes, another in backgrounds, and so on. He created a vast production line in which a large number of canvases would be worked on at the same time. When an important client visited the studio, Rubens would shoo his hired painters out for the day. While the client watched from a balcony, Rubens would work at an incredible pace, with unbelievable energy. The client would leave in awe of this prodigious man, who could paint so many masterpieces in so short a time.

This is the essence of the Law: Learn to get others to do the work for you while you take the credit, and you appear to be of godlike strength and power. If you think it important to do all the work yourself, you will never get far, and you will suffer the fate of the Balboas and Teslas of the world. Find people with the skills and creativity you lack. Either hire them, while putting your own name on top of theirs, or find a way to take their work and make it your own. Their creativity thus becomes yours, and you seem a genius to the world.

There is another application of this law that does not require the parasitic use of your contemporaries' labor: Use the past, a vast storehouse of

THE BLIND HEN

A hen who had lost her sight, and was accustomed to scratching up the earth in search of food, although blind, still continued to scratch away most diligently. Of what use was it to the industrious fool? Another sharpsighted hen who spared her tender feet never moved from her side, and enjoyed, without scratching, the fruit of the other's labor. For as often as the blind hen scratched up a barleycorn, her watchful companion devoured it.

FABLES,
GOTTHOLD LESSING,
1729-1781

knowledge and wisdom. Isaac Newton called this "standing on the shoulders of giants." He meant that in making his discoveries he had built on the achievements of others. A great part of his aura of genius, he knew, was attributable to his shrewd ability to make the most of the insights of ancient, medieval, and Renaissance scientists. Shakespeare borrowed plots, characterizations, and even dialogue from Plutarch, among other writers, for he knew that nobody surpassed Plutarch in the writing of subtle psychology and witty quotes. How many later writers have in their turn borrowed from—*plagiarized*—Shakespeare?

We all know how few of today's politicians write their own speeches. Their own words would not win them a single vote; their eloquence and wit, whatever there is of it, they owe to a speech writer. Other people do the work, they take the credit. The upside of this is that it is a kind of power that is available to everyone. Learn to use the knowledge of the past and you will look like a genius, even when you are really just a clever borrower.

Writers who have delved into human nature, ancient masters of strategy, historians of human stupidity and folly, kings and queens who have learned the hard way how to handle the burdens of power—their knowledge is gathering dust, waiting for you to come and stand on their shoulders. Their wit can be your wit, their skill can be your skill, and they will never come around to tell people how unoriginal you really are. You can slog through life, making endless mistakes, wasting time and energy trying to do things from your own experience. Or you can use the armies of the past. As Bismarck once said, "Fools say that they learn by experience. I prefer to profit by others' experience."

Image: The Vulture. Of all the creatures in
the jungle, he has it the easiest. The
hard work of others becomes his work;
their failure to survive becomes his
nourishment. Keep an eye on
the Vulture—while you are
hard at work, he is cir-
cling above. Do not
fight him, join
h i m .

Authority: There is much to be known, life is short, and life is not life without knowledge. It is therefore an excellent device to acquire knowledge from everybody. Thus, by the sweat of another's brow, you win the reputation of being an oracle. (Baltasar Gracián, 1601–1658)

REVERSAL

There are times when taking the credit for work that others have done is not the wise course: If your power is not firmly enough established, you will seem to be pushing people out of the limelight. To be a brilliant exploiter of talent your position must be unshakable, or you will be accused of deception.

Be sure you know when letting other people share the credit serves your purpose. It is especially important to not be greedy when you have a master above you. President Richard Nixon's historic visit to the People's Republic of China was originally his idea, but it might never have come off but for the deft diplomacy of Henry Kissinger. Nor would it have been as successful without Kissinger's skills. Still, when the time came to take credit, Kissinger adroitly let Nixon take the lion's share. Knowing that the truth would come out later, he was careful not to jeopardize his standing in the short term by hogging the limelight. Kissinger played the game expertly: He took credit for the work of those below him while graciously giving credit for his own labors to those above. That is the way to play the game.

MAKE OTHER PEOPLE

COME TO YOU—

USE BAIT IF NECESSARY

JUDGMENT

When you force the other person to act, you are the one in control. It is always better to make your opponent come to you, abandoning his own plans in the process. Lure him with fabulous gains—then attack. You hold the cards.

OBSERVANCE OF THE LAW

At the Congress of Vienna in 1814, the major powers of Europe gathered to carve up the remains of Napoleon's fallen Empire. The city was full of gaiety and the balls were the most splendid in memory. Hovering over the proceedings, however, was the shadow of Napoleon himself. Instead of being executed or exiled far away, he had been sent to the island of Elba, not far from the coast of Italy.

Even imprisoned on an island, a man as bold and creative as Napoleon Bonaparte made everyone nervous. The Austrians plotted to kill him on Elba, but decided it was too risky. Alexander I, Russia's temperamental czar, heightened the anxiety by throwing a fit during the congress when a part of Poland was denied him: "Beware, I shall loose the monster!" he threatened. Everyone knew he meant Napoleon. Of all the statesmen gathered in Vienna, only Talleyrand, Napoleon's former foreign minister, seemed calm and unconcerned. It was as if he knew something the others did not.

Meanwhile, on the island of Elba, Napoleon's life was a mockery of his previous glory. As Elba's "king," he had been allowed to form a court—there was a cook, a wardrobe mistress, an official pianist, and a handful of courtiers. All this was designed to humiliate Napoleon, and it seemed to work.

That winter, however, there occurred a series of events so strange and dramatic they might have been scripted in a play. Elba was surrounded by British ships, their cannons covering all possible exit points. Yet somehow, in broad daylight on 26 February 1815, a ship with nine hundred men on board picked up Napoleon and put to sea. The English gave chase but the ship got away. This almost impossible escape astonished the public throughout Europe, and terrified the statesmen at the Congress of Vienna.

Although it would have been safer to leave Europe, Napoleon not only chose to return to France, he raised the odds by marching on Paris with a tiny army, in hopes of recapturing the throne. His strategy worked—people of all classes threw themselves at his feet. An army under Marshal Ney sped from Paris to arrest him, but when the soldiers saw their beloved former leader, they changed sides. Napoleon was declared emperor again. Volunteers swelled the ranks of his new army. Delirium swept the country. In Paris, crowds went wild. The king who had replaced Napoleon fled the country.

For the next hundred days, Napoleon ruled France. Soon, however, the giddiness subsided. France was bankrupt, its resources nearly exhausted, and there was little Napoleon could do about this. At the Battle of Waterloo, in June of that year, he was finally defeated for good. This time his enemies had learned their lesson: They exiled him to the barren island of Saint Helena, off the west coast of Africa. There he had no more hope of escape.

Interpretation

Only years later did the facts of Napoleon's dramatic escape from Elba come to light. Before he decided to attempt this bold move, visitors to his court had told him that he was more popular in France than ever, and that the country would embrace him again. One of these visitors was Austria's General Koller, who convinced Napoleon that if he escaped, the European powers, England included, would welcome him back into power. Napoleon was tipped off that the English would let him go, and indeed his escape occurred in the middle of the afternoon, in full view of English spyglasses.

What Napoleon did not know was that there was a man behind it all, pulling the strings, and that this man was his former minister, Talleyrand. And Talleyrand was doing all this not to bring back the glory days but to crush Napoleon once and for all. Considering the emperor's ambition unsettling to Europe's stability, he had turned against him long ago. When Napoleon was exiled to Elba, Talleyrand had protested. Napoleon should be sent farther away, he argued, or Europe would never have peace. But no one listened.

Instead of pushing his opinion, Talleyrand bided his time. Working quietly, he eventually won over Castlereagh and Metternich, the foreign ministers of England and Austria.

Together these men baited Napoleon into escaping. Even Koller's visit, to whisper the promise of glory in the exile's ear, was part of the plan. Like a master cardplayer, Talleyrand figured everything out in advance. He knew Napoleon would fall into the trap he had set. He also foresaw that Napoleon would lead the country into a war, which, given France's weakened condition, could only last a few months. One diplomat in Vienna, who understood that Talleyrand was behind it all, said, "He has set the house ablaze in order to save it from the plague."

When I have laid bait for deer,
I don't shoot at the first doe that comes to sniff,
but wait until the whole herd has gathered round.
Otto von Bismarck, 1815–1898

KEYS TO POWER

How many times has this scenario played itself out in history: An aggressive leader initiates a series of bold moves that begin by bringing him much power. Slowly, however, his power reaches a peak, and soon everything turns against him. His numerous enemies band together; trying to maintain his power, he exhausts himself going in this direction and that, and inevitably he collapses. The reason for this pattern is that the aggressive person is rarely in full control. He cannot see more than a couple of moves ahead, cannot see the consequences of this bold move or that one. Because he is constantly being forced to react to the moves of his ever-growing host of enemies, and to the unforeseen consequences of his own rash actions, his aggressive energy is turned against him.

In the realm of power, you must ask yourself, what is the point of chasing here and there, trying to solve problems and defeat my enemies, if I never feel in control? Why am I always having to react to events instead of directing them? The answer is simple: Your idea of power is wrong. You have mistaken aggressive action for effective action. And most often the most effective action is to stay back, keep calm, and let others be frustrated by the traps you lay for them, playing for long-term power rather than quick victory.

Remember: The essence of power is the ability to keep the initiative, to get others to react to *your* moves, to keep your opponent and those around you on the defensive. When you make other people come to you, you suddenly become the one controlling the situation. And the one who has control has power. Two things must happen to place you in this position: You yourself must learn to master your emotions, and never to be influenced by anger; meanwhile, however, you must play on people's natural tendency to react angrily when pushed and baited. In the long run, the ability to make others come to you is a weapon far more powerful than any tool of aggression.

Study how Talleyrand, the master of the art, performed this delicate trick. First, he overcame the urge to try to convince his fellow statesmen that they needed to banish Napoleon far away. It is only natural to want to persuade people by pleading your case, imposing your will with words. But this often turns against you. Few of Talleyrand's contemporaries believed Napoleon was still a threat, so that if he had spent a lot of energy trying to convince them, he would only have made himself look foolish. Instead, he held his tongue and his emotions in check. Most important of all, he laid Napoleon a sweet and irresistible trap. He knew the man's weakness, his impetuosity, his need for glory and the love of the masses, and he played all this to perfection. When Napoleon went for the bait, there was no danger that he might succeed and turn the tables on Talleyrand, who better than anyone knew France's depleted state. And even had Napoleon been able to overcome these difficulties, the likelihood of his success would have been greater were he able to choose his time and place of action. By setting the proper trap, Talleyrand took the time and place into his own hands.

All of us have only so much energy, and there is a moment when our energies are at their peak. When you make the other person come to you, he wears himself out, wasting his energy on the trip. In the year 1905, Russia and Japan were at war. The Japanese had only recently begun to modernize their warships, so that the Russians had a stronger navy, but by spreading false information the Japanese marshal Togo Heihachiro baited the Russians into leaving their docks in the Baltic Sea, making them believe they could wipe out the Japanese fleet in one swift attack. The Russian fleet could not reach Japan by the quickest route—through the Strait of Gibraltar and then the Suez Canal into the Indian Ocean—because these were controlled by the British, and Japan was an ally of Great Britain. They had to go around the Cape of Good Hope, at the southern tip of Africa, adding over more than six thousand miles to the voyage. Once the fleet passed the Cape, the Japanese spread another false story: They were sailing to launch a counterattack. So the Russians made the entire journey to Japan on combat alert. By the time they arrived, their seamen were tense, exhausted, and overworked, while the Japanese had been waiting at their ease. Despite the odds and their lack of experience in modern naval warfare, the Japanese crushed the Russians.

One added benefit of making the opponent come to you, as the Japanese discovered with the Russians, is that it forces him to operate in your territory. Being on hostile ground will make him nervous and often he will rush his actions and make mistakes. For negotiations or meetings, it is always wise to lure others into your territory, or the territory of your choice. You have your bearings, while they see nothing familiar and are subtly placed on the defensive.

Manipulation is a dangerous game. Once someone suspects he is being manipulated, it becomes harder and harder to control him. But when you make your opponent come to you, you create the illusion that he is controlling the situation. He does not feel the strings that pull him, just as Napoleon imagined that he himself was the master of his daring escape and return to power.

Everything depends on the sweetness of your bait. If your trap is attractive enough, the turbulence of your enemies' emotions and desires will blind them to reality. The greedier they become, the more they can be led around.

The great nineteenth-century robber baron Daniel Drew was a master at playing the stock market. When he wanted a particular stock to be bought or sold, driving prices up or down, he rarely resorted to the direct approach. One of his tricks was to hurry through an exclusive club near Wall Street, obviously on his way to the stock exchange, and to pull out his customary red bandanna to wipe his perspiring brow. A slip of paper would fall from this bandanna that he would pretend not to notice. The club's members were always trying to foresee Drew's moves, and they would pounce on the paper, which invariably seemed to contain an inside tip on a stock. Word would spread, and members would buy or sell the stock in droves, playing perfectly into Drew's hands.

If you can get other people to dig their own graves, why sweat yourself? Pickpockets work this to perfection. The key to picking a pocket is knowing which pocket contains the wallet. Experienced pickpockets often ply their trade in train stations and other places where there is a clearly marked sign reading BEWARE OF PICKPOCKETS. Passersby seeing the sign invariably feel for their wallet to make sure it is still there. For the watching pickpockets, this is like shooting fish in a barrel. Pickpockets have even been known to place their own BEWARE OF PICKPOCKETS signs to ensure their success.

When you are making people come to you, it is sometimes better to let them know you are forcing their hand. You give up deception for overt manipulation. The psychological ramifications are profound: The person who makes others come to him appears powerful, and demands respect.

Filippo Brunelleschi, the great Renaissance artist and architect, was a great practitioner of the art of making others come to him as a sign of his power. On one occasion he had been engaged to repair the dome of the Santa Maria del Fiore cathedral in Florence. The commission was important and prestigious. But when the city officials hired a second man, Lorenzo Ghiberti, to work with Brunelleschi, the great artist brooded in secret. He knew that Ghiberti had gotten the job through his connections, and that he would do none of the work and get half the credit. At a critical moment of the construction, then, Brunelleschi suddenly developed a mysterious illness. He had to stop work, but pointed out to city officials that they had hired Ghiberti, who should have been able to continue the work on his own. Soon it became clear that Ghiberti was useless and the officials came begging to Brunelleschi. He ignored them, insisting that Ghiberti should finish the project, until finally they realized the problem: They fired Ghiberti.

By some miracle, Brunelleschi recovered within days. He did not have to throw a tantrum or make a fool of himself; he simply practiced the art of "making others come to you."

If on one occasion you make it a point of dignity that others must come to you and you succeed, they will continue to do so even after you stop trying.

Image: The Honeyed Bear Trap. The bear hunter does not chase his prey; a bear that knows it is hunted is nearly impossible to catch and is ferocious if cornered. Instead, the hunter lays traps baited with honey. He does not exhaust himself and risk his life in pursuit. He baits, then waits.

Authority: Good warriors make others come to them, and do not go to others. This is the principle of emptiness and fullness of others and self. When you induce opponents to come to you, then their force is always empty; as long as you do not go to them, your force is always full. Attacking emptiness with fullness is like throwing stones on eggs. (Zhang Yu, eleventh-century commentator on *The Art of War*)

REVERSAL

Although it is generally the wiser policy to make others exhaust themselves chasing you, there are opposite cases where striking suddenly and aggressively at the enemy so demoralizes him that his energies sink. Instead of making others come to you, you go to them, force the issue, take the lead. Fast attack can be an awesome weapon, for it forces the other person to react without the time to think or plan. With no time to think, people make errors of judgment, and are thrown on the defensive. This tactic is the obverse of waiting and baiting, but it serves the same function: You make your enemy respond on your terms.

Men like Cesare Borgia and Napoleon used the element of speed to intimidate and control. A rapid and unforeseen move is terrifying and demoralizing. You must choose your tactics depending on the situation. If you have time on your side, and know that you and your enemies are at least at equal strength, then deplete their strength by making them come to you. If time is against you—your enemies are weaker, and waiting will only give them the chance to recover—give them no such chance. Strike quickly and they have nowhere to go. As the boxer Joe Louis put it, "He can run, but he can't hide."

9

WIN THROUGH YOUR

ACTIONS, NEVER

THROUGH ARGUMENT

JUDGMENT

Any momentary triumph you think you have gained through argument is really a Pyrrhic victory: The resentment and ill will you stir up is stronger and lasts longer than any momentary change of opinion. It is much more powerful to get others to agree with you through your actions, without saying a word. Demonstrate, do not explicate.

TRANSGRESSION OF THE LAW

THE SULTAN AND
THE VIZIER

A vizier had served his
master for some thirty
years and was known
and admired for his
loyalty, truthfulness,
and devotion to God.
His honesty, however,
had made him many
enemies in the court,
who spread stories of
his duplicity and
perfidy. They worked
on the sultan day in
and day out until he too
came to distrust the
innocent vizier and
finally ordered the man
who had served him so
well to be put to death.
In this realm, those
condemned to death
were tied up and
thrown into the pen
where the sultan kept
his fiercest hunting
dogs. The dogs would
promptly tear the
victim to pieces.
Before being thrown to
the dogs, however, the
vizier asked for one last
request. "I would like
ten days' respite," he
said, "so that I can pay
my debts, collect any
money due to me,
return items that people
have put in my care,
and share out my goods
among the members of
my family and my chil-
dren and appoint a
guardian for them."
After receiving a guar-
antee that the vizier
would not try to escape,
the sultan granted this
request.
The vizier hurried
home, collected one
hundred gold pieces,
then paid a visit to the
huntsman who looked
after the sultan's

In 131 B.C., the Roman consul Publius Crassus Dives Mucianus, laying siege to the Greek town of Pergamus, found himself in need of a battering ram to force through the town's walls. He had seen a couple of hefty ship's masts in a shipyard in Athens a few days before, and he ordered that the larger of these be sent to him immediately. The military engineer in Athens who received the order felt certain that the consul really wanted the smaller of the masts. He argued endlessly with the soldiers who delivered the request: The smaller mast, he told them, was much better suited to the task. And indeed it would be easier to transport.

The soldiers warned the engineer that their master was not a man to argue with, but he insisted that the smaller mast would be the only one that would work with a machine that he was constructing to go with it. He drew diagram after diagram, and went so far as to say that he was the expert and they had no clue what they were talking about. The soldiers knew their leader and at last convinced the engineer that it would be better to swallow his expertise and obey.

After they left, though, the engineer thought about it some more. What was the point, he asked himself, in obeying an order that would lead to failure? And so he sent the smaller mast, confident that the consul would see how much more effective it was and reward him justly.

When the smaller mast arrived, Mucianus asked his soldiers for an explanation. They described to him how the engineer had argued endlessly for the smaller mast, but had finally promised to send the larger one. Mucianus went into a rage. He could not concentrate on the siege, or consider the importance of breaching the walls before the town received reinforcements. All he could think about was the impudent engineer, whom he ordered to be brought to him immediately.

Arriving a few days later, the engineer gladly explained to the consul, one more time, the reasons for the smaller mast. He went on and on, using the same arguments he had made with the soldiers. He said it was wise to listen to experts in these matters, and if the attack was only tried with the battering ram he had sent, the consul would not regret it. Mucianus let him finish, then had him stripped naked before the soldiers and flogged and scourged with rods until he died.

Interpretation

The engineer, whose name has not been recorded by history, had spent his life designing masts and pillars, and was respected as the finest engineer in a city that had excelled in the science. He knew that he was right. A smaller ram would allow more speed and carry more force. Larger is not necessarily better. Of course the consul would see his logic, and would eventually understand that science is neutral and reason superior. How could the consul possibly persist in his ignorance if the engineer showed him detailed diagrams and explained the theories behind his advice?

The military engineer was the quintessence of the Arguer, a type found everywhere among us. The Arguer does not understand that words are never neutral, and that by arguing with a superior he impugns the intelligence of one more powerful than he. He also has no awareness of the person he is dealing with. Since each man believes that he is right, and words will rarely convince him otherwise, the arguer's reasoning falls on deaf ears. When cornered, he only argues more, digging his own grave. Once he has made the other person feel insecure and inferior in his beliefs, the eloquence of Socrates could not save the situation.

It is not simply a question of avoiding an argument with those who stand above you. We all believe we are masters in the realm of opinions and reasoning. You must be careful, then: Learn to demonstrate the correctness of your ideas indirectly.

OBSERVANCE OF THE LAW

In 1502, in Florence, Italy, an enormous block of marble stood in the works department of the church of Santa Maria del Fiore. It had once been a magnificent piece of raw stone, but an unskillful sculptor had mistakenly bored a hole through it where there should have been a figure's legs, generally mutilating it. Piero Soderini, Florence's mayor, had contemplated trying to save the block by commissioning Leonardo da Vinci to work on it, or some other master, but had given up, since everyone agreed that the stone had been ruined. So, despite the money that had been wasted on it, it gathered dust in the dark halls of the church.

This was where things stood until some Florentine friends of the great Michelangelo decided to write to the artist, then living in Rome. He alone, they said, could do something with the marble, which was still magnificent raw material. Michelangelo traveled to Florence, examined the stone, and came to the conclusion that he could in fact carve a fine figure from it, by adapting the pose to the way the rock had been mutilated. Soderini argued that this was a waste of time—nobody could salvage such a disaster—but he finally agreed to let the artist work on it. Michelangelo decided he would depict a young David, sling in hand.

Weeks later, as Michelangelo was putting the final touches on the statue, Soderini entered the studio. Fancying himself a bit of a connoisseur, he studied the huge work, and told Michelangelo that while he thought it was magnificent, the nose, he judged, was too big. Michelangelo realized that Soderini was standing in a place right under the giant figure and did not have the proper perspective. Without a word, he gestured for Soderini to follow him up the scaffolding. Reaching the nose, he picked up his chisel, as well as a bit of marble dust that lay on the planks. With Soderini just a few feet below him on the scaffolding, Michelangelo started to tap lightly with the chisel, letting the bits of dust he had gathered in his hand to fall little by little. He actually did nothing to change the nose, but gave every appearance of working on it. After a few minutes of this charade he stood aside: "Look at it now." "I like it better," replied Soderini, "you've made it come alive."

dogs. He offered this man the one hundred gold pieces and said, "Let me look after the dogs for ten days." The huntsman agreed, and for the next ten days the vizier cared for the beasts with great attention, grooming them well and feeding them handsomely. By the end of the ten days they were eating out of his hand.

On the eleventh day the vizier was called before the sultan, the charges were repeated, and the sultan watched as the vizier was tied up and thrown to the dogs. Yet when the beasts saw him, they ran up to him with wagging tails. They nibbled affectionately at his shoulders and began playing with him. The sultan and the other witnesses were amazed, and the sultan asked the vizier why the dogs had spared his life. The vizier replied, "I have looked after these dogs for ten days. The sultan has seen the result for himself. I have looked after you for thirty years, and what is the result? I am condemned to death on the strength of accusations brought by my enemies." The sultan blushed with shame. He not only pardoned the vizier but gave him a fine set of clothes and handed over to him the men who had slandered his reputation. The noble vizier set them free and continued to treat them with kindness.

THE SUBTLE RUSE:
THE BOOK OF ARABIC
WISDOM AND GUILE,
THIRTEENTH CENTURY

Interpretation

Michelangelo knew that by changing the shape of the nose he might ruin the entire sculpture. Yet Soderini was a patron who prided himself on his aesthetic judgment. To offend such a man by arguing would not only gain Michelangelo nothing, it would put future commissions in jeopardy. Michelangelo was too clever to argue. His solution was to change Soderini's perspective (literally bringing him closer to the nose) without making him realize that this was the cause of his misperception.

Fortunately for posterity, Michelangelo found a way to keep the perfection of the statue intact while at the same time making Soderini believe he had improved it. Such is the double power of winning through actions rather than argument: No one is offended, and your point is proven.

KEYS TO POWER

In the realm of power you must learn to judge your moves by their long-term effects on other people. The problem in trying to prove a point or gain a victory through argument is that in the end you can never be certain how it affects the people you're arguing with: They may appear to agree with you politely, but inside they may resent you. Or perhaps something you said inadvertently even offended them—words have that insidious ability to be interpreted according to the other person's mood and insecurities. Even the best argument has no solid foundation, for we have all come to distrust the slippery nature of words. And days after agreeing with someone, we often revert to our old opinion out of sheer habit.

Understand this: Words are a dime a dozen. Everyone knows that in the heat of an argument, we will all say anything to support our cause. We will quote the Bible, refer to unverifiable statistics. Who can be persuaded by bags of air like that? Action and demonstration are much more powerful and meaningful. They are there, before our eyes, for us to see—"Yes, now the statue's nose does look just right." There are no offensive words, no possibility of misinterpretation. No one can argue with a demonstrated proof. As Baltasar Gracián remarks, "The truth is generally seen, rarely heard."

Sir Christopher Wren was England's version of the Renaissance man. He had mastered the sciences of mathematics, astronomy, physics, and physiology. Yet during his extremely long career as England's most celebrated architect he was often told by his patrons to make impractical changes in his designs. Never once did he argue or offend. He had other ways of proving his point.

In 1688 Wren designed a magnificent town hall for the city of Westminster. The mayor, however, was not satisfied; in fact he was nervous. He told Wren he was afraid the second floor was not secure, and that it could all come crashing down on his office on the first floor. He demanded that Wren add two stone columns for extra support. Wren, the consummate engineer, knew that these columns would serve no purpose, and that the mayor's fears were baseless. But build them he did, and the mayor was grateful. It was only years later that workmen on a high scaffold saw that the columns stopped just short of the ceiling.

They were dummies. But both men got what they wanted: The mayor could relax, and Wren knew posterity would understand that his original design worked and the columns were unnecessary.

The power of demonstrating your idea is that your opponents do not get defensive, and are therefore more open to persuasion. Making them literally and physically feel your meaning is infinitely more powerful than argument.

A heckler once interrupted Nikita Khrushchev in the middle of a speech in which he was denouncing the crimes of Stalin. "You were a colleague of Stalin's," the heckler yelled, "why didn't you stop him then?" Khrushschev apparently could not see the heckler and barked out, "Who said that?" No hand went up. No one moved a muscle. After a few seconds of tense silence, Khrushchev finally said in a quiet voice, "Now you know why I didn't stop him." Instead of just arguing that anyone facing Stalin was afraid, knowing that the slightest sign of rebellion would mean certain death, he had made them *feel* what it was like to face Stalin—had made them feel the paranoia, the fear of speaking up, the terror of confronting the leader, in this case Khrushchev. The demonstration was visceral and no more argument was necessary.

The most powerful persuasion goes beyond action into symbol. The power of a symbol—a flag, a mythic story, a monument to some emotional event—is that everyone understands you without anything being said. In 1975, when Henry Kissinger was engaged in some frustrating negotiations with the Israelis over the return of part of the Sinai desert that they had seized in the 1967 war, he suddenly broke off a tense meeting and decided to do some sight-seeing. He paid a visit to the ruins of the ancient fortress of Masada, known to all Israelis as the place where seven hundred Jewish warriors committed mass suicide in A.D. 73 rather than give in to the Roman troops besieging them. The Israelis instantly understood the message of Kissinger's visit: He was indirectly accusing them of courting mass suicide. Although the visit did not by itself change their minds, it made them think far more seriously than any direct warning would have. Symbols like this one carry great emotional significance.

When aiming for power, or trying to conserve it, always look for the indirect route. And also choose your battles carefully. If it does not matter in the long run whether the other person agrees with you—or if time and their own experience will make them understand what you mean—then it is best not even to bother with a demonstration. Save your energy and walk away.

honor and respect to him, too. In this way the Egyptians were persuaded to accept him as their master.

THE HISTORIES
HERODOTUS,
FIFTH CENTURY B.C.

GOD AND ABRAHAM

The Most High God had promised that He would not take Abraham's soul unless the man wanted to die and asked Him to do so. When Abraham's life was drawing to a close, and God determined to seize him, He sent an angel in the guise of a decrepit old man who was almost entirely incapacitated. The old man stopped outside Abraham's door and said to him, "Oh Abraham, I would like something to eat." Abraham was amazed to hear him say this. "Die," exclaimed Abraham. "It would be better for you than to go on living in that condition." Abraham always kept food ready at his home for passing guests. So he gave the old man a bowl containing broth and meat with bread crumbs. The old man sat down to eat. He swallowed laboriously, with great effort, and once when he took some food it dropped from his hand, scattering on the ground. "Oh Abraham," he said,

Image: The See-
saw. Up and down
and up and down
go the arguers,
getting nowhere
fast. Get off the
seesaw and show
them your mean-
ing without kick
ing or pushing.
Leave them at the
top and let gravity
bring them gently
to the ground.

Authority: Never argue. In society nothing must be discussed; give only results. (Benjamin Disraeli, 1804–1881)

REVERSAL

Verbal argument has one vital use in the realm of power: To distract and cover your tracks when you are practicing deception or are caught in a lie. In such cases it is to your advantage to argue with all the conviction you can muster. Draw the other person into an argument to distract them from your deceptive move. When caught in a lie, the more emotional and certain you appear, the less likely it seems that you are lying.

This technique has saved the hide of many a con artist. Once Count Victor Lustig, swindler par excellence, had sold dozens of suckers around the country a phony box with which he claimed to be able to copy money. Discovering their mistake, the suckers generally chose not to go the police, rather than risk the embarrassment of publicity. But one Sheriff Richards, of Remsen County, Oklahoma, was not the kind of man to accept being conned out of $10,000, and one morning he tracked Lustig down to a hotel in Chicago.

Lustig heard a knock on the door. When he opened it he was looking down the barrel of a gun. "What seems to be the problem?" he calmly asked. "You son of a bitch," yelled the sheriff, "I'm going to kill you. You conned me with that damn box of yours!" Lustig feigned confusion. "You mean it's not working?" he asked. "You know it's not working," replied the sheriff. "But that's impossible," said Lustig. "There's no way it couldn't be working. Did you operate it properly?" "I did exactly what you told me to do," said the sheriff. "No, you must have done something wrong," said Lustig. The argument went in circles. The barrel of the gun was gently lowered.

Lustig next went to phase two in the argument tactic: He poured out a whole bunch of technical gobbledygook about the box's operation, completely beguiling the sheriff, who now appeared less sure of himself and argued less forcefully. "Look," said Lustig, "I'll give you your money back right now. I'll also give you written instructions on how to work the machine and I'll come out to Oklahoma to make sure it's working properly. There's no way you can lose on that." The sheriff reluctantly agreed. To satisfy him totally, Lustig took out a hundred one-hundred-dollar bills and gave them to him, telling him to relax and have a fun weekend in Chicago. Calmer and a little confused, the sheriff finally left. Over the next few days Lustig checked the paper every morning. He finally found what he was looking for: A short article reporting Sheriff Richards's arrest, trial, and conviction for passing counterfeit notes. Lustig had won the argument; the sheriff never bothered him again.

INFECTION: AVOID THE

UNHAPPY AND UNLUCKY

JUDGMENT

You can die from someone else's misery—emotional states are as infectious as diseases. You may feel you are helping the drowning man but you are only precipitating your own disaster. The unfortunate sometimes draw misfortune on themselves; they will also draw it on you. Associate with the happy and fortunate instead.

TRANSGRESSION OF THE LAW

Born in Limerick, Ireland, in 1818, Marie Gilbert came to Paris in the 1840s to make her fortune as a dancer and performer. Taking the name Lola Montez (her mother was of distant Spanish descent), she claimed to be a flamenco dancer from Spain. By 1845 her career was languishing, and to survive she became a courtesan—quickly one of the more successful in Paris.

Only one man could salvage Lola's dancing career: Alexandre Dujarier, owner of the newspaper with the largest circulation in France, and also the newspaper's drama critic. She decided to woo and conquer him. Investigating his habits, she discovered that he went riding every morning. An excellent horsewoman herself, she rode out one morning and "accidentally" ran into him. Soon they were riding together every day. A few weeks later Lola moved into his apartment.

For a while the two were happy together. With Dujarier's help, Lola began to revive her dancing career. Despite the risk to his social standing, Dujarier told friends he would marry her in the spring. (Lola had never told him that she had eloped at age nineteen with an Englishman, and was still legally married.) Although Dujarier was deeply in love, his life started to slide downhill.

His fortunes in business changed and influential friends began to avoid him. One night Dujarier was invited to a party, attended by some of the wealthiest young men in Paris. Lola wanted to go too but he would not allow it. They had their first quarrel, and Dujarier attended the party by himself. There, hopelessly drunk, he insulted an influential drama critic, Jean-Baptiste Rosemond de Beauvallon, perhaps because of something the critic had said about Lola. The following morning Beauvallon challenged him to a duel. Beauvallon was one of the best pistol shots in France. Dujarier tried to apologize, but the duel took place, and he was shot and killed. Thus ended the life of one of the most promising young men of Paris society. Devastated, Lola left Paris.

In 1846 Lola Montez found herself in Munich, where she decided to woo and conquer King Ludwig of Bavaria. The best way to Ludwig, she discovered, was through his aide-de-camp, Count Otto von Rechberg, a man with a fondness for pretty girls. One day when the count was breakfasting at an outdoor café, Lola rode by on her horse, was "accidentally" thrown from the saddle, and landed at Rechberg's feet. The count rushed to help her and was enchanted. He promised to introduce her to Ludwig.

Rechberg arranged an audience with the king for Lola, but when she arrived in the anteroom, she could hear the king saying he was too busy to meet a favor-seeking stranger. Lola pushed aside the sentries and entered his room anyway. In the process, the front of her dress somehow got torn (perhaps by her, perhaps by one of the sentries), and to the astonishment of all, most especially the king, her bare breasts were brazenly exposed. Lola was granted her audience with Ludwig. Fifty-five hours later she made her debut on the Bavarian stage; the reviews were terrible, but that did not stop Ludwig from arranging more performances.

THE NUT AND THE CAMANILE

A nut found itself carried by a crow to the top of a tall campanile, and by falling into a crevice succeeded in escaping its dread fate. It then besought the wall to shelter it, by appealing to it by the grace of God, and praising its height, and the beauty and noble tone of its bells. "Alas," it went on, "as I have not been able to drop beneath the green branches of my old Father and to lie in the fallow earth covered by his fallen leaves, do you, at least, not abandon me. When I found myself in the beak of the cruel crow I made a vow, that if I escaped I would end my life in a little hole."
At these words, the wall, moved with compassion, was content to shelter the nut in the spot where it had fallen. Within a short time, the nut burst open: Its roots reached in between the crevices of the stones and began to push them apart; its shoots pressed up toward the sky. They soon rose above the building, and as the twisted roots grew thicker they began to thrust the walls apart and force the ancient stones from their old places. Then the wall, too late and in vain, bewailed the cause of its destruction, and in short time it fell in ruin.

LEONARDO DA VINCI, 1452–1519

Ludwig was, in his own words, "bewitched" by Lola. He started to appear in public with her on his arm, and then he bought and furnished an apartment for her on one of Munich's most fashionable boulevards. Although he had been known as a miser, and was not given to flights of fancy, he started to shower Lola with gifts and to write poetry for her. Now his favored mistress, she catapulted to fame and fortune overnight.

Lola began to lose her sense of proportion. One day when she was out riding, an elderly man rode ahead of her, a bit too slowly for her liking. Unable to pass him, she began to slash him with her riding crop. On another occasion she took her dog, unleashed, out for a stroll. The dog attacked a passerby, but instead of helping the man get the dog away, she whipped him with the leash. Incidents like this infuriated the stolid citizens of Bavaria, but Ludwig stood by Lola and even had her naturalized as a Bavarian citizen. The king's entourage tried to wake him to the dangers of the affair, but those who criticized Lola were summarily fired.

While Bavarians who had loved their king now outwardly disrespected him, Lola was made a countess, had a new palace built for herself, and began to dabble in politics, advising Ludwig on policy. She was the most powerful force in the kingdom. Her influence in the king's cabinet continued to grow, and she treated the other ministers with disdain. As a result, riots broke out throughout the realm. A once peaceful land was virtually in the grip of civil war, and students everywhere were chanting, *"Raus mit Lola!"*

By February of 1848, Ludwig was finally unable to withstand the pressure. With great sadness he ordered Lola to leave Bavaria immediately. She left, but not until she was paid off. For the next five weeks the Bavarians' wrath was turned against their formerly beloved king. In March of that year he was forced to abdicate.

Lola Montez moved to England. More than anything she needed respectability, and despite being married (she still had not arranged a divorce from the Englishman she had wed years before), she set her sights on George Trafford Heald, a promising young army officer who was the son of an influential barrister. Although he was ten years younger than Lola, and could have chosen a wife among the prettiest and wealthiest young girls of English society, Heald fell under her spell. They were married in 1849. Soon arrested on the charge of bigamy, she skipped bail, and she and Heald made their way to Spain. They quarreled horribly and on one occasion Lola slashed him with a knife. Finally, she drove him away. Returning to England, he found he had lost his position in the army. Ostracized from English society, he moved to Portugal, where he lived in poverty. After a few months his short life ended in a boating accident.

A few years later the man who published Lola Montez's autobiography went bankrupt.

In 1853 Lola moved to California, where she met and married a man named Pat Hull. Their relationship was as stormy as all the others, and she left Hull for another man. He took to drink and fell into a deep depression that lasted until he died, four years later, still a relatively young man.

At the age of forty-one, Lola gave away her clothes and finery and turned to God. She toured America, lecturing on religious topics, dressed in white and wearing a halolike white headgear. She died two years later, in 1861.

Interpretation

Lola Montez attracted men with her wiles, but her power over them went beyond the sexual. It was through the force of her character that she kept her lovers enthralled. Men were sucked into the maelstrom she churned up around her. They felt confused, upset, but the strength of the emotions she stirred also made them feel more alive.

As is often the case with infection, the problems would only arise over time. Lola's inherent instability would begin to get under her lovers' skin. They would find themselves drawn into her problems, but their emotional attachment to her would make them want to help her. This was the crucial point of the disease—for Lola Montez could not be helped. Her problems were too deep. Once the lover identified with them, he was lost. He would find himself embroiled in quarrels. The infection would spread to his family and friends, or, in the case of Ludwig, to an entire nation. The only solution would be to cut her off, or suffer an eventual collapse.

The infecting-character type is not restricted to women; it has nothing to do with gender. It stems from an inward instability that radiates outward, drawing disaster upon itself. There is almost a desire to destroy and unsettle. You could spend a lifetime studying the pathology of infecting characters, but don't waste your time—just learn the lesson. When you suspect you are in the presence of an infector, don't argue, don't try to help, don't pass the person on to your friends, or you will become enmeshed. Flee the infector's presence or suffer the consequences.

> *Yond Cassius has a lean and hungry look. He thinks too much. . . .*
> *I do not know the man I should avoid so soon as that spare Cassius. . . .*
> *Such men as he be never at heart's ease whiles they behold a greater*
> *than themselves, and therefore are they very dangerous.*
> Julius Ceasar, *William Shakespeare, 1564–1616*

KEYS TO POWER

Those misfortunates among us who have been brought down by circumstances beyond their control deserve all the help and sympathy we can give them. But there are others who are not born to misfortune or unhappiness, but who draw it upon themselves by their destructive actions and unsettling effect on others. It would be a great thing if we could raise them up, change their patterns, but more often than not it is their patterns that end up getting inside and changing us. The reason is simple—humans are extremely susceptible to the moods, emotions, and even the ways of thinking of those with whom they spend their time.

The incurably unhappy and unstable have a particularly strong infect-

Regard no foolish man as cultured, though you may reckon a gifted man as wise; and esteem no ignorant abstainer a true ascetic. Do not consort with fools, especially those who consider themselves wise. And be not self-satisfied with your own ignorance. Let your intercourse be only with men of good repute; for it is by such association that men themselves attain to good repute. Do you not observe how sesame-oil is mingled with roses or violets and how, when it has been for some time in association with roses or violets, it ceases to be sesame-oil and is called oil of roses or oil of violets?

A MIRROR FOR PRINCES, KAI KA'US IBN ISKANDAR, ELEVENTH CENTURY

ing power because their characters and emotions are so intense. They often present themselves as victims, making it difficult, at first, to see their miseries as self-inflicted. Before you realize the real nature of their problems you have been infected by them.

Understand this: In the game of power, the people you associate with are critical. The risk of associating with infectors is that you will waste valuable time and energy trying to free yourself. Through a kind of guilt by association, you will also suffer in the eyes of others. Never underestimate the dangers of infection.

There are many kinds of infector to be aware of, but one of the most insidious is the sufferer from chronic dissatisfaction. Cassius, the Roman conspirator against Julius Caesar, had the discontent that comes from deep envy. He simply could not endure the presence of anyone of greater talent. Probably because Caesar sensed the man's interminable sourness, he passed him up for the position of first praetorship, and gave the position to Brutus instead. Cassius brooded and brooded, his hatred for Caesar becoming pathological. Brutus himself, a devoted republican, disliked Caesar's dictatorship; had he had the patience to wait, he would have become the first man in Rome after Caesar's death, and could have undone the evil that the leader had wrought. But Cassius infected him with his own rancor, bending his ear daily with tales of Caesar's evil. He finally won Brutus over to the conspiracy. It was the beginning of a great tragedy. How many misfortunes could have been avoided had Brutus learned to fear the power of infection.

There is only one solution to infection: quarantine. But by the time you recognize the problem it is often too late. A Lola Montez overwhelms you with her forceful personality. Cassius intrigues you with his confiding nature and the depth of his feelings. How can you protect yourself against such insidious viruses? The answer lies in judging people on the effects they have on the world and not on the reasons they give for their prob-

Image: A Virus. Unseen, it

lems. Infectors can be recognized by the misfortune they draw on them-

enters your pores without

selves, their turbulent past, their long line of broken relationships, their un-

warning, spreading silently and

stable careers, and the very force of their character, which sweeps you up

slowly. Before you are aware of

and makes you lose your reason. Be forewarned by these signs of an infec-

the infection, it is deep inside you.

tor; learn to see the discontent in their eye. Most important of all, do not take pity. Do not enmesh yourself in trying to help. The infector will remain unchanged, but you will be unhinged.

The other side of infection is equally valid, and perhaps more readily understood: There are people who attract happiness to themselves by their good cheer, natural buoyancy, and intelligence. They are a source of pleasure, and you must associate with them to share in the prosperity they draw upon themselves.

This applies to more than good cheer and success: All positive qualities can infect us. Talleyrand had many strange and intimidating traits, but most agreed that he surpassed all Frenchmen in graciousness, aristocratic charm, and wit. Indeed he came from one of the oldest noble families in the country, and despite his belief in democracy and the French Republic, he retained his courtly manners. His contemporary Napoleon was in many ways the opposite—a peasant from Corsica, taciturn and ungracious, even violent.

There was no one Napoleon admired more than Talleyrand. He envied his minister's way with people, his wit and his ability to charm women, and as best he could, he kept Talleyrand around him, hoping to soak up the culture he lacked. There is no doubt that Napoleon changed as his rule continued. Many of the rough edges were smoothed by his constant association with Talleyrand.

Use the positive side of this emotional osmosis to advantage. If, for example, you are miserly by nature, you will never go beyond a certain limit; only generous souls attain greatness. Associate with the generous, then, and they will infect you, opening up everything that is tight and restricted in you. If you are gloomy, gravitate to the cheerful. If you are prone to isolation, force yourself to befriend the gregarious. Never associate with those who share your defects—they will reinforce everything that holds you back. Only create associations with positive affinities. Make this a rule of life and you will benefit more than from all the therapy in the world.

Authority: Recognize the fortunate so that you may choose their company, and the unfortunate so that you may avoid them. Misfortune is usually the crime of folly, and among those who suffer from it there is no malady more contagious: Never open your door to the least of misfortunes, for, if you do, many others will follow in its train.... Do not die of another's misery. (Baltasar Gracián, 1601–1658)

REVERSAL
This law admits of no reversal. Its application is universal. There is nothing to be gained by associating with those who infect you with their misery; there is only power and good fortune to be obtained by associating with the fortunate. Ignore this law at your peril.

LEARN TO KEEP PEOPLE

DEPENDENT ON YOU

JUDGMENT

To maintain your independence you must always be needed and wanted. The more you are relied on, the more freedom you have. Make people depend on you for their happiness and prosperity and you have nothing to fear. Never teach them enough so that they can do without you.

TRANSGRESSION OF THE LAW

Sometime in the Middle Ages, a mercenary soldier (a *condottiere*), whose name has not been recorded, saved the town of Siena from a foreign aggressor. How could the good citizens of Siena reward him? No amount of money or honor could possibly compare in value to the preservation of a city's liberty. The citizens thought of making the mercenary the lord of the city, but even that, they decided, wasn't recompense enough. At last one of them stood before the assembly called to debate this matter and said, "Let us kill him and then worship him as our patron saint." And so they did.

The Count of Carmagnola was one of the bravest and most successful of all the *condottieri*. In 1442, late in his life, he was in the employ of the city of Venice, which was in the midst of a long war with Florence. The count was suddenly recalled to Venice. A favorite of the people, he was received there with all kinds of honor and splendor. That evening he was to dine with the doge himself, in the doge's palace. On the way into the palace, however, he noticed that the guard was leading him in a different direction from usual. Crossing the famous Bridge of Sighs, he suddenly realized where they were taking him—to the dungeon. He was convicted on a trumped-up charge and the next day in the Piazza San Marco, before a horrified crowd who could not understand how his fate had changed so drastically, he was beheaded.

Many of the great *condottieri* of Renaissance Italy suffered the same fate as the patron saint of Siena and the Count of Carmagnola: They won battle after battle for their employers only to find themselves banished, imprisoned, or executed. The problem was not ingratitude; it was that there were so many other *condottieri* as able and valiant as they were. They were replaceable. Nothing was lost by killing them. Meanwhile, the older among them had grown powerful themselves, and wanted more and more money for their services. How much better, then, to do away with them and hire a younger, cheaper mercenary. That was the fate of the Count of Carmagnola, who had started to act impudently and independently. He had taken his power for granted without making sure that he was truly indispensable.

Such is the fate (to a less violent degree, one hopes) of those who do not make others dependent on them. Sooner or later someone comes along who can do the job as well as they can—someone younger, fresher, less expensive, less threatening.

Be the *only one* who can do what you do, and make the fate of those who hire you so entwined with yours that they cannot possibly get rid of you. Otherwise you will someday be forced to cross your own Bridge of Sighs.

OBSERVANCE OF THE LAW

When Otto von Bismarck became a deputy in the Prussian parliament in 1847, he was thirty-two years old and without an ally or friend. Looking

THE TWO HORSES

Two horses were carrying two loads. The front Horse went well, but the rear Horse was lazy. The men began to pile the rear Horse's load on the front Horse; when they had transferred it all, the rear Horse found it easy going, and he said to the front Horse: "Toil and sweat! The more you try, the more you have to suffer." When they reached the tavern, the owner said: "Why should I fodder two horses when I carry all on one? I had better give the one all the food it wants, and cut the throat of the other; at least I shall have the hide." And so he did.

FABLES,
LEO TOLSTOY,
1828–1910

*Then the Woman
laughed and set the Cat
a bowl of the warm
white milk and said, "O
Cat, you are as clever
as a man, but remem-
ber that your bargain
was not made with the
Man or the Dog, and I
do not know what they
will do when they come
home." "What is that to
me?" said the Cat. "If I
have my place in the
Cave by the fire and my
warm white milk three
times a day, I do not
care what the Man or
the Dog can do."
. . . And from that day
to this, Best Beloved,
three proper Men out
of five will always
throw things at a Cat
whenever they meet
him, and all proper
Dogs will chase him up
a tree. But the Cat
keeps his side of the
bargain too. He will kill
mice, and he will be
kind to Babies when he
is in the house, just as
long as they do not pull
his tail too hard. But
when he has done that,
and between times, and
when the moon gets up
and the night comes, he
is the Cat that walks by
himself, and all places
are alike to him. Then
he goes out to the Wet
Wild Woods or up the
Wet Wild Trees or on
the Wet Wild Roofs,
waving his wild tail
and walking by his
wild lone.*

JUST SO STORIES,
RUDYARD KIPLING,
1865–1936

around him, he decided that the side to ally himself with was not the parliament's liberals or conservatives, not any particular minister, and certainly not the people. It was with the king, Frederick William IV. This was
an odd choice to say the least, for Frederick was at a low point of his power.
A weak, indecisive man, he consistently gave in to the liberals in parliament; in fact he was spineless, and stood for much that Bismarck disliked,
personally and politically. Yet Bismarck courted Frederick night and day.
When other deputies attacked the king for his many inept moves, only Bismarck stood by him.

Finally, it all paid off: In 1851 Bismarck was made a minister in the
king's cabinet. Now he went to work. Time and again he forced the king's
hand, getting him to build up the military, to stand up to the liberals, to do
exactly as Bismarck wished. He worked on Frederick's insecurity about his
manliness, challenging him to be firm and to rule with pride. And he
slowly restored the king's powers until the monarchy was once again the
most powerful force in Prussia.

When Frederick died, in 1861, his brother William assumed the
throne. William disliked Bismarck intensely and had no intention of keeping him around. But he also inherited the same situation his brother had:
enemies galore, who wanted to nibble his power away. He actually considered abdicating, feeling he lacked the strength to deal with this dangerous
and precarious position. But Bismarck insinuated himself once again. He
stood by the new king, gave him strength, and urged him into firm and decisive action. The king grew dependent on Bismarck's strong-arm tactics to
keep his enemies at bay, and despite his antipathy toward the man, he soon
made him his prime minister. The two quarreled often over policy—
Bismarck was much more conservative—but the king understood his own
dependency. Whenever the prime minister threatened to resign, the king
gave in to him, time after time. It was in fact Bismarck who set state policy.

Years later, Bismarck's actions as Prussia's prime minister led the various German states to be united into one country. Now Bismarck finagled
the king into letting himself be crowned emperor of Germany. Yet it was
really Bismarck who had reached the heights of power. As right-hand man
to the emperor, and as imperial chancellor and knighted prince, he pulled
all the levers.

Interpretation

Most young and ambitious politicians looking out on the political landscape
of 1840s Germany would have tried to build a power base among those
with the most power. Bismarck saw different. Joining forces with the powerful can be foolish: They will swallow you up, just as the doge of Venice
swallowed up the Count of Carmagnola. No one will come to depend on
you if they are already strong. If you are ambitious, it is much wiser to seek
out weak rulers or masters with whom you can create a relationship of dependency. You become their strength, their intelligence, their spine. What
power you hold! If they got rid of you the whole edifice would collapse.

Necessity rules the world. People rarely act unless compelled to. If you create no need for yourself, then you will be done away with at first opportunity. If, on the other hand, you understand the Laws of Power and make others depend on you for their welfare, if you can counteract their weakness with your own "iron and blood," in Bismarck's phrase, then you will survive your masters as Bismarck did. You will have all the benefits of power without the thorns that come from being a master.

> *Thus a wise prince will think of ways to keep his citizens of every sort and under every circumstance dependent on the state and on him; and then they will always be trustworthy.*
> *Niccolò Machiavelli, 1469–1527*

KEYS TO POWER

The ultimate power is the power to get people to do as you wish. When you can do this without having to force people or hurt them, when they willingly grant you what you desire, then your power is untouchable. The best way to achieve this position is to create a relationship of dependence. The master requires your services; he is weak, or unable to function without you; you have enmeshed yourself in his work so deeply that doing away with you would bring him great difficulty, or at least would mean valuable time lost in training another to replace you. Once such a relationship is established you have the upper hand, the leverage to make the master do as you wish. It is the classic case of the man behind the throne, the servant of the king who actually controls the king. Bismarck did not have to bully either Frederick or William into doing his bidding. He simply made it clear that unless he got what he wanted he would walk away, leaving the king to twist in the wind. Both kings soon danced to Bismarck's tune.

Do not be one of the many who mistakenly believe that the ultimate form of power is independence. Power involves a relationship between people; you will always need others as allies, pawns, or even as weak masters who serve as your front. The completely independent man would live in a cabin in the woods—he would have the freedom to come and go as he pleased, but he would have no power. The best you can hope for is that others will grow so dependent on you that you enjoy a kind of reverse independence: Their need for you frees you.

Louis XI (1423–1483), the great Spider King of France, had a weakness for astrology. He kept a court astrologer whom he admired, until one day the man predicted that a lady of the court would die within eight days. When the prophecy came true, Louis was terrified, thinking that either the man had murdered the woman to prove his accuracy or that he was so versed in his science that his powers threatened Louis himself. In either case he had to be killed.

One evening Louis summoned the astrologer to his room, high in the castle. Before the man arrived, the king told his servants that when he gave

An extravagant young Vine, vainly ambitious of independence, and fond of rambling at large, despised the alliance of a stately elm that grew near, and courted her embraces. Having risen to some small height without any kind of support, she shot forth her flimsy branches to a very uncommon and superfluous length; calling on her neighbour to take notice how little she wanted his assistance. "Poor infatuated shrub," replied the elm, "how inconsistent is thy conduct! Wouldst thou be truly independent, thou shouldst carefully apply those juices to the enlargement of thy stem, which thou lavishest in vain upon unnecessary foliage. I shortly shall behold thee grovelling on the ground; yet countenanced, indeed, by many of the human race, who, intoxicated with vanity, have despised economy; and who, to support for a moment their empty boast of independence, have exhausted the very source of it in frivolous expenses."

FABLES,
ROBERT DODSLEY,
1703–1764

the signal they were to pick the astrologer up, carry him to the window, and hurl him to the ground, hundreds of feet below.

The astrologer soon arrived, but before giving the signal, Louis decided to ask him one last question: "You claim to understand astrology and to know the fate of others, so tell me what your fate will be and how long you have to live."

"I shall die just three days before Your Majesty," the astrologer replied. The king's signal was never given. The man's life was spared. The Spider King not only protected his astrologer for as long as he was alive, he lavished him with gifts and had him tended by the finest court doctors.

The astrologer survived Louis by several years, disproving his power of prophecy but proving his mastery of power.

This is the model: Make others dependent on you. To get rid of you might spell disaster, even death, and your master dares not tempt fate by finding out. There are many ways to obtain such a position. Foremost among them is to possess a talent and creative skill that simply cannot be replaced.

During the Renaissance, the major obstacle to a painter's success was finding the right patron. Michelangelo did this better than anyone else: His patron was Pope Julius II. But he and the pope quarreled over the building of the pope's marble tomb, and Michelangelo left Rome in disgust. To the amazement of those in the pope's circle, not only did the pope not fire him, he sought him out and in his own haughty way begged the artist to stay. Michelangelo, he knew, could find another patron, but he could never find another Michelangelo.

You do not have to have the talent of a Michelangelo; you do have to have a skill that sets you apart from the crowd. You should create a situation in which you can always latch on to another master or patron but your master cannot easily find another servant with your particular talent. And if, in reality, you are not actually indispensable, you must find a way to make it look as if you are. Having the appearance of specialized knowledge and skill gives you leeway in your ability to deceive those above you into thinking they cannot do without you. Real dependence on your master's part, however, leaves him more vulnerable to you than the faked variety, and it is always within your power to make your skill indispensable.

This is what is meant by the intertwining of fates: Like creeping ivy, you have wrapped yourself around the source of power, so that it would cause great trauma to cut you away. And you do not necessarily have to entwine yourself around the master; another person will do, as long as he or she too is indispensable in the chain.

One day Harry Cohn, president of Columbia Pictures, was visited in his office by a gloomy group of his executives. It was 1951, when the witch-hunt against Communists in Hollywood, carried on by the U.S. Congress's House Un-American Activities Committee, was at its height. The executives had bad news: One of their employees, the screenwriter John Howard Lawson, had been singled out as a Communist. They had to get rid of him right away or suffer the wrath of the committee.

Harry Cohn was no bleeding-heart liberal; in fact, he had always been a die-hard Republican.

His favorite politician was Benito Mussolini, whom he had once visited, and whose framed photo hung on his wall. If there was someone he hated Cohn would call him a "Communist bastard." But to the executives' amazement Cohn told them he would not fire Lawson. He did not keep the screenwriter on because he was a good writer—there were many good writers in Hollywood. He kept him because of a chain of dependence: Lawson was Humphrey Bogart's writer and Bogart was Columbia's star. If Cohn messed with Lawson he would ruin an immensely profitable relationship. That was worth more than the terrible publicity brought to him by his defiance of the committee.

Henry Kissinger managed to survive the many bloodlettings that went on in the Nixon White House not because he was the best diplomat Nixon could find—there were other fine negotiators—and not because the two men got along so well: They did not. Nor did they share their beliefs and politics. Kissinger survived because he entrenched himself in so many areas of the political structure that to do away with him would lead to chaos. Michelangelo's power was *intensive,* depending on one skill, his ability as an artist; Kissinger's was *extensive.* He got himself involved in so many aspects and departments of the administration that his involvement became a card in his hand. It also made him many allies. If you can arrange such a position for yourself, getting rid of you becomes dangerous—all sorts of interdependencies will unravel. Still, the intensive form of power provides more freedom than the extensive, because those who have it depend on no particular master, or particular position of power, for their security.

To make others dependent on you, one route to take is the secret-intelligence tactic. By knowing other people's secrets, by holding information that they wouldn't want broadcast, you seal your fate with theirs. You are untouchable. Ministers of secret police have held this position throughout the ages: They can make or break a king, or, as in the case of J. Edgar Hoover, a president. But the role is so full of insecurities and paranoia that the power it provides almost cancels itself out. You cannot rest at ease, and what good is power if it brings you no peace?

One last warning: Do not imagine that your master's dependence on you will make him love you. In fact, he may resent and fear you. But, as Machiavelli said, it is better to be feared than loved. Fear you can control; love, never. Depending on an emotion as subtle and changeable as love or friendship will only make you insecure. Better to have others depend on you out of fear of the consequences of losing you than out of love of your company.

Image: Vines with Many Thorns. Below, the roots grow deep and wide. Above, the vines push through bushes, entwine themselves around trees and poles and window ledges. To get rid of them would cost such toil and blood, it is easier to let them climb.

Authority: Make people depend on you. More is to be gained from such dependence than courtesy. He who has slaked his thirst, immediately turns his back on the well, no longer needing it. When dependence disappears, so does civility and decency, and then respect. The first lesson which experience should teach you is to keep hope alive but never satisfied, keeping even a royal patron ever in need of you. (Baltasar Gracián, 1601–1658)

REVERSAL

The weakness of making others depend on you is that you are in some measure dependent on them. But trying to move beyond that point means getting rid of those above you—it means standing alone, depending on no one. Such is the monopolistic drive of a J. P. Morgan or a John D. Rockefeller—to drive out all competition, to be in complete control. If you can corner the market, so much the better.

No such independence comes without a price. You are forced to isolate yourself. Monopolies often turn inward and destroy themselves from the internal pressure. They also stir up powerful resentment, making their enemies bond together to fight them. The drive for complete control is often ruinous and fruitless. Interdependence remains the law, independence a rare and often fatal exception. Better to place yourself in a position of mutual dependence, then, and to follow this critical law rather than look for its reversal. You will not have the unbearable pressure of being on top, and the master above you will in essence be your slave, for *he* will depend on *you*.

USE SELECTIVE HONESTY

AND GENEROSITY TO

DISARM YOUR VICTIM

JUDGMENT

One sincere and honest move will cover over dozens of dishonest ones. Open-hearted gestures of honesty and generosity bring down the guard of even the most suspicious people. Once your selective honesty opens a hole in their armor, you can deceive and manipulate them at will. A timely gift—a Trojan horse—will serve the same purpose.

OBSERVANCE OF THE LAW

FRANCESCO BORRI,
COURTIER CHARLATAN

*Francesco Giuseppe
Borri of Milan, whose
death in 1695 fell just
within the seventeenth
century ... was a fore-
runner of that special
type of charlatanical
adventurer, the cour-
tier or "cavalier"
impostor.... His real
period of glory began
after he moved to
Amsterdam. There he
assumed the title of
Medico Universale,
maintained a great
retinue, and drove
about in a coach with
six horses.... Patients
streamed to him, and
some invalids had
themselves carried in
sedan chairs all the way
from Paris to his place
in Amsterdam. Borri
took no payment for
his consultations: He
distributed great sums
among the poor and
was never known to
receive any money
through the post or
bills of exchange. As he
continued to live with
such splendor, never-
theless, it was presumed
that he possessed the
philosophers' stone.
Suddenly this benefac-
tor disappeared from
Amsterdam. Then it
was discovered that he
had taken with him
money and diamonds
that had been placed
in his charge.*

THE POWER OF
THE CHARLATAN,
GRETE DE FRANCESCO,
1939

Sometime in 1926, a tall, dapperly dressed man paid a visit to Al Capone, the most feared gangster of his time. Speaking with an elegant Continental accent, the man introduced himself as Count Victor Lustig. He promised that if Capone gave him $50,000 he could double it. Capone had more than enough funds to cover the "investment," but he wasn't in the habit of entrusting large sums to total strangers. He looked the count over: Something about the man was different—his classy style, his manner—and so Capone decided to play along. He counted out the bills personally and handed them to Lustig. "Okay, Count," said Capone. "Double it in sixty days like you said." Lustig left with the money, put it in a safe-deposit box in Chicago, then headed to New York, where he had several other money-making schemes in progress.

The $50,000 remained in the bank box untouched. Lustig made no effort to double it. Two months later he returned to Chicago, took the money from the box, and paid Capone another visit. He looked at the gangster's stony-faced bodyguards, smiled apologetically, and said, "Please accept my profound regrets, Mr. Capone. I'm sorry to report that the plan failed . . . I failed."

Capone slowly stood up. He glowered at Lustig, debating which part of the river to throw him in. But the count reached into his coat pocket, withdrew the $50,000, and placed it on the desk. "Here, sir, is your money, to the penny. Again, my sincere apologies. This is most embarrassing. Things didn't work out the way I thought they would. I would have loved to have doubled your money for you and for myself—Lord knows I need it—but the plan just didn't materialize."

Capone sagged back into his chair, confused. "I know you're a con man, Count," said Capone. "I knew it the moment you walked in here. I expected either one hundred thousand dollars or nothing. But this . . . getting my money back . . . well." "Again my apologies, Mr. Capone," said Lustig, as he picked up his hat and began to leave. "My God! You're honest!" yelled Capone. "If you're on the spot, here's five to help you along." He counted out five one-thousand-dollar bills out of the $50,000. The count seemed stunned, bowed deeply, mumbled his thanks, and left, taking the money.

The $5,000 was what Lustig had been after all along.

Interpretation

Count Victor Lustig, a man who spoke several languages and prided himself on his refinement and culture, was one of the great con artists of modern times. He was known for his audacity, his fearlessness, and, most important, his knowledge of human psychology. He could size up a man in minutes, discovering his weaknesses, and he had radar for suckers. Lustig knew that most men build up defenses against crooks and other troublemakers. The con artist's job is to bring those defenses down.

One sure way to do this is through an act of apparent sincerity and honesty. Who will distrust a person literally caught in the act of being honest? Lustig used selective honesty many times, but with Capone he went a step further. No normal con man would have dared such a con; he would have chosen his suckers for their meekness, for that look about them that says they will take their medicine without complaint. Con Capone and you would spend the rest of your life (whatever remained of it) afraid. But Lustig understood that a man like Capone spends his life mistrusting others. No one around him is honest or generous, and being so much in the company of wolves is exhausting, even depressing. A man like Capone yearns to be the recipient of an honest or generous gesture, to feel that not everyone has an angle or is out to rob him.

Lustig's act of selective honesty disarmed Capone because it was so unexpected. A con artist loves conflicting emotions like these, since the person caught up in them is so easily distracted and deceived.

Do not shy away from practicing this law on the Capones of the world. With a well-timed gesture of honesty or generosity, you will have the most brutal and cynical beast in the kingdom eating out of your hand.

Everything turns gray when I don't have at least one mark on the horizon.
Life then seems empty and depressing. I cannot understand honest men.
They lead desperate lives, full of boredom.
Count Victor Lustig, 1890–1947

KEYS TO POWER

The essence of deception is distraction. Distracting the people you want to deceive gives you the time and space to do something they won't notice. An act of kindness, generosity, or honesty is often the most powerful form of distraction because it disarms other people's suspicions. It turns them into children, eagerly lapping up any kind of affectionate gesture.

In ancient China this was called "giving before you take"—the giving makes it hard for the other person to notice the taking. It is a device with infinite practical uses. Brazenly taking something from someone is danger- ous, even for the powerful. The victim will plot revenge. It is also danger- ous simply to ask for what you need, no matter how politely: Unless the other person sees some gain for themselves, they may come to resent your neediness. Learn to give before you take. It softens the ground, takes the bite out of a future request, or simply creates a distraction. And the giving can take many forms: an actual gift, a generous act, a kind favor, an "hon- est" admission—whatever it takes.

Selective honesty is best employed on your first encounter with some- one. We are all creatures of habit, and our first impressions last a long time. If someone believes you are honest at the start of your relationship it takes a lot to convince them otherwise. This gives you room to maneuver.

Jay Gould, like Al Capone, was a man who distrusted everyone. By the time he was thirty-three he was already a multimillionaire, mostly through deception and strong-arming. In the late 1860s, Gould in- vested heavily in the Erie Railroad, then discovered that the market had been flooded with a vast amount of phony stock certificates for the company. He stood to lose a fortune and to suffer a lot of embarrassment.

In the midst of this crisis, a man named Lord John Gordon-Gordon offered to help. Gordon-Gordon, a Scottish lord, had apparently made a small fortune investing in railroads.

By hiring some handwriting experts Gordon-Gordon was able to prove to Gould that the culprits for the phony stock certificates were actually several top executives with the Erie Railroad itself. Gould was grateful. Gordon-Gordon then proposed that he and Gould join forces to buy up a controlling interest in Erie. Gould agreed. For a while the venture appeared to prosper. The two men were now good friends, and every time Gordon-Gordon came to Gould asking for money to buy more stock, Gould gave it to him. In 1873, however, Gordon-Gordon suddenly dumped all of his stock, making a fortune but drastically lowering the value of Gould's own holdings. Then he disappeared from sight.

Upon investigation, Gould found out that Gordon-Gordon's real name was John Crowningsfield, and that he was the bastard son of a merchant seaman and a London barmaid. There had been many clues before then that Gordon-Gordon was a con man, but his initial act of honesty and support had so blinded Gould that it took the loss of millions for him to see through the scheme.

A single act of honesty is often not enough. What is required is a reputation for honesty, built on a series of acts—but these can be quite inconsequential. Once this reputation is established, as with first impressions, it is hard to shake.

In ancient China, Duke Wu of Chêng decided it was time to take over the increasingly powerful kingdom of Hu. Telling no one of his plan, he married his daughter to Hu's ruler. He then called a council and asked his ministers, "I am considering a military campaign. Which country should we invade?" As he had expected, one of his ministers replied, "Hu should be invaded." The duke seemed angry, and said, "Hu is a sister state now. Why do you suggest invading her?" He had the minister executed for his impolitic remark. The ruler of Hu heard about this, and considering other tokens of Wu's honesty and the marriage with his daughter, he took no precautions to defend himself from Chêng. A few weeks later, Chêng forces swept through Hu and took the country, never to relinquish it.

Honesty is one of the best ways to disarm the wary, but it is not the only one. Any kind of noble, apparently selfless act will serve. Perhaps the best such act, though, is one of generosity. Few people can resist a gift, even from the most hardened enemy, which is why it is often the perfect way to disarm people. A gift brings out the child in us, instantly lowering our defenses. Although we often view other people's actions in the most cynical light, we rarely see the Machiavellian element of a gift, which quite often hides ulterior motives. A gift is the perfect object in which to hide a deceptive move.

Over three thousand years ago the ancient Greeks traveled across the sea to recapture the beautiful Helen, stolen away from them by Paris, and to destroy Paris's city, Troy. The siege lasted ten years, many heroes died, yet neither side had come close to victory. One day, the prophet Calchas assembled the Greeks.

"Stop battering away at these walls!" he told them. "You must find some other way, some ruse. We cannot take Troy by force alone. We must find some cunning stratagem." The cunning Greek leader Odysseus then came up with the idea of building a giant wooden horse, hiding soldiers inside it, then offering it to the Trojans as a gift. Neoptolemus, son of Achilles, was disgusted with this idea; it was unmanly. Better for thousands to die on the battlefield than to gain victory so deceitfully. But the soldiers, faced with a choice between manliness, honor, and another ten years of death, on the one hand and a quick victory on the other, chose the horse, which was promptly built. The trick was successful and Troy fell. One gift did more for the Greek cause than ten years of fighting.

> Image: The Trojan Horse. Your guile is hidden inside a magnificent gift that proves irresistible to your opponent. The walls open. Once inside, wreak havoc.

Selective kindness should also be part of your arsenal of deception. For years the ancient Romans had besieged the city of the Faliscans, always unsuccessfully. One day, however, when the Roman general Camillus was encamped outside the city, he suddenly saw a man leading some children toward him. The man was a Faliscan teacher, and the children, it turned out, were the sons and daughters of the noblest and wealthiest citizens of the town. On the pretense of taking these children out for a walk, he had led them straight to the Romans, offering them as hostages in hopes of ingratiating himself with Camillus, the city's enemy.

Camillus did not take the children hostage. He stripped the teacher, tied his hands behind his back, gave each child a rod, and let them whip him all the way back to the city. The gesture had an immediate effect on the Faliscans. Had Camillus used the children as hostages, some in the city would have voted to surrender. And even if the Faliscans had gone on fighting, their resistance would have been halfhearted. Camillus's refusal to take advantage of the situation broke down the Faliscans' resistance, and they surrendered. The general had calculated correctly. And in any case he had had nothing to lose: He knew that the hostage ploy would not have ended the war, at least not right away. By turning the situation around, he earned his enemy's trust and respect, disarming them. Selective kindness will often break down even the most stubborn foe: Aiming right for the heart, it corrodes the will to fight back.

Remember: By playing on people's emotions, calculated acts of kindness can turn a Capone into a gullible child. As with any emotional approach, the tactic must be practiced with caution: If people see through it, their disappointed feelings of gratitude and warmth will become the most violent hatred and distrust. Unless you can make the gesture seem sincere and heartfelt, do not play with fire.

REVERSAL

When you have a history of deceit behind you, no amount of honesty, generosity, or kindness will fool people. In fact it will only call attention to itself. Once people have come to see you as deceitful, to act honest all of a sudden is simply suspicious. In these cases it is better to play the rogue.

Count Lustig, pulling the biggest con of his career, was about to sell the Eiffel Tower to an unsuspecting industrialist who believed the government was auctioning it off for scrap metal. The industrialist was prepared to hand over a huge sum of money to Lustig, who had successfully impersonated a government official. At the last minute, however, the mark was suspicious. Something about Lustig bothered him. At the meeting in which he was to hand over the money, Lustig sensed his sudden distrust.

Leaning over to the industrialist, Lustig explained, in a low whisper, how low his salary was, how difficult his finances were, on and on. After a few minutes of this, the industrialist realized that Lustig was asking for a bribe. For the first time he relaxed. Now he knew he could trust Lustig: Since all government officials were dishonest, Lustig had to be real. The man forked over the money. By acting dishonest, Lustig seemed the real McCoy. In this case selective honesty would have had the opposite effect.

As the French diplomat Talleyrand grew older, his reputation as a master liar and deceiver spread. At the Congress of Vienna (1814–1815), he would spin fabulous stories and make impossible remarks to people who knew he had to be lying. His dishonesty had no purpose except to cloak the moments when he really was deceiving them. One day, for example, among friends, Talleyrand said with apparent sincerity, "In business one ought to show one's hand." No one who heard him could believe their ears: A man who never once in his life had shown his cards was telling other people to show theirs. Tactics like this made it impossible to distinguish Talleyrand's real deceptions from his fake ones. By embracing his reputation for dishonesty, he preserved his ability to deceive.

Nothing in the realm of power is set in stone. Overt deceptiveness will sometimes cover your tracks, even making you admired for the honesty of your dishonesty.

WHEN ASKING FOR HELP,

APPEAL TO PEOPLE'S

SELF-INTEREST,

NEVER TO THEIR MERCY

OR GRATITUDE

JUDGMENT

If you need to turn to an ally for help, do not bother to remind him of your past assistance and good deeds. He will find a way to ignore you. Instead, uncover something in your request, or in your alliance with him, that will benefit him, and emphasize it out of all proportion. He will respond enthusiastically when he sees something to be gained for himself.

In the early fourteenth century, a young man named Castruccio Castracani rose from the rank of common soldier to become lord of the great city of Lucca, Italy. One of the most powerful families in the city, the Poggios, had been instrumental in his climb (which succeeded through treachery and bloodshed), but after he came to power, they came to feel he had forgotten them. His ambition outweighed any gratitude he felt. In 1325, while Castruccio was away fighting Lucca's main rival, Florence, the Poggios conspired with other noble families in the city to rid themselves of this troublesome and ambitious prince.

Mounting an insurrection, the plotters attacked and murdered the governor whom Castruccio had left behind to rule the city. Riots broke out, and the Castruccio supporters and the Poggio supporters were poised to do battle. At the height of the tension, however, Stefano di Poggio, the oldest member of the family, intervened, and made both sides lay down their arms.

A peaceful man, Stefano had not taken part in the conspiracy. He had told his family it would end in a useless bloodbath. Now he insisted he should intercede on the family's behalf and persuade Castruccio to listen to their complaints and satisfy their demands. Stefano was the oldest and wisest member of the clan, and his family agreed to put their trust in his diplomacy rather than in their weapons.

When news of the rebellion reached Castruccio, he hurried back to Lucca. By the time he arrived, however, the fighting had ceased, through Stefano's agency, and he was surprised by the city's calm and peace. Stefano di Poggio had imagined that Castruccio would be grateful to him for his part in quelling the rebellion, so he paid the prince a visit. He explained how he had brought peace, then begged for Castruccio's mercy. He said that the rebels in his family were young and impetuous, hungry for power yet inexperienced; he recalled his family's past generosity to Castruccio. For all these reasons, he said, the great prince should pardon the Poggios and listen to their complaints. This, he said, was the only just thing to do, since the family had willingly laid down their arms and had always supported him.

Castruccio listened patiently. He seemed not the slightest bit angry or resentful. Instead, he told Stefano to rest assured that justice would prevail, and he asked him to bring his entire family to the palace to talk over their grievances and come to an agreement. As they took leave of one another, Castruccio said he thanked God for the chance he had been given to show his clemency and kindness. That evening the entire Poggio family came to the palace. Castruccio immediately had them imprisoned and a few days later all were executed, including Stefano.

Interpretation

Stefano di Poggio is the embodiment of all those who believe that the justice and nobility of their cause will prevail. Certainly appeals to justice and gratitude have occasionally succeeded in the past, but more often than not they have had dire consequences, especially in dealings with the Castruccios of the world. Stefano knew that the prince had risen to power through treachery and ruthlessness. This was a man, after all, who had put a close and devoted friend to death. When Castruccio was told that it had been a terrible wrong to kill such an old friend, he replied that he had executed not an old friend but a new enemy.

A man like Castruccio knows only force and self-interest. When the rebellion began, to end it and place oneself at his mercy was the most dangerous possible move. Even once Stefano di Poggio had made that fatal mistake, however, he still had options: He could have offered money to Castruccio, could have made promises for the future, could have pointed out what the Poggios could still contribute to Castruccio's power—their influence with the most influential families of Rome, for example, and the great marriage they could have brokered.

Instead Stefano brought up the past, and debts that carried no obligation. Not only is a man not obliged to be grateful, gratitude is often a terrible burden that he gladly discards. And in this case Castruccio rid himself of his obligations to the Poggios by eliminating the Poggios.

OBSERVANCE OF THE LAW

In 433 B.C., just before the Peloponnesian War, the island of Corcyra (later called Corfu) and the Greek city-state of Corinth stood on the brink of conflict. Both parties sent ambassadors to Athens to try to win over the Athenians to their side. The stakes were high, since whoever had Athens on his side was sure to win. And whoever won the war would certainly give the defeated side no mercy.

Corcyra spoke first. Its ambassador began by admitting that the island had never helped Athens before, and in fact had allied itself with Athens's enemies. There were no ties of friendship or gratitude between Corcyra and Athens. Yes, the ambassador admitted, he had come to Athens now out of fear and concern for Corcyra's safety. The only thing he could offer was an alliance of mutual interests. Corcyra had a navy only surpassed in size and strength by Athens's own; an alliance between the two states would create a formidable force, one that could intimidate the rival state of Sparta. That, unfortunately, was all Corcyra had to offer.

The representative from Corinth then gave a brilliant, passionate speech, in sharp contrast to the dry, colorless approach of the Corcyran. He talked of everything Corinth had done for Athens in the past. He asked how it would look to Athens's other allies if the city put an agreement with a former enemy over one with a present friend, one that had served Athens's interest loyally: Perhaps those allies would break their agreements with Athens if they saw that their loyalty was not valued. He referred to Hellenic law, and the need to repay Corinth for all its good deeds. He finally went on to list the many services Corinth had performed for Athens, and the importance of showing gratitude to one's friends.

After the speech, the Athenians debated the issue in an assembly. On

Most men are so thoroughly subjective that nothing really interests them but themselves. They always think of their own case as soon as ever any remark is made, and their whole attention is engrossed and absorbed by the merest chance reference to anything which affects them personally, be it never so remote.
ARTHUR SCHOPENHAUER, 1788–1860

the second round, they voted overwhelmingly to ally with Corcyra and drop Corinth.

Interpretation

History has remembered the Athenians nobly, but they were the preeminent realists of classical Greece. With them, all the rhetoric, all the emotional appeals in the world, could not match a good pragmatic argument, especially one that added to their power.

What the Corinthian ambassador did not realize was that his references to Corinth's past generosity to Athens only irritated the Athenians, subtly asking them to feel guilty and putting them under obligation. The Athenians couldn't care less about past favors and friendly feelings. At the same time, they knew that if their other allies thought them ungrateful for abandoning Corinth, these city-states would still be unlikely to break their ties to Athens, the preeminent power in Greece. Athens ruled its empire by force, and would simply compel any rebellious ally to return to the fold.

When people choose between talk about the past and talk about the future, a pragmatic person will always opt for the future and forget the past. As the Corcyrans realized, it is always best to speak pragmatically to a pragmatic person. And in the end, most people *are* in fact pragmatic—they will rarely act against their own self-interest.

> *It has always been a rule that the weak should be subject to the strong;*
> *and besides, we consider that we are worthy of our power. Up till the*
> *present moment you, too, used to think that we were; but now, after*
> *calculating your own interest, you are beginning to talk in terms of right*
> *and wrong. Considerations of this kind have never yet turned people aside*
> *from the opportunities of aggrandizement offered by superior strength.*
>
> Athenian representative to Sparta,
> quoted in The Peloponnesian War, Thucydides, c. 465–395 B.C.

KEYS TO POWER

In your quest for power, you will constantly find yourself in the position of asking for help from those more powerful than you. There is an art to asking for help, an art that depends on your ability to understand the person you are dealing with, and to not confuse your needs with theirs.

Most people never succeed at this, because they are completely trapped in their own wants and desires. They start from the assumption that the people they are appealing to have a selfless interest in helping them. They talk as if their needs mattered to these people—who probably couldn't care less. Sometimes they refer to larger issues: a great cause, or grand emotions such as love and gratitude. They go for the big picture when simple, everyday realities would have much more appeal. What they do not realize is that even the most powerful person is locked inside needs of his own, and that if you make no appeal to his self-interest, he merely sees you as desperate or, at best, a waste of time.

In the sixteenth century, Portuguese missionaries tried for years to convert the people of Japan to Catholicism, while at the same time Portugal had a monopoly on trade between Japan and Europe. Although the missionaries did have some success, they never got far among the ruling elite; by the beginning of the seventeenth century, in fact, their proselytizing had completely antagonized the Japanese emperor Ieyasu. When the Dutch began to arrive in Japan in great numbers, Ieyasu was much relieved. He needed Europeans for their know-how in guns and navigation, and here at last were Europeans who cared nothing for spreading religion—the Dutch wanted only to trade. Ieyasu swiftly moved to evict the Portuguese. From then on, he would only deal with the practical-minded Dutch.

Japan and Holland were vastly different cultures, but each shared a timeless and universal concern: self-interest. Every person you deal with is like another culture, an alien land with a past that has nothing to do with yours. Yet you can bypass the differences between you and him by appealing to his self-interest. Do not be subtle: You have valuable knowledge to share, you will fill his coffers with gold, you will make him live longer and happier. This is a language that all of us speak and understand.

A key step in the process is to understand the other person's psychology. Is he vain? Is he concerned about his reputation or his social standing? Does he have enemies you could help him vanquish? Is he simply motivated by money and power?

When the Mongols invaded China in the twelfth century, they threatened to obliterate a culture that had thrived for over two thousand years. Their leader, Genghis Khan, saw nothing in China but a country that lacked pasturing for his horses, and he decided to destroy the place, leveling all its cities, for "it would be better to exterminate the Chinese and let the grass grow." It was not a soldier, a general, or a king who saved the Chinese from devastation, but a man named Yelu Ch'u-Ts'ai. A foreigner himself, Ch'u-Ts'ai had come to appreciate the superiority of Chinese culture. He managed to make himself a trusted adviser to Genghis Khan, and persuaded him that he would reap riches out of the place if, instead of destroying it, he simply taxed everyone who lived there. Khan saw the wisdom in this and did as Ch'u-Ts'ai advised.

When Khan took the city of Kaifeng, after a long siege, and decided to massacre its inhabitants (as he had in other cities that had resisted him), Ch'u-Ts'ai told him that the finest craftsmen and engineers in China had fled to Kaifeng, and it would be better to put them to use. Kaifeng was spared. Never before had Genghis Khan shown such mercy, but then it really wasn't mercy that saved Kaifeng. Ch'u-Ts'ai knew Khan well. He was a barbaric peasant who cared nothing for culture, or indeed for anything other than warfare and practical results. Ch'u-Ts'ai chose to appeal to the only emotion that would work on such a man: greed.

Self-interest is the lever that will move people. Once you make them see how you can in some way meet their needs or advance their cause, their resistance to your requests for help will magically fall away. At each step on the way to acquiring power, you must train yourself to think your way inside the other person's mind, to see their needs and interests, to get rid of the screen of your own feelings that obscure the truth. Master this art and there will be no limits to what you can accomplish.

Image: A Cord that
Binds. The cord of
mercy and grati-
tude is threadbare,
and will break at
the first shock.
Do not throw
such a lifeline.
The cord of
mutual self-inter-
est is woven of
many fibers and
cannot easily be
severed. It will serve
you well for years.

Authority: The shortest and best way to make your fortune is to let people see clearly that it is in their interests
to promote yours. (Jean de La Bruyère, 1645–1696)

REVERSAL

Some people will see an appeal to their self-interest as ugly and ignoble. They actually prefer to be able to exercise charity, mercy, and justice, which are their ways of feeling superior to you: When you beg them for help, you emphasize their power and position. They are strong enough to need nothing from you except the chance to feel superior. This is the wine that intoxicates them. They are dying to fund your project, to introduce you to powerful people—provided, of course, that all this is done in public, and for a good cause (usually the more public, the better). Not everyone, then, can be approached through cynical self-interest. Some people will be put off by it, because they don't want to seem to be motivated by such things. They need opportunities to display their good heart.

Do not be shy. Give them that opportunity. It's not as if you are con-ning them by asking for help—it is really their pleasure to give, and to be seen giving. You must distinguish the differences among powerful people and figure out what makes them tick. When they ooze greed, do not appeal to their charity. When they want to look charitable and noble, do not ap-peal to their greed.

POSE AS A FRIEND,

WORK AS A SPY

JUDGMENT

Knowing about your rival is critical. Use spies to gather valuable information that will keep you a step ahead. Better still: Play the spy yourself. In polite social encounters, learn to probe. Ask indirect questions to get people to reveal their weaknesses and intentions. There is no occasion that is not an opportunity for artful spying.

OBSERVANCE OF THE LAW

Joseph Duveen was undoubtedly the greatest art dealer of his time—from 1904 to 1940 he almost single-handedly monopolized America's millionaire art-collecting market. But one prize plum eluded him: the industrialist Andrew Mellon. Before he died, Duveen was determined to make Mellon a client.

Duveen's friends said this was an impossible dream. Mellon was a stiff, taciturn man. The stories he had heard about the congenial, talkative Duveen rubbed him the wrong way—he had made it clear he had no desire to meet the man. Yet Duveen told his doubting friends, "Not only will Mellon buy from me but he will buy *only* from me." For several years he tracked his prey, learning the man's habits, tastes, phobias. To do this, he secretly put several of Mellon's staff on his own payroll, worming valuable information out of them. By the time he moved into action, he knew Mellon about as well as Mellon's wife did.

In 1921 Mellon was visiting London, and staying in a palatial suite on the third floor of Claridge's Hotel. Duveen booked himself into the suite just below Mellon's, on the second floor. He had arranged for his valet to befriend Mellon's valet, and on the fateful day he had chosen to make his move, Mellon's valet told Duveen's valet, who told Duveen, that he had just helped Mellon on with his overcoat, and that the industrialist was making his way down the corridor to ring for the lift.

Duveen's valet hurriedly helped Duveen with his own overcoat. Seconds later, Duveen entered the lift, and lo and behold, there was Mellon. "How do you do, Mr. Mellon?" said Duveen, introducing himself. "I am on my way to the National Gallery to look at some pictures." How uncanny—that was precisely where Mellon was headed. And so Duveen was able to accompany his prey to the one location that would ensure his success. He knew Mellon's taste inside and out, and while the two men wandered through the museum, he dazzled the magnate with his knowledge. Once again quite uncannily, they seemed to have remarkably similar tastes.

Mellon was pleasantly surprised: This was not the Duveen he had expected. The man was charming and agreeable, and clearly had exquisite taste. When they returned to New York, Mellon visited Duveen's exclusive gallery and fell in love with the collection. Everything, surprisingly enough, seemed to be precisely the kind of work he wanted to collect. For the rest of his life he was Duveen's best and most generous client.

Interpretation

A man as ambitious and competitive as Joseph Duveen left nothing to chance. What's the point of winging it, of just hoping you may be able to charm this or that client? It's like shooting ducks blindfolded. Arm yourself with a little knowledge and your aim improves.

Mellon was the most spectacular of Duveen's catches, but he spied on many a millionaire. By secretly putting members of his clients' household staffs on his own payroll, he would gain constant access to valuable information about their masters' comings and goings, changes in taste, and other such tidbits of information that would put him a step ahead. A rival of Duveen's who wanted to make Henry Frick a client noticed that whenever he visited this wealthy New Yorker, Duveen was there before him, as if he had a sixth sense. To other dealers Duveen seemed to be everywhere, and to know everything before they did. His powers discouraged and disheartened them, until many simply gave up going after the wealthy clients who could make a dealer rich.

Such is the power of artful spying: It makes you seem all-powerful, clairvoyant. Your knowledge of your mark can also make you seem charming, so well can you anticipate his desires. No one sees the source of your power, and what they cannot see they cannot fight.

> *Rulers see through spies, as cows through smell, Brahmins through*
> *scriptures and the rest of the people through their normal eyes.*
> Kautilya, Indian philosopher, third century B.C.

KEYS TO POWER

In the realm of power, your goal is a degree of control over future events. Part of the problem you face, then, is that people won't tell you all their thoughts, emotions, and plans. Controlling what they say, they often keep the most critical parts of their character hidden—their weaknesses, ulterior motives, obsessions. The result is that you cannot predict their moves, and are constantly in the dark. The trick is to find a way to probe them, to find out their secrets and hidden intentions, without letting them know what you are up to.

This is not as difficult as you might think. A friendly front will let you secretly gather information on friends and enemies alike. Let others consult the horoscope, or read tarot cards: You have more concrete means of seeing into the future.

The most common way of spying is to use other people, as Duveen did. The method is simple, powerful, but risky: You will certainly gather information, but you have little control over the people who are doing the work. Perhaps they will ineptly reveal your spying, or even secretly turn against you. It is far better to be the spy yourself, to pose as a friend while secretly gathering information.

The French politician Talleyrand was one of the greatest practitioners of this art. He had an uncanny ability to worm secrets out of people in polite conversation. A contemporary of his, Baron de Vitrolles, wrote, "Wit and grace marked his conversation. He possessed the art of concealing his thoughts or his malice beneath a transparent veil of insinuations, words that imply something more than they express. Only when necessary did he inject his own personality." The key here is Talleyrand's ability to suppress himself in the conversation, to make others talk endlessly about themselves and inadvertently reveal their intentions and plans.

If you have reason to
suspect that a person is
telling you a lie, look as
though you believed
every word he said.
This will give him
courage to go on; he
will become more
vehement in his
assertions, and in the
end betray himself.
Again, if you perceive
that a person is trying
to conceal something
from you, but with only
partial success, look as
though you did not
believe him. The oppo-
sition on your part will
provoke him into lead-
ing out his reserve of
truth and bringing the
whole force of it to
bear upon your
incredulity.
ARTHUR
SCHOPENHAUER,
1788–1860

Throughout Talleyrand's life, people said he was a superb conversa-
tionalist—yet he actually said very little. He never talked about his own
ideas; he got others to reveal theirs. He would organize friendly games of
charades for foreign diplomats, social gatherings where, however, he
would carefully weigh their words, cajole confidences out of them, and
gather information invaluable to his work as France's foreign minister. At
the Congress of Vienna (1814–1815) he did his spying in other ways: He
would blurt out what seemed to be a secret (actually something he had
made up), then watch his listeners' reactions. He might tell a gathering of
diplomats, for instance, that a reliable source had revealed to him that the
czar of Russia was planning to arrest his top general for treason. By watching the diplomats' reactions to this made-up story, he would know which
ones were most excited by the weakening of the Russian army—perhaps
their goverments had designs on Russia? As Baron von Stetten said,
"Monsieur Talleyrand fires a pistol into the air to see who will jump out the
window."

During social gatherings and innocuous encounters, pay attention.
This is when people's guards are down. By suppressing your own personality, you can make them reveal things. The brilliance of the maneuver is
that they will mistake your interest in them for friendship, so that you not
only learn, you make allies.

Nevertheless, you should practice this tactic with caution and care. If
people begin to suspect you are worming secrets out of them under the
cover of conversation, they will strictly avoid you. Emphasize friendly
chatter, not valuable information. Your search for gems of information cannot be too obvious, or your probing questions will reveal more about yourself and your intentions than about the information you hope to find.

A trick to try in spying comes from La Rochefoucauld, who wrote,
"Sincerity is found in very few men, and is often the cleverest of ruses—
one is sincere in order to draw out the confidence and secrets of the other."
By pretending to bare your heart to another person, in other words, you
make them more likely to reveal their own secrets. Give them a false confession and they will give you a real one. Another trick was identified by
the philosopher Arthur Schopenhauer, who suggested vehemently contradicting people you're in conversation with as a way of irritating them, stirring them up so that they lose some of the control over their words. In their
emotional reaction they will reveal all kinds of truths about themselves,
truths you can later use against them.

Another method of indirect spying is to test people, to lay little traps
that make them reveal things about themselves. Chosroes II, a notoriously
clever seventh-century king of the Persians, had many ways of seeing
through his subjects without raising suspicion. If he noticed, for instance,
that two of his courtiers had become particularly friendly, he would call
one of them aside and say he had information that the other was a traitor,
and would soon be killed. The king would tell the courtier he trusted him
more than anyone, and that he must keep this information secret. Then he

would watch the two men carefully. If he saw that the second courtier had not changed in his behavior toward the king, he would conclude that the first courtier had kept the secret, and he would quickly promote the man, later taking him aside to confess, "I meant to kill your friend because of certain information that had reached me, but, when I investigated the matter, I found it was untrue." If, on the other hand, the second courtier started to avoid the king, acting aloof and tense, Chosroes would know that the secret had been revealed. He would ban the second courtier from his court, letting him know that the whole business had only been a test, but that even though the man had done nothing wrong, he could no longer trust him. The first courtier, however, had revealed a secret, and him Chosroes would ban from his entire kingdom.

It may seem an odd form of spying that reveals not empirical information but a person's character. Often, however, it is the best way of solving problems before they arise.

By tempting people into certain acts, you learn about their loyalty, their honesty, and so on. And this kind of knowledge is often the most valuable of all: Armed with it, you can predict their actions in the future.

Image:
The Third Eye of
the Spy. In the land of
the two-eyed, the third eye
gives you the omniscience
of a god. You see further than
others, and you see deeper
into them. Nobody is
safe from the eye
but you.

Authority: Now, the reason a brilliant sovereign and a wise general conquer the enemy whenever they move, and their achievements surpass those of ordinary men, is their foreknowledge of the enemy situation. This "foreknowledge" cannot be elicited from spirits, nor from gods, nor by analogy with past events, nor by astrologic calculations. It must be obtained from men who know the enemy situation—from spies. (Sun-tzu, *The Art of War,* fourth century B.C.)

REVERSAL

Information is critical to power, but just as you spy on other people, you must be prepared for them to spy on you. One of the most potent weapons in the battle for information, then, is giving out false information. As Winston Churchill said, "Truth is so precious that she should always be attended by a bodyguard of lies." You must surround yourself with such a bodyguard, so that your truth cannot be penetrated. By planting the information of your choice, you control the game.

In 1944 the Nazis' rocket-bomb attacks on London suddenly escalated. Over two thousand V-1 flying bombs fell on the city, killing more than five thousand people and wounding many more. Somehow, however, the Germans consistently missed their targets. Bombs that were intended for Tower Bridge, or Piccadilly, would fall well short of the city, landing in the less populated suburbs. This was because, in fixing their targets, the Germans relied on secret agents they had planted in England. They did not know that these agents had been discovered, and that in their place, English-controlled agents were feeding them subtly deceptive information.

The bombs would hit farther and farther from their targets every time they fell. By the end of the campaign they were landing on cows in the country. By feeding people wrong information, then, you gain a potent advantage. While spying gives you a third eye, disinformation puts out one of your enemy's eyes. A cyclops, he always misses his target.

CRUSH YOUR

ENEMY TOTALLY

JUDGMENT

All great leaders since Moses have known that a feared enemy must be crushed completely. (Sometimes they have learned this the hard way.) If one ember is left alight, no matter how dimly it smolders, a fire will eventually break out. More is lost through stopping halfway than through total annihilation: The enemy will recover, and will seek revenge. Crush him, not only in body but in spirit.

TRANSGRESSION OF THE LAW

The remnants of an enemy can become active like those of a disease or fire. Hence, these should be exterminated completely. . . . One should never ignore an enemy, knowing him to be weak. He becomes dangerous in due course, like the spark of fire in a haystack.

KAUTILYA,
INDIAN PHILOSOPHER,
THIRD CENTURY B.C.

No rivalry between leaders is more celebrated in Chinese history than the struggle between Hsiang Yu and Liu Pang. These two generals began their careers as friends, fighting on the same side. Hsiang Yu came from the nobility; large and powerful, given to bouts of violence and temper, a bit dull-witted, he was yet a mighty warrior who always fought at the head of his troops. Liu Pang came from peasant stock. He had never been much of a soldier, and preferred women and wine to fighting; in fact, he was something of a scoundrel. But he was wily, and he had the ability to recognize the best strategists, keep them as his advisers, and listen to their advice. He had risen in the army through these strengths.

In 208 B.C., the king of Ch'u sent two massive armies to conquer the powerful kingdom of Ch'in. One army went north, under the generalship of Sung Yi, with Hsiang Yu second in command; the other, led by Liu Pang, headed straight toward Ch'in. The target was the kingdom's splendid capital, Hsien-yang. And Hsiang Yu, ever violent and impatient, could not stand the idea that Liu Pang would get to Hsien-yang first, and perhaps would assume command of the entire army.

At one point on the northern front, Hsiang's commander, Sung Yi, hesitated in sending his troops into battle. Furious, Hsiang entered Sung Yi's tent, proclaimed him a traitor, cut off his head, and assumed sole command of the army. Without waiting for orders, he left the northern front and marched directly on Hsien-yang. He felt certain he was the better soldier and general than Liu, but, to his utter astonishment, his rival, leading a smaller, swifter army, managed to reach Hsien-yang first. Hsiang had an adviser, Fan Tseng, who warned him, "This village headman [Liu Pang] used to be greedy only for riches and women, but since entering the capital he has not been led astray by wealth, wine, or sex. That shows he is aiming high."

THE TRAP AT
SINIGAGLIA

On the day Ramiro was executed, Cesare [Borgia] quit Cesena, leaving the mutilated body on the town square, and marched south. Three days later he arrived at Fano, where he received the envoys of the city of Ancona, who assured him of their loyalty. A messenger from Vitellozzo Vitelli announced that the little Adriatic port of Sinigaglia had surrendered to the condottieri *[mercenary soldiers]. Only the citadel, in charge of the Genoese Andrea Doria, still held out, and Doria refused to hand it over to anyone except Cesare himself. [Borgia] sent word that he would arrive the next day, which was just what the*

Fan Tseng urged Hsiang to kill his rival before it was too late. He told the general to invite the wily peasant to a banquet at their camp outside Hsien-yang and, in the midst of a celebratory sword dance, to have his head cut off. The invitation was sent; Liu fell for the trap, and came to the banquet. But Hsiang hesitated in ordering the sword dance, and by the time he gave the signal, Liu had sensed a trap, and managed to escape. "Bah!" cried Fan Tseng in disgust, seeing that Hsiang had botched the plot. "One cannot plan with a simpleton. Liu Pang will steal your empire yet and make us all his prisoners."

Realizing his mistake, Hsiang hurriedly marched on Hsien-yang, this time determined to hack off his rival's head. Liu was never one to fight when the odds were against him, and he abandoned the city. Hsiang captured Hsien-yang, murdered the young prince of Ch'in, and burned the city to the ground. Liu was now Hsiang's bitter enemy, and he pursued him for many months, finally cornering him in a walled city. Lacking food, his army in disarray, Liu sued for peace.

Again Fan Tseng warned Hsiang, "Crush him now! If you let him go again, you will be sorry later." But Hsiang decided to be merciful. He wanted to bring Liu back to Ch'u alive, and to force his former friend to acknowledge him as master. But Fan proved right: Liu managed to use the negotiations for his surrender as a distraction, and he escaped with a small army. Hsiang, amazed that he had yet again let his rival slip away, once more set out after Liu, this time with such ferocity that he seemed to have lost his mind. At one point, having captured Liu's father in battle, Hsiang stood the old man up during the fighting and yelled to Liu across the line of troops, "Surrender now, or I shall boil your father alive!" Liu calmly answered, "But we are sworn brothers. So my father is your father also. If you insist on boiling your own father, send me a bowl of the soup!" Hsiang backed down, and the struggle continued.

A few weeks later, in the thick of the hunt, Hsiang scattered his forces unwisely, and in a surprise attack Liu was able to surround his main garrison. For the first time the tables were turned. Now it was Hsiang who sued for peace. Liu's top adviser urged him to destroy Hsiang, crush his army, show no mercy. "To let him go would be like rearing a tiger—it will devour you later," the adviser said. Liu agreed.

Making a false treaty, he lured Hsiang into relaxing his defense, then slaughtered almost all of his army. Hsiang managed to escape. Alone and on foot, knowing that Liu had put a bounty on his head, he came upon a small group of his own retreating soldiers, and cried out, "I hear Liu Pang has offered one thousand pieces of gold and a fief of ten thousand families for my head. Let me do you a favor." Then he slit his own throat and died.

Interpretation

Hsiang Yu had proven his ruthlessness on many an occasion. He rarely hesitated in doing away with a rival if it served his purposes. But with Liu Pang he acted differently. He respected his rival, and did not want to defeat him through deception; he wanted to prove his superiority on the battlefield, even to force the clever Liu to surrender and to serve him. Every time he had his rival in his hands, something made him hesitate—a fatal sympathy with or respect for the man who, after all, had once been a friend and comrade in arms. But the moment Hsiang made it clear that he intended to do away with Liu, yet failed to accomplish it, he sealed his own doom. Liu would not suffer the same hesitation once the tables were turned.

This is the fate that faces all of us when we sympathize with our enemies, when pity, or the hope of reconciliation, makes us pull back from doing away with them. We only strengthen their fear and hatred of us. We have beaten them, and they are humiliated; yet we nurture these resentful vipers who will one day kill us. Power cannot be dealt with this way. It must be exterminated, crushed, and denied the chance to return to haunt us. This is all the truer with a former friend who has become an enemy. The law governing fatal antagonisms reads: Reconciliation is out of the question. Only one side can win, and it must win totally.

Liu Pang learned this lesson well. After defeating Hsiang Yu, this son

condottieri *wanted to hear. Once he reached Sinigaglia, Cesare would be an easy prey, caught between the citadel and their forces ringing the town. . . . The* condottieri *were sure they had military superiority, believing that the departure of the French troops had left Cesare with only a small force. In fact, according to Machiavelli, [Borgia] had left Cesena with ten thousand infantrymen and three thousand horse, taking pains to split up his men so that they would march along parallel routes before converging on Sinigaglia. The reason for such a large force was that he knew, from a confession extracted from Ramiro de Lorca, what the* condottieri *had up their sleeve. He therefore decided to turn their own trap against them. This was the masterpiece of trickery that the historian Paolo Giovio later called "the magnificent deceit." At dawn on December 31 [1502], Cesare reached the outskirts of Sinigaglia. . . . Led by Michelotto Corella, Cesare's advance guard of two hundred lances took up its position on the canal bridge. . . . This control of the bridge effectively prevented the conspirators' troops from withdrawing. . . . Cesare greeted the* condottieri *effusively and invited them to join him. . . . Michelotto*

had prepared the
Palazzo Bernardino
for Cesare's use, and
the duke invited the
condottieri *inside....*
Once indoors the men
were quietly arrested
by guards who crept up
from the rear....
[Cesare] gave orders
for an attack on
Vitelli's and Orsini's
soldiers in the outlying
areas.... That night,
while their troops were
being crushed, Miche-
lotto throttled Olive-
retto and Vitelli in the
Bernardino palace....
At one fell swoop,
[Borgia] had got rid of
his former generals and
worst enemies.

THE BORGIAS,
IVAN CLOULAS,
1989

To have ultimate
victory, you must be
ruthless.

NAPOLEON BONAPARTE,
1769–1821

of a farmer went on to become supreme commander of the armies of Ch'u. Crushing his next rival—the king of Ch'u, his own former leader—he crowned himself emperor, defeated everyone in his path, and went down in history as one of the greatest rulers of China, the immortal Han Kao-tsu, founder of the Han Dynasty.

Those who seek to achieve things should show no mercy.

Kautilya, Indian philosopher, third century B.C.

OBSERVANCE OF THE LAW

Wu Chao, born in A.D. 625, was the daughter of a duke, and as a beautiful young woman of many charms, she was accordingly attached to the harem of Emperor T'ai Tsung.

The imperial harem was a dangerous place, full of young concubines vying to become the emperor's favorite. Wu's beauty and forceful character quickly won her this battle, but, knowing that an emperor, like other powerful men, is a creature of whim, and that she could easily be replaced, she kept her eye on the future.

Wu managed to seduce the emperor's dissolute son, Kao Tsung, on the only possible occasion when she could find him alone: while he was relieving himself at the royal urinal. Even so, when the emperor died and Kao Tsung took over the throne, she still suffered the fate to which all wives and concubines of a deceased emperor were bound by tradition and law: Her head shaven, she entered a convent, for what was supposed to be the rest of her life. For seven years Wu schemed to escape. By communicating in secret with the new emperor, and by befriending his wife, the empress, she managed to get a highly unusual royal edict allowing her to return to the palace and to the royal harem. Once there, she fawned on the empress, while still sleeping with the emperor. The empress did not discourage this—she had yet to provide the emperor with an heir, her position was vulnerable, and Wu was a valuable ally.

In 654 Wu Chao gave birth to a child. One day the empress came to visit, and as soon as she had left, Wu smothered the newborn—her own baby. When the murder was discovered, suspicion immediately fell on the empress, who had been on the scene moments earlier, and whose jealous nature was known by all. This was precisely Wu's plan. Shortly thereafter, the empress was charged with murder and executed. Wu Chao was crowned empress in her place. Her new husband, addicted to his life of pleasure, gladly gave up the reins of government to Wu Chao, who was from then on known as Empress Wu.

Although now in a position of great power, Wu hardly felt secure. There were enemies everywhere; she could not let down her guard for one moment. Indeed, when she was forty-one, she began to fear that her beautiful young niece was becoming the emperor's favorite. She poisoned the woman with a clay mixed into her food. In 675 her own son, touted as the heir apparent, was poisoned as well. The next-eldest son—illegitimate, but now the crown prince—was exiled a little later on trumped-up charges. And when the emperor died, in 683, Wu managed to have the son after that declared unfit for the throne. All this meant that it was her youngest, most ineffectual son who finally became emperor. In this way she continued to rule.

Over the next five years there were innumerable palace coups. All of them failed, and all of the conspirators were executed. By 688 there was no one left to challenge Wu. She proclaimed herself a divine descendant of Buddha, and in 690 her wishes were finally granted: She was named Holy and Divine "Emperor" of China.

Wu became emperor because there was literally nobody left from the previous T'ang dynasty. And so she ruled unchallenged, for over a decade of relative peace. In 705, at the age of eighty, she was forced to abdicate.

Interpretation

All who knew Empress Wu remarked on her energy and intelligence. At the time, there was no glory available for an ambitious woman beyond a few years in the imperial harem, then a lifetime walled up in a convent. In Wu's gradual but remarkable rise to the top, she was never naive. She knew that any hesitation, any momentary weakness, would spell her end. If, every time she got rid of a rival a new one appeared, the solution was simple: She had to crush them all or be killed herself. Other emperors before her had followed the same path to the top, but Wu—who, as a woman, had next to no chance to gain power—had to be more ruthless still.

Empress Wu's forty-year reign was one of the longest in Chinese history. Although the story of her bloody rise to power is well known, in China she is considered one of the period's most able and effective rulers.

> A priest asked the dying Spanish statesman and general Ramón María Narváez
> (1800–1868), "Does your Excellency forgive all your enemies?" "I do not
> have to forgive my enemies," answered Narváez, "I have had them all shot."

KEYS TO POWER

It is no accident that the two stories illustrating this law come from China: Chinese history abounds with examples of enemies who were left alive and returned to haunt the lenient. "Crush the enemy" is a key strategic tenet of Sun-tzu, the fourth-century-B.C. author of *The Art of War*. The idea is simple: Your enemies wish you ill. There is nothing they want more than to eliminate you. If, in your struggles with them, you stop halfway or even three quarters of the way, out of mercy or hope of reconciliation, you only make them more determined, more embittered, and they will someday take revenge. They may act friendly for the time being, but this is only because you have defeated them. They have no choice but to bide their time.

The solution: Have no mercy. Crush your enemies as totally as they would crush you. Ultimately the only peace and security you can hope for from your enemies is their disappearance.

Mao Tse-tung, a devoted reader of Sun-tzu and of Chinese history generally, knew the importance of this law. In 1934 the Communist leader and some 75,000 poorly equipped soldiers fled into the desolate mountains of western China to escape Chiang Kai-shek's much larger army, in what has since been called the Long March.

Chiang was determined to eliminate every last Communist, and by a few years later Mao had less than 10,000 soldiers left. By 1937, in fact, when China was invaded by Japan, Chiang calculated that the Communists were no longer a threat. He chose to give up the chase and concentrate on the Japanese. Ten years later the Communists had recovered enough to rout Chiang's army. Chiang had forgotten the ancient wisdom of crushing the enemy; Mao had not. Chiang was pursued until he and his entire army fled to the island of Taiwan. Nothing remains of his regime in mainland China to this day.

The wisdom behind "crushing the enemy" is as ancient as the Bible: Its first practitioner may have been Moses, who learned it from God Himself, when He parted the Red Sea for the Jews, then let the water flow back over the pursuing Egyptians so that "not so much as one of them remained." When Moses returned from Mount Sinai with the Ten Commandments and found his people worshipping the Golden Calf, he had every last offender slaughtered. And just before he died, he told his followers, finally about to enter the Promised Land, that when they had defeated the tribes of Canaan they should "utterly destroy them . . . make no covenant with them, and show no mercy to them."

The goal of total victory is an axiom of modern warfare, and was codified as such by Carl von Clausewitz, the premier philosopher of war. Analyzing the campaigns of Napoleon, von Clausewitz wrote, "We do claim that direct annihilation of the enemy's forces must always be the *dominant consideration*. . . . Once a major victory is achieved there must be no talk of rest, of breathing space . . . but only of the pursuit, going for the enemy again, seizing his capital, attacking his reserves and anything else that might give his country aid and comfort." The reason for this is that after war come negotiation and the division of territory. If you have only won a partial victory, you will inevitably lose in negotiation what you have gained by war.

The solution is simple: Allow your enemies no options. Annihilate them and their territory is yours to carve. The goal of power is to control your enemies completely, to make them obey your will. You cannot afford to go halfway. If they have no options, they will be forced to do your bidding. This law has applications far beyond the battlefield. Negotiation is the insidious viper that will eat away at your victory, so give your enemies nothing to negotiate, no hope, no room to maneuver. They are crushed and that is that.

Realize this: In your struggle for power you will stir up rivalries and create enemies. There will be people you cannot win over, who will remain your enemies no matter what. But whatever wound you inflicted on them, deliberately or not, do not take their hatred personally. Just recognize that there is no possibility of peace between you, especially as long as you stay in power. If you let them stick around, they will seek revenge, as certainly as night follows day. To wait for them to show their cards is just silly; as Empress Wu understood, by then it will be too late.

Be realistic: With an enemy like this around, you will never be secure. Remember the lessons of history, and the wisdom of Moses and Mao: Never go halfway.

It is not, of course, a question of murder, it is a question of banishment. Sufficiently weakened and then exiled from your court forever, your enemies are rendered harmless. They have no hope of recovering, insinuating themselves and hurting you. And if they cannot be banished, at least understand that they are plotting against you, and pay no heed to whatever friendliness they feign. Your only weapon in such a situation is your own wariness. If you cannot banish them immediately, then plot for the best time to act.

Image: A Viper crushed beneath your foot but left alive, will rear up and bite you with a double dose of venom. An enemy that is left around is like a half-dead viper that you nurse back to health. Time makes the venom grow stronger.

Authority: For it must be noted, that men must either be caressed or else annihilated; they will revenge themselves for small injuries, but cannot do so for great ones; the injury therefore that we do to a man must be such that we need not fear his vengeance. (Niccolò Machiavelli, 1469–1527)

REVERSAL

This law should very rarely be ignored, but it does sometimes happen that it is better to let your enemies destroy themselves, if such a thing is possible, than to make them suffer by your hand. In warfare, for example, a good general knows that if he attacks an army when it is cornered, its soldiers will fight much more fiercely. It is sometimes better, then, to leave them an escape route, a way out. As they retreat, they wear themselves out, and are ultimately more demoralized by the retreat than by any defeat he might inflict on the battlefield. When you have someone on the ropes, then—but only when you are sure they have no chance of recovery—you might let them hang themselves. Let them be the agents of their own destruction. The result will be the same, and you won't feel half as bad.

Finally, sometimes by crushing an enemy, you embitter them so much that they spend years and years plotting revenge. The Treaty of Versailles had such an effect on the Germans. Some would argue that in the long run it would be better to show some leniency. The problem is, your leniency involves another risk—it may embolden the enemy, which still harbors a grudge, but now has some room to operate. It is almost always wiser to crush your enemy. If they plot revenge years later, do not let your guard down, but simply crush them again.

16

USE ABSENCE TO

INCREASE RESPECT

AND HONOR

JUDGMENT

Too much circulation makes the price go down: The more you are seen and heard from, the more common you appear. If you are already established in a group, temporary withdrawal from it will make you more talked about, even more admired. You must learn when to leave. Create value through scarcity.

TRANSGRESSION AND OBSERVANCE OF THE LAW

Sir Guillaume de Balaun was a troubadour who roamed the South of France in the Middle Ages, going from castle to castle, reciting poetry, and playing the perfect knight. At the castle of Javiac he met and fell in love with the beautiful lady of the house, Madame Guillelma de Javiac. He sang her his songs, recited his poetry, played chess with her, and little by little she in turn fell in love with him. Guillaume had a friend, Sir Pierre de Barjac, who traveled with him and who was also received at the castle. And Pierre too fell in love with a lady in Javiac, the gracious but temperamental Viernetta.

Then one day Pierre and Viernetta had a violent quarrel. The lady dismissed him, and he sought out his friend Guillaume to help heal the breach and get him back in her good graces. Guillaume was about to leave the castle for a while, but on his return, several weeks later, he worked his magic, and Pierre and the lady were reconciled. Pierre felt that his love had increased tenfold—that there was no stronger love, in fact, than the love that follows reconciliation. The stronger and longer the disagreement, he told Guillaume, the sweeter the feeling that comes with peace and rapprochement.

As a troubadour, Sir Guillaume prided himself on experiencing all the joys and sorrows of love. On hearing his friend's talk, he too wanted know the bliss of reconciliation after a quarrel. He therefore feigned great anger with Lady Guillelma, stopped sending her love letters, and abruptly left the castle and stayed away, even during the festivals and hunts. This drove the young lady wild.

Guillelma sent messengers to Guillaume to find out what had happened, but he turned the messengers away. He thought all this would make her angry, forcing him to plead for reconciliation as Pierre had. Instead, however, his absence had the opposite effect: It made Guillelma love him all the more. Now the lady pursued her knight, sending messengers and love notes of her own. This was almost unheard of—a lady never pursued her troubadour. And Guillaume did not like it. Guillelma's forwardness made him feel she had lost some of her dignity. Not only was he no longer sure of his plan, he was no longer sure of his lady.

Finally, after several months of not hearing from Guillaume, Guillelma gave up. She sent him no more messengers, and he began to wonder—perhaps she was angry? Perhaps the plan had worked after all? So much the better if she was. He would wait no more—it was time to reconcile. So he put on his best robe, decked the horse in its fanciest caparison, chose a magnificent helmet, and rode off to Javiac.

On hearing that her beloved had returned, Guillelma rushed to see him, knelt before him, dropped her veil to kiss him, and begged forgiveness for whatever slight had caused his anger. Imagine his confusion and despair—his plan had failed abysmally. She was not angry, she had never been angry, she was only deeper in love, and he would never experience the joy of reconciliation after a quarrel. Seeing her now, and still desperate to taste that joy, he decided to try one more time: He drove her away with harsh words and threatening gestures. She left, this time vowing never to see him again.

The next morning the troubadour regretted what he had done. He rode back to Javiac, but the lady would not receive him, and ordered her servants to chase him away, across the drawbridge and over the hill. Guillaume fled. Back in his chamber he collapsed and started to cry: He had made a terrible mistake. Over the next year, unable to see his lady, he experienced the absence, the terrible absence, that can only inflame love. He wrote one of his most beautiful poems, "My song ascends for mercy praying." And he sent many letters to Guillelma, explaining what he had done, and begging forgiveness.

After a great deal of this, Lady Guillelma, remembering his beautiful songs, his handsome figure, and his skills in dancing and falconry, found herself yearning to have him back. As penance for his cruelty, she ordered him to remove the nail from the little finger of his right hand, and to send it to her along with a poem describing his miseries.

He did as she asked. Finally Guillaume de Balaun was able to taste the ultimate sensation—a reconciliation even surpassing that of his friend Pierre.

Interpretation

Trying to discover the joys of reconciliation, Guillaume de Balaun inadvertently experienced the truth of the law of absence and presence. At the start of an affair, you need to heighten your presence in the eyes of the other. If you absent yourself too early, you may be forgotten. But once your lover's emotions are engaged, and the feeling of love has crystallized, absence inflames and excites. Giving no reason for your absence excites even more: The other person assumes he or she is at fault. While you are away, the lover's imagination takes flight, and a stimulated imagination cannot help but make love grow stronger. Conversely, the more Guillelma pursued Guillaume, the less he loved her—she had become too present, too accessible, leaving no room for *his* imagination and fancy, so that his feelings were suffocating. When she finally stopped sending messengers, he was able to breathe again, and to return to his plan.

What withdraws, what becomes scarce, suddenly seems to deserve our respect and honor. What stays too long, inundating us with its presence, makes us disdain it. In the Middle Ages, ladies were constantly putting their knights through trials of love, sending them on some long and arduous quest—all to create a pattern of absence and presence. Indeed, had Guillaume not left his lady in the first place, she might have been forced to send him away, creating an absence of her own.

> *Absence diminishes minor passions and inflames great ones,*
> *as the wind douses a candle and fans a fire.*
> *La Rochefoucauld, 1613–1680*

FIVE VIRTUES OF THE COCK

While serving under the Duke Ai of Lu, T'ien Jao, resenting his obscure position, said to his master, "I am going to wander far away like a snow goose."
"What do you mean by that?" inquired the Duke.
"Do you see the cock?" said T'ien Jao in reply. "Its crest is a symbol of civility; its powerful talons suggest strength; its daring to fight any enemy denotes courage; its instinct to invite others whenever food is obtained shows benevolence; and, last but not least, its punctuality in keeping the time through the night gives us an example of veracity. In spite, however, of these five virtues, the cock is daily killed to fill a dish on your table. Why? The reason is that it is found within our reach. On the other hand, the snow goose traverses in one flight a thousand li. Resting in your garden, it preys on your fishes and turtles and pecks your millet. Though devoid of any of the cock's five virtues, yet you prize this bird for the sake of its scarcity. This being so, I shall fly far like a snow goose."

ANCIENT CHINESE PARABLES, YU HSIU SEN, ED., 1974

OBSERVANCE OF THE LAW

For many centuries the Assyrians ruled upper Asia with an iron fist. In the eighth century B.C., however, the people of Medea (now northwestern Iran) revolted against them, and finally broke free. Now the Medes had to establish a new government. Determined to avoid any form of despotism, they refused to give ultimate power to any one man, or to establish a monarchy. Without a leader, however, the country soon fell into chaos, and fractured into small kingdoms, with village fighting against village.

In one such village lived a man named Deioces, who began to make a name for himself for fair dealing and the ability to settle disputes.

He did this so successfully, in fact, that soon any legal conflict in the area was brought to him, and his power increased. Throughout the land, the law had fallen into disrepute—the judges were corrupt, and no one entrusted their cases to the courts any more, resorting to violence instead. When news spread of Deioces' wisdom, incorruptibility, and unshakable impartiality, Medean villages far and wide turned to him to settle all manner of cases. Soon he became the sole arbiter of justice in the land.

At the height of his power, Deioces suddenly decided he had had enough. He would no longer sit in the chair of judgment, would hear no more suits, settle no more disputes between brother and brother, village and village. Complaining that he was spending so much time dealing with other people's problems that he had neglected his own affairs, he retired. The country once again descended into chaos. With the sudden withdrawal of a powerful arbiter like Deioces, crime increased, and contempt for the law was never greater. The Medes held a meeting of all the villages to decide how to get out of their predicament. "We cannot continue to live in this country under these conditions," said one tribal leader. "Let us appoint one of our number to rule so that we can live under orderly government, rather than losing our homes altogether in the present chaos."

And so, despite all that the Medes had suffered under the Assyrian despotism, they decided to set up a monarchy and name a king. And the man they most wanted to rule, of course, was the fair-minded Deioces. He was hard to convince, for he wanted nothing more to do with the villages' infighting and bickering, but the Medes begged and pleaded—without him the country had descended into a state of lawlessness. Deioces finally agreed.

Yet he also imposed conditions. An enormous palace was to be constructed for him, he was to be provided with bodyguards, and a capital city was to be built from which he could rule. All of this was done, and Deioces settled into his palace. In the center of the capital, the palace was surrounded by walls, and completely inaccessible to ordinary people. Deioces then established the terms of his rule: Admission to his presence was forbidden. Communication with the king was only possible through messengers. No one in the royal court could see him more than once a week, and then only by permission.

Deioces ruled for fifty-three years, extended the Medean empire, and established the foundation for what would later be the Persian empire, under his great-great-grandson Cyrus. During Deioces' reign, the people's respect for him gradually turned into a form of worship: He was not a mere mortal, they believed, but the son of a god.

Interpretation

Deioces was a man of great ambition. He determined early on that the country needed a strong ruler, and that he was the man for the job.

In a land plagued with anarchy, the most powerful man is the judge and arbiter. So Deioces began his career by making his reputation as a man of impeccable fairness.

At the height of his power as a judge, however, Deioces realized the truth of the law of absence and presence: By serving so many clients, he had become too noticeable, too available, and had lost the respect he had earlier enjoyed. People were taking his services for granted. The only way to regain the veneration and power he wanted was to withdraw completely, and let the Medes taste what life was like without him. As he expected, they came begging for him to rule.

Once Deioces had discovered the truth of this law, he carried it to its ultimate realization. In the palace his people had built for him, none could see him except a few courtiers, and those only rarely. As Herodotus wrote, "There was a risk that if they saw him habitually, it might lead to jealousy and resentment, and plots would follow; but if nobody saw him, the legend would grow that he was a being of a different order from mere men."

> *A man said to a Dervish: "Why do I not see you more often?" The Dervish replied, "Because the words 'Why have you not been to see me?' are sweeter to my ear than the words 'Why have you come again?'"*
> Mulla Jami,quoted in Idries Shah's Caravan of Dreams, 1968

KEYS TO POWER

Everything in the world depends on absence and presence. A strong presence will draw power and attention to you—you shine more brightly than those around you. But a point is inevitably reached where too much presence creates the opposite effect: The more you are seen and heard from, the more your value degrades. You become a habit. No matter how hard you try to be different, subtly, without your knowing why, people respect you less and less. At the right moment you must learn to withdraw yourself before they unconsciously push you away. It is a game of hide-and-seek.

The truth of this law can most easily be appreciated in matters of love and seduction. In the beginning stages of an affair, the lover's absence stimulates your imagination, forming a sort of aura around him or her. But this aura fades when you know too much—when your imagination no longer has room to roam. The loved one becomes a person like anyone else, a person whose presence is taken for granted. This is why the seventeenth-century French courtesan Ninon de Lenclos advised constant feints at withdrawal from one's lover. "Love never dies of starvation," she wrote, "but often of indigestion."

The moment you allow yourself to be treated like anyone else, it is too late—you are swallowed and digested. To prevent this you need to starve the other person of your presence. Force their respect by threatening them with the possibility that they will lose you for good; create a pattern of presence and absence.

Once you die, everything about you will seem different. You will be surrounded by an instant aura of respect. People will remember their criticisms of you, their arguments with you, and will be filled with regret and guilt. They are missing a presence that will never return. But you do not have to wait until you die: By completely withdrawing for a while, you create a kind of death before death. And when you come back, it will be as if you had come back from the dead—an air of resurrection will cling to you, and people will be relieved at your return. This is how Deioces made himself king.

Napoleon was recognizing the law of absence and presence when he said, "If I am often seen at the theater, people will cease to notice me." Today, in a world inundated with presence through the flood of images, the game of withdrawal is all the more powerful. We rarely know when to withdraw anymore, and nothing seems private, so we are awed by anyone who is able to disappear by choice. Novelists J. D. Salinger and Thomas Pynchon have created cultlike followings by knowing when to disappear.

Another, more everyday side of this law, but one that demonstrates its truth even further, is the law of scarcity in the science of economics. By withdrawing something from the market, you create instant value. In seventeenth-century Holland, the upper classes wanted to make the tulip more than just a beautiful flower—they wanted it to be a kind of status symbol. Making the flower scarce, indeed almost impossible to obtain, they sparked what was later called tulipomania. A single flower was now worth more than its weight in gold. In our own century, similarly, the art dealer Joseph Duveen insisted on making the paintings he sold as scarce and rare as possible. To keep their prices elevated and their status high, he bought up whole collections and stored them in his basement. The paintings that he sold became more than just paintings—they were fetish objects, their value increased by their rarity. "You can get all the pictures you want at fifty thousand dollars apiece—that's easy," he once said. "But to get pictures at a quarter of a million apiece—that wants doing!"

I m a g e:
The Sun. It can only be
appreciated by its absence.
The longer the days of rain, the
more the sun is craved. But too many
hot days and the sun overwhelms.
Learn to keep yourself obscure and
make people demand your return.

Extend the law of scarcity to your own skills. Make what you are offering the world rare and hard to find, and you instantly increase its value.

There always comes a moment when those in power overstay their welcome. We have grown tired of them, lost respect for them; we see them as no different from the rest of mankind, which is to say that we see them as rather worse, since we inevitably compare their current status in our eyes to their former one. There is an art to knowing when to retire. If it is done right, you regain the respect you had lost, and retain a part of your power.

The greatest ruler of the sixteenth century was Charles V. King of Spain, Hapsburg emperor, he governed an empire that at one point included much of Europe and the New World. Yet at the height of his power, in 1557, he retired to the monastery of Yuste. All of Europe was captivated by his sudden withdrawal; people who had hated and feared him suddenly called him great, and he came to be seen as a saint. In more recent times, the film actress Greta Garbo was never more admired than when she retired, in 1941. For some her absence came too soon—she was in her mid-thirties—but she wisely preferred to leave on her own terms, rather than waiting for her audience to grow tired of her.

Make yourself too available and the aura of power you have created around yourself will wear away. Turn the game around: Make yourself less accessible and you increase the value of your presence.

Authority:
Use absence to create
respect and esteem. If presence
diminishes fame, absence augments it.
A man who when absent is regarded as a
lion becomes when present something common and ridiculous. Talents lose their luster
if we become too familiar with them, for the
outer shell of the mind is more readily seen
than its rich inner kernel. Even the outstanding genius makes use of retirement so that
men may honor him and so that the
yearning aroused by his absence
may cause him to be esteemed.
(Baltasar Gracián,
1601–1658)

REVERSAL

This law only applies once a certain level of power has been attained. The need to withdraw only comes after you have established your presence; leave too early and you do not increase your respect, you are simply forgotten. When you are first entering onto the world's stage, create an image that is recognizable, reproducible, and is seen everywhere. Until that status is attained, absence is dangerous—instead of fanning the flames, it will extinguish them.

In love and seduction, similarly, absence is only effective once you have surrounded the other with your image, been seen by him or her everywhere. Everything must remind your lover of your presence, so that when you do choose to be away, the lover will always be thinking of you, will always be seeing you in his or her mind's eye.

Remember: In the beginning, make yourself not scarce but omnipresent. Only what is seen, appreciated, and loved will be missed in its absence.

KEEP OTHERS IN

SUSPENDED TERROR:

CULTIVATE AN AIR OF

UNPREDICTABILITY

JUDGMENT

Humans are creatures of habit with an insatiable need to see familiarity in other people's actions. Your predictability gives them a sense of control. Turn the tables: Be deliberately unpredictable. Behavior that seems to have no consistency or purpose will keep them off-balance, and they will wear themselves out trying to explain your moves. Taken to an extreme, this strategy can intimidate and terrorize.

OBSERVANCE OF THE LAW

In May of 1972, chess champion Boris Spassky anxiously awaited his rival Bobby Fischer in Reykjavík, Iceland. The two men had been scheduled to meet for the World Championship of Chess, but Fischer had not arrived on time and the match was on hold. Fischer had problems with the size of the prize money, problems with the way the money was to be distributed, problems with the logistics of holding the match in Iceland. He might back out at any moment.

Spassky tried to be patient. His Russian bosses felt that Fischer was humiliating him and told him to walk away, but Spassky wanted this match. He knew he could destroy Fischer, and nothing was going to spoil the greatest victory of his career. "So it seems that all our work may come to nothing," Spassky told a comrade. "But what can we do? It is Bobby's move. If he comes, we play. If he does not come, we do not play. A man who is willing to commit suicide has the initiative."

Fischer finally arrived in Reykjavík, but the problems, and the threat of cancellation, continued. He disliked the hall where the match was to be fought, he criticized the lighting, he complained about the noise of the cameras, he even hated the chairs in which he and Spassky were to sit. Now the Soviet Union took the initiative and threatened to withdraw their man.

The bluff apparently worked: After all the weeks of waiting, the endless and infuriating negotiations, Fischer agreed to play. Everyone was relieved, no one more than Spassky. But on the day of the official introductions, Fischer arrived very late, and on the day when the "Match of the Century" was to begin, he was late again. This time, however, the consequences would be dire: If he showed up *too* late he would forfeit the first game. What was going on? Was he playing some sort of mind game? Or was Bobby Fischer perhaps afraid of Boris Spassky? It seemed to the assembled grand masters, and to Spassky, that this young kid from Brooklyn had a terrible case of the jitters. At 5:09 Fischer showed up, exactly one minute before the match was to be canceled.

The first game of a chess tournament is critical, since it sets the tone for the months to come. It is often a slow and quiet struggle, with the two players preparing themselves for the war and trying to read each other's strategies. This game was different. Fischer made a terrible move early on, perhaps the worst of his career, and when Spassky had him on the ropes, he seemed to give up. Yet Spassky knew that Fischer *never* gave up. Even when facing checkmate, he fought to the bitter end, wearing the opponent down. This time, though, he seemed resigned. Then suddenly he broke out a bold move that put the room in a buzz. The move shocked Spassky, but he recovered and managed to win the game. But no one could figure out what Fischer was up to. Had he lost deliberately? Or was he rattled? Unsettled? Even, as some thought, insane?

After his defeat in the first game, Fischer complained all the more loudly about the room, the cameras, and everything else. He also failed to show up on time for the second game. This time the organizers had had enough: He was given a forfeit. Now he was down two games to none, a position from which no one had ever come back to win a chess championship. Fischer was clearly unhinged. Yet in the third game, as all those who witnessed it remember, he had a ferocious look in his eye, a look that clearly bothered Spassky. And despite the hole he had dug for himself, he seemed supremely confident. He did make what appeared to be another blunder, as he had in the first game—but his cocky air made Spassky smell a trap. Yet despite the Russian's suspicions, he could not figure out the trap, and before he knew it Fischer had checkmated him. In fact Fischer's unorthodox tactics had completely unnerved his opponent. At the end of the game, Fischer leaped up and rushed out, yelling to his confederates as he smashed a fist into his palm, "I'm crushing him with brute force!"

In the next games Fischer pulled moves that no one had seen from him before, moves that were not his style. Now Spassky started to make blunders. After losing the sixth game, he started to cry. One grand master said, "After this, Spassky's got to ask himself if it's safe to go back to Russia." After the eighth game Spassky decided he knew what was happening: Bobby Fischer was hypnotizing him. He decided not to look Fischer in the eye; he lost anyway.

After the fourteenth game he called a staff conference and announced, "An attempt is being made to control my mind." He wondered whether the orange juice they drank at the chess table could have been drugged. Maybe chemicals were being blown into the air. Finally Spassky went public, accusing the Fischer team of putting something in the chairs that was altering Spassky's mind. The KGB went on alert: Boris Spassky was embarrassing the Soviet Union!

The chairs were taken apart and X-rayed. A chemist found nothing unusual in them. The only things anyone found anywhere, in fact, were two dead flies in a lighting fixture. Spassky began to complain of hallucinations. He tried to keep playing, but his mind was unraveling. He could not go on. On September 2, he resigned. Although still relatively young, he never recovered from this defeat.

Interpretation

In previous games between Fischer and Spassky, Fischer had not fared well. Spassky had an uncanny ability to read his opponent's strategy and use it against him. Adaptable and patient, he would build attacks that would defeat not in seven moves but in seventy. He defeated Fischer every time they played because he saw much further ahead, and because he was a brilliant psychologist who never lost control. One master said, "He doesn't just look for the best move. He looks for the move that will disturb the man he is playing."

Fischer, however, finally understood that this was one of the keys to Spassky's success: He played on your predictability, defeated you at your own game. Everything Fischer did for the championship match was an attempt to put the initiative on his side and to keep Spassky off-balance. Clearly the endless waiting had an effect on Spassky's psyche. Most powerful of all, though, were Fischer's deliberate blunders and his appearance of having no clear strategy. In fact, he was doing everything he could to scramble his old patterns, even if it meant losing the first match and forfeiting the second.

Spassky was known for his sangfroid and levelheadedness, but for the first time in his life he could not figure out his opponent. He slowly melted down, until at the end *he* was the one who seemed insane.

Chess contains the concentrated essence of life: First, because to win you have to be supremely patient and farseeing; and second, because the game is built on patterns, whole sequences of moves that have been played before and will be played again, with slight alterations, in any one match. Your opponent analyzes the patterns you are playing and uses them to try to foresee your moves. Allowing him nothing predictable to base his strategy on gives you a big advantage. In chess as in life, when people cannot figure out what you are doing, they are kept in a state of terror—waiting, uncertain, confused.

> *Life at court is a serious, melancholy game of chess, which requires us to draw*
> *up our pieces and batteries, form a plan, pursue it, parry that of our*
> *adversary. Sometimes, however, it is better to take risks*
> *and play the most capricious, unpredictable move.*
> *Jean de La Bruyère, 1645–1696*

KEYS TO POWER

Nothing is more terrifying than the sudden and unpredictable. That is why we are so frightened by earthquakes and tornadoes: We do not know when they will strike. After one has occurred, we wait in terror for the next one. To a lesser degree, this is the effect that unpredictable human behavior has on us.

Animals behave in set patterns, which is why we are able to hunt and kill them. Only man has the capacity to consciously alter his behavior, to improvise and overcome the weight of routine and habit. Yet most men do not realize this power. They prefer the comforts of routine, of giving in to the animal nature that has them repeating the same compulsive actions time and time again. They do this because it requires no effort, and because they mistakenly believe that if they do not unsettle others, they will be left alone. Understand: A person of power instills a kind of fear by *deliberately* unsettling those around him to keep the initiative on his side. You sometimes need to strike without warning, to make others tremble when they least expect it. It is a device that the powerful have used for centuries.

Filippo Maria, the last of the Visconti dukes of Milan in fifteenth-century Italy, consciously did the opposite of what everyone expected of him. For instance, he might suddenly shower a courtier with attention, and then, once the man had come to expect a promotion to higher office, would suddenly start treating him with the utmost disdain. Confused, the man might leave the court, when the duke would suddenly recall him and start treating him well again. Doubly confused, the courtier would wonder whether his assumption that he would be promoted had become obvious, and offensive, to the duke, and would start to behave as if he no longer expected such honor. The duke would rebuke him for his lack of ambition and would send him away.

The secret of dealing with Filippo was simple: Do not presume to know what he wants. Do not try to guess what will please him. Never inject *your* will; just surrender to *his* will. Then wait to see what happens. Amidst the confusion and uncertainty he created, the duke ruled supreme, unchallenged and at peace.

Unpredictability is most often the tactic of the master, but the underdog too can use it to great effect. If you find yourself outnumbered or cornered, throw in a series of unpredictable moves. Your enemies will be so confused that they will pull back or make a tactical blunder.

In the spring of 1862, during the American Civil War, General Stonewall Jackson and a force of 4,600 Confederate soldiers were tormenting the larger Union forces in the Shenandoah Valley. Meanwhile, not far away, General George Brinton McClellan, heading a force of 90,000 Union soldiers, was marching south from Washington, D.C., to lay siege to Richmond, Virginia, the Confederate capital. As the weeks of the campaign went by, Jackson repeatedly led his soldiers out of the Shenandoah Valley, then back to it.

His movements made no sense. Was he preparing to help defend Richmond? Was he marching on Washington, now that McClellan's absence had left it unprotected? Was he heading north to wreak havoc up there? Why was his small force moving in circles?

Jackson's inexplicable moves made the Union generals delay the march on Richmond as they waited to figure out what he was up to. Meanwhile, the South was able to pour reinforcements into the town. A battle that could have crushed the Confederacy turned into a stalemate. Jackson used this tactic time and again when facing numerically superior forces. "Always mystify, mislead, and surprise the enemy, if possible," he said, ". . . such tactics will win every time and a small army may thus destroy a large one."

This law applies not only to war but to everyday situations. People are always trying to read the motives behind your actions and to use your predictability against you. Throw in a completely inexplicable move and you put them on the defensive. Because they do not understand you, they are unnerved, and in such a state you can easily intimidate them.

Pablo Picasso once remarked, "The best calculation is the absence of calculation. Once you have attained a certain level of recognition, others generally figure that when you do something, it's for an intelligent reason. So it's really foolish to plot out your movements too carefully in advance. You're better off acting capriciously."

For a while, Picasso worked with the art dealer Paul Rosenberg. At first he allowed him a fair amount of latitude in handling his paintings, then one day, for no apparent reason, he told the man he would no longer give him any work to sell. As Picasso explained, "Rosenberg would spend the next forty-eight hours trying to figure out why. Was I reserving things for some other dealer? I'd go on working and sleeping and Rosenberg would spend his time figuring. In two days he'd come back, nerves jangled, anxious, saying, 'After all, dear friend, you wouldn't turn me down if I offered you this much [naming a substantially higher figure] for those paintings rather than the price I've been accustomed to paying you, would you?'"

Unpredictability is not only a weapon of terror: Scrambling your patterns on a day-to-day basis will cause a stir around you and stimulate interest. People will talk about you, ascribe motives and explanations that have nothing to do with the truth, but that keep you constantly in their minds. In the end, the more capricious you appear, the more respect you will garner. Only the terminally subordinate act in a predictable manner.

Image: The Cyclone. A wind that cannot be foreseen. Sudden shifts in the barometer, inexplicable changes in direction and velocity. There is no defense: A cyclone sows terror and confusion.

Authority: The enlightened ruler is so mysterious that he seems to dwell nowhere, so inexplicable that no one can seek him. He reposes in nonaction above, and his ministers tremble below. (Han-fei-tzu, Chinese philosopher, third century B.C.)

REVERSAL

Sometimes predictability can work in your favor: By creating a pattern for people to be familiar and comfortable with, you can lull them to sleep. They have prepared everything according to their preconceived notions about you. You can use this in several ways: First, it sets up a smoke screen, a comfortable front behind which you can carry on deceptive actions. Second, it allows you on rare occasions to do something completely against the pattern, unsettling your opponent so deeply he will fall to the ground without being pushed.

In 1974 Muhammad Ali and George Foreman were scheduled to fight for the world heavyweight boxing championship. Everyone knew what would happen: Big George Foreman would try to land a knockout punch while Ali would dance around him, wearing him out. That was Ali's way of fighting, his pattern, and he had not changed it in more than ten years. But in this case it seemed to give Foreman the advantage: He had a devastating punch, and if he waited, sooner or later Ali would have to come to him. Ali, the master strategist, had other plans: In press conferences before the big fight, he said he was going to change his style and punch it out with Foreman. No one, least of all Foreman, believed this for a second. That plan would be suicide on Ali's part; he was playing the comedian, as usual. Then, before the fight, Ali's trainer loosened the ropes around the ring, something a trainer would do if his boxer were intending to slug it out. But no one believed this ploy; it had to be a setup.

To everyone's amazement, Ali did exactly what he had said he would do. As Foreman waited for him to dance around, Ali went right up to him and slugged it out. He completely upset his opponent's strategy. At a loss, Foreman ended up wearing himself out, not by chasing Ali but by throwing punches wildly, and taking more and more counterpunches. Finally, Ali landed a dramatic right cross that knocked out Foreman. The habit of assuming that a person's behavior will fit its previous patterns is so strong that not even Ali's announcement of a strategy change was enough to upset it. Foreman walked into a trap—the trap he had been told to expect.

A warning: Unpredictability can work against you sometimes, especially if you are in a subordinate position. There are times when it is better to let people feel comfortable and settled around you than to disturb them. Too much unpredictability will be seen as a sign of indecisiveness, or even of some more serious psychic problem. Patterns are powerful, and you can terrify people by disrupting them. Such power should only be used judiciously.

DO NOT BUILD FORTRESSES

TO PROTECT YOURSELF—

ISOLATION IS DANGEROUS

JUDGMENT

The world is dangerous and enemies are everywhere—everyone has to protect themselves. A fortress seems the safest. But isolation exposes you to more dangers than it protects you from—it cuts you off from valuable information, it makes you conspicuous and an easy target. Better to circulate among people, find allies, mingle. You are shielded from your enemies by the crowd.

TRANSGRESSION OF THE LAW

Ch'in Shih Huang Ti, the first emperor of China (221–210 B.C.), was the mightiest man of his day. His empire was vaster and more powerful than that of Alexander the Great. He had conquered all of the kingdoms surrounding his own kingdom of Ch'in and unified them into one massive realm called China. But in the last years of his life, few, if anyone, saw him.

The emperor lived in the most magnificent palace built to that date, in the capital of Hsien-yang. The palace had 270 pavilions; all of these were connected by secret underground passageways, allowing the emperor to move through the palace without anyone seeing him. He slept in a different room every night, and anyone who inadvertently laid eyes on him was instantly beheaded. Only a handful of men knew his whereabouts, and if they revealed it to anyone, they, too, were put to death.

The first emperor had grown so terrified of human contact that when he had to leave the palace he traveled incognito, disguising himself carefully. On one such trip through the provinces, he suddenly died. His body was borne back to the capital in the emperor's carriage, with a cart packed with salted fish trailing behind it to cover up the smell of the rotting corpse—no one was to know of his death. He died alone, far from his wives, his family, his friends, and his courtiers, accompanied only by a minister and a handful of eunuchs.

Interpretation

Shih Huang Ti started off as the king of Ch'in, a fearless warrior of unbridled ambition. Writers of the time described him as a man with "a waspish nose, eyes like slits, the voice of a jackal, and the heart of a tiger or wolf." He could be merciful sometimes, but more often he "swallowed men up without a scruple." It was through trickery and violence that he conquered the provinces surrounding his own and created China, forging a single nation and culture out of many. He broke up the feudal system, and to keep an eye on the many members of the royal families that were scattered across the realm's various kingdoms, he moved 120,000 of them to the capital, where he housed the most important courtiers in the vast palace of Hsien-yang. He consolidated the many walls on the borders and built them into the Great Wall of China. He standardized the country's laws, its written language, even the size of its cartwheels.

As part of this process of unification, however, the first emperor outlawed the writings and teachings of Confucius, the philosopher whose ideas on the moral life had already become virtually a religion in Chinese culture. On Shih Huang Ti's order, thousands of books relating to Confucius were burned, and anyone who quoted Confucius was to be beheaded. This made many enemies for the emperor, and he grew constantly afraid, even paranoid. The executions mounted. A contemporary, the writer Hanfei-tzu, noted that "Ch'in has been victorious for four generations, yet has lived in constant terror and apprehension of destruction."

As the emperor withdrew deeper and deeper into the palace to protect

THE MASQUE OF THE
RED DEATH

The "Red Death" had long devastated the country. No pestilence had ever been so fatal, or so hideous. Blood was its Avatar and its seal—the redness and horror of blood. There were sharp pains, and sudden dizziness, and then profuse bleeding at the pores, with dissolution. . . . And the whole seizure, progress, and termination of the disease, were the incidents of half an hour.
But the Prince Prospero was happy and dauntless and sagacious. When his dominions were half-depopulated, he summoned to his presence a thousand hale and light-hearted friends from among the knights and dames of his court, and with these retired to the deep seclusion of one of his castellated abbeys. This was an extensive and magnificent structure, the creation of the prince's own eccentric yet august taste. A strong and lofty wall girdled it in. This wall had gates of iron. The courtiers, having entered, brought furnaces and massy hammers and welded the bolts. They resolved to leave means neither of ingress nor egress to the sudden impulses of despair or of frenzy from within. The abbey was amply provisioned. With such

himself, he slowly lost control of the realm. Eunuchs and ministers enacted political policies without his approval or even his knowledge; they also plotted against him. By the end, he was emperor in name only, and was so isolated that barely anyone knew he had died. He had probably been poi- soned by the same scheming ministers who encouraged his isolation.

That is what isolation brings: Retreat into a fortress and you lose con- tact with the sources of your power. You lose your ear for what is happen- ing around you, as well as a sense of proportion. Instead of being safer, you cut yourself off from the kind of knowledge on which your life depends. Never enclose yourself so far from the streets that you cannot hear what is happening around you, including the plots against you.

OBSERVANCE OF THE LAW

Louis XIV had the palace of Versailles built for him and his court in the 1660s, and it was like no other royal palace in the world. As in a beehive, everything revolved around the royal person. He lived surrounded by the nobility, who were allotted apartments nestled around his, their closeness to him dependent on their rank. The king's bedroom occupied the literal center of the palace and was the focus of everyone's attention. Every morn- ing the king was greeted in this room by a ritual known as the *lever*.

At eight A.M., the king's first valet, who slept at the foot of the royal bed, would awaken His Majesty. Then pages would open the door and admit those who had a function in the *lever*. The order of their entry was precise: First came the king's illegitimate sons and his grandchildren, then the princes and princesses of the blood, and then his physician and sur- geon. There followed the grand officers of the wardrobe, the king's official reader, and those in charge of entertaining the king. Next would arrive var- ious government officials, in ascending order of rank. Last but not least came those attending the *lever* by special invitation. By the end of the cere- mony, the room would be packed with well over a hundred royal atten- dants and visitors.

The day was organized so that all the palace's energy was directed at and passed through the king. Louis was constantly attended by courtiers and officials, all asking for his advice and judgment. To all their questions he usually replied, "I shall see."

As Saint-Simon noted, "If he turned to someone, asked him a ques- tion, made an insignificant remark, the eyes of all present were turned on this person. It was a distinction that was talked of and increased prestige." There was no possibility of privacy in the palace, not even for the king— every room communicated with another, and every hallway led to larger rooms where groups of nobles gathered constantly. Everyone's actions were interdependent, and nothing and no one passed unnoticed: "The king not only saw to it that all the high nobility was present at his court," wrote Saint-Simon, "he demanded the same of the minor nobility. At his *lever* and *coucher,* at his meals, in his gardens of Versailles, he always looked about him, noticing everything. He was offended if the most distinguished nobles did not live permanently at court, and those who showed themselves never or hardly ever, incurred his full displeasure. If one of these desired something, the king would say proudly: 'I do not know him,' and the judgment was irrevocable."

Interpretation

Louis XIV came to power at the end of a terrible civil war, the Fronde. A principal instigator of the war had been the nobility, which deeply resented the growing power of the throne and yearned for the days of feudalism, when the lords ruled their own fiefdoms and the king had little authority over them. The nobles had lost the civil war, but they remained a fractious, resentful lot.

The construction of Versailles, then, was far more than the decadent whim of a luxury-loving king. It served a crucial function: The king could keep an eye and an ear on everyone and everything around him. The once proud nobility was reduced to squabbling over the right to help the king put on his robes in the morning. There was no possibility here of privacy—no possibility of isolation. Louis XIV very early grasped the truth that for a king to isolate himself is gravely dangerous. In his absence, conspiracies will spring up like mushrooms after rain, animosities will crystallize into factions, and rebellion will break out before he has the time to react. To combat this, sociability and openness must not only be encouraged, they must be formally organized and channeled.

These conditions at Versailles lasted for Louis's entire reign, some fifty years of relative peace and tranquillity. Through it all, not a pin dropped without Louis hearing it.

Solitude is dangerous to reason, without being favorable to virtue. . . .
Remember that the solitary mortal is certainly luxurious,
probably superstitious, and possibly mad.
Dr. Samuel Johnson, 1709–1784

KEYS TO POWER

Machiavelli makes the argument that in a strictly military sense a fortress is invariably a mistake. It becomes a symbol of power's isolation, and is an easy target for its builders' enemies. Designed to defend you, fortresses actually cut you off from help and cut into your flexibility. They may appear impregnable, but once you retire to one, everyone knows where you are; and a siege does not have to succeed to turn your fortress into a prison. With their small and confined spaces, fortresses are also extremely vulnerable to the plague and contagious diseases. In a strategic sense, the isolation of a fortress provides no protection, and actually creates more problems than it solves.

was made so nearly to resemble the countenance of a stiffened corpse that the closest scrutiny must have had difficulty in detecting the cheat. And yet all this might have been endured, if not approved, by the mad revellers around. But the mummer had gone so far as to assume the type of the Red Death. His vesture was dabbled in blood—*and his broad brow, with all the features of the face, was sprinkled with the scarlet horror. . . .*

. . . A throng of the revellers at once threw themselves into the black apartment, and, seizing the mummer, whose tall figure stood erect and motionless within the shadow of the ebony clock, gasped in unutterable horror at finding the grave cerements and corpse-like mask, which they handled with so violent a rudeness, untenanted by any tangible form. And now was acknowledged the presence of the Red Death. He had come like a thief in the night. And one by one dropped the revellers in the blood-bedewed halls of their revel, and died each in the despairing posture of his fall. And the life of the ebony clock went out with that of the last of the gay. And the flames of the tripods expired. And Darkness and Decay and the Red Death held illimitable dominion over all.

THE MASQUE OF THE RED DEATH,
EDGAR ALLAN POE,
1809–1849

Because humans are social creatures by nature, power depends on social interaction and circulation. To make yourself powerful you must place yourself at the center of things, as Louis XIV did at Versailles. All activity should revolve around you, and you should be aware of everything happening on the street, and of anyone who might be hatching plots against you. The danger for most people comes when they feel threatened. In such times they tend to retreat and close ranks, to find security in a kind of fortress. In doing so, however, they come to rely for information on a smaller and smaller circle, and lose perspective on events around them. They lose maneuverability and become easy targets, and their isolation makes them paranoid. As in warfare and most games of strategy, isolation often precedes defeat and death.

In moments of uncertainty and danger, you need to fight this desire to turn inward. Instead, make yourself more accessible, seek out old allies and make new ones, force yourself into more and more different circles. This has been the trick of powerful people for centuries.

The Roman statesman Cicero was born into the lower nobility, and had little chance of power unless he managed to make a place for himself among the aristocrats who controlled the city. He succeeded brilliantly, identifying everyone with influence and figuring out how they were connected to one another. He mingled everywhere, knew everyone, and had such a vast network of connections that an enemy here could easily be counterbalanced by an ally there.

The French statesman Talleyrand played the game the same way. Although he came from one of the oldest aristocratic families in France, he made a point of always staying in touch with what was happening in the streets of Paris, allowing him to foresee trends and troubles. He even got a certain pleasure out of mingling with shady criminal types, who supplied him with valuable information. Every time there was a crisis, a transition of power—the end of the Directory, the fall of Napoleon, the abdication of Louis XVIII—he was able to survive and even thrive, because he never closed himself up in a small circle but always forged connections with the new order.

This law pertains to kings and queens, and to those of the highest power: The moment you lose contact with your people, seeking security in isolation, rebellion is brewing. Never imagine yourself so elevated that you can afford to cut yourself off from even the lowest echelons. By retreating to a fortress, you make yourself an easy target for your plotting subjects, who view your isolation as an insult and a reason for rebellion.

Since humans are such social creatures, it follows that the social arts that make us pleasant to be around can be practiced only by constant exposure and circulation. The more you are in contact with others, the more graceful and at ease you become. Isolation, on the other hand, engenders an awkwardness in your gestures, and leads to further isolation, as people start avoiding you.

In 1545 Duke Cosimo I de' Medici decided that to ensure the immortality of his name he would commission frescoes for the main chapel of the church of San Lorenzo in Florence. He had many great painters to choose from, and in the end he picked Jacopo da Pontormo. Getting on in years, Pontormo wanted to make these frescoes his chef d'oeuvre and legacy. His first decision was to close the chapel off with walls, partitions, and blinds. He wanted no one to witness the creation of his masterpiece, or to steal his ideas. He would outdo Michelangelo himself. When some young men broke into the chapel out of curiosity, Jacopo sealed it off even further.

Pontormo filled the chapel's ceiling with biblical scenes—the Creation, Adam and Eve, Noah's ark, on and on. At the top of the middle wall he painted Christ in his majesty, raising the dead on Judgment Day. The artist worked on the chapel for eleven years, rarely leaving it, since he had developed a phobia for human contact and was afraid his ideas would be stolen.

Pontormo died before completing the frescoes, and none of them has survived. But the great Renaissance writer Vasari, a friend of Pontormo's who saw the frescoes shortly after the artist's death, left a description of what they looked like. There was a total lack of proportion. Scenes bumped against scenes, figures in one story being juxtaposed with those in another, in maddening numbers. Pontormo had become obsessed with detail but had lost any sense of the overall composition. Vasari left off his description of the frescoes by writing that if he continued, "I think I would go mad and become entangled in this painting, just as I believe that in the eleven years of time Jacopo spent on it, he entangled himself and anyone else who saw it." Instead of crowning Pontormo's career, the work became his undoing.

These frescoes were visual equivalents of the effects of isolation on the human mind: a loss of proportion, an obsession with detail combined with an inability to see the larger picture, a kind of extravagant ugliness that no longer communicates. Clearly, isolation is as deadly for the creative arts as for the social arts. Shakespeare is the most famous writer in history because, as a dramatist for the popular stage, he opened himself up to the masses, making his work accessible to people no matter what their education and taste. Artists who hole themselves up in their fortress lose a sense of proportion, their work communicating only to their small circle. Such art remains cornered and powerless.

Finally, since power is a human creation, it is inevitably increased by contact with other people. Instead of falling into the fortress mentality, view the world in the following manner: It is like a vast Versailles, with every room communicating with another. You need to be permeable, able to float in and out of different circles and mix with different types. That kind of mobility and social contact will protect you from plotters, who will be unable to keep secrets from you, and from your enemies, who will be unable to isolate you from your allies. Always on the move, you mix and mingle in the rooms of the palace, never sitting or settling in one place. No hunter can fix his aim on such a swift-moving creature.

Image: The Fortress. High
up on the hill, the citadel becomes a symbol of all that is
hateful in power and authority.
The citizens of the town betray
you to the first enemy that comes.
Cut off from communication and intelligence, the citadel falls with ease.

Authority: A good and wise prince, desirous of maintaining that
character, and to avoid giving the opportunity to his sons to become oppressive, will never build fortresses, so that they may
place their reliance upon the good will of their subjects, and not
upon the strength of citadels. (Niccolò Machiavelli, 1469–1527)

REVERSAL

It is hardly ever right and propitious to choose isolation. Without keeping
an ear on what is happening in the streets, you will be unable to protect
yourself. About the only thing that constant human contact cannot facili-
tate is thought. The weight of society's pressure to conform, and the lack of
distance from other people, can make it impossible to think clearly about
what is going on around you. As a temporary recourse, then, isolation can
help you to gain perspective. Many a serious thinker has been produced in
prisons, where we have nothing to do but think. Machiavelli could write
The Prince only once he found himself in exile and isolated on a farm far
from the political intrigues of Florence.

The danger is, however, that this kind of isolation will sire all kinds of
strange and perverted ideas. You may gain perspective on the larger picture, but you lose a sense of your own smallness and limitations. Also, the
more isolated you are, the harder it is to break out of your isolation when
you choose to—it sinks you deep into its quicksand without your noticing.
If you need time to think, then, choose isolation only as a last resort, and
only in small doses. Be careful to keep your way back into society open.

KNOW WHO YOU'RE

DEALING WITH—

DO NOT OFFEND THE

WRONG PERSON

JUDGMENT

There are many different kinds of people in the world, and you can never assume that everyone will react to your strategies in the same way. Deceive or outmaneuver some people and they will spend the rest of their lives seeking revenge. They are wolves in lambs' clothing. Choose your victims and opponents carefully, then—never offend or deceive the wrong person.

OPPONENTS, SUCKERS, AND VICTIMS: Preliminary Typology

In your rise to power you will come across many breeds of opponent, sucker, and victim. The highest form of the art of power is the ability to distinguish the wolves from the lambs, the foxes from the hares, the hawks from the vultures. If you make this distinction well, you will succeed without needing to coerce anyone too much. But if you deal blindly with whomever crosses your path, you will have a life of constant sorrow, if you even live that long. Being able to recognize types of people, and to act accordingly, is critical. The following are the five most dangerous and difficult types of mark in the jungle, as identified by artists—con and otherwise—of the past.

The Arrogant and Proud Man. Although he may initially disguise it, this man's touchy pride makes him very dangerous. Any perceived slight will lead to a vengeance of overwhelming violence. You may say to yourself, "But I only said such-and-such at a party, where everyone was drunk. . . ." It does not matter. There is no sanity behind his overreaction, so do not waste time trying to figure him out. If at any point in your dealings with a person you sense an oversensitive and overactive pride, flee. Whatever you are hoping for from him isn't worth it.

The Hopelessly Insecure Man. This man is related to the proud and arrogant type, but is less violent and harder to spot. His ego is fragile, his sense of self insecure, and if he feels himself deceived or attacked, the hurt will simmer. He will attack you in bites that will take forever to get big enough for you to notice. If you find you have deceived or harmed such a man, disappear for a long time. Do not stay around him or he will nibble you to death.

Mr. Suspicion. Another variant on the breeds above, this is a future Joe Stalin. He sees what he wants to see—usually the worst—in other people, and imagines that everyone is after him. Mr. Suspicion is in fact the least dangerous of the three: Genuinely unbalanced, he is easy to deceive, just as Stalin himself was constantly deceived. Play on his suspicious nature to get him to turn against other people. But if you do become the target of his suspicions, watch out.

The Serpent with a Long Memory. If hurt or deceived, this man will show no anger on the surface; he will calculate and wait. Then, when he is in a position to turn the tables, he will exact a revenge marked by a cold-blooded shrewdness. Recognize this man by his calculation and cunning in the different areas of his life. He is usually cold and unaffectionate. Be doubly careful of this snake, and if you have somehow injured him, either crush him completely or get him out of your sight.

The Plain, Unassuming, and Often Unintelligent Man. Ah, your ears prick up when you find such a tempting victim. But this man is a lot harder to deceive than you imagine. Falling for a ruse often takes intelligence and imagination—a sense of the possible rewards. The blunt man will not take the bait because he does not recognize it. He is that unaware. The danger with this man is not that he will harm you or seek revenge, but merely that he will waste your time, energy, resources, and even your sanity in trying to deceive him. Have a test ready for a mark—a joke, a story. If his reaction is utterly literal, this is the type you are dealing with. Continue at your own risk.

TRANSGRESSIONS OF THE LAW

Transgression I

In the early part of the thirteenth century, Muhammad, the shah of Khwarezm, managed after many wars to forge a huge empire, extending west to present-day Turkey and south to Afghanistan. The empire's center was the great Asian capital of Samarkand. The shah had a powerful, well-trained army, and could mobilize 200,000 warriors within days.

In 1219 Muhammad received an embassy from a new tribal leader to the east, Genghis Khan. The embassy included all sorts of gifts to the great Muhammad, representing the finest goods from Khan's small but growing Mongol empire. Genghis Khan wanted to reopen the Silk Route to Europe, and offered to share it with Muhammad, while promising peace between the two empires.

Muhammad did not know this upstart from the east, who, it seemed to him, was extremely arrogant to try to talk as an equal to one so clearly his superior. He ignored Khan's offer. Khan tried again: This time he sent a caravan of a hundred camels filled with the rarest articles he had plundered from China. Before the caravan reached Muhammad, however, Inalchik, the governor of a region bordering on Samarkand, seized it for himself, and executed its leaders.

Genghis Khan was sure that this was a mistake—that Inalchik had acted without Muhammad's approval. He sent yet another mission to Muhammad, reiterating his offer and asking that the governor be punished. This time Muhammad himself had one of the ambassadors beheaded, and sent the other two back with shaved heads—a horrifying insult in the Mongol code of honor. Khan sent a message to the shah: "You have chosen war. What will happen will happen, and what it is to be we know not; only God knows." Mobilizing his forces, in 1220 he attacked Inalchik's province, where he seized the capital, captured the governor, and ordered him executed by having molten silver poured into his eyes and ears.

Over the next year, Khan led a series of guerrilla-like campaigns against the shah's much larger army. His method was totally novel for the time—his soldiers could move very fast on horseback, and had mastered the art of firing with bow and arrow while mounted. The speed and flexibility of his forces allowed him to deceive Muhammad as to his intentions and the directions of his movements. Eventually he managed first to sur-

prison, and put Aguirre on the beast. . . . The beast was driven on, and he received the lashes. . . ."

When freed, Aguirre announced his intention of killing the official who had sentenced him, the alcalde Esquivel. Esquivel's term of office expired and he fled to Lima, three hundred twenty leagues away, but within fifteen days Aguirre had tracked him there. The frightened judge journeyed to Quito, a trip of four hundred leagues, and in twenty days Aguirre arrived.

"When Esquivel heard of his presence," according to Garcilaso, "he made another journey of five hundred leagues to Cuzco; but in a few days Aguirre also arrived, having travelled on foot and without shoes, saying that a whipped man has no business to ride a horse, or to go where he would be seen by others. In this way, Aguirre followed his judge for three years, and four months." Wearying of the pursuit, Esquivel remained at Cuzco, a city so sternly governed that he felt he would be safe from Aguirre. He took a house near the cathedral and never ventured outdoors without a sword and a dagger. "However, on a certain Monday, at noon, Aguirre entered his house, and having walked all over it, and having traversed a corridor, a saloon, a chamber, and an inner

round Samarkand, then to seize it. Muhammad fled, and a year later died, his vast empire broken and destroyed. Genghis Khan was sole master of Samarkand, the Silk Route, and most of northern Asia.

Interpretation

Never assume that the person you are dealing with is weaker or less important than you are. Some men are slow to take offense, which may make you misjudge the thickness of their skin, and fail to worry about insulting them. But should you offend their honor and their pride, they will overwhelm you with a violence that seems sudden and extreme given their slowness to anger. If you want to turn people down, it is best to do so politely and respectfully, even if you feel their request is impudent or their offer ridiculous. Never reject them with an insult until you know them better; you may be dealing with a Genghis Khan.

Transgression II

In the late 1910s some of the best swindlers in America formed a con-artist ring based in Denver, Colorado. In the winter months they would spread across the southern states, plying their trade. In 1920 Joe Furey, a leader of the ring, was working his way through Texas, making hundreds of thousands of dollars with classic con games. In Fort Worth, he met a sucker named J. Frank Norfleet, a cattleman who owned a large ranch. Norfleet fell for the con. Convinced of the riches to come, he emptied his bank account of $45,000 and handed it over to Furey and his confederates. A few days later they gave him his "millions," which turned out to be a few good dollars wrapped around a packet of newspaper clippings.

Furey and his men had worked such cons a hundred times before, and the sucker was usually so embarrassed by his gullibility that he quietly learned his lesson and accepted the loss. But Norfleet was not like other suckers. He went to the police, who told him there was little they could do. "Then I'll go after those people myself," Norfleet told the detectives. "I'll get them, too, if it takes the rest of my life." His wife took over the ranch as Norfleet scoured the country, looking for others who had been fleeced in the same game. One such sucker came forward, and the two men identified one of the con artists in San Francisco, and managed to get him locked up. The man committed suicide rather than face a long term in prison.

Norfleet kept going. He tracked down another of the con artists in Montana, roped him like a calf, and dragged him through the muddy streets to the town jail. He traveled not only across the country but to England, Canada, and Mexico in search of Joe Furey, and also of Furey's right-hand man, W. B. Spencer. Finding Spencer in Montreal, Norfleet chased him through the streets. Spencer escaped but the rancher stayed on his trail and caught up with him in Salt Lake City. Preferring the mercy of the law to Norfleet's wrath, Spencer turned himself in.

Norfleet found Furey in Jacksonville, Florida, and personally hauled him off to face justice in Texas. But he wouldn't stop there: He continued on to Denver, determined to break up the entire ring. Spending not only large sums of money but another year of his life in the pursuit, he managed to put all of the con ring's leaders behind bars. Even some he didn't catch had grown so terrified of him that they too turned themselves in.

After five years of hunting, Norfleet had single-handedly destroyed the country's largest confederation of con artists. The effort bankrupted him and ruined his marriage, but he died a satisfied man.

Interpretation

Most men accept the humiliation of being conned with a sense of resignation. They learn their lesson, recognizing that there is no such thing as a free lunch, and that they have usually been brought down by their own greed for easy money. Some, however, refuse to take their medicine. Instead of reflecting on their own gullibility and avarice, they see themselves as totally innocent victims.

Men like this may seem to be crusaders for justice and honesty, but they are actually immoderately insecure. Being fooled, being conned, has activated their self-doubt, and they are desperate to repair the damage. Were the mortgage on Norfleet's ranch, the collapse of his marriage, and the years of borrowing money and living in cheap hotels worth his revenge over his embarrassment at being fleeced? To the Norfleets of the world, overcoming their embarrassment is worth any price.

All people have insecurities, and often the best way to deceive a sucker is to play upon his insecurities. But in the realm of power, everything is a question of degree, and the person who is decidedly more insecure than the average mortal presents great dangers. Be warned: If you practice deception or trickery of any sort, study your mark well. Some people's insecurity and ego fragility cannot tolerate the slightest offense. To see if you are dealing with such a type, test them first—make, say, a mild joke at their expense. A confident person will laugh; an overly insecure one will react as if personally insulted. If you suspect you are dealing with this type, find another victim.

Transgression III

In the fifth century B.C., Ch'ung-erh, the prince of Ch'in (in present-day China), had been forced into exile. He lived modestly—even, sometimes, in poverty—waiting for the time when he could return home and resume his princely life. Once he was passing through the state of Cheng, where the ruler, not knowing who he was, treated him rudely. The ruler's minister, Shu Chan, saw this and said, "This man is a worthy prince. May Your Highness treat him with great courtesy and thereby place him under an obligation!" But the ruler, able to see only the prince's lowly station, ignored this advice and insulted the prince again. Shu Chan again warned his master, saying, "If Your Highness cannot treat Ch'ung-erh with courtesy, you should put him to death, to avoid calamity in the future." The ruler only scoffed.

Years later, the prince was finally able to return home, his circumstances greatly changed. He did not forget who had been kind to him, and who had been insolent, during his years of poverty. Least of all did he forget his treatment at the hands of the ruler of Cheng. At his first opportunity he assembled a vast army and marched on Cheng, taking eight cities, destroying the kingdom, and sending the ruler into an exile of his own.

Interpretation

You can never be sure who you are dealing with. A man who is of little importance and means today can be a person of power tomorrow. We forget a lot in our lives, but we rarely forget an insult.

How was the ruler of Cheng to know that Prince Ch'ung-erh was an ambitious, calculating, cunning type, a serpent with a long memory? There was really no way for him to know, you may say—but since there was no way, it would have been better not to tempt the fates by finding out. There is nothing to be gained by insulting a person unnecessarily. Swallow the impulse to offend, even if the other person seems weak. The satisfaction is meager compared to the danger that someday he or she will be in a position to hurt you.

Transgression IV

The year of 1920 had been a particularly bad one for American art dealers. Big buyers—the robber-baron generation of the previous century—were getting to an age where they were dying off like flies, and no new millionaires had emerged to take their place. Things were so bad that a number of the major dealers decided to pool their resources, an unheard-of event, since art dealers usually get along like cats and dogs.

Joseph Duveen, art dealer to the richest tycoons of America, was suffering more than the others that year, so he decided to go along with this alliance. The group now consisted of the five biggest dealers in the country. Looking around for a new client, they decided that their last best hope was Henry Ford, then the wealthiest man in America. Ford had yet to venture into the art market, and he was such a big target that it made sense for them to work together.

The dealers decided to assemble a list, "The 100 Greatest Paintings in the World" (all of which they happened to have in stock), and to offer the lot of them to Ford. With one purchase he could make himself the world's greatest collector. The consortium worked for weeks to produce a magnificent object: a three-volume set of books containing beautiful reproductions of the paintings, as well as scholarly texts accompanying each picture. Next they made a personal visit to Ford at his home in Dearborn, Michigan. There they were surprised by the simplicity of his house: Mr. Ford was obviously an extremely unaffected man.

Ford received them in his study. Looking through the book, he expressed astonishment and delight. The excited dealers began imagining the millions of dollars that would shortly flow into their coffers. Finally, however, Ford looked up from the book and said, "Gentlemen, beautiful books like these, with beautiful colored pictures like these, must cost an awful lot!" "But Mr. Ford!" exclaimed Duveen, "we don't expect you to *buy* these books. We got them up especially for you, to show you the pictures. These books are a present to you." Ford seemed puzzled. "Gentlemen," he said, "it is extremely nice of you, but I really don't see how I can accept a beautiful, expensive present like this from strangers." Duveen explained to Ford that the reproductions in the books showed paintings they had hoped to sell to him. Ford finally understood. "But gentlemen," he exclaimed, "what would I want with the original pictures when the ones right here in these books are so beautiful?"

Interpretation

Joseph Duveen prided himself on studying his victims and clients in advance, figuring out their weaknesses and the peculiarities of their tastes before he ever met them. He was driven by desperation to drop this tactic just once, in his assault on Henry Ford. It took him months to recover from his misjudgment, both mentally and monetarily. Ford was the unassuming plain-man type who just isn't worth the bother. He was the incarnation of those literal-minded folk who do not possess enough imagination to be deceived. From then on, Duveen saved his energies for the Mellons and Morgans of the world—men crafty enough for him to entrap in his snares.

KEYS TO POWER

The ability to measure people and to know who you're dealing with is the most important skill of all in gathering and conserving power. Without it you are blind: Not only will you offend the wrong people, you will choose the wrong types to work on, and will think you are flattering people when you are actually insulting them. Before embarking on any move, take the measure of your mark or potential opponent. Otherwise you will waste time and make mistakes. Study people's weaknesses, the chinks in their armor, their areas of both pride and insecurity. Know their ins and outs before you even decide whether or not to deal with them.

Two final words of caution: First, in judging and measuring your opponent, never rely on your instincts. You will make the greatest mistakes of all if you rely on such inexact indicators. Nothing can substitute for gathering concrete knowledge. Study and spy on your opponent for however long it takes; this will pay off in the long run.

Second, never trust appearances. Anyone with a serpent's heart can use a show of kindness to cloak it; a person who is blustery on the outside is often really a coward. Learn to see through appearances and their contradictions. Never trust the version that people give of themselves—it is utterly unreliable.

Image: The Hunter. He does not lay the same trap for a wolf as for a fox. He does not set bait where no one will take it. He knows his prey thoroughly, its habits and hideaways, and hunts accordingly.

Authority: Be convinced, that there are no persons so insignificant and inconsiderable, but may, some time or other, have it in their power to be of use to you; which they certainly will not, if you have once shown them contempt. Wrongs are often forgiven, but contempt never is. Our pride remembers it for ever. (Lord Chesterfield, 1694–1773)

REVERSAL
What possible good can come from ignorance about other people? Learn to tell the lions from the lambs or pay the price. Obey this law to its fullest extent; it has no reversal—do not bother looking for one.

20

DO NOT COMMIT

TO ANYONE

JUDGMENT

It is the fool who always rushes to take sides. Do not commit to any side or cause but yourself. By maintaining your independence, you become the master of others— playing people against one another, making them pursue you.

PART I: DO NOT COMMIT TO ANYONE, BUT BE COURTED BY ALL

If you allow people to feel they possess you to any degree, you lose all power over them. By not committing your affections, they will only try harder to win you over. Stay aloof and you gain the power that comes from their attention and frustrated desire. Play the Virgin Queen: Give them hope but never satisfaction.

OBSERVANCE OF THE LAW

When Queen Elizabeth I ascended the throne of England, in 1558, there was much to-do about her finding a husband. The issue was debated in Parliament, and was a main topic of conversation among Englishmen of all classes; they often disagreed as to whom she should marry, but everyone thought she should marry as soon as possible, for a queen must have a king, and must bear heirs for the kingdom. The debates raged on for years. Meanwhile the most handsome and eligible bachelors in the realm—Sir Robert Dudley, the Earl of Essex, Sir Walter Raleigh—vied for Elizabeth's hand. She did not discourage them, but she seemed to be in no hurry, and her hints as to which man might be her favorite often contradicted each other. In 1566, Parliament sent a delegation to Elizabeth urging her to marry before she was too old to bear children. She did not argue, nor did she discourage the delegation, but she remained a virgin nonetheless.

The delicate game that Elizabeth played with her suitors slowly made her the subject of innumerable sexual fantasies and the object of cultish worship. The court physician, Simon Forman, used his diary to describe his dreams of deflowering her. Painters represented her as Diana and other goddesses. The poet Edmund Spenser and others wrote eulogies to the Virgin Queen. She was referred to as "the world's Empresse," "that virtuous Virgo" who rules the world and sets the stars in motion. In conversation with her, her many male suitors would employ bold sexual innuendo, a dare that Elizabeth did not discourage. She did all she could to stir their interest and simultaneously keep them at bay.

Throughout Europe, kings and princes knew that a marriage with Elizabeth would seal an alliance between England and any nation. The king of Spain wooed her, as did the prince of Sweden and the archduke of Austria. She politely refused them all.

The great diplomatic issue of Elizabeth's day was posed by the revolt of the Flemish and Dutch Lowlands, which were then possessions of Spain. Should England break its alliance with Spain and choose France as its main ally on the Continent, thereby encouraging Flemish and Dutch independence? By 1570 it had come to seem that an alliance with France would be England's wisest course. France had two eligible men of noble blood, the dukes of Anjou and Alençon, brothers of the French king. Would either of them marry Elizabeth? Both had advantages, and Elizabeth kept the hopes of both alive. The issue simmered for years. The duke of Anjou made several visits to England, kissed Elizabeth in public, even called her by pet names; she appeared to requite his affections. Meanwhile, as she flirted with the two brothers, a treaty was signed that sealed peace between France and England. By 1582 Elizabeth felt she could break off the courtship. In the case of the duke of Anjou in particular, she did so with great relief: For the sake of diplomacy she had allowed herself to be courted by a man whose presence she could not stand and whom she found physically repulsive. Once peace between France and England was secure, she dropped the unctuous duke as politely as she could.

By this time Elizabeth was too old to bear children. She was accordingly able to live the rest of her life as she desired, and she died the Virgin Queen. She left no direct heir, but ruled through a period of incomparable peace and cultural fertility.

Interpretation

Elizabeth had good reason not to marry: She had witnessed the mistakes of Mary Queen of Scots, her cousin. Resisting the idea of being ruled by a woman, the Scots expected Mary to marry and marry wisely. To wed a foreigner would be unpopular; to favor any particular noble house would open up terrible rivalries. In the end Mary chose Lord Darnley, a Catholic. In doing so she incurred the wrath of Scotland's Protestants, and endless turmoil ensued.

Elizabeth knew that marriage can often lead to a female ruler's undoing: By marrying and committing to an alliance with one party or nation, the queen becomes embroiled in conflicts that are not of her choosing, conflicts which may eventually overwhelm her or lead her into a futile war. Also, the husband becomes the de facto ruler, and often tries to do away with his wife the queen, as Darnley tried to get rid of Mary. Elizabeth learned the lesson well. She had two goals as a ruler: to avoid marriage and to avoid war. She managed to combine these goals by dangling the possibility of marriage in order to forge alliances. The moment she committed to any single suitor would have been the moment she lost her power. She had to emanate mystery and desirability, never discouraging anyone's hopes but never yielding.

Through this lifelong game of flirting and withdrawing, Elizabeth dominated the country and every man who sought to conquer her. As the center of attention, she was in control. Keeping her independence above all, Elizabeth protected her power and made herself an object of worship.

I would rather be a beggar and single than a queen and married.
Queen Elizabeth I, 1533–1603

KEYS TO POWER

Since power depends greatly on appearances, you must learn the tricks that will enhance your image. Refusing to commit to a person or group is one of these. When you hold yourself back, you incur not anger but a kind of respect. You instantly seem powerful because you make yourself un-graspable, rather than succumbing to the group, or to the relationship, as most people do. This aura of power only grows with time: As your reputation for independence grows, more and more people will come to desire you, wanting to be the one who gets you to commit. Desire is like a virus: If we see that someone is desired by other people, we tend to find this person desirable too.

The moment you commit, the magic is gone. You become like every-one else. People will try all kinds of underhanded methods to get you to commit. They will give you gifts, shower you with favors, all to put you under obligation. Encourage the attention, stimulate their interest, but do not commit at any cost. Accept the gifts and favors if you so desire, but be careful to maintain your inner aloofness. You cannot inadvertently allow yourself to feel obligated to anyone.

Remember, though: The goal is not to put people off, or to make it seem that you are incapable of commitment. Like the Virgin Queen, you need to stir the pot, excite interest, lure people with the possibility of having you. You have to bend to their attention occasionally, then—but never too far.

The Greek soldier and statesman Alcibiades played this game to per-fection. It was Alcibiades who inspired and led the massive Athenian ar-mada that invaded Sicily in 414 B.C. When envious Athenians back home tried to bring him down by accusing him of trumped-up charges, he de-fected to the enemy, the Spartans, instead of facing a trial back home. Then, after the Athenians were defeated at Syracuse, he left Sparta for Persia, even though the power of Sparta was now on the rise. Now, however, both the Athenians and the Spartans courted Alcibiades because of his influence with the Persians; and the Persians showered him with honors because of his power over the Athenians and the Spartans. He made promises to every side but committed to none, and in the end he held all the cards.

If you aspire to power and influence, try the Alcibiades tactic: Put yourself in the middle between competing powers. Lure one side with the promise of your help; the other side, always wanting to outdo its enemy, will pursue you as well. As each side vies for your attention, you will im-mediately seem a person of great influence and desirability. More power will accrue to you than if you had rashly committed to one side. To perfect this tactic you need to keep yourself inwardly free from emotional entan-glements, and to view all those around you as pawns in your rise to the top. You cannot let yourself become the lackey for any cause.

In the midst of the 1968 U.S. presidential election, Henry Kissinger made a phone call to Richard Nixon's team. Kissinger had been allied with Nelson Rockefeller, who had unsuccessfully sought the Republican nomina-tion. Now Kissinger offered to supply the Nixon camp with valuable inside information on the negotiations for peace in Vietnam that were then going on in Paris. He had a man on the negotiating team keeping him informed of the latest developments. The Nixon team gladly accepted his offer.

At the same time, however, Kissinger also approached the Democratic nominee, Hubert Humphrey, and offered his aid. The Humphrey people asked him for inside information on Nixon and he supplied it. "Look," Kissinger told Humphrey's people, "I've hated Nixon for years." In fact he had no interest in either side. What he really wanted was what he got: the promise of a high-level cabinet post from both Nixon and Humphrey. Whichever man won the election, Kissinger's career was secure.

The winner, of course, was Nixon, and Kissinger duly went on to his cabinet post. Even so, he was careful never to appear too much of a Nixon man. When Nixon was reelected in 1972, men much more loyal to him than Kissinger were fired. Kissinger was also the only Nixon high official to survive Watergate and serve under the next president, Gerald Ford. By maintaining a little distance he thrived in turbulent times.

Those who use this strategy often notice a strange phenomenon: People who rush to the support of others tend to gain little respect in the process, for their help is so easily obtained, while those who stand back find themselves besieged with supplicants. Their aloofness is powerful, and everyone wants them on their side.

When Picasso, after early years of poverty, had become the most successful artist in the world, he did not commit himself to this dealer or that dealer, although they now besieged him from all sides with attractive offers and grand promises. Instead, he appeared to have no interest in their services; this technique drove them wild, and as they fought over him his prices only rose. When Henry Kissinger, as U.S. secretary of state, wanted to reach détente with the Soviet Union, he made no concessions or conciliatory gestures, but courted China instead. This infuriated and also scared the Soviets—they were already politically isolated and feared further isolation if the United States and China came together. Kissinger's move pushed them to the negotiating table. The tactic has a parallel in seduction: When you want to seduce a woman, Stendhal advises, court her sister first.

Stay aloof and people will come to you. It will become a challenge for them to win your affections. As long as you imitate the wise Virgin Queen and stimulate their hopes, you will remain a magnet of attention and desire.

Image:
The Virgin Queen.
The center of attention, desire, and worship. Never succumbing to one suitor or the other, the Virgin Queen keeps them all revolving around her like planets, unable to leave her orbit but never getting any closer to her.

Authority: Do not commit yourself to anybody or anything, for that is to be a slave, a slave to every man. . . . Above all, keep yourself free of commitments and obligations—they are the device of another to get you into his power. . . . (Baltasar Gracián, 1601–1658)

PART II: DO NOT COMMIT TO ANYONE— STAY ABOVE THE FRAY

Do not let people drag you into their petty fights and squabbles. Seem interested and supportive, but find a way to remain neutral; let others do the fighting while you stand back, watch and wait. When the fighting parties are good and tired they will be ripe for the picking. You can make it a practice, in fact, to stir up quarrels between other people, and then offer to mediate, gaining power as the go-between.

OBSERVANCE OF THE LAW

THE KITES, THE
CROWS, AND THE FOX

The kites and the crows made an agreement among themselves that they should go halves in everything obtained in the forest. One day they saw a fox that had been wounded by hunters lying helpless under a tree, and gathered round it. The crows said, "We will take the upper half of the fox." "Then we will take the lower half," said the kites. The fox laughed at this, and said, "I always thought the kites were superior in creation to the crows; as such they must get the upper half of my body, of which my head, with the brain and other delicate things in it, forms a portion." "Oh, yes, that is right," said the kites, "we will have that part of the fox." "Not at all," said the crows, "we must have it, as already agreed." Then a war arose between the rival parties, and a great many fell on both sides, and the remaining few escaped with difficulty. The fox continued there for some days,

In the late fifteenth century, the strongest city-states in Italy—Venice, Florence, Rome, and Milan—found themselves constantly squabbling. Hovering above their struggles were the nations of France and Spain, ready to grab whatever they could from the weakened Italian powers. And trapped in the middle was the small state of Mantua, ruled by the young Duke Gianfrancesco Gonzaga. Mantua was strategically located in northern Italy, and it seemed only a matter of time before one of the powers swallowed it up and it ceased to exist as an independent kingdom.

Gonzaga was a fierce warrior and a skilled commander of troops, and he became a kind of mercenary general for whatever side paid him best. In the year 1490, he married Isabella d'Este, daughter of the ruler of another small Italian duchy, Ferrara. Since he now spent most of his time away from Mantua, it fell to Isabella to rule in his stead.

Isabella's first true test as ruler came in 1498, when King Louis XII of France was preparing armies to attack Milan. In their usual perfidious fashion, the Italian states immediately looked for ways to profit from Milan's difficulties. Pope Alexander VI promised not to intervene, thereby giving the French carte blanche. The Venetians signaled that they would not help Milan, either—and in exchange for this, they hoped the French would give them Mantua. The ruler of Milan, Lodovico Sforza, suddenly found himself alone and abandoned. He turned to Isabella d'Este, one of his closest friends (also rumored to be his lover), and begged her to persuade Duke Gonzaga to come to his aid. Isabella tried, but her husband balked, for he saw Sforza's cause as hopeless. And so, in 1499, Louis swooped down on Milan and took it with ease.

Isabella now faced a dilemma: If she stayed loyal to Lodovico, the French would now move against her. But if, instead, she allied herself with France, she would make enemies elsewhere in Italy, compromising Mantua once Louis eventually withdrew. And if she looked to Venice or Rome for help, they would simply swallow up Mantua under the cloak of coming to her aid. Yet she had to do something. The mighty king of France was breathing down her neck: She decided to befriend him, as she had befriended Lodovico Sforza before him—with alluring gifts, witty, intelligent letters, and the possibility of her company, for Isabella was famous as a woman of incomparable beauty and charm.

In 1500 Louis invited Isabella to a great party in Milan to celebrate his victory. Leonardo da Vinci built an enormous mechanical lion for the affair: When the lion opened its mouth, it spewed fresh lilies, the symbols of French royalty. At the party Isabella wore one of her celebrated dresses (she had by far the largest wardrobe of any of the Italian princesses), and just as she had hoped, she charmed and captivated Louis, who ignored all the other ladies vying for his attention. She soon became his constant companion, and in exchange for her friendship he pledged to protect Mantua's independence from Venice.

As one danger receded, however, another, more worrying one arose, this time from the south, in the form of Cesare Borgia. Starting in 1500, Borgia had marched steadily northward, gobbling up all the small kingdoms in his path in the name of his father, Pope Alexander. Isabella understood Cesare perfectly: He could be neither trusted nor in any way offended. He had to be cajoled and kept at arm's length. Isabella began by sending him gifts—falcons, prize dogs, perfumes, and dozens of masks, which she knew he always wore when he walked the streets of Rome. She sent messengers with flattering greetings (although these messengers also acted as her spies). At one point Cesare asked if he could house some troops in Mantua; Isabella managed to dissuade him politely, knowing full well that once the troops were quartered in the city, they would never leave.

Even while Isabella was charming Cesare, she convinced everyone around her to take care never to utter a harsh word about him, since he had spies everywhere and would use the slightest pretext for invasion. When Isabella had a child, she asked Cesare to be the godfather. She even dangled in front of him the possibility of a marriage between her family and his. Somehow it all worked, for although elsewhere he seized everything in his path, he spared Mantua.

In 1503 Cesare's father, Alexander, died, and a few years later the new pope, Julius II, went to war to drive the French troops from Italy. When the ruler of Ferrara—Alfonso, Isabella's brother—sided with the French, Julius decided to attack and humble him. Once again Isabella found herself in the middle: the pope on one side, the French and her brother on the other. She dared not ally herself with either, but to offend either would be equally disastrous. Again she played the double game at which she had become so expert. On the one hand she got her husband Gonzaga to fight for the pope, knowing he would not fight very hard. On the other she let French troops pass through Mantua to come to Ferrara's aid. While she publicly complained that the French had "invaded" her territory, she privately supplied them with valuable information. To make the invasion plausible to Julius, she even had the French pretend to plunder Mantua. It worked once again: The pope left Mantua alone.

In 1513, after a lengthy siege, Julius defeated Ferrara, and the French troops withdrew. Worn out by the effort, the pope died a few months later. With his death, the nightmarish cycle of battles and petty squabbles began to repeat itself.

leisurely feeding on the dead kites and crows, and then left the place hale and hearty, observing, "The weak benefit by the quarrels of the mighty."

INDIAN FABLES

Men of great abilities are slow to act, for it is easier to avoid occasions for committing yourself than to come well out of a commitment. Such occasions test your judgment; it is safer to avoid them than to emerge victorious from them. One obligation leads to a greater one, and you come very near to the brink of disaster.

BALTASAR GRACIÁN, 1601–1658

A great deal changed in Italy during Isabella's reign: Popes came and went, Cesare Borgia rose and then fell, Venice lost its empire, Milan was invaded, Florence fell into decline, and Rome was sacked by the Hapsburg Emperor Charles V. Through all this, tiny Mantua not only survived but thrived, its court the envy of Italy. Its wealth and sovereignty would remain intact for a century after Isabella's death, in 1539.

Interpretation

Isabella d'Este understood Italy's political situation with amazing clarity: Once you took the side of any of the forces in the field, you were doomed. The powerful would take you over, the weak would wear you down. Any new alliance would lead to a new enemy, and as this cycle stirred up more conflict, other forces would be dragged in, until you could no longer extricate yourself. Eventually you would collapse from exhaustion.

Isabella steered her kingdom on the only course that would bring her safely through. She would not allow herself to lose her head through loyalty to a duke or a king. Nor would she try to stop the conflict that raged around her—that would only drag her into it. And in any case the conflict was to her advantage. If the various parties were fighting to the death, and exhausting themselves in the process, they were in no position to gobble up Mantua. The source of Isabella's power was her clever ability to seem interested in the affairs and interests of each side, while actually committing to no one but herself and her kingdom.

Once you step into a fight that is not of your own choosing, you lose all initiative. The combatants' interests become your interests; you become their tool. Learn to control yourself, to restrain your natural tendency to take sides and join the fight. Be friendly and charming to each of the combatants, then step back as they collide. With every battle they grow weaker, while you grow stronger with every battle you avoid.

> *When the snipe and the mussel struggle, the fisherman gets the benefit.*
> *Ancient Chiness saying*

KEYS TO POWER

To succeed in the game of power, you have to master your emotions. But even if you succeed in gaining such self-control, you can never control the temperamental dispositions of those around you. And this presents a great danger. Most people operate in a whirlpool of emotions, constantly reacting, churning up squabbles and conflicts. Your self-control and autonomy will only bother and infuriate them. They will try to draw you into the whirlpool, begging you to take sides in their endless battles, or to make peace for them. If you succumb to their emotional entreaties, little by little you will find *your* mind and time occupied by *their* problems. Do not allow whatever compassion and pity you possess to suck you in. You can never win in this game; the conflicts can only multiply.

On the other hand, you cannot completely stand aside, for that would cause needless offense. To play the game properly, you must seem interested in other people's problems, even sometimes appear to take their side. But while you make outward gestures of support, you must maintain your inner energy and sanity by keeping your emotions disengaged. No matter how hard people try to pull you in, never let your interest in their affairs and petty squabbles go beyond the surface. Give them gifts, listen with a sympathetic look, even occasionally play the charmer—but inwardly keep both the friendly kings and the perfidious Borgias at arm's length. By refusing to commit and thus maintaining your autonomy you retain the initiative: Your moves stay matters of your own choosing, not defensive reactions to the push-and-pull of those around you.

Slowness to pick up your weapons can be a weapon itself, especially if you let other people exhaust themselves fighting, then take advantage of their exhaustion. In ancient China, the kingdom of Chin once invaded the kingdom of Hsing. Huan, the ruler of a nearby province, thought he should rush to Hsing's defense, but his adviser counseled him to wait: "Hsing is not yet going to ruin," he said, "and Chin is not yet exhausted. If Chin is not exhausted, [we] cannot become very influential. Moreover, the merit of supporting a state in danger is not as great as the virtue of reviving a ruined one." The adviser's argument won the day, and as he had predicted, Huan later had the glory both of rescuing Hsing from the brink of destruction and then of conquering an exhausted Chin. He stayed out of the fighting until the forces engaged in it had worn each other down, at which point it was safe for him to intervene.

That is what holding back from the fray allows you: time to position yourself to take advantage of the situation once one side starts to lose. You can also take the game a step further, by promising your support to both sides in a conflict while maneuvering so that the one to come out ahead in the struggle is you. This was what Castruccio Castracani, ruler of the Italian town of Lucca in the fourteenth century, did when he had designs on the town of Pistoia. A siege would have been expensive, costing both lives and money, but Castruccio knew that Pistoia contained two rival factions, the Blacks and the Whites, which hated one another. He negotiated with the Blacks, promising to help them against the Whites; then, without their knowledge, he promised the Whites he would help them against the Blacks. And Castruccio kept his promises—he sent an army to a Black-controlled gate to the city, which the sentries of course welcomed in. Meanwhile another of his armies entered through a White-controlled gate. The two armies united in the middle, occupied the town, killed the leaders of both factions, ended the internal war, and took Pistoia for Castruccio.

Preserving your autonomy gives you options when people come to blows—you can play the mediator, broker the peace, while really securing your own interests. You can pledge support to one side and the other may have to court you with a higher bid. Or, like Castruccio, you can appear to take both sides, then play the antagonists against each other.

Oftentimes when a conflict breaks out, you are tempted to side with the stronger party, or the one that offers you apparent advantages in an al-

THE PRICE OF ENVY

While a poor woman stood in the marketplace selling cheeses, a cat came along and carried off a cheese. A dog saw the pilferer and tried to take the cheese away from him. The cat stood up to the dog. So they pitched into each other. The dog barked and snapped; the cat spat and scratched, but they could bring the battle to no decision.

"Let's go to the fox and have him referee the matter," the cat finally suggested.

"Agreed," said the dog. So they went to the fox. The fox listened to their arguments with a judicious air.

"Foolish animals," he chided them, "why carry on like that? If both of you are willing, I'll divide the cheese in two and you'll both be satisfied."

"Agreed," said the cat and the dog.

So the fox took out his knife and cut the cheese in two, but, instead of cutting it lengthwise, he cut it in the width.

"My half is smaller!" protested the dog. The fox looked judiciously through his spectacles at the dog's share.

"You're right, quite right!" he decided. So he went and bit off a piece of the cat's share.

"That will make it even!" he said. When the cat saw what the fox did she began to yowl:

liance. This is risky business. First, it is often difficult to foresee which side will prevail in the long run. But even if you guess right and ally yourself with the stronger party, you may find yourself swallowed up and lost, or conveniently forgotten, when they become victors. Side with the weaker, on the other hand, and you are doomed. But play a waiting game and you cannot lose.

In France's July Revolution of 1830, after three days of riots, the statesman Talleyrand, now elderly, sat by his Paris window, listening to the pealing bells that signaled the riots were over. Turning to an assistant, he said, "Ah, the bells! We're winning." "Who's 'we,' *mon prince?*" the assistant asked. Gesturing for the man to keep quiet, Talleyrand replied, "Not a word! I'll tell you who we are tomorrow." He well knew that only fools rush into a situation—that by committing too quickly you lose your maneuverability. People also respect you less: Perhaps tomorrow, they think, you will commit to another, different cause, since you gave yourself so easily to this one. Good fortune is a fickle god and will often pass from one side to the other. Commitment to one side deprives you of the advantage of time and the luxury of waiting. Let others fall in love with this group or that; for your part don't rush in, don't lose your head.

Finally, there are occasions when it is wisest to drop all pretense of appearing supportive and instead to trumpet your independence and self-reliance. The aristocratic pose of independence is particularly important for those who need to gain respect. George Washington recognized this in his work to establish the young American republic on firm ground. As president, Washington avoided the temptation of making an alliance with France or England, despite the pressure on him to do so. He wanted the country to earn the world's respect through its independence. Although a treaty with France might have helped in the short term, in the long run he knew it would be more effective to establish the nation's autonomy. Europe would have to see the United States as an equal power.

Remember: You have only so much energy and so much time. Every moment wasted on the affairs of others subtracts from your strength. You may be afraid that people will condemn you as heartless, but in the end, maintaining your independence and self-reliance will gain you more respect and place you in a position of power from which you can choose to help others on your own initiative.

Image: A Thicket of Shrubs. In the forest, one shrub latches on to another, entangling its neighbor with its thorns, the thicket slowly extending its impenetrable domain. Only what keeps its distance and stands apart can grow and rise above the thicket.

Authority: Regard it as more courageous not to become involved in an engagement than to win in battle, and where there is already one interfering fool, take care that there shall not be two. (Baltasar Gracian, 1601-1658)

REVERSAL

Both parts of this law will turn against you if you take it too far. The game proposed here is delicate and difficult. If you play too many parties against one another, they will see through the maneuver and will gang up on you. If you keep your growing number of suitors waiting too long, you will inspire not desire but distrust. People will start to lose interest. Eventually you may find it worthwhile to commit to one side—if only for appearances' sake, to prove you are capable of attachment.

Even then, however, the key will be to maintain your inner independence—to keep yourself from getting emotionally involved. Preserve the unspoken option of being able to leave at any moment and reclaim your freedom if the side you are allied with starts to collapse. The friends you made while you were being courted will give you plenty of places to go once you jump ship.

PLAY A SUCKER TO CATCH

A SUCKER—SEEM DUMBER

THAN YOUR MARK

JUDGMENT

No one likes feeling stupider than the next person. The trick, then, is to make your victims feel smart—and not just smart, but smarter than you are. Once convinced of this, they will never suspect that you may have ulterior motives.

OBSERVANCE OF THE LAW

In the winter of 1872, the U.S. financier Asbury Harpending was visiting London when he received a cable: A diamond mine had been discovered in the American West. The cable came from a reliable source—William Ralston, owner of the Bank of California—but Harpending nevertheless took it as a practical joke, probably inspired by the recent discovery of huge diamond mines in South Africa. True, when reports had first come in of gold being discovered in the western United States, everyone had been skeptical, and those had turned out to be true. But a diamond mine in the West! Harpending showed the cable to his fellow financier Baron Rothschild (one of the richest men in the world), saying it must be a joke. The baron, however, replied, "Don't be too sure about that. America is a very large country. It has furnished the world with many surprises already. Perhaps it has others in store." Harpending promptly took the first ship back to the States.

When Harpending reached San Francisco, there was an excitement in the air recalling the Gold Rush days of the late 1840s. Two crusty prospectors named Philip Arnold and John Slack had been the ones to find the diamond mine. They had not divulged its location, in Wyoming, but had led a highly respected mining expert to it several weeks back, taking a circular route so he could not guess his whereabouts. Once there, the expert had watched as the miners dug up diamonds. Back in San Francisco the expert had taken the gems to various jewelers, one of whom had estimated their worth at $1.5 million.

Harpending and Ralston now asked Arnold and Slack to accompany them back to New York, where the jeweler Charles Tiffany would verify the original estimates. The prospectors responded uneasily—they smelled a trap: How could they trust these city slickers? What if Tiffany and the financiers managed to steal the whole mine out from under them? Ralston tried to allay their fears by giving them $100,000 and placing another $300,000 in escrow for them. If the deal went through, they would be paid an additional $300,000. The miners agreed.

The little group traveled to New York, where a meeting was held at the mansion of Samuel L. Barlow. The cream of the city's aristocracy was in attendance—General George Brinton McClellan, commander of the Union forces in the Civil War; General Benjamin Butler; Horace Greeley, editor of the newspaper the *New York Tribune;* Harpending; Ralston; and Tiffany. Only Slack and Arnold were missing—as tourists in the city, they had decided to go sight-seeing.

When Tiffany announced that the gems were real and worth a fortune, the financiers could barely control their excitement. They wired Rothschild and other tycoons to tell them about the diamond mine and inviting them to share in the investment. At the same time, they also told the prospectors that they wanted one more test: They insisted that a mining expert of their choosing accompany Slack and Arnold to the site to verify its wealth. The prospectors reluctantly agreed. In the meantime, they said,

Now, there is nothing of which a man is prouder than of intellectual ability, for it is this that gives him his commanding place in the animal world. It is an exceedingly rash thing to let anyone see that you are decidedly superior to him in this respect, and to let other people see it too.... Hence, while rank and riches may always reckon upon deferential treatment in society, that is something which intellectual ability can never expect: To be ignored is the greatest favour shown to it; and if people notice it at all, it is because they regard it as a piece of impertinence, or else as something to which its possessor has no legitimate right, and upon which he dares to pride himself; and in retaliation and revenge for his conduct, people secretly try and humiliate him in some other way; and if they wait to do this, it is only for a fitting opportunity. A man may be as humble as possible in his demeanour, and yet hardly ever get people to overlook his crime in standing intellectually above them. In the Garden of Roses, Sadi makes the remark: "You should know that foolish people are a hundredfold more averse to meeting the wise than the wise are indisposed for the company of the foolish."

they had to return to San Francisco. The jewels that Tiffany had examined they left with Harpending for safekeeping.

Several weeks later, a man named Louis Janin, the best mining expert in the country, met the prospectors in San Francisco. Janin was a born skeptic who was determined to make sure that the mine was not a fraud. Accompanying Janin were Harpending, and several other interested financiers. As with the previous expert, the prospectors led the team through a complex series of canyons, completely confusing them as to their whereabouts. Arriving at the site, the financiers watched in amazement as Janin dug the area up, leveling anthills, turning over boulders, and finding emeralds, rubies, sapphires, and most of all diamonds. The dig lasted eight days, and by the end, Janin was convinced: He told the investors that they now possessed the richest field in mining history. "With a hundred men and proper machinery," he told them, "I would guarantee to send out one million dollars in diamonds every thirty days."

Returning to San Francisco a few days later, Ralston, Harpending, and company acted fast to form a $10 million corporation of private investors. First, however, they had to get rid of Arnold and Slack. That meant hiding their excitement—they certainly did not want to reveal the field's real value. So they played possum. Who knows if Janin is right, they told the prospectors, the mine may not be as rich as we think. This just made the prospectors angry. Trying a different tactic, the financiers told the two men that if they insisted on having shares in the mine, they would end up being fleeced by the unscrupulous tycoons and investors who would run the corporation; better, they said, to take the $700,000 already offered—an enormous sum at the time—and put their greed aside. This the prospectors seemed to understand, and they finally agreed to take the money, in return signing the rights to the site over to the financiers, and leaving maps to it.

News of the mine spread like wildfire. Prospectors fanned out across Wyoming. Meanwhile Harpending and group began spending the millions they had collected from their investors, buying equipment, hiring the best men in the business, and furnishing luxurious offices in New York and San Francisco.

A few weeks later, on their first trip back to the site, they learned the hard truth: Not a single diamond or ruby was to be found. It was all a fake. They were ruined. Harpending had unwittingly lured the richest men in the world into the biggest scam of the century.

Interpretation

Arnold and Slack pulled off their stupendous con not by using a fake engineer or bribing Tiffany: All of the experts had been real. All of them honestly believed in the existence of the mine and in the value of the gems. What had fooled them all was nothing else than Arnold and Slack themselves. The two men seemed to be such rubes, such hayseeds, so naive, that no one for an instant had believed them capable of an audacious scam. The prospectors had simply observed the law of appearing more stupid than the mark—the deceiver's First Commandment.

The logistics of the con were quite simple. Months before Arnold and Slack announced the "discovery" of the diamond mine, they traveled to Europe, where they purchased some real gems for around $12,000 (part of the money they had saved from their days as gold miners). They then salted the "mine" with these gems, which the first expert dug up and brought to San Francisco. The jewelers who had appraised these stones, including Tiffany himself, had gotten caught up in the fever and had grossly overestimated their value. Then Ralston gave the prospectors $100,000 as security, and immediately after their trip to New York they simply went to Amsterdam, where they bought sacks of uncut gems, before returning to San Francisco. The second time they salted the mine, there were many more jewels to be found.

The effectiveness of the scheme, however, rested not on tricks like these but on the fact that Arnold and Slack played their parts to perfection. On their trip to New York, where they mingled with millionaires and tycoons, they played up their clodhopper image, wearing pants and coats a size or two too small and acting incredulous at everything they saw in the big city. No one believed that these country simpletons could possibly be conning the most devious, unscrupulous financiers of the time. And once Harpending, Ralston, and even Rothschild accepted the mine's existence, anyone who doubted it was questioning the intelligence of the world's most successful businessmen.

In the end, Harpending's reputation was ruined and he never recovered; Rothschild learned his lesson and never fell for another con; Slack took his money and disappeared from view, never to be found. Arnold simply went home to Kentucky. After all, his sale of his mining rights had been legitimate; the buyers had taken the best advice, and if the mine had run out of diamonds, that was their problem. Arnold used the money to greatly enlarge his farm and open up a bank of his own.

KEYS TO POWER

The feeling that someone else is more intelligent than we are is almost intolerable. We usually try to justify it in different ways: "He only has book knowledge, whereas I have real knowledge." "Her parents paid for her to get a good education. If my parents had had as much money, if I had been as privileged. . . ." "He's not as smart as he thinks." Last but not least: "She may know her narrow little field better than I do, but beyond that she's really not smart at all. Even Einstein was a boob outside physics."

Given how important the idea of intelligence is to most people's vanity, it is critical never inadvertently to insult or impugn a person's brain power. That is an unforgivable sin. But if you can make this iron rule work for you, it opens up all sorts of avenues of deception. Subliminally reassure people that they are more intelligent than you are, or even that you are a bit of a moron, and you can run rings around them. The feeling of intellectual superiority you give them will disarm their suspicion-muscles.

In 1865 the Prussian councillor Otto von Bismarck wanted Austria to sign a certain treaty. The treaty was totally in the interests of Prussia and against the interests of Austria, and Bismarck would have to strategize to get the Austrians to agree to it. But the Austrian negotiator, Count Blome, was an avid cardplayer. His particular game was quinze, and he often said that he could judge a man's character by the way he played quinze. Bismarck knew of this saying of Blome's.

The night before the negotiations were to begin, Bismarck innocently engaged Blome in a game of quinze. The Prussian would later write, "That was the very last time I ever played quinze. I played so recklessly that everyone was astonished. I lost several thousand talers [the currency of the time], but I succeeded in fooling [Blome], for he believed me to be more venturesome than I am and I gave way." Besides appearing reckless, Bismarck also played the witless fool, saying ridiculous things and bumbling about with a surplus of nervous energy.

All this made Blome feel he had gathered valuable information. He knew that Bismarck was aggressive—the Prussian already had that reputation, and the way he played had confirmed it. And aggressive men, Blome knew, can be foolish and rash. Accordingly, when the time came to sign the treaty, Blome thought he had the advantage. A heedless fool like Bismarck, he thought, is incapable of cold-blooded calculation and deception, so he only glanced at the treaty before signing it—he failed to read the fine print. As soon as the ink was dry, a joyous Bismarck exclaimed in his face, "Well, I could never have believed that I should find an Austrian diplomat willing to sign that document!"

The Chinese have a phrase, "Masquerading as a swine to kill the tiger." This refers to an ancient hunting technique in which the hunter clothes himself in the hide and snout of a pig, and mimics its grunting. The mighty tiger thinks a pig is coming his way, and lets it get close, savoring the prospect of an easy meal. But it is the hunter who has the last laugh.

Masquerading as a swine works wonders on those who, like tigers, are arrogant and overconfident: The easier they think it is to prey on you, the more easily you can turn the tables. This trick is also useful if you are ambitious yet find yourself low in the hierarchy: Appearing less intelligent than you are, even a bit of a fool, is the perfect disguise. Look like a harmless pig and no one will believe you harbor dangerous ambitions. They may even promote you since you seem so likable, and subservient. Claudius before he became emperor of Rome, and the prince of France who later became Louis XIII, used this tactic when those above them suspected they might have designs on the throne. By playing the fool as young men, they were left alone. When the time came for them to strike, and to act with vigor and decisiveness, they caught everyone off-guard.

Intelligence is the obvious quality to downplay, but why stop there? Taste and sophistication rank close to intelligence on the vanity scale; make people feel they are more sophisticated than you are and their guard will come down. As Arnold and Slack knew, an air of complete naiveté can work wonders. Those fancy financiers were laughing at them behind their backs, but who laughed loudest in the end? In general, then, always make people believe they are smarter and more sophisticated than you are. They will keep you around because you make them feel better about themselves, and the longer you are around, the more opportunities you will have to deceive them.

Image:
The Opossum. In playing
dead, the opossum plays stupid.
Many a predator has therefore left it
alone. Who could believe that such an
ugly, unintelligent, nervous little creature
could be capable of such deception?

Authority: Know how to make use of stupidity: The wisest man plays this card at times. There are occasions when the highest wisdom consists in appearing not to know—you must not be ignorant but capable of playing it. It is not much good being wise among fools and sane among lunatics. He who poses as a fool is not a fool. The best way to be well received by all is to clothe yourself in the skin of the dumbest of brutes. (Baltasar Gracián, 1601–1658)

REVERSAL
To reveal the true nature of your intelligence rarely pays; you should get in the habit of downplaying it at all times. If people inadvertently learn the truth—that you are actually much smarter than you look—they will admire you more for being discreet than for making your brilliance show. At the start of your climb to the top, of course, you cannot play too stupid: You may want to let your bosses know, in a subtle way, that you are smarter than the competition around you. As you climb the ladder, however, you should to some degree try to dampen your brilliance.

There is, however, one situation where it pays to do the opposite—when you can cover up a deception with a show of intelligence. In matters of smarts as in most things, appearances are what count. If you seem to have authority and knowledge, people will believe what you say. This can be very useful in getting you out of a scrape.

The art dealer Joseph Duveen was once attending a soirée at the New York home of a tycoon to whom he had recently sold a Dürer painting for a high price. Among the guests was a young French art critic who seemed extremely knowledgeable and confident. Wanting to impress this man, the tycoon's daughter showed him the Dürer, which had not yet been hung. The critic studied it for a time, then finally said, "You know, I don't think this Dürer is right." He followed the young woman as she hurried to tell her father what he had said, and listened as the magnate, deeply unsettled, turned to Duveen for reassurance. Duveen just laughed. "How very amusing," he said. "Do you realize, young man, that at least twenty other art experts here and in Europe have been taken in too, and have said that painting isn't genuine? And now you've made the same mistake." His confident tone and air of authority intimidated the Frenchman, who apologized for his mistake.

Duveen knew that the art market was flooded with fakes, and that many paintings had been falsely ascribed to old masters. He tried his best to distinguish the real from the fake, but in his zeal to sell he often overplayed a work's authenticity. What mattered to him was that the buyer believed he had bought a Dürer, and that Duveen himself convinced everyone of his "expertness" through his air of irreproachable authority. Thus, it is important to be able to play the professor when necessary and never impose such an attitude for its own sake.

22

USE THE SURRENDER

TACTIC: TRANSFORM

WEAKNESS INTO POWER

JUDGMENT

When you are weaker, never fight for honor's sake; choose surrender instead. Surrender gives you time to recover, time to torment and irritate your conqueror, time to wait for his power to wane. Do not give him the satisfaction of fighting and defeating you—surrender first. By turning the other cheek you infuriate and unsettle him. Make surrender a tool of power.

TRANSGRESSION OF THE LAW

The island of Melos is strategically situated in the heart of the Mediterranean. In classical times, the city of Athens dominated the sea and coastal
areas around Greece, but Sparta, in the Peloponnese, had been Melos's
original colonizer. During the Peloponnesian War, then, the Melians refused to ally themselves with Athens and remained loyal to Mother Sparta.
In 416 B.C. the Athenians sent an expedition against Melos. Before launch-
ing an all-out attack, however, they dispatched a delegation to persuade the
Melians to surrender and become an ally rather than suffer devastation and
defeat.

"You know as well as we do," the delegates said, "that the standard of
justice depends on the equality of power to compel, and that in fact the
strong do what they have the power to do and the weak accept what they
have to accept." When the Melians responded that this denied the notion
of fair play, the Athenians said that those in power determined what was
fair and what was not. The Melians argued that this authority belonged to
the gods, not to mortals. "Our opinion of the gods and our knowledge of
men," replied a member of the Athenian delegation, "lead us to conclude
that it is a general and necessary law of nature to rule whatever one can."

The Melians would not budge. Sparta, they insisted, would come to
their defense. The Athenians countered that the Spartans were a conservative, practical people, and would not help Melos because they had nothing
to gain and a lot to lose by doing so.

Finally the Melians began to talk of honor and the principle of resisting
brute force. "Do not be led astray by a false sense of honor," said the Athenians. "Honor often brings men to ruin when they are faced with an obvious danger that somehow affects their pride. There is nothing disgraceful in
giving way to the greatest city in Hellas when she is offering you such reasonable terms." The debate ended. The Melians discussed the issue among
themselves, and decided to trust in the aid of the Spartans, the will of the
gods, and the rightness of their cause. They politely declined the Athenians'
offer.

A few days later the Athenians invaded Melos. The Melians fought
nobly, even without the Spartans, who did not come to their rescue. It took
several attempts before the Athenians could surround and besiege their
main city, but the Melians finally surrendered. The Athenians wasted no
time—they put to death all the men of military age that they could capture,
they sold the women and children as slaves, and they repopulated the island with their own colonists. Only a handful of Melians survived.

Interpretation

The Athenians were one of the most eminently practical people in history,
and they made the most practical argument they could with the Melians:
When you are weaker, there is nothing to be gained by fighting a useless
fight. No one comes to help the weak—by doing so they would only put
themselves in jeopardy. The weak are alone and must submit. Fighting

gives you nothing to gain but martyrdom, and in the process a lot of people who do not believe in your cause will die.

Weakness is no sin, and can even become a strength if you learn how to play it right. Had the Melians surrendered in the first place, they would have been able to sabotage the Athenians in subtle ways, or might have gotten what they could have out of the alliance and then left it when the Athenians themselves were weakened, as in fact happened several years later. Fortunes change and the mighty are often brought down. Surrender conceals great power: Lulling the enemy into complacency, it gives you time to recoup, time to undermine, time for revenge. Never sacrifice that time in exchange for honor in a battle that you cannot win.

Weak people never give way when they ought to.
Cardinal de Retz, 1613–1679

OBSERVANCE OF THE LAW

Sometime in the 1920s the German writer Bertolt Brecht became a convert to the cause of Communism. From then on his plays, essays, and poems reflected his revolutionary fervor, and he generally tried to make his ideological statements as clear as possible. When Hitler came to power in Germany, Brecht and his Communist colleagues became marked men. He had many friends in the United States—Americans who sympathized with his beliefs, as well as fellow German intellectuals who had fled Hitler. In 1941, accordingly, Brecht emigrated to the United States, and chose to settle in Los Angeles, where he hoped to make a living in the film business.

Over the next few years Brecht wrote screenplays with a pointedly anticapitalist slant. He had little success in Hollywood, so in 1947, the war having ended, he decided to return to Europe. That same year, however, the U.S. Congress's House Un-American Activities Committee began its investigation into supposed Communist infiltration in Hollywood. It began to gather information on Brecht, who had so openly espoused Marxism, and on September 19, 1947, only a month before he had planned to leave the United States, he received a subpoena to appear before the committee. In addition to Brecht, a number of other writers, producers, and directors were summoned to appear as well, and this group came to be known as the Hollywood 19.

Before going to Washington, the Hollywood 19 met to decide on a plan of action. Their approach would be confrontational. Instead of answering questions about their membership, or lack of it, in the Communist Party, they would read prepared statements that would challenge the authority of the committee and argue that its activities were unconstitutional. Even if this strategy meant imprisonment, it would gain publicity for their cause.

Brecht disagreed. What good was it, he asked, to play the martyr and gain a little public sympathy if in the process they lost the ability to stage their plays and sell their scripts for years to come? He felt certain they were

Voltaire was living in exile in London at a time when anti-French sentiment was at its highest. One day walking through the streets, he found himself surrounded by an angry crowd. "Hang him. Hang the Frenchman," they yelled. Voltaire calmly addressed the mob with the following words: "Men of England! You wish to kill me because I am a Frenchman. Am I not punished enough in not being born an Englishman?" The crowd cheered his thoughtful words, and escorted him safely back to his lodgings.

THE LITTLE, BROWN BOOK OF ANECDOTES, CLIFTON FADIMAN, ED., 1985

all more intelligent than the members of the committee. Why lower themselves to the level of their opponents by arguing with them? Why not outfox the committee by appearing to surrender to it while subtly mocking it? The Hollywood 19 listened to Brecht politely, but decided to stick to their plan, leaving Brecht to go his own way.

The committee finally summoned Brecht on October 30. They expected him to do what others among the Hollywood 19 who had testified before him had done: Argue, refuse to answer questions, challenge the committee's right to hold its hearing, even yell and hurl insults. Much to their surprise, however, Brecht was the very picture of congeniality. He wore a suit (something he rarely did), smoked a cigar (he had heard that the committee chairman was a passionate cigar smoker), answered their questions politely, and generally deferred to their authority.

Unlike the other witnesses, Brecht answered the question of whether he belonged to the Communist Party: He was not a member, he said, which happened to be the truth. One committee member asked him, "Is it true you have written a number of revolutionary plays?" Brecht had written many plays with overt Communist messages, but he responded, "I have written a number of poems and songs and plays in the fight against Hitler and, of course, they can be considered, therefore, as revolutionary because I, of course, was for the overthrow of that government." This statement went unchallenged.

Brecht's English was more than adequate, but he used an interpreter throughout his testimony, a tactic that allowed him to play subtle games with language. When committee members found Communist leanings in lines from English editions of his poems, he would repeat the lines in German for the interpreter, who would then retranslate them; and somehow they would come out innocuous. At one point a committee member read one of Brecht's revolutionary poems out loud in English, and asked him if he had written it. "No," he responded, "I wrote a German poem, which is very different from this." The author's elusive answers baffled the committee members, but his politeness and the way he yielded to their authority made it impossible for them to get angry with him.

After only an hour of questioning, the committee members had had enough. "Thank you very much," said the chairman, "You are a good example to the [other] witnesses." Not only did they free him, they offered to help him if he had any trouble with immigration officials who might detain him for their own reasons. The following day, Brecht left the United States, never to return.

Interpretation

The Hollywood 19's confrontational approach won them a lot of sympathy, and years later they gained a kind of vindication in public opinion. But they were also blacklisted, and lost valuable years of profitable working time. Brecht, on the other hand, expressed his disgust at the committee more indirectly. It was not that he changed his beliefs or compromised his values; instead, during his short testimony, he kept the upper hand by appearing to yield while all the time running circles around the committee with vague responses, outright lies that went unchallenged because they were wrapped in enigmas, and word games. In the end he kept the freedom to continue his revolutionary writing (as opposed to suffering imprisonment or detainment in the United States), even while subtly mocking the committee and its authority with his pseudo-obedience.

Keep in mind the following: People trying to make a show of their authority are easily deceived by the surrender tactic. Your outward sign of submission makes them feel important; satisfied that you respect them, they become easier targets for a later counterattack, or for the kind of indirect ridicule used by Brecht. Measuring your power over time, never sacrifice long-term maneuverability for the short-lived glories of martyrdom.

When the great lord passes, the wise peasant bows deeply and silently farts.
Ethiopian proverb

KEYS TO POWER

What gets us into trouble in the realm of power is often our own overreaction to the moves of our enemies and rivals. That overreaction creates problems we would have avoided had we been more reasonable. It also has an endless rebound effect, for the enemy then overreacts as well, much as the Athenians did to the Melians. It is always our first instinct to react, to meet aggression with some other kind of aggression. But the next time someone pushes you and you find yourself starting to react, try this: Do not resist or fight back, but yield, turn the other cheek, bend. You will find that this often neutralizes their behavior—they expected, even wanted you to react with force and so they are caught off-guard and confounded by your lack of resistance. By yielding, you in fact control the situation, because your surrender is part of a larger plan to lull them into believing they have defeated you.

This is the essence of the surrender tactic: Inwardly you stay firm, but outwardly you bend. Deprived of a reason to get angry, your opponents will often be bewildered instead. And they are unlikely to react with more violence, which would demand a reaction from you. Instead you are allowed the time and space to plot the countermoves that will bring them down. In the battle of the intelligent against the brutal and the aggressive, the surrender tactic is the supreme weapon. It does require self-control: Those who genuinely surrender give up their freedom, and may be crushed by the humiliation of their defeat. You have to remember that you only *appear* to surrender, like the animal that plays dead to save its hide.

We have seen that it can be better to surrender than to fight; faced with a more powerful opponent and a sure defeat, it is often also better to surrender than to run away. Running away may save you for the time being, but the aggressor will eventually catch up with you. If you surrender instead, you have an opportunity to coil around your enemy and strike with your fangs from close up.

In 473 B.C., in ancient China, King Goujian of Yue suffered a horrible defeat from the ruler of Wu in the battle of Fujiao. Goujian wanted to flee, but he had an adviser who told him to surrender and to place himself in the service of the ruler of Wu, from which position he could study the man and plot his revenge. Deciding to follow this advice, Goujian gave the ruler all of his riches, and went to work in his conqueror's stables as the lowest servant. For three years he humbled himself before the ruler, who then, finally satisfied of his loyalty, allowed him to return home. Inwardly, however, Goujian had spent those three years gathering information and plotting revenge. When a terrible drought struck Wu, and the kingdom was weakened by inner turmoil, he raised an army, invaded, and won with ease. That is the power behind surrender: It gives you the time and the flexibility to plot a devastating counterblow. Had Goujian run away, he would have lost this chance.

When foreign trade began to threaten Japanese independence in the mid–nineteenth century, the Japanese debated how to defeat the foreigners. One minister, Hotta Masayoshi, wrote a memorandum in 1857 that influenced Japanese policy for years to come: "I am therefore convinced that our policy should be to conclude friendly alliances, to send ships to foreign countries everywhere and conduct trade, to copy the foreigners where they are at their best and so repair our own shortcomings, to foster our national strength and complete our armaments, and so *gradually* subject the foreigners to our influence until in the end all the countries of the world know the blessings of perfect tranquillity and our hegemony is acknowledged throughout the globe." This is a brilliant application of the Law: Use surrender to gain access to your enemy. Learn his ways, insinuate yourself with him slowly, outwardly conform to his customs, but inwardly maintain your own culture. Eventually you will emerge victorious, for while he considers you weak and inferior, and takes no precautions against you, you are using the time to catch up and surpass him. This soft, permeable form of invasion is often the best, for the enemy has nothing to react against, prepare for, or resist. And had Japan resisted Western influence by force, it might well have suffered a devastating invasion that would have permanently altered its culture.

Surrender can also offer a way of mocking your enemies, of turning their power against them, as it did for Brecht. Milan Kundera's novel *The Joke,* based on the author's experiences in a penal camp in Czechoslovakia, tells the story of how the prison guards organized a relay race, guards against prisoners. For the guards this was a chance to show off their physical superiority. The prisoners knew they were expected to lose, so they went out of their way to oblige—miming exaggerated exertion while barely moving, running a few yards and collapsing, limping, jogging ever so slowly while the guards raced ahead at full speed. Both by joining the race and by losing it, they had obliged the guards obediently; but their "overobedience" had mocked the event to the point of ruining it. Overobedience—surrender—was here a way to demonstrate superiority in a reverse manner. Resistance would have engaged the prisoners in the cycle of violence, lowering them to the guards' level. *Overobeying* the guards, however, made them ridiculous, yet they could not rightly punish the prisoners, who had only done what they asked.

Power is always in flux—since the game is by nature fluid, and an arena of constant struggle, those with power almost always find themselves eventually on the downward swing. If you find yourself temporarily weakened, the surrender tactic is perfect for raising yourself up again—it disguises your ambition; it teaches you patience and self-control, key skills in the game; and it puts you in the best possible position for taking advantage of your oppressor's sudden slide. If you run away or fight back, in the long run you cannot win. If you surrender, you will almost always emerge victorious.

Image: An Oak Tree. The oak that resists the wind loses its branches one by one, and with nothing left to protect it, the trunk finally snaps. The oak that bends lives longer, its trunk growing wider, its roots deeper and more tenacious.

Authority: Ye have heard that it hath been said, An eye for an eye and a tooth for a tooth: But I say unto you, That ye resist not evil: but whosoever shall smite thee on thy right cheek, turn to him the other also. And if any man will sue thee at the law, and take away thy coat, let them have thy cloak also. And whosoever shall compel thee to go a mile, go with him twain. (Jesus Christ, in *Matthew* 5:38–41)

REVERSAL

The point of surrendering is to save your hide for a later date when you can reassert yourself. It is precisely to avoid martyrdom that one surrenders, but there are times when the enemy will not relent, and martyrdom seems the only way out. Furthermore, if you are willing to die, others may gain power and inspiration from your example.

Yet martyrdom, surrender's reversal, is a messy, inexact tactic, and is as violent as the aggression it combats. For every famous martyr there are thousands more who have inspired neither a religion nor a rebellion, so that if martyrdom does sometimes grant a certain power, it does so unpredictably. More important, you will not be around to enjoy that power, such as it is. And there is finally something selfish and arrogant about martyrs, as if they felt their followers were less important than their own glory.

When power deserts you, it is best to ignore this Law's reversal. Leave martyrdom alone: The pendulum will swing back your way eventually, and you should stay alive to see it.

CONCENTRATE

YOUR FORCES

JUDGMENT

Conserve your forces and energies by keeping them concentrated at their strongest point. You gain more by finding a rich mine and mining it deeper, than by flitting from one shallow mine to another—intensity defeats extensity every time. When looking for sources of power to elevate you, find the one key patron, the fat cow who will give you milk for a long time to come.

TRANSGRESSION OF THE LAW

In China in the early sixth century B.C., the kingdom of Wu began a war with the neighboring northern provinces of the Middle Kingdom. Wu was a growing power, but it lacked the great history and civilization of the Middle Kingdom, for centuries the center of Chinese culture. By defeating the Middle Kingdom, the king of Wu would instantly raise his status.

The war began with great fanfare and several victories, but it soon bogged down. A victory on one front would leave the Wu armies vulnerable on another. The king's chief minister and adviser, Wu Tzu-hsiu, warned him that the barbarous state of Yueh, to the south, was beginning to notice the kingdom of Wu's problems and had designs to invade. The king only laughed at such worries—one more big victory and the great Middle Kingdom would be his.

In the year 490, Wu Tzu-hsiu sent his son away to safety in the kingdom of Ch'i. In doing so he sent the king a signal that he disapproved of the war, and that he believed the king's selfish ambition was leading Wu to ruin. The king, sensing betrayal, lashed out at his minister, accusing him of a lack of loyalty and, in a fit of anger, ordered him to kill himself. Wu Tzu-hsiu obeyed his king, but before he plunged the knife into his chest, he cried, "Tear out my eyes, oh King, and fix them on the gate of Wu, so that I may see the triumphant entry of Yueh."

As Wu Tzu-hsiu had predicted, within a few years a Yueh army passed beneath the gate of Wu. As the barbarians surrounded the palace, the king remembered his minister's last words—and felt the dead man's disembodied eyes watching his disgrace. Unable to bear his shame, the king killed himself, "covering his face so that he would not have to meet the reproachful gaze of his minister in the next world."

Interpretation

The story of Wu is a paradigm of all the empires that have come to ruin by overreaching. Drunk with success and sick with ambition, such empires expand to grotesque proportions and meet a ruin that is total. This is what happened to ancient Athens, which lusted for the faraway island of Sicily and ended up losing its empire. The Romans stretched the boundaries of their empire to encompass vast territories; in doing so they increased their vulnerability, and the chances of invasion from yet another barbarian tribe. Their useless expansion led their empire into oblivion.

For the Chinese, the fate of the kingdom of Wu serves as an elemental lesson on what happens when you dissipate your forces on several fronts, losing sight of distant dangers for the sake of present gain. "If you are not in danger," says Sun-tzu, "do not fight." It is almost a physical law: What is bloated beyond its proportions inevitably collapses. The mind must not wander from goal to goal, or be distracted by success from its sense of purpose and proportion. What is concentrated, coherent, and connected to its past has power. What is dissipated, divided, and distended rots and falls to the ground. The bigger it bloats, the harder it falls.

THE GOOSE AND
THE HORSE

A goose who was plucking grass upon a common thought herself affronted by a horse who fed near her; and, in hissing accents, thus addressed him: "I am certainly a more noble and perfect animal than you, for the whole range and extent of your faculties is confined to one element. I can walk upon the ground as well as you; I have, besides, wings, with which I can raise myself in the air; and when I please, I can sport on ponds and lakes, and refresh myself in the cool waters. I enjoy the different powers of a bird, a fish, and a quadruped." The horse, snorting somewhat disdainfully, replied: "It is true you inhabit three elements, but you make no very distinguished figure in any one of them. You fly, indeed; but your flight is so heavy and clumsy, that you have no right to put yourself on a level with the lark or the swallow. You can swim on the surface of the waters, but you cannot live in them as fishes do; you cannot find your food in that element, nor glide smoothly along the bottom of the waves. And when you walk, or rather waddle, upon the ground, with your broad feet and your long neck stretched out,

OBSERVANCE OF THE LAW

The Rothschild banking family had humble beginnings in the Jewish ghetto of Frankfurt, Germany. The city's harsh laws made it impossible for Jews to mingle outside the ghetto, but the Jews had turned this into a virtue—it made them self-reliant, and zealous to preserve their culture at all costs. Mayer Amschel, the first of the Rothschilds to accumulate wealth by lending money, in the late eighteenth century, well understood the power that comes from this kind of concentration and cohesion.

First, Mayer Amschel allied himself with one family, the powerful princes of Thurn und Taxis. Instead of spreading his services out, he made himself these princes' primary banker. Second, he entrusted none of his business to outsiders, using only his children and close relatives. The more unified and tight-knit the family, the more powerful it would become. Soon Mayer Amschel's five sons were running the business. And when Mayer Amschel lay dying, in 1812, he refused to name a principal heir, instead setting up all of his sons to continue the family tradition, so that they would stay united and would resist the dangers of diffusion and of infiltration by outsiders.

Once Mayer Amschel's sons controlled the family business, they decided that the key to wealth on a larger scale was to secure a foothold in the finances of Europe as a whole, rather than being tied to any one country or prince. Of the five brothers, Nathan had already opened up shop in London. In 1813 James moved to Paris. Amschel remained in Frankfurt, Salomon established himself in Vienna, and Karl, the youngest son, went to Naples. With each sphere of influence covered, they could tighten their hold on Europe's financial markets.

This widespread network, of course, opened the Rothschilds to the very danger of which their father had warned them: diffusion, division, dissension. They avoided this danger, and established themselves as the most powerful force in European finance and politics, by once again resorting to the strategy of the ghetto—excluding outsiders, concentrating their forces. The Rothschilds established the fastest courier system in Europe, allowing them to get news of events before all their competitors. They held a virtual monopoly on information. And their internal communications and correspondence were written in Frankfurt Yiddish, and in a code that only the brothers could decipher. There was no point in stealing this information— no one could understand it. "Even the shewdest bankers cannot find their way through the Rothschild maze," admitted a financier who had tried to infiltrate the clan.

In 1824 James Rothschild decided it was time to get married. This presented a problem for the Rothschilds, since it meant incorporating an outsider into the Rothschild clan, an outsider who could betray its secrets. James therefore decided to marry within the family, and chose the daughter of his brother Salomon. The brothers were ecstatic—this was the perfect solution to their marriage problems. James's choice now became the family policy: Two years later, Nathan married off his daughter to

hissing at everyone who passes by, you bring upon yourself the derision of all beholders. I confess that I am only formed to move upon the ground; but how graceful is my make! How well turned my limbs! How highly finished my body! How great my strength! How astonishing my speed! I had much rather be confined to one element, and be admired in that, than be a goose in all!"

FABLES FROM BOCCACCIO AND CHAUCER, DR. JOHN AIKIN, 1747–1822

Beware of dissipating your powers; strive constantly to concentrate them. Genius thinks it can do whatever it sees others doing, but it is sure to repent of every ill-judged outlay.

JOHANN VON GOETHE, 1749–1832

Salomon's son. In the years to come, the five brothers arranged eighteen matches among their children, sixteen of these being contracted between first cousins.

"We are like the mechanism of a watch: Each part is essential," said brother Salomon. As in a watch, every part of the business moved in concert with every other, and the inner workings were invisible to the world, which only saw the movement of the hands. While other rich and powerful families suffered irrecoverable downturns during the tumultous first half of the nineteenth century, the tight-knit Rothschilds managed not only to preserve but to expand their unprecedented wealth.

Interpretation

The Rothschilds were born in strange times. They came from a place that had not changed in centuries, but lived in an age that gave birth to the Industrial Revolution, the French Revolution, and an endless series of upheavals. The Rothchilds kept the past alive, resisted the patterns of dispersion of their era and for this are emblematic of the law of concentration.

No one represents this better than James Rothschild, the son who established himself in Paris. In his lifetime James witnessed the defeat of Napoleon, the restoration of the Bourbon monarchy, the bourgeois monarchy of Orléans, the return to a republic, and finally the enthronement of Napoleon III. French styles and fashions changed at a relentless pace during all this turmoil. Without appearing to be a relic of the past, James steered his family as if the ghetto lived on within them. He kept alive his clan's inner cohesion and strength. Only through such an anchoring in the past was the family able to thrive amidst such chaos. Concentration was the foundation of the Rothschilds' power, wealth, and stability.

> *The best strategy is always to be very strong; first in general, then*
> *at the decisive point. . . . There is no higher and simpler law of strategy*
> *than that of keeping one's forces concentrated. . . . In short the*
> *first principle is: act with the utmost concentration.*
> On War, *Carl von Clauservitz, 1780–1831*

KEYS TO POWER

The world is plagued by greater and greater division—within countries, political groups, families, even individuals. We are all in a state of total distraction and diffusion, hardly able to keep our minds in one direction before we are pulled in a thousand others. The modern world's level of conflict is higher than ever, and we have internalized it in our own lives.

The solution is a form of retreat inside ourselves, to the past, to more concentrated forms of thought and action. As Schopenhauer wrote, "Intellect is a magnitude of intensity, not a magnitude of extensity." Napoleon knew the value of concentrating your forces at the enemy's weakest spot—

it was the secret of his success on the battlefield. But his willpower and his mind were equally modeled on this notion. Single-mindedness of purpose, total concentration on the goal, and the use of these qualities against people less focused, people in a state of distraction—such an arrow will find its mark every time and overwhelm the enemy.

Casanova attributed his success in life to his ability to concentrate on a single goal and push at it until it yielded. It was his ability to give himself over completely to the women he desired that made him so intensely seductive. For the weeks or months that one of these women lived in his orbit, he thought of no one else. When he was imprisoned in the treacherous "leads" of the doge's palace in Venice, a prison from which no one had ever escaped, he concentrated his mind on the single goal of escape, day after day. A change of cells, which meant that months of digging had all been for naught, did not discourage him; he persisted and eventually escaped. "I have always believed," he later wrote, "that when a man gets it into his head to do something, and when he exclusively occupies himself in that design, he must succeed, whatever the difficulties. That man will become Grand Vizier or Pope."

Concentrate on a single goal, a single task, and beat it into submission. In the world of power you will constantly need help from other people, usually those more powerful than you. The fool flits from one person to another, believing that he will survive by spreading himself out. It is a corollary of the law of concentration, however, that much energy is saved, and more power is attained, by affixing yourself to a single, appropriate source of power. The scientist Nikola Tesla ruined himself by believing that he somehow maintained his independence by not having to serve a single master. He even turned down J. P. Morgan, who offered him a rich contract. In the end, Tesla's "independence" meant that he could depend on no single patron, but was always having to toady up to a dozen of them. Later in his life he realized his mistake.

All the great Renaissance painters and writers wrestled with this problem, none more so than the sixteenth-century writer Pietro Aretino. Throughout his life Aretino suffered the indignities of having to please this prince and that. At last, he had had enough, and decided to woo Charles V, promising the emperor the services of his powerful pen. He finally discovered the freedom that came from attachment to a single source of power. Michelangelo found this freedom with Pope Julius II, Galileo with the Medicis. In the end, the single patron appreciates your loyalty and becomes dependent on your services; in the long run the master serves the slave.

Finally, power itself always exists in concentrated forms. In any organization it is inevitable for a small group to hold the strings. And often it is not those with the titles. In the game of power, only the fool flails about without fixing his target. You must find out who controls the operations, who is the real director behind the scenes. As Richelieu discovered at the beginning of his rise to the top of the French political scene during the early seventeenth century, it was not King Louis XIII who decided things, it was the king's mother. And so he attached himself to her, and catapulted through the ranks of the courtiers, all the way to the top.

It is enough to strike oil once—your wealth and power are assured for a lifetime.

Image: The Arrow. You cannot hit two targets
with one arrow. If your thoughts stray, you
miss the enemy's heart. Mind and
arrow must become one. Only
with such concentration of
mental and physical
power can your arrow
hit the target and
pierce the
heart.

Authority: Prize intensity more than extensity. Perfection re-
sides in quality, not quantity. Extent alone never rises above
mediocrity, and it is the misfortune of men with wide general
interests that while they would like to have their finger in every
pie, they have one in none. Intensity gives eminence, and rises
to the heroic in matters sublime. (Baltasar Gracián, 1601–1658)

REVERSAL

There are dangers in concentration, and moments when dispersion is the proper tactical move. Fighting the Nationalists for control of China, Mao Tse-tung and the Communists fought a protracted war on several fronts, using sabotage and ambush as their main weapons. Dispersal is often suit-able for the weaker side; it is, in fact, a crucial principle of guerrilla warfare. When fighting a stronger army, concentrating your forces only makes you an easier target—better to dissolve into the scenery and frustrate your enemy with the elusiveness of your presence.

Tying yourself to a single source of power has one preeminent danger: If that person dies, leaves, or falls from grace, you suffer. This is what hap-pened to Cesare Borgia, who derived his power from his father, Pope Alexander VI. It was the pope who gave Cesare armies to fight with and wars to wage in his name. When he suddenly died (perhaps from poison),

Cesare was as good as dead. He had made far too many enemies over the years, and was now without his father's protection. In cases when you may need protection, then, it is often wise to entwine yourself around several sources of power. Such a move would be especially prudent in periods of great tumult and violent change, or when your enemies are numerous. The more patrons and masters you serve the less risk you run if one of them falls from power. Such dispersion will even allow you to play one off against the other. Even if you concentrate on the single source of power, you still must practice caution, and prepare for the day when your master or patron is no longer there to help you.

Finally, being too single-minded in purpose can make you an intolerable bore, especially in the arts. The Renaissance painter Paolo Uccello was so obsessed with perspective that his paintings look lifeless and contrived. Whereas Leonardo da Vinci interested himself in everything—architecture, painting, warfare, sculpture, mechanics. Diffusion was the source of his power. But such genius is rare, and the rest of us are better off erring on the side of intensity.

PLAY THE PERFECT

COURTIER

JUDGMENT

The perfect courtier thrives in a world where everything revolves around power and political dexterity. He has mastered the art of indirection; he flatters, yields to superiors, and asserts power over others in the most oblique and graceful manner. Learn and apply the laws of courtiership and there will be no limit to how far you can rise in the court.

COURT SOCIETY

It is a fact of human nature that the structure of a court society forms itself around power. In the past, the court gathered around the ruler, and had many functions: Besides keeping the ruler amused, it was a way to solidify the hierarchy of royalty, nobility, and the upper classes, and to keep the nobility both subordinate and close to the ruler, so that he could keep an eye on them. The court serves power in many ways, but most of all it glorifies the ruler, providing him with a microcosmic world that must struggle to please him.

To be a courtier was a dangerous game. A nineteenth-century Arab traveler to the court of Darfur, in what is now Sudan, reported that courtiers there had to do whatever the sultan did: If he were injured, they had to suffer the same injury; if he fell off his horse during a hunt, they fell, too. Mimicry like this appeared in courts all over the world. More troublesome was the danger of displeasing the ruler—one wrong move spelled death or exile. The successful courtier had to walk a tightrope, pleasing but not pleasing too much, obeying but somehow distinguishing himself from the other courtiers, while also never distinguishing himself so far as to make the ruler insecure.

Great courtiers throughout history have mastered the science of manipulating people. They make the king feel more kingly; they make everyone else fear their power. They are magicians of appearance, knowing that most things at court are judged by how they seem. Great courtiers are gracious and polite; their aggression is veiled and indirect. Masters of the word, they never say more than necessary, getting the most out of a compliment or hidden insult. They are magnets of pleasure—people want to be around them because they know how to please, yet they neither fawn nor humiliate themselves. Great courtiers become the king's favorites, enjoying the benefits of that position. They often end up more powerful than the ruler, for they are wizards in the accumulation of influence.

Many today dismiss court life as a relic of the past, a historical curiosity. They reason, according to Machiavelli, "as though heaven, the sun, the elements, and men had changed the order of their motions and power, and were different from what they were in ancient times." There may be no more Sun Kings but there are still plenty of people who believe the sun revolves around them. The royal court may have more or less disappeared, or at least lost its power, but courts and courtiers still exist because power still exists. A courtier is rarely asked to fall off a horse anymore, but the laws that govern court politics are as timeless as the laws of power. There is much to be learned, then, from great courtiers past and present.

THE LAWS OF COURT POLITICS

Avoid Ostentation. It is never prudent to prattle on about yourself or call too much attention to your actions. The more you talk about your deeds the more suspicion you cause. You also stir up enough envy among your peers to induce treachery and backstabbing. Be careful, ever so careful, in trumpeting your own achievements, and always talk less about yourself than about other people. Modesty is generally preferable.

Practice Nonchalance. Never seem to be working too hard. Your talent must appear to flow naturally, with an ease that makes people take you for a genius rather than a workaholic. Even when something demands a lot of sweat, make it look effortless—people prefer to not see your blood and toil, which is another form of ostentation. It is better for them to marvel at how gracefully you have achieved your accomplishment than to wonder why it took so much work.

Be Frugal with Flattery. It may seem that your superiors cannot get enough flattery, but too much of even a good thing loses its value. It also stirs up suspicion among your peers. Learn to flatter indirectly—by downplaying your own contribution, for example, to make your master look better.

Arrange to Be Noticed. There is a paradox: You cannot display yourself too brazenly, yet you must also get yourself noticed. In the court of Louis XIV, whoever the king decided to look at rose instantly in the court hierarchy. You stand no chance of rising if the ruler does not notice you in the swamp of courtiers. This task requires much art. It is often initially a matter of being seen, in the literal sense. Pay attention to your physical appearance, then, and find a way to create a distinctive—a *subtly* distinctive—style and image.

Alter Your Style and Language According to the Person You Are Dealing With. The pseudo-belief in equality—the idea that talking and acting the same way with everyone, no matter what their rank, makes you somehow a paragon of civilization—is a terrible mistake. Those below you will take it as a form of condescension, which it is, and those above you will be offended, although they may not admit it. You must change your style and your way of speaking to suit each person. This is not lying, it is acting, and acting is an art, not a gift from God. Learn the art. This is also true for the great variety of cultures found in the modern court: *Never* assume that your criteria of behavior and judgment are universal. Not only is an inability to adapt to another culture the height of barbarism, it puts you at a disadvantage.

Never Be the Bearer of Bad News. The king kills the messenger who brings bad news: This is a cliché but there is truth to it. You must struggle and if necessary lie and cheat to be sure that the lot of the bearer of bad news falls on a colleague, never on you. Bring only good news and your approach will gladden your master.

Never Affect Friendliness and Intimacy with Your Master. He does not want a friend for a subordinate, he wants a subordinate. Never approach him in an easy, friendly way, or act as if you are on the best of terms—that is *his* prerogative. If *he* chooses to deal with you on this level, assume a wary chumminess. Otherwise err in the opposite direction, and make the distance between you clear.

Never Criticize Those Above You Directly. This may seem obvious, but there are often times when some sort of criticism is necessary—to say nothing, or to give no advice, would open you to risks of another sort. You must learn, however, to couch your advice and criticism as indirectly and as politely as possible. Think twice, or three times, before deciding you have made them sufficiently circuitous. Err on the side of subtlety and gentleness.

Be Frugal in Asking Those Above You for Favors. Nothing irritates a master more than having to reject someone's request. It stirs up guilt and resentment. Ask for favors as rarely as possible, and know when to stop. Rather than making yourself the supplicant, it is always better to earn your favors, so that the ruler bestows them willingly. Most important: Do not ask for favors on another person's behalf, least of all a friend's.

Never Joke About Appearances or Taste. A lively wit and a humorous disposition are essential qualities for a good courtier, and there are times when vulgarity is appropriate and engaging. But avoid any kind of joke about appearance or taste, two highly sensitive areas, especially with those above you. Do not even try it when you are away from them. You will dig your own grave.

Do Not Be the Court Cynic. Express admiration for the good work of others. If you constantly criticize your equals or subordinates some of that criticism will rub off on you, hovering over you like a gray cloud wherever you go. People will groan at each new cynical comment, and you will irritate them. By expressing modest admiration for other people's achievements, you paradoxically call attention to your own. The ability to express wonder and amazement, and seem like you mean it, is a rare and dying talent, but one still greatly valued.

Be Self-observant. The mirror is a miraculous invention; without it you would commit great sins against beauty and decorum. You also need a mirror for your actions. This can sometimes come from other people telling you what they see in you, but that is not the most trustworthy method: *You* must be the mirror, training your mind to try to see yourself as others see you. Are you acting too obsequious? Are you trying too hard to please? Do you seem desperate for attention, giving the impression that you are on the decline? Be observant about yourself and you will avoid a mountain of blunders.

Master Your Emotions. As an actor in a great play, you must learn to cry and laugh on command and when it is appropriate. You must be able both to disguise your anger and frustration and to fake your contentment and agreement. You must be the master of your own face. Call it lying if you like; but if you prefer to not play the game and to always be honest and up-front, do not complain when others call you obnoxious and arrogant.

Fit the Spirit of the Times. A slight affectation of a past era can be charming, as long as you choose a period at least twenty years back; wear-ing the fashions of ten years ago is ludicrous, unless you enjoy the role of court jester. Your spirit and way of thinking must keep up with the times, even if the times offend your sensibilities. Be too forward-thinking, how-ever, and no one will understand you. It is never a good idea to stand out too much in this area; you are best off at least being able to mimic the spirit of the times.

Be a Source of Pleasure. This is critical. It is an obvious law of human nature that we will flee what is unpleasant and distasteful, while charm and the promise of delight will draw us like moths to a flame. Make yourself the flame and you will rise to the top. Since life is otherwise so full of unpleas-antness and pleasure so scarce, you will be as indispensable as food and drink. This may seem obvious, but what is obvious is often ignored or un-appreciated. There are degrees to this: Not everyone can play the role of favorite, for not everyone is blessed with charm and wit. But we can all control our unpleasant qualities and obscure them when necessary.

> *A man who knows the court is master of his gestures, of his eyes and*
> *of his face; he is profound, impenetrable; he dissimulates bad offices,*
> *smiles at his enemies, controls his irritation, disguises his passions,*
> *belies his heart, speaks and acts against his feelings.*
> Jean de La Bruyère, 1645–1696

SCENES OF COURT LIFE: Exemplary Deeds and Fatal Mistakes

Scene I

Alexander the Great, conqueror of the Mediterranean basin and the Mid-dle East through to India, had had the great Aristotle as his tutor and men-tor, and throughout his short life he remained devoted to philosophy and his master's teachings. He once complained to Aristotle that during his long campaigns he had no one with whom he could discuss philosophical matters. Aristotle responded by suggesting that he take Callisthenes, a for-mer pupil of Aristotle's and a promising philosopher in his own right, along on the next campaign.

Aristotle had schooled Callisthenes in the skills of being a courtier, but the young man secretly scoffed at them. He believed in pure philosophy, in unadorned words, in speaking the naked truth. If Alexander loved learning so much, Callisthenes thought, he could not object to one who spoke his mind. During one of Alexander's major campaigns, Callisthenes spoke his mind one too many times and Alexander had him put to death.

Interpretation

In court, honesty is a fool's game. Never be so self-absorbed as to believe that the master is interested in your criticisms of him, no matter how accurate they are.

Scene II

Beginning in the Han Dynasty two thousand years ago, Chinese scholars compiled a series of writings called the *21 Histories,* an official biography of each dynasty, including stories, statistics, census figures, and war chronicles. Each history also contained a chapter called "Unusual Events," and here, among the listings of earthquakes and floods, there would sometimes suddenly appear descriptions of such bizarre manifestations as two-headed sheep, geese flying backward, stars suddenly appearing in different parts of the sky, and so on. The earthquakes could be historically verified, but the monsters and weird natural phenomena were clearly inserted on purpose, and invariably occurred in clusters. What could this mean?

The Chinese emperor was considered more than a man—he was a force of nature. His kingdom was the center of the universe, and everything revolved around him. He embodied the world's perfection. To criticize him or any of his actions would have been to criticize the divine order. No minister or courtier dared approach the emperor with even the slightest cautionary word. But emperors were fallible and the kingdom suffered greatly by their mistakes. Inserting sightings of strange phenomena into the court chronicles was the only way to warn them. The emperor would read of geese flying backward and moons out of orbit, and realize that he was being cautioned. His actions were unbalancing the universe and needed to change.

Interpretation

For Chinese courtiers, the problem of how to give the emperor advice was an important issue. Over the years, thousands of them had died trying to warn or counsel their master. To be made safely, their criticisms had to be indirect—yet if they were *too* indirect they would not be heeded. The chronicles were their solution: Identify no one person as the source of criticism, make the advice as impersonal as possible, but let the emperor know the gravity of the situation.

Your master is no longer the center of the universe, but he still imagines that everything revolves around him. When you criticize him he sees the person criticizing, not the criticism itself. Like the Chinese courtiers, you must find a way to disappear behind the warning. Use symbols and other indirect methods to paint a picture of the problems to come, without putting your neck on the line.

Scene III

Early in his career, the French architect Jules Mansart received commissions to design minor additions to Versailles for King Louis XIV. For each design he would draw up his plans, making sure they followed Louis's instructions closely. He would then present them to His Majesty.

The courtier Saint-Simon described Mansart's technique in dealing with the king: "His particular skill was to show the king plans that purposely included something imperfect about them, often dealing with the gardens, which were not Mansart's specialty. The king, as Mansart expected, would put his finger exactly on the problem and propose how to solve it, at which point Mansart would exclaim for all to hear that he would never have seen the problem that the king had so masterfully found and solved; he would burst with admiration, confessing that next to the king he was but a lowly pupil." At the age of thirty, having used these methods time and time again, Mansart received a prestigious royal commission: Although he was less talented and experienced than a number of other French designers, he was to take charge of the enlargement of Versailles. He was the king's architect from then on.

Interpretation

As a young man, Mansart had seen how many royal craftsmen in the service of Louis XIV had lost their positions not through a lack of talent but through a costly social blunder. He would not make that mistake. Mansart always strove to make Louis feel better about himself, to feed the king's vanity as publicly as possible.

Never imagine that skill and talent are all that matter. In court the courtier's art is more important than his talent; never spend so much time on your studies that you neglect your social skills. And the greatest skill of all is the ability to make the master look more talented than those around him.

Scene IV

Jean-Baptiste Isabey had become the unofficial painter of the Napoleonic court. During the Congress of Vienna in 1814, after Napoleon, defeated, had been imprisoned on the island of Elba, the participants in these meetings, which were to decide the fate of Europe, invited Isabey to immortalize the historic events in an epic painting.

When Isabey arrived in Vienna, Talleyrand, the main negotiator for the French, paid the artist a visit. Considering his role in the proceedings, the statesman explained, he expected to occupy center stage in the painting. Isabey cordially agreed. A few days later the Duke of Wellington, the main negotiator for the English, also approached Isabey, and said much the same thing that Talleyrand had. The ever polite Isabey agreed that the great duke should indeed be the center of attention.

Back in his studio, Isabey pondered the dilemma. If he gave the spotlight to either of the two men, he could create a diplomatic rift, stirring up all sorts of resentment at a time when peace and concord were critical.

When the painting was finally unveiled, however, both Talleyrand and Wellington felt honored and satisfied. The work depicts a large hall filled with diplomats and politicians from all over Europe. On one side the Duke of Wellington enters the room, and all eyes are turned toward him; he is the "center" of attention. In the very center of the painting, meanwhile, sits Talleyrand.

Interpretation

It is often very difficult to satisfy the master, but to satisfy two masters in one stroke takes the genius of a great courtier. Such predicaments are common in the life of a courtier: By giving attention to one master, he displeases another. You must find a way to navigate this Scylla and Charybdis safely. Masters must receive their due; never inadvertently stir up the resentment of one in pleasing another.

Scene V

George Brummell, also known as Beau Brummell, made his mark in the late 1700s by the supreme elegance of his appearance, his popularization of shoe buckles (soon imitated by all the dandies), and his clever way with words. His London house was *the* fashionable spot in town, and Brummell was the authority on all matters of fashion. If he disliked your footwear, you immediately got rid of it and bought whatever *he* was wearing. He perfected the art of tying a cravat; Lord Byron was said to spend many a night in front of the mirror trying to figure out the secret behind Brummell's perfect knots.

One of Brummell's greatest admirers was the Prince of Wales, who fancied himself a fashionable young man. Becoming attached to the prince's court (and provided with a royal pension), Brummell was soon so sure of his own authority there that he took to joking about the prince's weight, referring to his host as Big Ben. Since trimness of figure was an important quality for a dandy, this was a withering criticism. At dinner once, when the service was slow, Brummell said to the prince, "Do ring, Big Ben." The prince rang, but when the valet arrived he ordered the man to show Brummell the door and never admit him again.

Despite falling into the prince's disfavor, Brummell continued to treat everyone around him with the same arrogance. Without the Prince of Wales' patronage to support him, he sank into horrible debt, but he maintained his insolent manners, and everyone soon abandoned him. He died in the most pitiable poverty, alone and deranged.

Interpretation

Beau Brummell's devastating wit was one of the qualities that endeared him to the Prince of Wales. But not even he, the arbiter of taste and fashion, could get away with a joke about the prince's appearance, least of all to his face. Never joke about a person's plumpness, even indirectly—and particularly when he is your master. The poorhouses of history are filled with people who have made such jokes at their master's expense.

Scene VI

Pope Urban VIII wanted to be remembered for his skills in writing poetry, which unfortunately were mediocre at best. In 1629 Duke Francesco d'Este, knowing the pope's literary pretensions, sent the poet Fulvio Testi as his ambassador to the Vatican. One of Testi's letters to the duke reveals why he was chosen: "Once our discussion was over, I kneeled to depart, but His Holiness made a signal and walked to another room where he sleeps, and after reaching a small table, he grabbed a bundle of papers and thus, turning to me with a smiling face, he said: 'We want Your Lordship to listen to some of our compositions.' And, in fact, he read me two very long Pindaric poems, one in praise of the most holy Virgin, and the other one about Countess Matilde."

We do not know exactly what Testi thought of these very long poems, since it would have been dangerous for him to state his opinion freely, even in a letter. But he went on to write, "I, following the mood, commented on each line with the needed praise, and, after having kissed His Holiness's foot for such an unusual sign of benevolence [the reading of the poetry], I left." Weeks later, when the duke himself visited the pope, he managed to recite entire verses of the pope's poetry and praised it enough to make the pope "so jubilant he seemed to lose his mind."

Interpretation

In matters of taste you can never be too obsequious with your master. Taste is one of the ego's prickliest parts; never impugn or question the master's taste—his poetry is sublime, his dress impeccable, and his manner the model for all.

Scene VII

One afternoon in ancient China, Chao, ruler of Han from 358 to 333 B.C., got drunk and fell asleep in the palace gardens. The court crown-keeper, whose sole task was to look after the ruler's head apparel, passed through the gardens and saw his master sleeping without a coat. Since it was getting cold, the crown-keeper placed his own coat over the ruler, and left.

When Chao awoke and saw the coat upon him, he asked his attendants, "Who put more clothes on my body?" "The crown-keeper," they replied. The ruler immediately called for his official coat-keeper and had him punished for neglecting his duties. He also called for the crown-keeper, whom he had beheaded.

Interpretation

Do not overstep your bounds. Do what you are assigned to do, to the best of your abilities, and never do more. To think that by doing more you are doing better is a common blunder. It is never good to seem to be trying too hard—it is as if you were covering up some deficiency. Fulfilling a task that has not been asked of you just makes people suspicious. If you are a crown-keeper, be a crown-keeper. Save your excess energy for when you are not in the court.

Scene VIII

One day, for amusement, the Italian Renaissance painter Fra Filippo Lippi (1406–1469) and some friends went sailing in a small boat off Ancona. There they were captured by two Moorish galleys, which hauled them off in chains to Barbary, where they were sold as slaves. For eighteen long months Filippo toiled with no hope of returning to Italy.

On several occasions Filippo saw the man who had bought him pass by, and one day he decided to sketch this man's portrait, using burnt coal—charcoal—from the fire. Still in his chains, he found a white wall, where he drew a full-length likeness of his owner in Moorish clothing. The owner soon heard about this, for no one had seen such skill in drawing before in these parts; it seemed like a miracle, a gift from God. The drawing so pleased the owner that he instantly gave Filippo his freedom and employed him in his court. All the big men on the Barbary coast came to see the magnificent color portraits that Fra Filippo then proceeded to do, and finally, in gratitude for the honor in this way brought upon him, Filippo's owner returned the artist safely to Italy.

Interpretation

We who toil for other people have all in some way been captured by pirates and sold into slavery. But like Fra Filippo (if to a lesser degree), most of us possess some gift, some talent, an ability to do something better than other people. Make your master a gift of your talents and you will rise above other courtiers. Let him take the credit if necessary, it will only be temporary: Use him as a stepping stone, a way of displaying your talent and eventually buying your freedom from enslavement.

Scene IX

Alfonso I of Aragon once had a servant who told the king that the night before he had had a dream: Alfonso had given him a gift of weapons, horses, and clothes. Alfonso, a generous, lordly man, decided it would be amusing to make this dream come true, and promptly gave the servant exactly these gifts.

A little while later, the same servant announced to Alfonso that he had had yet another dream, and in this one Alfonso had given him a considerable pile of gold florins. The king smiled and said, "Don't believe in dreams from now on; they lie."

Interpretation

In his treatment of the servant's first dream, Alfonso remained in control. By making a dream come true, he claimed a godlike power for himself, if in a mild and humorous way. In the second dream, however, all appearance of magic was gone; this was nothing but an ugly con game on the servant's part. Never ask for too much, then, and know when to stop. It is the master's prerogative to give—to give when he wants and what he wants, and to do so without prompting. Do not give him the chance to reject your requests. Better to win favors by deserving them, so that they are bestowed without your asking.

Scene X

The great English landscape painter J. M. W. Turner (1775–1851) was known for his use of color, which he applied with a brilliance and a strange iridescence. The color in his paintings was so striking, in fact, that other artists never wanted his work hung next to theirs: It inevitably made everything around it seem dull.

The painter Sir Thomas Lawrence once had the misfortune of seeing Turner's masterpiece *Cologne* hanging in an exhibition between two works of his own. Lawrence complained bitterly to the gallery owner, who gave him no satisfaction: After all, *someone's* paintings had to hang next to Turner's. But Turner heard of Lawrence's complaint, and before the exhibition opened, he toned down the brilliant golden sky in *Cologne,* making it as dull as the colors in Lawrence's works. A friend of Turner's who saw the painting approached the artist with a horrified look: "What have you done to your picture!" he said. "Well, poor Lawrence was so unhappy," Turner replied, "and it's only lampblack. It'll wash off after the exhibition."

Interpretation

Many of a courtier's anxieties have to do with the master, with whom most dangers lie. Yet it is a mistake to imagine that the master is the only one to determine your fate. Your equals and subordinates play integral parts also. A court is a vast stew of resentments, fears, and powerful envy. You have to placate everyone who might someday harm you, deflecting their resentment and envy and diverting their hostility onto other people.

Turner, eminent courtier, knew that his good fortune and fame depended on his fellow painters as well as on his dealers and patrons. How many of the great have been felled by envious colleagues! Better temporarily to dull your brilliance than to suffer the slings and arrows of envy.

Scene XI

Winston Churchill was an amateur artist, and after World War II his paintings became collector's items. The American publisher Henry Luce, in fact, creator of *Time* and *Life* magazines, kept one of Churchill's landscapes hanging in his private office in New York.

On a tour through the United States once, Churchill visited Luce in his office, and the two men looked at the painting together. The publisher remarked, "It's a good picture, but I think it needs something in the foreground—a sheep, perhaps." Much to Luce's horror, Churchill's secretary called the publisher the next day and asked him to have the painting sent to England. Luce did so, mortified that he had perhaps offended the former prime minister. A few days later, however, the painting was shipped back, but slightly altered: a single sheep now grazed peacefully in the foreground.

Interpretation

In stature and fame, Churchill stood head and shoulders above Luce, but Luce was certainly a man of power, so let us imagine a slight equality between them. Still, what did Churchill have to fear from an American publisher? Why bow to the criticism of a dilettante?

A court—in this case the entire world of diplomats and international statesmen, and also of the journalists who court them—is a place of mutual dependence. It is unwise to insult or offend the taste of people of power, even if they are below or equal to you. If a man like Churchill can swallow the criticisms of a man like Luce, he proves himself a courtier without peer. (Perhaps his correction of the painting implied a certain condescension as well, but he did it so subtly that Luce did not perceive any slight.) Imitate Churchill: Put in the sheep. It is always beneficial to play the obliging courtier, even when you are not serving a master.

THE DELICATE GAME OF COURTIERSHIP: A Warning

Talleyrand was the consummate courtier, especially in serving his master Napoleon. When the two men were first getting to know each other, Napoleon once said in passing, "I shall come to lunch at your house one of these days." Talleyrand had a house at Auteuil, in the suburbs of Paris. "I should be delighted, *mon général*," the minister replied, "and since my house is close to the Bois de Boulogne, you will be able to amuse yourself with a bit of shooting in the afternoon."

"I do not like shooting," said Napoleon, "But I love hunting. Are there any boars in the Bois de Boulogne?" Napoleon came from Corsica, where boar hunting was a great sport. By asking if there were boars in a Paris park, he showed himself still a provincial, almost a rube. Talleyrand did not laugh, however, but he could not resist a practical joke on the man who was now his master in politics, although not in blood and nobility, since Talleyrand came from an old aristocratic family. To Napoleon's question, then, he simply replied, "Very few, *mon général,* but I dare say you will manage to find one."

It was arranged that Napoleon would arrive at Talleyrand's house the following day at seven A.M. and would spend the morning there. The "boar hunt" would take place in the afternoon. Throughout the morning the excited general talked nothing but boar hunting. Meanwhile, Talleyrand secretly had his servants go to the market, buy two enormous black pigs, and take them to the great park.

After lunch, the hunters and their hounds set off for the Bois de Boulogne. At a secret signal from Talleyrand, the servants loosed one of the pigs. "I see a boar," Napoleon cried joyfully, jumping onto his horse to give chase. Talleyrand stayed behind. It took half an hour of galloping through the park before the "boar" was finally captured. At the moment of triumph, however, Napoleon was approached by one of his aides, who knew the creature could not possibly be a boar, and feared the general would be ridiculed once the story got out: "Sir," he told Napoleon, "you realize of course that this is not a boar but a pig."

Flying into a rage, Napoleon immediately set off at a gallop for Talleyrand's house. He realized along the way that he would now be the butt of many a joke, and that exploding at Talleyrand would only make him more ridiculous; it would be better to make a show of good humor. Still, he did not hide his displeasure well.

Talleyrand decided to try to soothe the general's bruised ego. He told Napoleon not to go back to Paris yet—he should again go hunting in the park. There were many rabbits there, and hunting them had been a favorite pastime of Louis XVI. Talleyrand even offered to let Napoleon use a set of guns that had once belonged to Louis. With much flattery and cajolery, he once again got Napoleon to agree to a hunt.

The party left for the park in the late afternoon. Along the way, Napoleon told Talleyrand, "I'm not Louis XVI, I surely won't kill even one rabbit." Yet that afternoon, strangely enough, the park was teeming with rabbits. Napoleon killed at least fifty of them, and his mood changed from anger to satisfaction. At the end of his wild shooting spree, however, the same aide approached him and whispered in his ear, "To tell the truth, sir, I am beginning to believe these are not wild rabbits. I suspect that rascal Talleyrand has played another joke on us." (The aide was right: Talleyrand had in fact sent his servants back to the market, where they had purchased dozens of rabbits and then had released them in the Bois de Boulogne.)

Napoleon immediately mounted his horse and galloped away, this time returning straight to Paris. He later threatened Talleyrand, warned him not to tell a soul what had happened; if he became the laughingstock of Paris, there would be hell to pay.

It took months for Napoleon to be able to trust Talleyrand again, and he never totally forgave him his humiliation.

Interpretation

Courtiers are like magicians: They deceptively play with appearances, only letting those around them see what they want them to see. With so much deception and manipulation afoot, it is essential to keep people from seeing your tricks and glimpsing your sleight of hand.

Talleyrand was normally the Grand Wizard of Courtiership, and but for Napoleon's aide, he probably would have gotten away completely with both pleasing his master and having a joke at the general's expense. But courtiership is a subtle art, and overlooked traps and inadvertent mistakes can ruin your best tricks. Never risk being caught in your maneuvers; never let people see your devices. If that happens you instantly pass in people's perceptions from a courtier of great manners to a loathsome rogue. It is a delicate game you play; apply the utmost attention to covering your tracks, and never let your master unmask you.

RE-CREATE YOURSELF

JUDGMENT

Do not accept the roles that society foists on you. Re-create yourself by forging a new identity, one that commands attention and never bores the audience. Be the master of your own image rather than letting others define it for you. Incorporate dramatic devices into your public gestures and actions—your power will be enhanced and your character will seem larger than life.

Julius Caesar made his first significant mark on Roman society in 65 B.C., when he assumed the post of *aedile,* the official in charge of grain distribution and public games. He began his entrance into the public eye by organizing a series of carefully crafted and well-timed spectacles—wild-beast hunts, extravagant gladiator shows, theatrical contests. On several occasions, he paid for these spectacles out of his own pocket. To the common man, Julius Caesar became indelibly associated with these much-loved events. As he slowly rose to attain the position of consul, his popularity among the masses served as the foundation of his power. He had created an image of himself as a great public showman.

In 49 B.C., Rome was on the brink of a civil war between rival leaders, Caesar and Pompey. At the height of the tension, Caesar, an addict of the stage, attended a theatrical performance, and afterward, lost in thought, he wandered in the darkness back to his camp at the Rubicon, the river that divides Italy from Gaul, where he had been campaigning. To march his army back into Italy across the Rubicon would mean the beginning of a war with Pompey.

Before his staff Caesar argued both sides, forming the options like an actor on stage, a precursor of Hamlet. Finally, to put his soliloquy to an end, he pointed to a seemingly innocent apparition at the edge of the river—a very tall soldier blasting a call on a trumpet, then going across a bridge over the Rubicon—and pronounced, "Let us accept this as a sign from the Gods and follow where they beckon, in vengeance on our double-dealing enemies. The die is cast." All of this he spoke portentously and dramatically, gesturing toward the river and looking his generals in the eye. He knew that these generals were uncertain in their support, but his oratory overwhelmed them with a sense of the drama of the moment, and of the need to seize the time. A more prosaic speech would never have had the same effect. The generals rallied to his cause; Caesar and his army crossed the Rubicon and by the following year had vanquished Pompey, making Caesar dictator of Rome.

In warfare, Caesar always played the leading man with gusto. He was as skilled a horseman as any of his soldiers, and took pride in outdoing them in feats of bravery and endurance. He entered battle astride the strongest mount, so that his soldiers would see him in the thick of battle, urging them on, always positioning himself in the center, a godlike symbol of power and a model for them to follow. Of all the armies in Rome, Caesar's was the most devoted and loyal. His soldiers, like the common people who had attended his entertainments, had come to identify with him and with his cause.

After the defeat of Pompey, the entertainments grew in scale. Nothing like them had ever been seen in Rome. The chariot races became more spectacular, the gladiator fights more dramatic, as Caesar staged fights to the death among the Roman nobility. He organized enormous mock naval battles on an artificial lake. Plays were performed in every Roman ward. A

The man who intends to make his fortune in this ancient capital of the world [Rome] must be a chameleon susceptible of reflecting the colors of the atmosphere that surrounds him—a Proteus apt to assume every form, every shape. He must be supple, flexible, insinuating, close, inscrutable, often base, sometimes sincere, sometimes perfidious, always concealing a part of his knowledge, indulging in but one tone of voice, patient, a perfect master of his own countenance, as cold as ice when any other man would be all fire; and if unfortunately he is not religious at heart—a very common occurrence for a soul possessing the above requisites— he must have religion in his mind, that is to say, on his face, on his lips, in his manners; he must suffer quietly, if he be an honest man, the necessity of knowing himself an arrant hypocrite. The man whose soul would loathe such a life should leave Rome and seek his fortune elsewhere. I do not know whether I am praising or excusing myself, but of all those qualities I possessed but one— namely, flexibility.

MEMOIRS,
GIOVANNI CASANOVA,
1725–1798

giant new theater was built that sloped dramatically down the Tarpeian Rock. Crowds from all over the empire flocked to these events, the roads to Rome lined with visitors' tents. And in 45 B.C., timing his entry into the city for maximum effect and surprise, Caesar brought Cleopatra back to Rome after his Egyptian campaign, and staged even more extravagant public spectacles.

These events were more than devices to divert the masses; they dramatically enhanced the public's sense of Caesar's character, and made him seem larger than life. Caesar was the master of his public image, of which he was forever aware. When he appeared before crowds he wore the most spectacular purple robes. He would be upstaged by no one. He was notoriously vain about his appearance—it was said that one reason he enjoyed being honored by the Senate and people was that on these occasions he could wear a laurel wreath, hiding his baldness. Caesar was a masterful orator. He knew how to say a lot by saying a little, intuited the moment to end a speech for maximum effect. He never failed to incorporate a surprise into his public appearances—a startling announcement that would heighten their drama.

Immensely popular among the Roman people, Caesar was hated and feared by his rivals. On the ides of March—March 15—in the year 44 B.C., a group of conspirators led by Brutus and Cassius surrounded him in the senate and stabbed him to death. Even dying, however, he kept his sense of drama. Drawing the top of his gown over his face, he let go of the cloth's lower part so that it draped his legs, allowing him to die covered and decent. According to the Roman historian Suetonius, his final words to his old friend Brutus, who was about to deliver a second blow, were in Greek, and as if rehearsed for the end of a play: "You too, my child?"

Interpretation

The Roman theater was an event for the masses, attended by crowds unimaginable today. Packed into enormous auditoriums, the audience would be amused by raucous comedy or moved by high tragedy. Theater seemed to contain the essence of life, in its concentrated, dramatic form. Like a religious ritual, it had a powerful, instant appeal to the common man.

Julius Caesar was perhaps the first public figure to understand the vital link between power and theater. This was because of his own obsessive interest in drama. He sublimated this interest by making himself an actor and director on the world stage. He said his lines as if they had been scripted; he gestured and moved through a crowd with a constant sense of how he appeared to his audience. He incorporated surprise into his repertoire, building drama into his speeches, staging into his public appearances. His gestures were broad enough for the common man to grasp them instantly. He became immensely popular.

Caesar set the ideal for all leaders and people of power. Like him, you must learn to enlarge your actions through dramatic techniques such as surprise, suspense, the creation of sympathy, and symbolic identification. Also like him, you must be constantly aware of your audience—of what will please them and what will bore them. You must arrange to place yourself at the center, to command attention, and never to be upstaged at any cost.

OBSERVANCE OF THE LAW II

In the year 1831, a young woman named Aurore Dupin Dudevant left her husband and family in the provinces and moved to Paris. She wanted to be a writer; marriage, she felt, was worse than prison, for it left her neither the time nor the freedom to pursue her passion. In Paris she would establish her independence and make her living by writing.

Soon after Dudevant arrived in the capital, however, she had to confront certain harsh realities. To have any degree of freedom in Paris you had to have money. For a woman, money could only come through marriage or prostitution. No woman had ever come close to making a living by writing. Women wrote as a hobby, supported by their husbands, or by an inheritance. In fact when Dudevant first showed her writing to an editor, he told her, "You should make babies, Madame, not literature."

Clearly Dudevant had come to Paris to attempt the impossible. In the end, though, she came up with a strategy to do what no woman had ever done—a strategy to re-create herself completely, forging a public image of her own making. Women writers before her had been forced into a ready-made role, that of the second-rate artist who wrote mostly for other women. Dudevant decided that if she had to play a role, she would turn the game around: She would play the part of a man.

In 1832 a publisher accepted Dudevant's first major novel, *Indiana*. She had chosen to publish it under a pseudonym, "George Sand," and all of Paris assumed this impressive new writer was male. Dudevant had sometimes worn men's clothes before creating "George Sand" (she had always found men's shirts and riding breeches more comfortable); now, as a public figure, she exaggerated the image. She added long men's coats, gray hats, heavy boots, and dandyish cravats to her wardrobe. She smoked cigars and in conversation expressed herself like a man, unafraid to dominate the conversation or to use a saucy word.

This strange "male/female" writer fascinated the public. And unlike other women writers, Sand found herself accepted into the clique of male artists. She drank and smoked with them, even carried on affairs with the most famous artists of Europe—Musset, Liszt, Chopin. It was she who did the wooing, and also the abandoning—she moved on at her discretion.

Those who knew Sand well understood that her male persona protected her from the public's prying eyes. Out in the world, she enjoyed playing the part to the extreme; in private she remained herself. She also realized that the character of "George Sand" could grow stale or predictable, and to avoid this she would every now and then dramatically alter the character she had created; instead of conducting affairs with famous men, she would begin meddling in politics, leading demonstrations, inspiring student rebellions. No one would dictate to her the limits of the character she had created. Long after she died, and after most people had stopped reading her novels, the larger-than-life theatricality of that character has continued to fascinate and inspire.

Interpretation

Throughout Sand's public life, acquaintances and other artists who spent time in her company had the feeling they were in the presence of a man. But in her journals and to her closest friends, such as Gustave Flaubert, she confessed that she had no desire to be a man, but was playing a part for public consumption. What she really wanted was the power to determine her own character. She refused the limits her society would have set on her. She did not attain her power, however, by being herself; instead she created a persona that she could constantly adapt to her own desires, a persona that attracted attention and gave her presence.

Understand this: The world wants to assign you a role in life. And once you accept that role you are doomed. Your power is limited to the tiny amount allotted to the role you have selected or have been forced to assume. An actor, on the other hand, plays many roles. Enjoy that protean power, and if it is beyond you, at least forge a new identity, one of your own making, one that has had no boundaries assigned to it by an envious and resentful world. This act of defiance is Promethean: It makes you responsible for your own creation.

Your new identity will protect you from the world precisely because it is not "you"; it is a costume you put on and take off. You need not take it personally. And your new identity sets you apart, gives you theatrical presence. Those in the back rows can see you and hear you. Those in the front rows marvel at your audacity.

Do not people talk in society of a man being a great actor? They do not mean by that that he feels, but that he excels in simulating, though he feels nothing.
Denis Diderot, 1713–1784

KEYS TO POWER

The character you seem to have been born with is not necessarily who you are; beyond the characteristics you have inherited, your parents, your friends, and your peers have helped to shape your personality. The Promethean task of the powerful is to take control of the process, to stop allowing others that ability to limit and mold them. Remake yourself into a character of power. Working on yourself like clay should be one of your greatest and most pleasurable life tasks. It makes you in essence an artist— an artist creating yourself.

In fact, the idea of self-creation comes from the world of art. For thousands of years, only kings and the highest courtiers had the freedom to shape their public image and determine their own identity. Similarly, only kings and the wealthiest lords could contemplate their own image in art, and consciously alter it. The rest of mankind played the limited role that society demanded of them, and had little self-consciousness.

A shift in this condition can be detected in Velázquez's painting *Las Meninas,* made in 1656. The artist appears at the left of the canvas, standing before a painting that he is in the process of creating, but that has its back to us—we cannot see it. Beside him stands a princess, her attendants, and one of the court dwarves, all watching him work. The people posing for the painting are not directly visible, but we can see them in tiny reflections in a mirror on the back wall—the king and queen of Spain, who must be sitting somewhere in the foreground, outside the picture.

The painting represents a dramatic change in the dynamics of power and the ability to determine one's own position in society. For Velázquez, the artist, is far more prominently positioned than the king and queen. In a sense he is more powerful than they are, since he is clearly the one controlling the image—*their* image. Velázquez no longer saw himself as the slavish, dependent artist. He had remade himself into a man of power. And indeed the first people other than aristocrats to play openly with their image in Western society were artists and writers, and later on dandies and bohemians. Today the concept of self-creation has slowly filtered down to the rest of society, and has become an ideal to aspire to. Like Velázquez, you must demand for yourself the power to determine your position in the painting, and to create your own image.

The first step in the process of self-creation is self-consciousness—being aware of yourself as an actor and taking control of your appearance and emotions. As Diderot said, the bad actor is the one who is always sincere. People who wear their hearts on their sleeves out in society are tiresome and embarrassing. Their sincerity notwithstanding, it is hard to take them seriously. Those who cry in public may temporarily elicit sympathy, but sympathy soon turns to scorn and irritation at their self-obsessiveness—they are crying to get attention, we feel, and a malicious part of us wants to deny them the satisfaction.

Good actors control themselves better. They can *play* sincere and heartfelt, can affect a tear and a compassionate look at will, but they don't have to feel it. They externalize emotion in a form that others can understand. Method acting is fatal in the real world. No ruler or leader could possibly play the part if all of the emotions he showed had to be real. So learn self-control. Adopt the plasticity of the actor, who can mold his or her face to the emotion required.

The second step in the process of self-creation is a variation on the George Sand strategy: the creation of a memorable character, one that compels attention, that stands out above the other players on the stage. This was the game Abraham Lincoln played. The homespun, common country man, he knew, was a kind of president that America had never had but would delight in electing. Although many of these qualities came naturally to him, he played them up—the hat and clothes, the beard. (No president before him had worn a beard.) Lincoln was also the first president to use photographs to spread his image, helping to create the icon of the "homespun president."

Good drama, however, needs more than an interesting appearance, or a single stand-out moment. Drama takes place over time—it is an unfolding event. Rhythm and timing are critical. One of the most important elements in the rhythm of drama is suspense. Houdini for instance, could sometimes complete his escape acts in seconds—but he drew them out to minutes, to make the audience sweat.

The key to keeping the audience on the edge of their seats is letting events unfold slowly, then speeding them up at the right moment, according to a pattern and tempo that you control. Great rulers from Napoleon to Mao Tse-tung have used theatrical timing to surprise and divert their public. Franklin Delano Roosevelt understood the importance of staging political events in a particular order and rhythm.

At the time of his 1932 presidential election, the United States was in the midst of a dire economic crisis. Banks were failing at an alarming rate. Shortly after winning the election, Roosevelt went into a kind of retreat. He said nothing about his plans or his cabinet appointments. He even refused to meet the sitting president, Herbert Hoover, to discuss the transition. By the time of Roosevelt's inauguration the country was in a state of high anxiety.

In his inaugural address, Roosevelt shifted gears. He made a powerful speech, making it clear that he intended to lead the country in a completely new direction, sweeping away the timid gestures of his predecessors. From then on the pace of his speeches and public decisions—cabinet appointments, bold legislation—unfolded at an incredibly rapid rate. The period after the inauguration became known as the "Hundred Days," and its success in altering the country's mood partly stemmed from Roosevelt's clever pacing and use of dramatic contrast. He held his audience in suspense, then hit them with a series of bold gestures that seemed all the more momentous because they came from nowhere. You must learn to orchestrate events in a similar manner, never revealing all your cards at once, but unfolding them in a way that heightens their dramatic effect.

Besides covering a multitude of sins, good drama can also confuse and deceive your enemy. During World War II, the German playwright Bertolt Brecht worked in Hollywood as a screenwriter. After the war he was called before the House Committee on Un-American Activities for his supposed Communist sympathies. Other writers who had been called to testify planned to humiliate the committee members with an angry emotional stand. Brecht was wiser: He would play the committee like a violin, charming them while fooling them as well. He carefully rehearsed his responses, and brought along some props, notably a cigar on which he puffed away, knowing the head of the committee liked cigars. And indeed he proceeded to beguile the committee with well-crafted responses that were ambiguous, funny, and double-edged. Instead of an angry, heartfelt tirade, he ran circles around them with a staged production, and they let him off scot-free.

Other dramatic effects for your repertoire include the beau geste, an action at a climactic moment that symbolizes your triumph or your boldness. Caesar's dramatic crossing of the Rubicon was a *beau geste*—a move that dazzled the soldiers and gave him heroic proportions. You must also appreciate the importance of stage entrances and exits. When Cleopatra first met Caesar in Egypt, she arrived rolled up in a carpet, which she arranged to have unfurled at his feet. George Washington twice left power with flourish and fanfare (first as a general, then as a president who refused to sit for a third term), showing he knew how to make the moment count, dramatically and symbolically. Your own entrances and exits should be crafted and planned as carefully.

Remember that overacting can be counterproductive—it is another way of spending too much effort trying to attract attention. The actor Richard Burton discovered early in his career that by standing totally still onstage, he drew attention to himself and away from the other actors. It is less what you do that matters, clearly, than how you do it—your gracefulness and imposing stillness on the social stage count for more than overdoing your part and moving around too much.

Finally: Learn to play many roles, to be whatever the moment requires. Adapt your mask to the situation—be protean in the faces you wear. Bismarck played this game to perfection: To a liberal he was a liberal, to a hawk he was a hawk. He could not be grasped, and what cannot be grasped cannot be consumed.

I m a g e :
The Greek Sea-God Proteus.
His power came from his ability to
change shape at will, to be whatever the
moment required. When Menelaus, brother
of Agamemnon, tried to seize him, Proteus
transformed himself into a lion, then a serpent, a
panther, a boar, running water, and finally a leafy tree.

Authority: Know how to be all things to all men. A discreet Proteus—a scholar among scholars, a saint among saints. That is the art of winning over everyone, for like attracts like. Take note of temperaments and adapt yourself to that of each person you meet—follow the lead of the serious and jovial in turn, changing your mood discreetly. (Baltasar Gracián, 1601–1658)

REVERSAL

There can really be no reversal to this critical law: Bad theater is bad theater. Even appearing natural requires art—in other words, acting. Bad acting only creates embarrassment. Of course you should not be *too* dramatic—avoid the histrionic gesture. But that is simply bad theater anyway, since it violates centuries-old dramatic laws against overacting. In essence there is no reversal to this law.

KEEP YOUR HANDS CLEAN

JUDGMENT

You must seem a paragon of civility and efficiency: Your hands are never soiled by mistakes and nasty deeds. Maintain such a spotless appearance by using others as scapegoats and cat's-paws to disguise your involvement.

PART I: CONCEAL YOUR MISTAKES—
HAVE A SCAPEGOAT AROUND TO TAKE THE BLAME

Our good name and reputation depend more on what we conceal than on what we reveal. Everyone makes mistakes, but those who are truly clever manage to hide them, and to make sure someone else is blamed. A convenient scapegoat should always be kept around for such moments.

OBSERVANCE OF THE LAW I

Near the end of the second century A.D., as China's mighty Han Empire slowly collapsed, the great general and imperial minister Ts'ao Ts'ao emerged as the most powerful man in the country. Seeking to extend his power base and to rid himself of the last of his rivals, Ts'ao Ts'ao began a campaign to take control of the strategically vital Central Plain. During the siege of a key city, he slightly miscalculated the timing for supplies of grain to arrive from the capital. As he waited for the shipment to come in, the army ran low on food, and Ts'ao Ts'ao was forced to order the chief of commissariat to reduce its rations.

Ts'ao Ts'ao kept a tight rein on the army, and ran a network of informers. His spies soon reported that the men were complaining, grumbling that he was living well while they themselves had barely enough to eat. Perhaps Ts'ao Ts'ao was keeping the food for himself, they murmured. If the grumbling spread, Ts'ao Ts'ao could have a mutiny on his hands. He summoned the chief of commissariat to his tent.

"I want to ask you to lend me something, and you must not refuse," Ts'ao Ts'ao told the chief. "What is it?" the chief replied. "I want the loan of your head to show to the troops," said Ts'ao Ts'ao. "But I've done nothing wrong!" cried the chief. "I know," said Ts'ao Ts'ao with a sigh, "but if I do not put you to death, there will be a mutiny. Do not grieve—after you're gone, I'll look after your family." Put this way, the request left the chief no choice, so he resigned himself to his fate and was beheaded that very day. Seeing his head on public display, the soldiers stopped grumbling. Some saw through Ts'ao Ts'ao's gesture, but kept quiet, stunned and intimidated by his violence. And most accepted his version of who was to blame, preferring to believe in his wisdom and fairness than in his incompetence and cruelty.

Interpretation

Ts'ao Ts'ao came to power in an extremely tumultuous time. In the struggle for supremacy in the crumbling Han Empire, enemies had emerged from all sides. The battle for the Central Plain had proven more difficult than he imagined, and money and provisions were a constant concern. No wonder that under such stress, he had forgotten to order supplies in time.

Once it became clear that the delay was a critical mistake, and that the army was seething with mutiny, Ts'ao Ts'ao had two options: apology and excuses, or a scapegoat. Understanding the workings of power and the im-

CHELM JUSTICE

A great calamity befell the town of Chelm one day. The town cobbler murdered one of his customers. So he was brought before the judge, who sentenced him to die by hanging. When the verdict was read a townsman arose and cried out, "If your Honor pleases—you have sentenced to death the town cobbler! He's the only one we've got. If you hang him who will mend our shoes?" "Who? Who?" cried all the people of Chelm with one voice.
The judge nodded in agreement and reconsidered his verdict. "Good people of Chelm," he said, "what you say is true. Since we have only one cobbler it would be a great wrong against the community to let him die. As there are two roofers in the town let one of them be hanged instead."

A TREASURY OF JEWISH FOLKLORE,
NATHAN AUSUBEL, ED.,
1948

portance of appearances as he did, Ts'ao Ts'ao did not hesitate for a moment: He shopped around for the most convenient head and had it served up immediately.

Occasional mistakes are inevitable—the world is just too unpredictable. People of power, however, are undone not by the mistakes they make, but by the way they deal with them. Like surgeons, they must cut away the tumor with speed and finality. Excuses and apologies are much too blunt tools for this delicate operation; the powerful avoid them. By apologizing you open up all sorts of doubts about your competence, your intentions, any other mistakes you may not have confessed. Excuses satisfy no one and apologies make everyone uncomfortable. The mistake does not vanish with an apology; it deepens and festers. Better to cut it off instantly, distract attention from yourself, and focus attention on a convenient scapegoat before people have time to ponder your responsibility or your possible incompetence.

I would rather betray the whole world than let the world betray me.
General Ts'ao Ts'ao, c.A.D., 155–220

OBSERVANCE OF THE LAW II

For several years Cesare Borgia campaigned to gain control of large parts of Italy in the name of his father, Pope Alexander. In the year 1500 he managed to take Romagna, in northern Italy. The region had for years been ruled by a series of greedy masters who had plundered its wealth for themselves. Without police or any disciplining force, it had descended into lawlessness, whole areas being ruled by robbers and feuding families. To establish order, Cesare appointed a lieutenant general of the region—Remirro de Orco, "a cruel and vigorous man," according to Niccolò Machiavelli. Cesare gave de Orco absolute powers.

With energy and violence, de Orco established a severe, brutal justice in Romagna, and soon rid it of almost all of its lawless elements. But in his zeal he sometimes went too far, and after a couple of years the local population resented and even hated him. In December of 1502, Cesare took decisive action. He first let it be known that he had not approved of de Orco's cruel and violent deeds, which stemmed from the lieutenant's brutal nature. Then, on December 22, he imprisoned de Orco in the town of Cesena, and the day after Christmas the townspeople awoke to find a strange spectacle in the middle of the piazza: de Orco's headless body, dressed in a lavish suit with a purple cape, the head impaled beside it on a pike, the bloody knife and executioner's block laid out beside the head. As Machiavelli concluded his comments on the affair, "The ferocity of this scene left the people at once stunned and satisfied."

Interpretation

Cesare Borgia was a master player in the game of power. Always planning several moves ahead, he set his opponents the cleverest traps. For this Machiavelli honored him above all others in *The Prince*.

Cesare foresaw the future with amazing clarity in Romagna: Only brutal justice would bring order to the region. The process would take several years, and at first the people would welcome it. But it would soon make many enemies, and the citizens would come to resent the imposition of such unforgiving justice, especially by outsiders. Cesare himself, then, could not be seen as the agent of this justice—the people's hatred would cause too many problems in the future. And so he chose the one man who could do the dirty work, knowing in advance that once the task was done he would have to display de Orco's head on a pike. The scapegoat in this case had been planned from the beginning.

With Ts'ao Ts'ao, the scapegoat was an entirely innocent man; in the Romagna, he was the offensive weapon in Cesare's arsenal that let him get the dirty work done without bloodying his own hands. With this second kind of scapegoat it is wise to separate yourself from the hatchet man at some point, either leaving him dangling in the wind or, like Cesare, even making yourself the one to bring him to justice. Not only are you free of involvement in the problem, you can appear as the one who cleaned it up.

> *The Athenians regularly maintained a number of degraded and useless*
> *beings at the public expense; and when any calamity, such as plague,*
> *drought, or famine, befell the city . . . [these scapegoats] were led about . . .*
> *and then sacrificed, apparently by being stoned outside the city.*
> The Golden Bough, *Sir James George Frazer, 1854–1941*

KEYS TO POWER

The use of scapegoats is as old as civilization itself, and examples of it can be found in cultures around the world. The main idea behind these sacrifices is the shifting of guilt and sin to an outside figure—object, animal, or man—which is then banished or destroyed. The Hebrews used to take a live goat (hence the term "scapegoat") upon whose head the priest would lay both hands while confessing the sins of the Children of Israel. Having thus had those sins transferred to it, the beast would be led away and abandoned in the wilderness. With the Athenians and the Aztecs, the scapegoat was human, often a person fed and raised for the purpose. Since famine and plague were thought to be visited on humans by the gods, in punishment for wrongdoing, the people suffered not only from the famine and plague themselves but from blame and guilt. They freed themselves of guilt by transferring it to an innocent person, whose death was intended to satisfy the divine powers and banish the evil from their midst.

It is an extremely human response to not look inward after a mistake or crime, but rather to look outward and to affix blame and guilt on a convenient object. When the plague was ravaging Thebes, Oedipus looked everywhere for its cause, everywhere except inside himself and his own sin of incest, which had so offended the gods and occasioned the plague. This profound need to exteriorize one's guilt, to project it on another person or object, has an immense power, which the clever know how to harness. Sacrifice is a ritual, perhaps the most ancient ritual of all; ritual too is a well-spring of power. In the killing of de Orco, note Cesare's symbolic and ritualistic display of his body. By framing it in this dramatic way he focused guilt outward. The citizens of Romagna responded instantly. Because it comes so naturally to us to look outward rather than inward, we readily accept the scapegoat's guilt.

The bloody sacrifice of the scapegoat seems a barbaric relic of the past, but the practice lives on to this day, if indirectly and symbolically; since power depends on appearances, and those in power must seem never to make mistakes, the use of scapegoats is as popular as ever. What modern leader will take responsibility for his blunders? He searches out others to blame, a scapegoat to sacrifice. When Mao Tse-tung's Cultural Revolution failed miserably, he made no apologies or excuses to the Chinese people; instead, like Ts'ao Ts'ao before him, he offered up scapegoats, including his own personal secretary and high-ranking member of the Party, Ch'en Po-ta.

Franklin D. Roosevelt had a reputation for honesty and fairness. Throughout his career, however, he faced many situations in which being the nice guy would have spelled political disaster—yet he could not be seen as the agent of any foul play. For twenty years, then, his secretary, Louis Howe, played the role de Orco had. *He* handled the backroom deals, the manipulation of the press, the underhanded campaign maneuvers. And whenever a mistake was committed, or a dirty trick contradicting Roosevelt's carefully crafted image became public, Howe served as the scapegoat, and never complained.

Besides conveniently shifting blame, a scapegoat can serve as a warning to others. In 1631 a plot was hatched to oust France's Cardinal Richelieu from power, a plot that became known as "The Day of the Dupes." It almost succeeded, since it involved the upper echelons of government, including the queen mother. But through luck and his own connivances, Richelieu survived.

One of the key conspirators was a man named Marillac, the keeper of the seals. Richelieu could not imprison him without implicating the queen mother, an extremely dangerous tactic, so he targeted Marillac's brother, a marshal in the army. This man had no involvement in the plot. Richelieu, however, afraid that other conspiracies might be in the air, especially in the army, decided to set an example. He tried the brother on trumped-up charges and had him executed. In this way he indirectly punished the real perpetrator, who had thought himself protected, and warned any future conspirators that he would not shrink from sacrificing the innocent to protect his own power.

In fact it is often wise to choose the most innocent victim possible as a sacrificial goat. Such people will not be powerful enough to fight you, and their naive protests may be seen as protesting too much—may be seen, in other words, as a sign of their guilt. Be careful, however, not to create a martyr. It is important that *you* remain the victim, the poor leader betrayed by the incompetence of those around you. If the scapegoat appears too weak and his punishment too cruel, you may end up the victim of your own device. Sometimes you should find a more powerful scapegoat—one who will elicit less sympathy in the long run.

In this vein, history has time and again shown the value of using a close associate as a scapegoat. This is known as the "fall of the favorite." Most kings had a personal favorite at court, a man whom they singled out, sometimes for no apparent reason, and lavished with favors and attention. But this court favorite could serve as a convenient scapegoat in case of a threat to the king's reputation. The public would readily believe in the scapegoat's guilt—why would the king sacrifice his favorite unless he were guilty? And the other courtiers, resentful of the favorite anyway, would rejoice at his downfall. The king, meanwhile, would rid himself of a man who by that time had probably learned too much about him, perhaps becoming arrogant and even disdainful of him. Choosing a close associate as a scapegoat has the same value as the "fall of the favorite." You may lose a friend or aide, but in the long-term scheme of things, it is more important to hide your mistakes than to hold on to someone who one day will probably turn against you. Besides, you can always find a new favorite to take his place.

Image: The Innocent Goat. On the Day of Atonement, the high priest brings the goat into the temple, places his hands on its head, and confesses the people's sins, transferring guilt to the guiltless beast, which is then led to the wilderness and abandoned, the people's sins and blame vanishing with him.

Authority: Folly consists not in committing Folly, but in being incapable of concealing it. All men make mistakes, but the wise conceal the blunders they have made, while fools make them public. Reputation depends more on what is hidden than on what is seen. If you can't be good, be careful. (Baltasar Gracián, 1601–1658)

PART II: MAKE USE OF THE CAT'S-PAW

In the fable, the Monkey grabs the paw of his friend, the Cat, and uses it to fish chestnuts out of the fire, thus getting the nuts he craves, without hurting himself.

If there is something unpleasant or unpopular that needs to be done, it is far too risky for you to do the work yourself. You need a cat's-paw— someone who does the dirty, dangerous work for you. The cat's-paw grabs what you need, hurts whom you need hurt, and keeps people from noticing that you are the one responsible. Let someone else be the executioner, or the bearer of bad news, while you bring only joy and glad tidings.

OBSERVANCE OF THE LAW I

In 59 B.C., the future queen Cleopatra of Egypt, then ten years old, witnessed the overthrow and banishment of her father, Ptolemy XII, at the hand of his elder daughters—her own sisters. One of the daughters, Berenice, emerged as the leader of the rebellion, and to ensure that she would now rule Egypt alone, she imprisoned her other sisters and murdered her own husband. This may have been necessary as a practical step to secure her rule. But that a member of the royal family, a queen no less, would so overtly exact such violence on her own family horrified her subjects and stirred up powerful opposition. Four years later this opposition was able to return Ptolemy to power, and he promptly had Berenice and the other elder sisters beheaded.

In 51 B.C. Ptolemy died, leaving four remaining children as heirs. As was the tradition in Egypt, the eldest son, Ptolemy XIII (only ten at the time), married the elder sister, Cleopatra (now eighteen), and the couple took the throne together as king and queen. None of the four children felt satisfied with this; everyone, including Cleopatra, wanted more power. A struggle emerged between Cleopatra and Ptolemy, each trying to push the other to the side.

In 48 B.C., with the help of a government faction that feared Cleopatra's ambitions, Ptolemy was able to force his sister to flee the country, leaving himself as sole ruler. In exile, Cleopatra schemed. She wanted to rule alone and to restore Egypt to its past glory, a goal she felt none of her other siblings could achieve; yet as long as they were alive, she could not realize her dream. And the example of Berenice had made it clear that no one would serve a queen who was seen murdering her own kind. Even Ptolemy XIII had not dared murder Cleopatra, although he knew she would plot against him from abroad.

Within a year after Cleopatra's banishment, the Roman dictator Julius Caesar arrived in Egypt, determined to make the country a Roman colony. Cleopatra saw her chance: Reentering Egypt in disguise, she traveled hundreds of miles to reach Caesar in Alexandria. Legend has it that she had herself smuggled into his presence rolled up inside a carpet, which was gracefully unfurled at his feet, revealing the young queen. Cleopatra immediately went to work on the Roman. She appealed to his love of spectacle and his interest in Egyptian history, and poured on her feminine charms. Caesar soon succumbed and restored Cleopatra to the throne.

Cleopatra's siblings seethed—she had outmaneuvered them. Ptolemy XIII would not wait to see what happened next: From his palace in Alexandria, he summoned a great army to march on the city and attack Caesar. In response, Caesar immediately put Ptolemy and the rest of the family under house arrest. But Cleopatra's younger sister Arsinoe escaped from the palace and placed herself at the head of the approaching Egyptian troops, proclaiming herself queen of Egypt. Now Cleopatra finally saw her chance: She convinced Caesar to release Ptolemy from house arrest, under the agreement that he would broker a truce. Of course she knew he would do the opposite—that he would fight Arsinoe for control of the Egyptian army. But this was to Cleopatra's benefit, for it would divide the royal family. Better still, it would give Caesar the chance to defeat and kill her siblings in battle.

Reinforced by troops from Rome, Caesar swiftly defeated the rebels. In the Egyptians' retreat, Ptolemy drowned in the Nile. Caesar captured Arsinoe and had her sent to Rome as a prisoner. He also executed the numerous enemies who had conspired against Cleopatra, and imprisoned others who had opposed her. To reinforce her position as uncontested queen, Cleopatra now married the only sibling left, Ptolemy XIV—only eleven at the time, and the weakest of the lot. Four years later Ptolemy mysteriously died, of poison.

In 41 B.C., Cleopatra employed on a second Roman leader, Marc Antony, the same tactics she had used so well on Julius Caesar. After seducing him, she hinted to him that her sister Arsinoe, still a prisoner in Rome, had conspired to destroy him. Marc Antony believed her and promptly had Arsinoe executed, thereby getting rid of the last of the siblings who had posed such a threat to Cleopatra.

Interpretation

Legend has it that Cleopatra succeeded through her seductive charms, but in reality her power came from an ability to get people to do her bidding without realizing they were being manipulated. Caesar and Antony not only rid her of her most dangerous siblings—Ptolemy XIII and Arsinoe— they decimated *all* of her enemies, in both the government and the military. The two men became her cat's-paws. They entered the fire for her, did the ugly but necessary work, while shielding her from appearing as the destroyer of her siblings and fellow Egyptians. And in the end, both men acquiesced to her desire to rule Egypt not as a Roman colony but as an independent allied kingdom. And they did all this for her without realizing how she had manipulated them. This was persuasion of the subtlest and most powerful kind.

THE CROW-HEN, THE COBRA, AND THE JACKAL

Once upon a time there was a crow and his wife who had built a nest in a banyan tree. A big snake crawled into the hollow trunk and ate up the chicks as they were hatched. The crow did not want to move, since he loved the tree dearly. So he went to his friend the jackal for advice. A plan of action was devised. The crow and his wife flew about in implementation. As the wife approached a pond, she saw the women of the king's court bathing, with pearls, necklaces, gems, garments, and a golden chain laying on the shore. The crow-hen seized the golden chain in her beak and flew toward the banyan tree with the eunuchs in pursuit. When she reached the tree, she dropped the chain into the hole. As the kings'

A queen must never dirty her hands with ugly tasks, nor can a king appear in public with blood on his face. Yet power cannot survive without the constant squashing of enemies—there will always be dirty little tasks that have to be done to keep you on the throne. Like Cleopatra, you need a cat's-paw.

This will usually be a person from outside your immediate circle, who will therefore be unlikely to realize how he or she is being used. You will find these dupes everywhere—people who enjoy doing you favors, especially if you throw them a minimal bone or two in exchange. But as they accomplish tasks that may seem to them innocent enough, or at least completely justified, they are actually clearing the field for you, spreading the information you feed them, undermining people they do not realize are your rivals, inadvertently furthering your cause, dirtying their hands while yours remain spotless.

OBSERVANCE OF THE LAW II

In the late 1920s, civil war broke out in China as the Nationalist and Communist parties battled for control of the country. In 1927 Chiang Kai-shek, the Nationalist leader, vowed to kill every last Communist, and over the next few years he nearly accomplished his task, pushing his enemies hard until, in 1934–1935, he forced them into the Long March, a six-thousand-mile retreat from the southeast to the remote northwest, through harsh terrain, in which most of their ranks were decimated. In late 1936 Chiang planned one last offensive to wipe them out, but he was caught in a mutiny: His own soldiers captured him and turned him over to the Communists. Now he could only expect the worst.

Meanwhile, however, the Japanese began an invasion of China, and much to Chiang's surprise, instead of killing him the Communist leader, Mao Tse-tung, proposed a deal: The Communists would let him go, and would recognize him as commander of their forces as well as his, if he would agree to fight alongside them against their common enemy. Chiang had expected torture and execution; now he could not believe his luck. How soft these Reds had become. Without having to fight a rearguard action against the Communists, he knew he could beat the Japanese, and then a few years down the line he would turn around and destroy the Reds with ease. He had nothing to lose and everything to gain by agreeing to their terms.

The Communists proceeded to fight the Japanese in their usual fashion, with hit-and-run guerrilla tactics, while the Nationalists fought a more conventional war. Together, after several years, they succeeded in evicting the Japanese. Now, however, Chiang finally understood what Mao had really planned. His own army had met the brunt of the Japanese artillery, was greatly weakened, and would take a few years to recover. The Communists, meanwhile, had not only avoided any direct hits from the Japanese, they had used the time to recoup their strength, and to spread out and gain pockets of influence all over China. As soon as the war against the Japanese ended, the civil war started again—but this time the Communists enveloped the weakened Nationalists and slowly beat them into submission. The Japanese had served as Mao's cat's-paw, inadvertently ploughing the fields for the Communists and making possible their victory over Chiang Kai-shek.

Interpretation

Most leaders who had taken as powerful an enemy as Chiang Kai-shek prisoner would have made sure to kill him. But in doing so they would have lost the chance Mao exploited. Without the experienced Chiang as leader of the Nationalists, the fight to drive the Japanese out might have lasted much longer, with devastating results. Mao was far too clever to let anger spoil the chance to kill two birds with one stone. In essence, Mao used two cat's-paws to help him attain total victory. First, he cleverly baited Chiang into taking charge of the war against the Japanese. Mao knew the Nationalists led by Chiang would do most of the hard fighting and would succeed in pushing the Japanese out of China, if they did not have to concern themselves with fighting the Communists at the same time. The Nationalists, then, were the first cat's-paw, used to evict the Japanese. But Mao also knew that in the process of leading the war against the invaders, the Japanese artillery and air support would decimate the conventional forces of the Nationalists, doing damage it could take the Communists decades to inflict. Why waste time and lives if the Japanese could do the job quickly? It was this wise policy of using one cat's-paw after another that allowed the Communists to prevail.

There are two uses of the cat's-paw: to save appearances, as Cleopatra did, and to save energy and effort. The latter case in particular demands that you plan several moves in advance, realizing that a temporary move backward (letting Chiang go, say) can lead to a giant leap forward. If you are temporarily weakened and need time to recover, it will often serve you well to use those around you both as a screen to hide your intentions and as a cat's-paw to do your work for you. Look for a powerful third party who shares an enemy with you (if for different reasons), then take advantage of their superior power to deal blows which would have cost you much more energy, since you are weaker. You can even gently guide them into hostilities. Always search out the overly aggressive as potential cat's-paws—they are often more than willing to get into a fight, and you can choose just the right fight for your purposes.

OBSERVANCE OF THE LAW III

Kuriyama Daizen was an adept of Cha-no-yu (Hot Water for Tea, the Japanese tea ceremony) and a student of the teachings of the great tea master Sen no Rikyu. Around 1620 Daizen learned that a friend of his, Hoshino Soemon, had borrowed a large sum of money (300 ryo) to help a

The news of Omar's conversion to Islam was spread everywhere. And that was just what he intended.

THE SUBTLE RUSE: THE BOOK OF ARABIC WISDOM AND GUILE, THIRTEENTH CENTURY

A FOOL AND A WISE MAN

A wise man,
walking alone,
Was being bothered by
a fool throwing stones
at his head.
Turning to face him,
he said:
"My dear chap, well
thrown!
Please accept these
few francs.
You've worked hard
enough to get more
than mere thanks.
Every effort deserves
its reward.
But see that man over
there? He can afford
More than I can.
Present him with some
of your stones: they'll
earn a good wage."
Lured by the bait,
the stupid man
Ran off to repeat
the outrage
On the other worthy
citizen.
This time he wasn't
paid in money
for his stones.
Up rushed
serving-men,
And seized him and
thrashed him and
broke all his bones.
In the courts of kings
there are pests like this,
devoid of sense:
They'll make their

THE INDIAN BIRD

*A merchant kept a bird
in a cage. He was going
to India, the land from
which the bird came,
and asked it whether he
could bring anything
back for it. The bird
asked for its freedom,
but was refused. So he
asked the merchant to
visit a jungle in India
and announce his
captivity to the free
birds who were there.
The merchant did so,
and no sooner had he
spoken when a wild
bird, just like his own,
fell senseless out of a
tree on to the ground.
The merchant thought
that this must be a rela-
tive of his own bird,
and felt sad that he
should have caused this
death.
When he got home, the
bird asked him whether
he had brought good
news from India.
"No," said the
merchant, "I fear that
my news is bad. One of*

relative who had fallen into debt. But although Soemon had managed to bail out his relative, he had simply displaced the burden onto himself. Daizen knew Soemon well—he neither cared nor understood much about money, and could easily get into trouble through slowness in repaying the loan, which had been made by a wealthy merchant called Kawachiya Sanemon. Yet if Daizen offered to help Soemon pay back the loan, he would refuse, out of pride, and might even be offended.

One day Daizen visited his friend, and after touring the garden and looking at Soemon's prized peonies, they retired to his reception room. Here Daizen saw a painting by the master Kano Tennyu. "Ah," Daizen exclaimed, "a splendid piece of painting. . . . I don't know when I have seen anything I like better." After several more bouts of praise, Soemon had no choice: "Well," he said, "since you like it so much, I hope you will do me the favor of accepting it."

At first Daizen refused, but when Soemon insisted he gave in. The next day Soemon in turn received a package from Daizen. Inside it was a beautiful and delicate vase, which Daizen, in an accompanying note, asked his friend to accept as a token of his appreciation for the painting that Soemon had so graciously given him the day before. He explained that the vase had been made by Sen no Rikyu himself, and bore an inscription from Emperor Hideyoshi. If Soemon did not care for the vase, Daizen suggested, he might make a gift of it to an adherent of Cha-no-yu—perhaps the merchant Kawachiya Sanemon, who had often expressed a desire to possess it. "I hear," Daizen continued, "he has a fine piece of fancy paper [the 300-ryo I.O.U.] which you would much like. It is possible you might arrange an exchange."

Realizing what his gracious friend was up to, Soemon took the vase to the wealthy lender. "However did you get this," exclaimed Sanemon, when Soemon showed him the vase. "I have often heard of it, but this is the first time I have ever seen it. It is such a treasure that it is never allowed outside the gate!" He instantly offered to exchange the debt note for the flower vase, and to give Soemon 300 ryo more on top of it. But Soemon, who did not care for money, only wanted the debt note back, and Sanemon gladly gave it to him. Then Soemon immediately hurried to Daizen's house to thank him for his clever support.

Interpretation

Kuriyama Daizen understood that the granting of a favor is never simple: If it is done with fuss and obviousness, its receiver feels burdened by an obligation. This may give the doer a certain power, but it is a power that will eventually self-destruct, for it will stir up resentment and resistance. A favor done indirectly and elegantly has ten times more power. Daizen knew a direct approach would only have offended Soemon. By letting his friend give him the painting, however, he made Soemon feel that he too had pleased his friend with a gift. In the end, all three parties emerged from the encounter feeling fulfilled in their own way.

In essence, Daizen made himself the cat's-paw, the tool to take the chestnuts out of the fire. He must have felt some pain in losing the vase, but he gained not only the painting but, more important, the power of the courtier. The courtier uses his gloved hand to soften any blows against him, disguise his scars, and make the act of rescue more elegant and clean. By helping others, the courtier eventually helps himself. Daizen's example provides the paradigm for every favor done between friends and peers: never impose your favors. Search out ways to make yourself the cat's-paw, indirectly extricating your friends from distress without imposing yourself or making them feel obligated to you.

One should not be too straightforward. Go and see the forest.
The straight trees are cut down, the crooked ones are left standing.
Kautilya, Indian philosopher, third century B.C.

KEYS TO POWER

As a leader you may imagine that constant diligence, and the appearance of working harder than anyone else, signify power. Actually, though, they have the opposite effect: They imply weakness. Why are you working so hard? Perhaps you are incompetent, and have to put in extra effort just to keep up; perhaps you are one of those people who does not know how to delegate, and has to meddle in everything. The truly powerful, on the other hand, seem never to be in a hurry or overburdened. While others work their fingers to the bone, they take their leisure. They know how to find the right people to put in the effort while they save their energy and keep their hands out of the fire. Similarly, you may believe that by taking on the dirty work yourself, involving yourself directly in unpleasant actions, you impose your power and instill fear. In fact you make yourself look ugly, and abusive of your high position. Truly powerful people keep their hands clean. Only good things surround them, and the only announcements they make are of glorious achievements.

You will often find it necessary, of course, to expend energy, or to effect an evil but necessary action. But you must never appear to be this action's agent. Find a cat's-paw. Develop the arts of finding, using, and, in time, getting rid of these people when their cat's-paw role has been fulfilled.

On the eve of an important river battle, the great third-century Chinese strategist Chuko Liang found himself falsely accused of secretly working for the other side. As proof of his loyalty, his commander ordered him to produce 100,000 arrows for the army within three days, or be put to death. Instead of trying to manufacture the arrows, an impossible task, Liang took a dozen boats and had bundles of straw lashed to their sides. In the late afternoon, when mist always blanketed the river, he floated the boats toward the enemy camp. Fearing a trap from the wily Chuko Liang, the enemy did not attack the barely visible boats with boats of their own,

your relations collapsed and fell at my feet when I mentioned your captivity."
As soon as these words were spoken the merchant's bird collapsed and fell to the bottom of the cage. "The news of his kinsman's death has killed him, too," thought the merchant. Sorrowfully he picked up the bird and put it on the windowsill. At once the bird revived and flew to a nearby tree. "Now you know," the bird said, "that what you thought was disaster was in fact good news for me. And how the message, the suggestion of how to behave in order to free myself, was transmitted to me through you, my captor." And he flew away, free at last.

TALES OF THE DERVISHES, IDRIES SHAH, 1967

*At the turn of the year,
when kings take the
field, David sent Joab
out with his other offi-
cers and all the Israelite
forces, and they
ravaged Ammon and
laid siege to Rabbah,
while David remained
in Jerusalem. One
evening David got up
from his couch and, as
he walked about on the
roof of the palace, he
saw from there a
woman bathing and
she was very beautiful.
He sent to inquire who
she was, and the answer
came, "It must be
Bathsheba, daughter of
Eliam and wife of
Uriah the Hittite. . . ."
David wrote a letter to
Joab and sent Uriah
with it. He wrote in the
letter: "Put Uriah
opposite the enemy
where the fighting is
fiercest and then fall
back, and leave him to
meet his death." . . .
Joab . . . stationed
Uriah at a point where
he knew they would
put up a stout fight. The
men of the city sallied
out and engaged Joab,
and some of David's
guards fell; Uriah the
Hittite was also killed.
Joab sent David a
dispatch with all the
news of the battle. . . .
When Uriah's wife
heard that her husband
was dead, she mourned
for him; and when the
period of mourning
was over, David sent
for her and brought her
into his house. She
became his wife and
bore him a son.*

OLD TESTAMENT,
2 SAMUEL, 11–12

but showered them with arrows from the bank. As Liang's boats inched closer, they redoubled the rain of arrows, which stuck in the thick straw. After several hours, the men hiding on board sailed the vessels quickly downstream, where Chuko Liang met them and collected his 100,000 arrows.

Chuko Liang would never do work that others could do for him—he was always thinking up tricks like this one. The key to planning such a strategy is the ability to think far ahead, to imagine ways in which other people can be baited into doing the job for you.

An essential element in making this strategy work is to disguise your goal, shrouding it in mystery, like the strange enemy boats appearing dimly in the mist. When your rivals cannot be sure what you are after, they will react in ways that often work against them in the long run. In fact they will become your cat's-paws. If you disguise your intentions, it is much easier to guide them into moves that accomplish exactly what you want done, but prefer not to do yourself. This may require planning several moves in advance, like a billiard ball that bounces off the sides a few times before heading into the right pocket.

The early-twentieth-century American con artist Yellow Kid Weil knew that no matter how skillfully he homed in on the perfect wealthy sucker, if he, a stranger, approached this man directly, the sucker might become suspicious. So Weil would find someone the sucker already knew to serve as a cat's-paw—someone lower on the totem pole who was himself an unlikely target, and would therefore be less suspicious. Weil would interest this man in a scheme promising incredible wealth. Convinced the scheme was for real, the cat's-paw would often suggest, without prompting, that his boss or wealthy friend should get involved: Having more cash to invest, this man would increase the size of the pot, making bigger bucks for all concerned. The cat's-paw would then involve the wealthy sucker who had been Weil's target all along, but who would not suspect a trap, since it was his trusty subordinate who had roped him in. Devices like this are often the best way to approach a person of power: Use an associate or subordinate to hook you up with your primary target. The cat's-paw establishes your credibility and shields you from the unsavory appearance of being too pushy in your courtship.

The easiest and most effective way to use a cat's-paw is often to plant information with him that he will then spread to your primary target. False or planted information is a powerful tool, especially if spread by a dupe whom no one suspects. You will find it very easy to play innocent and disguise yourself as the source.

The strategic therapist Dr. Milton H. Erickson would often encounter among his patients a married couple in which the wife wanted the therapy but the husband absolutely refused it. Rather than wasting energy trying to deal with the man directly, Dr. Erickson would see the wife alone, and as she talked he would interject interpretations of the husband's behavior that he knew would rile the husband up if he heard them. Sure enough, the wife would tell her husband what the doctor had said. After a few weeks the husband would be so furious he would insist on joining his wife in the sessions so he could set the doctor straight.

Finally, you may well find cases in which deliberately offering yourself as the cat's-paw will ultimately gain you great power. This is the ruse of the perfect courtier. Its symbol is Sir Walter Raleigh, who once placed his own cloak on the muddy ground so that Queen Elizabeth would not sully her shoes. As the instrument that protects a master or peer from unpleasantness or danger, you gain immense respect, which sooner or later will pay dividends. And remember: If you can make your assistance subtle and gracious rather than boastful and burdensome, your recompense will be that much the more satisfying and powerful.

Image: The Cat's-Paw.
It has long claws to grab
things. It is soft and
padded. Take hold of the cat
and use its paw to pluck
things out of the fire, to claw
your enemy, to play with the
mouse before devouring it.
Sometimes you hurt the
cat, but most often it
doesn't feel a thing.

Authority: Do everything pleasant yourself, everything unpleasant through third parties. By adopting the first course you win favor, by taking the second you deflect ill will. Important affairs often require rewards and punishments. Let only the good come from you and the evil from others. (Baltasar Gracián, 1601–1658)

REVERSAL

The cat's-paw and the scapegoat must be used with extreme caution and delicacy. They are like screens that hide your own involvement in dirty work from the public; if at any moment the screen is lifted and you are seen as the manipulator, the puppet master, the whole dynamic turns around—your hand will be seen everywhere, and you will be blamed for misfortunes you may have had nothing to do with. Once the truth is revealed, events will snowball beyond your control.

In 1572, Queen Catherine de' Médicis of France conspired to do away with Gaspard de Coligny, an admiral in the French navy and a leading member of the Huguenot (French Protestant) community. Coligny was close to Catherine's son, Charles IX, and she feared his growing influence on the young king. So she arranged for a member of the Guise family, one of the most powerful royal clans in France, to assassinate him.

Secretly, however, Catherine had another plan: She wanted the Huguenots to blame the Guises for killing one of their leaders, and to take revenge. With one blow, she would erase or injure two threatening rivals, Coligny and the Guise family. Yet both plans went awry. The assassin missed his target, only wounding Coligny; knowing Catherine as his enemy, he strongly suspected it was she who had set up the attack on him, and he told the king so. Eventually the failed assassination and the arguments that ensued from it set off a chain of events that led to a bloody civil war between Catholics and Protestants, culminating in the horrifying Massacre of St. Bartholomew's Eve, in which thousands of Protestants were killed.

If you have to use a cat's-paw or a scapegoat in an action of great consequence, be very careful: Too much can go wrong. It is often wiser to use such dupes in more innocent endeavors, where mistakes or miscalculations will cause no serious harm.

Finally, there are moments when it is advantageous to not disguise your involvement or responsibility, but rather to take the blame yourself for some mistake. If you have power and are secure in it, you should sometimes play the penitent: With a sorrowful look, you ask for forgiveness from those weaker than you. It is the ploy of the king who makes a show of his own sacrifices for the good of the people. Similarly, upon occasion you may want to appear as the agent of punishment in order to instill fear and trembling in your subordinates. Instead of the cat's-paw you show your own mighty hand as a threatening gesture. Play such a card sparingly. If you play it too often, fear will turn into resentment and hatred. Before you know it, such emotions will spark a vigorous opposition that will someday bring you down. Get in the habit of using a cat's-paw—it is far safer.

27

PLAY ON PEOPLE'S NEED

TO BELIEVE TO CREATE A

CULTLIKE FOLLOWING

JUDGMENT

People have an overwhelming desire to believe in something. Become the focal point of such desire by offering them a cause, a new faith to follow. Keep your words vague but full of promise; emphasize enthusiasm over rationality and clear thinking. Give your new disciples rituals to perform, ask them to make sacrifices on your behalf. In the absence of organized religion and grand causes, your new belief system will bring you untold power.

THE SCIENCE OF CHARLATANISM,
OR HOW TO CREATE A CULT IN FIVE EASY STEPS

It was to the charlatan's advantage that the individuals predisposed to credulity should multiply, that the groups of his adherents should enlarge to mass proportions, guaranteeing an ever greater scope for his triumphs. And this was in fact to occur, as science was popularized, from the Renaissance on down through succeeding centuries. With the immense growth of knowledge and its spread through printing in modern times, the mass of the half educated, the eagerly gullible prey of the quack, also increased, became indeed a majority; real power could be based on their wishes, opinions, preferences, and rejections. The charlatan's empire accordingly widened with the modern dissemination of knowledge; since he operated on the basis of science, however much he perverted it, producing gold with a technique borrowed from chemistry and his wonderful balsams with the apparatus of medicine, he could not appeal to an entirely ignorant folk. The illiterate would be protected against his absurdities by their healthy common sense. His choicest audience would be composed of the semiliterate, those who had exchanged their common sense for a little distorted information and had

In searching, as you must, for the methods that will gain you the most power for the least effort, you will find the creation of a cultlike following one of the most effective. Having a large following opens up all sorts of possibilities for deception; not only will your followers worship you, they will defend you from your enemies and will voluntarily take on the work of enticing others to join your fledgling cult. This kind of power will lift you to another realm: You will no longer have to struggle or use subterfuge to enforce your will. You are adored and can do no wrong.

You might think it a gargantuan task to create such a following, but in fact it is fairly simple. As humans, we have a desperate need to believe in something, anything. This makes us eminently gullible: We simply cannot endure long periods of doubt, or of the emptiness that comes from a lack of something to believe in. Dangle in front of us some new cause, elixir, get-rich-quick scheme, or the latest technological trend or art movement and we leap from the water as one to take the bait. Look at history: The chronicles of the new trends and cults that have made a mass following for themselves could fill a library. After a few centuries, a few decades, a few years, a few months, they generally look ridiculous, but at the time they seem so attractive, so transcendental, so divine.

Always in a rush to believe in something, we will manufacture saints and faiths out of nothing. Do not let this gullibility go to waste: Make yourself the object of worship. Make people form a cult around you.

The great European charlatans of the sixteenth and seventeenth centuries mastered the art of cultmaking. They lived, as we do now, in a time of transformation: Organized religion was on the wane, science on the rise. People were desperate to rally around a new cause or faith. The charlatans had begun by peddling health elixirs and alchemic shortcuts to wealth. Moving quickly from town to town, they originally focused on small groups—until, by accident, they stumbled on a truth of human nature: The larger the group they gathered around themselves, the easier it was to deceive.

The charlatan would station himself on a high wooden platform (hence the term "mountebank") and crowds would swarm around him. In a group setting, people were more emotional, less able to reason. Had the charlatan spoken to them individually, they might have found him ridiculous, but lost in a crowd they got caught up in a communal mood of rapt attention. It became impossible for them to find the distance to be skeptical. Any deficiencies in the charlatan's ideas were hidden by the zeal of the mass. Passion and enthusiasm swept through the crowd like a contagion, and they reacted violently to anyone who dared to spread a seed of doubt. Both consciously studying this dynamic over decades of experiment and spontaneously adapting to these situations as they happened, the charlatans perfected the science of attracting and holding a crowd, molding the crowd into followers and the followers into a cult.

The gimmicks of the charlatans may seem quaint today, but there are thousands of charlatans among us still, using the same tried-and-true methods their predecessors refined centuries ago, only changing the names of their elixirs and modernizing the look of their cults. We find these latter-day charlatans in all arenas of life—business, fashion, politics, art. Many of them, perhaps, are following in the charlatan tradition without having any knowledge of its history, but you can be more systematic and deliberate. Simply follow the five steps of cultmaking that our charlatan ancestors perfected over the years.

Step 1: Keep It Vague; Keep It Simple. To create a cult you must first attract attention. This you should do not through actions, which are too clear and readable, but through words, which are hazy and deceptive. Your initial speeches, conversations, and interviews must include two elements: on the one hand the promise of something great and transformative, and on the other a total vagueness. This combination will stimulate all kinds of hazy dreams in your listeners, who will make their own connections and see what they want to see.

To make your vagueness attractive, use words of great resonance but cloudy meaning, words full of heat and enthusiasm. Fancy titles for simple things are helpful, as are the use of numbers and the creation of new words for vague concepts. All of these create the impression of specialized knowledge, giving you a veneer of profundity. By the same token, try to make the subject of your cult new and fresh, so that few will understand it. Done right, the combination of vague promises, cloudy but alluring concepts, and fiery enthusiasm will stir people's souls and a group will form around you.

Talk *too* vaguely and you have no credibility. But it is more dangerous to be specific. If you explain in detail the benefits people will gain by following your cult, you will be expected to satisfy them.

As a corollary to its vagueness your appeal should also be simple. Most people's problems have complex causes: deep-rooted neurosis, interconnected social factors, roots that go way back in time and are exceedingly hard to unravel. Few, however, have the patience to deal with this; most people want to hear that a simple solution will cure their problems. The ability to offer this kind of solution will give you great power and build you a following. Instead of the complicated explanations of real life, return to the primitive solutions of our ancestors, to good old country remedies, to mysterious panaceas.

Step 2: Emphasize the Visual and the Sensual over the Intellectual. Once people have begun to gather around you, two dangers will present themselves: boredom and skepticism. Boredom will make people go elsewhere; skepticism will allow them the distance to think rationally about whatever it is you are offering, blowing away the mist you have artfully created and revealing your ideas for what they are. You need to amuse the bored, then, and ward off the cynics.

encountered science and education at some time, though briefly and unsuccessfully. . . . The great mass of mankind has always been predisposed to marvel at mysteries, and this was especially true at certain historic periods when the secure foundations of life seemed shaken and old values, economic or spiritual, long accepted as certainties, could no longer be relied upon. Then the numbers of the charlatan's dupes multiplied—the "self killers," as a seventeenth-century Englishman called them.

THE POWER OF THE CHARLATAN, GRETE DE FRANCESCO, 1939

THE OWL WHO WAS GOD

Once upon a starless midnight there was an owl who sat on the branch of an oak tree. Two ground moles tried to slip quietly by, unnoticed. "You!" said the owl. "Who?" they quavered, in fear and astonishment, for they could not believe it was possible for anyone to see them in that thick darkness. "You two!" said the owl. The moles hurried away and told the other creatures of the field and forest that the owl was the greatest and wisest of all animals because he could see in the dark

The best way to do this is through theater, or other devices of its kind. Surround yourself with luxury, dazzle your followers with visual splendor, fill their eyes with spectacle. Not only will this keep them from seeing the ridiculousness of your ideas, the holes in your belief system, it will also attract more attention, more followers. Appeal to all the senses: Use incense for scent, soothing music for hearing, colorful charts and graphs for the eye. You might even tickle the mind, perhaps by using new technological gadgets to give your cult a pseudo-scientific veneer—as long as you do not make anyone really think. Use the exotic—distant cultures, strange customs—to create theatrical effects, and to make the most banal and ordinary affairs seem signs of something extraordinary.

Step 3: Borrow the Forms of Organized Religion to Structure the Group. Your cultlike following is growing; it is time to organize it. Find a way both elevating and comforting. Organized religions have long held unquestioned authority for large numbers of people, and continue to do so in our supposedly secular age. And even if the religion itself has faded some, its forms still resonate with power. The lofty and holy associations of organized religion can be endlessly exploited. Create rituals for your followers; organize them into a hierarchy, ranking them in grades of sanctity, and giving them names and titles that resound with religious overtones; ask them for sacrifices that will fill your coffers and increase your power. To emphasize your gathering's quasi-religious nature, talk and act like a prophet. You are not a dictator, after all; you are a priest, a guru, a sage, a shaman, or any other word that hides your real power in the mist of religion.

Step 4: Disguise Your Source of Income. Your group has grown, and you have structured it in a churchlike form. Your coffers are beginning to fill with your followers' money. Yet you must never be seen as hungry for money and the power it brings. It is at this moment that you must disguise the source of your income.

Your followers want to believe that if they follow you all sorts of good things will fall into their lap. By surrounding yourself with luxury you become living proof of the soundness of your belief system. Never reveal that your wealth actually comes from your followers' pockets; instead, make it seem to come from the truth of your methods. Followers will copy your each and every move in the belief that it will bring them the same results, and their imitative enthusiasm will blind them to the charlatan nature of your wealth.

Step 5: Set Up an Us-Versus-Them Dynamic. The group is now large and thriving, a magnet attracting more and more particles. If you are not careful, though, inertia will set in, and time and boredom will demagnetize the group. To keep your followers united, you must now do what all religions and belief systems have done: create an us-versus-them dynamic.

First, make sure your followers believe they are part of an exclusive club, unified by a bond of common goals. Then, to strengthen this bond, manufacture the notion of a devious enemy out to ruin you. There is a force of nonbelievers that will do anything to stop you. Any outsider who tries to reveal the charlatan nature of your belief system can now be described as a member of this devious force.

If you have no enemies, invent one. Given a straw man to react against, your followers will tighten and cohere. They have your cause to believe in and infidels to destroy.

OBSERVANCES OF THE LAW

Observance I

In the year 1653, a twenty-seven-year-old Milan man named Francesco Giuseppe Borri claimed to have had a vision. He went around town telling one and all that the archangel Michael had appeared to him and announced that he had been chosen to be the *capitano generale* of the Army of the New Pope, an army that would seize and revitalize the world. The archangel had further revealed that Borri now had the power to see people's souls, and that he would soon discover the philosopher's stone—a long-sought-after substance that could change base metals into gold. Friends and acquaintances who heard Borri explain the vision, and who witnessed the change that had come over him, were impressed, for Borri had previously devoted himself to a life of wine, women, and gambling. Now he gave all that up, plunging himself into the study of alchemy and talking only of mysticism and the occult.

The transformation was so sudden and miraculous, and Borri's words were so filled with enthusiasm, that he began to create a following. Unfortunately the Italian Inquisition began to notice him as well—they prosecuted anyone who delved into the occult—so he left Italy and began to wander Europe, from Austria to Holland, telling one and all that "to those who follow me all joy shall be granted." Wherever Borri stayed he attracted followers. His method was simple: He spoke of his vision, which had grown more and more elaborate, and offered to "look into" the soul of anyone who believed him (and they were many). Seemingly in a trance, he would stare at this new follower for several minutes, then claim to have seen the person's soul, degree of enlightenment, and potential for spiritual greatness. If what he saw showed promise, he would add the person to his growing order of disciples, an honor indeed.

The cult had six degrees, into which the disciples were assigned according to what Borri had glimpsed in their souls. With work and total devotion to the cult they could graduate to a higher degree. Borri—whom they called "His Excellency," and "Universal Doctor"—demanded from them the strictest vows of poverty. All the goods and moneys they possessed had to be turned over to him. But they did not mind handing over their property, for Borri had told them, "I shall soon bring my chemical

of tremendous importance. "He's God!" screamed a Plymouth Rock hen. And the others took up the cry "He's God!" So they followed him wherever he went and when he began to bump into things they began to bump into things, too. Finally he came to a concrete highway and he started up the middle of it and all the other creatures followed him. Presently a hawk, who was acting as outrider, observed a truck coming toward them at fifty miles an hour, and he reported to the secretary bird and the secretary bird reported to the owl. "There's danger ahead," said the secretary bird. "To wit?" said the owl. The secretary bird told him. "Aren't you afraid?" He asked. "Who?" said the owl calmly, for he could not see the truck. "He's God!" cried all the creatures again, and they were still crying "He's God!" when the truck hit them and ran them down. Some of the animals were merely injured, but most of them, including the owl, were killed. Moral: You can fool too many of the people too much of the time.

THE THURBER CARNIVAL, JAMES THURBER, 1894–1961

Given his growing wealth, Borri began to change his style of living. Renting the most splendid apartment in the city into which he had temporarily settled, he would furnish it with fabulous furniture and accessories, which he had begun to collect. He would drive through the city in a coach studded with jewels, with six magnificent black horses at its head. He never stayed too long in one place, and when he disappeared, saying he had more souls to gather into his flock, his reputation only grew in his absence. He became famous, although in fact he had never done a single concrete thing.

From all over Europe, the blind, the crippled, and the desperate came to visit Borri, for word had spread that he had healing powers. He asked no fee for his services, which only made him seem more marvelous, and indeed some claimed that in this or that city he had performed a miracle cure. By only hinting at his accomplishments, he encouraged people's imaginations to blow them up to fantastic proportions. His wealth, for example, actually came from the vast sums he was collecting from his increasingly select group of rich disciples; yet it was presumed that he had in fact perfected the philosopher's stone. The Church continued to pursue him, denouncing him for heresy and witchcraft, and Borri's response to these charges was a dignified silence; this only enhanced his reputation and made his followers more passionate. Only the great are persecuted, after all; how many understood Jesus Christ in his own time? Borri did not have to say a word—his followers now called the Pope the Antichrist.

And so Borri's power grew and grew, until one day he left the city of Amsterdam (where he had settled for a while), absconding with huge sums of borrowed money and diamonds that had been entrusted to him. (He claimed to be able to remove the flaws from diamonds through the power of his gifted mind.) Now he was on the run. The Inquisition eventually caught up with him, and for the last twenty years of his life he was imprisoned in Rome. But so great was the belief in his occult powers that to his dying day he was visited by wealthy believers, including Queen Christina of Sweden. Supplying him with money and materials, these visitors allowed him to continue his search for the elusive philosopher's stone.

Interpretation

Before he formed his cult, Borri seems to have stumbled on a critical discovery. Tiring of his life of debauchery, he had decided to give it up and to devote himself to the occult, a genuine interest of his. He must have noticed, however, that when he alluded to a mystical experience (rather than physical exhaustion) as the source of his conversion, people of all classes wanted to hear more. Realizing the power he could gain by ascribing the change to something external and mysterious, he went further with his manufactured visions. The grander the vision, and the more sacrifices he asked for, the more appealing and believable his story seemed to become.

Remember: People are not interested in the truth about change. They

To become the founder of a new religion one must be psychologically infallible in one's knowledge of a certain average type of souls who have not yet recognized that they belong together.
FRIEDRICH NIETZSCHE, 1844–1900

Men are so simple of mind, and so much dominated by their immediate needs, that a deceitful man will always find plenty who are ready to be deceived.
NICCOLÒ MACHIAVELLI, 1469–1527

THE TEMPLE OF HEALTH

[In the late 1780s] the Scottish quack James Graham . . . was winning a large following and great riches in London. . . . [Graham] maintained a show of great scientific technique. In 1772 . . . he had visited Philadelphia, where he met Benjamin Franklin and became interested in the latter's experiments with electricity. These appear to have inspired the apparatus in the "Temple of Health,"

do not want to hear that it has come from hard work, or from anything as banal as exhaustion, boredom, or depression; they are dying to believe in something romantic, otherworldly. They want to hear of angels and out-of-body experiences. Indulge them. Hint at the mystical source of some personal change, wrap it in ethereal colors, and a cultlike following will form around you. Adapt to people's needs: The messiah must mirror the desires of his followers. And always *aim* high. The bigger and bolder your illusion, the better.

Observance II

In the mid-1700s, word spread in Europe's fashionable society of a Swiss country doctor named Michael Schüppach who practiced a different kind of medicine: He used the healing powers of nature to perform miraculous cures. Soon well-to-do people from all over the Continent, their ailments both serious and mild, were making the trek to the alpine village of Langnau, where Schüppach lived and worked. Trudging through the mountains, these visitors witnessed the most dramatic natural landscapes that Europe has to offer. By the time they reached Langnau, they were already feeling transformed and on their way to health.

Schüppach, who had become known as simply the "Mountain Doctor," had a small pharmacy in town. This place became quite a scene: Crowds of people from many different countries would cram the small room, its walls lined with colorful bottles filled with herbal cures. Where most doctors of the time prescribed foul-tasting concoctions that bore incomprehensible Latin titles (as medicines often do still), Schüppach's cures had names such as "The Oil of Joy," "Little Flower's Heart," or "Against the Monster," and they tasted sweet and pleasing.

Visitors to Langnau would have to wait patiently for a visit with the Mountain Doctor, because every day some eighty messengers would arrive at the pharmacy bearing flasks of urine from all over Europe. Schüppach claimed he could diagnose what ailed you simply by looking at a sample of your urine and reading a written description of your ailment. (Naturally he read the description very carefully before prescribing a cure.) When he finally had a spare minute (the urine samples took up much of his time), he would call the visitor into his office in the pharmacy. He would then examine this person's urine sample, explaining that its appearance would tell him everything he needed to know. Country people had a sense for these things, he would say—their wisdom came from living a simple, godly life with none of the complications of urban living. This personal consultation would also include a discussion as to how one might bring one's soul more into harmony with nature.

Schüppach had devised many forms of treatment, each profoundly unlike the usual medical practices of the time. He was a believer, for instance, in electric shock therapy. To those who wondered whether this was in keeping with his belief in the healing power of nature, he would explain that electricity is a natural phenomenon; he was merely imitating the

the fabulous establishment he opened in London for the sale of his elixirs. . . . In the chief room, where he received patients, stood "the largest air pump in the world" to assist him in his "philosophical investigations" into disease, and also a "stupendous metallic conductor," a richly gilded pedestal surrounded with retorts and vials of "etherial and other essences." . . . According to J. Ennemoser, who published a history of magic in 1844 at Leipzig, Graham's "house . . . united the useful with the pleasurable. Everywhere the utmost magnificence was displayed. Even in the outer court, averred an eye-witness, it seemed as though art, invention, and riches had been exhausted. On the side walls in the chambers an arc-shaped glow was provided by artificial electric light; star rays darted forth; transparent glasses of all colors were placed with clever selection and much taste. All this, the same eyewitness assures us, was ravishing and exalted the imagination to the highest degree." Visitors were given a printed sheet of rules for healthy living. In the Great Apollo Apartment they might join in mysterious rituals, accompanied by chants: "Hail, Vital Air, aethereal! Magnetic Magic, hail!" And while they hailed the

power of lightning. One of his patients claimed to be inhabited by seven devils. The doctor cured him with electrical shocks, and as he administered these he exclaimed that he could see the devils flying out of the man's body, one by one. Another man claimed to have swallowed a hay wagon and its driver, which were causing him massive pains in the chest. The Mountain Doctor listened patiently, claimed to be able to hear the crack of a whip in the man's belly, promised to cure him, and gave him a sedative and a purgative. The man fell asleep on a chair outside the pharmacy. As soon as he awoke he vomited, and as he vomited a hay wagon sped past him (the Mountain Doctor had hired it for the occasion), the crack of its whip making him feel that somehow he had indeed expelled it under the doctor's care.

Over the years, the Mountain Doctor's fame grew. He was consulted by the powerful—even the writer Goethe made the trek to his village—and he became the center of a cult of nature in which everything natural was considered worthy of worship. Schüppach was careful to create effects that would entertain and inspire his patients. A professor who visited him once wrote, "One stands or sits in company, one plays cards, sometimes with a young woman; now a concert is given, now a lunch or supper, and now a little ballet is presented. With a very happy effect, the freedom of nature is everywhere united with the pleasures of the beau monde, and if the doctor is not able to heal any diseases, he can at least cure hypochondria and the vapors."

Interpretation

Schüppach had begun his career as an ordinary village doctor. He would sometimes use in his practice some of the village remedies he had grown up with, and apparently he noticed some results, for soon these herbal tinctures and natural forms of healing became his specialty. And in fact his natural form of healing did have profound psychological effects on his patients. Where the normal drugs of the time created fear and pain, Schüppach's treatments were comfortable and soothing. The resulting improvement in the patient's mood was a critical element in the cures he brought about. His patients believed so deeply in his skills that they willed themselves into health. Instead of scoffing at their irrational explanations for their ailments, Schüppach used their hypochondria to make it seem that he had effected a great cure.

The case of the Mountain Doctor teaches us valuable lessons in the creation of a cultlike following. First, you must find a way to engage people's will, to make their belief in your powers strong enough that they imagine all sorts of benefits. Their belief will have a self-fulfilling quality, but you must make sure that it is you, rather than their own will, who is seen as the agent of transformation. Find the belief, cause, or fantasy that will make them believe with a passion and they will imagine the rest, worshipping you as healer, prophet, genius, whatever you like.

Second, Schüppach teaches us the everlasting power of belief in nature, and in simplicity. Nature, in reality, is full of much that is terrifying—poisonous plants, fierce animals, sudden disasters, plagues. Belief in the healing, comforting quality of nature is really a constructed myth, a romanticism. But the appeal to nature can bring you great power, especially in complicated and stressful times.

This appeal, however, must be handled right. Devise a kind of theater of nature in which you, as the director, pick and choose the qualities that fit the romanticism of the times. The Mountain Doctor played the part to perfection, playing up his homespun wisdom and wit, and staging his cures as dramatic pieces. He did not make himself one with nature; instead he molded nature into a cult, an artificial construction. To create a "natural" effect you actually have to work hard, making nature theatrical and delightfully pagan. Otherwise no one will notice. Nature too must follow trends and be progressive.

Observance III

In 1788, at the age of fifty-five, the doctor and scientist Franz Mesmer was at a crossroads. He was a pioneer in the study of animal magnetism—the belief that animals contain magnetic matter, and that a doctor or specialist can effect miraculous cures by working on this charged substance—but in Vienna, where he lived, his theories had met with scorn and ridicule from the medical establishment. In treating women for convulsions, Mesmer claimed to have worked a number of cures, his proudest achievement being the restoration of sight to a blind girl. But another doctor who examined the young girl said she was as blind as ever, an assessment with which she herself agreed. Mesmer countered that his enemies were out to slander him by winning her over to their side. This claim only elicited more ridicule. Clearly the sober-minded Viennese were the wrong audience for his theories, and so he decided to move to Paris and start again.

Renting a splendid apartment in his new city, Mesmer decorated it appropriately. Stained glass in most of the windows created a religious feeling, and mirrors on all the walls produced an hypnotic effect. The doctor advertised that in his apartment he would give demonstrations of the powers of animal magnetism, inviting the diseased and melancholic to feel its powers. Soon Parisians of all classes (but mostly women, who seemed more attracted to the idea than men did) were paying for entry to witness the miracles that Mesmer promised.

Inside the apartment, the scents of orange blossom and exotic incense wafted through special vents. As the initiates filtered into the salon where the demonstrations took place, they heard harp music and the lulling sounds of a female vocalist coming from another room. In the center of the salon was a long oval container filled with water that Mesmer claimed had been magnetized. From holes in the container's metal lid protruded long movable iron rods. The visitors were instructed to sit around the container, place these magnetized rods on the body part that gave them pains or problems, and then hold hands with their neighbors, sitting as close as possible to one another to help the magnetic force pass between their bodies. Sometimes, too, they were attached to each other by cords.

Mesmer would leave the room, and "assistant magnetizers"—all hand-

In the town of Tarnopol lived a man by the name of Reb Feivel. One day, as he sat in his house deeply absorbed in his Talmud, he heard a loud noise outside. When he went to the window he saw a lot of little pranksters. "Up to some new piece of mischief, no doubt," he thought.

"Children, run quickly to the synagogue," he cried, leaning out and improvising the first story that occurred to him. "You'll see there a sea monster, and what a monster! It's a creature with five feet, three eyes, and a beard like that of a goat, only it's green!"

And sure enough the children scampered off and Reb Feivel returned to his studies. He smiled into his beard as he thought of the trick he had played on those little rascals. It wasn't long before his studies were interrupted again, this time by running footsteps. When he went to the window he saw several Jews running.

"Where are you running?" he called out.

"To the synagogue!" answered the Jews. "Haven't you heard? There's a sea monster, there's a creature with five legs, three eyes, and a beard like that of a goat, only it's green!" Reb Feivel laughed with glee, thinking of the trick he had played,

and sat down again to
his Talmud.
But no sooner had he
begun to concentrate
when suddenly he
heard a dinning tumult
outside. And what did
he see? A great crowd
of men, women and
children, all running
toward the synagogue.
"What's up?" he cried,
sticking his head out of
the window.
"What a question!
Why, don't you know?"
they answered. "Right
in front of the syna-
gogue there's a sea
monster. It's a creature
with five legs, three
eyes, and a beard like
that of a goat, only
it's green!"
And as the crowd
hurried by, Reb Feivel
suddenly noticed that
the rabbi himself was
among them.
"Lord of the world!"
he exclaimed. "If the
rabbi himself is
running with them
surely there must be
something happening.
Where there's smoke
there's fire!"
Without further
thought Reb Feivel
grabbed his hat, left his
house, and also
began running.
"Who can tell?" he
muttered to himself as
he ran, all out of
breath, toward the
synagogue.

A TREASURY OF
JEWISH FOLKLORE,
NATHAN AUSUBEL, ED.,
1948

some and strapping young men—would enter with jars of magnetized water that they would sprinkle on the patients, rubbing the healing fluid on their bodies, massaging it into their skin, moving them toward a trancelike state. And after a few minutes a kind of delirium would overcome the women. Some would sob, some would shriek and tear their hair, others would laugh hysterically. At the height of the delirium Mesmer would reenter the salon, dressed in a flowing silk robe embroidered with golden flowers and carrying a white magnetic rod. Moving around the container, he would stroke and soothe the patients until calm was restored. Many women would later attribute the strange power he had on them to his piercing look, which, they thought, was exciting or quieting the magnetic fluids in their bodies.

Within months of his arrival in Paris, Mesmer became the rage. His supporters included Marie-Antoinette herself, the queen of France, wife of Louis XVI. As in Vienna, he was condemned by the official faculty of medicine, but it did not matter. His growing following of pupils and patients paid him handsomely.

Mesmer expanded his theories to proclaim that all humanity could be brought into harmony through the power of magnetism, a concept with much appeal during the French Revolution. A cult of Mesmerism spread across the country; in many towns, "Societies of Harmony" sprang up to experiment with magnetism. These societies eventually became notorious: They tended to be led by libertines who would turn their sessions into a kind of group orgy.

At the height of Mesmer's popularity, a French commission published a report based on years of testing the theory of animal magnetism. The conclusion: Magnetism's effects on the body actually came from a kind of group hysteria and autosuggestion. The report was well documented, and ruined Mesmer's reputation in France. He left the country and went into retirement. Only a few years later, however, imitators sprang up all over Europe and the cult of Mesmerism spread once again, its believers more numerous than ever.

Interpretation

Mesmer's career can be broken into two parts. When still in Vienna, he clearly believed in the validity of his theory, and did all he could to prove it. But his growing frustration and the disapproval of his colleagues made him adopt another strategy. First he moved to Paris, where no one knew him, and where his extravagant theories found a more fruitful soil. Then he appealed to the French love of theater and spectacle, making his apartment into a kind of magical world in which a sensory overload of smells, sights, and sounds entranced his customers. Most important, from now on he practiced his magnetism only on a group. The group provided the setting in which the magnetism would have its proper effect, one believer infecting the other, overwhelming any individual doubter.

Mesmer thus passed from being a confirmed advocate of magnetism to the role of a charlatan using every trick in the book to captivate the public. The biggest trick of all was to play on the repressed sexuality that bubbles under the surface of any group setting. In a group, a longing for social unity, a longing older than civilization, cries out to be awakened. This desire may be subsumed under a unifying cause, but beneath it is a repressed sexuality that the charlatan knows how to exploit and manipulate for his own purposes.

This is the lesson that Mesmer teaches us: Our tendency to doubt, the distance that allows us to reason, is broken down when we join a group. The warmth and infectiousness of the group overwhelm the skeptical individual. This is the power you gain by creating a cult. Also, by playing on people's repressed sexuality, you lead them into mistaking their excited feelings for signs of your mystical strength. You gain untold power by working on people's unrealized desire for a kind of promiscuous and pagan unity.

Remember too that the most effective cults mix religion with science. Take the latest technological trend or fad and blend it with a noble cause, a mystical faith, a new form of healing. People's interpretations of your hybrid cult will run rampant, and they will attribute powers to you that you had never even thought to claim.

Image: The Magnet. An unseen force draws objects to it, which in turn become magnetized themselves, drawing other pieces to them, the magnetic power of the whole constantly increasing. But take away the original magnet and it all falls apart. Become the magnet, the invisible force that attracts people's imaginations and holds them together. Once they have clustered around you, no power can wrest them away.

Authority: The charlatan achieves his great power by simply opening a possibility for men to believe what they already want to believe. . . . The credulous cannot keep at a distance; they crowd around the wonder worker, entering his personal aura, surrendering themselves to illusion with a heavy solemnity, like cattle. (Grete de Francesco)

REVERSAL

One reason to create a following is that a group is often easier to deceive than an individual, and turns over to you that much more power. This comes, however, with a danger: If at any moment the group sees through you, you will find yourself facing not one deceived soul but an angry crowd that will tear you to pieces as avidly as it once followed you. The charlatans constantly faced this danger, and were always ready to move out of town as it inevitably became clear that their elixirs did not work and their ideas were sham. Too slow and they paid with their lives. In playing with the crowd, you are playing with fire, and must constantly keep an eye out for any sparks of doubt, any enemies who will turn the crowd against you. When you play with the emotions of a crowd, you have to know how to adapt, attuning yourself instantaneously to all of the moods and desires that a group will produce. Use spies, be on top of everything, and keep your bags packed.

For this reason you may often prefer to deal with people one by one. Isolating them from their normal milieu can have the same effect as putting them in a group—it makes them more prone to suggestion and intimidation. Choose the right sucker and if he eventually sees through you he may prove easier to escape than a crowd.

28

ENTER ACTION

WITH BOLDNESS

JUDGMENT

If you are unsure of a course of action, do not attempt it. Your doubts and hesitations will infect your execution. Timidity is dangerous: Better to enter with boldness. Any mistakes you commit through audacity are easily corrected with more audacity. Everyone admires the bold; no one honors the timid.

*The path of pleasure
never leads to glory!
The prodigious
achievements of
Hercules were the
result of high adven-
ture, and though there
is little, either in fable
or history, to show that
he had any rivals, still it
is recorded that a
knight errant, in
company with a fellow
adventurer, sought his
fortune in a romantic
country. He had not
traveled far when his
companion observed a
post, on which was
written the following
inscription: "Brave
adventurer, if you have
a desire to discover that
which has never been
seen by any knight
errant, you have only
to pass this torrent, and
then take in your arms
an elephant of stone
and carry it in one
breath to the summit of
this mountain, whose
noble head seems
blended with the sky."
"But," said the knight's
companion, "the water
may be deep as well as
rapid, and though,
notwithstanding, we
should pass it, why
should we be encum-
bered with the
elephant? What a
ridiculous undertak-
ing!" And philosophi-
cally and with nice
calculation, he
observed that the
elephant might be
carried four steps; but
for conveying it to the
top of the mountain in
one breath, that was
not in the power of a
mortal, unless it should*

BOLDNESS AND HESITATION: A Brief Psychological Comparison
Boldness and hesitation elicit very different psychological responses in their targets: Hesitation puts obstacles in your path, boldness eliminates them. Once you understand this, you will find it essential to overcome your natural timidity and practice the art of audacity. The following are among the most pronounced psychological effects of boldness and timidity.

The Bolder the Lie the Better. We all have weaknesses, and our efforts are never perfect. But entering action with boldness has the magical effect of hiding our deficiencies. Con artists know that the bolder the lie, the more convincing it becomes. The sheer audacity of the story makes it more credible, distracting attention from its inconsistencies. When putting together a con or entering any kind of negotiation, go further than you planned. Ask for the moon and you will be surprised how often you get it.

Lions Circle the Hesitant Prey. People have a sixth sense for the weaknesses of others. If, in a first encounter, you demonstrate your willingness to compromise, back down, and retreat, you bring out the lion even in people who are not necessarily bloodthirsty. Everything depends on perception, and once you are seen as the kind of person who quickly goes on the defensive, who is willing to negotiate and be amenable, you will be pushed around without mercy.

Boldness Strikes Fear; Fear Creates Authority. The bold move makes you seem larger and more powerful than you are. If it comes suddenly, with the stealth and swiftness of a snake, it inspires that much more fear. By intimidating with a bold move, you establish a precedent: in every subsequent encounter, people will be on the defensive, in terror of your next strike.

Going Halfway with Half a Heart Digs the Deeper Grave. If you enter an action with less than total confidence, you set up obstacles in your own path. When a problem arises you will grow confused, seeing options where there are none and inadvertently creating more problems still. Retreating from the hunter, the timid hare scurries more easily into his snares.

Hesitation Creates Gaps, Boldness Obliterates Them. When you take time to think, to hem and haw, you create a gap that allows others time to think as well. Your timidity infects people with awkward energy, elicits embarrassment. Doubt springs up on all sides.

Boldness destroys such gaps. The swiftness of the move and the energy of the action leave others no space to doubt and worry. In seduction, hesitation is fatal—it makes your victim conscious of your intentions. The bold move crowns seduction with triumph: It leaves no time for reflection.

Audacity Separates You from the Herd. Boldness gives you presence and makes you seem larger than life. The timid fade into the wallpaper, the bold draw attention, and what draws attention draws power. We cannot keep our eyes off the audacious—we cannot wait to see their next bold move.

OBSERVANCES OF THE LAW

Observance I

In May of 1925, five of the most successful dealers in the French scrap-metal business found themselves invited to an "official" but "highly confidential" meeting with the deputy director general of the Ministry of Post and Telegraphs at the Hotel Crillon, then the most luxurious hotel in Paris. When the businessmen arrived, it was the director general himself, a Monsieur Lustig, who met them in a swank suite on the top floor.

The businessmen had no idea why they had been summoned to this meeting, and they were bursting with curiosity. After drinks, the director explained. "Gentlemen," he said, "this is an urgent matter that requires complete secrecy. The government is going to have to tear down the Eiffel Tower." The dealers listened in stunned silence as the director explained that the tower, as recently reported in the news, desperately needed repairs. It had originally been meant as a temporary structure (for the Exposition of 1889), its maintenance costs had soared over the years, and now, in a time of a fiscal crisis, the government would have to spend millions to fix it. Many Parisians considered the Eiffel Tower an eyesore and would be delighted to see it go. Over time, even the tourists would forget about it—it would live on in photographs and postcards. "Gentlemen," Lustig said, "you are all invited to make the government an offer for the Eiffel Tower."

He gave the businessmen sheets of government stationery filled with figures, such as the tonnage of the tower's metal. Their eyes popped as they calculated how much they could make from the scrap. Then Lustig led them to a waiting limo, which brought them to the Eiffel Tower. Flashing an official badge, he guided them through the area, spicing his tour with amusing anecdotes. At the end of the visit he thanked them and asked them to have their offers delivered to his suite within four days.

Several days after the offers were submitted, one of the five, a Monsieur P., received notice that his bid was the winner, and that to secure the sale he should come to the suite at the hotel within two days, bearing a certified check for more than 250,000 francs (the equivalent today of about $1,000,000)—a quarter of the total price. On delivery of the check, he would receive the documents confirming his ownership of the Eiffel Tower. Monsieur P. was excited—he would go down in history as the man who had bought and torn down the infamous landmark. But by the time he arrived at the suite, check in hand, he was beginning to have doubts about the whole affair. Why meet in a hotel instead of a government building? Why hadn't he heard from other officials? Was this a hoax, a scam? As he listened to Lustig discuss the arrangements for the scrapping of the tower, he hesitated, and contemplated backing out.

be the dwarf figure of an elephant, fit only to be placed on the top of a stick; and then what honor would there be in such an adventure? "There is," said he, "some deception in this writing. It is an enigma only fit to amuse a child. I shall therefore leave you and your elephant." The reasoner then departed; but the adventurous man rushed with his eyes closed across the water; neither depth nor violence prevented him, and according to the inscription he saw the elephant lying on the opposite bank. He took it and carried it to the top of the hill, where he saw a town. A shriek from the elephant alarmed the people of the city, who rose in arms; but the adventurer, nothing daunted, was determined to die a hero. The people, however, were awed by his presence, and he was astonished to hear them proclaim him successor to their king, who had recently died. Great enterprises are only achieved by adventurous spirits. They who calculate with too great nicety every difficulty and obstacle which is likely to lie in their way, lose that time in hesitation, which the more daring seize and render available to the loftiest purposes.
FABLES,
JEAN DE LA FONTAINE,
1621–1695

Suddenly, however, he realized that the director had changed his tone. Instead of talking about the tower, he was complaining about his low salary, about his wife's desire for a fur coat, about how galling it was to work hard and be unappreciated. It dawned on Monsieur P. that this high government official was asking for a bribe. The effect on him, though, was not outrage but relief. Now he was sure that Lustig was for real, since in all of his previous encounters with French bureaucrats, they had inevitably asked for a little greasing of the palm. His confidence restored, Monsieur P. slipped the director several thousand francs in bills, then handed him the certified check. In return he received the documentation, including an impressive-looking bill of sale. He left the hotel, dreaming of the profits and fame to come.

Over the next few days, however, as Monsieur P. waited for correspondence from the government, he began to realize that something was amiss. A few telephone calls made it clear that there was no deputy director general Lustig, and there were no plans to destroy the Eiffel Tower: He had been bilked of over 250,000 francs!

Monsieur P. never went to the police. He knew what kind of reputation he would get if word got out that he had fallen for one of the most absurdly audacious cons in history. Besides the public humiliation, it would have been business suicide.

Interpretation

Had Count Victor Lustig, con artist extraordinaire, tried to sell the Arc de Triomphe, a bridge over the Seine, a statue of Balzac, no one would have believed him. But the Eiffel Tower was just too large, too improbable to be part of a con job. In fact it was so improbable that Lustig was able to return to Paris six months later and "resell" the Eiffel Tower to a different scrap-iron dealer, and for a higher price—a sum in francs equivalent today to over $1,500,000!

Largeness of scale deceives the human eye. It distracts and awes us, and is so self-evident that we cannot imagine there is any illusion or deception afoot. Arm yourself with bigness and boldness—stretch your deceptions as far as they will go and then go further. If you sense that the sucker has suspicions, do as the intrepid Lustig did: Instead of backing down, or lowering his price, he simply raised his price higher, by asking for and getting a bribe. Asking for more puts the other person on the defensive, cuts out the nibbling effect of compromise and doubt, and overwhelms with its boldness.

Observance II

On his deathbed in 1533, Vasily III, the Grand Duke of Moscow and ruler of a semi-united Russia, proclaimed his three-year-old son, Ivan IV, as his successor. He appointed his young wife, Helena, as regent until Ivan reached his majority and could rule on his own. The aristocracy—the boyars—secretly rejoiced: For years the dukes of Moscow had been trying to extend their authority over the boyars' turf. With Vasily dead, his heir a mere three years old, and a young woman in charge of the dukedom, the boyars would be able to roll back the dukes' gains, wrest control of the state, and humiliate the royal family.

Aware of these dangers, young Helena turned to her trusted friend Prince Ivan Obolensky to help her rule. But after five years as regent she suddenly died—poisoned by a member of the Shuisky family, the most fearsome boyar clan. The Shuisky princes seized control of the government and threw Obolensky in prison, where he starved to death. At the age of eight, Ivan was now a despised orphan, and any boyar or family member who took an interest in him was immediately banished or killed.

And so Ivan roamed the palace, hungry, ill clothed, and often in hiding from the Shuiskys, who treated him roughly when they saw him. On some days they would search him out, clothe him in royal robes, hand him a scepter, and set him on the throne—a kind of mock ritual in which they lampooned his royal pretensions. Then they would shoo him away. One evening several of them chased the Metropolitan—the head of the Russian church—through the palace, and he sought refuge in Ivan's room; the boy watched in horror as the Shuiskys entered, hurled insults, and beat the Metropolitan mercilessly.

Ivan had one friend in the palace, a boyar named Vorontsov who consoled and advised him. One day, however, as he, Vorontsov, and the newest Metropolitan conferred in the palace refectory, several Shuiskys burst in, beat up Vorontsov, and insulted the Metropolitan by tearing and treading on his robes. Then they banished Vorontsov from Moscow.

Throughout all this Ivan maintained a strict silence. To the boyars it seemed that their plan had worked: The young man had turned into a terrified and obedient idiot. They could ignore him now, even leave him alone. But on the evening of December 29, 1543, Ivan, now thirteen, asked Prince Andrei Shuisky to come to his room. When the prince arrived, the room was filled with palace guards. Young Ivan then pointed his finger at Andrei and ordered the guards to arrest him, have him killed, and throw his body to the bloodhounds in the royal kennel. Over the next few days Ivan had all of Andrei's close associates arrested and banished. Caught off-guard by his sudden boldness, the boyars now stood in mortal terror of this youth, the future Ivan the Terrible, who had planned and waited for five years to execute this one swift and bold act that would secure his power for decades to come.

Interpretation

The world is full of boyars—men who despise you, fear your ambition, and jealously guard their shrinking realms of power. You need to establish your authority and gain respect, but the moment the boyars sense your growing boldness, they will act to thwart you. This is how Ivan met such a situation: He lay low, showing neither ambition nor discontent. He waited, and when the time came he brought the palace guards over to his side. The guards had come to hate the cruel Shuiskys. Once they agreed to Ivan's plan, he struck with the swiftness of a snake, pointing his finger at Shuisky and giving him no time to react.

Negotiate with a boyar and you create opportunities for him. A small

city, he stopped a passing gentleman. "Hello, my friend! Who is the richest man in town?" "Poor countryman! Don't you know Byôn-ssi, the millionaire? His glittering tile-roofed house pierced by twelve gates is just over there." Huh Saeng bent his steps to the rich man's house. Having entered the big gate, he flung the guest-room door open and addressed the host: "I need 10,000 yang for capital for my commercial business and I want you to lend me the money." "Alright, sir. Where shall I send the money?" "To the Ansông Market in care of a commission merchant." "Very well, sir. I will draw on Kim, who does the biggest commission business in the Ansông Market. You'll get the money there." "Good-bye, sir." When Huh Saeng was gone, all the other guests in the room asked Byôn-ssi why he gave so much money to a beggarlike stranger whose family name was unknown to him. But the rich man replied with a triumphant face: "Even though he was in ragged clothes, he spoke clearly to the point without betraying shame or inferiority, unlike common people who want to borrow money for a bad debt. Such a man as he is either mad or self-confident in doing business. But judging from his dauntless eyes and booming voice he

compromise becomes the toehold he needs to tear you apart. The sudden bold move, without discussion or warning, obliterates these toeholds, and builds your authority. You terrify doubters and despisers and gain the confidence of the many who admire and glorify those who act boldly.

Observance III

In 1514 the twenty-two-year-old Pietro Aretino was working as a lowly assistant scullion to a wealthy Roman family. He had ambitions of greatness as a writer, to enflame the world with his name, but how could a mere lackey hope to realize such dreams?

That year Pope Leo X received from the king of Portugal an embassy that included many gifts, most prominent among them a great elephant, the first in Rome since imperial times. The pontiff adored this elephant and showered it with attention and gifts. But despite his love and care, the elephant, which was called Hanno, became deathly ill. The pope summoned doctors, who administered a five-hundred-pound purgative to the elephant, but all to no avail. The animal died and the pope went into mourning. To console himself he summoned the great painter Raphael and ordered him to create a life-sized painting of Hanno above the animal's tomb, bearing the inscription, "What nature took away, Raphael has with his art restored."

Over the next few days, a pamphlet circulated throughout Rome that caused great merriment and laughter. Entitled "The Last Will and Testament of the Elephant Hanno," it read, in part, "To my heir the Cardinal Santa Croce, I give my knees, so that he can imitate my genuflections. . . . To my heir Cardinal Santi Quattro, I give my jaws, so that he can more readily devour all of Christ's revenues. . . . To my heir Cardinal Medici, I give my ears, so that he can hear everyone's doings. . . ." To Cardinal Grassi, who had a reputation for lechery, the elephant bequeathed the appropriate, oversized part of his own anatomy.

On and on the anonymous pamphlet went, sparing none of the great in Rome, not even the pope. With each one it took aim at their best-known weakness. The pamphlet ended with verse, "See to it that Aretino is your friend / For he is a bad enemy to have. / His words alone could ruin the high pope / So God guard everyone from his tongue."

Interpretation

With one short pamphlet, Aretino, son of a poor shoemaker and a servant himself, hurled himself to fame. Everyone in Rome rushed to find out who this daring young man was. Even the pope, amused by his audacity, sought him out and ended up giving him a job in the papal service. Over the years he came to be known as the "Scourge of Princes," and his biting tongue earned him the respect and fear of the great, from the king of France to the Hapsburg emperor.

The Aretino strategy is simple: When you are as small and obscure as David was, you must find a Goliath to attack. The larger the target, the more attention you gain. The bolder the attack, the more you stand out from the crowd, and the more admiration you earn. Society is full of those who think daring thoughts but lack the guts to print and publicize them. Voice what the public feels—the expression of shared feelings is always powerful. Search out the most prominent target possible and sling your boldest shot. The world will enjoy the spectacle, and will honor the under-dog—you, that is—with glory and power.

KEYS TO POWER

Most of us are timid. We want to avoid tension and conflict and we want to be liked by all. We may contemplate a bold action but we rarely bring it to life. We are terrified of the consequences, of what others might think of us, of the hostility we will stir up if we dare go beyond our usual place.

Although we may disguise our timidity as a concern for others, a de-sire not to hurt or offend them, in fact it is the opposite—we are really self-absorbed, worried about ourselves and how others perceive us. Boldness, on the other hand, is outer-directed, and often makes people feel more at ease, since it is less self-conscious and less repressed.

This can be seen most clearly in seduction. All great seducers succeed through effrontery. Casanova's boldness was not revealed in a daring ap-proach to the woman he desired, or in intrepid words to flatter her; it con-sisted in his ability to surrender himself to her completely and to make her believe he would do anything for her, even risk his life, which in fact he sometimes did. The woman on whom he lavished this attention under-stood that he held nothing back from her. This was infinitely more flatter-ing than compliments. At no point during the seduction would he show hesitation or doubt, simply because he never felt it.

Part of the charm of being seduced is that it makes us feel engulfed, temporarily outside of ourselves and the usual doubts that permeate our lives. The moment the seducer hesitates, the charm is broken, because we become aware of the process, of their deliberate effort to seduce us, of their self-consciousness. Boldness directs attention outward and keeps the illusion alive. It never induces awkwardness or embarrassment. And so we admire the bold, and prefer to be around them, because their self-confidence infects us and draws us outside our own realm of inwardness and reflection.

Few are born bold. Even Napoleon had to cultivate the habit on the battlefield, where he knew it was a matter of life and death. In social set-tings he was awkward and timid, but he overcame this and practiced bold-ness in every part of his life because he saw its tremendous power, how it could literally enlarge a man (even one who, like Napoleon, was in fact conspicuously small). We also see this change in Ivan the Terrible: A harm-less boy suddenly transforms himself into a powerful young man who com-mands authority, simply by pointing a finger and taking bold action.

You must practice and develop your boldness. You will often find uses for it. The best place to begin is often the delicate world of negotiation, particularly those discussions in which you are asked to set your own price. How often we put ourselves down by asking for too little. When Christopher Columbus proposed that the Spanish court finance his voyage to the Americas, he also made the insanely bold demand that he be called "Grand Admiral of the Ocean." The court agreed. The price he set was the price he received—he demanded to be treated with respect, and so he was. Henry Kissinger too knew that in negotiation, bold demands work better than starting off with piecemeal concessions and trying to meet the other person halfway. Set your value high, and then, as Count Lustig did, set it higher.

Understand: If boldness is not natural, neither is timidity. It is an acquired habit, picked up out of a desire to avoid conflict. If timidity has taken hold of you, then, root it out. Your fears of the consequences of a bold action are way out of proportion to reality, and in fact the consequences of timidity are worse. Your value is lowered and you create a self-fulfilling cycle of doubt and disaster. Remember: The problems created by an audacious move can be disguised, even remedied, by more and greater audacity.

Image: The Lion and the Hare. The lion creates no gaps in his way—his movements are too swift, his jaws too quick and powerful. The timid hare will do anything to escape danger, but in its haste to retreat and flee, it backs into traps, hops smack into its enemies' jaws.

Authority: I certainly think that it is better to be impetuous than cautious, for fortune is a woman, and it is necessary, if you wish to master her, to conquer her by force; and it can be seen that she lets herself be overcome by the bold rather than by those who proceed coldly. And therefore, like a woman, she is always a friend to the young, because they are less cautious, fiercer, and master her with greater audacity. (Niccolò Machiavelli, 1469–1527)

REVERSAL

Boldness should never be the strategy behind all of your actions. It is a tactical instrument, to be used at the right moment. Plan and think ahead, and make the final element the bold move that will bring you success. In other words, since boldness is a learned response, it is also one that you learn to control and utilize at will. To go through life armed only with audacity would be tiring and also fatal. You would offend too many people, as is proven by those who cannot control their boldness. One such person was Lola Montez; her audacity brought her triumphs and led to her seduction of the king of Bavaria. But since she could never rein in her boldness, it also led to her downfall—in Bavaria, in England, wherever she turned. It crossed the border between boldness and the appearance of cruelty, even insanity. Ivan the Terrible suffered the same fate: When the power of boldness brought him success, he stuck to it, to the point where it became a lifelong pattern of violence and sadism. He lost the ability to tell when boldness was appropriate and when it was not.

Timidity has no place in the realm of power; you will often benefit, however, by being able to feign it. At that point, of course, it is no longer timidity but an offensive weapon: You are luring people in with your show of shyness, all the better to pounce on them boldly later.

PLAN ALL THE WAY

TO THE END

JUDGMENT

The ending is everything. Plan all the way to it, taking into account all the possible consequences, obstacles, and twists of fortune that might reverse your hard work and give the glory to others. By planning to the end you will not be overwhelmed by circumstances and you will know when to stop. Gently guide fortune and help determine the future by thinking far ahead.

TRANSGRESSION OF THE LAW

In 1510 a ship set out from the island of Hispaniola (now Haiti and the Dominican Republic) for Venezuela, where it was to rescue a besieged Spanish colony. Several miles out of port, a stowaway climbed out of a provision chest: Vasco Núñez de Balboa, a noble Spaniard who had come to the New World in search of gold but had fallen into debt and had escaped his creditors by hiding in the chest.

Balboa had been obsessed with gold ever since Columbus had returned to Spain from his voyages with tales of a fabulous but as yet undiscovered kingdom called El Dorado. Balboa was one of the first adventurers to come in search of Columbus's land of gold, and he had decided from the beginning that he would be the one to find it, through sheer audacity and single-mindedness. Now that he was free of his creditors, nothing would stop him.

Unfortunately the ship's owner, a wealthy jurist named Francisco Fernández de Enciso, was furious when told of the stowaway, and he ordered that Balboa be left on the first island they came across. Before they found any island, however, Enciso received news that the colony he was to rescue had been abandoned. This was Balboa's chance. He told the sailors of his previous voyages to Panama, and of the rumors he had heard of gold in the area. The excited sailors convinced Enciso to spare Balboa's life, and to establish a colony in Panama. Weeks later they named their new settlement "Darien."

Darien's first governor was Enciso, but Balboa was not a man to let others steal the initiative. He campaigned against Enciso among the sailors, who eventually made it clear that they preferred him as governor. Enciso fled to Spain, fearing for his life. Months later, when a representative of the Spanish crown arrived to establish himself as the new, official governor of Darien, he was turned away. On his return voyage to Spain, this man drowned; the drowning was accidental, but under Spanish law, Balboa had murdered the governor and usurped his position.

Balboa's bravado had got him out of scrapes before, but now his hopes of wealth and glory seemed doomed. To lay claim to El Dorado, should he discover it, he would need the approval of the Spanish king—which, as an outlaw, he would never receive. There was only one solution. Panamanian Indians had told Balboa of a vast ocean on the other side of the Central American isthmus, and had said that by traveling south upon this western coast, he would reach a fabulous land of gold, called by a name that to his ears sounded like "Biru." Balboa decided he would cross the treacherous jungles of Panama and become the first European to bathe his feet in this new ocean. From there he would march on El Dorado. If he did this on Spain's behalf, he would obtain the eternal gratitude of the king, and would secure his own reprieve—only he had to act before Spanish authorities came to arrest him.

In 1513, then, Balboa set out, with 190 soldiers. Halfway across the isthmus (some ninety miles wide at that point), only sixty soldiers re-

There are very few men—and they are the exceptions—who are able to think and feel beyond the present moment.

CARL VON CLAUSEWITZ, 1780-1831

THE TWO FROGS

Two frogs dwelt in the same pool. The pool being dried up under the summer's heat, they left it, and set out together to seek another home. As they went along they chanced to pass a deep well, amply supplied with water, on seeing which one of the frogs said to the other: "Let us descend and make our abode in this well, it will furnish us with shelter and food." The other replied with greater caution: "But suppose the water should fail us, how can we get out again from so great a depth?" Do nothing without a regard to the consequences.

FABLES,
AESOP,
SIXTH CENTURY B.C.

mained, many having succumbed to the harsh conditions—the blood-sucking insects, the torrential rainfall, fever. Finally, from a mountaintop, Balboa became the first European to lay eyes on the Pacific Ocean. Days later he marched in his armor into its waters, bearing the banner of Castile and claiming all its seas, lands, and islands in the name of the Spanish throne.

Indians from the area greeted Balboa with gold, jewels, and precious pearls, the like of which he had never seen. When he asked where these had come from, the Indians pointed south, to the land of the Incas. But Balboa had only a few soldiers left. For the moment, he decided, he should return to Darien, send the jewels and gold to Spain as a token of good will, and ask for a large army to aid him in the conquest of El Dorado.

When news reached Spain of Balboa's bold crossing of the isthmus, his discovery of the western ocean, and his planned conquest of El Dorado, the former criminal became a hero. He was instantly proclaimed governor of the new land. But before the king and queen received word of his discovery, they had already sent a dozen ships, under the command of a man named Pedro Arias Dávila, "Pedrarias," with orders to arrest Balboa for murder and to take command of the colony. By the time Pedrarias arrived in Panama, he had learned that Balboa had been pardoned, and that he was to share the governorship with the former outlaw.

All the same, Balboa felt uneasy. Gold was his dream, El Dorado his only desire. In pursuit of this goal he had nearly died many times over, and to share the wealth and glory with a newcomer would be intolerable. He also soon discovered that Pedrarias was a jealous, bitter man, and equally unhappy with the situation. Once again, the only solution for Balboa was to seize the initiative by proposing to cross the jungle with a larger army, carrying ship-building materials and tools. Once on the Pacific coast, he would create an armada with which to conquer the Incas. Surprisingly enough, Pedrarias agreed to the plan—perhaps sensing it would never work. Hundreds died in this second march through the jungle, and the timber they carried rotted in the torrential rains. Balboa, as usual, was undaunted—no power in the world could thwart his plan—and on arriving at the Pacific he began to cut down trees for new lumber. But the men remaining to him were too few and too weak to mount an invasion, and once again Balboa had to return to Darien.

Pedrarias had in any case invited Balboa back to discuss a new plan, and on the outskirts of the settlement, the explorer was met by Francisco Pizarro, an old friend who had accompanied him on his first crossing of the isthmus. But this was a trap: Leading one hundred soldiers, Pizarro surrounded his former friend, arrested him, and returned him to Pedrarias, who tried him on charges of rebellion. A few days later Balboa's head fell into a basket, along with those of his most trusted followers. Years later Pizarro himself reached Peru, and Balboa's deeds were forgotten.

Interpretation

Most men are ruled by the heart, not the head. Their plans are vague, and when they meet obstacles they improvise. But improvisation will only bring you as far as the next crisis, and is never a substitute for thinking several steps ahead and planning to the end.

Balboa had a dream of glory and wealth, and a vague plan to reach it. Yet his bold deeds, and his discovery of the Pacific, are largely forgotten, for he committed what in the world of power is the ultimate sin: He went part way, leaving the door open for others to take over. A real man of power would have had the prudence to see the dangers in the distance—the rivals who would want to share in the conquests, the vultures that would hover once they heard the word "gold." Balboa should have kept his knowledge of the Incas secret until after he had conquered Peru. Only then would his wealth, and his head, have been secure. Once Pedrarias arrived on the scene, a man of power and prudence would have schemed to kill or imprison him, and to take over the army he had brought for the conquest of Peru. But Balboa was locked in the moment, always reacting emotionally, never thinking ahead.

What good is it to have the greatest dream in the world if others reap the benefits and the glory? Never lose your head over a vague, open-ended dream—plan to the end.

OBSERVANCE OF THE LAW

In 1863 the Prussian premier Otto von Bismarck surveyed the chessboard of European power as it then stood. The main players were England, France, and Austria. Prussia itself was one of several states in the loosely allied German Federation. Austria, dominant member of the Federation, made sure that the other German states remained weak, divided and submissive. Bismarck believed that Prussia was destined for something far greater than servant boy to Austria.

This is how Bismarck played the game. His first move was to start a war with lowly Denmark, in order to recover the former Prussian lands of Schleswig-Holstein. He knew that these rumblings of Prussian independence might worry France and England, so he enlisted Austria in the war, claiming that he was recovering Schleswig-Holstein for their benefit. In a few months, after the war was decided, Bismarck demanded that the newly conquered lands be made part of Prussia. The Austrians of course were furious, but they compromised: First they agreed to give the Prussians Schleswig, and a year later they sold them Holstein. The world began to see that Austria was weakening and that Prussia was on the rise.

Bismarck's next move was his boldest: In 1866 he convinced King William of Prussia to withdraw from the German Federation, and in doing so to go to war with Austria itself. King William's wife, his son the crown prince, and the princes of the other German kingdoms vehemently opposed such a war. But Bismarck, undaunted, succeeded in forcing the conflict, and Prussia's superior army defeated the Austrians in the brutally

He who asks fortune-
tellers the future
unwittingly forfeits an
inner, intimation of
coming events that is a
thousand times more
exact than anything
they may say.
WALTER BENJAMIN,
1892–1940

short Seven Weeks War. The king and the Prussian generals then wanted
to march on Vienna, taking as much land from Austria as possible. But
Bismarck stopped them—now he presented himself as on the side of
peace. The result was that he was able to conclude a treaty with Austria
that granted Prussia and the other German states total autonomy. Bismarck could now position Prussia as the dominant power in Germany and
the head of a newly formed North German Confederation.

The French and the English began to compare Bismarck to Attila the
Hun, and to fear that he had designs on all of Europe. Once he had started
on the path to conquest, there was no telling where he would stop. And,
indeed, three years later Bismarck provoked a war with France. First he
appeared to give his permission to France's annexation of Belgium, then
at the last moment he changed his mind. Playing a cat-and-mouse game,
he infuriated the French emperor, Napoleon III, and stirred up his own
king against the French. To no one's surprise, war broke out in 1870. The
newly formed German federation enthusiastically joined in the war
on France, and once again the Prussian military machine and its allies
destroyed the enemy army in a matter of months. Although Bismarck
opposed taking any French land, the generals convinced him that Alsace-
Lorraine would become part of the federation.

Now all of Europe feared the next move of the Prussian monster, led
by Bismarck, the "Iron Chancellor." And in fact a year later Bismarck
founded the German Empire, with the Prussian king as the newly
crowned emperor and Bismarck himself a prince. But then something
strange happened: Bismarck instigated no more wars. And while the other
European powers grabbed up land for colonies in other continents, he severely limited Germany's colonial acquisitions. He did not want more
land for Germany, but more security. For the rest of his life he struggled to
maintain peace in Europe and to prevent further wars. Everybody assumed he had changed, mellowing with the years. They had failed to understand: This was the final move of his original plan.

Interpretation

There is a simple reason why most men never know when to come off the
attack: They form no concrete idea of their goal. Once they achieve victory they only hunger for more. To stop—to aim for a goal and then keep
to it—seems almost inhuman, in fact; yet nothing is more critical to the
maintenance of power. The person who goes too far in his triumphs creates a reaction that inevitably leads to a decline. The only solution is to
plan for the long run. Foresee the future with as much clarity as the gods
on Mount Olympus, who look through the clouds and see the ends of all
things.

From the beginning of his career in politics, Bismarck had one goal:
to form an independent German state led by Prussia. He instigated the
war with Denmark not to conquer territory but to stir up Prussian nation-
alism and unite the country. He incited the war with Austria only to gain

Prussian independence. (This was why he refused to grab Austrian territory.) And he fomented the war with France to unite the German kingdoms against a common enemy, and thus to prepare for the formation of a united Germany.

Once this was achieved, Bismarck stopped. He never let triumph go to his head, was never tempted by the siren call of more. He held the reins tightly, and whenever the generals, or the king, or the Prussian people demanded new conquests, he held them back. Nothing would spoil the beauty of his creation, certainly not a false euphoria that pushed those around him to attempt to go past the end that he had so carefully planned.

> *Experience shows that, if one foresees from far away the designs to be*
> *undertaken, one can act with speed when the moment comes to execute them.*
> *Cardinal Richelieu, 1585-1642*

KEYS TO POWER

According to the cosmology of the ancient Greeks, the gods were thought to have complete vision into the future. They saw everything to come, right down to the intricate details. Men, on the other hand, were seen as victims of fate, trapped in the moment and their emotions, unable to see beyond immediate dangers. Those heroes, such as Odysseus, who were able to look beyond the present and plan several steps ahead, seemed to defy fate, to approximate the gods in their ability to determine the future. The comparison is still valid—those among us who think further ahead and patiently bring their plans to fruition seem to have a godlike power.

Because most people are too imprisoned in the moment to plan with this kind of foresight, the ability to ignore immediate dangers and pleasures translates into power. It is the power of being able to overcome the natural human tendency to react to things as they happen, and instead to train oneself to step back, imagining the larger things taking shape beyond one's immediate vision. Most people believe that they are in fact aware of the future, that they are planning and thinking ahead. They are usually deluded: What they are really doing is succumbing to their desires, to what they want the future to be. Their plans are vague, based on their imaginations rather than their reality. They may believe they are thinking all the way to the end, but they are really only focusing on the happy ending, and deluding themselves by the strength of their desire.

In 415 B.C., the ancient Athenians attacked Sicily, believing their expedition would bring them riches, power, and a glorious ending to the sixteen-year Peloponnesian War. They did not consider the dangers of an invasion so far from home; they did not foresee that the Sicilians would fight all the harder since the battles were in their own homeland, or that all of Athens's enemies would band together against them, or that war would break out on several fronts, stretching their forces way too thin. The Sicilian expedition was a complete disaster, leading to the destruction of one of the greatest civilizations of all time. The Athenians were led into this disaster by their hearts, not their minds. They saw only the chance of glory, not the dangers that loomed in the distance.

Cardinal de Retz, the seventeenth-century Frenchman who prided himself on his insights into human schemes and why they mostly fail, analyzed this phenomenon. In the course of a rebellion he spearheaded against the French monarchy in 1651, the young king, Louis XIV, and his court had suddenly left Paris and established themselves in a palace outside the capital. The presence of the king so close to the heart of the revolution had been a tremendous burden on the revolutionaries, and they breathed a sigh of relief. This later proved their downfall, however, since the court's absence from Paris gave it much more room to maneuver. "The most ordinary cause of people's mistakes," Cardinal de Retz later wrote, "is their being too much frightened at the present danger, and not enough so at that which is remote."

The dangers that are remote, that loom in the distance—if we can see them as they take shape, how many mistakes we avoid. How many plans we would instantly abort if we realized we were avoiding a small danger only to step into a larger one. So much of power is not what you do but what you do not do—the rash and foolish actions that you refrain from before they get you into trouble. Plan in detail before you act—do not let vague plans lead you into trouble. Will this have unintended consequences? Will I stir up new enemies? Will someone else take advantage of my labors? Unhappy endings are much more common than happy ones—do not be swayed by the happy ending in your mind.

The French elections of 1848 came down to a struggle between Louis-Adolphe Thiers, the man of order, and General Louis Eugène Cavaignac, the rabble-rouser of the right. When Thiers realized he was hopelessly behind in this high-stakes race, he searched desperately for a solution. His eye fell on Louis Bonaparte, grand-nephew of the great general Napoleon, and a lowly deputy in the parliament. This Bonaparte seemed a bit of an imbecile, but his name alone could get him elected in a country yearning for a strong ruler. He would be Thiers's puppet and eventually would be pushed offstage. The first part of the plan worked to perfection, and Napoleon was elected by a large margin. The problem was that Thiers had not foreseen one simple fact: This "imbecile" was in fact a man of enormous ambition. Three years later he dissolved parliament, declared himself emperor, and ruled France for another eighteen years, much to the horror of Thiers and his party.

The ending is everything. It is the end of the action that determines who gets the glory, the money, the prize. Your conclusion must be crystal clear, and you must keep it constantly in mind. You must also figure out how to ward off the vultures circling overhead, trying to live off the carcass of your creation. And you must anticipate the many possible crises that will tempt you to improvise. Bismarck overcame these dangers because he planned to the end, kept on course through every crisis, and never let others steal the glory. Once he had reached his stated goal, he withdrew into his shell like a turtle. This kind of self-control is godlike.

When you see several steps ahead, and plan your moves all the way to the end, you will no longer be tempted by emotion or by the desire to improvise. Your clarity will rid you of the anxiety and vagueness that are the primary reasons why so many fail to conclude their actions success-fully. You see the ending and you tolerate no deviation.

Image:
The Gods on
Mount Olympus.
Looking down on
human actions from the
clouds, they see in advance the
endings of all the great dreams that
lead to disaster and tragedy. And
they laugh at our inability to see beyond
the moment, and at how we delude ourselves.

Authority: How much easier it is never to get in than to get yourself out! We should act contrary to the reed which, when it first appears, throws up a long straight stem but afterwards, as though it were ex-hausted . . . makes several dense knots, indicating that it no longer has its original vigor and drive. We must rather begin gently and coolly, saving our breath for the encounter and our vigorous thrusts for finishing off the job. In their beginnings it is we who guide affairs and hold them in our power; but so often once they are set in motion, it is they which guide us and sweep us along. (Montaigne, 1533–1592)

REVERSAL

It is a cliché among strategists that your plan must include alternatives and have a degree of flexibility. That is certainly true. If you are locked into a plan too rigidly, you will be unable to deal with sudden shifts of fortune. Once you have examined the future possibilities and decided on your target, you must build in alternatives and be open to new routes toward your goal.

Most people, however, lose less from overplanning and rigidity than from vagueness and a tendency to improvise constantly in the face of circumstance. There is no real purpose in contemplating a reversal to this Law, then, for no good can come from refusing to think far into the future and planning to the end. If you are clear- and far-thinking enough, you will understand that the future is uncertain, and that you must be open to adaptation. Only having a clear objective and a far-reaching plan allows you that freedom.

30

MAKE YOUR

ACCOMPLISHMENTS

SEEM EFFORTLESS

JUDGMENT

Your actions must seem natural and executed with ease. All the toil and practice that go into them, and also all the clever tricks, must be concealed. When you act, act effortlessly, as if you could do much more. Avoid the temptation of revealing how hard you work—it only raises questions. Teach no one your tricks or they will be used against you.

OBSERVANCE OF THE LAW 1

The Japanese tea ceremony called Cha-no-yu ("Hot Water for Tea") has origins in ancient times, but it reached its peak of refinement in the six-teenth century under its most renowned practitioner, Sen no Rikyu. Al-though not from a noble family, Rikyu rose to great power, becoming the preferred tea master of the Emperor Hideyoshi, and an important adviser on aesthetic and even political matters. For Rikyu, the secret of success consisted in appearing natural, concealing the effort behind one's work.

One day Rikyu and his son went to an acquaintance's house for a tea ceremony. On the way in, the son remarked that the lovely antique-look-ing gate at their host's house gave it an evocatively lonely appearance. "I don't think so," replied his father, "it looks as though it had been brought from some mountain temple a long way off, and as if the labor required to import it must have cost a lot of money." If the owner of the house had put this much effort into one gate, it would show in his tea ceremony—and in-deed Sen no Rikyu had to leave the ceremony early, unable to endure the affectation and effort it inadvertently revealed.

On another evening, while having tea at a friend's house, Rikyu saw his host go outside, hold up a lantern in the darkness, cut a lemon off a tree, and bring it in. This charmed Rikyu—the host needed a relish for the dish he was serving, and had spontaneously gone outside to get one. But when the man offered the lemon with some Osaka rice cake, Rikyu realized that he had planned the cutting of the lemon all along, to go with this expensive delicacy. The gesture no longer seemed spontaneous—it was a way for the host to prove his cleverness. He had accidentally revealed how hard he was trying. Having seen enough, Rikyu politely declined the cake, excused himself, and left.

Emperor Hideyoshi once planned to visit Rikyu for a tea ceremony. On the night before he was to come, snow began to fall. Thinking quickly, Rikyu laid round cushions that fit exactly on each of the stepping-stones that led through the garden to his house. Just before dawn, he rose, saw that it had stopped snowing, and carefully removed the cushions. When Hideyoshi arrived, he marveled at the simple beauty of the sight—the per-fectly round stepping stones, unencumbered by snow—and noticed how it called no attention to the manner in which Rikyu had accomplished it, but only to the polite gesture itself.

After Sen no Rikyu died, his ideas had a profound influence on the practice of the tea ceremony. The Tokugawa shogun Yorinobu, son of the great Emperor Ieyasu, was a student of Rikyu's teachings. In his garden he had a stone lantern made by a famous master, and Lord Sakai Tadakatsu asked if he could come by one day to see it. Yorinobu replied that he would be honored, and commanded his gardeners to put everything in order for the visit. These gardeners, unfamiliar with the precepts of Cha-no-yu, thought the stone lantern misshapen, its windows being too small for the present taste. They had a local workman enlarge the windows. A few days before Lord Sakai's visit, Yorinobu toured the garden. When he saw the altered windows he exploded with rage, ready to impale on his sword the fool who had ruined the lantern, upsetting its natural grace and destroying the whole purpose of Lord Sakai's visit.

When Yorinobu calmed down, however, he remembered that he had originally bought two of the lanterns, and that the second was in his garden on the island of Kishu. At great expense, he hired a whale boat and the finest rowers he could find, ordering them to bring the lantern to him within two days—a difficult feat at best. But the sailors rowed day and night, and with the luck of a good wind they arrived just in time. To Yorinobu's delight, this stone lantern was more magnificent than the first, for it had stood untouched for twenty years in a bamboo thicket, acquiring a brilliant antique appearance and a delicate covering of moss. When Lord Sakai arrived, later that same day, he was awed by the lantern, which was more magnificent than he had imagined—so graceful and at one with the elements. Fortunately he had no idea what time and effort it had cost Yorinobu to create this sublime effect.

Interpretation

To Sen no Rikyu, the sudden appearance of something naturally, almost accidentally graceful was the height of beauty. This beauty came without warning and seemed effortless. Nature created such things by its own laws and processes, but men had to create their effects through labor and contrivance. And when they showed the effort of producing the effect, the effect was spoiled. The gate came from too far away, the cutting of the lemon looked contrived.

You will often have to use tricks and ingenuity to create your effects—the cushions in the snow, the men rowing all night—but your audience must never suspect the work or the thinking that has gone into them. Nature does not reveal its tricks, and what imitates nature by appearing effortless approximates nature's power.

OBSERVANCE OF THE LAW II

The great escape artist Harry Houdini once advertised his act as "The Impossible Possible." And indeed those who witnessed his dramatic escapes felt that what he did onstage contradicted commonsense ideas of human capacity.

One evening in 1904, an audience of 4,000 Londoners filled a theater to watch Houdini accept a challenge: to escape from a pair of manacles billed as the strongest ever invented. They contained six sets of locks and nine tumblers in each cuff; a Birmingham maker had spent five years constructing them. Experts who examined them said they had never seen anything so intricate, and this intricacy was thought to make them impossible to escape.

The crowd watched the experts secure the manacles on Houdini's wrists. Then the escape artist entered a black cabinet on stage. The minutes

swallows over willow trees. When Masamune saw the finished work he was as overjoyed at the artist's skill as he had previously been annoyed at the apparent mess he was making of the screens.

CHA-NO-YU: THE JAPANESE TEA CEREMONY A. L. SADLER, 1962

THE WRESTLING MASTER

There was once a wrestling master who was versed in 360 feints and holds. He took a special liking to one of his pupils, to whom he taught 359 of them over a period of time. Somehow he never got around to the last trick. As months went by the young man became so proficient in the art that he bested everyone who dared to face him in the ring. He was so proud of his prowess that one day he boasted before the sultan that he could readily whip his master, were it not out of respect for his age and gratitude for his tutelage.

The sultan became incensed at this irreverence and ordered an immediate match with the royal court in attendance.

At the gong the youth barged forward with a lusty yell, only to be confronted with the unfamiliar 360th feint.

went by; the more time passed, the more certain it seemed that these manacles would be the first to defeat him. At one point he emerged from the cabinet, and asked that the cuffs be temporarily removed so that he could take off his coat—it was hot inside. The challengers refused, suspecting his request was a trick to find out how the locks worked. Undeterred, and without using his hands, Houdini managed to lift the coat over his shoulders, turn it inside out, remove a penknife from his vest pocket with his teeth, and, by moving his head, cut the coat off his arms. Freed from the coat, he stepped back into the cabinet, the audience roaring with approval at his grace and dexterity.

Finally, having kept the audience waiting long enough, Houdini emerged from the cabinet a second time, now with his hands free, the manacles raised high in triumph. To this day no one knows how he managed the escape. Although he had taken close to an hour to free himself, he had never looked concerned, had shown no sign of doubt. Indeed it seemed by the end that he had drawn out the escape as a way to heighten the drama, to make the audience worry—for there was no other sign that the performance had been anything but easy. The complaint about the heat was equally part of the act. The spectators of this and other Houdini performances must have felt he was toying with them: These manacles are nothing, he seemed to say, I could have freed myself a lot sooner, and from a lot worse.

Over the years, Houdini escaped from the chained carcass of an embalmed "sea monster" (a half octopus, half whalelike beast that had beached near Boston); he had himself sealed inside an enormous envelope from which he emerged without breaking the paper; he passed through brick walls; he wriggled free from straitjackets while dangling high in the air; he leaped from bridges into icy waters, his hands manacled and his legs in chains; he had himself submerged in glass cases full of water, hands padlocked, while the audience watched in amazement as he worked himself free, struggling for close to an hour apparently without breathing. Each time he seemed to court certain death yet survived with superhuman aplomb. Meanwhile, he said nothing about his methods, gave no clues as to how he accomplished any of his tricks—he left his audiences and critics speculating, his power and reputation enhanced by their struggles with the inexplicable. Perhaps the most baffling trick of all was making a ten-thousand-pound elephant disappear before an audience's eyes, a feat he repeated on stage for over nineteen weeks. No one has ever really explained how he did this, for in the auditorium where he performed the trick, there was simply nowhere for an elephant to hide.

The effortlessness of Houdini's escapes led some to think he used occult forces, his superior psychic abilities giving him special control over his body. But a German escape artist named Kleppini claimed to know Houdini's secret: He simply used elaborate gadgets. Kleppini also claimed to have defeated Houdini in a handcuff challenge in Holland.

Houdini did not mind all kinds of speculation floating around about his methods, but he would not tolerate an outright lie, and in 1902 he challenged Kleppini to a handcuff duel. Kleppini accepted. Through a spy, he found out the secret word to unlock a pair of French combination-lock cuffs that Houdini liked to use. His plan was to choose these cuffs to escape from onstage. This would definitely debunk Houdini—his "genius" simply lay in his use of mechanical gadgets.

On the night of the challenge, just as Kleppini had planned, Houdini offered him a choice of cuffs and he selected the ones with the combination lock. He was even able to disappear with them behind a screen to make a quick test, and reemerged seconds later, confident of victory.

Acting as if he sensed fraud, Houdini refused to lock Kleppini in the cuffs. The two men argued and began to fight, even wrestling with each other onstage. After a few minutes of this, an apparently angry, frustrated Houdini gave up and locked Kleppini in the cuffs. For the next few minutes Kleppini strained to get free. Something was wrong—minutes earlier he had opened the cuffs behind the screen; now the same code no longer worked. He sweated, racking his brains. Hours went by, the audience left, and finally an exhausted and humiliated Kleppini gave up and asked to be released.

The cuffs that Kleppini himself had opened behind the screen with the word *"C-L-E-F-S"* (French for "keys") now clicked open only with the word *"F-R-A-U-D."* Kleppini never figured out how Houdini had accomplished this uncanny feat.

Keep the extent of your abilities unknown. The wise man does not allow his knowledge and abilities to be sounded to the bottom, if he desires to be honored by all. He allows you to know them but not to comprehend them. No one must know the extent of his abilities, lest he be disappointed. No one ever has an opportunity of fathoming him entirely. For guesses and doubts about the extent of his talents arouse more veneration than accurate knowledge of them, be they ever so great.

BALTASAR GRACIÁN, 1601–1658

Interpretation

Although we do not know for certain how Houdini accomplished many of his most ingenious escapes, one thing is clear: It was not the occult, or any kind of magic, that gave him his powers, but hard work and endless practice, all of which he carefully concealed from the world. Houdini never left anything to chance—day and night he studied the workings of locks, researched centuries-old sleight-of-hand tricks, pored over books on mechanics, whatever he could use. Every moment not spent researching he spent working his body, keeping himself exceptionally limber, and learning how to control his muscles and his breathing.

Early on in Houdini's career, an old Japanese performer whom he toured with taught him an ancient trick: how to swallow an ivory ball, then bring it back up. He practiced this endlessly with a small peeled potato tied to a string—up and down he would manipulate the potato with his throat muscles, until they were strong enough to move it without the string. The organizers of the London handcuff challenge had searched Houdini's body thoroughly beforehand, but no one could check the inside of his throat, where he could have concealed small tools to help him escape. Even so, Kleppini was fundamentally wrong: It was not Houdini's tools but his practice, work, and research that made his escapes possible.

Kleppini, in fact, was completely outwitted by Houdini, who set the whole thing up. He let his opponent learn the code to the French cuffs, then baited him into choosing those cuffs onstage. Then, during the two men's tussle, the dexterous Houdini was able to change the code to *"F-R-A-U-D."* He had spent weeks practicing this trick, but the audience saw none of the sweat and toil behind the scenes. Nor was Houdini ever nervous; he induced nervousness in others. (He deliberately dragged out the time it would take to escape, as a way of heightening the drama, and making the audience squirm.) His escapes from death, always graceful and easy, made him look like a superman.

As a person of power, you must research and practice endlessly before appearing in public, onstage or anywhere else. Never expose the sweat and labor behind your poise. Some think such exposure will demonstrate their diligence and honesty, but it actually just makes them look weaker—as if anyone who practiced and worked at it could do what they had done, or as if they weren't really up to the job. Keep your effort and your tricks to yourself and you seem to have the grace and ease of a god. One never sees the source of a god's power revealed; one only sees its effects.

> *A line [of poetry] will take us hours maybe;*
> *Yet if it does not seem a moment's thought,*
> *Our stitching and unstitching has been naught.*
> Adam's Curse, *William Butler Yeats, 1865–1939*

KEYS TO POWER

Humanity's first notions of power came from primitive encounters with nature—the flash of lightning in the sky, a sudden flood, the speed and ferocity of a wild animal. These forces required no thinking, no planning—they awed us by their sudden appearance, their gracefulness, and their power over life and death. And this remains the kind of power we have always wanted to imitate. Through science and technology we have re-created the speed and sublime power of nature, but something is missing: Our machines are noisy and jerky, they reveal their effort. Even the very best creations of technology cannot root out our admiration for things that move easily and effortlessly. The power of children to bend us to their will comes from a kind of seductive charm that we feel in the presence of a creature less reflective and more graceful than we are. We cannot return to such a state, but if we can create the appearance of this kind of ease, we elicit in others the kind of primitive awe that nature has always evoked in humankind.

One of the first European writers to expound on this principle came from that most unnatural of environments, the Renaissance court. In *The Book of the Courtier,* published in 1528, Baldassare Castiglione describes the highly elaborate and codified manners of the perfect court citizen. And yet, Castiglione explains, the courtier must execute these gestures with what he calls *sprezzatura,* the capacity to make the difficult seem easy. He urges the courtier to "practice in all things a certain nonchalance which conceals all artistry and makes whatever one says or does seem uncontrived and effortless." We all admire the achievement of some unusual feat, but if it is accomplished naturally and gracefully, our admiration increases tenfold— "whereas . . . to labor at what one is doing and . . . to make bones over it, shows an extreme lack of grace and causes everything, whatever its worth, to be discounted."

Much of the idea of *sprezzatura* came from the world of art. All the great Renaissance artists carefully kept their works under wraps. Only the finished masterpiece could be shown to the public. Michelangelo forbade even popes to view his work in process. A Renaissance artist was always careful to keep his studios shut to patrons and public alike, not out of fear of imitation, but because to see the making of the works would mar the magic of their effect, and their studied atmosphere of ease and natural beauty.

The Renaissance painter Vasari, also the first great art critic, ridiculed the work of Paolo Uccello, who was obsessed with the laws of perspective. The effort Uccello spent on improving the appearance of perspective was too obvious in his work—it made his paintings ugly and labored, overwhelmed by the effort of their effects. We have the same response when we watch performers who put too much effort into their act: Seeing them trying so hard breaks the illusion. It also makes us uncomfortable. Calm, graceful performers, on the other hand, set us at ease, creating the illusion that they are not acting but being natural and themselves, even when everything they are doing involves labor and practice.

The idea of *sprezzatura* is relevant to all forms of power, for power depends vitally on appearances and the illusions you create. Your public actions are like artworks: They must have visual appeal, must create anticipation, even entertain. When you reveal the inner workings of your creation, you become just one more mortal among others. What is understandable is not awe-inspiring—we tell ourselves we could do as well if we had the money and time. Avoid the temptation of showing how clever you are—it is far more clever to conceal the mechanisms of your cleverness.

Talleyrand's application of this concept to his daily life greatly enhanced the aura of power that surrounded him. He never liked to work too hard, so he made others do the work for him—the spying, the research, the detailed analyses. With all this labor at his disposal, he himself never seemed to strain. When his spies revealed that a certain event was about to take place, he would talk in social conversation as if he *sensed* its imminence. The result was that people thought he was clairvoyant. His short pithy statements and witticisms always seemed to summarize a situation perfectly, but they were based on much research and thought. To those in government, including Napoleon himself, Talleyrand gave the impression of immense power—an effect entirely dependent on the apparent ease with which he accomplished his feats.

There is another reason for concealing your shortcuts and tricks:

When you let this information out, you give people ideas they can use against you. You lose the advantages of keeping silent. We tend to want the world to know what we have done—we want our vanity gratified by having our hard work and cleverness applauded, and we may even want sympathy for the hours it has taken to reach our point of artistry. Learn to control this propensity to blab, for its effect is often the opposite of what you expected. Remember: The more mystery surrounds your actions, the more awesome your power seems. You appear to be the only one who can do what you do—and the appearance of having an exclusive gift is immensely powerful. Finally, because you achieve your accomplishments with grace and ease, people believe that you could always do more if you tried harder. This elicits not only admiration but a touch of fear. Your powers are untapped—no one can fathom their limits.

Image: The Racehorse. From up close we would see the
strain, the effort to control the horse, the labored, painful
breathing. But from the distance where we sit and watch, it
is all gracefulness, flying through the air. Keep others at a
distance and they will only see the ease with which you move.

Authority: For whatever action [nonchalance] accompanies, no
matter how trivial it is, it not only reveals the skill of the person
doing it but also very often causes it to be considered far greater
than it really is. This is because it makes the onlookers believe that
a man who performs well with so much facility must possess even
greater skill than he does. (Baldassare Castiglione, 1478–1529)

REVERSAL

The secrecy with which you surround your actions must seem lighthearted in spirit. A zeal to conceal your work creates an unpleasant, almost paranoiac impression: you are taking the game too seriously. Houdini was careful to make the concealment of his tricks seem a game, all part of the show. Never show your work until it is finished, but if you put too much effort into keeping it under wraps you will be like the painter Pontormo, who spent the last years of his life hiding his frescoes from the public eye and only succeeded in driving himself mad. Always keep your sense of humor about yourself.

There are also times when revealing the inner workings of your projects can prove worthwhile. It all depends on your audience's taste, and on the times in which you operate. P. T. Barnum recognized that his public wanted to feel involved in his shows, and that understanding his tricks delighted them, partly, perhaps, because implicitly debunking people who kept their sources of power hidden from the masses appealed to America's democratic spirit. The public also appreciated the showman's humor and honesty. Barnum took this to the extreme of publicizing his own humbuggery in his popular autobiography, written when his career was at its height.

As long as the *partial* disclosure of tricks and techniques is carefully planned, rather than the result of an uncontrollable need to blab, it is the ultimate in cleverness. It gives the audience the illusion of being superior and involved, even while much of what you do remains concealed from them.

31

CONTROL THE OPTIONS:

GET OTHERS TO PLAY WITH

THE CARDS YOU DEAL

JUDGMENT

The best deceptions are the ones that seem to give the other person a choice: Your victims feel they are in control, but are actually your puppets. Give people options that come out in your favor whichever one they choose. Force them to make choices between the lesser of two evils, both of which serve your purpose. Put them on the horns of a dilemma: They are gored wherever they turn.

OBSERVANCE OF THE LAW I

From early in his reign, Ivan IV, later known as Ivan the Terrible, had to confront an unpleasant reality: The country desperately needed reform, but he lacked the power to push it through. The greatest limit to his authority came from the boyars, the Russian princely class that dominated the country and terrorized the peasantry.

In 1553, at the age of twenty-three, Ivan fell ill. Lying in bed, nearing death, he asked the boyars to swear allegiance to his son as the new czar. Some hesitated, some even refused. Then and there Ivan saw he had no power over the boyars. He recovered from his illness, but he never forgot the lesson: The boyars were out to destroy him. And indeed in the years to come, many of the most powerful of them defected to Russia's main enemies, Poland and Lithuania, where they plotted their return and the overthrow of the czar. Even one of Ivan's closest friends, Prince Andrey Kurbski, suddenly turned against him, defecting to Lithuania in 1564, and becoming the strongest of Ivan's enemies.

When Kurbski began raising troops for an invasion, the royal dynasty seemed suddenly more precarious than ever. With émigré nobles fomenting invasion from the west, Tartars bearing down from the east, and the boyars stirring up trouble within the country, Russia's vast size made it a nightmare to defend. In whatever direction Ivan struck, he would leave himself vulnerable on the other side. Only if he had absolute power could he deal with this many-headed Hydra. And he had no such power.

Ivan brooded until the morning of December 3, 1564, when the citizens of Moscow awoke to a strange sight. Hundreds of sleds filled the square before the Kremlin, loaded with the czar's treasures and with provisions for the entire court. They watched in disbelief as the czar and his court boarded the sleds and left town. Without explaining why, he established himself in a village south of Moscow. For an entire month a kind of terror gripped the capital, for the Muscovites feared that Ivan had abandoned them to the bloodthirsty boyars. Shops closed up and riotous mobs gathered daily. Finally, on January 3 of 1565, a letter arrived from the czar, explaining that he could no longer bear the boyars' betrayals and had decided to abdicate once and for all.

Read aloud in public, the letter had a startling effect: Merchants and commoners blamed the boyars for Ivan's decision, and took to the streets, terrifying the nobility with their fury. Soon a group of delegates representing the church, the princes, and the people made the journey to Ivan's village, and begged the czar, in the name of the holy land of Russia, to return to the throne. Ivan listened but would not change his mind. After days of hearing their pleas, however, he offered his subjects a choice: Either they grant him absolute powers to govern as he pleased, with no interference from the boyars, or they find a new leader.

Faced with a choice between civil war and the acceptance of despotic power, almost every sector of Russian society "opted" for a strong czar, calling for Ivan's return to Moscow and the restoration of law and order. In

The German Chancellor Bismarck, enraged at the constant criticisms from Rudolf Virchow (the German pathologist and liberal politician), had his seconds call upon the scientist to challenge him to a duel. "As the challenged party, I have the choice of weapons," said Virchow, "and I choose these." He held aloft two large and apparently identical sausages. "One of these," he went on, "is infected with deadly germs; the other is perfectly sound. Let His Excellency decide which one he wishes to eat, and I will eat the other." Almost immediately the message came back that the chancellor had decided to cancel the duel.

THE LITTLE, BROWN BOOK OF ANECDOTES, CLIFTON FADIMAN, ED., 1985

February, with much celebration, Ivan returned to Moscow. The Russians could no longer complain if he behaved dictatorially—they had given him this power themselves.

Interpretation

Ivan the Terrible faced a terrible dilemma: To give in to the boyars would lead to certain destruction, but civil war would bring a different kind of ruin. Even if Ivan came out of such a war on top, the country would be devastated and its divisions would be stronger than ever. His weapon of choice in the past had been to make a bold, offensive move. Now, however, that kind of move would turn against him—the more boldly he confronted his enemies, the worse the reactions he would spark.

The main weakness of a show of force is that it stirs up resentment and eventually leads to a response that eats at your authority. Ivan, immensely creative in the use of power, saw clearly that the only path to the kind of victory he wanted was a false withdrawal. He would not force the country over to his position, he would give it "options": either his abdication, and certain anarchy, or his accession to absolute power. To back up his move, he made it clear that he preferred to abdicate: "Call my bluff," he said, "and watch what happens." No one called his bluff. By withdrawing for just a month, he showed the country a glimpse of the nightmares that would follow his abdication—Tartar invasions, civil war, ruin. (All of these did eventually come to pass after Ivan's death, in the infamous "Time of the Troubles.")

Withdrawal and disappearance are classic ways of controlling the options. You give people a sense of how things will fall apart without you, and you offer them a "choice": I stay away and you suffer the consequences, or I return under circumstances that I dictate. In this method of controlling people's options, they choose the option that gives you power because the alternative is just too unpleasant. You force their hand, but indirectly: They seem to have a choice. Whenever people feel they have a choice, they walk into your trap that much more easily.

OBSERVANCE OF THE LAW II

As a seventeenth-century French courtesan, Ninon de Lenclos found that her life had certain pleasures. Her lovers came from royalty and aristocracy, and they paid her well, entertained her with their wit and intellect, satisfied her rather demanding sensual needs, and treated her almost as an equal. Such a life was infinitely preferable to marriage. In 1643, however, Ninon's mother died suddenly, leaving her, at the age of twenty-three, totally alone in the world—no family, no dowry, nothing to fall back upon. A kind of panic overtook her and she entered a convent, turning her back on her illustrious lovers. A year later she left the convent and moved to Lyons. When she finally reappeared in Paris, in 1648, lovers and suitors flocked to her door in greater numbers than ever before, for she was the wittiest and

THEE LIAR

Once upon a time there was a king of Armenia, who, being of a curious turn of mind and in need of some new diversion, sent his heralds throughout the land to make the following proclamation: "Hear this! Whatever man among you can prove himself the most outrageous liar in Armenia shall receive an apple made of pure gold from the hands of His Majesty the King!" People began to swarm to the palace from every town and hamlet in the country, people of all ranks and conditions, princes, merchants, farmers, priests, rich and poor, tall and short, fat and thin. There was no lack of liars in the land, and each one told his tale to the king. A ruler, however, has heard practically every sort of lie, and none of those now told him convinced the king that he had listened to the best of them. The king was beginning to grow tired of his new sport and was thinking of calling the whole contest off without declaring a winner, when there appeared before him a poor, ragged man, carrying a large earthenware pitcher under his arm. "What can I do for you?" asked His Majesty. "Sire!" said the poor man, slightly bewil-

most spirited courtesan of the time and her presence had been greatly missed.

Ninon's followers quickly discovered, however, that she had changed her old way of doing things, and had set up a new system of options. The dukes, seigneurs, and princes who wanted to pay for her services could continue to do so, but they were no longer in control—she would sleep with them when she wanted, according to her whim. All their money bought them was a possibility. If it was her pleasure to sleep with them only once a month, so be it.

Those who did not want to be what Ninon called a *payeur* could join the large and growing group of men she called her *martyrs*—men who visited her apartment principally for her friendship, her biting wit, her lute-playing, and the company of the most vibrant minds of the period, including Molière, La Rochefoucauld, and Saint-Évremond. The *martyrs,* too, however, entertained a possibility: She would regularly select from them a *favori,* a man who would become her lover without having to pay, and to whom she would abandon herself completely for as long as she so desired—a week, a few months, rarely longer. A *payeur* could not become a *favori,* but a *martyr* had no guarantee of becoming one, and indeed could remain disappointed for an entire lifetime. The poet Charleval, for example, never enjoyed Ninon's favors, but never stopped coming to visit—he did not want to do without her company.

As word of this system reached polite French society, Ninon became the object of intense hostility. Her reversal of the position of the courtesan scandalized the queen mother and her court. Much to their horror, however, it did not discourage her male suitors—indeed it only increased their numbers and intensified their desire. It became an honor to be a *payeur,* helping Ninon to maintain her lifestyle and her glittering salon, accompanying her sometimes to the theater, and sleeping with her when she chose. Even more distinguished were the *martyrs,* enjoying her company without paying for it and maintaining the hope, however remote, of some day becoming her *favori.* That possibility spurred on many a young nobleman, as word spread that none among the courtesans could surpass Ninon in the art of love. And so the married and the single, the old and the young, entered her web and chose one of the two options presented to them, both of which amply satisfied her.

Interpretation

The life of the courtesan entailed the possibility of a power that was denied a married woman, but it also had obvious perils. The man who paid for the courtesan's services in essence owned her, determining when he could possess her and when, later on, he would abandon her. As she grew older, her options narrowed, as fewer men chose her. To avoid a life of poverty she had to amass her fortune while she was young. The courtesan's legendary greed, then, reflected a practical necessity, yet also lessened her allure, since the illusion of being desired is important to men, who are often alien-

dered. "Surely you remember? You owe me a pot of gold, and I have come to collect it."
"You are a perfect liar, sir!" exclaimed the king. "I owe you no money!"
"A perfect liar, am I?" said the poor man. "Then give me the golden apple!"
The king, realizing that the man was trying to trick him, started to hedge.
"No, no! You are not a liar!"
"Then give me the pot of gold you owe me, sire," said the man.
The king saw the dilemma. He handed over the golden apple.

ARMENIAN FOLK-TALES AND FABLES, RETOLD BY CHARLES DOWNING, 1993

ated if their partner is too interested in their money. As the courtesan aged, then, she faced a most difficult fate.

Ninon de Lenclos had a horror of any kind of dependence. She early on tasted a kind of equality with her lovers, and she would not settle into a system that left her such distasteful options. Strangely enough, the system she devised in its place seemed to satisfy her suitors as much as it did her. The *payeurs* may have had to pay, but the fact that Ninon would only sleep with them when she wanted to gave them a thrill unavailable with every other courtesan: She was yielding out of her own desire. The *martyrs'* avoidance of the taint of having to pay gave them a sense of superiority; as members of Ninon's fraternity of admirers, they also might some day experience the ultimate pleasure of being her *favori*. Finally, Ninon did not force her suitors into either category. They could "choose" which side they preferred—a freedom that left them a vestige of masculine pride.

Such is the power of giving people a choice, or rather the illusion of one, for they are playing with cards you have dealt them. Where the alternatives set up by Ivan the Terrible involved a certain risk—one option would have led to his losing his power—Ninon created a situation in which every option redounded to her favor. From the *payeurs* she received the money she needed to run her salon. And from the *martyrs* she gained the ultimate in power: She could surround herself with a bevy of admirers, a harem from which to choose her lovers.

The system, though, depended on one critical factor: the possibility, however remote, that a *martyr* could become a *favori*. The illusion that riches, glory, or sensual satisfaction may someday fall into your victim's lap is an irresistible carrot to include in your list of choices. That hope, however slim, will make men accept the most ridiculous situations, because it leaves them the all-important option of a dream. The illusion of choice, married to the possibility of future good fortune, will lure the most stubborn sucker into your glittering web.

KEYS TO POWER

Words like "freedom," "options," and "choice" evoke a power of possibility far beyond the reality of the benefits they entail. When examined closely, the choices we have—in the marketplace, in elections, in our jobs—tend to have noticeable limitations: They are often a matter of a choice simply between A and B, with the rest of the alphabet out of the picture. Yet as long as the faintest mirage of choice flickers on, we rarely focus on the missing options. We "choose" to believe that the game is fair, and that we have our freedom. We prefer not to think too much about the depth of our liberty to choose.

This unwillingness to probe the smallness of our choices stems from the fact that too much freedom creates a kind of anxiety. The phrase "unlimited options" sounds infinitely promising, but unlimited options would actually paralyze us and cloud our ability to choose. Our limited range of choices comforts us.

This supplies the clever and cunning with enormous opportunities for deception. For people who are choosing between alternatives find it hard to believe they are being manipulated or deceived; they cannot see that you are allowing them a small amount of free will in exchange for a much more powerful imposition of your own will. Setting up a narrow range of choices, then, should always be a part of your deceptions. There is a saying: If you can get the bird to walk into the cage on its own, it will sing that much more prettily.

The following are among the most common forms of "controlling the options":

Color the Choices. This was a favored technique of Henry Kissinger. As President Richard Nixon's secretary of state, Kissinger considered himself better informed than his boss, and believed that in most situations he could make the best decision on his own. But if he tried to determine policy, he would offend or perhaps enrage a notoriously insecure man. So Kissinger would propose three or four choices of action for each situation, and would present them in such a way that the one he preferred always seemed the best solution compared to the others. Time after time, Nixon fell for the bait, never suspecting that he was moving where Kissinger pushed him. This is an excellent device to use on the insecure master.

Force the Resister. One of the main problems faced by Dr. Milton H. Erickson, a pioneer of hypnosis therapy in the 1950s, was the relapse. His patients might seem to be recovering rapidly, but their apparent susceptibility to the therapy masked a deep resistance: They would soon relapse into old habits, blame the doctor, and stop coming to see him. To avoid this, Erickson began *ordering* some patients to have a relapse, to make themselves feel as bad as when they first came in—to go back to square one. Faced with this option, the patients would usually "choose" to avoid the relapse— which, of course, was what Erickson really wanted.

This is a good technique to use on children and other willful people who enjoy doing the opposite of what you ask them to: Push them to "choose" what you want them to do by appearing to advocate the opposite.

Alter the Playing Field. In the 1860s, John D. Rockefeller set out to create an oil monopoly. If he tried to buy up the smaller oil companies they would figure out what he was doing and fight back. Instead, he began secretly buying up the railway companies that transported the oil. When he then attempted to take over a particular company, and met with resistance, he reminded them of their dependence on the rails. Refusing them shipping, or simply raising their fees, could ruin their business. Rockefeller altered the playing field so that the only options the small oil producers had were the ones he gave them.

In this tactic your opponents know their hand is being forced, but it doesn't matter. The technique is effective against those who resist at all costs.

The Shrinking Options. The late-nineteenth-century art dealer Ambroise Vollard perfected this technique.

Customers would come to Vollard's shop to see some Cézannes. He would show three paintings, neglect to mention a price, and pretend to doze off. The visitors would have to leave without deciding. They would usually come back the next day to see the paintings again, but this time Vollard would pull out less interesting works, pretending he thought they were the same ones. The baffled customers would look at the new offerings, leave to think them over, and return yet again. Once again the same thing would happen: Vollard would show paintings of lesser quality still. Finally the buyers would realize they had better grab what he was showing them, because tomorrow they would have to settle for something worse, perhaps at even higher prices.

A variation on this technique is to raise the price every time the buyer hesitates and another day goes by. This is an excellent negotiating ploy to use on the chronically indecisive, who will fall for the idea that they are getting a better deal today than if they wait till tomorrow.

The Weak Man on the Precipice. The weak are the easiest to maneuver by controlling their options. Cardinal de Retz, the great seventeenth-century provocateur, served as an unofficial assistant to the Duke of Orléans, who was notoriously indecisive. It was a constant struggle to convince the duke to take action—he would hem and haw, weigh the options, and wait till the last moment, giving everyone around him an ulcer. But Retz discovered a way to handle him: He would describe all sorts of dangers, exaggerating them as much as possible, until the duke saw a yawning abyss in every direction except one: the one Retz was pushing him to take.

This tactic is similar to "Color the Choices," but with the weak you have to be more aggressive. Work on their emotions—use fear and terror to propel them into action. Try reason and they will always find a way to procrastinate.

Brothers in Crime. This is a classic con-artist technique: You attract your victims to some criminal scheme, creating a bond of blood and guilt between you. They participate in your deception, commit a crime (or think they do—see the story of Sam Geezil in Law 3), and are easily manipulated. Serge Stavisky, the great French con artist of the 1920s, so entangled the government in his scams and swindles that the state did not dare to prosecute him, and "chose" to leave him alone. It is often wise to implicate in your deceptions the very person who can do you the most harm if you fail. Their involvement can be subtle—even a hint of their involvement will narrow their options and buy their silence.

The Horns of a Dilemma. This idea was demonstrated by General William Sherman's infamous march through Georgia during the American Civil War. Although the Confederates knew what direction Sherman was heading in, they never knew if he would attack from the left or the right, for he divided his army into two wings—and if the rebels retreated from one wing they found themselves facing the other. This is a classic trial lawyer's technique: The lawyer leads the witnesses to decide between two possible explanations of an event, both of which poke a hole in their story. They have to answer the lawyer's questions, but whatever they say they hurt themselves. The key to this move is to strike quickly: Deny the victim the time to think of an escape. As they wriggle between the horns of the dilemma, they dig their own grave.

Understand: In your struggles with your rivals, it will often be necessary for you to hurt them. And if you are clearly the agent of their punishment, expect a counterattack—expect revenge. If, however, they seem *to themselves* to be the agents of their own misfortune, they will submit quietly. When Ivan left Moscow for his rural village, the citizens asking him to return agreed to his demand for absolute power. Over the years to come, they resented him less for the terror he unleashed on the country, because, after all, they had granted him his power themselves. This is why it is always good to allow your victims their choice of poison, and to cloak your involvement in providing it to them as far as possible.

Image: The Horns of the Bull. The bull backs you into the corner with its horns—not a single horn, which you might be able to escape, but a pair of horns that trap you within their hold. Run right or run left—either way you move into their piercing ends and are gored.

Authority: For the wounds and every other evil that men inflict upon themselves spontaneously, and of their own choice, are in the long run less painful than those inflicted by others. (Niccolò Machiavelli, 1469–1527)

REVERSAL

Controlling the options has one main purpose: to disguise yourself as the agent of power and punishment. The tactic works best, then, for those whose power is fragile, and who cannot operate too openly without incurring suspicion, resentment, and anger. Even as a general rule, however, it is rarely wise to be seen as exerting power directly and forcefully, no matter how secure or strong you are. It is usually more elegant and more effective to give people the illusion of choice.

On the other hand, by limiting other people's options you sometimes limit your own. There are situations in which it is to your advantage to allow your rivals a large degree of freedom: As you watch them operate, you give yourself rich opportunities to spy, gather information, and plan your deceptions. The nineteenth-century banker James Rothschild liked this method: He felt that if he tried to control his opponents' movements, he lost the chance to observe their strategy and plan a more effective course. The more freedom he allowed them in the short term, the more forcefully he could act against them in the long run.

PLAY TO PEOPLE'S

FANTASIES

JUDGMENT

The truth is often avoided because it is ugly and unpleasant. Never appeal to truth and reality unless you are prepared for the anger that comes from disenchantment. Life is so harsh and distressing that people who can manufacture romance or conjure up fantasy are like oases in the desert: Everyone flocks to them. There is great power in tapping into the fantasies of the masses.

The city-state of Venice was prosperous for so long that its citizens felt their small republic had destiny on its side. In the Middle Ages and High Renaissance, its virtual monopoly on trade to the east made it the wealthiest city in Europe. Under a beneficent republican government, Venetians enjoyed liberties that few other Italians had ever known. Yet in the sixteenth century their fortunes suddenly changed. The opening of the New World transferred power to the Atlantic side of Europe—to the Spanish and Portuguese, and later the Dutch and English. Venice could not compete economically and its empire gradually dwindled. The final blow was the devastating loss of a prized Mediterranean possession, the island of Cyprus, captured from Venice by the Turks in 1570.

Now noble families went broke in Venice, and banks began to fold. A kind of gloom and depression settled over the citizens. They had known a glittering past—had either lived through it or heard stories about it from their elders. The closeness of the glory years was humiliating. The Venetians half believed that the goddess Fortune was only playing a joke on them, and that the old days would soon return. For the time being, though, what could they do?

In 1589 rumors began to swirl around Venice of the arrival not far away of a mysterious man called "Il Bragadino," a master of alchemy, a man who had won incredible wealth through his ability, it was said, to multiply gold through the use of a secret substance. The rumor spread quickly because a few years earlier, a Venetian nobleman passing through Poland had heard a learned man prophesy that Venice would recover her past glory and power if she could find a man who understood the alchemic art of manufacturing gold. And so, as word reached Venice of the gold this Bragadino possessed—he clinked gold coins continuously in his hands, and golden objects filled his palace—some began to dream: Through him, their city would prosper again.

Members of Venice's most important noble families accordingly went together to Brescia, where Bragadino lived. They toured his palace and watched in awe as he demonstrated his gold-making abilities, taking a pinch of seemingly worthless minerals and transforming it into several ounces of gold dust. The Venetian senate prepared to debate the idea of extending an official invitation to Bragadino to stay in Venice at the city's expense, when word suddenly reached them that they were competing with the Duke of Mantua for his services. They heard of a magnificent party in Bragadino's palace for the duke, featuring garments with golden buttons, gold watches, gold plates, and on and on. Worried they might lose Bragadino to Mantua, the senate voted almost unanimously to invite him to Venice, promising him the mountain of money he would need to continue living in his luxurious style—but only if he came right away.

Late that year the mysterious Bragadino arrived in Venice. With his piercing dark eyes under thick brows, and the two enormous black mastiffs that accompanied him everywhere, he was forbidding and impressive. He took up residence in a sumptuous palace on the island of the Giudecca, with the republic funding his banquets, his expensive clothes, and all his other whims. A kind of alchemy fever spread through Venice. On street corners, hawkers would sell coal, distilling apparatus, bellows, how-to books on the subject. Everyone began to practice alchemy—everyone except Bragadino.

The alchemist seemed to be in no hurry to begin manufacturing the gold that would save Venice from ruin. Strangely enough this only increased his popularity and following; people thronged from all over Europe, even Asia, to meet this remarkable man. Months went by, with gifts pouring in to Bragadino from all sides. Still he gave no sign of the miracle that the Venetians confidently expected him to produce. Eventually the citizens began to grow impatient, wondering if he would wait forever. At first the senators warned them not to hurry him—he was a capricious devil, who needed to be cajoled. Finally, though, the nobility began to wonder too, and the senate came under pressure to show a return on the city's ballooning investment.

Bragadino had only scorn for the doubters, but he responded to them. He had, he said, already deposited in the city's mint the mysterious substance with which he multiplied gold. He could use this substance up all at once, and produce double the gold, but the more slowly the process took place, the more it would yield. If left alone for seven years, sealed in a casket, the substance would multiply the gold in the mint thirty times over. Most of the senators agreed to wait to reap the gold mine Bragadino promised. Others, however, were angry: seven more years of this man living royally at the public trough! And many of the common citizens of Venice echoed these sentiments. Finally the alchemist's enemies demanded he produce a proof of his skills: a substantial amount of gold, and soon.

Lofty, apparently devoted to his art, Bragadino responded that Venice, in its impatience, had betrayed him, and would therefore lose his services. He left town, going first to nearby Padua, then, in 1590, to Munich, at the invitation of the Duke of Bavaria, who, like the entire city of Venice, had known great wealth but had fallen into bankruptcy through his own profligacy, and hoped to regain his fortune through the famous alchemist's services. And so Bragadino resumed the comfortable arrangement he had known in Venice, and the same pattern repeated itself.

Interpretation

The young Cypriot Mamugnà had lived in Venice for several years before reincarnating himself as the alchemist Bragadino. He saw how gloom had settled on the city, how everyone was hoping for a redemption from some indefinite source. While other charlatans mastered everyday cons based on sleight of hand, Mamugnà mastered human nature. With Venice as his target from the start, he traveled abroad, made some money through his alchemy scams, and then returned to Italy, setting up shop in Brescia. There he created a reputation that he knew would spread to Venice. From a distance, in fact, his aura of power would be all the more impressive.

At first Mamugnà did not use vulgar demonstrations to convince peo-

formerly strangled his wife and son. A courtier thought fit to inform the bereaved monarch, and even affirmed that he had seen the stag laugh. The rage of a king, says Solomon, is terrible, and especially that of a lion-king. "Pitiful forester!" he exclaimed, "darest thou laugh when all around are dissolved in tears? We will not soil our royal claws with thy profane blood! Do thou, brave wolf, avenge our queen, by immolating this traitor to her august manes." Hereupon the stag replied: "Sire, the time for weeping is passed; grief is here superfluous. Your revered spouse appeared to me but now, reposing on a bed of roses; I instantly recognized her. 'Friend,' said she to me, 'have done with this funereal pomp, cease these useless tears. I have tasted a thousand delights in the Elysian fields, conversing with those who are saints like myself. Let the king's despair remain for some time unchecked, it gratifies me.'" Scarcely had he spoken, when every one shouted: "A miracle! a miracle!" The stag, instead of being punished, received a handsome gift. Do but entertain a king with dreams, flatter him, and tell him a few pleasant fantastic lies: whatever his indignation against you may be, he will swallow the bait, and make you his dearest friend.

FABLES,
JEAN DE LA FONTAINE,
1621–1695

ple of his alchemic skill. His sumptuous palace, his opulent garments, the clink of gold in his hands, all these provided a superior argument to anything rational. And these established the cycle that kept him going: His obvious wealth confirmed his reputation as an alchemist, so that patrons like the Duke of Mantua gave him money, which allowed him to live in wealth, which reinforced his reputation as an alchemist, and so on. Only once this reputation was established, and dukes and senators were fighting over him, did he resort to the trifling necessity of a demonstration. By then, however, people were easy to deceive: They wanted to believe. The Venetian senators who watched him multiply gold wanted to believe so badly that they failed to notice the glass pipe up his sleeve, from which he slipped gold dust into his pinches of minerals. Brilliant and capricious, he was the alchemist of their fantasies—and once he had created an aura like this, no one noticed his simple deceptions.

Such is the power of the fantasies that take root in us, especially in times of scarcity and decline. People rarely believe that their problems arise from their own misdeeds and stupidity. Someone or something out there is to blame—the other, the world, the gods—and so salvation comes from the outside as well. Had Bragadino arrived in Venice armed with a detailed analysis of the reasons behind the city's economic decline, and of the hard-nosed steps that it could take to turn things around, he would have been scorned. The reality was too ugly and the solution too painful—mostly the kind of hard work that the citizens' ancestors had mustered to create an empire. Fantasy, on the other hand—in this case the romance of alchemy—was easy to understand and infinitely more palatable.

To gain power, you must be a source of pleasure for those around you—and pleasure comes from playing to people's fantasies. Never promise a gradual improvement through hard work; rather, promise the moon, the great and sudden transformation, the pot of gold.

No man need despair of gaining converts to the most extravagant
hypothesis who has art enough to represent it in favorable colors.
David Hume, 1711–1776

KEYS TO POWER

Fantasy can never operate alone. It requires the backdrop of the humdrum and the mundane. It is the oppressiveness of reality that allows fantasy to take root and bloom. In sixteenth-century Venice, the reality was one of decline and loss of prestige. The corresponding fantasy described a sudden recovery of past glories through the miracle of alchemy. While the reality only got worse, the Venetians inhabited a happy dream world in which their city restored its fabulous wealth and power overnight, turning dust into gold.

The person who can spin a fantasy out of an oppressive reality has access to untold power. As you search for the fantasy that will take hold of the masses, then, keep your eye on the banal truths that weigh heavily on us all. Never be distracted by people's glamorous portraits of themselves and their lives; search and dig for what really imprisons them. Once you find that, you have the magical key that will put great power in your hands.

Although times and people change, let us examine a few of the oppressive realities that endure, and the opportunities for power they provide:

The Reality: Change is slow and gradual. It requires hard work, a bit of luck, a fair amount of self-sacrifice, and a lot of patience.
The Fantasy: A sudden transformation will bring a total change in one's fortunes, bypassing work, luck, self-sacrifice, and time in one fantastic stroke.

This is of course the fantasy par excellence of the charlatans who prowl among us to this day, and was the key to Bragadino's success. Promise a great and total change—from poor to rich, sickness to health, misery to ecstasy—and you will have followers.

How did the great sixteenth-century German quack Leonhard Thurneisser become the court physician for the Elector of Brandenburg without ever studying medicine? Instead of offering amputations, leeches, and foul-tasting purgatives (the medicaments of the time), Thurneisser offered sweet-tasting elixirs and promised instant recovery. Fashionable courtiers especially wanted his solution of "drinkable gold," which cost a fortune. If some inexplicable illness assailed you, Thurneisser would consult a horoscope and prescribe a talisman. Who could resist such a fantasy—health and well-being without sacrifice and pain!

The Reality: The social realm has hard-set codes and boundaries. We understand these limits and know that we have to move within the same familiar circles, day in and day out.
The Fantasy: We can enter a totally new world with different codes and the promise of adventure.

In the early 1700s, all London was abuzz with talk of a mysterious stranger, a young man named George Psalmanazar. He had arrived from what was to most Englishmen a fantastical land: the island of Formosa (now Taiwan), off the coast of China. Oxford University engaged Psalmanazar to teach the island's language; a few years later he translated the Bible into Formosan, then wrote a book—an immediate best-seller—on Formosa's history and geography. English royalty wined and dined the young man, and everywhere he went he entertained his hosts with wondrous stories of his homeland, and its bizarre customs.

After Psalmanazar died, however, his will revealed that he was in fact merely a Frenchman with a rich imagination. Everything he had said about Formosa—its alphabet, its language, its literature, its entire culture—he had invented. He had built on the English public's ignorance of the place to concoct an elaborate story that fulfilled their desire for the exotic and strange. British culture's rigid control of people's dangerous dreams gave him the perfect opportunity to exploit their fantasy.

The fantasy of the exotic, of course, can also skirt the sexual. It must not come too close, though, for the physical hinders the power of fantasy; it can be seen, grasped, and then tired of—the fate of most courtesans. The bodily charms of the mistress only whet the master's appetite for more and different pleasures, a new beauty to adore. To bring power, fantasy must remain to some degree unrealized, literally unreal. The dancer Mata Hari, for instance, who rose to public prominence in Paris before World War I, had quite ordinary looks. Her power came from the fantasy she created of being strange and exotic, unknowable and indecipherable. The taboo she worked with was less sex itself than the breaking of social codes.

Another form of the fantasy of the exotic is simply the hope for relief from boredom. Con artists love to play on the oppressiveness of the working world, its lack of adventure. Their cons might involve, say, the recovery of lost Spanish treasure, with the possible participation of an alluring Mexican señorita and a connection to the president of a South American country—anything offering release from the humdrum.

The Reality: Society is fragmented and full of conflict.
The Fantasy: People can come together in a mystical union of souls.

In the 1920s the con man Oscar Hartzell made a quick fortune out of the age-old Sir Francis Drake swindle—basically promising any sucker who happened to be surnamed "Drake" a substantial share of the long-lost "Drake treasure," to which Hartzell had access. Thousands across the Midwest fell for the scam, which Hartzell cleverly turned into a crusade against the government and everyone else who was trying to keep the Drake fortune out of the rightful hands of its heirs. There developed a mystical union of the oppressed Drakes, with emotional rallies and meetings. Promise such a union and you can gain much power, but it is a dangerous power that can easily turn against you. This is a fantasy for demagogues to play on.

The Reality: Death. The dead cannot be brought back, the past cannot be changed.
The Fantasy: A sudden reversal of this intolerable fact.

This con has many variations, but requires great skill and subtlety.

The beauty and importance of the art of Vermeer have long been recognized, but his paintings are small in number, and are extremely rare. In the 1930s, though, Vermeers began to appear on the art market. Experts were called on to verify them, and pronounced them real. Possession of these new Vermeers would crown a collector's career. It was like the resurrection of Lazarus: In a strange way, Vermeer had been brought back to life. The past had been changed.

Only later did it come out that the new Vermeers were the work of a middle-aged Dutch forger named Han van Meegeren. And he had chosen

Vermeer for his scam because he understood fantasy: The paintings would seem real precisely because the public, and the experts as well, so desperately wanted to believe they were.

Remember: The key to fantasy is distance. The distant has allure and promise, seems simple and problem free. What you are offering, then, should be ungraspable. Never let it become oppressively familiar; it is the mirage in the distance, withdrawing as the sucker approaches. Never be too direct in describing the fantasy—keep it vague. As a forger of fantasies, let your victim come close enough to see and be tempted, but keep him far away enough that he stays dreaming and desiring.

Image: The
Moon. Unattainable,
always changing shape,
disappearing and reappear-
ing. We look at it, imagine,
wonder, and pine—never familiar, continuous provoker
of dreams. Do not offer
the obvious. Promise
the moon.

Authority: A lie is an allurement, a fabrication, that can be embell-
ished into a fantasy. It can be clothed in the raiments of a mystic
conception. Truth is cold, sober fact, not so comfortable to absorb.
A lie is more palatable. The most detested person in the world is
the one who always tells the truth, who never romances. . . .
I found it far more interesting and profitable to romance than to
tell the truth. (Joseph Weil, a.k.a. "The Yellow Kid," 1875–1976)

REVERSAL

If there is power in tapping into the fantasies of the masses, there is also danger. Fantasy usually contains an element of play—the public half realizes it is being duped, but it keeps the dream alive anyway, relishing the entertainment and the temporary diversion from the everyday that you are providing. So keep it light—never come too close to the place where you are actually expected to produce results. That place may prove extremely hazardous.

After Bragadino established himself in Munich, he found that the sober-minded Bavarians had far less faith in alchemy than the temperamental Venetians. Only the duke really believed in it, for he needed it desperately to rescue him from the hopeless mess he was in. As Bragadino played his familiar waiting game, accepting gifts and expecting patience, the public grew angry. Money was being spent and was yielding no results. In 1592 the Bavarians demanded justice, and eventually Bragadino found himself swinging from the gallows. As before, he had promised and had not delivered, but this time he had misjudged the forbearance of his hosts, and his inability to fulfill their fantasy proved fatal.

One last thing: Never make the mistake of imagining that fantasy is always fantastical. It certainly contrasts with reality, but reality itself is sometimes so theatrical and stylized that fantasy becomes a desire for simple things. The image Abraham Lincoln created of himself, for example, as a homespun country lawyer with a beard, made him the common man's president.

P. T. Barnum created a successful act with Tom Thumb, a dwarf who dressed up as famous leaders of the past, such as Napoleon, and lampooned them wickedly. The show delighted everyone, right up to Queen Victoria, by appealing to the fantasy of the time: Enough of the vainglorious rulers of history, the common man knows best. Tom Thumb reversed the familiar pattern of fantasy in which the strange and unknown becomes the ideal. But the act still obeyed the Law, for underlying it was the fantasy that the simple man is without problems, and is happier than the powerful and the rich.

Both Lincoln and Tom Thumb played the commoner but carefully maintained their distance. Should you play with such a fantasy, you too must carefully cultivate distance and not allow your "common" persona to become too familiar or it will not project as fantasy.

LAW

33

DISCOVER EACH

MAN'S THUMBSCREW

JUDGMENT

Everyone has a weakness, a gap in the castle wall. That weakness is usually an insecurity, an uncontrollable emotion or need; it can also be a small secret pleasure. Either way, once found, it is a thumbscrew you can turn to your advantage.

FINDING THE THUMBSCREW: A Strategic Plan of Action

THE LION THE
CHAMOIS, AND THE FOX

A lion was chasing a
chamois along a valley.
He had all but caught
it, and with longing
eyes was anticipating a
certain and a satisfying
repast. It seemed as if it
were utterly impossible
for the victim to escape;
for a deep ravine
appeared to bar the
way for both the hunter
and the hunted. But the
nimble chamois, gath-,
ering together all its
strength, shot like an
arrow from a bow
across the chasm, and
stood still on the rocky
cliff on the other side.
Our lion pulled up
short. But at that
moment a friend of his
happened to be near at
hand. That friend was
the fox.
"What!" said he, "with
your strength and
agility, is it possible
that you will yield to a
feeble chamois? You
have only to will, and
you will be able to
work wonders. Though
the abyss be deep, yet, if
you are only in earnest,
I am certain you will
clear it. Surely you can
confide in my disinter-
ested friendship. I
would not expose your
life to danger if I were
not so well aware of
your strength and
dexterity."
The lion's blood waxed
hot, and began to boil
in his veins. He flung
himself with all his
might into space. But
he could not clear the
chasm; so down he
tumbled headlong, and
was killed by the fall.

We all have resistances. We live with a perpetual armor around ourselves to defend against change and the intrusive actions of friends and rivals. We would like nothing more than to be left to do things our own way. Constantly butting up against these resistances will cost you a lot of energy. One of the most important things to realize about people, though, is that they all have a weakness, some part of their psychological armor that will *not* resist, that will bend to your will if you find it and push on it. Some people wear their weaknesses openly, others disguise them. Those who disguise them are often the ones most effectively undone through that one chink in their armor.

In planning your assault, keep these principles in mind:

Pay Attention to Gestures and Unconscious Signals. As Sigmund Freud remarked, "No mortal can keep a secret. If his lips are silent, he chatters with his fingertips; betrayal oozes out of him at every pore." This is a critical concept in the search for a person's weakness—it is revealed by seemingly unimportant gestures and passing words.

The key is not only what you look for but where and how you look. Everyday conversation supplies the richest mine of weaknesses, so train yourself to listen. Start by always seeming interested—the appearance of a sympathetic ear will spur anyone to talk. A clever trick, often used by the nineteenth-century French statesman Talleyrand, is to appear to open up to the other person, to share a secret with them. It can be completely made up, or it can be real but of no great importance to you—the important thing is that it should *seem* to come from the heart. This will usually elicit a response that is not only as frank as yours but more genuine—a response that reveals a weakness.

If you suspect that someone has a particular soft spot, probe for it indirectly. If, for instance, you sense that a man has a need to be loved, openly flatter him. If he laps up your compliments, no matter how obvious, you are on the right track. Train your eye for details—how someone tips a waiter, what delights a person, the hidden messages in clothes. Find people's idols, the things they worship and will do anything to get—perhaps you can be the supplier of their fantasies. Remember: Since we all try to hide our weaknesses, there is little to be learned from our conscious behavior. What oozes out in the little things outside our conscious control is what you want to know.

Find the Helpless Child. Most weaknesses begin in childhood, before the self builds up compensatory defenses. Perhaps the child was pampered or indulged in a particular area, or perhaps a certain emotional need went unfulfilled; as he or she grows older, the indulgence or the deficiency may be buried but never disappears. Knowing about a childhood need gives you a powerful key to a person's weakness.

One sign of this weakness is that when you touch on it the person will often act like a child. Be on the lookout, then, for any behavior that should have been outgrown. If your victims or rivals went without something important, such as parental support, when they were children, supply it, or its facsimile. If they reveal a secret taste, a hidden indulgence, indulge it. In either case they will be unable to resist you.

Look for Contrasts. An overt trait often conceals its opposite. People who thump their chests are often big cowards; a prudish exterior may hide a lascivious soul; the uptight are often screaming for adventure; the shy are dying for attention. By probing beyond appearances, you will often find people's weaknesses in the opposite of the qualities they reveal to you.

Find the Weak Link. Sometimes in your search for weaknesses it is not what but who that matters. In today's versions of the court, there is often someone behind the scenes who has a great deal of power, a tremendous influence over the person superficially on top. These behind-the-scenes powerbrokers are the group's weak link: Win their favor and you indirectly influence the king. Alternatively, even in a group of people acting with the appearance of one will—as when a group under attack closes ranks to resist an outsider—there is always a weak link in the chain. Find the one person who will bend under pressure.

Fill the Void. The two main emotional voids to fill are insecurity and unhappiness. The insecure are suckers for any kind of social validation; as for the chronically unhappy, look for the roots of their unhappiness. The insecure and the unhappy are the people least able to disguise their weaknesses. The ability to fill their emotional voids is a great source of power, and an indefinitely prolongable one.

Feed on Uncontrollable Emotions. The uncontrollable emotion can be a paranoid fear—a fear disproportionate to the situation—or any base motive such as lust, greed, vanity, or hatred. People in the grip of these emotions often cannot control themselves, and you can do the controlling for them.

OBSERVANCES OF THE LAW

Observance I

In 1615 the thirty-year-old bishop of Luçon, later known as Cardinal Richelieu, gave a speech before representatives of the three estates of France—clergy, nobility, and commoners. Richelieu had been chosen to serve as the mouthpiece for the clergy—an immense responsibility for a man still young and not particularly well known. On all of the important issues of the day, the speech followed the Church line. But near the end of it Richelieu did something that had nothing to do with the Church and everything to do with his career. He turned to the throne of the fifteen-year-old King Louis XIII, and to the Queen Mother Marie de' Médicis, who sat beside

Then what did his dear friend do? He cautiously made his way down to the bottom of the ravine, and there, out in the open space and the free air, seeing that the lion wanted neither flattery nor obedience now, he set to work to pay the last sad rites to his dead friend, and in a month picked his bones clean.

FABLES,
IVAN KRILOFF,
1768–1844

IRVING LAZAR

[Hollywood super-agent] Irving Paul Lazar was once anxious to sell [studio mogul] Jack L. Warner a play. "I had a long meeting with him today," Lazar explained [to screen-writer Garson Kanin], "but I didn't mention it, I didn't even bring it up."
"Why not?" I asked.
"Because I'm going to wait until the weekend after next, when I go to Palm Springs."
"I don't understand."
"You don't? I go to Palm Springs every weekend, but Warner isn't going this week-end. He's got a preview or something. So he's not coming down till the next weekend, so that's when I'm going to bring it up."
"Irving, I'm more and

A year later the queen mother appointed Richelieu secretary of state for foreign affairs, an incredible coup for the young bishop. He had now entered the inner circle of power, and he studied the workings of the court as if it were the machinery of a watch. An Italian, Concino Concini, was the queen mother's favorite, or rather her lover, a role that made him perhaps the most powerful man in France. Concini was vain and foppish, and Richelieu played him perfectly—attending to him as if *he* were the king. Within months Richelieu had become one of Concini's favorites. But something happened in 1617 that turned everything upside down: the young king, who up until then had shown every sign of being an idiot, had Concini murdered and his most important associates imprisoned. In so doing Louis took command of the country with one blow, sweeping the queen mother aside.

Had Richelieu played it wrong? He had been close to both Concini and Marie de Médicis, whose advisers and ministers were now all out of favor, some even arrested. The queen mother herself was shut up in the Louvre, a virtual prisoner. Richelieu wasted no time. If everyone was deserting Marie de Médicis, he would stand by her. He knew Louis could not get rid of her, for the king was still very young, and had in any case always been inordinately attached to her. As Marie's only remaining powerful friend, Richelieu filled the valuable function of liaison between the king and his mother. In return he received her protection, and was able to survive the palace coup, even to thrive. Over the next few years the queen mother grew still more dependent on him, and in 1622 she repaid him for his loyalty: Through the intercession of her allies in Rome, Richelieu was elevated to the powerful rank of cardinal.

By 1623 King Louis was in trouble. He had no one he could trust to advise him, and although he was now a young man instead of a boy, he remained childish in spirit, and affairs of state came hard to him. Now that he had taken the throne, Marie was no longer the regent and theoretically had no power, but she still had her son's ear, and she kept telling him that Richelieu was his only possible savior. At first Louis would have none of it—he hated the cardinal with a passion, only tolerating him out of love for Marie. In the end, however, isolated in the court and crippled by his own indecisiveness, he yielded to his mother and made Richelieu first his chief councilor and later prime minister.

Now Richelieu no longer needed Marie de Médicis. He stopped visiting and courting her, stopped listening to her opinions, even argued with her and opposed her wishes. Instead he concentrated on the king, making himself indispensable to his new master. All the previous premiers, understanding the king's childishness, had tried to keep him out of trouble; the shrewd Richelieu played him differently, deliberately pushing him into one ambitious project after another, such as a crusade against the Huguenots and finally an extended war with Spain. The immensity of these projects only made the king more dependent on his powerful premier, the only man able to keep order in the realm. And so, for the next eighteen years, Richelieu, exploiting the king's weaknesses, governed and molded France according to his own vision, unifying the country and making it a strong European power for centuries to come.

Interpretation

Richelieu saw everything as a military campaign, and no strategic move was more important to him than discovering his enemy's weaknesses and applying pressure to them. As early as his speech in 1615, he was looking for the weak link in the chain of power, and he saw that it was the queen mother. Not that Marie was obviously weak—she governed both France and her son; but Richelieu saw that she was really an insecure woman who needed constant masculine attention. He showered her with affection and respect, even toadying up to her favorite, Concini. He knew the day would come when the king would take over, but he also recognized that Louis loved his mother dearly and would always remain a child in relation to her. The way to control Louis, then, was not by gaining his favor, which could change overnight, but by gaining sway over his mother, for whom his affection would never change.

Once Richelieu had the position he desired—prime minister—he discarded the queen mother, moving on to the next weak link in the chain: the king's own character. There was a part of him that would always be a helpless child in need of higher authority. It was on the foundation of the king's weakness that Richelieu established his own power and fame.

Remember: When entering the court, find the weak link. The person in control is often not the king or queen; it is someone behind the scenes—the favorite, the husband or wife, even the court fool. This person may have more weaknesses than the king himself, because his power depends on all kinds of capricious factors outside his control.

Finally, when dealing with helpless children who cannot make decisions, play on their weakness and push them into bold ventures. They will have to depend on you even more, for you will become the adult figure whom they rely on to get them out of scrapes and to safety.

Observance II

In December of 1925, guests at the swankiest hotel in Palm Beach, Florida, watched with interest as a mysterious man arrived in a Rolls-Royce driven by a Japanese chauffeur. Over the next few days they studied this handsome man, who walked with an elegant cane, received telegrams at all hours, and only engaged in the briefest of conversations. He was a count, they heard, Count Victor Lustig, and he came from one of the wealthiest families in Europe—but this was all they could find out.

Imagine their amazement, then, when Lustig one day walked up to one of the least distinguished guests in the hotel, a Mr. Herman Loller,

French perfumer. Do
you like it?"
"I love it," she replied.
The following day I
went through my
effects and found two
empty bottles. Both had
come from France, but
were empty. I went to a
downtown department
store and purchased
ten ounces of Coty's
"April Violets." I
poured this into the
two French bottles,
carefully sealed them,
wrapped them in
tissue paper.
That evening I dropped
by the banker's home
and presented the two
bottles to his wife.
"They were especially
put up for me in
Cologne," I told her.
The next day the
banker called at my
hotel. His wife was
enraptured by the
perfume. She consid-
ered it the most
wonderful, the most
exotic fragrance she
had ever used. I did not
tell the banker he could
get all he wanted right
in Omaha.
"She said," the banker
added, "that I was
fortunate to be associ-
ated with a man like
you." From then on his
attitude was changed,
for he had complete
faith in his wife's judg-
ment. . . . He parted
with $350,000. This,
incidentally was my
biggest [con] score.
"YELLOW KID" WEIL,
1875–1976

head of an engineering company, and entered into conversation with him. Loller had made his fortune only recently, and forging social connections was very important to him. He felt honored and somewhat intimidated by this sophisticated man, who spoke perfect English with a hint of a foreign accent. Over the days to come, the two became friends.

Loller of course did most of the talking, and one night he confessed that his business was doing poorly, with more troubles ahead. In return, Lustig confided in his new friend that he too had serious money problems—Communists had seized his family estate and all its assets. He was too old to learn a trade and go to work. Luckily he had found an an-swer—"a money-making machine." "You counterfeit?" Loller whispered in half-shock. No, Lustig replied, explaining that through a secret chemical process, his machine could duplicate any paper currency with complete ac-curacy. Put in a dollar bill and six hours later you had two, both perfect. He proceeded to explain how the machine had been smuggled out of Europe, how the Germans had developed it to undermine the British, how it had supported the count for several years, and on and on. When Loller insisted on a demonstration, the two men went to Lustig's room, where the count produced a magnificent mahogany box fitted with slots, cranks, and dials. Loller watched as Lustig inserted a dollar bill in the box. Sure enough, early the following morning Lustig pulled out two bills, still wet from the chemicals.

Lustig gave the notes to Loller, who immediately took the bills to a local bank—which accepted them as genuine. Now the businessman fever-ishly begged Lustig to sell him a machine. The count explained that there was only one in existence, so Loller made him a high offer: $25,000, then a considerable amount (more than $400,000 in today's terms). Even so, Lustig seemed reluctant: He did not feel right about making his friend pay so much. Yet finally he agreed to the sale. After all, he said, "I suppose it matters little what you pay me. You are, after all, going to recover the amount within a few days by duplicating your own bills." Making Loller swear never to reveal the machine's existence to other people, Lustig ac-cepted the money. Later the same day he checked out of the hotel. A year later, after many futile attempts at duplicating bills, Loller finally went to the police with the story of how Count Lustig had conned him with a pair of dollar bills, some chemicals, and a worthless mahogany box.

Interpretation

Count Lustig had an eagle eye for other people's weaknesses. He saw them in the smallest gesture. Loller, for instance, overtipped waiters, seemed nervous in conversation with the concierge, talked loudly about his busi-ness. His weakness, Lustig knew, was his need for social validation and for the respect that he thought his wealth had earned him. He was also chroni-cally insecure. Lustig had come to the hotel to hunt for prey. In Loller he homed in on the perfect sucker—a man hungering for someone to fill his psychic voids.

In offering Loller his friendship, then, Lustig knew he was offering him the immediate respect of the other guests. As a count, Lustig was also offering the newly rich businessman access to the glittering world of old wealth. And for the coup de grâce, he apparently owned a machine that would rescue Loller from his worries. It would even put him on a par with Lustig himself, who had also used the machine to maintain his status. No wonder Loller took the bait.

Remember: When searching for suckers, always look for the dissatisfied, the unhappy, the insecure. Such people are riddled with weaknesses and have needs that you can fill. Their neediness is the groove in which you place your thumbnail and turn them at will.

Observance III

In the year 1559, the French king Henri II died in a jousting exhibition. His son assumed the throne, becoming Francis II, but in the background stood Henri's wife and queen, Catherine de' Médicis, a woman who had long ago proven her skill in affairs of state. When Francis died the next year, Catherine took control of the country as regent to her next son in line of succession, the future Charles IX, a mere ten years old at the time.

The main threats to the queen's power were Antoine de Bourbon, king of Navarre, and his brother, Louis, the powerful prince of Condé, both of whom could claim the right to serve as regent instead of Catherine, who, after all, was Italian—a foreigner. Catherine quickly appointed Antoine lieutenant general of the kingdom, a title that seemed to satisfy his ambition. It also meant that he had to remain in court, where Catherine could keep an eye on him. Her next move proved smarter still: Antoine had a notorious weakness for young women, so she assigned one of her most attractive maids of honor, Louise de Rouet, to seduce him. Now Antoine's intimate, Louise reported all of his actions to Catherine. The move worked so brilliantly that Catherine assigned another of her maids to Prince Condé, and thus was formed her *escadron volant*—"flying squadron"—of young girls whom she used to keep the unsuspecting males in the court under her control.

In 1572 Catherine married off her daughter, Marguerite de Valois, to Henri, the son of Antoine and the new king of Navarre. To put a family that had always struggled against her so close to power was a dangerous move, so to make sure of Henri's loyalty she unleashed on him the loveliest member of her "flying squadron," Charlotte de Beaune Semblançay, baroness of Sauves. Catherine did this even though Henri was married to her daughter. Within weeks, Marguerite de Valois wrote in her memoirs, "Mme. de Sauves so completely ensnared my husband that we no longer slept together, nor even conversed."

The baroness was an excellent spy and helped to keep Henri under Catherine's thumb. When the queen's youngest son, the Duke of Alençon, grew so close to Henri that she feared the two might plot against her, she assigned the baroness to him as well. This most infamous member of the flying squadron quickly seduced Alençon, and soon the two young men fought over her and their friendship quickly ended, along with any danger of a conspiracy.

And while I am on the subject, there is another fact that deserves mention. It is this. A man shows his character just in the way in which he deals with trifles—for then he is off his guard. This will often afford a good opportunity of observing the boundless egoism of a man's nature, and his total lack of consideration for others; and if these defects show themselves in small things, or merely in his general demeanour, you will find that they also underlie his action in matters of importance, although he may disguise the fact. This is an opportunity which should not be missed. If in the little affairs of every day—the trifles of life . . .—a man is inconsiderate and seeks only what is advantageous or convenient to himself, to the prejudice of others' rights; if he appropriates to himself that which belongs to all alike, you may be sure there is no justice in his heart, and that he would be a scoundrel on a wholesale scale, only that law and compulsion bind his hands.

ARTHUR
SCHOPENHAUER,
1788–1860

Interpretation

THE BATTLE AT
PHARSALIA

*When the two armies
[Julius Caesar's and
Pompey's] were come
into Pharsalia, and
both encamped there,
Pompey's thoughts ran
the same way as they
had done before,
against fighting.... But
those who were about
him were greatly confi-
dent of success ... as if
they had already
conquered.... The
cavalry especially were
obstinate for fighting,
being splendidly armed
and bravely mounted,
and valuing themselves
upon the fine horses
they kept, and upon
their own handsome
persons; as also upon
the advantage of their
numbers, for they were
five thousand against
one thousand of
Caesar's. Nor were the
numbers of the infantry
less disproportionate,
there being forty-five
thousand of Pompey's
against twenty-two
thousand of the enemy.
[The next day] whilst
the infantry was thus
sharply engaged in the
main battle, on the
flank Pompey's horse
rode up confidently,
and opened [his
cavalry's] ranks very
wide, that they might
surround the right wing
of Caesar. But before
they engaged, Caesar's
cohorts rushed out and
attacked them, and did
not dart their javelins
at a distance, nor strike
at the thighs and legs,
as they usually did in
close battle, but aimed
at their faces. For thus*

Catherine had seen very early on the sway that a mistress has over a man of power: Her own husband, Henri II, had kept one of the most infamous mistresses of them all, Diane de Poitiers. What Catherine learned from the experience was that a man like her husband wanted to feel he could win a woman over without having to rely on his status, which he had inherited rather than earned. And such a need contained a huge blind spot: As long as the woman began the affair by acting as if she had been conquered, the man would fail to notice that as time passed the mistress had come to hold power over him, as Diane de Poitiers did over Henri. It was Catherine's strategy to turn this weakness to her advantage, using it as a way to conquer and control men. All she had to do was unleash the loveliest women in the court, her "flying squadron," on men whom she knew shared her husband's vulnerability.

Remember: Always look for passions and obsessions that cannot be controlled. The stronger the passion, the more vulnerable the person. This may seem surprising, for passionate people look strong. In fact, however, they are simply filling the stage with their theatricality, distracting people from how weak and helpless they really are. A man's need to conquer women actually reveals a tremendous helplessness that has made suckers out of them for thousands of years. Look at the part of a person that is most visible—their greed, their lust, their intense fear. These are the emotions they cannot conceal, and over which they have the least control. And what people cannot control, you can control for them.

Observance IV

Arabella Huntington, wife of the great late-nineteenth-century railroad magnate Collis P. Huntington, came from humble origins and always struggled for social recognition among her wealthy peers. When she gave a party in her San Francisco mansion, few of the social elite would show up; most of them took her for a gold digger, not their kind. Because of her husband's fabulous wealth, art dealers courted her, but with such condescension they obviously saw her as an upstart. Only one man of consequence treated her differently: the dealer Joseph Duveen.

For the first few years of Duveen's relationship with Arabella, he made no effort to sell expensive art to her. Instead he accompanied her to fine stores, chatted endlessly about queens and princesses he knew, on and on. At last, she thought, a man who treated her as an equal, even a superior, in high society. Meanwhile, if Duveen did not try to sell art to her, he did subtly educate her in his aesthetic ideas—namely, that the best art was the most expensive art. And after Arabella had soaked up his way of seeing things, Duveen would act as if she always had exquisite taste, even though before she met him her aesthetics had been abysmal.

When Collis Huntington died, in 1900, Arabella came into a fortune. She suddenly started to buy expensive paintings, by Rembrandt and Velázquez, for example—and only from Duveen. Years later Duveen sold her Gainsborough's *Blue Boy* for the highest price ever paid for a work of art at the time, an astounding purchase for a family that previously had shown little interest in collecting.

Interpretation

Joseph Duveen instantly understood Arabella Huntington and what made her tick: She wanted to feel important, at home in society. Intensely insecure about her lower-class background, she needed confirmation of her new social status. Duveen waited. Instead of rushing into trying to persuade her to collect art, he subtly went to work on her weaknesses. He made her feel that she deserved his attention not because she was the wife of one of the wealthiest men in the world but because of her own special character—and this completely melted her. Duveen never condescended to Arabella; rather than lecturing to her, he instilled his ideas in her indirectly. The result was one of his best and most devoted clients, and also the sale of *The Blue Boy*.

People's need for validation and recognition, their need to feel important, is the best kind of weakness to exploit. First, it is almost universal; second, exploiting it is so very easy. All you have to do is find ways to make people feel better about their taste, their social standing, their intelligence. Once the fish are hooked, you can reel them in again and again, for years—you are filling a positive role, giving them what they cannot get on their own. They may never suspect that you are turning them like a thumbscrew, and if they do they may not care, because you are making them feel better about themselves, and that is worth any price.

Observance V

In 1862 King William of Prussia named Otto von Bismarck premier and minister for foreign affairs. Bismarck was known for his boldness, his ambition—and his interest in strengthening the military. Since William was surrounded by liberals in his government and cabinet, politicians who already wanted to limit his powers, it was quite dangerous for him to put Bismarck in this sensitive position. His wife, Queen Augusta, had tried to dissuade him, but although she usually got her way with him, this time William stuck to his guns.

Only a week after becoming prime minister, Bismarck made an impromptu speech to a few dozen ministers to convince them of the need to enlarge the army. He ended by saying, "The great questions of the time will be decided, not by speeches and resolutions of majorities, but by iron and blood." His speech was immediately disseminated throughout Germany. The queen screamed at her husband that Bismarck was a barbaric militarist who was out to usurp control of Prussia, and that William had to fire him. The liberals in the government agreed with her. The outcry was so vehement that William began to be afraid he would end up on a scaffold, like Louis XVI of France, if he kept Bismarck on as prime minister.

Bismarck knew he had to get to the king before it was too late. He also knew he had blundered, and should have tempered his fiery words. Yet as he contemplated his strategy, he decided not to apologize but to do the exact opposite. Bismarck knew the king well.

Caesar had instructed them, in hopes that young gentlemen, who had not known much of battles and wounds, but came wearing their hair long, in the flower of their age and height of their beauty, would be more apprehensive of such blows, and not care for hazarding both a danger at present and a blemish for the future. And so it proved, for they were so far from bearing the stroke of the javelins, that they could not stand the sight of them, but turned about, and covered their faces to secure them. Once in disorder, presently they turned about to fly; and so most shamefully ruined all. For those who had beat them back at once outflanked the infantry, and falling on their rear, cut them to pieces. Pompey, who commanded the other wing of the army, when he saw his cavalry thus broken and flying, was no longer himself, nor did he now remember that he was Pompey the Great, but, like one whom some god had deprived of his senses, retired to his tent without speaking a word, and there sat to expect the event, till the whole army was routed.

THE LIFE OF JULIUS CAESAR, PLUTARCH, c. A.D. 46–120

When the two men met, William, predictably, had been worked into a tizzy by the queen. He reiterated his fear of being guillotined. But Bismarck only replied, "Yes, then we shall be dead! We must die sooner or later, and could there be a more respectable way of dying? I should die fighting for the cause of my king and master. Your Majesty would die sealing with your own blood your royal rights granted by God's grace. Whether upon the scaffold or upon the battlefield makes no difference to the glorious staking of body and life on behalf of rights granted by God's grace!" On he went, appealing to William's sense of honor and the majesty of his position as head of the army. How could the king allow people to push him around? Wasn't the honor of Germany more important than quibbling over words? Not only did the prime minister convince the king to stand up to both his wife and his parliament, he persuaded him to build up the army—Bismarck's goal all along.

Interpretation

Bismarck knew the king felt bullied by those around him. He knew that William had a military background and a deep sense of honor, and that he felt ashamed at his cravenness before his wife and his government. William secretly yearned to be a great and mighty king, but he dared not express this ambition because he was afraid of ending up like Louis XVI. Where a show of courage often conceals a man's timidity, William's timidity concealed his need to show courage and thump his chest.

Bismarck sensed the longing for glory beneath William's pacifist front, so he played to the king's insecurity about his manhood, finally pushing him into three wars and the creation of a German empire. Timidity is a potent weakness to exploit. Timid souls often yearn to be their opposite—to be Napoleons. Yet they lack the inner strength. You, in essence, can become their Napoleon, pushing them into bold actions that serve your needs while also making them dependent on you. Remember: Look to the opposites and never take appearances at face value.

Image: The Thumbscrew. Your enemy has secrets that he guards, thinks thoughts he will not reveal. But they come out in ways he cannot help. It is there somewhere, a groove of weakness on his head, at his heart, over his belly. Once you find the groove, put your thumb in it and turn him at will.

Authority: Find out each man's thumbscrew. 'Tis the art of setting their wills in action. It needs more skill than resolution. You must know where to get at anyone. Every volition has a special motive which varies according to taste. All men are idolaters, some of fame, others of self-interest, most of pleasure. Skill consists in knowing these idols in order to bring them into play. Knowing any man's mainspring of motive you have as it were the key to his will. (Baltasar Gracián, 1601–1658)

REVERSAL

Playing on people's weakness has one significant danger: You may stir up an action you cannot control.

In your games of power you always look several steps ahead and plan accordingly. And you exploit the fact that other people are more emotional and incapable of such foresight. But when you play on their vulnerabilities, the areas over which they have least control, you can unleash emotions that will upset your plans. Push timid people into bold action and they may go too far; answer their need for attention or recognition and they may need more than you want to give them. The helpless, childish element you are playing on can turn against you.

The more emotional the weakness, the greater the potential danger. Know the limits to this game, then, and never get carried away by your control over your victims. You are after power, not the thrill of control.

BE ROYAL IN YOUR OWN FASHION: ACT LIKE A KING TO BE TREATED LIKE ONE

JUDGMENT

The way you carry yourself will often determine how you are treated: In the long run, appearing vulgar or common will make people disrespect you. For a king respects himself and inspires the same sentiment in others. By acting regally and confident of your powers, you make yourself seem destined to wear a crown.

TRANSGRESSION OF THE LAW

In July of 1830, a revolution broke out in Paris that forced the king, Charles X, to abdicate. A commission of the highest authorities in the land gathered to choose a successor, and the man they picked was Louis-Philippe, the Duke of Orléans.

From the beginning it was clear that Louis-Philippe would be a different kind of king, and not just because he came from a different branch of the royal family, or because he had not inherited the crown but had been given it, by a commission, putting his legitimacy in question. Rather it was that he disliked ceremony and the trappings of royalty; he had more friends among the bankers than among the nobility; and his style was not to create a new kind of royal rule, as Napoleon had done, but to downplay his status, the better to mix with the businessmen and middle-class folk who had called him to lead. Thus the symbols that came to be associated with Louis-Philippe were neither the scepter nor the crown, but the gray hat and umbrella with which he would proudly walk the streets of Paris, as if he were a bourgeois out for a stroll. When Louis-Philippe invited James Rothschild, the most important banker in France, to his palace, he treated him as an equal. And unlike any king before him, not only did he talk business with Monsieur Rothschild but that was literally all he talked, for he loved money and had amassed a huge fortune.

As the reign of the "bourgeois king" plodded on, people came to despise him. The aristocracy could not endure the sight of an unkingly king, and within a few years they turned on him. Meanwhile the growing class of the poor, including the radicals who had chased out Charles X, found no satisfaction in a ruler who neither acted as a king nor governed as a man of the people. The bankers to whom Louis-Philippe was the most beholden soon realized that it was they who controlled the country, not he, and they treated him with growing contempt. One day, at the start of a train trip organized for the royal family, James Rothschild actually berated him—and in public—for being late. Once the king had made news by treating the banker as an equal; now the banker treated the king as an inferior.

Eventually the workers' insurrections that had brought down Louis-Philippe's predecessor began to reemerge, and the king put them down with force. But what was he defending so brutally? Not the institution of the monarchy, which he disdained, nor a democratic republic, which his rule prevented. What he was really defending, it seemed, was his own fortune, and the fortunes of the bankers—not a way to inspire loyalty among the citizenry.

In early 1848, Frenchmen of all classes began to demonstrate for electoral reforms that would make the country truly democratic. By February the demonstrations had turned violent. To assuage the populace, Louis-Philippe fired his prime minister and appointed a liberal as a replacement. But this created the opposite of the desired effect: The people sensed they could push the king around. The demonstrations turned into a full-fledged revolution, with gunfire and barricades in the streets.

Never lose your self-respect, nor be too familiar with yourself when you are alone. Let your integrity itself be your own standard of rectitude, and be more indebted to the severity of your own judgment of yourself than to all external precepts. Desist from unseemly conduct, rather out of respect for your own virtue than for the strictures of external authority. Come to hold yourself in awe, and you will have no need of Seneca's imaginary tutor.

BALTASAR GRACIÁN, 1601–1658

On the night of February 23, a crowd of Parisians surrounded the palace. With a suddenness that caught everyone by surprise, Louis-Philippe abdicated that very evening and fled to England. He left no successor, nor even the suggestion of one—his whole government folded up and dissolved like a traveling circus leaving town.

Interpretation

Louis-Philippe consciously dissolved the aura that naturally pertains to kings and leaders. Scoffing at the symbolism of grandeur, he believed a new world was dawning, where rulers should act and be like ordinary citizens. He was right: A new world, without kings and queens, was certainly on its way. He was profoundly wrong, however, in predicting a change in the dynamics of power.

The bourgeois king's hat and umbrella amused the French at first, but soon grew irritating. People knew that Louis-Philippe was not really like them at all—that the hat and umbrella were essentially a kind of trick to encourage them in the fantasy that the country had suddenly grown more equal. Actually, though, the divisions of wealth had never been greater. The French expected their ruler to be a bit of a showman, to have some presence. Even a radical like Robespierre, who had briefly come to power during the French Revolution fifty years earlier, had understood this, and certainly Napoleon, who had turned the revolutionary republic into an imperial regime, had known it in his bones. Indeed as soon as Louis-Philippe fled the stage, the French revealed their true desire: They elected Napoleon's grand-nephew president. He was a virtual unknown, but they hoped he would re-create the great general's powerful aura, erasing the awkward memory of the "bourgeois king."

Powerful people may be tempted to affect a common-man aura, trying to create the illusion that they and their subjects or underlings are basically the same. But the people whom this false gesture is intended to impress will quickly see through it. They understand that they are not being given more power—that it only *appears* as if they shared in the powerful person's fate. The only kind of common touch that works is the kind affected by Franklin Roosevelt, a style that said the president shared values and goals with the common people even while he remained a patrician at heart. He never pretended to erase his distance from the crowd.

Leaders who try to dissolve that distance through a false chumminess gradually lose the ability to inspire loyalty, fear, or love. Instead they elicit contempt. Like Louis-Philippe, they are too uninspiring even to be worth the guillotine—the best they can do is simply vanish in the night, as if they were never there.

OBSERVANCE OF THE LAW

When Christopher Columbus was trying to find funding for his legendary voyages, many around him believed he came from the Italian aristocracy. This view was passed into history through a biography written after the explorer's death by his son, which describes him as a descendant of a Count

Colombo of the Castle of Cuccaro in Montferrat. Colombo in turn was said to be descended from the legendary Roman general Colonius, and two of his first cousins were supposedly direct descendants of an emperor of Constantinople. An illustrious background indeed. But it was nothing more than illustrious fantasy, for Columbus was actually the son of Domenico Colombo, a humble weaver who had opened a wine shop when Christopher was a young man, and who then made his living by selling cheese.

Columbus himself had created the myth of his noble background, because from early on he felt that destiny had singled him out for great things, and that he had a kind of royalty in his blood. Accordingly he acted as if he were indeed descended from noble stock. After an uneventful career as a merchant on a commercial vessel, Columbus, originally from Genoa, settled in Lisbon. Using the fabricated story of his noble background, he married into an established Lisbon family that had excellent connections with Portuguese royalty.

Through his in-laws, Columbus finagled a meeting with the king of Portugal, João II, whom he petitioned to finance a westward voyage aimed at discovering a shorter route to Asia. In return for announcing that any discoveries he achieved would be made in the king's name, Columbus wanted a series of rights: the title Grand Admiral of the Oceanic Sea; the office of viceroy over any lands he found; and 10 percent of the future commerce with such lands. All of these rights were to be hereditary and for all time. Columbus made these demands even though he had previously been a mere merchant, he knew almost nothing about navigation, he could not work a quadrant, and he had never led a group of men. In short he had absolutely no qualifications for the journey he proposed. Furthermore, his petition included no details as to how he would accomplish his plans, just vague promises.

When Columbus finished his pitch, João II smiled: He politely declined the offer, but left the door open for the future. Here Columbus must have noticed something he would never forget: Even as the king turned down the sailor's demands, he treated them as legitimate. He neither laughed at Columbus nor questioned his background and credentials. In fact the king was impressed by the boldness of Columbus's requests, and clearly felt comfortable in the company of a man who acted so confidently. The meeting must have convinced Columbus that his instincts were correct: By asking for the moon, he had instantly raised his own status, for the king assumed that unless a man who set such a high price on himself were mad, which Columbus did not appear to be, he must somehow be worth it.

A few years later Columbus moved to Spain. Using his Portuguese connections, he moved in elevated circles at the Spanish court, receiving subsidies from illustrious financiers and sharing tables with dukes and princes. To all these men he repeated his request for financing for a voyage to the west—and also for the rights he had demanded from João II. Some, such as the powerful duke of Medina, wanted to help, but could not, since they lacked the power to grant him the titles and rights he wanted. But Columbus would not back down. He soon realized that only one person

HIPPOCLEIDES AT SICYON

In the next generation the family became much more famous than before through the distinction conferred upon it by Cleisthenes the master of Sicyon. Cleisthenes . . . had a daughter, Agarista, whom he wished to marry to the best man in all Greece. So during the Olympic games, in which he had himself won the chariot race, he had a public announcement made, to the effect that any Greek who thought himself good enough to become Cleisthenes' son-in-law should present himself in Sicyon within sixty days—or sooner if he wished—because he intended, within the year following the sixtieth day, to betroth his daughter to her future husband. Cleisthenes had had a race-track and a wrestling-ring specially made for his purpose, and presently the suitors began to arrive— every man of Greek nationality who had something to be proud of either in his country or in himself. . . . Cleisthenes began by asking each [of the numerous suitors] in turn to name his country and parentage; then he kept them in his house for a year, to get to know them well, entering into conversation with them sometimes singly, sometimes all together, and testing each of them for his

could meet his demands: Queen Isabella. In 1487 he finally managed a meeting with the queen, and although he could not convince her to finance the voyage, he completely charmed her, and became a frequent guest in the palace.

In 1492 the Spanish finally expelled the Moorish invaders who cen-turies earlier had seized parts of the country. With the wartime burden on her treasury lifted, Isabella felt she could finally respond to the demands of her explorer friend, and she decided to pay for three ships, equipment, the salaries of the crews, and a modest stipend for Columbus. More important, she had a contract drawn up that granted Columbus the titles and rights on which he had insisted. The only one she denied—and only in the contract's fine print—was the 10 percent of all revenues from any lands discovered: an absurd demand, since he wanted no time limit on it. (Had the clause been left in, it would eventually have made Columbus and his heirs the wealthiest family on the planet. Columbus never read the fine print.)

Satisfied that his demands had been met, Columbus set sail that same year in search of the passage to Asia. (Before he left he was careful to hire the best navigator he could find to help him get there.) The mission failed to find such a passage, yet when Columbus petitioned the queen to finance an even more ambitious voyage the following year, she agreed. By then she had come to see Columbus as destined for great things.

Interpretation

As an explorer Columbus was mediocre at best. He knew less about the sea than did the average sailor on his ships, could never determine the lati-tude and longitude of his discoveries, mistook islands for vast continents, and treated his crew badly. But in one area he was a genius: He knew how to sell himself. How else to explain how the son of a cheese vendor, a low-level sea merchant, managed to ingratiate himself with the highest royal and aristocratic families?

Columbus had an amazing power to charm the nobility, and it all came from the way he carried himself. He projected a sense of confidence that was completely out of proportion to his means. Nor was his confidence the aggressive, ugly self-promotion of an upstart—it was a quiet and calm self-assurance. In fact it was the same confidence usually shown by the no-bility themselves. The powerful in the old-style aristocracies felt no need to prove or assert themselves; being noble, they knew they always deserved more, and asked for it. With Columbus, then, they felt an instant affinity, for he carried himself just the way they did—elevated above the crowd, destined for greatness.

Understand: It is within your power to set your own price. How you carry yourself reflects what you think of yourself. If you ask for little, shuf-fle your feet and lower your head, people will assume this reflects your character. But this behavior is not you—it is only how you have chosen to present yourself to other people. You can just as easily present the Colum-bus front: buoyancy, confidence, and the feeling that you were born to wear a crown.

With all great deceivers there is a noteworthy occurrence to which they owe their power. In the actual act of deception they are overcome by belief in themselves: it is this which then speaks so miraculously and compellingly to those around them.

Friedrich Nietzsche, 1844–1900

KEYS TO POWER

As children, we start our lives with great exuberance, expecting and demanding everything from the world. This generally carries over into our first forays into society, as we begin our careers. But as we grow older the rebuffs and failures we experience set up boundaries that only get firmer with time. Coming to expect less from the world, we accept limitations that are really self-imposed. We start to bow and scrape and apologize for even the simplest of requests. The solution to such a shrinking of horizons is to deliberately force ourselves in the opposite direction—to downplay the failures and ignore the limitations, to make ourselves demand and expect as much as the child. To accomplish this, we must use a particular strategy upon ourselves. Call it the Strategy of the Crown.

The Strategy of the Crown is based on a simple chain of cause and effect: If we believe we are destined for great things, our belief will radiate outward, just as a crown creates an aura around a king. This outward radiance will infect the people around us, who will think we must have reasons to feel so confident. People who wear crowns seem to feel no inner sense of the limits to what they can ask for or what they can accomplish. This too radiates outward. Limits and boundaries disappear. Use the Strategy of the Crown and you will be surprised how often it bears fruit. Take as an example those happy children who ask for whatever they want, and get it. Their high expectations are their charm. Adults enjoy granting their wishes—just as Isabella enjoyed granting the wishes of Columbus.

Throughout history, people of undistinguished birth—the Theodoras of Byzantium, the Columbuses, the Beethovens, the Disraelis—have managed to work the Strategy of the Crown, believing so firmly in their own greatness that it becomes a self-fulfilling prophecy. The trick is simple: Be overcome by your self-belief. Even while you know you are practicing a kind of deception on yourself, act like a king. You are likely to be treated as one.

The crown may separate you from other people, but it is up to you to make that separation real: You have to act differently, demonstrating your distance from those around you. One way to emphasize your difference is to always act with dignity, no matter the circumstance. Louis-Philippe gave no sense of being different from other people—he was the banker king. And the moment his subjects threatened him, he caved in. Everyone sensed this and pounced. Lacking regal dignity and firmness of purpose, Louis-Philippe seemed an impostor, and the crown was easily toppled from his head.

Regal bearing should not be confused with arrogance. Arrogance may seem the king's entitlement, but in fact it betrays insecurity. It is the very opposite of a royal demeanor.

Hippocleides, climbing on to it, danced first some Laconian dances, next some Attic ones, and ended by standing on his head and beating time with his legs in the air. The Laconian and Attic dances were bad enough; but Cleisthenes, though he already loathed the thought of having a son-in-law like that, nevertheless restrained himself and managed to avoid an outburst; but when he saw Hippocleides beating time with his legs, he could bear it no longer. "Son of Tisander," he cried, "you have danced away your marriage."

THE HISTORIES, HERODOTUS, FIFTH CENTURY B.C.

Haile Selassie, ruler of Ethiopia for forty or so years beginning in 1930, was once a young man named Lij Tafari. He came from a noble family, but there was no real chance of him coming to power, for he was far down the line of succession from the king then on the throne, Menelik II. Nevertheless, from an early age he exhibited a self-confidence and a royal bearing that surprised everyone around him.

At the age of fourteen, Tafari went to live at the court, where he immediately impressed Menelik and became his favorite. Tafari's grace under fire, his patience, and his calm self-assurance fascinated the king. The other young nobles, arrogant, blustery, and envious, would push this slight, bookish teenager around. But he never got angry—that would have been a sign of insecurity, to which he would not stoop. There were already people around him who felt he would someday rise to the top, for he acted as if he were already there.

Years later, in 1936, when the Italian Fascists had taken over Ethiopia and Tafari, now called Haile Selassie, was in exile, he addressed the League of Nations to plead his country's case. The Italians in the audience heckled him with vulgar abuse, but he maintained his dignified pose, as if completely unaffected. This elevated him while making his opponents look even uglier. Dignity, in fact, is invariably the mask to assume under difficult circumstances: It is as if nothing can affect you, and you have all the time in the world to respond. This is an extremely powerful pose.

A royal demeanor has other uses. Con artists have long known the value of an aristocratic front; it either disarms people and makes them less suspicious, or else it intimidates them and puts them on the defensive—and as Count Victor Lustig knew, once you put a sucker on the defensive he is doomed. The con man Yellow Kid Weil, too, would often assume the trappings of a man of wealth, along with the nonchalance that goes with them. Alluding to some magical method of making money, he would stand aloof, like a king, exuding confidence as if he really were fabulously rich. The suckers would beg to be in on the con, to have a chance at the wealth that he so clearly displayed.

Finally, to reinforce the inner psychological tricks involved in projecting a royal demeanor, there are outward strategies to help you create the effect. First, the Columbus Strategy: Always make a bold demand. Set your price high and do not waver. Second, in a dignified way, go after the highest person in the building. This immediately puts you on the same plane as the chief executive you are attacking. It is the David and Goliath Strategy: By choosing a great opponent, you create the appearance of greatness.

Third, give a gift of some sort to those above you. This is the strategy of those who have a patron: By giving your patron a gift, you are essentially saying that the two of you are equal. It is the old con game of giving so that you can take. When the Renaissance writer Pietro Aretino wanted the Duke of Mantua as his next patron, he knew that if he was slavish and sycophantic, the duke would think him unworthy; so he approached the duke with gifts, in this case paintings by the writer's good friend Titian.

Accepting the gifts created a kind of equality between duke and writer: The duke was put at ease by the feeling that he was dealing with a man of his own aristocratic stamp. He funded Aretino generously. The gift strategy is subtle and brilliant because you do not beg: You ask for help in a dignified way that implies equality between two people, one of whom just happens to have more money.

Remember: It is up to you to set your own price. Ask for less and that is just what you will get. Ask for more, however, and you send a signal that you are worth a king's ransom. Even those who turn you down respect you for your confidence, and that respect will eventually pay off in ways you cannot imagine.

Image: The Crown. Place it upon your head and you assume a different pose—tranquil yet radiating assurance. Never show doubt, never lose your dignity beneath the crown, or it will not fit. It will seem to be destined for one more worthy. Do not wait for a coronation; the greatest emperors crown themselves.

Authority: Everyone should be royal after his own fashion. Let all your actions, even though they are not those of a king, be, in their own sphere, worthy of one. Be sublime in your deeds, lofty in your thoughts; and in all your doings show that you deserve to be a king even though you are not one in reality. (Baltasar Gracián, 1601–1658)

REVERSAL

The idea behind the assumption of regal confidence is to set yourself apart from other people, but if you take this too far it will be your undoing. Never make the mistake of thinking that you elevate yourself by humiliating people. Also, it is never a good idea to loom too high above the crowd—you make an easy target. And there are times when an aristocratic pose is eminently dangerous.

Charles I, king of England during the 1640s, faced a profound public disenchantment with the institution of monarchy. Revolts erupted throughout the country, led by Oliver Cromwell. Had Charles reacted to the times with insight, supporting reforms and making a show of sacrificing some of his power, history might have been different. Instead he reverted to an even more regal pose, seeming outraged by the assault on his power and on the divine institution of monarchy. His stiff kingliness offended people and spurred on their revolts. And eventually Charles lost his head, literally. Understand: You are radiating confidence, not arrogance or disdain.

Finally, it is true that you can sometimes find some power through affecting a kind of earthy vulgarity, which will prove amusing by its extremeness. But to the extent that you win this game by going beyond the limits, separating yourself from other people by appearing even more vulgar than they are, the game is dangerous: There will always be people more vulgar than you, and you will easily be replaced the following season by someone younger and worse.

35

MASTER THE ART

OF TIMING

JUDGMENT

Never seem to be in a hurry—hurrying betrays a lack of control over yourself, and over time. Always seem patient, as if you know that everything will come to you eventually. Become a detective of the right moment; sniff out the spirit of the times, the trends that will carry you to power. Learn to stand back when the time is not yet ripe, and to strike fiercely when it has reached fruition.

OBSERVANCE OF THE LAW

Starting out in life as a nondescript French seminary-school teacher, Joseph Fouché wandered from town to town for most of the decade of the 1780s, teaching mathematics to young boys. Yet he never completely committed himself to the church, never took his vows as a priest—he had bigger plans. Patiently waiting for his chance, he kept his options open. And when the French Revolution broke out, in 1789, Fouché waited no longer: He got rid of his cassock, grew his hair long, and became a revolutionary. For this was the spirit of the times. To miss the boat at this critical moment could have spelt disaster. Fouché did not miss the boat: Befriending the revolutionary leader Robespierre, he quickly rose in the rebel ranks. In 1792 the town of Nantes elected Fouché to be its representative to the National Convention (created that year to frame a new constitution for a French republic).

When Fouché arrived in Paris to take his seat at the convention, a violent rift had broken out between the moderates and the radical Jacobins. Fouché sensed that in the long run neither side would emerge victorious. Power rarely ends up in the hands of those who start a revolution, or even of those who further it; power sticks to those who bring it to a conclusion. That was the side Fouché wanted to be on.

His sense of timing was uncanny. He started as a moderate, for moderates were in the majority. When the time came to decide on whether or not to execute Louis XVI, however, he saw that the people were clamoring for the king's head, so he cast the deciding vote—for the guillotine. Now he had become a radical. Yet as tensions came to the boil in Paris, he foresaw the danger of being too closely associated with any one faction, so he accepted a position in the provinces, where he could lie low for a while. A few months later he was assigned to the post of proconsul in Lyons, where he oversaw the execution of dozens of aristocrats. At a certain moment, however, he called a halt to the killings, sensing that the mood of the country was turning—and despite the blood already on his hands, the citizens of Lyons hailed him as a savior from what had become known as the Terror.

So far Fouché had played his cards brilliantly, but in 1794 his old friend Robespierre recalled him to Paris to account for his actions in Lyons. Robespierre had been the driving force behind the Terror. He had sent heads on both the right and the left rolling, and Fouché, whom he no longer trusted, seemed destined to provide the next head. Over the next few weeks, a tense struggle ensued: While Robespierre railed openly against Fouché, accusing of him dangerous ambitions and calling for his arrest, the crafty Fouché worked more indirectly, quietly gaining support among those who were beginning to tire of Robespierre's dictatorial control. Fouché was playing for time. He knew that the longer he survived, the more disaffected citizens he could rally against Robespierre. He had to have broad support before he moved against the powerful leader. He rallied support among both the moderates and the Jacobins, playing on the widespread fear of Robespierre—everyone was afraid of being the next to go to the guillotine. It all came to fruition on July 27: The convention

SERTORIUS'S LESSON

Sertorius's strength was now rapidly increasing, for all the tribes between the Ebro and the Pyrenees came over to his side, and troops came flocking daily to join him from every quarter. At the same time he was troubled by the lack of discipline and the overconfidence of these newly arrived barbarians, who would shout at him to attack the enemy and had no patience with his delaying tactics, and he therefore tried to win them over by argument. But when he saw that they were discontented and persisted in pressing their demands regardless of the circumstances, he let them have their way and allowed them to engage the enemy; he hoped that they would suffer a severe defeat without being completely crushed, and that this would make them better disposed to obey his orders in future. The event turned out as he expected and Sertorius came to their rescue, provided a rallying point for the fugitives, and led them safely back to his camp. His next step was to revive their dejected spirits, and so a few days later he summoned a general assembly. Before it he produced two horses, one of them old and enfeebled, the other large and lusty and

turned against Robespierre, shouting down his usual lengthy speech. He was quickly arrested, and a few days later it was Robespierre's head, not Fouché's, that fell into the basket.

When Fouché returned to the convention after Robespierre's death, he played his most unexpected move: Having led the conspiracy against Robespierre, he was expected to sit with the moderates, but lo and behold, he once again changed sides, joining the radical Jacobins. For perhaps the first time in his life he aligned himself with the minority. Clearly he sensed a reaction stirring: He knew that the moderate faction that had executed Robespierre, and was now about to take power, would initiate a new round of the Terror, this time against the radicals. In siding with the Jacobins, then, Fouché was sitting with the martyrs of the days to come—the people who would be considered blameless in the troubles that were on their way. Taking sides with what was about to become the losing team was a risky gambit, of course, but Fouché must have calculated he could keep his head long enough to quietly stir up the populace against the moderates and watch them fall from power. And indeed, although the moderates did call for his arrest in December of 1795, and would have sent him to the guillotine, too much time had passed. The executions had become unpopular with the people, and Fouché survived the swing of the pendulum one more time.

A new government took over, the Directoire. It was not, however, a Jacobin government, but a moderate one—more moderate than the government that had reimposed the Terror. Fouché, the radical, had kept his head, but now he had to keep a low profile. He waited patiently on the sidelines for several years, allowing time to soften any bitter feelings against him, then he approached the Directoire and convinced them he had a new passion: intelligence-gathering. He became a paid spy for the government, excelled at the job, and in 1799 was rewarded by being made minister of police. Now he was not just empowered but required to extend his spying to every corner of France—a responsibility that would greatly reinforce his natural ability to sniff out where the wind was blowing. One of the first social trends he detected, in fact, came in the person of Napoleon, a brash young general whose destiny he right away saw was entwined with the future of France. When Napoleon unleashed a coup d'état, on November 9, 1799, Fouché pretended to be asleep. Indeed he slept the whole day. For this indirect assistance—it might have been thought his job, after all, to prevent a military coup—Napoleon kept him on as minister of police in the new regime.

Over the next few years, Napoleon came to rely on Fouché more and more. He even gave this former revolutionary a title, duke of Otranto, and rewarded him with great wealth. By 1808, however, Fouché, always attuned to the times, sensed that Napoleon was on the downswing. His futile war with Spain, a country that posed no threat to France, was a sign that he was losing a sense of proportion. Never one to be caught on a sinking ship, Fouché conspired with Talleyrand to bring about Napoleon's downfall. Al-

possessing a flowing tail, which was remarkable for the thickness and beauty of its hair. By the side of the weak horse stood a tall strong man, and by the side of the powerful horse a short man of mean physique. At a signal the strong man seized the tail of his horse and tried with all his strength to pull it towards him, as if to tear it off, while the weak man began to pull the hairs one by one from the tail of the strong horse.

The strong man, after tugging with all his might to no purpose and causing the spectators a great deal of amusement in the process, finally gave up the attempt, while the weak man quickly and with very little trouble stripped his horse's tail completely bare. Then Sertorius rose to his feet and said, "Now you can see, my friends and allies, that perseverance is more effective than brute strength, and that there are many difficulties that cannot be overcome if you try to do everything at once, but which will yield if you master them little by little. The truth is that a steady continuous effort is irresistible, for this is the way in which Time captures and subdues the greatest powers on earth. Now Time, you should remember, is a good friend and ally to those who use their intelligence to choose the right moment, but a most dangerous enemy

to those who rush into
action at the wrong
one."

LIFE OF SERTORIUS,
PLUTARCH,
C. A.D. 46–120

though the conspiracy failed—Talleyrand was fired; Fouché stayed, but was kept on a tight leash—it publicized a growing discontent with the emperor, who seemed to be losing control. By 1814 Napoleon's power had crumbled and allied forces finally conquered him.

The next government was a restoration of the monarchy, in the form of King Louis XVIII, brother of Louis XVI. Fouché, his nose always sniffing the air for the next social shift, knew Louis would not last long—he had none of Napoleon's flair. Fouché once again played his waiting game, lying low, staying away from the spotlight. Sure enough, in February of 1815, Napoleon escaped from the island of Elba, where he had been imprisoned. Louis XVIII panicked: His policies had alienated the citizenry, who were clamoring for Napoleon's return. So Louis turned to the one man who could maybe have saved his hide, Fouché, the former radical who had sent his brother, Louis XVI, to the guillotine, but was now one of the most popular and widely admired politicians in France. Fouché, however, would not side with a loser: He refused Louis's request for help by pretending that his help was unnecessary—by swearing that Napoleon would never return to power (although he knew otherwise). A short time later, of course, Napoleon and his new citizen army were closing in on Paris.

Seeing his reign about to collapse, feeling that Fouché had betrayed him, and certain that he did not want this powerful and able man on Napoleon's team, King Louis ordered the minister's arrest and execution. On March 16, 1815, policemen surrounded Fouché's coach on a Paris boulevard. Was this finally his end? Perhaps, but not immediately: Fouché told the police that an ex-member of government could not be arrested on the street. They fell for the story and allowed him to return home. Later that day, though, they came to his house and once again declared him under arrest. Fouché nodded—but would the officers be so kind as allow a gentleman to wash and to change his clothes before leaving his house for the last time? They gave their permission, Fouché left the room, and the minutes went by. Fouché did not return. Finally the policemen went into the next room—where they saw a ladder against an open window, leading down to the garden below.

That day and the next the police combed Paris for Fouché, but by then Napoleon's cannons were audible in the distance and the king and all the king's men had to flee the city. As soon as Napoleon entered Paris, Fouché came out of hiding. He had cheated the executioner once again. Napoleon greeted his former minister of police and gladly restored him to his old post. During the 100 days that Napoleon remained in power, until Waterloo, it was essentially Fouché who governed France. After Napoleon fell, Louis XVIII returned to the throne, and like a cat with nine lives, Fouché stayed on to serve in yet another government—by then his power and influence had grown so great that not even the king dared challenge him.

Interpretation

In a period of unprecedented turmoil, Joseph Fouché thrived through his mastery of the art of timing. He teaches us a number of key lessons.

Mr. Shih had two sons:
one loved learning; the
other war. The first
expounded his moral
teachings at the
admiring court of Ch'i
and was made a tutor,
while the second talked
strategy at the bellicose
court of Ch'u and was
made a general. The
impecunious Mr. Meng,
hearing of these
successes, sent his own
two sons out to follow
the example of the
Shih boys. The first
expounded his moral
teachings at the court
of Ch'in, but the King
of Ch'in said: "At
present the states are
quarreling violently
and every prince is
busy arming his troops
to the teeth. If I
followed this prig's
pratings we should
soon be annihilated."
So he had the fellow
castrated. Meanwhile,
the second brother
displayed his military
genius at the court of
Wei. But the King of
Wei said: "Mine is a
weak state. If I relied
on force instead of
diplomacy, we should
soon be wiped out. If,
on the other hand, I let
this fire-eater go, he
will offer his services to
another state and then

First, it is critical to recognize the spirit of the times. Fouché always looked two steps ahead, found the wave that would carry him to power, and rode it. You must always work with the times, anticipate twists and turns, and never miss the boat. Sometimes the spirit of the times is obscure: Recognize it not by what is loudest and most obvious in it, but by what lies hidden and dormant. Look forward to the Napoleons of the future rather than holding on to the ruins of the past.

Second, recognizing the prevailing winds does not necessarily mean running with them. Any potent social movement creates a powerful reaction, and it is wise to anticipate what that reaction will be, as Fouché did after the execution of Robespierre. Rather than ride the cresting wave of the moment, wait for the tide's ebb to carry you back to power. Upon occasion bet on the reaction that is brewing, and place yourself in the vanguard of it.

Finally, Fouché had remarkable patience. Without patience as your sword and shield, your timing will fail and you will inevitably find yourself a loser. When the times were against Fouché, he did not struggle, get emotional, or strike out rashly. He kept his cool and maintained a low profile, patiently building support among the citizenry, the bulwark in his next rise to power. Whenever he found himself in the weaker position, he played for time, which he knew would always be his ally if he was patient. Recognize the moment, then, to hide in the grass or slither under a rock, as well as the moment to bare your fangs and attack.

> *Space we can recover, time never.*
> *Napoleon Bonaparte, 1769–1821*

KEYS TO POWER

Time is an artificial concept that we ourselves have created to make the limitlessness of eternity and the universe more bearable, more human. Since we have constructed the concept of time, we are also able to mold it to some degree, to play tricks with it. The time of a child is long and slow, with vast expanses; the time of an adult whizzes by frighteningly fast. Time, then, depends on perception, which, we know, can be willfully altered. This is the first thing to understand in mastering the art of timing. If the inner turmoil caused by our emotions tends to make time move faster, it follows that once we control our emotional responses to events, time will move much more slowly. This altered way of dealing with things tends to lengthen our perception of future time, opens up possibilities that fear and anger close off, and allows us the patience that is the principal requirement in the art of timing.

There are three kinds of time for us to deal with; each presents problems that can be solved with skill and practice. First there is *long time:* the drawn-out, years-long kind of time that must be managed with patience and gentle guidance. Our handling of long time should be mostly defensive—this is the art of not reacting impulsively, of waiting for opportunity.

we shall be in trouble."
So he had the fellow's feet cut off. Both families did exactly the same thing, but one timed it right, the other wrong. Thus success depends not on ratiocination but on rhythm.

LIEH TZU, QUOTED IN THE CHINESE LOOKING GLASS, DENNIS BLOODWORTH, 1967

The sultan [of Persia] had sentenced two men to death. One of them, knowing how much the sultan loved his stallion, offered to teach the horse to fly within a year in return for his life. The sultan, fancying himself as the rider of the only flying horse in the world, agreed. The other prisoner looked at his friend in disbelief. "You know horses don't fly. What made you come up with a crazy idea like that? You're only postponing the inevitable." "Not so," said the [first prisoner]. "I have actually given myself four chances for freedom. First, the sultan might die during the year. Second, I might die. Third, the horse might die. And fourth . . . I might teach the horse to fly!"

THE CRAFT OF POWER, R. G. H. SIU, 1979

Next there is *forced time:* the short-term time that we can manipulate as an offensive weapon, upsetting the timing of our opponents. Finally there is *end time,* when a plan must be executed with speed and force. We have waited, found the moment, and must not hesitate.

Long Time. The famous seventeenth-century Ming painter Chou Yung relates a story that altered his behavior forever. Late one winter afternoon he set out to visit a town that lay across the river from his own town. He was bringing some important books and papers with him and had commissioned a young boy to help him carry them. As the ferry neared the other side of the river, Chou Yung asked the boatman if they would have time to get to the town before its gates closed, since it was a mile away and night was approaching. The boatman glanced at the boy, and at the bundle of loosely tied papers and books—"Yes," he replied, "if you do not walk too fast."

As they started out, however, the sun was setting. Afraid of being locked out of the town at night, prey to local bandits, Chou and the boy walked faster and faster, finally breaking into a run. Suddenly the string around the papers broke and the documents scattered on the ground. It took them many minutes to put the packet together again, and by the time they had reached the city gates, it was too late.

When you force the pace out of fear and impatience, you create a nest of problems that require fixing, and you end up taking much longer than if you had taken your time. Hurriers may occasionally get there quicker, but papers fly everywhere, new dangers arise, and they find themselves in constant crisis mode, fixing the problems that they themselves have created. Sometimes not acting in the face of danger is your best move—you wait, you deliberately slow down. As time passes it will eventually present opportunities you had not imagined.

Waiting involves controlling not only your own emotions but those of your colleagues, who, mistaking action for power, may try to push you into making rash moves. In your rivals, on the other hand, you can encourage this same mistake: If you let them rush headlong into trouble while you stand back and wait, you will soon find ripe moments to intervene and pick up the pieces. This wise policy was the principal strategy of the great early-seventeenth-century emperor Tokugawa Ieyasu of Japan. When his predecessor, the headstrong Hideyoshi, whom he served as a general, staged a rash invasion of Korea, Ieyasu did not involve himself. He knew the invasion would be a disaster and would lead to Hideyoshi's downfall. Better to stand patiently on the sidelines, *even for many years,* and then be in position to seize power when the time is right—exactly what Ieyasu did, with great artistry.

You do not deliberately slow time down to live longer, or to take more pleasure in the moment, but the better to play the game of power. First, when your mind is uncluttered by constant emergencies you will see further into the future. Second, you will be able to resist the baits that people

A fisherman in the month of May stood angling on the bank of the Thames with an artificial fly. He threw his bait with so much art, that a young trout was rushing toward it, when she was prevented by her mother. "Never," said she, "my child, be too precipitate, where there is a possibility of danger. Take due time to consider, before you risk an action that may be fatal. How know you whether yon appearance be indeed a fly, or the snare of an enemy? Let someone else make the experiment before you. If it be a fly, he will very probably elude the first attack: and the second may be made, if not with success, at least with safety." She had no sooner spoken, than a gudgeon seized the pretended fly, and became an example to the giddy daughter of the importance of her mother's counsel.

FABLES,
ROBERT DODSLEY,
1703–1764

dangle in front of you, and will keep yourself from becoming another impatient sucker. Third, you will have more room to be flexible. Opportunities will inevitably arise that you had not expected and would have missed had you forced the pace. Fourth, you will not move from one deal to the next without completing the first one. To build your power's foundation can take years; make sure that foundation is secure. Do not be a flash in the pan—success that is built up slowly and surely is the only kind that lasts.

Finally, slowing time down will give you a perspective on the times you live in, letting you take a certain distance and putting you in a less emotionally charged position to see the shapes of things to come. Hurriers will often mistake surface phenomena for a real trend, seeing only what they want to see. How much better to see what is really happening, even if it is unpleasant or makes your task harder.

Forced Time. The trick in forcing time is to upset the timing of others—to make them hurry, to make them wait, to make them abandon their own pace, to distort their perception of time. By upsetting the timing of your opponent while you stay patient, you open up time for yourself, which is half the game.

In 1473 the great Turkish sultan Mehmed the Conqueror invited negotiations with Hungary to end the off-and-on war the two countries had waged for years. When the Hungarian emissary arrived in Turkey to start the talks, Turkish officials humbly apologized—Mehmed had just left Istanbul, the capital, to battle his longtime foe, Uzun Hasan. But he urgently wanted peace with Hungary, and had asked that the emissary join him at the front.

When the emissary arrived at the site of the fighting, Mehmed had already left it, moving eastward in pursuit of his swift foe. This happened several times. Wherever the emissary stopped, the Turks lavished gifts and banquets on him, in pleasurable but time-consuming ceremonies. Finally Mehmed defeated Uzun and met with the emissary. Yet his terms for peace with Hungary were excessively harsh. After a few days, the negotiations ended, and the usual stalemate remained in place. But this was fine with Mehmed. In fact he had planned it that way all along: Plotting his campaign against Uzun, he had seen that diverting his armies to the east would leave his western flank vulnerable. To prevent Hungary from taking advantage of his weakness and his preoccupation elsewhere, he first dangled the lure of peace before his enemy, then made them wait—all on his own terms.

Making people wait is a powerful way of forcing time, as long as they do not figure out what you are up to. You control the clock, they linger in limbo—and rapidly come unglued, opening up opportunities for you to strike. The opposite effect is equally powerful: You make your opponents hurry. Start off your dealings with them slowly, then suddenly apply pressure, making them feel that everything is happening at once. People who lack the time to think will make mistakes—so set their deadlines for them.

This was the technique Machiavelli admired in Cesare Borgia, who, during negotiations, would suddenly press vehemently for a decision, upsetting his opponent's timing and patience. For who would dare make Cesare wait?

Joseph Duveen, the famous art dealer, knew that if he gave an indecisive buyer like John D. Rockefeller a deadline—the painting had to leave the country, another tycoon was interested in it—the client would buy just in time. Freud noticed that patients who had spent years in psychoanalysis without improvement would miraculously recover just in time if he fixed a definite date for the end of the therapy. Jacques Lacan, the famous French psychoanalyst, used a variation on this tactic—he would sometimes end the customary hour session of therapy after only ten minutes, without warning. After this happened several times, the patient would realize that he had better make maximum use of the time, rather than wasting much of the hour with a lot of talk that meant nothing. The deadline, then, is a powerful tool. Close off the vistas of indecision and force people to make up their damn minds or get to the point—never let them make you play on their excruciating terms. Never give them time.

Magicians and showmen are experts in forcing time. Houdini could often wriggle free of handcuffs in minutes, but he would draw the escape out to an hour, making the audience sweat, as time came to an apparent standstill. Magicians have always known that the best way to alter our perception of time is often to slow down the pace. Creating suspense brings time to a terrifying pause: The slower the magician's hands move, the easier it is to create the illusion of speed, making people think the rabbit has appeared instantaneously. The great nineteenth-century magician Jean-Eugène Robert-Houdin took explicit notice of this effect: "The more slowly a story is told," he said, "the shorter it seems."

Going slower also makes what you are doing more interesting—the audience yields to your pace, becomes entranced. It is a state in which time whizzes delightfully by. You must practice such illusions, which share in the hypnotist's power to alter perceptions of time.

End Time. You can play the game with the utmost artistry—waiting patiently for the right moment to act, putting your competitors off their form by messing with their timing—but it won't mean a thing unless you know how to finish. Do not be one of those people who look like paragons of patience but are actually just afraid to bring things to a close: Patience is worthless unless combined with a willingness to fall ruthlessly on your opponent at the right moment. You can wait as long as necessary for the conclusion to come, but when it comes it must come quickly. Use speed to paralyze your opponent, cover up any mistakes you might make, and impress people with your aura of authority and finality.

With the patience of a snake charmer, you draw the snake out with calm and steady rhythms. Once the snake is out, though, would you dangle your foot above its deadly head? There is never a good reason to allow the slightest hitch in your endgame. Your mastery of timing can really only be judged by how you work with end time—how you quickly change the pace and bring things to a swift and definitive conclusion.

Image: The Hawk. Patiently and silently it circles the sky, high
above, all-seeing with its powerful eyes. Those below have
no awareness that they are being tracked. Suddenly,
when the moment arrives, the hawk swoops
down with a speed that cannot be defended against; before its prey
knows what has happened,
the bird's viselike talons
have carried it
up into the
sky.

Authority: There is a tide in the affairs of men, / Which, taken at the flood, leads on to fortune; / Omitted, all the voyage of their life / Is bound in shallows and in miseries. (*Julius Caesar,* William Shakespeare, 1564–1616)

REVERSAL
There is no power to be gained in letting go of the reins and adapting to whatever time brings. To some degree you must guide time or you will be its merciless victim. There is accordingly no reversal to this law.

36

DISDAIN THINGS

YOU CANNOT HAVE:

IGNORING THEM IS

THE BEST REVENGE

JUDGMENT

By acknowledging a petty problem you give it existence and credibility. The more attention you pay an enemy, the stronger you make him; and a small mistake is often made worse and more visible when you try to fix it. It is sometimes best to leave things alone. If there is something you want but cannot have, show contempt for it. The less interest you reveal, the more superior you seem.

TRANSGRESSION OF THE LAW

The Mexican rebel leader Pancho Villa started out as the chief of a gang of bandits, but after revolution broke out in Mexico in 1910, he became a kind of folk hero—robbing trains and giving the money to the poor, leading daring raids, and charming the ladies with romantic escapades. His exploits fascinated Americans—he seemed a man from another era, part Robin Hood, part Don Juan. After a few years of bitter fighting, however, General Carranza emerged as the victor in the Revolution; the defeated Villa and his troops went back home, to the northern state of Chihuahua. His army dwindled and he turned to banditry again, damaging his popularity. Finally, perhaps out of desperation, he began to rail against the United States, the gringos, whom he blamed for his troubles.

In March of 1916, Pancho Villa raided Columbus, New Mexico. Rampaging through the town, he and his gang killed seventeen American soldiers and civilians. President Woodrow Wilson, like many Americans, had admired Villa; now, however, the bandit needed to be punished. Wilson's advisers urged him to send troops into Mexico to capture Villa. For a power as large as the United States, they argued, not to strike back at an army that had invaded its territory would send the worst kind of signal. Furthermore, they continued, many Americans saw Wilson as a pacifist, a principle the public doubted as a response to violence; he needed to prove his mettle and manliness by ordering the use of force.

The pressure on Wilson was strong, and before the month was out, with the approval of the Carranza government, he sent an army of ten thousand soldiers to capture Pancho Villa. The venture was called the Punitive Expedition, and its leader was the dashing General John J. Pershing, who had defeated guerrillas in the Philippines and Native Americans in the American Southwest. Certainly Pershing could find and overpower Pancho Villa.

The Punitive Expedition became a sensational story, and carloads of U.S. reporters followed Pershing into action. The campaign, they wrote, would be a test of American power. The soldiers carried the latest in weaponry, communicated by radio, and were supported by reconnaissance from the air.

In the first few months, the troops split up into small units to comb the wilds of northern Mexico. The Americans offered a $50,000 reward for information leading to Villa's capture. But the Mexican people, who had been disillusioned with Villa when he had returned to banditry, now idolized him for facing this mighty American army. They began to give Pershing false leads: Villa had been seen in this village, or in that mountain hideaway, airplanes would be dispatched, troops would scurry after them, and no one would ever see him. The wily bandit seemed to be always one step ahead of the American military.

By the summer of that year, the expedition had swelled to 123,000 men. They suffered through the stultifying heat, the mosquitoes, the wild terrain. Trudging over a countryside in which they were already resented,

THE FOX AND THE GRAPES

*A starving fox ...
saw a cluster
Of luscious-looking
grapes of purplish
luster
Dangling above him on
a trellis-frame.
He would have dearly
liked them for his
lunch,
But when he tried and
failed to reach the
bunch:
"Ah well, it's more than
likely they're not
sweet—
Good only for green
fools to eat!"*

*Wasn't he wise to say
they were unripe
Rather than whine
and gripe?*

FABLES,
JEAN DE LA FONTAINE,
1621–1695

*Once when G. K.
Chesterton's economic
views were abused in
print by George
Bernard Shaw, his
friends waited in vain
for him to reply.
Historian Hilaire
Belloc reproached him.
"My dear Belloc,"
Chesterton said, "I
have answered him.
To a man of Shaw's
wit, silence is the one
unbearable repartee."*

THE LITTLE, BROWN
BOOK OF ANECDOTES,
CLIFTON FADIMAN, ED.,
1985

they infuriated both the local people and the Mexican government. At one point Pancho Villa hid in a mountain cave to recover from a gunshot wound he received in a skirmish with the Mexican army; looking down from his aerie, he could watch Pershing lead the exhausted American troops back and forth across the mountains, never getting any closer to their goal.

All the way into winter, Villa played his cat-and-mouse game. Americans came to see the affair as a kind of slapstick farce—in fact they began to admire Villa again, respecting his resourcefulness in eluding a superior force. In January of 1917, Wilson finally ordered Pershing's withdrawal. As the troops made their way back to American territory, rebel forces pursued them, forcing the U.S. Army to use airplanes to protect its rear flanks. The Punitive Expedition was being punished itself—it had turned into a retreat of the most humiliating sort.

Interpretation

Woodrow Wilson organized the Punitive Expedition as a show of force: He would teach Pancho Villa a lesson and in the process show the world that no one, large or small, could attack the mighty United States and get away with it. The expedition would be over in a few weeks, and Villa would be forgotten.

That was not how it played out. The longer the expedition took, the more it focused attention on the Americans' incompetence and on Villa's cleverness. Soon what was forgotten was not Villa but the raid that had started it all. As a minor annoyance became an international embarrassment, and the enraged Americans dispatched more troops, the imbalance between the size of the pursuer and the size of the pursued—who still managed to stay free—made the affair a joke. And in the end this white elephant of an army had to lumber out of Mexico, humiliated. The Punitive Expedition did the opposite of what it set out to do: It left Villa not only free but more popular than ever.

What could Wilson have done differently? He could have pressured the Carranza government to catch Villa for him. Alternatively, since many Mexicans had tired of Villa before the Punitive Expedition began, he could have worked quietly with them and won their support for a much smaller raid to capture the bandit. He could have organized a trap on the American side of the border, anticipating the next raid. Or he could have ignored the matter altogether for the time being, waiting for the Mexicans themselves to do away with Villa of their own accord.

Remember: You *choose* to let things bother you. You can just as easily choose not to notice the irritating offender, to consider the matter trivial and unworthy of your interest. That is the powerful move. What you do not react to cannot drag you down in a futile engagement. Your pride is not involved. The best lesson you can teach an irritating gnat is to consign it to oblivion by ignoring it. If it is impossible to ignore (Pancho Villa had in fact killed American citizens), then conspire in secret to do away with it, but

THE ASS AND
THE GRADENER

An ass had once by some accident lost his tail, which was a grievous affliction to him; and he was everywhere seeking after it, being fool enough to think he could get it set on again. He passed through a meadow, and afterwards got into a garden. The gardener seeing him, and not able to endure the mischief he was doing in trampling down his plants, fell into a violent rage, ran to the ass, and never standing on the ceremony of a pillory, cut off both his ears, and beat him out of the ground. Thus the ass, who bemoaned the loss of his tail, was in far greater affliction when he saw himself without ears.

FABLES,
PILPAY,
INDIA,
FOURTH CENTURY

THE PRODIGY OX

Once, when the Toku-daiji minister of the right was chief of the imperial police, he was holding a meeting of his staff at the middle gate when an ox belonging to an official named Akikane got loose and wandered into the ministry building. It climbed up on

never inadvertently draw attention to the bothersome insect that will go away or die on its own. If you waste time and energy in such entanglements, it is your own fault. Learn to play the card of disdain and turn your back on what cannot harm you in the long run.

Just think—it cost your government $130 million to try to get me. I took them over rough, hilly country. Sometimes for fifty miles at a stretch they had no water. They had nothing but the sun and mosquitoes. . . . And nothing was gained.
Pancho Villa, 1878–1923

OBSERVANCE OF THE LAW

In the year 1527, King Henry VIII of England decided he had to find a way to get rid of his wife, Catherine of Aragon. Catherine had failed to produce a son, a male heir who would ensure the continuance of his dynasty, and Henry thought he knew why: He had read in the Bible the passage, "And if a man shall take his brother's wife, it is an unclean thing: he hath uncovered his brother's nakedness; they shall be childless." Before marrying Henry, Catherine had married his older brother Arthur, but Arthur had died five months later. Henry had waited an appropriate time, then had married his brother's widow.

Catherine was the daughter of King Ferdinand and Queen Isabella of Spain, and by marrying her Henry had kept alive a valuable alliance. Now, however, Catherine had to assure him that her brief marriage with Arthur had never been consummated. Otherwise Henry would view their relationship as incestuous and their marriage as null and void. Catherine insisted that she had remained a virgin through her marriage to Arthur, and Pope Clement VII supported her by giving his blessing to the union, which he could not have done had he considered it incestuous. Yet after years of marriage to Henry, Catherine had failed to produce a son, and in the early 1520s she had entered menopause. To the king this could only mean one thing: She had lied about her virginity, their union was incestuous, and God had punished them.

There was another reason why Henry wanted to get rid of Catherine: He had fallen in love with a younger woman, Anne Boleyn. Not only was he in love with her, but if he married her he could still hope to sire a legitimate son. The marriage to Catherine had to be annulled. For this, however, Henry had to apply to the Vatican. But Pope Clement would never annul the marriage.

By the summer of 1527, rumors spread throughout Europe that Henry was about to attempt the impossible—to annul his marriage against Clement's wishes. Catherine would never abdicate, let alone voluntarily enter a nunnery, as Henry had urged her. But Henry had his own strategy: He stopped sleeping in the same bed with Catherine, since he considered her his sister-in-law, not his lawful wife. He insisted on calling her Princess

the dais where the chief was seated and lay there, chewing its cud. Everyone was sure that this was some grave portent, and urged that the ox be sent to a yin-yang diviner. However, the prime minister, the father of the minister of the right, said, "An ox has no discrimination. It has legs—there is nowhere it won't go. It does not make sense to deprive an underpaid official of the wretched ox he needs in order to attend court." He returned the ox to its owner and changed the matting on which it had lain. No untoward event of any kind occurred afterward. They say that if you see a prodigy and do not treat it as such, its character as a prodigy is destroyed.

ESSAYS IN IDLENESS,
KENKŌ,
JAPAN,
FOURTEENTH CENTURY

Dowager of Wales, her title as Arthur's widow. Finally, in 1531, he banished her from court and shipped her off to a distant castle. The pope ordered him to return her to court, on pain of excommunication, the most severe penalty a Catholic could suffer. Henry not only ignored this threat, he insisted that his marriage to Catherine had been dissolved, and in 1533 he married Anne Boleyn.

Clement refused to recognize the marriage, but Henry did not care. He no longer recognized the pope's authority, and proceeded to break with the Roman Catholic Church, establishing the Church of England in its stead, with the king as the head of the new church. And so, not surprisingly, the newly formed Church of England proclaimed Anne Boleyn England's rightful queen.

The pope tried every threat in the book, but nothing worked. Henry simply ignored him. Clement fumed—no one had ever treated him so contemptuously. Henry had humiliated him and he had no power of recourse. Even excommunication (which he constantly threatened but never carried out) would no longer matter.

Catherine too felt the devastating sting of Henry's disdain. She tried to fight back, but in appealing to Henry her words fell on deaf ears, and soon they fell on no one's. Isolated from the court, ignored by the king, mad with anger and frustration, Catherine slowly deteriorated, and finally died in January of 1536, from a cancerous tumor of the heart.

Interpretation

When you pay attention to a person, the two of you become partners of sorts, each moving in step to the actions and reactions of the other. In the process you lose your initiative. It is a dynamic of all interactions: By acknowledging other people, even if only to fight with them, you open yourself to their influence. Had Henry locked horns with Catherine, he would have found himself mired in endless arguments that would have weakened his resolve and eventually worn him down. (Catherine was a strong, stubborn woman.) Had he set out to convince Clement to change his verdict on the marriage's validity, or tried to compromise and negotiate with him, he would have gotten bogged down in Clement's favorite tactic: playing for time, promising flexibility, but actually getting what popes always got— their way.

Henry would have none of this. He played a devastating power game—total disdain. By ignoring people you cancel them out. This unsettles and infuriates them—but since they have no dealings with you, there is nothing they can do.

This is the offensive aspect of the law. Playing the card of contempt is immensely powerful, for it lets you determine the conditions of the conflict. The war is waged on your terms. This is the ultimate power pose: You are the king, and you ignore what offends you. Watch how this tactic infuriates people—half of what they do is to get your attention, and when you withhold it from them, they flounder in frustration.

KEYS TO POWER

Desire often creates paradoxical effects: The more you want something, the more you chase after it, the more it eludes you. The more interest you show, the more you repel the object of your desire. This is because your interest is too strong—it makes people awkward, even fearful. Uncontrollable desire makes you seem weak, unworthy, pathetic.

You need to turn your back on what you want, show your contempt and disdain. This is the kind of powerful response that will drive your targets crazy. They will respond with a desire of their own, which is simply to have an effect on you—perhaps to possess you, perhaps to hurt you. If they want to possess you, you have successfully completed the first step of seduction. If they want to hurt you, you have unsettled them and made them play by your rules (see Laws 8 and 39 on baiting people into action).

Contempt is the prerogative of the king. Where his eyes turn, what he decides to see, is what has reality; what he ignores and turns his back on is as good as dead. That was the weapon of King Louis XIV—if he did not like you, he acted as if you were not there, maintaining his superiority by cutting off the dynamic of interaction. This is the power you have when you play the card of contempt, periodically showing people that you can do without them.

If choosing to ignore enhances your power, it follows that the opposite approach—commitment and engagement—often weakens you. By paying undue attention to a puny enemy, *you* look puny, and the longer it takes you to crush such an enemy, the larger the enemy seems. When Athens set out to conquer the island of Sicily, in 415 B.C., a giant power was attacking a tiny one. Yet by entangling Athens in a long-drawn-out conflict, Syracuse, Sicily's most important city-state, was able to grow in stature and confidence. Finally defeating Athens, it made itself famous for centuries to come. In recent times, President John F. Kennedy made a similar mistake in his attitude to Fidel Castro of Cuba: His failed invasion at the Bay of Pigs, in 1961, made Castro an international hero.

A second danger: If you succeed in crushing the irritant, or even if you merely wound it, you create sympathy for the weaker side. Critics of Franklin D. Roosevelt complained bitterly about the money his administration spent on government projects, but their attacks had no resonance with the public, who saw the president as working to end the Great Depression. His opponents thought they had an example that would show just how wasteful he had become: his dog, Fala, which he lavished with favors and attention. Critics railed at his insensitivity—spending taxpayers' money on a dog while so many Americans were still in poverty. But Roosevelt had a response: How *dare* his critics attack a defenseless little dog?

His speech in defense of Fala was one of the most popular he ever gave. In this case, the weak party involved was the president's dog and the attack backfired—in the long run, it only made the president more sympathetic, since many people will naturally side with the "underdog," just as the American public came to sympathize with the wily but outnumbered Pancho Villa.

It is tempting to want to fix our mistakes, but the harder we try, the worse we often make them. It is sometimes more politic to leave them alone. In 1971, when the *New York Times* published the Pentagon Papers, a group of government documents about the history of U.S. involvement in Indochina, Henry Kissinger erupted into a volcanic rage. Furious about the Nixon administration's vulnerability to this kind of damaging leak, he made recommendations that eventually led to the formation of a group called the Plumbers to plug the leaks. This was the unit that later broke into Democratic Party offices in the Watergate Hotel, setting off the chain of events that led to Nixon's downfall. In reality the publication of the Pentagon Papers was not a serious threat to the administration, but Kissinger's reaction made it a big deal. In trying to fix one problem, he created another: a paranoia for security that in the end was much more destructive to the government. Had he ignored the Pentagon Papers, the scandal they had created would eventually have blown over.

Instead of inadvertently focusing attention on a problem, making it seem worse by publicizing how much concern and anxiety it is causing you, it is often far wiser to play the contemptuous aristocrat, not deigning to acknowledge the problem's existence. There are several ways to execute this strategy.

First there is the sour-grapes approach. If there is something you want but that you realize you cannot have, the worst thing you can do is draw attention to your disappointment by complaining about it. An infinitely more powerful tactic is to act as if it never really interested you in the first place. When the writer George Sand's supporters nominated her to be the first female member of the Académie Française, in 1861, Sand quickly saw that the academy would never admit her. Instead of whining, though, she claimed she had no interest in belonging to this group of worn-out, overrated, out-of-touch windbags. Her disdain was the perfect response: Had she shown her anger at her exclusion, she would have revealed how much it meant to her. Instead she branded the academy a club of old men—and why should she be angry or disappointed at not having to spend her time with them? Crying "sour grapes" is sometimes seen as a reflection of the weak; it is actually the tactic of the powerful.

Second, when you are attacked by an inferior, deflect people's attention by making it clear that the attack has not even registered. Look away, or answer sweetly, showing how little the attack concerns you. Similarly, when you yourself have committed a blunder, the best response is often to make less of your mistake by treating it lightly.

The Japanese emperor Go-Saiin, a great disciple of the tea ceremony, owned a priceless antique tea bowl that all the courtiers envied. One day a guest, Dainagon Tsunehiro, asked if he could carry the tea bowl into the light, to examine it more closely. The bowl rarely left the table, but the emperor was in good spirits and he consented. As Dainagon carried the bowl to the railing of the verandah, however, and held it up to the light, it slipped from his hands and fell on a rock in the garden below, smashing into tiny fragments.

The emperor of course was furious. "It was indeed most clumsy of me to let it drop in this way," said Dainagon, with a deep bow, "but really there is not much harm done. This Ido tea-bowl is a very old one and it is impossible to say how much longer it would have lasted, but anyhow it is not a thing of any public use, so I think it rather fortunate that it has broken thus." This surprising response had an immediate effect: The emperor calmed down. Dainagon neither sniveled nor overapologized, but signaled his own worth and power by treating his mistake with a touch of disdain. The emperor had to respond with a similar aristocratic indifference; his anger had made him seem low and petty—an image Dainagon was able to manipulate.

Among equals this tactic might backfire: Your indifference could make you seem callous. But with a master, if you act quickly and without great fuss, it can work to great effect: You bypass his angry response, save him the time and energy he would waste by brooding over it, and allow him the opportunity to display his own lack of pettiness publicly.

If we make excuses and denials when we are caught in a mistake or a deception, we stir the waters and make the situation worse. It is often wiser to play things the opposite way. The Renaissance writer Pietro Aretino often boasted of his aristocratic lineage, which was, of course, a fiction, since he was actually the son of a shoemaker. When an enemy of his finally revealed the embarrassing truth, word quickly spread, and soon all of Venice (where he lived at the time) was aghast at Aretino's lies. Had he tried to defend himself, he would have only dragged himself down. His response was masterful: He announced that he was indeed the son of a shoemaker, but this only proved his greatness, since he had risen from the lowest stratum of society to its very pinnacle. From then on he never mentioned his previous lie, trumpeting instead his new position on the matter of his ancestry.

Remember: The powerful responses to niggling, petty annoyances and irritations are contempt and disdain. Never show that something has affected you, or that you are offended—that only shows you have acknowledged a problem. Contempt is a dish that is best served cold and without affectation.

Image:
The Tiny
Wound.

It is small but painful and irritating. You
try all sorts of medicaments, you complain, you scratch and pick at the scab.
Doctors only make it worse, transforming
the tiny wound into a grave matter. If only
you had left the wound alone, letting time
heal it and freeing yourself of worry.

Authority: Know how to play the card of contempt. It is the most politic
kind of revenge. For there are many of whom we should have known
nothing if their distinguished opponents had taken no notice of them.
There is no revenge like oblivion, for it is the entombment of the unworthy in the dust of their own nothingness. (Baltasar Gracián, 1601–1658)

REVERSAL

You must play the card of contempt with care and delicacy. Most small
troubles will vanish on their own if you leave them be; but some will grow
and fester unless you attend to them. Ignore a person of inferior stature and
the next time you look he has become a serious rival, and your contempt
has made him vengeful as well. The great princes of Renaissance Italy
chose to ignore Cesare Borgia at the outset of his career as a young general
in the army of his father, Pope Alexander VI. By the time they paid attention it was too late—the cub was now a lion, gobbling up chunks of Italy.
Often, then, while you show contempt publicly you will also need to keep
an eye on the problem privately, monitoring its status and making sure it
goes away. Do not let it become a cancerous cell.

Develop the skill of sensing problems when they are still small and
taking care of them before they become intractable. Learn to distinguish
between the potentially disastrous and the mildly irritating, the nuisance
that will quietly go away on its own. In either case, though, never completely take your eye off it. As long as it is alive it can smolder and spark
into life.

CREATE COMPELLING

SPECTACLES

JUDGMENT

Striking imagery and grand symbolic gestures create the aura of power—everyone responds to them. Stage spectacles for those around you, then, full of arresting visuals and radiant symbols that heighten your presence. Dazzled by appearances, no one will notice what you are really doing.

OBSERVANCE OF THE LAW I

ANTONY AND CLEOPATRA

She relied above all upon her physical presence and the spell and enchantment which it could create. . . . She came sailing up the river Cydnus in a barge with a poop of gold, its purple sails billowing in the wind, while her rowers caressed the water with oars of silver which dipped in time to the music of the flute, accompanied by pipes and lutes. Cleopatra herself reclined beneath a canopy of cloth of gold, dressed in the character of Aphrodite, as we see her in paintings, while on either side to complete the picture stood boys costumed as Cupids who cooled her with their fans. Instead of a crew the barge was lined with the most beautiful of her waiting-women attired as Nereids and Graces, some at the rudders, others at the tackle of the sails, and all the while an indescribably rich perfume, exhaled from innumerable censers, was wafted from the vessel to the riverbanks. Great multitudes accompanied this royal progress, some of them following the queen on both sides of the river from its very mouth, while others hurried down from the city of Tarsus to gaze at the sight. Gradually the crowds drifted away from the marketplace,

In the early 1780s, word spread through Berlin of the strange and spectacular medical practice of a Dr. Weisleder. He performed his miracles in an enormous converted beer hall, outside which Berliners began to notice ever longer lines of people—the blind, the lame, anyone with an illness incurable by normal medicine. When it leaked out that the doctor worked by exposing the patient to the rays of the moon, he soon became dubbed The Moon Doctor of Berlin.

Sometime in 1783, it was reported that Dr. Weisleder had cured a well-to-do woman of a terrible ailment. He suddenly became a celebrity. Previously only the poorest Berliners had been seen waiting outside the beer hall in their rags; now magnificent carriages were parked outside, and gentlemen in frock coats, and ladies with enormous coiffures, lined the street as sunset drew near. Even folk with the mildest of ailments came, out of sheer curiosity. As they waited in line, the poorer clients would explain to the gentlemen and ladies that the doctor only practiced when the moon was in its increscent phase. Many would add that they themselves had already been exposed to the healing powers he called forth from the rays of the moon. Even those who felt cured kept coming back, drawn by this powerful experience.

Inside the beer hall, a strange and stirring spectacle greeted the visitor: Packed into the entrance hall was a crowd of all classes and ethnic backgrounds, a veritable Tower of Babel. Through tall windows on the northern side of the hall, silvery moonlight poured in at odd angles. The doctor and his wife, who, it seemed, was also able to effect the cure, practiced on the second floor, which was reached by a stairway, at the end of the hall. As the line edged closer to the stairs, the sick would hear shouts and cries from above, and word would spread of, perhaps, a blind gentleman suddenly able to see.

Once upstairs, the line would fork in two directions, toward a northern room for the doctor, a southern one for his wife, who worked only on the ladies. Finally, after hours of anticipation and waiting in line, the gentlemen patients would be led before the amazing doctor himself, an elderly man with a few stalks of wild gray hair and an air of nervous energy. He would take the patient (let us say a young boy, brought in by his father), uncover the afflicted body part, and lift the boy up to the window, which faced the light of the moon. He would rub the site of the injury or illness, mumble something unintelligible, look knowingly at the moon, and then, after collecting his fee, send the boy and his father on their way. Meanwhile, in the south-facing room, his wife would be doing the same with the ladies—which was odd, really, since the moon cannot appear in two places at once; it cannot have been visible, in other words, from both windows. Apparently the mere thought, idea, and symbol of the moon were enough, for the ladies did not complain, and would later remark confidently that the wife of the Moon Doctor had the same healing powers as he.

Interpretation

Dr. Weisleder may have known nothing about medicine, but he understood human nature. He recognized that people do not always want words, or rational explanations, or demonstrations of the powers of science; they want an immediate appeal to their emotions. Give them that and they will do the rest—such as imagine they can be healed by the light reflected from a rock a quarter million miles away. Dr. Weisleder had no need of pills, or of lengthy lectures on the moon's power, or of any silly gadgetry to amplify its rays. He understood that the simpler the spectacle the better—just the moonlight pouring in from the side, the stairway leading to the heavens, and the rays of the moon, whether directly visible or not. Any added effects might have made it seem that the moon was not strong enough on its own. And the moon *was* strong enough—it was a magnet for fantasies, as it has been throughout history. Simply by associating himself with the image of the moon, the doctor gained power.

Remember: Your search for power depends on shortcuts. You must always circumvent people's suspicions, their perverse desire to resist your will. Images are an extremely effective shortcut: Bypassing the head, the seat of doubt and resistance, they aim straight for the heart. Overwhelming the eyes, they create powerful associations, bringing people together and stirring their emotions. With the white light of the moon in their eyes, your targets are blinded to the deceptions you practice.

OBSERVANCE OF THE LAW II

In 1536 the future king Henri II of France took his first mistress, Diane de Poitiers. Diane was thirty-seven at the time, and was the widow of the grand seneschal of Normandy. Henri, meanwhile, was a sprightly lad of seventeen, who was just beginning to sow his wild oats. At first their union seemed merely platonic, with Henri showing an intensely spiritual devotion to Diane. But it soon became clear that he loved her in every way, preferring her bed to that of his young wife, Catherine de' Médicis.

In 1547 King Francis died and Henri ascended to the throne. This new situation posed perils for Diane de Poitiers. She had just turned forty-eight, and despite her notorious cold baths and rumored youth potions, she was beginning to show her age; now that Henri was king, perhaps he would return to the queen's bed, and do as other kings had done—choose mistresses from the bevy of beauties who made the French court the envy of Europe. He was, after all, only twenty-eight, and cut a dashing figure. But Diane did not give up so easily. She would continue to enthrall her lover, as she had enthralled him for the past eleven years.

Diane's secret weapons were symbols and images, to which she had always paid great attention. Early on in her relationship with Henri, she had created a motif by intertwining her initials with his, to symbolize their union. The idea worked like a charm: Henri put this insignia everywhere—on his royal robes, on monuments, on churches, on the facade of the

between two things by following the hidden detours of their causal connexions, thought makes a leap and discovers their relation not in the connexion of cause and effects, but in a connexion of signification. . . . Symbolist thought permits an infinity of relations between things. Each thing may denote a number of distinct ideas by its different special qualities, and a quality may have several symbolic meanings. The highest conceptions have symbols by the thousand. Nothing is too humble to represent and glory the sublime. The walnut signifies Christ: the sweet kernel is His divine nature, the green and pulpy outer peel is His humanity, the wooden shell between is the cross. Thus all things raise his thoughts to the eternal. . . . Every precious stone, besides its natural splendour sparkles with the brilliance of its symbolic values. The assimilation of roses and virginity is much more than a poetic comparison, for it reveals their common essence. As each notion arises in the mind the logic of symbolism creates an harmony of ideas.

THE WANING OF THE MIDDLE AGES, JOHAN HUIZINGA, 1928

Louvre, then the royal palace in Paris. Diane's favorite colors were black and white, which she wore exclusively, and wherever it was possible the insignia appeared in these colors. Everyone recognized the symbol and its meaning. Soon after Henri took the throne, however, Diane went still further: She decided to identify herself with the Roman goddess Diana, her namesake. Diana was the goddess of the hunt, the traditional royal pastime and the particular passion of Henri. Equally important, in Renaissance art she symbolized chastity and purity. For a woman like Diane to identify herself with this goddess would instantly call up those images in the court, giving her an air of respectability. Symbolizing her "chaste" relationship with Henri, it would also set her apart from the adulterous liaisons of royal mistresses past.

To effect this association, Diane began by completely transforming her castle at Anet. She razed the building's structure and in its place erected a magnificent Doric-columned edifice modeled after a Roman temple. It was made in white Normandy stone flecked with black silex, reproducing Diane's trademark colors of black and white. The insignia of her and Henri's initials appeared on the columns, the doors, the windows, the carpet. Meanwhile, symbols of Diana—crescent moons, stags, and hounds—adorned the gates and facade. Inside, enormous tapestries depicting episodes in the life of the goddess lay on the floors and hung on the walls. In the garden stood the famous Goujon sculpture *Diane Chasseresse,* which is now in the Louvre, and which had an uncanny resemblance to Diane de Poitiers. Paintings and other depictions of Diana appeared in every corner of the castle.

Anet overwhelmed Henri, who soon was trumpeting the image of Diane de Poitiers as a Roman goddess. In 1548, when the couple appeared together in Lyons for a royal celebration, the townspeople welcomed them with a *tableau vivant* depicting a scene with Diana the huntress. France's greatest poet of the period, Pierre de Ronsard, began to write verses in honor of Diana—indeed a kind of cult of Diana sprang up, all inspired by the king's mistress. It seemed to Henri that Diane had given herself a kind of divine aura, and as if he were destined to worship her for the rest of his life. And until his death, in 1559, he did remain faithful to her—making her a duchess, giving her untold wealth, and displaying an almost religious devotion to his first and only mistress.

Interpretation

Diane de Poitiers, a woman from a modest bourgeois background, managed to captivate Henri for over twenty years. By the time he died she was well into her sixties, yet his passion for her only increased with the years. She knew the king well. He was not an intellectual but a lover of the outdoors—he particularly loved jousting tournaments, with their bright pennants, brilliantly caparisoned horses, and beautifully dressed women. Henri's love of visual splendor seemed childlike to Diane, and she played on this weakness of his at every opportunity.

Most astute of all was Diane's appropriation of the goddess Diana. Here she took the game beyond physical imagery into the realm of the psychic symbol. It was quite a feat to transform a king's mistress into an emblem of power and purity, but she managed it. Without the resonance of the goddess, Diane was merely an aging courtesan. With the imagery and symbolism of Diana on her shoulders, she seemed a mythic force, destined for greatness.

You too can play with images like these, weaving visual clues into an encompassing gestalt, as Diane did with her colors and her insignia. Establish a trademark like these to set yourself apart. Then take the game further: Find an image or symbol from the past that will neatly fit your situation, and put it on your shoulders like a cape. It will make you seem larger than life.

> *Because of the light it shines on the other stars which make up a kind of court around it, because of the just and equal distribution of its rays to all alike, because of the good it brings to all places, producing life, joy and action, because of its constancy from which it never varies, I chose the sun as the most magnificent image to represent a great leader.*
>
> Louis XIV, the Sun King, 1638–1715

KEYS TO POWER

Using words to plead your case is risky business: Words are dangerous instruments, and often go astray. The words people use to persuade us virtually invite us to reflect on them with words of our own; we mull them over, and often end up believing the opposite of what they say. (That is part of our perverse nature.) It also happens that words offend us, stirring up associations unintended by the speaker.

The visual, on the other hand, short-circuits the labyrinth of words. It strikes with an emotional power and immediacy that leave no gaps for reflection and doubt. Like music, it leaps right over rational, reasonable thoughts. Imagine the Moon Doctor trying to make a case for his medical practice, trying to convince the unconverted by telling them about the healing powers of the moon, and about his own special connection to a distant object in the sky. Fortunately for him, he was able to create a compelling spectacle that made words unnecessary. The moment his patients entered the beer hall, the image of the moon spoke eloquently enough.

Understand: Words put you on the defensive. If you have to explain yourself your power is already in question. The image, on the other hand, imposes itself as a given. It discourages questions, creates forceful associations, resists unintended interpretations, communicates instantly, and forges bonds that transcend social differences. Words stir up arguments and divisions; images bring people together. They are the quintessential instruments of power.

The symbol has the same force, whether it is visual (the statue of

There was a man named Sakamotoya Hechigwan who lived in upper Kyoto.... When [Emperor] Hideyoshi gave his great Cha-no-yu [tea ceremony] meeting at Kitano in the tenth month of 1588, Hechigwan set up a great red umbrella nine feet across mounted on a stick seven feet high. The circumference of the handle he surrounded for about two feet by a reed fence in such a way that the rays of the sun were reflected from it and diffused the colour of the umbrella all around. This device pleased Hideyoshi so much that he remitted Hechigwan's taxes as a reward.

CHA-NO-YU: THE JAPANESE TEA CEREMONY, A. L. SADLER, 1962

Diana) or a verbal description of something visual (the words "the Sun King"). The symbolic object stands for something else, something abstract (such as the image "Diana" standing for chastity). The abstract concept—purity, patriotism, courage, love—is full of emotional and powerful associations. The symbol is a shortcut of expression, containing dozens of meanings in one simple phrase or object. The symbol of the Sun King, as explained by Louis XIV, can be read on many layers, but the beauty of it is that its associations required no explanation, spoke immediately to his subjects, distinguished him from all other kings, and conjured up a kind of majesty that went far beyond the words themselves. The symbol contains untold power.

The first step in using symbols and images is to understand the primacy of sight among the senses. Before the Renaissance, it has been argued, sight and the other senses—taste, touch, and so on—operated on a relatively equal plane. Since then, however, the visual has come to dominate the others, and is the sense we most depend on and trust. As Gracián said, "The truth is generally seen, rarely heard." When the Renaissance painter Fra Filippo Lippi was a captured slave among the Moors, he won his freedom by sketching a drawing of his master on a white wall with a piece of charcoal; when the owner saw the drawing, he instantly understood the power of a man who could make such images, and let Fra Lippi go. That one image was far more powerful than any argument the artist could have made with words.

Never neglect the way you arrange things visually. Factors like color, for example, have enormous symbolic resonance. When the con artist Yellow Kid Weil created a newsletter touting the phony stocks he was peddling, he called it the "Red Letter Newsletter" and had it printed, at considerable expense, in red ink. The color created a sense of urgency, power, and good fortune. Weil recognized details like these as keys to deception—as do modern advertisers and mass-marketers. If you use "gold" in the title of anything you are trying to sell, for example, print it in gold. Since the eye predominates, people will respond more to the color than to the word.

The visual contains great emotional power. The Roman emperor Constantine worshipped the sun as a god for most of his life; one day, though, he looked up at the sun, and saw a cross superimposed on it. The vision of the cross over the sun proved to him the ascendancy of the new religion, and he converted not just himself but the whole Roman Empire to Christianity soon thereafter. All the preaching and proselytizing in the world could not have been as powerful. Find and associate yourself with the images and symbols that will communicate in this immediate way today, and you will have untold power.

Most effective of all is a new combination—a fusion of images and symbols that have not been seen together before, but that through their association clearly demonstrate your new idea, message, religion. The creation of new images and symbols out of old ones in this way has a poetic effect—viewers' associations run rampant, giving them a sense of participation.

Visual images often appear in a sequence, and the order in which they appear creates a symbol. The first to appear, for instance, symbolizes power; the image at the center seems to have central importance.

Near the end of World War II, orders came down from General Eisenhower that American troops were to lead the way into Paris after its liberation from the Nazis. The French general Charles de Gaulle, however, realized that this sequence would imply that the Americans now commanded the fate of France. Through much manipulation, de Gaulle made certain that he and the French Second Armored Division would appear at the head of the liberating force. The strategy worked: After he had successfully pulled off this stunt, the Allies started treating him as the new leader of an independent France. De Gaulle knew that a leader has to locate himself literally at the head of his troops. This visual association is crucial to the emotional response that he needs to elicit.

Things change in the game of symbols: It is probably no longer possible to pose as a "sun king," or to wrap the mantle of Diana around you. Yet you can associate yourself with such symbols more indirectly. And, of course, you can make your own mythology out of figures from more recent history, people who are comfortably dead but still powerfully associative in the public eye. The idea is to give yourself an aura, a stature that your normal banal appearance simply will not create. By herself Diane de Poitiers had no such radiant powers; she was as human and ordinary as most of us. But the symbol elevated her above the human lot, and made her seem divine.

Using symbols also has a courtier-like effect, since they are often gentler than brutish words. The psychotherapist Dr. Milton H. Erickson always tried to find symbols and images that would communicate to the patient in ways that words could not. When dealing with a severely troubled patient, he would not question him directly but would talk about something irrelevant, such as driving through the desert in Arizona, where he practiced in the 1950s. In describing this he would eventually come to an appropriate symbol for what he suspected was the man's problem. If he felt the patient was isolated, say, Dr. Erickson would talk of a single ironwood tree, and how its isolation left it battered by the winds. Making an emotional connection with the tree as a symbol, the patient would open up more readily to the doctor's probing.

Use the power of symbols as a way to rally, animate, and unite your troops or team. During the rebellion against the French crown in 1648, those loyal to the king disparaged the rebels by comparing them to the slingshots (in French, *frondes*) that little boys use to frighten big boys. Cardinal de Retz decided to turn this disparaging term into the rebels' symbol: The uprising was now known as the *Fronde,* and the rebels as *frondeurs.* They began to wear sashes in their hats that symbolized the slingshot, and the word became their rallying cry. Without it the rebellion might well have petered out. Always find a symbol to represent your cause—the more emotional associations, the better.

The best way to use images and symbols is to organize them into a grand spectacle that awes people and distracts them from unpleasant realities. This is easy to do: People love what is grand, spectacular, and larger than life. Appeal to their emotions and they will flock to your spectacle in hordes. The visual is the easiest route to their hearts.

Image:
The Cross and the
Sun. Crucifixion and
total radiance. With one
imposed over the other, a
new reality takes shape—
a new power is in the
ascendant. The sym-
bol—no explanation
necessary.

Authority: The people are always impressed by the superficial appearance of things.... The [prince] should, at fitting times of the year, keep the people occupied and distracted with festivities and spectacles. (Niccolò Machiavelli, 1469–1527)

REVERSAL

No power is made available by ignoring images and symbols. There is no possible reversal to this law.

38

THINK AS YOU LIKE

BUT BEHAVE LIKE

OTHERS

JUDGMENT

If you make a show of going against the times, flaunting your unconventional ideas and unorthodox ways, people will think that you only want attention and that you look down upon them. They will find a way to punish you for making them feel inferior. It is far safer to blend in and nurture the common touch. Share your original- ity only with tolerant friends and those who are sure to appreciate your uniqueness.

TRANSGRESSION OF THE LAW

Around the year 478 B.C., the city of Sparta sent an expedition to Persia led by the young Spartan nobleman Pausanias. The city-states of Greece had recently fought off a mighty invasion from Persia, and now Pausanias, along with allied ships from Athens, had orders to punish the invaders and win back the islands and coastal towns that the Persians had occupied. Both the Athenians and the Spartans had great respect for Pausanias—he had proven himself as a fearless warrior, with a flair for the dramatic.

With amazing speed, Pausanias and his troops took Cyprus, then moved on to the mainland of Asia Minor known as the Hellespont and captured Byzantium (modern-day Istanbul). Now master of part of the Persian empire, Pausanias began to show signs of behavior that went beyond his normal flamboyance. He appeared in public wearing pomades in his hair and flowing Persian robes, and accompanied by a bodyguard of Egyptians. He held lavish banquets in which he sat in the Persian manner and demanded to be entertained. He stopped seeing his old friends, entered into communication with the Persian King Xerxes, and all in all affected the style and manner of a Persian dictator.

Clearly power and success had gone to Pausanias's head. His army—Athenians and Spartans alike—at first thought this a passing fancy: He had always been a bit exaggerated in his gestures. But when he flaunted his disdain for the Greeks' simple way of life, and insulted the common Greek soldier, they began to feel he had gone too far. Although there was no concrete evidence for this, rumors spread that he had gone over to the other side, and that he dreamed of becoming a kind of Greek Xerxes. To quell the possibility of mutiny, the Spartans relieved Pausanias of his command and called him home.

Pausanias, however, continued to dress in the Persian style, even in Sparta. After a few months he independently hired a trireme and returned to the Hellespont, telling his compatriots he was going to continue the fight against the Persians. Actually, however, he had different plans—to make himself ruler of all Greece, with the aid of Xerxes himself. The Spartans declared him a public enemy and sent a ship to capture him. Pausanias surrendered, certain that he could clear himself of the charges of treason. It did come out during the trial that during his reign as commander he had offended his fellow Greeks time and again, erecting monuments, for instance, in his own name, rather than in those of the cities whose troops had fought alongside him, as was the custom. Yet Pausanias proved right: Despite the evidence of his numerous contacts with the enemy, the Spartans refused to imprison a man of such noble birth, and let him go.

Now thinking himself untouchable, Pausanias hired a messenger to take a letter to Xerxes, but the messenger instead took the letter to the Spartan authorities. These men wanted to find out more, so they had the messenger arrange to meet Pausanias in a temple where they could hide and listen behind a partition. What Pausanias said shocked them—they had never heard such contempt for their ways spoken so brazenly by one of their own—and they made arrangements for his immediate arrest.

On his way home from the temple, Pausanias got word of what had happened. He ran to another temple to hide, but the authorities followed him there and placed sentries all around. Pausanias refused to surrender. Unwilling to forcibly remove him from the sacred temple, the authorities kept him trapped inside, until he eventually died of starvation.

Interpretation

At first glance it might seem that Pausanias simply fell in love with another culture, a phenomenon as old as time. Never comfortable with the asceticism of the Spartans, he found himself enthralled by the Persian love of luxury and sensual pleasure. He put on Persian robes and perfumes with a sense of deliverance from Greek discipline and simplicity.

This is how it appears when people adopt a culture in which they were not raised. Often, however, there is also something else at play: People who flaunt their infatuation with a different culture are expressing a disdain and contempt for their own. They are using the outward appearance of the exotic to separate themselves from the common folk who unquestioningly follow the local customs and laws, and to express their sense of superiority. Otherwise they would act with more dignity, showing respect for those who do not share their desires. Indeed their need to show their difference so dramatically often makes them disliked by the people whose beliefs they challenge, indirectly and subtly, perhaps, but offensively nonetheless.

As Thucydides wrote of Pausanias, "By his contempt for the laws and his imitation of foreign ways he had made himself very widely suspected of being unwilling to abide by normal standards." Cultures have norms that reflect centuries of shared beliefs and ideals. Do not expect to scoff at such things with impunity. You will be punished somehow, even if just through isolation—a position of real powerlessness.

Many of us, like Pausanias, feel the siren call of the exotic, the foreign. Measure and moderate this desire. Flaunting your pleasure in alien ways of thinking and acting will reveal a different motive—to demonstrate your superiority over your fellows.

OBSERVANCE OF THE LAW

During the late sixteenth century, a violent reaction against the Protestant Reformation erupted in Italy. The Counter-Reformation, as it was called, included its own version of the Inquisition to root out all deviations from the Catholic Church. Among its victims was the scientist Galileo, but an important thinker who suffered even greater persecution was the Dominican monk and philosopher Tommaso Campanella.

A follower of the materialist doctrine of the Roman philosopher Epicurus, Campanella did not believe in miracles, or in heaven and hell. The Church had promoted such superstitions, he wrote, to control the common folk by keeping them in fear. Such ideas verged on atheism, and Campanella expressed them incautiously. In 1593 the Inquisition threw him

WHEN THE WATERS WERE CHANGED

Once upon a time Khidr, the teacher of Moses, called upon mankind with a warning. At a certain date, he said, all the water in the world which had not been specially hoarded, would disappear. It would then be renewed, with different water, which would drive men mad.

Only one man listened to the meaning of this advice. He collected water and went to a secure place where he stored it, and waited for the water to change its character.

On the appointed date the streams stopped running, the wells went dry, and the man who had listened, seeing this

into prison for his heretical beliefs. Six years later, as a form of partial release, he was confined to a monastery in Naples.

Southern Italy was controlled by Spain at the time, and in Naples Campanella became involved in a plot to fight and throw out these invaders. His hope was to establish an independent republic based on his own ideas of utopia. The leaders of the Italian Inquisition, working with their Spanish counterparts, had him imprisoned again. This time they also tortured him, to discover the true nature of his impious beliefs: He was subjected to the infamous *la veglia*, a torture in which he was suspended by his arms in a squatting position a few inches above a seat studded with spikes. The posture was impossible to sustain, and in time the victim would end up sitting on the spikes, which would tear his flesh at the slightest contact.

During these years, however, Campanella learned something about power. Facing the prospect of execution for heresy, he changed his strategy: He would not renounce his beliefs, yet he knew he had to disguise their outward appearance.

To save his life, Campanella feigned madness. He let his inquisitors imagine that his beliefs stemmed from an incontrollable unsoundness of mind. For a while the tortures continued, to see if his insanity was faked, but in 1603 his sentence was commuted to life in prison. The first four years of this he spent chained to a wall in an underground dungeon. Despite such conditions, he continued to write—although no longer would he be so foolish as to express his ideas directly.

One book of Campanella's, *The Hispanic Monarchy,* promoted the idea that Spain had a divine mission to expand its powers around the world, and offered the Spanish king practical, Machiavelli-type advice for achieving this. Despite his own interest in Machiavelli, the book in general presented ideas completely the opposite to his own. *The Hispanic Monarchy* was in fact a ploy, an attempt to show his conversion to orthodoxy in the boldest manner possible. It worked: In 1626, six years after its publication, the pope finally let Campanella out of prison.

Shortly after gaining his freedom, Campanella wrote *Atheism Conquered,* a book attacking free-thinkers, Machiavellians, Calvinists, and heretics of all stripes. The book is written in the form of debates in which heretics express their beliefs and are countered by arguments for the superiority of Catholicism. Campanella had obviously reformed—his book made that clear. Or did it?

The arguments in the mouths of the heretics had never before been expressed with such verve and freshness. Pretending to present their side only to knock it down, Campanella actually summarized the case against Catholicism with striking passion. When he argued the other side, supposedly *his* side, on the other hand, he resorted to stale clichés and convoluted rationales. Brief and eloquent, the heretics' arguments seemed bold and sincere. The lengthy arguments for Catholicism seemed tiresome and unconvincing.

Catholics who read the book found it disturbing and ambiguous, but they could not claim it was heretical, or that Campanella should be returned to prison. His defense of Catholicism, after all, used arguments they had used themselves. Yet in the years to come, *Atheism Conquered* became a bible for atheists, Machiavellians and libertines who used the arguments Campanella had put in their mouths to defend their dangerous ideas. Combining an outward display of conformity with an expression of his true beliefs in a way that his sympathizers would understand, Campanella showed that he had learned his lesson.

Interpretation

In the face of awesome persecution, Campanella devised three strategic moves that saved his hide, freed him from prison, and allowed him to continue to express his beliefs. First he feigned madness—the medieval equivalent of disavowing responsibility for one's actions, like blaming one's parents today. Next he wrote a book that expressed the exact opposite of his own beliefs. Finally, and most brilliantly of all, he disguised his ideas while insinuating them at the same time. It is an old but powerful trick: You pretend to disagree with dangerous ideas, but in the course of your disagreement you give those ideas expression and exposure. You seem to conform to the prevailing orthodoxy, but those who know will understand the irony involved. You are protected.

It is inevitable in society that certain values and customs lose contact with their original motives and become oppressive. And there will always be those who rebel against such oppression, harboring ideas far ahead of their time. As Campanella was forced to realize, however, there is no point in making a display of your dangerous ideas if they only bring you suffering and persecution. Martyrdom serves no purpose—better to live on in an oppressive world, even to thrive in it. Meanwhile find a way to express your ideas subtly for those who understand you. Laying your pearls before swine will only bring you trouble.

> *For a long time I have not said what I believed, nor do I ever believe*
> *what I say, and if indeed sometimes I do happen to tell the truth,*
> *I hide it among so many lies that it is hard to find.*
> *Niccolò Machiavelli, in a letter to Francesco Guicciardini, May 17, 1521*

KEYS TO POWER

We all tell lies and hide our true feelings, for complete free expression is a social impossibility. From an early age we learn to conceal our thoughts, telling the prickly and insecure what we know they want to hear, watching carefully lest we offend them. For most of us this is natural—there are ideas and values that most people accept, and it is pointless to argue. We believe what we want to, then, but on the outside we wear a mask.

There are people, however, who see such restraints as an intolerable infringement on their freedom, and who have a need to prove the superi-

THE CITIZEN AND
THE TRAVELLER

*"Look around you,"
said the citizen. "This is
the largest market in
the world."
"Oh surely not," said
the traveller.
"Well, perhaps not
the largest," said the
citizen, "but much
the best."
"You are certainly
wrong there," said the
traveller. "I can tell
you...."
They buried the
stranger in the dusk.*

FABLES,
ROBERT LOUIS
STEVENSON, 1850–1894

ority of their values and beliefs. In the end, though, their arguments convince only a few and offend a great deal more. The reason arguments do not work is that most people hold their ideas and values without thinking about them. There is a strong emotional content in their beliefs: They really do not want to have to rework their habits of thinking, and when you challenge them, whether directly through your arguments or indirectly through your behavior, they are hostile.

Wise and clever people learn early on that they can display conventional behavior and mouth conventional ideas without having to believe in them. The power these people gain from blending in is that of being left alone to have the thoughts they want to have, and to express them to the people they want to express them to, without suffering isolation or ostracism. Once they have established themselves in a position of power, they can try to convince a wider circle of the correctness of their ideas—perhaps working indirectly, using Campanella's strategies of irony and insinuation.

In the late fourteenth century, the Spanish began a massive persecution of the Jews, murdering thousands and driving others out of the country. Those who remained in Spain were forced to convert. Yet over the next three hundred years, the Spanish noticed a phenomenon that disturbed them: Many of the converts lived their outward lives as Catholics, yet somehow managed to retain their Jewish beliefs, practicing the religion in private. Many of these so-called Marranos (originally a derogatory term, being the Spanish for "pig") attained high levels of government office, married into the nobility, and gave every appearance of Christian piety, only to be discovered late in life as practicing Jews. (The Spanish Inquisition was specifically commissioned to ferret them out.) Over the years they mastered the art of dissimulation, displaying crucifixes liberally, giving generous gifts to churches, even occasionally making anti-Semitic remarks—and all the while maintaining their inner freedom and beliefs.

*If Machiavelli had had
a prince for disciple,
the first thing he would
have recommended
him to do would have
been to write a book
against Machiavellism.*

VOLTAIRE,
1694–1778

In society, the Marranos knew, outward appearances are what matter. This remains true today. The strategy is simple: As Campanella did in writing *Atheism Conquered,* make a show of blending in, even going so far as to be the most zealous advocate of the prevailing orthodoxy. If you stick to conventional appearances in public few will believe you think differently in private.

Do not be so foolish as to imagine that in our own time the old orthodoxies are gone. Jonas Salk, for instance, thought science had gotten past politics and protocol. And so, in his search for a polio vaccine, he broke all the rules—going public with a discovery before showing it to the scientific community, taking credit for the vaccine without acknowledging the scientists who had paved the way, making himself a star. The public may have loved him but scientists shunned him. His disrespect for his community's orthodoxies left him isolated, and he wasted years trying to heal the breach, and struggling for funding and cooperation.

Bertolt Brecht underwent a modern form of Inquisition—the House

Un-American Activities Committee—and approached it with considerable canniness. Having worked off and on in the American film industry during World War II, in 1947 Brecht was summoned to appear before the committee to answer questions on his suspected Communist sympathies. Other writers called before the committee made a point of attacking its members, and of acting as belligerently as possible in order to gain sympathy for themselves. Brecht, on the other hand, who had actually worked steadfastly for the Communist cause, played the opposite game: He answered questions with ambiguous generalities that defied easy interpretation. Call it the Campanella strategy. Brecht even wore a suit—a rare event for him— and made a point of smoking a cigar during the proceedings, knowing that a key committee member had a passion for cigars. In the end he charmed the committee members, who let him go scot-free.

Brecht then moved to East Germany, where he encountered a different kind of Inquisition. Here the Communists were in power, and they criticized his plays as decadent and pessimistic. He did not argue with them, but made small changes in the performance scripts to shut them up. Meanwhile he managed to preserve the published texts as written. His outward conformity in both cases gave him the freedom to work unhindered, without having to change his thinking. In the end, he made his way safely through dangerous times in different countries through the use of little dances of orthodoxy, and proved he was more powerful than the forces of repression.

Not only do people of power avoid the offenses of Pausanias and Salk, they also learn to play the clever fox and feign the common touch. This has been the ploy of con artists and politicians throughout the centuries. Leaders like Julius Caesar and Franklin D. Roosevelt have overcome their natural aristocratic stance to cultivate a familiarity with the common man. They have expressed this familiarity in little gestures, often symbolic, to show the people that their leaders share popular values, despite their different status.

The logical extension of this practice is the invaluable ability to be all things to all people. When you go into society, leave behind your own ideas and values, and put on the mask that is most appropriate for the group in which you find yourself. Bismarck played this game successfully for years—there were people who vaguely understood what he was up to, but not clearly enough that it mattered. People will swallow the bait because it flatters them to believe that you share their ideas. They will not take you as a hypocrite if you are careful—for how can they accuse you of hypocrisy if you do not let them know exactly what you stand for? Nor will they see you as lacking in values. Of course you have values—the values you share with them, while in their company.

> Authority: Do not give dogs what is holy; and do not throw your pearls before swine, lest they trample them under foot and turn to attack you. (Jesus Christ, Matthew 7:6)

**Image:
The Black
Sheep.** The herd shuns the
black sheep, uncertain
whether or not it belongs
with them. So it straggles behind, or wanders away from
the herd, where it is cornered
by wolves and promptly devoured. Stay with the herd—
there is safety in numbers. Keep
your differences in your
thoughts and not in your fleece.

REVERSAL

The only time it is worth standing out is when you already stand out—
when you have achieved an unshakable position of power, and can display
your difference from others as a sign of the distance between you. As president of the United States, Lyndon Johnson would sometimes hold meetings while he sat on the toilet. Since no one else either could or would
claim such a "privilege," Johnson was showing people that he did not have
to observe the protocols and niceties of others. The Roman emperor
Caligula played the same game: He would wear a woman's negligee, or a
bathrobe, to receive important visitors. He even went so far as to have his
horse elected consul. But it backfired, for the people hated Caligula, and
his gestures eventually brought his overthrow. The truth is that even those
who attain the heights of power would be better off at least affecting the
common touch, for at some point they may need popular support.

Finally, there is always a place for the gadfly, the person who successfully defies custom and mocks what has grown lifeless in a culture. Oscar
Wilde, for example, achieved considerable social power on this foundation: He made it clear that he disdained the usual ways of doing things, and
when he gave public readings his audiences not only expected him to insult them but welcomed it. We notice, however, that his eccentric role
eventually destroyed him. Even had he come to a better end, remember
that he possessed an unusual genius: Without his gift to amuse and delight,
his barbs would simply have offended people.

LAW

39

STIR UP WATERS

TO CATCH FISH

JUDGMENT

Anger and emotion are strategically counterproductive. You must always stay calm and objective. But if you can make your enemies angry while staying calm yourself, you gain a decided advantage. Put your enemies off-balance: Find the chink in their vanity through which you can rattle them and you hold the strings.

TRANSGRESSION OF THE LAW

ITAKURA SHIGEMUNE
GRINDS HIS OWN TEA

*The Kyoto Shoshidai
Itakura Suwo-no-kami
Shigemune was very
fond of Cha-no-yu
(the tea ceremony), and
used to grind his own
tea while sitting in the
court as judge. And the
reason was this. He
once asked a friend of
his who was his
companion in Cha-no-
yu, a tea merchant
named Eiki, to tell him
frankly what was the
public opinion about
him. "Well," said Eiki,
"they say that you get
irritated with those who
don't give their
evidence very clearly
and scold them, and so
people are afraid to
bring lawsuits before
you and if they do, the
truth does not come
out."
"Ah, I am glad you
have told me that,"
replied Shigemune, "for
now that I consider it, I
have fallen into the
habit of speaking
sharply to people in
this way, and no doubt
humble folk and those
who are not ready in
speech get flurried and
are unable to put their
case in the best light.
I will see to it that this
does not occur in the
future." So after this he
had a tea mill placed
before him in court and
in front of it the paper-
covered shoji were
drawn to, and Shige-
mune sat behind them
and ground the tea and
thus kept his mind
calm while he heard
the cases. And he could*

In January of 1809, an agitated and anxious Napoleon hurried back to Paris from his Spanish wars. His spies and confidants had confirmed a rumor that his foreign minister Talleyrand had conspired against him with Fouché, the minister of police. Immediately on arriving in the capital the shocked emperor summoned his ministers to the palace. Following them into the meeting right after their arrival, he began pacing up and down, and started rambling vaguely about plotters working against him, speculators bringing down the stock market, legislators delaying his policies—and his own ministers undermining him.

As Napoleon talked, Talleyrand leaned on the mantelpiece, looking completely indifferent. Facing Talleyrand directly, Napoleon announced, "For these ministers, treason has begun when they permit themselves to doubt." At the word "treason" the ruler expected his minister to be afraid. But Talleyrand only smiled, calm and bored.

The sight of a subordinate apparently serene in the face of charges that could get him hanged pushed Napoleon to the edge. There were ministers, he said, who wanted him dead, and he took a step closer to Talleyrand—who stared back at him unfazed. Finally Napoleon exploded. "You are a coward," he screamed in Talleyrand's face, "a man of no faith. Nothing is sacred to you. You would sell your own father. I have showered you with riches and yet there is nothing you would not do to hurt me." The other ministers looked at each other in disbelief—they had never seen this fearless general, the conqueror of most of Europe, so unhinged.

"You deserve to be broken like glass," Napoleon continued, stamping. "I have the power to do it, but I have too much contempt for you to bother. Why didn't I have you hanged from the gates of the Tuileries? But there is still time for that." Yelling, almost out of breath, his face red, his eyes bulging, he went on, "You, by the way, are nothing but shit in a silk stocking. . . . What about your wife? You never told me that San Carlos was your wife's lover?" "Indeed, sire, it did not occur to me that this information had any bearing on Your Majesty's glory or my own," said Talleyrand calmly, completely unflustered. After a few more insults, Napoleon walked away. Talleyrand slowly crossed the room, moving with his characteristic limp. As an attendant helped him with his cloak, he turned to his fellow ministers (all afraid they would never see him again), and said, "What a pity, gentlemen, that so great a man should have such bad manners."

Despite his anger, Napoleon did not arrest his foreign minister. He merely relieved him of his duties and banished him from the court, believing that for this man humiliation would be punishment enough. He did not realize that word had quickly spread of his tirade—of how the emperor had completely lost control of himself, and how Talleyrand had essentially humiliated him by maintaining his composure and dignity. A page had been turned: For the first time people had seen the great emperor lose his cool under fire. A feeling spread that he was on the way down. As Talleyrand later said, "This is the beginning of the end."

Interpretation

This was indeed the beginning of the end. Waterloo was still six years ahead, but Napoleon was on a slow descent to defeat, crystallizing in 1812 with his disastrous invasion of Russia. Talleyrand was the first to see the signs of his decline, especially in the irrational war with Spain. Sometime in 1808, the minister decided that for the future peace of Europe, Napoleon had to go. And so he conspired with Fouché.

It is possible that the conspiracy was never anything more than a ploy—a device to push Napoleon over the edge. For it is hard to believe that two of the most practical men in history would only go halfway in their plotting. They may have been only stirring the waters, trying to goad Napoleon into a misstep. And indeed, what they got was the tantrum that laid out his loss of control for all to see. In fact, Napoleon's soon-famous blowup that afternoon had a profoundly negative effect on his public image.

This is the problem with the angry response. At first it may strike fear and terror, but only in some, and as the days pass and the storm clears, other responses emerge—embarrassment and uneasiness about the shouter's capacity for going out of control, and resentment of what has been said. Losing your temper, you always make unfair and exaggerated accusations. A few such tirades and people are counting the days until you are gone.

In the face of a conspiracy against him, a conspiracy between his two most important ministers, Napoleon certainly had a right to feel angry and anxious. But by responding so angrily, and so publicly, he only demonstrated his frustration. To show your frustration is to show that you have lost your power to shape events; it is the helpless action of the child who resorts to a hysterical fit to get his way. The powerful never reveal this kind of weakness.

There were a number of things Napoleon could have done in this situation. He could have thought about the fact that two eminently sensible men had had reason to turn against him, and could have listened and learned from them. He could have tried to win them back to him. He could even have gotten rid of them, making their imprisonment or death an ominous display of his power. No tirades, no childish fits, no embarrassing after-effects—just a quiet and definitive severing of ties.

Remember: Tantrums neither intimidate nor inspire loyalty. They only create doubts and uneasiness about your power. Exposing your weakness, these stormy eruptions often herald a fall.

OBSERVANCE OF THE LAW

By the late 1920s, Haile Selassie had nearly achieved his goal of assuming total control over Ethiopia, a country he felt needed strong and unified leadership. As regent to the empress Zauditu (stepdaughter of the late queen) and heir to the throne, Selassie had spent several years weakening the power of Ethiopia's various warlords. Now only one real obstacle stood

easily see whether his composure was ruffled or not by looking at the tea, which would not fall evenly ground to the proper consistency if he got excited. And so justice was done impartially and people went away from his court satisfied.

CHA-NO-YU:
THE JAPANESE TEA
CEREMONY
A. L. SADLER,
1962

If possible, no animosity should be felt for anyone. . . . To speak angrily to a person, to show your hatred by what you say or by the way you look, is an unnecessary proceeding—dangerous, foolish, ridiculous, and vulgar.
Anger or hatred should never be shown otherwise than in what you do; and feelings will be all the more effective in action, in so far as you avoid the exhibition of them in any other way. It is only the cold-blooded animals whose bite is poisonous.

ARTHUR
SCHOPENHAUER,
1788–1860

in his way: the empress and her husband, Ras Gugsa. Selassie knew the royal couple hated him and wanted to get rid of him, so to cut short their plotting he made Gugsa the governor of the northern province of Begemeder, forcing him to leave the capital, where the empress lived.

For several years Gugsa played the loyal administrator. But Selassie did not trust him: He knew that Gugsa and the empress were plotting revenge. As time passed and Gugsa made no move, the chances of a plot only increased. Selassie knew what he had to do: draw Gugsa out, get under his skin, and push him into action before he was ready.

For several years, a northern tribe, the Azebu Gallas, had been in virtual rebellion against the throne, robbing and pillaging local villages and refusing to pay taxes. Selassie had done nothing to stop them, letting them grow stronger. Finally, in 1929, he ordered Ras Gugsa to lead an army against these disobedient tribesmen. Gugsa agreed, but inwardly he seethed—he had no grudge against the Azebu Gallas, and the demand that he fight them hurt his pride. He could not disobey the order, but as he worked to put together an army, he began to spread an ugly rumor—that Selassie was in cahoots with the pope, and planned to convert the country to Roman Catholicism and make it a colony of Italy. Gugsa's army swelled, and some of the tribes from which its soldiers came secretly agreed to fight Selassie. In March of 1930 an enormous force of 35,000 men began to march, not on the Azebu Gallas but south, toward the capital of Addis Ababa. Made confident by his growing strength, Gugsa now openly led a holy war to depose Selassie and put the country back in the hands of true Christians.

He did not see the trap that had been laid for him. Before Selassie had ordered Gugsa to fight the Azebu Gallas, he had secured the support of the Ethiopian church. And before the revolt got underway, he had bribed several of Gugsa's key allies not to show up for battle. As the rebel army marched south, airplanes flew overhead dropping leaflets announcing that the highest church officials had recognized Selassie as the true Christian leader of Ethiopia, and that they had excommunicated Gugsa for fomenting a civil war. These leaflets severely blunted the emotions behind the holy crusade. And as battle loomed and the support that Gugsa's allies had promised him failed to show up, soldiers began to flee or defect.

When the battle came, the rebel army quicky collapsed. Refusing to surrender, Ras Gugsa was killed in the fighting. The empress, distraught over her husband's death, died a few days later. On April 30, Selassie issued a formal proclamation announcing his new title: Emperor of Ethiopia.

Interpretation

Haile Selassie always saw several moves ahead. He knew that if he let Ras Gugsa decide the time and place of the revolt, the danger would be much greater than if he forced Gugsa to act on Selassie's terms. So he goaded him into rebellion by offending his manly pride, asking him to fight people he had no quarrel with on behalf of a man he hated. Thinking everything out

THE MONKEY AND
THE WASP

A monkey, whilst munching a ripe pear, was pestered by the bare-faced importunities of a wasp, who, nolens volens, would have a part. After threatening the monkey with his anger if he further hesitated to submit to his demand, he settled on the fruit; but was as soon knocked off by the monkey. The irritable wasp now had recourse to invective—and, after using the most insulting language, which the other calmly listened to, he so worked himself up into violent passion that, losing all consideration of the penalty, he flew to the face of the monkey, and stung him with such rage that he was unable to extricate his weapon, and was compelled to tear himself away, leaving it in the wound—thus entailing on himself a lingering death, accompanied by pains much greater than those he had inflicted.

FABLES,
JONATHAN BIRCH,
1783–1847

ahead, Selassie made sure that Gugsa's rebellion would come to nothing, and that he could use it to do away with his last two enemies.

This is the essence of the Law: When the waters are still, your opponents have the time and space to plot actions that they will initiate and control. So stir the waters, force the fish to the surface, get them to act before they are ready, steal the initiative. The best way to do this is to play on uncontrollable emotions—pride, vanity, love, hate. Once the water is stirred up, the little fish cannot help but rise to the bait. The angrier they become, the less control they have, and finally they are caught in the whirlpool you have made, and they drown.

> *A sovereign should never launch an army out of anger,*
> *a leader should never start a war out of wrath.*
> Sun-tzu, fourth century B.C.

KEYS TO POWER

Angry people usually end up looking ridiculous, for their response seems out of proportion to what occasioned it. They have taken things too seriously, exaggerating the hurt or insult that has been done to them. They are so sensitive to slight that it becomes comical how much they take personally. More comical still is their belief that their outbursts signify power. The truth is the opposite: Petulance is not power, it is a sign of helplessness. People may temporarily be cowed by your tantrums, but in the end they lose respect for you. They also realize they can easily undermine a person with so little self-control.

The answer, however, is not to repress our angry or emotional responses. For repression drains us of energy and pushes us into strange behavior. Instead we have to change our perspective: We have to realize that nothing in the social realm, and in the game of power, is personal.

Everyone is caught up in a chain of events that long predates the present moment. Our anger often stems from problems in our childhood, from the problems of our parents which stem from their own childhood, on and on. Our anger also has roots in the many interactions with others, the accumulated disappointments and heartaches that we have suffered. An individual will often appear as the instigator of our anger but it is much more complicated, goes far beyond what that individual did to us. If a person explodes with anger at you (and it seems out of proportion to what you did to them), you must remind yourself that it is not exclusively directed at you—do not be so vain. The cause is much larger, goes way back in time, involves dozens of prior hurts, and is actually not worth the bother to understand. Instead of seeing it as a personal grudge, look at the emotional outburst as a disguised power move, an attempt to control or punish you cloaked in the form of hurt feelings and anger.

This shift of perspective will let you play the game of power with more clarity and energy. Instead of overreacting, and becoming ensnared in peo-

DITCH HIGH PRIEST

Kin'yo, an officer of the second rank, had a brother called the High Priest Ryogaku, an extremely bad-tempered man. Next to his monastery grew a large nettle-tree which occasioned the nick-name people gave him, the Nettle-tree High Priest. "That name is outrageous," said the high priest, and cut down the tree. The stump still being left, people referred to him now as the Stump High Priest. More furious than ever, Ryogaku had the stump dug up and thrown away, but this left a big ditch. People now called him the Ditch High Priest.

ESSAYS IN IDLENESS,
KENKŌ,
JAPAN,
FOURTEENTH CENTURY

ple's emotions, you will turn their loss of control to your advantage: You keep your head while they are losing theirs.

During an important battle in the War of the Three Kingdoms, in the third century A.D., advisers to the commander Ts'ao Ts'ao discovered documents showing that certain of his generals had conspired with the enemy, and urged him to arrest and execute them. Instead he ordered the documents burned and the matter forgotten. At this critical moment in the battle, to get upset or demand justice would have reverberated against him: An angry action would have called attention to the generals' disloyalty, which would have harmed the troops' morale. Justice could wait—he would deal with the generals in time. Ts'ao Ts'ao kept his head and made the right decision.

Compare this to Napoleon's response to Talleyrand: Instead of taking the conspiracy personally, the emperor should have played the game like Ts'ao Ts'ao, carefully weighing the consequences of any action he took. The more powerful response in the end would have been to ignore Talleyrand, or to bring the minister gradually back to his side and punish him later.

Anger only cuts off our options, and the powerful cannot thrive without options. Once you train yourself not to take matters personally, and to control your emotional responses, you will have placed yourself in a position of tremendous power: Now you can play with the emotional responses of other people. Stir the insecure into action by impugning their manhood, and by dangling the prospect of an easy victory before their faces. Do as Houdini did when challenged by the less successful escape artist Kleppini: Reveal an apparent weakness (Houdini let Kleppini steal the combination for a pair of cuffs) to lure your opponent into action. Then you can beat him with ease. With the arrogant too you can appear weaker than you are, taunting them into a rash action.

Sun Pin, commander of the armies of Ch'i and loyal disciple of Suntzu, once led his troops against the armies of Wei, which outnumbered him two to one. "Let us light a hundred thousand fires when our army enters Wei," suggested Sun Pin, "fifty thousand on the next day, and only thirty thousand on the third." On the third day the Wei general exclaimed, "I knew the men of Ch'i were cowards, and after only three days more than half of them have deserted!" So, leaving behind his slow-moving heavy infantry, the general decided to seize the moment and move swiftly on the Ch'i camp with a lightly armed force. Sun Pin's troops retreated, luring Wei's army into a narrow pass, where they ambushed and destroyed them. With the Wei general dead and his forces decimated, Sun Pin now easily defeated the rest of his army.

In the face of a hot-headed enemy, finally, an excellent response is no response. Follow the Talleyrand tactic: Nothing is as infuriating as a man who keeps his cool while others are losing theirs. If it will work to your advantage to unsettle people, affect the aristocratic, bored pose, neither mocking nor triumphant but simply indifferent. This will light their fuse.

When they embarrass themselves with a temper tantrum, you will have gained several victories, one of these being that in the face of their childishness you have maintained your dignity and composure.

Image: The Pond of Fish. The waters
are clear and calm, and the fish are well below the surface.
Stir the waters and they emerge. Stir it some more and they get
angry, rising to the surface, biting whatever comes near—
including a freshly baited hook.

Authority: If your opponent is of a hot temper, try to irritate him. If he is arrogant, try to encourage his egotism. . . . One who is skilled at making the enemy move does so by creating a situation according to which the enemy will act; he entices the enemy with something he is certain to take. He keeps the enemy on the move by holding out bait and then attacks him with picked troops. (Sun-tzu, fourth century B.C.)

REVERSAL

When playing with people's emotions you have to be careful. Study the enemy beforehand: Some fish are best left at the bottom of the pond.

The leaders of the city of Tyre, capital of ancient Phoenicia, felt confident they could withstand Alexander the Great, who had conquered the Orient but had not attacked their city, which stood well protected on the water. They sent ambassadors to Alexander saying that although they would recognize him as emperor they would not allow him or his forces to enter Tyre. This of course enraged him, and he immediately mounted a siege. For four months the city withstood him, and finally he decided that the struggle was not worth it, and that he would come to terms with the Tyrians. But they, feeling that they had already baited Alexander and gotten away with it, and confident that they could withstand him, refused to negotiate—in fact they killed his messengers.

This pushed Alexander over the edge. Now it did not matter to him how long the siege lasted or how large an army it needed; he had the resources, and would do whatever it took. He remounted his assault so strenuously that he captured Tyre within days, burned it to the ground, and sold its people into slavery.

You can bait the powerful and get them to commit and divide their forces as Sun Pin did, but test the waters first. Find the gap in their strength. If there is no gap—if they are impossibly strong—you have nothing to gain and everything to lose by provoking them. Choose carefully whom you bait, and never stir up the sharks.

Finally there are times when a well-timed burst of anger can do you good, but your anger must be manufactured and under your control. Then you can determine exactly how and on whom it will fall. Never stir up reactions that will work against you in the long run. And use your thunderbolts rarely, to make them the more intimidating and meaningful. Whether purposefully staged or not, if your outbursts come too often, they will lose their power.

DESPISE THE

FREE LUNCH

JUDGMENT

What is offered for free is dangerous—it usually involves either a trick or a hidden obligation. What has worth is worth paying for. By paying your own way you stay clear of gratitude, guilt, and deceit. It is also often wise to pay the full price—there is no cutting corners with excellence. Be lavish with your money and keep it circulating, for generosity is a sign and a magnet for power.

MONEY AND POWER

In the realm of power, everything must be judged by its cost, and everything has a price. What is offered for free or at bargain rates often comes with a psychological price tag—complicated feelings of obligation, compromises with quality, the insecurity those compromises bring, on and on. The powerful learn early to protect their most valuable resources: independence and room to maneuver. By paying the full price, they keep themselves free of dangerous entanglements and worries.

Being open and flexible with money also teaches the value of strategic generosity, a variation on the old trick of "giving when you are about to take." By giving the appropriate gift, you put the recipient under obligation. Generosity softens people up—to be deceived. By gaining a reputation for liberality, you win people's admiration while distracting them from your power plays. By strategically spreading your wealth, you charm the other courtiers, creating pleasure and making valuable allies.

Look at the masters of power—the Caesars, the Queen Elizabeths, the Michelangelos, the Medicis: Not a miser among them. Even the great con artists spend freely to swindle. Tight purse strings are unattractive—when engaged in seduction, Casanova would give completely not only of himself but of his wallet. The powerful understand that money is psychologically charged, and that it is also a vessel of politeness and sociability. They make the human side of money a weapon in their armory.

For everyone able to play with money, thousands more are locked in a self-destructive refusal to use money creatively and strategically. These types represent the opposite pole to the powerful, and you must learn to recognize them—either to avoid their poisonous natures or to turn their inflexibility to your advantage:

The Greedy Fish. The greedy fish take the human side out of money. Cold and ruthless, they see only the lifeless balance sheet; viewing others solely as either pawns or obstructions in their pursuit of wealth, they trample on people's sentiments and alienate valuable allies. No one wants to work with the greedy fish, and over the years they end up isolated, which often proves their undoing.

Greedy fish are the con artist's bread and butter: Lured by the bait of easy money, they swallow the ruse hook, line, and sinker. They are easy to deceive, for they spend so much time dealing with numbers (not with people) that they become blind to psychology, including their own. Either avoid them before they exploit you or play on their greed to your gain.

The Bargain Demon. Powerful people judge everything by what it costs, not just in money but in time, dignity, and peace of mind. And this is exactly what Bargain Demons cannot do. Wasting valuable time digging for bargains, they worry endlessly about what they could have gotten elsewhere for a little less. On top of that, the bargain item they do buy is often shabby; perhaps it needs costly repairs, or will have to be replaced twice as

---

BURIED TREASURE

Many weak-minded persons in cities hope to discover property under the surface of the earth and to make some profit from it. In the Maghrib there are many Berber "students" who are unable to make a living by natural ways and means. They approach well-to-do people with papers that have torn margins and contain either non-Arabic writing or what they claim to be the translation of a document written by the owner of buried treasures, giving the clue to the hiding place. In this way, they try to get their sustenance by [persuading the well-to-do] to send them out to dig and hunt for treasure. Occasionally, one of these treasure hunters displays strange information or some remarkable trick of magic with which he fools people into believing his other claims, although, in fact, he knows nothing of magic and its procedures. . . . The things that have been said about [treasure hunting] have no scientific basis, nor are they based upon [factual] information. It should be realized that although treasures are found, this happens rarely and by chance, not by systematic search. . . . Those who are deluded or afflicted by these things must take refuge in God

fast as a high-quality item. The costs of these pursuits—not always in money (though the price of a bargain is often deceptive) but in time and peace of mind—discourage normal people from undertaking them, but for the Bargain Demon the bargain is an end in itself.

These types might seem to harm only themselves, but their attitudes are contagious: Unless you resist them they will infect you with the insecure feeling that you should have looked harder to find a cheaper price. Don't argue with them or try to change them. Just mentally add up the cost, in time and inner peace if not in hidden financial expense, of the irrational pursuit of a bargain.

The Sadist. Financial sadists play vicious power games with money as a way of asserting their power. They might, for example, make you wait for money that is owed you, promising you that the check is in the mail. Or if they hire you to work for them, they meddle in every aspect of the job, haggling and giving you ulcers. Sadists seem to think that paying for something gives them the right to torture and abuse the seller. They have no sense of the courtier element in money. If you are unlucky enough to get involved with this type, accepting a financial loss may be better in the long run than getting entangled in their destructive power games.

The Indiscriminate Giver. Generosity has a definite function in power: It attracts people, softens them up, makes allies out of them. But it has to be used strategically, with a definite end in mind. Indiscriminate Givers, on the other hand, are generous because they want to be loved and admired by all. And their generosity is so indiscriminate and needy that it may not have the desired effect: If they give to one and all, why should the recipient feel special? Attractive as it may seem to make an Indiscriminate Giver your mark, in any involvement with this type you will often feel burdened by their insatiable emotional needs.

TRANSGRESSIONS OF THE LAW

Transgression I

After Francisco Pizarro conquered Peru, in 1532, gold from the Incan Empire began to pour into Spain, and Spaniards of all classes started dreaming of the instant riches to be had in the New World. The story soon spread of an Indian chief to the east of Peru who once each year would ritually cover himself in gold dust and dive into a lake. Soon word of mouth transformed *El Dorado*, the "Golden Man," into an empire called El Dorado, wealthier than the Incan, where the streets were paved and the buildings inlaid with gold. This elaboration of the story did not seem implausible, for surely a chief who could afford to waste gold dust in a lake must rule a golden empire. Soon Spaniards were searching for El Dorado all over northern South America.

from their inability to make a living and their laziness in this respect. They should not occupy themselves with absurdities and untrue stories.

THE MUQADDIMAH,
IBN KHALDŪN,
1332–1406

THE MISER

A miser, to make sure of his property, sold all that he had and converted it into a great lump of gold, which he hid in a hole in the ground, and went continually to visit and inspect it. This roused the curiosity of one of his workmen, who, suspecting that there was a treasure, when his master's back was turned, went to the spot, and stole it away. When the miser returned and found the place empty, he wept and tore his hair. But a neighbor who saw him in this extravagant grief, and learned the cause of it, said: "Fret thyself no longer, but take a stone and put it in the same place, and think that it is your lump of gold; for, as you never meant to use it, the one will do you as much good as the other."
The worth of money is not in its possession, but in its use.

FABLES,
AESOP,
SIXTH CENTURY B.C.

In February of 1541, the largest expedition yet in this venture, led by Pizarro's brother Gonzalo, left Quito, in Ecuador. Resplendent in their armors and colorful silks, 340 Spaniards headed east, along with 4,000 Indians to carry supplies and serve as scouts, 4,000 swine, dozens of llamas, and close to 1,000 dogs. But the expedition was soon hit by torrential rain, which rotted its gear and spoiled its food. Meanwhile, as Gonzalo Pizarro questioned the Indians they met along the way, those who seemed to be withholding information, or who had not even heard of the fabulous kingdom, he would torture and feed to the dogs. Word of the Spaniards' murderousness spread quickly among the Indians, who realized that the only way to avoid Gonzalo's wrath was to make up stories about El Dorado and send him as far away as possible. As Gonzalo and his men followed the leads the Indians gave them, then, they were only led farther into deep jungle.

The explorers' spirits sagged. Their uniforms had long since shredded; their armor rusted and they threw it away; their shoes were torn to pieces, forcing them to walk barefoot; the Indian slaves they had set out with had either died or deserted them; they had eaten not only the swine but the hunting dogs and llamas. They lived on roots and fruit. Realizing that they could not continue this way, Pizarro decided to risk river travel, and a barge was built out of rotting wood. But the journey down the treacherous Napo River proved no easier. Setting up camp on the river's edge, Gonzalo sent scouts ahead on the barge to find Indian settlements with food. He waited and waited for the scouts to return, only to find out they had decided to desert the expedition and continue down the river on their own.

The rain continued without end. Gonzalo's men forgot about El Dorado; they wanted only to return to Quito. Finally, in August of 1542, a little over a hundred men, from an expedition originally numbering in the thousands, managed to find their way back. To the residents of Quito they seemed to have emerged from hell itself, wrapped in tatters and skins, their bodies covered in sores, and so emaciated as to be unrecognizable. For over a year and a half they had marched in an enormous circle, two thousand miles by foot. The vast sums of money invested in the expedition had yielded nothing—no sign of El Dorado and no sign of gold.

Interpretation

Even after Gonzalo Pizarro's disaster, the Spaniards launched expedition after expedition in search of El Dorado. And like Pizarro the conquistadors would burn and loot villages, torture Indians, endure unimaginable hardships, and get no closer to gold. The money they spent on such expeditions cannot be calculated; yet despite the futility of the search, the lure of the fantasy endured.

Not only did the search for El Dorado cost millions of lives—both Indian and Spanish—it helped bring the ruin of the Spanish empire. Gold became Spain's obsession. The gold that did find its way back to Spain—and a lot did—was reinvested in more expeditions, or in the purchase of luxuries, rather than in agriculture or any other productive endeavor. Whole Spanish towns were depopulated as their menfolk left to hunt gold. Farms fell into ruin, and the army had no recruits for its European wars. By the end of the seventeenth century, the entire country had shrunk by more than half of its population; the city of Madrid had gone from a population of 400,000 to 150,000. With diminishing returns from its efforts over so many years, Spain fell into a decline from which it never recovered.

Power requires self-discipline. The prospect of wealth, particularly easy, sudden wealth, plays havoc with the emotions. The suddenly rich believe that more is always possible. The free lunch, the money that will fall into your lap, is just around the corner.

In this delusion the greedy neglect everything power really depends on: self-control, the goodwill of others, and so on. Understand: With one exception—death—no lasting change in fortune comes quickly. Sudden wealth rarely lasts, for it is built on nothing solid. Never let lust for money lure you out of the protective and enduring fortress of real power. Make power your goal and money will find its way to you. Leave El Dorado for suckers and fools.

Transgression II

In the early eighteenth century, no one stood higher in English society than the Duke and Duchess of Marlborough. The duke, having led successful campaigns against the French, was considered Europe's premier general and strategist. And his wife, the duchess, after much maneuvering, had established herself as the favorite of Queen Anne, who became ruler of England in 1702. In 1704 the duke's triumph at the Battle of Blenheim made him the toast of England, and to honor him the queen awarded him a large plot of land in the town of Woodstock, and the funds to create a great palace there. Calling his planned home the Palace of Blenheim, the duke chose as his architect the young John Vanbrugh, a kind of Renaissance man who wrote plays as well as designed buildings. And so construction began, in the summer of 1705, with much fanfare and great hopes.

Vanbrugh had a dramatist's sense of architecture. His palace was to be a monument to Marlborough's brilliance and power, and was to include artificial lakes, enormous bridges, elaborate gardens, and other fantastical touches. From day one, however, the duchess could not be pleased: She thought Vanbrugh was wasting money on yet another stand of trees; she wanted the palace finished as soon as possible. The duchess tortured Vanbrugh and his workmen on every detail. She was consumed with petty matters; although the government was paying for Blenheim, she counted every penny. Eventually her grumbling, about Blenheim and other things too, created an irreparable rift between her and Queen Anne, who, in 1711, dismissed her from the court, ordering her to vacate her apartments at the royal palace. When the duchess left (fuming over the loss of her position, and also of her royal salary), she emptied the apartment of every fixture down to the brass doorknobs.

Over the next ten years, work on Blenheim would stop and start, as the funds became harder to procure from the government. The duchess thought Vanbrugh was out to ruin her. She quibbled over every carload of stone and bushel of lime, counted every extra yard of iron railing or foot of wainscot, hurling abuse at the wasteful workmen, contractors, and surveyors. Marlborough, old and weary, wanted nothing more than to settle into the palace in his last years, but the project became bogged down in a swamp of litigation, the workmen suing the duchess for wages, the duchess suing the architect right back. In the midst of this interminable wrangling, the duke died. He had never spent a night in his beloved Blenheim.

After Marlborough's death, it became clear that he had a vast estate, worth over £2 million—more than enough to pay for finishing the palace. But the duchess would not relent: She held back Vanbrugh's wages as well as the workmen's, and finally had the architect dismissed. The man who took his place finished Blenheim in a few years, following Vanbrugh's designs to the letter. Vanbrugh died in 1726, locked out of the palace by the duchess, unable to set foot in his greatest creation. Foreshadowing the romantic movement, Blenheim had started a whole new trend in architecture, but had given its creator a twenty-year nightmare.

Interpretation

For the Duchess of Marlborough, money was a way to play sadistic power games. She saw the loss of money as a symbolic loss of power. With Vanbrugh her contortions went deeper still: He was a great artist, and she envied his power to create, to attain a fame outside her reach. She may not have had his gifts, but she did have the money to torture and abuse him over the pettiest details—to ruin his life.

This kind of sadism, however, bears an awful price. It made construction that should have lasted ten years take twenty. It poisoned many a relationship, alienated the duchess from the court, deeply pained the duke (who wanted only to live peacefully in Blenheim), created endless lawsuits, and took years off Vanbrugh's life. Finally, too, posterity had the last word: Vanbrugh is recognized as a genius while the duchess is forever remembered for her consummate cheapness.

The powerful must have grandeur of spirit—they can never reveal any pettiness. And money is the most visible arena in which to display either grandeur or pettiness. Best spend freely, then, and create a reputation for generosity, which in the end will pay great dividends. Never let financial details blind you to the bigger picture of how people perceive you. Their resentment will cost you in the long run. And if you want to meddle in the work of creative people under your hire, at least pay them well. Your money will buy their submission better than your displays of power.

OBSERVANCES OF THE LAW

Observance I

Pietro Aretino, son of a lowly shoemaker, had catapulted himself into fame as a writer of biting satires. But like every Renaissance artist, he needed to find a patron who would give him a comfortable lifestyle while not interfering with his work. In 1528 Aretino decided to attempt a new strategy in the patronage game. Leaving Rome, he established himself in Venice, where few had heard of him. He had a fair amount of money he had managed to save, but little else. Soon after he moved into his new home, however, he threw open its doors to rich and poor, regaling them with banquets and amusements. He befriended each and every gondolier, tipping them royally. In the streets, he spread his money liberally, giving it away to beggars, orphans, washerwomen. Among the city's commoners, word quickly spread that Aretino was more than just a great writer, he was a man of power—a kind of lord.

Artists and men of influence soon began to frequent Aretino's house. Within a few years he made himself a celebrity; no visiting dignitary would think of leaving Venice without paying him a call. His generosity had cost him most of his savings, but had bought him influence and a good name— a cornerstone in the foundation of power. Since in Renaissance Italy as elsewhere the ability to spend freely was the privilege of the rich, the aristocracy thought Aretino had to be a man of influence, since he spent money like one. And since the influence of a man of influence is worth buying, Aretino became the recipient of all sorts of gifts and moneys. Dukes and duchesses, wealthy merchants, and popes and princes competed to gain his favor, and showered him with all kinds of presents.

Aretino's spending habits, of course, were strategic, and the strategy worked like a charm. But for real money and comfort he needed a great patron's bottomless pockets. Having surveyed the possibilities, he eventually set his sights on the extremely wealthy Marquis of Mantua, and wrote an epic poem that he dedicated to the marquis. This was a common practice of writers looking for patronage: In exchange for a dedication they would get a small stipend, enough to write yet another poem, so that they spent their lives in a kind of constant servility. Aretino, however, wanted power, not a measly wage. He might dedicate a poem to the marquis, but he would offer it to him as a gift, implying by doing so that he was not a hired hack looking for a stipend but that he and the marquis were equals.

Aretino's gift-giving did not stop there: As a close friend of two of Venice's greatest artists, the sculptor Jacopo Sansovino and the painter Titian, he convinced these men to participate in his gift-giving scheme. Aretino had studied the marquis before going to work on him, and knew his taste inside and out; he was able to advise Sansovino and Titian what subject matter would please the marquis most. When he then sent a Sansovino sculpture and a Titian painting to the marquis as gifts from all three of them, the man was beside himself with joy.

Over the next few months, Aretino sent other gifts—swords, saddles, the glass that was a Venetian specialty, things he knew the marquis prized. Soon he, Titian, and Sansovino began to receive gifts from the marquis in return. And the strategy went further: When the son-in-law of a friend of Aretino's found himself in jail in Mantua, Aretino was able to get the marquis to arrange his release. Aretino's friend, a wealthy merchant, was a man of great influence in Venice; by turning the goodwill he had built up

years passed by after this promise, and Pharaoh, doomed to ruin, continued to live in all his magnificence. Moses was impatient for God to destroy Pharaoh quickly, and he could not endure to wait any longer. So he fasted for forty days and went to Mount Sinai, and in his communing with god he said, "O Lord, Thou didst promise that Thou wouldst destroy Pharaoh, and still he has forsaken none of his blasphemies and pretensions. So when wilt Thou destroy him?"

A voice came from The Truth saying, "O Moses, you want Me to destroy Pharaoh as quickly as possible, but a thousand times a thousand of My servants want Me never to do so, because they partake of his bounty and enjoy tranquillity under his rule. By My power I swear that as long as he provides abundant food and comfort for My creatures, I shall not destroy him."

Moses said, "Then when will Thy promise be fulfilled?" God said, "My promise will be fulfilled when he withholds his provision from My creatures. If ever he begins to lessen his bounty, know that his hour is drawing near."

It chanced that one day Pharaoh said to Haman, "Moses has gathered the Sons of Israel about him and is causing us disquiet. We know not what will be

the issue of his affair
with us. We must keep
our stores full lest at
any time we be without
resources. So we must
halve our daily rations
and keep the saving in
reserve." He deducted
2,000 sheep, 200 cows,
and a 100 camels, and
similarly every two or
three days reduced the
ration. Moses then
knew that the promise
of The Truth was near
to fulfillment, for excessive economy is a sign
of decline and a bad
omen. The masters of
tradition say that on
the day when Pharaoh
was drowned only two
ewes had been killed in
his kitchen.
Nothing is better than
generosity. . . . If a man
is rich and desires,
without a royal charter,
to act like a lord; if he
wants men to humble
themselves before him,
to revere him and call
him lord and prince,
then tell him every day
to spread a table with
victuals. All those who
have acquired renown
in the world, have
gained it mainly
through hospitality,
while the miserly and
avaricious are despised
in both worlds.
THE BOOK OF
GOVERNMENT OR
RULES FOR KINGS,
NIZAM AL-MULK,
ELEVENTH CENTURY

with the marquis to use, Aretino had now bought this man's indebtedness, too, and he in turn would help Aretino when he could. The circle of influence was growing wider. Time and again, Aretino was able to cash in on the immense political power of the marquis, who also helped him in his many court romances.

Eventually, however, the relationship became strained, as Aretino came to feel that the marquis should have requited his generosity better. But he would not lower himself to begging or whining: Since the exchange of gifts between the two men had made them equals, it would not seem right to bring up money. He simply withdrew from the marquis's circle and hunted for other wealthy prey, settling first on the French king Francis, then the Medicis, the Duke of Urbino, Emperor Charles V, and more. In the end, having many patrons meant he did not have to bow to any of them, and his power seemed comparable to that of a great lord.

Interpretation

Aretino understood two fundamental properties of money: First, that it has to circulate to bring power. What money should buy is not lifeless objects but power over people. By keeping money in constant circulation, Aretino bought an ever-expanding circle of influence that in the end more than compensated him for his expenses.

Second, Aretino understood the key property of the gift. To give a gift is to imply that you and the recipient are equals at the very least, or that you are the recipient's superior. A gift also involves an indebtedness or obligation; when friends, for instance, offer you something for free, you can be sure they expect something in return, and that to get it they are making you feel indebted. (The mechanism may or may not be entirely conscious on their part, but this is how it works.)

Aretino avoided such encumbrances on his freedom. Instead of acting like a menial who expects the powerful to pay his way in life, he turned the whole dynamic around; instead of being indebted to the powerful, he made the powerful indebted to him. This was the point of his gift-giving, a ladder that carried him to the highest social levels. By the end of his life he had become the most famous writer in Europe.

Understand: Money may determine power relationships, but those relationships need not depend on the amount of money you have; they also depend on the way you use it. Powerful people give freely, buying influence rather than things. If you accept the inferior position because you have no fortune yet, you may find yourself in it forever. Play the trick that Aretino played on Italy's aristocracy: Imagine yourself an equal. Play the lord, give freely, open your doors, circulate your money, and create the facade of power through an alchemy that transforms money into influence.

Observance II

Soon after Baron James Rothschild made his fortune in Paris in the early 1820s, he faced his most intractable problem: How could a Jew and a German, a total outsider to French society, win the respect of the xenophobic French upper classes? Rothschild was a man who understood power—he knew that his fortune would bring him status, but that if he remained socially alienated neither his status nor his fortune would last. So he looked at the society of the time and asked what would win their hearts.

Charity? The French couldn't care less. Political influence? He already had that, and if anything it only made people more suspicious of him. The one weak spot, he decided, was boredom. In the period of the restoration of the monarchy, the French upper classes were bored. So Rothschild began to spend astounding sums of money on entertaining them. He hired the best architects in France to design his gardens and ballroom; he hired Marie-Antoine Carême, the most celebrated French chef, to prepare the most lavish parties Paris had ever witnessed; no Frenchman could resist, even if the parties were given by a German Jew. Rothschild's weekly soirées began to attract bigger and bigger numbers. Over the next few years he won the only thing that would secure an outsider's power: social acceptance.

Interpretation

Strategic generosity is always a great weapon in building a support base, particularly for the outsider. But the Baron de Rothschild was cleverer still: He knew it was his money that had created the barrier between him and the French, making him look ugly and untrustworthy. The best way to overcome this was literally to waste huge sums, a gesture to show he valued French culture and society over money. What Rothschild did resembled the famous potlatch feasts of the American Northwest: By periodically destroying its wealth in a giant orgy of festivals and bonfires, an Indian tribe would symbolize its power over other tribes. The base of its power was not money but its ability to spend, and its confidence in a superiority that would restore to it all that the potlatch had destroyed.

In the end, the baron's soirées reflected his desire to mingle not just in France's business world but in its society. By wasting money on his potlatches, he hoped to demonstrate that his power went beyond money into the more precious realm of culture. Rothschild may have won social acceptance by spending money, but the support base he gained was one that money alone could not buy. To secure his fortune he had to "waste" it. That is strategic generosity in a nutshell—the ability to be flexible with your wealth, putting it to work, not to buy objects, but to win people's hearts.

Observance III

The Medicis of Renaissance Florence had built their immense power on the fortune they had made in banking. But in Florence, centuries-old republic that it was, the idea that money bought power went against all the city's proud democratic values. Cosimo de' Medici, the first of the family to gain great fame, worked around this by keeping a low profile. He never flaunted his wealth. But by the time his grandson Lorenzo came of age, in the 1470s, the family's wealth was too large, and their influence too noticeable, to be disguised any longer.

Lorenzo solved the problem in his own way by developing the strategy of distraction that has served people of wealth ever since: He became

THE FLAME-COLORED CLOAK

During the campaign of Cambyses in Egypt, a great many Greeks visited that country for one reason or another: some, as was to be expected, for trade, some to serve in the army, others, no doubt, out of mere curiosity, to see what they could see. Amongst the sightseers was Aeaces's son Syloson, the exiled brother of Polycrates of Samos. While he was in Egypt, Syloson had an extraordinary stroke of luck: he was hanging about the streets of Memphis dressed in a flame-colored cloak, when Darius, who at that time was a member of Cambyses's guard and not yet of any particular importance, happened to catch sight of him and, seized with a sudden longing to possess the cloak, came up to Syloson and made him an offer for it.
His extreme anxiety to get it was obvious enough to Syloson, who was inspired to say: "I am not selling this for any money, but if you must have it, I will give it to you for free." Darius thereupon thanked him warmly and took it. Syloson at the moment merely thought he had lost it by his foolish good nature; then came the death of Cambyses and the revolt of the seven against the Magus, and Darius ascended the throne. Syloson now

the most illustrious patron of the arts that history has ever known. Not only did he spend lavishly on paintings, he created Italy's finest apprentice schools for young artists. It was in one of these schools that the young Michelangelo first caught the attention of Lorenzo, who invited the artist to come and live in his house. He did the same with Leonardo da Vinci. Once under his wing, Michelangelo and Leonardo requited his generosity by becoming loyal artists in his stable.

Whenever Lorenzo faced an enemy, he would wield the weapon of patronage. When Pisa, Florence's traditional enemy, threatened to rebel against it in 1472, Lorenzo placated its people by pouring money into its university, which had once been its pride and joy but had long ago lost its luster. The Pisans had no defense against this insidious maneuver, which simultaneously fed their love of culture and blunted their desire for battle.

Interpretation

Lorenzo undoubtedly loved the arts, but his patronage of artists had a practical function as well, of which he was keenly aware. In Florence at the time, banking was perhaps the least admired way of making money, and was certainly not a respected source of power. The arts were at the other pole, the pole of quasi-religious transcendence. By spending on the arts, Lorenzo diluted people's opinions of the ugly source of his wealth, disguising himself in nobility. There is no better use of strategic generosity than that of distracting attention from an unsavory reality and wrapping oneself in the mantle of art or religion.

Observance IV

Louis XIV had an eagle eye for the strategic power of money. When he came to the throne, the powerful nobility had recently proven a thorn in the monarchy's side, and seethed with rebelliousness. So he impoverished these aristocrats by making them spend enormous sums on maintaining their position in the court. Making them dependent on royal largesse for their livelihood, he had them in his claws.

Next Louis brought the nobles to their knees with strategic generosity. It would work like this: Whenever he noticed a stubborn courtier whose influence he needed to gain, or whose troublemaking he needed to squelch, he would use his vast wealth to soften the soil. First he would ignore his victim, making the man anxious. Then the man would suddenly find that his son had been given a well-paid post, or that funds had been spent liberally in his home region, or that he had been given a painting he had long coveted. Presents would flow from Louis's hands. Finally, weeks or months later, Louis would ask for the favor he had needed all along. A man who had once vowed to do anything to stop the king would find he had lost the desire to fight. A straightforward bribe would have made him rebellious; this was far more insidious. Facing hardened earth in which nothing could take root, Louis loosened the soil before he planted his seeds.

Interpretation

Louis understood that there is a deep-rooted emotional element in our attitude to money, an element going back to childhood. When we are children, all kinds of complicated feelings about our parents center around gifts; we see the giving of a gift as a sign of love and approval. And that emotional element never goes away. The recipients of gifts, financial or otherwise, are suddenly as vulnerable as children, especially when the gift comes from someone in authority. They cannot help opening up; their will is loosened, as Louis loosened the soil.

To succeed best, the gift should come out of the blue. It should be remarkable for the fact that a gift like it has never been given before, or for being preceded by a cold shoulder from the giver. The more often you give to particular people, the blunter this weapon becomes. If they don't take your gifts for granted, becoming monsters of ingratitude, they will resent what appears to be charity. The sudden, unexpected, one-time gift will not spoil your children; it will keep them under your thumb.

Observance V

The antique dealer Fushimiya, who lived in the city of Edo (former name for Tokyo) in the seventeenth century, once made a stop at a village teahouse. After enjoying a cup of tea, he spent several minutes scrutinizing the cup, which he eventually paid for and took away with him. A local artisan, watching this, waited until Fushimiya left the shop, then approached the old woman who owned the teahouse and asked her who this man was. She told him it was Japan's most famous connoisseur, antique dealer to the lord of Izumo. The artisan ran out of the shop, caught up with Fushimiya, and begged him to sell him the cup, which must clearly be valuable if Fushimiya judged it so. Fushimiya laughed heartily: "It's just an ordinary cup of Bizen ware," he explained, "and it is not valuable at all. The reason I was looking at it was that the steam seemed to hang about it strangely and I wondered if there wasn't a leak somewhere." (Devotees of the Tea Ceremony were interested in any odd or accidental beauty in nature.) Since the artisan still seemed so excited about it, Fushimiya gave him the cup for free.

The artisan took the cup around, trying to find an expert who would appraise it at a high price, but since all of them recognized it as an ordinary teacup he got nowhere. Soon he was neglecting his own business, thinking only of the cup and the fortune it could bring. Finally he went to Edo to talk to Fushimiya at his shop. There the dealer, realizing that he had inadvertently caused this man pain by making him believe the cup had great worth, paid him 100 ryo (gold pieces) for the cup as a kindness. The cup was indeed mediocre, but he wanted to rid the artisan of his obsession, while also allowing him to feel that his effort had not been wasted. The artisan thanked him and went on his way.

Soon word spread of Fushimiya's purchase of the teacup. Every dealer in Japan clamored for him to sell it, since a cup he had bought for 100 ryo must be worth much more. He tried to explain the circumstances in which he had bought the cup, but the dealers could not be dissuaded. Fushimiya finally relented and put the cup up for sale.

During the auction, two buyers simultaneously bid 200 ryo for the teacup, and then began to fight over who had bid first. Their fighting

never regret that you once did a favor to Darius the son of Hystaspes." "My lord," replied Syloson, "do not give me gold or silver, but recover Samos for me, my native island, which now since Oroetes killed my brother Polycrates is in the hands of one of our servants. Let Samos be your gift to me—but let no man in the island be killed or enslaved." Darius consented to Syloson's request, and dispatched a force under the command of Otanes, one of the seven, with orders to do everything that Syloson had asked.

THE HISTORIES, HERODOTUS, FIFTH CENTURY B.C.

Money is never spent to so much advantage as when you have been cheated out of it; for at one stroke you have purchased prudence.

ARTHUR SCHOPENHAUER, 1788–1860

*Kung-yi Hsiu, premier
of Lu, was fond of fish.
Therefore, people in
the whole country
conscientiously bought
fish, which they
presented to him.
However, Kung-yi
would not accept the
presents. Against such a
step his younger
brother remonstrated
with him and said:
"You like fish, indeed.
Why don't you accept
the present of fish?" In
reply, he said: "It is
solely because I like
fish that I would not
accept the fish they
gave me.
Indeed, if I accept the
fish, I will be placed
under an obligation to
them. Once placed
under an obligation to
them, I will some time
have to bend the law. If
I bend the law, I will be
dismissed from the
premiership. After
being dismissed from
the premiership, I
might not be able to
supply myself with fish.
On the contrary, if I do
not accept the fish from
them and am not
dismissed the premier-
ship, however fond of
fish, I can always
supply myself
with fish."

HAN-FEI-TZU,
CHINESE PHILOSOPHER,
THIRD CENTURY B.C.*

tipped over a table and the teacup fell to the ground and broke into several pieces. The auction was clearly over. Fushimiya glued and mended the cup, then stored it away, thinking the affair finished. Years later, however, the great tea master Matsudaira Fumai visited the store, and asked to see the cup, which by then had become legendary. Fumai examined it. "As a piece," he said, "it is not up to much, but a Tea Master prizes sentiment and association more than intrinsic value." He bought the cup for a high sum. A glued-together work of less than ordinary craftsmanship had become one of the most famous objects in Japan.

Interpretation

The story shows, first, an essential aspect of money: That it is humans who have created it and humans who instill it with meaning and value. Second, with objects as with money, what the courtier most values are the sentiments and emotions embedded in them—these are what make them worth having. The lesson is simple: The more your gifts and your acts of generosity play with sentiment, the more powerful they are. The object or concept that plays with a charged emotion or hits a chord of sentiment has more power than the money you squander on an expensive yet lifeless present.

Observance VI

Akimoto Suzutomo, a wealthy adherent of the tea ceremony, once gave his page 100 ryo (gold pieces) and instructed him to purchase a tea bowl offered by a particular dealer. When the page saw the bowl, he doubted it was worth that much, and after much bargaining got the price reduced to 95 ryo. Days later, after Suzutomo had put the bowl to use, the page proudly told him what he had done.

"What an ignoramus you are!" replied Suzutomo. "A tea bowl that anyone asks 100 pieces of gold for can only be a family heirloom, and a thing like that is only sold when the family is pressed for money. And in that case they will be hoping to find someone who will give even 150 pieces for it. So what sort of fellow is it who does not consider their feelings? Quite apart from that, a curio that you give 100 ryo for is something worth having, but one that has only cost 95 gives a mean impression. So never let me see that tea bowl again!" And he had the bowl locked away, and never took it out.

Interpretation

When you insist on paying less, you may save your five ryo, but the insult you cause and the cheap impression you create will cost you in reputation, which is the thing the powerful prize above all. Learn to pay the full price—it will save you a lot in the end.

Observance VII

Sometime near the beginning of the seventeenth century in Japan, a group of generals whiled away the time before a big battle by staging an incense-smelling competition. Each participant anted up a prize for the contest's winners—bows, arrows, saddles, and other items a warrior would covet.

The great Lord Date Masamune happened to pass by and was induced to participate. For a prize, he offered the gourd that hung from his belt. Everyone laughed, for no one wanted to win this cheap item. A retainer of the host finally accepted the gourd.

When the party broke up, however, and the generals were chatting outside the tent, Masamune brought over his magnificent horse and gave it to the retainer. "There," he said, "a horse has come out of the gourd." The stunned generals suddenly regretted their scorn at Masamune's gift.

Interpretation

Masamune understood the following: Money gives its possessor the ability to give pleasure to others. The more you can do this, the more you attract admiration. When you make a horse come out of a gourd, you give the ultimate demonstration of your power.

I took money only from those who could afford it and were willing to go in with me in schemes they fancied would fleece others. They wanted money for its own sake. I wanted it for the luxuries and pleasures it would afford me. They were seldom concerned with human nature. They knew little—and cared less—about their fellow men. If they had been keener students of human nature, if they had given more time to companionship with their fellows and less to the chase of the almighty dollar, they wouldn't have been such easy marks.

"YELLOW KID" WEIL, 1875–1976

Image: The River. To protect yourself or to save the resource, you dam it up. Soon, however, the waters become dank and pestilent. Only the foulest forms of life can live in such stagnant waters; nothing travels on them, all commerce stops. Destroy the dam. When water flows and circulates, it generates abundance, wealth, and power in ever larger circles. The River must flood periodically for good things to flourish.

Authority: The great man who is a miser is a great fool, and a man in high places can have no vice so harmful as avarice. A miserly man can conquer neither lands nor lordships, for he does not have a plentiful supply of friends with whom he may work his will. Whoever wants to have friends must not love his possessions but must acquire friends by means of fair gifts; for in the same way that the lodestone subtly draws iron to itself, so the gold and silver that a man gives attract the hearts of men. (*The Romance of the Rose,* Guillaume de Lorris, c. 1200–1238)

REVERSAL

The powerful never forget that what is offered for free is inevitably a trick. Friends who offer favors without asking for payment will later want something far dearer than the money you would have paid them. The bargain has hidden problems, both material and psychological. Learn to pay, then, and to pay well.

On the other hand, this Law offers great opportunities for swindling and deception if you apply it from the other side. Dangling the lure of a free lunch is the con artist's stock in trade.

No man was better at this than the most successful con artist of our age, Joseph Weil, a.k.a. "The Yellow Kid." The Yellow Kid learned early that what made his swindles possible was his fellow humans' greed. "This desire to get something for nothing," he once wrote, "has been very costly to many people who have dealt with me and with other con men. . . . When people learn—as I doubt they will—that they can't get something for nothing, crime will diminish and we shall all live in greater harmony." Over the years Weil devised many ways to seduce people with the prospect of easy money. He would hand out "free" real estate—who could resist such an offer?—and then the suckers would learn they had to pay $25 to register the sale. Since the land was free, it seemed worth the high fee, and the Yellow Kid would make thousands of dollars on the phony registration. In exchange he would give his suckers a phony deed. Other times, he would tell suckers about a fixed horse race, or a stock that would earn 200 percent in a few weeks. As he spun his stories he would watch the sucker's eyes open wide at the thought of a free lunch.

The lesson is simple: Bait your deceptions with the possibility of easy money. People are essentially lazy, and want wealth to fall in their lap rather than to work for it. For a small sum, sell them advice on how to make millions (P. T. Barnum did this later in life), and that small sum will become a fortune when multiplied by thousands of suckers. Lure people in with the prospect of easy money and you have the room to work still more deceptions on them, since greed is powerful enough to blind your victims to anything. And as the Yellow Kid said, half the fun is teaching a moral lesson: Greed does not pay.

41

AVOID STEPPING INTO

A GREAT MAN'S SHOES

JUDGMENT

What happens first always appears better and more original than what comes after. If you succeed a great man or have a famous parent, you will have to accomplish double their achievements to outshine them. Do not get lost in their shadow, or stuck in a past not of your own making: Establish your own name and identity by changing course. Slay the overbearing father, disparage his legacy, and gain power by shining in your own way.

THE EXCELLENCE
OF BEING FIRST

*Many would have
shone like the very
phoenix in their occu-
pations if others had
not preceded them.
Being first is a great
advantage; with
eminence, twice as
good. Deal the first
hand and you will win
the upper ground. . . .
Those who go first
win fame by right of
birth, and those who
follow are like second
sons, contenting them-
selves with meager
portions. . . .
Solomon opted wisely
for pacifism, yielding
warlike things to his
father. By changing
course he found it
easier to become a
hero. . . .
And our great Philip II
governed the entire
world from the throne
of his prudence, aston-
ishing the ages. If his
unconquered father
was a model of energy,
Philip was a paradigm
of prudence. . . . This
sort of novelty has
helped the well-advised
win a place in the roll
of the great.
Without leaving their
own art, the ingenious
leave the common path
and take, even in
professions gray with
age, new steps toward
eminence. Horace
yielded epic poetry to
Virgil, and Martial the
lyric to Horace. Terence
opted for comedy,
Persius for satire, each
hoping to be first in his
genre. Bold fancy never
succumbed to facile
imitation.*

A POCKET MIRROR
FOR HEROES,
BALTASAR GRACIÁN,
TRANSLATED BY
CHRISTOPHER MAURER,
1996

When Louis XIV died, in 1715, after a glorious fifty-five-year reign, all eyes focused on his great-grandson and chosen successor, the future Louis XV. Would the boy, only five at the time, prove as great a leader as the Sun King? Louis XIV had transformed a country on the verge of civil war into the preeminent power in Europe. The last years of his reign had been diffi-cult—he had been old and tired—but it was hoped that the child would de-velop into the kind of strong ruler who would reinvigorate the land and add to the firm foundation that Louis XIV had laid.

To this end the child was given the best minds of France as his tutors, men who would instruct him in the arts of statecraft, in the methods that the Sun King had perfected. Nothing was neglected in his education. But when Louis XV came to the throne, in 1726, a sudden change came over him: He no longer had to study or please others or prove himself. He stood alone at the top of a great country, with wealth and power at his command. He could do as he wished.

In the first years of his reign, Louis gave himself over to pleasure, leav-ing the government in the hands of a trusted minister, André-Hercule de Fleury. This caused little concern, for he was a young man who needed to sow his wild oats, and de Fleury was a good minister. But it slowly became clear that this was more than a passing phase. Louis had no interest in gov-erning. His main worry was not France's finances, or a possible war with Spain, but boredom. He could not stand being bored, and when he was not hunting deer, or chasing young girls, he whiled away his time at the gam-bling tables, losing huge sums in a single night.

The court, as usual, reflected the tastes of the ruler. Gambling and lav-ish parties became the obsession. The courtiers had no concern with the fu-ture of France—they poured their energies into charming the king, angling for titles that would bring them life pensions, and for cabinet positions de-manding little work but paying huge salaries. Parasites flocked to the court, and the state's debts swelled.

In 1745 Louis fell in love with Madame de Pompadour, a woman of middle-class origin who had managed to rise through her charms, her intel-ligence, and a good marriage. Madame de Pompadour became the official royal mistress; she also became France's arbiter of taste and fashion. But the Madame had political ambitions as well, and she eventually emerged as the country's unofficial prime minister—it was she, not Louis, who wielded hiring-and-firing power over France's most important ministers.

As he grew older Louis only needed more diversion. On the grounds of Versailles he built a brothel, Parc aux Cerfs, which housed some of the prettiest young girls of France. Underground passages and hidden stair-cases gave Louis access at all hours. After Madame de Pompadour died, in 1764, she was succeeded as royal mistress by Madame du Barry, who soon came to dominate the court, and who, like de Pompadour before her, began to meddle in affairs of state. If a minister did not please her he would find himself fired. All of Europe was aghast when du Barry, the daughter of a baker, managed to arrange the firing of Étienne de Choiseul, the foreign minister and France's most able diplomat. He had shown her too little respect. As time went by, swindlers and charlatans made their nests in Versailles, and enticed Louis's interest in astrology, the occult, and fraudulent business deals. The young and pampered teenager who had taken over France years before had only grown worse with age.

The motto that became attached to Louis's reign was *"Après moi, le déluge"*—"After me the flood," or, Let France rot after I am gone. And indeed when Louis did go, in 1774, worn out by debauchery, his country and his own finances were in horrible disarray. His grandson Louis XVI inherited a realm in desperate need of reform and a strong leader. But Louis XVI was even weaker than his grandfather, and could only watch as the country descended into revolution. In 1792 the republic introduced by the French Revolution declared the end of the monarchy, and gave the king a new name, "Louis the Last." A few months later he kneeled on the guillotine, his about-to-be-severed head stripped of all the radiance and power that the Sun King had invested in the crown.

Interpretation

From a country that had descended into civil war in the late 1640s, Louis XIV forged the mightiest realm in Europe. Great generals would tremble in his presence. A cook once made a mistake in preparing a dish and committed suicide rather than face the king's wrath. Louis XIV had many mistresses, but their power ended in the bedroom. He filled his court with the most brilliant minds of the age. The symbol of his power was Versailles: Refusing to accept the palace of his forefathers, the Louvre, he built his own palace in what was then the middle of nowhere, symbolizing that this was a new order he had founded, one without precedent. He made Versailles the centerpiece of his reign, a place that all the powerful of Europe envied and visited with a sense of awe. In essence, Louis took a great void—the decaying monarchy of France—and filled it with his own symbols and radiant power.

Louis XV, on the other hand, symbolizes the fate of all those who inherit something large or who follow in a great man's footsteps. It would seem easy for a son or successor to build on the grand foundation left for them, but in the realm of power the opposite is true. The pampered, indulged son almost always squanders the inheritance, for he does not start with the father's need to fill a void. As Machiavelli states, necessity is what impels men to take action, and once the necessity is gone, only rot and decay are left. Having no need to increase his store of power, Louis XV inevitably succumbed to inertia. Under him, Versailles, the symbol of the Sun King's authority, became a pleasure palace of incomparable banality, a kind of Las Vegas of the Bourbon monarchy. It came to represent all that the oppressed peasantry of France hated about their king, and during the Revolution they looted it with glee.

Louis XV had only one way out of the trap awaiting the son or successor of a man like the Sun King: to psychologically begin from nothing, to

Cimon's sympathies
were strongly with the
nobles and that Cimon
was the idol of the aris-
tocratic party, Pericles
began to ingratiate
himself with the people,
partly for self-preserva-
tion and partly by way
of securing power
against his rival.
He now entered upon
a new mode of life.
He was never to be
seen walking in any
street except the one
which led to the
market-place and the
council chamber.

THE LIFE OF PERICLES,
PLUTARCH,
c. A.D. 46–120

denigrate the past and his inheritance, and to move in a totally new direction, creating his own world. Assuming you have the choice, it would be
better to avoid the situation altogether, to place yourself where there is a
vacuum of power, where you can be the one to bring order out of chaos
without having to compete with another star in the sky. Power depends on
appearing larger than other people, and when you are lost in the shadow of
the father, the king, the great predecessor, you cannot possibly project such
a presence.

> But when they began to make sovereignty hereditary, the children quickly
> degenerated from their fathers; and, so far from trying to equal their father's
> virtues, they considered that a prince had nothing else to do than to excel
> all the rest in idleness, indulgence, and every other variety of pleasure.
> Niccolò Machiavelli, 1469–1527

OBSERVANCE OF THE LAW

Alexander the Great had a dominant passion as a young man—an intense
dislike for his father, King Philip of Macedonia. He hated Philip's cunning,
cautious style of ruling, his bombastic speeches, his drinking and whoring,
and his love of wrestling and of other wastes of time. Alexander knew he
had to make himself the very opposite of his domineering father: He would
force himself to be bold and reckless, he would control his tongue and be a
man of few words, and he would not lose precious time in pursuit of pleasures that brought no glory. Alexander also resented the fact that Philip
had conquered most of Greece: "My father will go on conquering till there
is nothing extraordinary left for me to do," he once complained. While
other sons of powerful men were content to inherit wealth and live a life of
leisure, Alexander wanted only to outdo his father, to obliterate Philip's
name from history by surpassing his accomplishments.

Alexander itched to show others how superior he was to his father. A
Thessalian horse-dealer once brought a prize horse named Bucephalus to
sell to Philip. None of the king's grooms could get near the horse—it was
far too savage—and Philip berated the merchant for bringing him such a
useless beast. Watching the whole affair, Alexander scowled and commented, "What a horse they are losing for want of skill and spirit to manage him!" When he had said this several times, Philip had finally had
enough, and challenged him to take on the horse. He called the merchant
back, secretly hoping his son would have a nasty fall and learn a bitter lesson. But Alexander was the one to teach the lesson: Not only did he mount
Bucephalus, he managed to ride him at full gallop, taming the horse that
would later carry him all the way to India. The courtiers applauded wildly,
but Philip seethed inside, seeing not a son but a rival to his power.

Alexander's defiance of his father grew bolder. One day the two men
had a heated argument before the entire court, and Philip drew his sword
as if to strike his son; having drunk too much wine, however, the king
stumbled. Alexander pointed at his father and jeered, "Men of Macedonia,

THE LIFE OF PIETRO
PERUGINO, PAINTER
c. 1450-1523

How beneficial poverty
may sometimes be to
those with talent, and
how it may serve as a
powerful goad to make
them perfect or excel-
lent in whatever occu-
pation they might
choose, can be seen
very clearly in the
actions of Pietro
Perugino. Wishing by
means of his ability to
attain some respectable
rank, after leaving
disastrous calamities
behind in Perugia and
coming to Florence, he
remained there many
months in poverty,
sleeping in a chest,
since he had no other
bed; he turned night
into day, and with the
greatest zeal continu-
ally applied himself to

see there the man who is preparing to pass from Europe to Asia. He cannot pass from one table to another without falling."

When Alexander was eighteen, a disgruntled courtier murdered Philip. As word of the regicide spread through Greece, city after city rose up in rebellion against their Macedonian rulers. Philip's advisers counseled Alexander, now the king, to proceed cautiously, to do as Philip had done and conquer through cunning. But Alexander would do things his way: He marched to the furthest reaches of the kingdom, suppressed the rebellious towns, and reunited the empire with brutal efficiency.

As a young rebel grows older, his struggle against the father often wanes, and he gradually comes to resemble the very man he had wanted to defy. But Alexander's loathing of his father did not end with Philip's death. Once he had consolidated Greece, he set his eyes on Persia, the prize that had eluded his father, who had dreamed of conquering Asia. If he defeated the Persians, Alexander would finally surpass Philip in glory and fame.

Alexander crossed into Asia with an army of 35,000 to face a Persian force numbering over a million. Before engaging the Persians in battle he passed through the town of Gordium. Here, in the town's main temple, there stood an ancient chariot tied with cords made of the rind of the cornel tree. Legend had it that any man who could undo these cords—the Gordian knot—would rule the world. Many had tried to untie the enormous and intricate knot, but none had succeeded. Alexander, seeing he could not possibly untie the knot with his bare hands, took out his sword and with one slash cut it in half. This symbolic gesture showed the world that he would not do as others, but would blaze his own path.

Against astounding odds, Alexander conquered the Persians. Most expected him to stop there—it was a great triumph, enough to secure his fame for eternity. But Alexander had the same relationship to his own deeds as he had to his father: His conquest of Persia represented the past, and he wanted never to rest on past triumphs, or to allow the past to outshine the present. He moved on to India, extending his empire beyond all known limits. Only his disgruntled and weary soldiers prevented him from going farther.

Interpretation

Alexander represents an extremely uncommon type in history: the son of a famous and successful man who manages to surpass the father in glory and power. The reason this type is uncommon is simple: The father most often manages to amass his fortune, his kingdom, because he begins with little or nothing. A desperate urge impels him to succeed—he has nothing to lose by cunning and impetuousness, and has no famous father of his own to compete against. This kind of man has reason to believe in himself—to believe that his way of doing things is the best, because, after all, it worked for him.

When a man like this has a son, he becomes domineering and oppressive, imposing his lessons on the son, who is starting off life in circumstances totally different from those in which the father himself began.

the study of his profession. After painting had become second nature to him, Pietro's only pleasure was always to be working in his craft and constantly to be painting. And because he always had the dread of poverty before his eyes, he did things to make money which he probably would not have bothered to do had he not been forced to support himself. Perhaps wealth would have closed to him and his talent the path to excellence just as poverty had opened it up to him, but need spurred him on since he desired to rise from such a miserable and lowly position—if not perhaps to the summit and supreme height of excellence, then at least to a point where he could have enough to live on. For this reason, he took no notice of cold, hunger, discomfort, inconvenience, toil or shame if he could only live one day in ease and repose; and he would always say—and as if it were a proverb— that after bad weather, good weather must follow, and that during the good weather houses must be built for shelter in times of need.

LIVES OF THE ARTISTS, GIORGIO VASARI, 1511–1574

Instead of allowing the son to go in a new direction, the father will try to put him in his own shoes, perhaps secretly wishing the boy will fail, as Philip half wanted to see Alexander thrown from Bucephalus. Fathers envy their sons' youth and vigor, after all, and their desire is to control and dominate. The sons of such men tend to become cowed and cautious, terrified of losing what their fathers have gained.

The son will never step out of his father's shadow unless he adopts the ruthless strategy of Alexander: disparage the past, create your own kingdom, put the father in the shadows instead of letting him do the same to you. If you cannot materially start from ground zero—it would be foolish to renounce an inheritance—you can at least begin from ground zero psychologically, by throwing off the weight of the past and charting a new direction. Alexander instinctively recognized that privileges of birth are impediments to power. Be merciless with the past, then—not only with your father and his father but with your own earlier achievements. Only the weak rest on their laurels and dote on past triumphs; in the game of power there is never time to rest.

KEYS TO POWER

In many ancient kingdoms, for example Bengal and Sumatra, after the king had ruled for several years his subjects would execute him. This was done partly as a ritual of renewal, but also to prevent him from growing too powerful—for the king would generally try to establish a permanent order, at the expense of other families and of his own sons. Instead of protecting the tribe and leading it in times of war, he would attempt to dominate it. And so he would be beaten to death, or executed in an elaborate ritual. Now that he was no longer around for his honors to go to his head, he could be worshipped as a god. Meanwhile the field had been cleared for a new and youthful order to establish itself.

The ambivalent, hostile attitude towards the king or father figure also finds expression in legends of heroes who do not know their father. Moses, the archetypal man of power, was found abandoned among the bulrushes and never knew his parents; without a father to compete with him or limit him, he could attain the heights of power. Hercules had no earthly father—he was the son of the god Zeus. Later in his life Alexander the Great spread the story that the god Jupiter Ammon had sired him, not Philip of Macedon. Legends and rituals like these eliminate the human father because he symbolizes the destructive power of the past.

The past prevents the young hero from creating his own world—he must do as his father did, even after that father is dead or powerless. The hero must bow and scrape before his predecessor and yield to tradition and precedent. What had success in the past must be carried over to the present, even though circumstances have greatly changed. The past also weighs the hero down with an inheritance that he is terrified of losing, making him timid and cautious.

Power depends on the ability to fill a void, to occupy a field that has been cleared of the dead weight of the past. Only after the father figure has been properly done away with will you have the necessary space to create and establish a new order. There are several strategies you can adopt to accomplish this—variations on the execution of the king that disguise the violence of the impulse by channeling it in socially acceptable forms.

Perhaps the simplest way to escape the shadow of the past is simply to belittle it, playing on the timeless antagonism between the generations, stirring up the young against the old. For this you need a convenient older figure to pillory. Mao Tse-tung, confronting a culture that fiercely resisted change, played on the suppressed resentment against the overbearing presence of the venerable Confucius in Chinese culture. John F. Kennedy knew the dangers of getting lost in the past; he radically distinguished his presidency from that of his predecessor, Dwight D. Eisenhower, and also from the preceding decade, the 1950s, which Eisenhower personified. Kennedy, for instance, would not play the dull and fatherly game of golf— a symbol of retirement and privilege, and Eisenhower's passion. Instead he played football on the White House lawn. In every aspect his administration represented vigor and youth, as opposed to the stodgy Eisenhower. Kennedy had discovered an old truth: The young are easily set against the old, since they yearn to make their own place in the world and resent the shadow of their fathers.

The distance you establish from your predecessor often demands some symbolism, a way of advertising itself publicly. Louis XIV, for example, created such symbolism when he rejected the traditional palace of the French kings and built his own palace of Versailles. King Philip II of Spain did the same when he created his center of power, the palace of El Escorial, in what was then the middle of nowhere. But Louis carried the game further: He would not be a king like his father or earlier ancestors, he would not wear a crown or carry a scepter or sit on a throne, he would establish a new kind of imposing authority with symbols and rituals of its own. Louis made his ancestors' rituals into laughable relics of the past. Follow his example: Never let yourself be seen as following your predecessor's path. If you do you will never surpass him. You must physically demonstrate your difference, by establishing a style and symbolism that sets you apart.

The Roman emperor Augustus, successor to Julius Caesar, understood this thoroughly. Caesar had been a great general, a theatrical figure whose spectacles kept the Romans entertained, an international emissary seduced by the charms of Cleopatra—a larger-than-life figure. So Augustus, despite his own theatrical tendencies, competed with Caesar not by trying to outdo him but by differentiating himself from him: He based his power on a return to Roman simplicity, an austerity of both style and substance. Against the memory of Caesar's sweeping presence Augustus posed a quiet and manly dignity.

The problem with the overbearing predecessor is that he fills the vistas before you with symbols of the past. You have no room to create your own name. To deal with this situation you need to hunt out the vacuums—those

cant that [nineteenth-century chess champion Paul] Morphy's soaring odyssey into the higher realms of chess began just a year after the unexpectedly sudden death of his father, which had been a great shock to him, and we may surmise that his brilliant effort of sublimation was, like Shakespeare's Hamlet *and Freud's* The Interpretation of Dreams, *a reaction to this critical event.... Something should now be said about the reception Morphy's successes met with, for they were of such a kind as to raise the question whether his subsequent collapse may not have been influenced through his perhaps belonging to the type that Freud has described under the name of* Die am Erfolge scheitern *("Those wrecked by success").... Couched in more psychological language, was Morphy affrighted at his own presumptuousness when the light of publicity was thrown on [his great success?] Freud has pointed out that the people who break under the strain of too great success do so because they can endure it only in imagination, not in reality. To castrate the father in a dream is a very different matter from doing it in reality. The real situation provokes the unconscious guilt in its full force, and the penalty may be mental collapse.*

THE PROBLEM OF PAUL MORPHY,
ERNEST JONES,
1951

areas in culture that have been left vacant and in which you can become the first and principal figure to shine.

When Pericles of Athens was about to launch a career as a statesman, he looked for the one thing that was missing in Athenian politics. Most of the great politicians of his time had allied themselves with the aristocracy; indeed Pericles himself had aristocratic tendencies. Yet he decided to throw in his hat with the city's democratic elements. The choice had nothing to do with his personal beliefs, but it launched him on a brilliant career. Out of necessity he became a man of the people. Instead of competing in an arena filled with great leaders both past and present, he would make a name for himself where no shadows could obscure his presence.

When the painter Diego de Velázquez began his career, he knew he could not compete in refinement and technique with the great Renaissance painters who had come before him. Instead he chose to work in a style that by the standards of the time seemed coarse and rough, in a way that had never been seen before. And in this style he excelled. There were members of the Spanish court who wanted to demonstrate their own break with the past; the newness of Velázquez's style thrilled them. Most people are afraid to break so boldly with tradition, but they secretly admire those who can break up the old forms and reinvigorate the culture. This is why there is so much power to be gained from entering vacuums and voids.

There is a kind of stubborn stupidity that recurs throughout history, and is a strong impediment to power: The superstitious belief that if the person before you succeeded by doing A, B, and C, you can re-create their success by doing the same thing. This cookie-cutter approach will seduce the uncreative, for it is easy, and appeals to their timidity and their laziness. But circumstances never repeat themselves exactly.

When General Douglas MacArthur assumed command of American forces in the Philippines during World War II, an assistant handed him a book containing the various precedents established by the commanders before him, the methods that had been successful for them. MacArthur asked the assistant how many copies there were of this book. Six, the assistant answered. "Well," the general replied, "you get all those six copies together and burn them—every one of them. I'll not be bound by precedents. Any time a problem comes up, I'll make the decision at once—immediately." Adopt this ruthless strategy toward the past: Burn all the books, and train yourself to react to circumstances as they happen.

You may believe that you have separated yourself from the predecessor or father figure, but as you grow older you must be eternally vigilant lest you become the father you had rebelled against. As a young man, Mao Tse-tung disliked his father and in the struggle against him found his own identity and a new set of values. But as he aged, his father's ways crept back in. Mao's father had valued manual work over intellect; Mao had scoffed at this as a young man, but as he grew older he unconsciously returned to his father's views and echoed such outdated ideas by forcing a whole generation of Chinese intellectuals into manual labor, a nightmarish mistake that cost his regime dearly. Remember: You are your own father. Do not let yourself spend years creating yourself only to let your guard down and allow the ghost of the past—father, habit, history—to sneak back in.

Finally, as noted in the story of Louis XV, plenitude and prosperity tend to make us lazy and inactive: When our power is secure we have no need to act. This is a serious danger, especially for those who achieve success and power at an early age. The playwright Tennessee Williams, for instance, found himself skyrocketed from obscurity to fame by the success of *The Glass Menagerie.* "The sort of life which I had had previous to this popular success," he later wrote, "was one that required endurance, a life of clawing and scratching, but it was a good life because it was the sort of life for which the human organism is created. I was not aware of how much vital energy had gone into this struggle until the struggle was removed. This was security at last. I sat down and looked about me and was suddenly very depressed." Williams had a nervous breakdown, which may in fact have been necessary for him: Pushed to the psychological edge, he could start writing with the old vitality again, and he produced *A Streetcar Named Desire.* Fyodor Dostoyevsky, similarly, whenever he wrote a successful novel, would feel that the financial security he had gained made the act of creation unnecessary. He would take his entire savings to the casino and would not leave until he had gambled away his last penny. Once reduced to poverty he could write again.

It is not necessary to go to such extremes, but you must be prepared to return to square one psychologically rather than growing fat and lazy with prosperity. Pablo Picasso could deal with success, but only by constantly changing the style of his painting, often breaking completely with what had made him successful before. How often our early triumphs turn us into a kind of caricature of ourselves. Powerful people recognize these traps; like Alexander the Great, they struggle constantly to re-create themselves. The father must not be allowed to return; he must be slain at every step of the way.

Image: The Father. He casts a giant shadow over his children, keeping them in thrall long after he is gone by tying them to the past, squashing their youthful spirit, and forcing them down the same tired path he followed himself. His tricks are many. At every crossroads you must slay the father and step out of his shadow.

Authority: Beware of stepping into a great man's shoes—you will have to accomplish twice as much to surpass him. Those who follow are taken for imitators. No matter how much they sweat, they will never shed that burden. It is an uncommon skill to find a new path for excellence, a modern route to celebrity. There are many roads to singularity, not all of them well traveled. The newest ones can be arduous, but they are often shortcuts to greatness. (Baltasar Gracián, 1601–1658)

REVERSAL

The shadow of a great predecessor could be used to advantage if it is chosen as a trick, a tactic that can be discarded once it has brought you power. Napoleon III used the name and legend of his illustrious grand-uncle Napoleon Bonaparte to help him become first president and then emperor of France. Once on the throne, however, he did not stay tied to the past; he quickly showed how different his reign would be, and was careful to keep the public from expecting him to attain the heights that Bonaparte had attained.

The past often has elements worth appropriating, qualities that would be foolish to reject out of a need to distinguish yourself. Even Alexander the Great recognized and was influenced by his father's skill in organizing an army. Making a display of doing things differently from your predecessor can make you seem childish and in fact out of control, unless your actions have a logic of their own.

Joseph II, son of the Austrian empress Maria Theresa, made a show of doing the exact opposite of his mother—dressing like an ordinary citizen, staying in inns instead of palaces, appearing as the "people's emperor." Maria Theresa, on the other hand, had been regal and aristocratic. The problem was that she had also been beloved, an empress who ruled wisely after years of learning the hard way. If you have the kind of intelligence and instinct that will point you in the right direction, playing the rebel will not be dangerous. But if you are mediocre, as Joseph II was in comparison to his mother, you are better off learning from your predecessor's knowledge and experience, which are based on something real.

Finally, it is often wise to keep an eye on the young, your future rivals in power. Just as you try to rid yourself of your father, they will soon play the same trick on you, denigrating everything you have accomplished. Just as you rise by rebelling against the past, keep an eye on those rising from below, and never give them the chance to do the same to you.

The great Baroque artist and architect Pietro Bernini was a master at sniffing out younger potential rivals and keeping them in his shadow. One day a young stonemason named Francesco Borromini showed Bernini his architectural sketches. Recognizing his talent immediately, Bernini instantly hired Borromini as his assistant, which delighted the young man but was actually only a tactic to keep him close at hand, so that he could play psychological games on him and create in him a kind of inferiority complex. And indeed, despite Borromini's brilliance, Bernini has the greater fame. His strategy with Borromini he made a lifelong practice: Fearing that the great sculptor Alessandro Algardi, for example, would eclipse him in fame, he arranged it so that Algardi could only find work as his assistant. And any assistant who rebelled against Bernini and tried to strike out on his own would find his career ruined.

42

STRIKE THE SHEPHERD

AND THE SHEEP

WILL SCATTER

JUDGMENT

Trouble can often be traced to a single strong individual—the stirrer, the arrogant underling, the poisoner of goodwill. If you allow such people room to operate, others will succumb to their influence. Do not wait for the troubles they cause to multiply, do not try to negotiate with them—they are irredeemable. Neutralize their influence by isolating or banishing them. Strike at the source of the trouble and the sheep will scatter.

OBSERVANCE OF THE LAW I

Near the end of the sixth century B.C., the city-state of Athens overthrew the series of petty tyrants who had dominated its politics for decades. It established instead a democracy that was to last over a century, a democracy that became the source of its power and its proudest achievement. But as the democracy evolved, so did a problem the Athenians had never faced: How to deal with those who did not concern themselves with the cohesion of a small city surrounded by enemies, who did not work for its greater glory, but thought of only themselves and their own ambitions and petty intrigues? The Athenians understood that these people, if left alone, would sow dissension, divide the city into factions, and stir up anxieties, all of which could lead to the ruin of their democracy.

Violent punishment no longer suited the new, civilized order that Athens had created. Instead the citizens found another, more satisfying, and less brutal way to deal with the chronically selfish: Every year they would gather in the marketplace and write on a piece of earthenware, an *ostrakon,* the name of an individual they wanted to see banished from the city for ten years. If a particular name appeared on six thousand ballots, that person would instantly be exiled. If no one received six thousand votes, the person with the most *ostraka* recording his name would suffer the ten-year "ostracism." This ritual expulsion became a kind of festival— what a joy to be able to banish those irritating, anxiety-inducing individuals who wanted to rise above the group they should have served.

In 490 B.C., Aristides, one of the great generals of Athenian history, helped defeat the Persians at the battle of Marathon. Meanwhile, off the battlefield, his fairness as a judge had earned him the nickname "The Just." But as the years went by the Athenians came to dislike him. He made such a show of his righteousness, and this, they believed, disguised his feelings of superiority and scorn for the common folk. His omnipresence in Athenian politics became obnoxious; the citizens grew tired of hearing him called "The Just." They feared that this was just the type of man—judgmental, haughty—who would eventually stir up fierce divisions among them. In 482 B.C., despite Aristides' invaluable expertise in the continuing war with the Persians, they collected the *ostraka* and had him banished.

After Aristides' ostracism, the great general Themistocles emerged as the city's premier leader. But his many honors and victories went to his head, and he too became arrogant and overbearing, constantly reminding the Athenians of his triumphs in battle, the temples he had built, the dangers he had fended off. He seemed to be saying that without him the city would come to ruin. And so, in 472 B.C., Themistocles' name was filled in on the *ostraka* and the city was rid of his poisonous presence.

The greatest political figure in fifth-century Athens was undoubtedly Pericles. Although several times threatened with ostracism, he avoided that fate by maintaining close ties with the people. Perhaps he had learned a lesson as a child from his favorite tutor, the incomparable Damon, who excelled above all other Athenians in his intelligence, his musical skills, and his rhetorical abilities. It was Damon who had trained Pericles in the arts of ruling. But he, too, suffered ostracism, for his superior airs and his insulting manner toward the commoners stirred up too much resentment.

Toward the end of the century there lived a man named Hyperbolus. Most writers of the time describe him as the city's most worthless citizen: He did not care what anyone thought of him, and slandered whomever he disliked. He amused some, but irritated many more. In 417 B.C., Hyperbolus saw an opportunity to stir up anger against the two leading politicians of the time, Alcibiades and Nicias. He hoped that one of the two would be ostracized and that he would rise in that man's place. His campaign seemed likely to succeed: The Athenians disliked Alcibiades' flamboyant and carefree lifestyle, and were wary of Nicias' wealth and aloofness. They seemed certain to ostracize one or the other. But Alcibiades and Nicias, although they were otherwise enemies, pooled their resources and managed to turn the ostracism on Hyperbolus instead. His obnoxiousness, they argued, could only be terminated by banishment.

Earlier sufferers of ostracism had been formidable, powerful men. Hyperbolus, however, was a low buffoon, and with his banishment the Athenians felt that ostracism had been degraded. And so they ended the practice that for nearly a hundred years had been one of the keys to keeping the peace within Athens.

Interpretation

The ancient Athenians had social instincts unknown today—the passage of centuries has blunted them. Citizens in the true sense of the word, the Athenians sensed the dangers posed by asocial behavior, and saw how such behavior often disguises itself in other forms: the holier-than-thou attitude that silently seeks to impose its standards on others; overweening ambition at the expense of the common good; the flaunting of superiority; quiet scheming; terminal obnoxiousness. Some of these behaviors would eat away at the city's cohesion by creating factions and sowing dissension, others would ruin the democratic spirit by making the common citizen feel inferior and envious. The Athenians did not try to reeducate people who acted in these ways, or to absorb them somehow into the group, or to impose a violent punishment that would only create other problems. The solution was quick and effective: Get rid of them.

Within any group, trouble can most often be traced to a single source, the unhappy, chronically dissatisfied one who will always stir up dissension and infect the group with his or her ill ease. Before you know what hit you the dissatisfaction spreads. Act before it becomes impossible to disentangle one strand of misery from another, or to see how the whole thing started. First, recognize troublemakers by their overbearing presence, or by their complaining nature. Once you spot them do not try to reform them or appease them—that will only make things worse. Do not attack them, whether directly or indirectly, for they are poisonous in nature and will work underground to destroy you. Do as the Athenians did: Banish them before it is too late. Separate them from the group before they become the eye of a whirlpool. Do not give them time to stir up anxieties and sow discontent; do not give them room to move. Let one person suffer so that the rest can live in peace.

> When the tree falls, the monkeys scatter.
> *Chiness saying*

OBSERVANCE OF THE LAW II

In 1296 the cardinals of the Catholic Church met in Rome to select a new pope. They chose Cardinal Gaetani, for he was incomparably shrewd; such a man would make the Vatican a great power. Taking the name Boniface VIII, Gaetani soon proved he deserved the cardinals' high opinion of him: He plotted his moves carefully in advance, and stopped at nothing to get his way. Once in power, Boniface quickly crushed his rivals and unified the Papal States. The European powers began to fear him, and sent delegates to negotiate with him. The German King Albrecht of Austria even yielded some territory to Boniface. All was proceeding according to the pope's plan.

One piece did not fall into place, however, and that was Tuscany, the richest part of Italy. If Boniface could conquer Florence, Tuscany's most powerful city, the region would be his. But Florence was a proud republic, and would be hard to defeat. The pope had to play his cards skillfully.

Florence was divided by two rival factions, the Blacks and the Whites. The Whites were the merchant families that had recently and quickly risen to power and wealth; the Blacks were the older money. Because of their popularity with the people, the Whites retained control of the city, to the Blacks' increasing resentment. The feud between the two grew steadily more bitter.

Here Boniface saw his chance: He would plot to help the Blacks take over the city, and Florence would be in his pocket. And as he studied the situation he began to focus on one man, Dante Alighieri, the celebrated writer, poet, and ardent supporter of the Whites. Dante had always been interested in politics. He believed passionately in the republic, and often chastised his fellow citizens for their lack of spine. He also happened to be the city's most eloquent public speaker. In 1300, the year Boniface began plotting to take over Tuscany, Dante's fellow citizens had voted him in to Florence's highest elected position, making him one of the city's six priors. During his six-month term in the post, he had stood firmly against the Blacks and against all of the pope's attempts to sow disorder.

By 1301, however, Boniface had a new plan: He called in Charles de Valois, powerful brother of the king of France, to help bring order to Tuscany. As Charles marched through northern Italy, and Florence seethed with anxiety and fear, Dante quickly emerged as the man who could rally

THE WOLVES AND THE SHEEP

Once upon a time, the wolves sent an embassy to the sheep, desiring that there might be peace between them for the time to come. "Why," said they, "should we be for ever waging this deadly strife? Those wicked dogs are the cause of all; they are incessantly barking at us, and provoking us. Send them away, and there will be no longer any obstacle to our eternal friendship and peace." The silly sheep listened, the dogs were dismissed, and the flock, thus deprived of their best protectors, became an easy prey to their treacherous enemy.

FABLES,
AESOP,
SIXTH CENTURY B.C.

the people, arguing vehemently against appeasement and working desperately to arm the citizens and to organize resistance against the pope and
his puppet French prince. By hook or by crook, Boniface had to neutralize
Dante. And so, even as on the one hand he threatened Florence with
Charles de Valois, on the other he held out the olive branch, the possibility of negotiations, hoping Dante would take the bait. And indeed the Florentines decided to send a delegation to Rome and try to negotiate a
peace. To head the mission, predictably, they chose Dante.

Some warned the poet that the wily pope was setting up a trap to lure
him away, but Dante went to Rome anyway, arriving as the French army
stood before the gates of Florence. He felt sure that his eloquence and reason would win the pope over and save the city. Yet when the pope met the
poet and the Florentine delegates, he instantly intimidated them, as he did
so many. "Fall on your knees before me!" he bellowed at their first meeting. "Submit to me! I tell you that in all truth I have nothing in my heart
but to promote your peace." Succumbing to his powerful presence, the
Florentines listened as the pope promised to look after their interests. He
then advised them to return home, leaving one of their members behind
to continue the talks. Boniface signaled that the man to stay was to be
Dante. He spoke with the utmost politeness, but in essence it was an order.

And so Dante remained in Rome. And while he and the pope continued their dialogue, Florence fell apart. With no one to rally the Whites,
and with Charles de Valois using the pope's money to bribe and sow dissension, the Whites disintegrated, some arguing for negotiations, others
switching sides. Facing an enemy now divided and unsure of itself, the
Blacks easily destroyed them within weeks, exacting violent revenge on
them. And once the Blacks stood firmly in power, the pope finally dismissed Dante from Rome.

The Blacks ordered Dante to return home to face accusations and
stand trial. When the poet refused, the Blacks condemned him to be
burned to death if he ever set foot in Florence again. And so Dante began
a miserable life of exile, wandering through Italy, disgraced in the city that
he loved, never to return to Florence, even after his death.

Interpretation

Boniface knew that if he only had a pretext to lure Dante away, Florence
would crumble. He played the oldest card in the book—threatening with
one hand while holding out the olive branch with the other—and Dante
fell for it. Once the poet was in Rome, the pope kept him there for as long
as it took. For Boniface understood one of the principal precepts in the
game of power: One resolute person, one disobedient spirit, can turn a
flock of sheep into a den of lions. So he isolated the troublemaker. Without the backbone of the city to keep them together, the sheep quickly
scattered.

Learn the lesson: Do not waste your time lashing out in all directions
at what seems to be a many-headed enemy. Find the one head that mat-

ters—the person with willpower, or smarts, or, most important of all, charisma. Whatever it costs you, lure this person away, for once he is absent his powers will lose their effect. His isolation can be physical (banishment or absence from the court), political (narrowing his base of support), or psychological (alienating him from the group through slander and insinuation). Cancer begins with a single cell; excise it before it spreads beyond cure.

KEYS TO POWER

In the past, an entire nation would be ruled by a king and his handful of ministers. Only the elite had any power to play with. Over the centuries, power has gradually become more and more diffused and democratized. This has created, however, a common misperception that groups no longer have centers of power—that power is spread out and scattered among many people. Actually, however, power has changed in its numbers but not in its essence. There may be fewer mighty tyrants commanding the power of life and death over millions, but there remain thousands of petty tyrants ruling smaller realms, and enforcing their will through indirect power games, charisma, and so on. In every group, power is concentrated in the hands of one or two people, for this is one area in which human nature will never change: People will congregate around a single strong personality like planets orbiting a sun.

To labor under the illusion that this kind of power center no longer exists is to make endless mistakes, waste energy and time, and never hit the target. Powerful people never waste time. Outwardly they may play along with the game—pretending that power is shared among many—but inwardly they keep their eyes on the inevitable few in the group who hold the cards. These are the ones they work on. When troubles arise, they look for the underlying cause, the single strong character who started the stirring and whose isolation or banishment will settle the waters again.

In his family-therapy practice, Dr. Milton H. Erickson found that if the family dynamic was unsettled and dysfunctional there was inevitably one person who was the stirrer, the troublemaker. In his sessions he would symbolically isolate this rotten apple by seating him or her apart from the others, if only by a few feet. Slowly the other family members would see the physically separate person as the source of their difficulty. Once you recognize who the stirrer is, pointing it out to other people will accomplish a great deal. Understanding who controls the group dynamic is a critical realization. Remember: Stirrers thrive by hiding in the group, disguising their actions among the reactions of others. Render their actions visible and they lose their power to upset.

A key element in games of strategy is isolating the enemy's power. In chess you try to corner the king. In the Chinese game of go you try to isolate the enemy's forces in small pockets, rendering them immobile and ineffectual. It is often better to isolate your enemies than to destroy them—you seem less brutal. The result, though, is the same, for in the game of power, isolation spells death.

The most effective form of isolation is somehow to separate your victims from their power base. When Mao Tse-tung wanted to eliminate an enemy in the ruling elite, he did not confront the person directly; he silently and stealthily worked to isolate the man, divide his allies and turn them away from him, shrink his support. Soon the man would vanish on his own.

Presence and appearance have great import in the game of power. To seduce, particularly in the beginning stages, you need to be constantly present, or create the feeling that you are; if you are often out of sight, the charm will wear off. Queen Elizabeth's prime minister, Robert Cecil, had two main rivals: the queen's favorite, the Earl of Essex, and her former favorite, Sir Walter Raleigh. He contrived to send them both on a mission against Spain; with them away from the court he managed to wrap his tentacles around the queen, secure his position as her top adviser and weaken her affection for Raleigh and the earl. The lesson here is twofold: First, your absence from the court spells danger for you, and you should never leave the scene in a time of turmoil, for your absence can both symbolize and induce a loss of power; second, and on the other hand, luring your enemies away from the court at critical moments is a great ploy.

Isolation has other strategic uses. When trying to seduce people, it is often wise to isolate them from their usual social context. Once isolated they are vulnerable to you, and your presence becomes magnified. Similarly, con artists often look for ways to isolate their marks from their normal social milieux, steering them into new environments in which they are no longer comfortable. Here they feel weak, and succumb to deception more easily. Isolation, then, can prove a powerful way of bringing people under your spell to seduce or swindle them.

You will often find powerful people who have alienated themselves from the group. Perhaps their power has gone to their heads, and they consider themselves superior; perhaps they have lost the knack of communicating with ordinary folk. Remember: This makes them vulnerable. Powerful though they be, people like this can be turned to use.

The monk Rasputin gained his power over Czar Nicholas and Czarina Alexandra of Russia through their tremendous isolation from the people. Alexandra in particular was a foreigner, and especially alienated from everyday Russians; Rasputin used his peasant origins to insinuate himself into her good graces, for she desperately wanted to communicate with her subjects. Once in the court's inner circle, Rasputin made himself indispensable and attained great power. Heading straight for the center, he aimed for the one figure in Russia who commanded power (the czarina dominated her husband), and found he had no need to isolate her for the work was already done. The Rasputin strategy can bring you great power: Always search out people who hold high positions yet who find themselves isolated on the board. They are like apples falling into your lap, easily seduced, and able to catapult you into power yourself.

Finally, the reason you strike at the shepherd is because such an action will dishearten the sheep beyond any rational measure. When Hernando Cortés and Francisco Pizarro led their tiny forces against the Aztec and Incan empires, they did not make the mistake of fighting on several fronts, nor were they intimidated by the numbers arrayed against them; they captured the kings, Moctezuma and Atahualpa. Vast empires fell into their hands. With the leader gone the center of gravity is gone; there is nothing to revolve around and everything falls apart. Aim at the leaders, bring them down, and look for the endless opportunities in the confusion that will ensue.

Image: A Flock of Fatted Sheep. Do not waste precious time trying to steal a sheep or two; do not risk life and limb by setting upon the dogs that guard the flock. Aim at the shepherd. Lure him away and the dogs will follow. Strike him down and the flock will scatter—you can pick them off one by one.

Authority: If you draw a bow, draw the strongest. If you use an arrow, use the longest. To shoot a rider, first shoot his horse. To catch a gang of bandits, first capture its leader. Just as a country has its border, so the killing of men has its limits. If the enemy's attack can be stopped [with a blow to the head], why have any more dead and wounded than necessary? (Chinese poet Tu Fu, Tang dynasty, eighth century)

REVERSAL

"Any harm you do to a man should be done in such a way that you need not fear his revenge," writes Machiavelli. If you act to isolate your enemy, make sure he lacks the means to repay the favor. If you apply this Law, in other words, apply it from a position of superiority, so that you have nothing to fear from his resentment.

Andrew Johnson, Abraham Lincoln's successor as U.S. president, saw Ulysses S. Grant as a troublesome member of his government. So he isolated Grant, as a prelude to forcing him out. This only enraged the great general, however, who responded by forming a support base in the Republican party and going on to become the next president. It would have been far wiser to keep a man like Grant in the fold, where he could do less harm, than to make him revengeful. And so you may often find it better to keep people on your side, where you can watch them, than to risk creating an angry enemy. Keeping them close, you can secretly whittle away at their support base, so that when the time comes to cut them loose they will fall fast and hard without knowing what hit them.

43

WORK ON THE HEARTS

AND MINDS OF OTHERS

JUDGMENT

Coercion creates a reaction that will eventually work against you. You must seduce others into wanting to move in your direction. A person you have seduced becomes your loyal pawn. And the way to seduce others is to operate on their individual psychologies and weaknesses. Soften up the resistant by working on their emotions, playing on what they hold dear and what they fear. Ignore the hearts and minds of others and they will grow to hate you.

TRANSGRESSION OF THE LAW

CYRUS'S RUSE

Thinking of the means by which he could most effectively persuade the Persians to revolt, [Cyrus's] deliberations led him to adopt the following plan, which he found best suited to his purpose. He wrote on a roll of parchment that Astyages had appointed him to command the Persian army; then he summoned an assembly of the Persians, opened the roll in their presence and read out what he had written. "And now, he added, I have an order for you: every man is to appear on parade with a billhook...." The order was obeyed. All the men assembled with their billhooks, and Cyrus's next command was that before the day was out they should clear a certain piece of rough land full of thorn-bushes, about eighteen or twenty furlongs square. This too was done, whereupon Cyrus issued the further order that they should present themselves again on the following day, after having taken a bath. Meanwhile, Cyrus collected and slaughtered all his father's goats, sheep, and oxen in preparation for entertaining the whole Persian army at a banquet, together with the best wine and bread he could procure. The next day the guests assembled, and were

Near the end of the reign of Louis XV, all of France seemed desperate for change. When the king's grandson and chosen successor, the future Louis XVI, married the fifteen-year-old daughter of the empress of Austria, the French caught a glimpse of the future that seemed hopeful. The young bride, Marie-Antoinette, was beautiful and full of life. She instantly changed the mood of the court, which was rank with Louis XV's debaucheries; even the common people, who had yet to see her, talked excitedly of Marie-Antoinette. The French had grown disgusted with the series of mistresses who had dominated Louis XV, and they looked forward to serving their new queen. In 1773, when Marie-Antoinette publicly rode through the streets of Paris for the first time, applauding crowds swarmed around her carriage. "How fortunate," she wrote her mother, "to be in a position in which one can gain widespread affection at so little cost."

In 1774 Louis XV died and Louis XVI took the throne. As soon as Marie-Antoinette became queen she abandoned herself to the pleasures she loved the most—ordering and wearing the most expensive gowns and jewelry in the realm; sporting the most elaborate hair in history, her sculpted coiffures rising as much as three feet above her head; and throwing a constant succession of masked balls and fêtes. All of these whims she paid for on credit, never concerning herself with the cost or who paid the bills.

Marie-Antoinette's greatest pleasure was the creation and designing of a private Garden of Eden at the Petit Trianon, a château on the grounds of Versailles with its own woods. The gardens at the Petit Trianon were to be as "natural" as possible, including moss applied by hand to the trees and rocks. To heighten the pastoral effect, the queen employed peasant milk-maids to milk the finest-looking cows in the realm; launderers and cheese-makers in special peasant outfits she helped design; shepherds to tend sheep with silk ribbons around their necks. When she inspected the barns, she would watch her milkmaids squeezing milk into porcelain vases made at the royal ceramic works. To pass the time, Marie-Antoinette would gather flowers in the woods around the Petit Trianon, or watch her "good peasants" doing their "chores." The place became a separate world, its community limited to her chosen favorites.

With each new whim, the cost of maintaining the Petit Trianon soared. Meanwhile, France itself was deteriorating: There was famine and wide-spread discontent. Even socially insulated courtiers seethed with resentment—the queen treated them like children. Only her favorites mattered, and these were becoming fewer and fewer. But Marie-Antoinette did not concern herself with this. Not once throughout her reign did she read a minister's report. Not once did she tour the provinces and rally the people to her side. Not once did she mingle among the Parisians, or receive a delegation from them. She did none of these things because as queen she felt the people owed her their affection, and she was not required to love them in return.

In 1784 the queen became embroiled in a scandal. As part of an elaborate swindle, the most expensive diamond necklace in Europe had been purchased under her name, and during the swindlers' trial her lavish lifestyle became public: People heard about the money she spent on jewels and dresses and masked dances. They gave her the nickname "Madame Deficit," and from then on she became the focus of the people's growing resentment. When she appeared in her box at the opera the audience greeted her with hisses. Even the court turned against her. For while she had been running up her huge expenditures, the country was headed for ruin.

Five years later, in 1789, an unprecedented event took place: the beginning of the French Revolution. The queen did not worry—let the people have their little rebellion, she seemed to think; it would soon quiet down and she would be able to resume her life of pleasure. That year the people marched on Versailles, forcing the royal family to quit the palace and take residence in Paris. This was a triumph for the rebels, but it offered the queen an opportunity to heal the wounds she had opened and establish contact with the people. The queen, however, had not learned her lesson: Not once would she leave the palace during her stay in Paris. Her subjects could rot in hell for all she cared.

In 1792 the royal couple was moved from the palace to a prison, as the revolution officially declared the end of the monarchy. The following year Louis XVI was tried, found guilty, and guillotined. As Marie-Antoinette awaited the same fate, hardly a soul came to her defense—not one of her former friends in the court, not one of Europe's other monarchs (who, as members of their own countries' royal families, had all the reason in the world to show that revolution did not pay), not even her own family in Austria, including her brother, who now sat on the throne. She had become the world's pariah. In October of 1793, she finally knelt at the guillotine, unrepentant and defiant to the bitter end.

Interpretation

From early on, Marie-Antoinette acquired the most dangerous of attitudes: As a young princess in Austria she was endlessly flattered and cajoled. As the future queen of the French court she was the center of everyone's attention. She never learned to charm or please other people, to become attuned to their individual psychologies. She never had to work to get her way, to use calculation or cunning or the arts of persuasion. And like everyone who is indulged from an early age, she evolved into a monster of insensitivity.

Marie-Antoinette became the focus of an entire country's dissatisfaction because it is so infuriating to meet with a person who makes no effort to seduce you or attempt to persuade you, even if only for the purpose of deception. And do not imagine that she represents a bygone era, or that she is even rare. Her type is today more common than ever. Such types live in their own bubble—they seem to feel they are born kings and queens, and that attention is owed them. They do not consider anyone else's nature, but bulldoze over people with the self-righteous arrogance of a Marie-Antoinette. Pampered and indulged as children, as adults they still believe

told to sit down on the grass and enjoy themselves. After the meal Cyrus asked them which they preferred— yesterday's work or today's amusement; and they replied that it was indeed a far cry from the previous day's misery to their present pleasures. This was the answer which Cyrus wanted; he seized upon it at once and proceeded to lay bare what he had in mind. "Men of Persia," he said, "listen to me: obey my orders, and you will be able to enjoy a thousand pleasures as good as this without ever turning your hands to menial labor; but, if you disobey, yesterday's task will be the pattern of innumerable others you will be forced to perform. Take my advice and win your freedom. I am the man destined to undertake your liberation, and it is my belief that you are a match for the Medes in war as in everything else. It is the truth I tell you. Do not delay, but fling off the yoke of Astyages at once."

The Persians had long resented their subjection to the Medes. At last they had found a leader, and welcomed with enthusiasm the prospect of liberty.... On the present occasion the Persians under Cyrus rose against the Medes and from then onwards were masters of Asia.

THE HISTORIES,
HERODOTUS,
FIFTH CENTURY B.C..

that everything must come to them; convinced of their own charm, they make no effort to charm, seduce, or gently persuade.

In the realm of power, such attitudes are disastrous. At all times you must attend to those around you, gauging their particular psychology, tailoring your words to what you know will entice and seduce them. This requires energy and art. The higher your station, the greater the need to remain attuned to the hearts and minds of those below you, creating a base of support to maintain you at the pinnacle. Without that base, your power will teeter, and at the slightest change of fortune those below will gladly assist in your fall from grace.

OBSERVANCE OF THE LAW

In A.D. 225, Chuko Liang, master strategist and chief minister to the ruler of Shu in ancient China, confronted a dangerous situation. The kingdom of Wei had mounted an all-out attack on Shu from the north. More dangerous still, Wei had formed an alliance with the barbarous states to the south of Shu, led by King Menghuo. Chuko Liang had to deal with this second menace from the south before he could hope to fend off Wei in the north.

As Chuko Liang prepared to march south against the barbarians, a wise man in his camp offered him advice. It would be impossible, this man said, to pacify the region by force. Liang would probably beat Menghuo, but as soon as he headed north again to deal with Wei, Menghuo would reinvade. "It is better to win hearts," said the wise man, "than cities; better to battle with hearts than with weapons. I hope you will succeed in winning the hearts of these people." "You read my thoughts," responded Chuko Liang.

As Liang expected, Menghuo launched a powerful attack. But Liang laid a trap and managed to capture a large part of Menghuo's army, including the king himself. Instead of punishing or executing his prisoners, however, he separated the soldiers from their king, had their shackles removed, regaled them with food and wine, and then addressed them. "You are all upright men," he said. "I believe you all have parents, wives, and children waiting for you at home. They are doubtless shedding bitter tears at your fate. I am going to release you, so that you can return home to your loved ones and comfort them." The men thanked Liang with tears in their eyes; then he sent for Menghuo. "If I release you," asked Liang, "what will you do?" "I will pull my army together again," answered the king, "and lead it against you to a decisive battle. But if you capture me a second time, I will bow to your superiority." Not only did Liang order Menghuo released, he gave him a gift of a horse and saddle. When angry lieutenants wondered why he did this, Liang told them, "I can capture that man as easily as I can take something out of my pocket. I am trying to win his heart. When I do, peace will come of itself here in the south."

As Menghuo had said he would, he attacked again. But his own officers, whom Liang had treated so well, rebelled against him, captured him, and turned him over to Liang, who asked him again the same question as before. Menghuo replied that he had not been beaten fairly, but merely betrayed by his own officers; he would fight again, but if captured a third time he would bow to Liang's superiority.

Over the following months Liang outwitted Menghuo again and again, capturing him a third, a fourth, and a fifth time. On each occasion Menghuo's troops grew more dissatisfied. Liang had treated them with respect; they had lost their heart for fighting. But every time Chuko Liang asked Menghuo to yield, the great king would come up with another excuse: You tricked me, I lost through bad luck, on and on. If you capture me again, he would promise, I swear I will not betray you. And so Liang would let him go.

When he captured Menghuo for the sixth time, he asked the king the same question again. "If you capture me a seventh time," the king replied, "I shall give you my loyalty and never rebel again." "Very well," said Liang. "But if I capture you again, I will not release you."

Now Menghuo and his soldiers fled to a far corner of their kingdom, the region of Wuge. Defeated so many times, Menghuo had only one hope left: He would ask the help of King Wutugu of Wuge, who had an immense and ferocious army. Wutugu's warriors wore an armor of tightly woven vines soaked in oil, then dried to an impenetrable hardness. With Menghuo at his side, Wutugu marched this mighty army against Liang, and this time the great strategist seemed frightened, leading his men in a hurried retreat. But he was merely leading Wutugu into a trap: He cornered the king's men in a narrow valley, then lit fires set all around them. When the fires reached the soldiers Wutugu's whole army burst into flame—the oil in their armor, of course, being highly flammable. All of them perished.

Liang had managed to separate Menghuo and his entourage from the carnage in the valley, and the king found himself a captive for the seventh time. After this slaughter Liang could not bear to face his prisoner again. He sent a messenger to the captured king: "He has commissioned me to release you. Mobilize another army against him, if you can, and try once more to defeat him." Sobbing, the king fell to the ground, crawled to Liang on his hands and knees, and prostrated himself at his feet. "Oh great minister," cried Menghuo, "yours is the majesty of Heaven. We men of the south will never again offer resistance to your rule." "Do you now yield?" asked Liang. "I, my sons, and my grandsons are deeply moved by Your Honor's boundless, life-giving mercy. How could we not yield?"

Liang honored Menghuo with a great banquet, reestablished him on the throne, restored his conquered lands to his rule, then returned north with his army, leaving no occupying force. Liang never came back—he had no need to: Menghuo had become his most devoted and unshakable ally.

Interpretation

Chuko Liang had two options: Try to defeat the barbarians in the south with one crushing blow, or patiently and slowly win them to his side over time. Most people more powerful than their enemy grab the first option and never consider the second, but the truly powerful think far ahead: The

The men who have changed the universe have never gotten there by working on leaders, but rather by moving the masses. Working on leaders is the method of intrigue and only leads to secondary results. Working on the masses, however, is the stroke of genius that changes the face of the world.
NAPOLEON BONAPARTE, 1769–1821

LIFE OF ALEXANDER THE GREAT

This long and painful pursuit of Darius—for in eleven days he marched 33 hundred furlongs—harassed his soldiers so that most of them were ready to give it up, chiefly for want of water. While they were in this distress, it happened that some Macedonians who had fetched water in skins upon their mules from a river they had found out came about noon to the place where Alexander was, and seeing him almost choked with thirst, presently filled a helmet and offered it him. . . . Then he took the helmet into his hands, and looking round about, when he saw all those who were near him stretching their heads out and looking earnestly after the drink, he returned it again with thanks

without tasting a
drop of it.
"For," said he, "if I
alone should drink, the
rest will be out of
heart." The soldiers no
sooner took notice of
his temperance and
magnanimity upon this
occasion, but they one
and all cried out to him
to lead them forward
boldly, and began
whipping on their
horses. For whilst they
had such a king they
said they defied both
weariness and thirst,
and looked upon them-
selves to be little less
than immortal.

THE LIFE OF
ALEXANDER THE GREAT,
PLUTARCH,
c. A.D. 46–120

first option may be quick and easy, but over time it brews ugly emotions in the hearts of the vanquished. Their resentment turns to hatred; such animosity keeps you on edge—you spend your energy protecting what you have gained, growing paranoid and defensive. The second option, though more difficult, not only brings you peace of mind, it converts a potential enemy into a pillar of support.

In all your encounters, take a step back—take the time to calculate and attune yourself to your targets' emotional makeup and psychological weaknesses. Force will only strengthen their resistance. With most people the heart is the key: They are like children, ruled by their emotions. To soften them up, alternate harshness with mercy. Play on their basic fears, and also their loves—freedom, family, etc. Once you break them down, you will have a lifelong friend and fiercely loyal ally.

Governments saw men only in mass; but our men, being irregulars, were not formations, but individuals. . . . Our kingdoms lay in each man's mind.
Seven Pillars of Wisdom, *T.E. Lawrence, 1888–1935*

KEYS TO POWER

In the game of power, you are surrounded by people who have absolutely no reason to help you unless it is in their interest to do so. And if you have nothing to offer their self-interest, you are likely to make them hostile, for they will see in you just one more competitor, one more waster of their time. Those that overcome this prevailing coldness are the ones who find the key that unlocks the stranger's heart and mind, seducing him into their corner, if necessary softening him up for a punch. But most people never learn this side of the game. When they meet someone new, rather than stepping back and probing to see what makes this person unique, they talk about themselves, eager to impose their own willpower and prejudices. They argue, boast, and make a show of their power. They may not know it but they are secretly creating an enemy, a resister, because there is no more infuriating feeling than having your individuality ignored, your own psychology unacknowledged. It makes you feel lifeless and resentful.

Remember: The key to persuasion is softening people up and breaking them down, gently. Seduce them with a two-pronged approach: Work on their emotions and play on their intellectual weaknesses. Be alert to both what separates them from everyone else (their individual psychology) and what they share with everyone else (their basic emotional responses). Aim at the primary emotions—love, hate, jealousy. Once you move their emotions you have reduced their control, making them more vulnerable to persuasion.

When Chuko Liang wanted to dissuade an important general of a rival kingdom from entering into an alliance with Ts'ao Ts'ao, Liang's dreaded enemy, he did not detail Ts'ao Ts'ao's cruelty, or attack him on moral grounds. Instead Liang suggested that Ts'ao Ts'ao was really after the general's beautiful young wife. This hit the general in the gut, and won him over. Mao Tse-tung similarly always appealed to popular emotions, and spoke in the simplest terms. Educated and well-read himself, in his speeches he used visceral metaphors, voicing the public's deepest anxieties and encouraging them to vent their frustrations in public meetings. Rather than arguing the practical aspects of a particular program, he would describe how it would affect them on the most primitive, down-to-earth level. Do not believe that this approach works only with the illiterate and unschooled—it works on one and all. All of us are mortal and face the same dreadful fate, and all of us share the desire for attachment and belonging. Stir up these emotions and you captivate our hearts.

The best way to do this is with a dramatic jolt, of the kind that Chuko Liang created when he fed and released prisoners who expected only the worst from him. Shaking them to the core, he softened their hearts. Play on contrasts like this: Push people to despair, then give them relief. If they expect pain and you give them pleasure, you win their hearts. Creating pleasure of any kind, in fact, will usually bring you success, as will allaying fears and providing or promising security.

Symbolic gestures are often enough to win sympathy and goodwill. A gesture of self-sacrifice, for example—a show that you suffer as those around you do—will make people identify with you, even if your suffering is symbolic or minor and theirs is real. When you enter a group, make a gesture of goodwill; soften the group up for the harsher actions that will follow later.

When T. E. Lawrence was fighting the Turks in the deserts of the Middle East during World War I, he had an epiphany: It seemed to him that conventional warfare had lost its value. The old-fashioned soldier was lost in the enormous armies of the time, in which he was ordered about like a lifeless pawn. Lawrence wanted to turn this around. For him, every soldier's mind was a kingdom he had to conquer. A committed, psychologically motivated soldier would fight harder and more creatively than a puppet.

Lawrence's perception is still more true in the world today, where so many of us feel alienated, anonymous, and suspicious of authority, all of which makes overt power plays and force even more counterproductive and dangerous. Instead of manipulating lifeless pawns, make those on your side convinced and excited by the cause you have enlisted them in; this will not only make your work easier but it will also give you more leeway to deceive them later on. And to accomplish this you need to deal with their individual psychologies. Never clumsily assume that the tactic that worked on one person will necessarily work on another. To find the key that will motivate them, first get them to open up. The more they talk, the more they reveal about their likes and dislikes—the handles and levers to move them with.

The quickest way to secure people's minds is by demonstrating, as simply as possible, how an action will benefit them. Self-interest is the strongest motive of all: A great cause may capture minds, but once the first flush of excitement is over, interest will flag—unless there is something to be gained. Self-interest is the solider foundation. The causes that work best use a noble veneer to cover a blatant appeal to self-interest; the cause seduces but the self-interest secures the deal.

The people who are best at appealing to people's minds are often artists, intellectuals, and those of a more poetic nature. This is because ideas are most easily communicated through metaphors and imagery. It is always good policy, then, to have in your pocket at least one artist or intellectual who can appeal concretely to people's minds. Kings have always kept a stable of writers in their barn: Frederick the Great had his Voltaire (until they quarreled and separated), Napoleon won over Goethe. Conversely, Napoleon III's alienation of writers such as Victor Hugo, whom he exiled from France, contributed to his growing unpopularity and eventual downfall. It is dangerous, then, to alienate those who have powers of expression, and useful to pacify and exploit them.

Finally, learn to play the numbers game. The wider your support base the stronger your power. Understanding that one alienated, disaffected soul can spark a blaze of discontent, Louis XIV made sure to endear himself to the lowest members of his staff. You too must constantly win over more allies on all levels—a time will inevitably come when you will need them.

Image:
The Keyhole.
People build
walls to keep you
out; never force
your way in — you
will find only more
walls within walls.
There are doors in
these walls, doors to
the heart and mind, and
they have tiny key-
holes. Peer through the
keyhole, find the key
that opens the door,
and you have access
to their will with
no ugly signs
of forced
entry.

Authority: The difficulties in the way of persuasion lie in my knowing the heart of the persuaded in order thereby to fit my wording into it. . . . For this reason, whoever attempts persuasion before the throne, must carefully observe the sovereign's feelings of love and hate, his secret wishes and fears, before he can conquer his heart. (Han-fei-tzu, Chinese philosopher, third century B.C.)

REVERSAL

There is no possible reversal to this Law.

DISARM AND INFURIATE

WITH THE MIRROR EFFECT

JUDGMENT

The mirror reflects reality, but it is also the perfect tool for deception: When you mirror your enemies, doing exactly as they do, they cannot figure out your strategy. The Mirror Effect mocks and humiliates them, making them over-react. By holding up a mirror to their psyches, you seduce them with the illusion that you share their values; by holding up a mirror to their actions, you teach them a lesson. Few can resist the power of the Mirror Effect.

MIRROR EFFECTS: Preliminary Typology

Mirrors have the power to disturb us. Gazing at our reflection in the mirror, we most often see what we want to see—the image of ourselves with which we are most comfortable. We tend not to look too closely, ignoring the wrinkles and blemishes. But if we do look hard at the reflected image, we sometimes feel that we are seeing ourselves as others see us, as a person among other people, an object rather than a subject. That feeling makes us shudder—we see ourselves, but from the outside, minus the thoughts, spirit, and soul that fill our consciousness. We are a thing.

In using Mirror Effects we symbolically re-create this disturbing power by mirroring the actions of other people, mimicking their movements to unsettle and infuriate them. Made to feel mocked, cloned, objectlike, an image without a soul, they get angry. Or do the same thing slightly differently and they might feel disarmed—you have perfectly reflected their wishes and desires. This is the narcissistic power of mirrors. In either case, the Mirror Effect unsettles your targets, whether angering or entrancing them, and in that instant you have the power to manipulate or seduce them. The Effect contains great power because it operates on the most primitive emotions.

There are four main Mirror Effects in the realm of power:

The Neutralizing Effect. In ancient Greek mythology, the Gorgon Medusa had serpents for hair, protruding tongue, massive teeth, and a face so ugly that anyone who gazed at her was turned into stone, out of fright. But the hero Perseus managed to slay Medusa by polishing his bronze shield into a mirror, then using the reflection in the mirror to guide him as he crept up and cut off her head without looking at her directly. If the shield in this instance was a mirror, the mirror also was a kind of shield: Medusa could not see Perseus, she saw only her own reflected actions, and behind this screen the hero stole up and destroyed her.

This is the essence of the Neutralizing Effect: Do what your enemies do, following their actions as best you can, and they cannot see what you are up to—they are blinded by your mirror. Their strategy for dealing with you depends on your reacting to them in a way characteristic of you; neutralize it by playing a game of mimicry with them. The tactic has a mocking, even infuriating effect. Most of us remember the childhood experience of someone teasing us by repeating our words exactly—after a while, usually not long, we wanted to punch them in the face. Working more subtly as an adult, you can still unsettle your opponents this way; shielding your own strategy with the mirror, you lay invisible traps, or push your opponents into the trap they planned for you.

This powerful technique has been used in military strategy since the days of Sun-tzu; in our own time it often appears in political campaigning. It is also useful for disguising those situations in which you have no particular strategy yourself. This is the Warrior's Mirror.

A reverse version of the Neutralizing Effect is the Shadow: You shadow your opponents' every move without their seeing you. Use the Shadow to gather information that will neutralize their strategy later on, when you will be able to thwart their every move. The Shadow is effective because to follow the movements of others is to gain valuable insights into their habits and routines. The Shadow is the preeminent device for detectives and spies.

The Narcissus Effect. Gazing at an image in the waters of a pond, the Greek youth Narcissus fell in love with it. And when he found out that the image was his own reflection, and that he therefore could not consummate his love, he despaired and drowned himself. All of us have a similar problem: We are profoundly in love with ourselves, but since this love excludes a love object outside ourselves, it remains continuously unsatisfied and unfulfilled. The Narcissus Effect plays on this universal narcissism: You look deep into the souls of other people; fathom their inmost desires, their values, their tastes, their spirit; and you reflect it back to them, making yourself into a kind of mirror image. Your ability to reflect their psyche gives you great power over them; they may even feel a tinge of love.

This is simply the ability to mimic another person not physically, but psychologically, and it is immensely powerful because it plays upon the unsatisfied self-love of a child. Normally, people bombard us with *their* experiences, *their* tastes. They hardly ever make the effort to see things through our eyes. This is annoying, but it also creates great opportunity: If you can show you understand another person by reflecting their inmost feelings, they will be entranced and disarmed, all the more so because it happens so rarely. No one can resist this feeling of being harmoniously reflected in the outside world, even though you might well be manufacturing it for their benefit, and for deceptive purposes of your own.

The Narcissus Effect works wonders in both social life and business; it gives us both the Seducer's and the Courtier's Mirror.

The Moral Effect. The power of verbal argument is extremely limited, and often accomplishes the opposite of what is intended. As Gracián remarks, "The truth is generally seen, rarely heard." The Moral Effect is a perfect way to demonstrate your ideas through action. Quite simply, you teach others a lesson by giving them a taste of their own medicine.

In the Moral Effect, you mirror what other people have done to you, and do so in a way that makes them realize you are doing to them exactly what they did to you. You make them *feel* that their behavior has been unpleasant, as opposed to hearing you complain and whine about it, which only gets their defenses up. And as they feel the result of their actions mirrored back at them, they realize in the profoundest sense how they hurt or punish others with their unsocial behavior. You objectify the qualities you want them to feel ashamed of and create a mirror in which they can gaze at their follies and learn a lesson about themselves. This technique is often used by educators, psychologists, and anyone who has to deal with unpleasant and unconscious behavior. This is the Teacher's Mirror. Whether or not there is actually anything wrong with the way people have treated you, however, it can often be to your advantage to reflect it back to them in a way that makes them feel guilty about it.

The Hallucinatory Effect. Mirrors are tremendously deceptive, for they create a sense that you are looking at the real world. Actually, though, you are only staring at a piece of glass, which, as everyone knows, cannot show the world exactly as it is: Everything in a mirror is reversed. When Alice goes through the looking glass in Lewis Carroll's book, she enters a world that is back-to-front, and more than just visually.

The Hallucinatory Effect comes from creating a perfect copy of an object, a place, a person. This copy acts as a kind of dummy—people take it for the real thing, because it has the physical appearance of the real thing. This is the preeminent technique of con artists, who strategically mimic the real world to deceive you. It also has applications in any arena that requires camouflage. This is the Deceiver's Mirror.

OBSERVANCES OF MIRROR EFFECTS

Observance I

In February of 1815, the emperor Napoleon escaped from the island of Elba, where he had been imprisoned by the allied forces of Europe, and returned to Paris in a march that stirred the French nation, rallying troops and citizens of all classes to his side and chasing his successor, King Louis XVIII, off the throne. By March, however, having reestablished himself in power, he had to face the fact that France's situation had gravely changed. The country was devastated, he had no allies among the other European nations, and his most loyal and important ministers had deserted him or left the country. Only one man remained from the old regime—Joseph Fouché, his former minister of police.

Napoleon had relied on Fouché to do his dirty work throughout his previous reign, but he had never been able to figure his minister out. He kept a corps of agents to spy on all of his ministers, so that he would always have an edge on them, but no one had gotten anything on Fouché. If suspected of some misdeed, the minister would not get angry or take the accusation personally—he would submit, nod, smile, and change colors chameleonlike, adapting to the requirements of the moment. At first this had seemed somewhat pleasant and charming, but after a while it frustrated Napoleon, who felt outdone by this slippery man. At one time or another he had fired all of his most important ministers, including Talleyrand, but he never touched Fouché. And so, in 1815, back in power and in need of help, he felt he had no choice but to reappoint Fouché as his minister of police.

Several weeks into his new reign, Napoleon's spies told him they be-

*One day Mr. Fox
decided to fork out
And invite old Mrs.
Stork out.
The dinner wasn't
elaborate—
Being habitually mean,
He didn't go in for
haute cuisine—
In fact it consisted of a
shallow plate
Of thin gruel.
Within a minute
Our joker had lapped
his plate clean;
Meanwhile his guest,
fishing away with
her beak,
Got not a morsel in it.
To pay him back for
this cruel Practical
joke, the stork invited
The fox to dinner the
following week.
"I should be
delighted,"
He replied;
"When it comes to
friends I never stand
upon pride."
Punctually on the
day he ran
To his hostess's house
and at once began
Praising everything:
"What taste! What chic!
And the food—done
just to a turn!"
Then sat down with a
hearty appetite
(Foxes are always
ready to eat)
And savored the deli-
cious smell of meat.
It was minced meat and
served—to serve
him right!—
In a long-necked,
narrow-mouthed urn.
The stork, easily
stooping,
Enjoyed her fill
With her long bill;
His snout, though,*

lieved Fouché was in secret contact with ministers of foreign countries, including Metternich of Austria. Afraid that his most valuable minister was
betraying him to his enemies, Napoleon had to find out the truth before it
was too late. He could not confront Fouché directly—in person the man
was as slippery as an eel. He needed hard proof.

This seemed to come in April, when the emperor's private police captured a Viennese gentleman who had come to Paris to pass information on
to Fouché. Ordering the man brought before him, Napoleon threatened to
shoot him then and there unless he confessed; the man broke down and
admitted he had given Fouché a letter from Metternich, written in invisible
ink, arranging for a secret meeting of special agents in Basel. Napoleon accordingly ordered one of his own agents to infiltrate this meeting. If Fouché
was indeed planning to betray him, he would finally be caught red-handed
and would hang.

Napoleon waited impatiently for the agent's return, but to his bewil-
derment the agent showed up days later reporting that he had heard nothing that would implicate Fouché in a conspiracy. In fact it seemed that the
other agents present suspected Fouché of double-crossing *them,* as if he
were working for Napoleon all along. Napoleon did not believe this for an
instant—Fouché had somehow outwitted him again.

The following morning Fouché visited Napoleon, and remarked, "By
the way, sire, I never told you that I had a letter from Metternich a few
days ago; my mind was so full of things of greater moment. Besides, his
emissary omitted to give me the powder needed to make the writing legi-
ble. . . . Here at length is the letter." Sure that Fouché was toying with him,
Napoleon exploded, "You are a traitor, Fouché! I ought to have you
hanged." He continued to harangue Fouché, but could not fire him without
proof. Fouché only expressed amazement at the emperor's words, but inwardly he smiled, for all along he had been playing a mirroring game.

Interpretation

Fouché had known for years that Napoleon kept on top of those around
him by spying on them day and night. The minister had survived this game
by having his own spies spy on Napoleon's spies, thus neutralizing any action Napoleon might take against him. In the case of the meeting in Basel,
he even turned the tables: Knowing about Napoleon's double agent, he set
it up so that it would appear as if Fouché were a loyal double agent too.

Fouché gained power and flourished in a period of great tumult by
mirroring those around him. During the French Revolution he was a radical Jacobin; after the Terror he became a moderate republican; and under
Napoleon he became a committed imperialist whom Napoleon ennobled
and made the duke of Otranto. If Napoleon took up the weapon of digging
up dirt on people, Fouché made sure he had the dirt on Napoleon, as well
as on everyone else. This also allowed him to predict the emperor's plans
and desires, so that he could echo his boss's sentiments before he had even
uttered them. Shielding his actions with a mirror strategy, Fouché could
also plot offensive moves without being caught in the act.

This is the power of mirroring those around you. First, you give people the feeling that you share their thoughts and goals. Second, if they suspect you have ulterior motives, the mirror shields you from them, preventing them from figuring out your strategy. Eventually this will infuriate and unsettle them. By playing the double, you steal their thunder, suck away their initiative, make them feel helpless. You also gain the ability to choose when and how to unsettle them—another avenue to power. And the mirror saves you mental energy: simply echoing the moves of others gives you the space you need to develop a strategy of your own.

being the wrong shape and size, He had to return to his den Empty-bellied, tail dragging, ears drooping, As red in the face as a fox who's been caught by a hen.

SELECTED FABLES,
JEAN DE LA FONTAINE,
1621–1695

Observance II

Early on in his career, the ambitious statesman and general Alcibiades of Athens (450–404 B.C.) fashioned a formidable weapon that became the source of his power. In every encounter with others, he would sense their moods and tastes, then carefully tailor his words and actions to mirror their inmost desires. He would seduce them with the idea that their values were superior to everyone else's, and that his goal was to model himself on them or help them realize their dreams. Few could resist his charm.

The first man to fall under his spell was the philosopher Socrates. Alcibiades represented the opposite of the Socratic ideal of simplicity and uprightness: He lived lavishly and was completely unprincipled. Whenever he met Socrates, however, he mirrored the older man's sobriety, eating simply, accompanying Socrates on long walks, and talking only of philosophy and virtue. Socrates was not completely fooled—he was not unaware of Alcibiades' other life. But that only made him vulnerable to a logic that flattered him: Only in my presence, he felt, does this man submit to a virtuous influence; only I have such power over him. This feeling intoxicated Socrates, who became Alcibiades' fervent admirer and supporter, one day even risking his own life to rescue the young man in battle.

The Athenians considered Alcibiades their greatest orator, for he had an uncanny ability to tune in to his audience's aspirations, and mirror their desires. He made his greatest speeches in support of the invasion of Sicily, which he thought would bring great wealth to Athens and limitless glory to himself. The speeches gave expression to young Athenians' thirst to conquer lands for themselves, rather than living off the victories of their ancestors. But he also tailored his words to reflect older men's nostalgia for the glory years when Athens led the Greeks against Persia, and then went on to create an empire. All Athens now dreamed of conquering Sicily; Alcibiades' plan was approved, and he was made the expedition's commander.

While Alcibiades was leading the invasion of Sicily, however, certain Athenians fabricated charges against him of profaning sacred statues. He knew his enemies would have him executed if he returned home, so at the last minute he deserted the Athenian fleet and defected to Athens's bitter enemy, Sparta. The Spartans welcomed this great man to their side, but they knew his reputation and were wary of him. Alcibiades loved luxury; the Spartans were a warrior people who worshipped austerity, and they were afraid he would corrupt their youth. But much to their relief, the Al-

THE PURLOINED LETTER

When I wish to find out how wise, or how stupid, or how good, or how wicked is any one, or what are his thoughts at the moment, I fashion the expression of my face, as accurately as possible, in accordance with the expression of his, and then wait to see what thoughts or sentiments arise in my mind or heart, as if to match or correspond with the expression.

EDGAR ALLAN POE,
1809–1849

LORENZO DE' MEDICI
SEDUCES THE POPE

*Lorenzo [de' Medici]
lost no opportunity of
increasing the respect
which Pope Innocent
now felt for him and of
gaining his friendship,
if possible his affection.
He took the trouble to
discover the Pope's
tastes and indulged
them accordingly. He
sent him . . . casks of
his favourite wine. . . .
He sent him courteous,
flattering letters in
which he assured him,
when the Pope was ill,
that he felt his suffer-
ings as though they
were his own, in which
he encouraged him
with such fortifying
statements as "a Pope
is what he wills to be,"
and in which, as
though incidentally, he
included his views on
the proper course of
papal policies. Innocent
was gratified by
Lorenzo's attentions
and convinced by his
arguments. . . . So
completely, indeed, did
he come to share his
opinions that, as the
disgruntled Ferrarese
ambassador put it,
"the Pope sleeps with
the eyes of the Magnifi-
cent Lorenzo."*

THE HOUSE
OF MEDICI:
ITS RISE AND FALL,
CHRISTOPHER HIBBERT,
1980

cibiades who arrived in Sparta was not at all what they expected: He wore his hair untrimmed (as they did), took cold baths, ate coarse bread and black broth, and wore simple clothes. To the Spartans this signified that he had come to see their way of life as superior to the Athenian; greater than they were, he had *chosen* to be a Spartan rather than being born one, and should thus be honored above all others. They fell under his spell and gave him great powers. Unfortunately Alcibiades rarely knew how to rein in his charm—he managed to seduce the king of Sparta's wife and make her pregnant. When this became public he once more had to flee for his life.

This time Alcibiades defected to Persia, where he suddenly went from Spartan simplicity to embracing the lavish Persian lifestyle down to the last detail. It was of course immensely flattering to the Persians to see a Greek of Alcibiades' stature prefer their culture over his own, and they showered him with honors, land, and power. Once seduced by the mirror, they failed to notice that behind this shield Alcibiades was playing a double game, se-cretly helping the Athenians in their war with Sparta and thus reingratiat-ing himself with the city to which he desperately wanted to return, and which welcomed him back with open arms in 408 B.C.

Interpretation

Early in his political career, Alcibiades made a discovery that changed his whole approach to power: He had a colorful and forceful personality, but when he argued his ideas strongly with other people he would win over a few while at the same time alienating many more. The secret to gaining as-cendancy over large numbers, he came to believe, was not to impose his colors but to absorb the colors of those around him, like a chameleon. Once people fell for the trick, the deceptions he went on to practice would be invisible to them.

Understand: Everyone is wrapped up in their own narcissistic shell. When you try to impose your own ego on them, a wall goes up, resistance is increased. By mirroring them, however, you seduce them into a kind of narcissistic rapture: They are gazing at a double of their own soul. This double is actually manufactured in its entirety by you. Once you have used the mirror to seduce them, you have great power over them.

It is worth noting, however, the dangers in the promiscuous use of the mirror. In Alcibiades' presence people felt larger, as if their egos had been doubled. But once he left, they felt empty and diminished, and when they saw him mirroring completely different people as totally as he had mir-rored them, they felt not just diminished but betrayed. Alcibiades' overuse of the Mirror Effect made whole peoples feel used, so that he constantly had to flee from one place to another. Indeed Alcibiades so angered the Spartans that they finally had him murdered. He had gone too far. The Se-ducer's Mirror must be used with caution and discrimination.

Observance III

In 1652 the recently widowed Baroness Mancini moved her family from Rome to Paris, where she could count on the influence and protection of her brother Cardinal Mazarin, the French prime minister. Of the baroness's five daughters, four dazzled the court with their beauty and high spirits. These infamously charming nieces of Cardinal Mazarin became known as the Mazarinettes, and soon found themselves invited to all the most important court functions.

One daughter, Marie Mancini, did not share this good fortune, for she lacked the beauty and grace of her sisters—who, along with her mother and even Cardinal Mazarin, eventually came to dislike her, for they felt she spoiled the family image. They tried to persuade her to enter a convent, where she would be less of an embarrassment, but she refused. Instead she applied herself to her studies, learning Latin and Greek, perfecting her French, and practicing her musical skills. On the rare occasions when the family would let her attend court affairs, she trained herself to be an artful listener, sizing people up for their weaknesses and hidden desires. And when she finally met the future King Louis XIV, in 1657 (Louis was seventeen years old, Marie eighteen), she decided that to spite her family and uncle, she would find a way to make this young man fall in love with her.

This was a seemingly impossible task for such a plain-looking girl, but Marie studied the future king closely. She noticed that her sisters' frivolity did not please him, and she sensed that he loathed the scheming and petty politicking that went on all around him. She saw that he had a romantic nature—he read adventure novels, insisted on marching at the head of his armies, and had high ideals and a passion for glory. The court did not feed these fantasies of his; it was a banal, superficial world that bored him.

The key to Louis's heart, Marie saw, would be to construct a mirror reflecting his fantasies and his youthful yearnings for glory and romance. To begin with she immersed herself in the romantic novels, poems, and plays that she knew the young king read voraciously. When Louis began to engage her in conversation, to his delight she would talk of the things that stirred his soul—not this fashion or that piece of gossip, but rather courtly love, the deeds of great knights, the nobility of past kings and heroes. She fed his thirst for glory by creating an image of an august, superior king whom he could aspire to become. She stirred his imagination.

As the future Sun King spent more and more time in Marie's presence, it eventually became clear that he had fallen in love with the least likely young woman of the court. To the horror of her sisters and mother, he showered Marie Mancini with attention. He brought her along on his military campaigns, and made a show of stationing her where she could watch as he marched into battle. He even promised Marie that he would marry her and make her queen.

Mazarin, however, would never allow the king to marry his niece, a woman who could bring France no diplomatic or royal alliances. Louis had to marry a princess of Spain or Austria. In 1658 Louis succumbed to the pressure and agreed to break off the first romantic involvement of his life. He did so with much regret, and at the end of his life he acknowledged that he never loved anyone as much as Marie Mancini.

Wittgenstein had an extraordinary gift for divining the thoughts of the person with whom he was engaged in discussion. While the other struggled to put his thought into words, Wittgenstein would perceive what it was and state it for him. This power of his, which sometimes seemed uncanny, was made possible, I am sure, by his own prolonged and continuous researches.

LUDWIG WITTGENSTEIN:
A MEMOIR,
NORMAN MALCOLM,
1958

The doctor should be opaque to his patients, and like a mirror, should show them nothing but what is shown to him.

SIGMUND FREUD,
1856–1939

Interpretation

Marie Mancini played the seducer's game to perfection. First, she took a step back, to study her prey. Seduction often fails to get past the first step because it is too aggressive; the first move must always be a retreat. By studying the king from a distance Marie saw what distinguished him from others—his high ideals, romantic nature, and snobbish disdain for petty politics. Marie's next step was to make a mirror for these hidden yearnings on Louis's part, letting him glimpse what he himself could be—a godlike king!

This mirror had several functions: Satisfying Louis's ego by giving him a double to look at, it also focused on him so exclusively as to give him the feeling that Marie existed for him alone. Surrounded by a pack of scheming courtiers who only had their own self-interest at heart, he could not fail to be touched by this devotional focus. Finally Marie's mirror set up an ideal for him to live up to: the noble knight of the medieval court. To a soul both romantic and ambitious, nothing could be more intoxicating than to have someone hold up an idealized reflection of him. In effect it was Marie Mancini who created the image of the Sun King—indeed Louis later admitted the enormous part she had played in fashioning his radiant self-image.

This is the power of the Seducer's Mirror: By doubling the tastes and ideals of the target, it shows your attention to his or her psychology, an attention more charming than any aggressive pursuit. Find out what sets the other person apart, then hold up the mirror that will reflect it and bring it out of them. Feed their fantasies of power and greatness by reflecting their ideals, and they will succumb.

Observance IV

In 1538, with the death of his mother, Helena, the eight-year-old future czar Ivan IV (or Ivan the Terrible) of Russia became an orphan. For the next five years he watched as the princely class, the boyars, terrorized the country. Now and then, to mock the young Ivan, they would make him wear a crown and scepter and place him on the throne. When the little boy's feet dangled over the edge of the chair, they would laugh and lift him off it, handing him from man to man in the air, making him feel his helplessness compared to them.

When Ivan was thirteen, he boldly murdered the boyar leader and ascended to the throne. For the next few decades he struggled to subdue the boyars' power, but they continued to defy him. By 1575 his efforts to transform Russia and defeat its enemies had exhausted him. Meanwhile, his subjects were complaining bitterly about his endless wars, his secret police, the unvanquished and oppressive boyars. His own ministers began to question his moves. Finally he had had enough. In 1564 he had temporarily abandoned the throne, forcing his subjects to call him back to power. Now he took the strategy a step further, and abdicated.

To take his place Ivan elevated a general of his, Simeon Bekbulatovich, to the throne. But although Simeon had recently converted to Christianity, he was by birth a Tartar, and his enthronement was an insult to Ivan's subjects, since Russians looked down on the Tartars as inferiors and infidels. Yet Ivan ordered that all Russians, including the boyars, pledge obedience to their new ruler. And while Simeon moved into the Kremlin, Ivan lived in a humble house on Moscow's outskirts, from which he would sometimes visit the palace, bow before the throne, sit among the other boyars, and humbly petition Simeon for favors.

Over time it became clear that Simeon was a kind of king's double. He dressed like Ivan, and acted like Ivan, but he had no real power, since no one would really obey him. The boyars at the court who were old enough to remember taunting Ivan when he was a boy, by placing him on the throne, saw the connection: They had made Ivan feel like a weak pretender, so now he mirrored them by placing a weak pretender of his own on the throne.

For two long years Ivan held the mirror of Simeon up to the Russian people. The mirror said: Your whining and disobedience have made me a czar with no real power, so I will reflect back to you a czar with no real power. You have treated me disrespectfully, so I will do the same to you, making Russia the laughingstock of the world. In 1577, in the name of the Russian people, the chastised boyars once again begged Ivan to return to the throne, which he did. He lived as czar until his death, in 1584, and the conspiracies, complaining, and second-guessing disappeared along with Simeon.

Interpretation

In 1564, after threatening to abdicate, Ivan had been granted absolute powers. But these powers had slowly been chipped away as every sector of society—the boyars, the church, the government—vied for more control. Foreign wars had exhausted the country, internal bickering had increased, and Ivan's attempts to respond had been met with scorn. Russia had turned into a kind of boisterous classroom in which the pupils laughed openly at the teacher. If he raised his voice or complained, he only met more resistance. He had to teach them a lesson, give them a taste of their own medicine. Simeon Bekbulatovich was the mirror he used to do so.

After two years in which the throne had been an object of ridicule and disgust, the Russian people learned their lesson. They wanted their czar back, conceding to him all the dignity and respect that the position should always have commanded. For the rest of his reign, Russia and Ivan got along fine.

Understand: People are locked in their own experiences. When you whine about some insensitivity on their part, they may seem to understand, but inwardly they are untouched and even more resistant. The goal of power is always to lower people's resistance to you. For this you need tricks, and one trick is to teach them a lesson.

Instead of haranguing people verbally, then, create a kind of mirror of their behavior. In doing so you leave them two choices: They can ignore you, or they can start to think about themselves. And even if they ignore you, you will have planted a seed in their unconscious that will eventually take root. When you mirror their behavior, incidentally, do not be afraid to add a touch of caricature and exaggeration, as Ivan did by enthroning a Tartar—it is the little spice in the soup that will open their eyes and make them see the ridiculousness in their own actions.

Observance V

Dr. Milton H. Erickson, a pioneer in strategic psychotherapy, would often educate his patients powerfully but indirectly by creating a kind of mirror effect. Constructing an analogy to make patients see the truth on their own, he would bypass their resistance to change. When Dr. Erickson treated married couples complaining of sexual problems, for instance, he often found that psychotherapy's tradition of direct confrontation and problem-airing only heightened the spouses' resistance and sharpened their differences. Instead, he would draw a husband and wife out on other topics, often banal ones, trying to find an analogy for the sexual conflict.

In one couple's first session, the pair were discussing their eating habits, especially at dinner. The wife preferred the leisurely approach—a drink before the meal, some appetizers, and then a small main course, all at a slow, civilized pace. This frustrated the husband—he wanted to get dinner over quickly and to dig right into the main course, the bigger the better. As the conversation continued, the couple began to catch glimpses of an analogy to their problems in bed. The moment they made this connection, however, Dr. Erickson would change the subject, carefully avoiding a discussion of the real problem.

The couple thought Erickson was just getting to know them and would deal with the problem directly the next time he saw them. But at the end of this first session, Dr. Erickson directed them to arrange a dinner a few nights away that would combine each person's desire: The wife would get the slow meal, including time spent bonding, and the husband would get the big dishes he wanted to eat. Without realizing they were acting under the doctor's gentle guidance, the couple would walk into a mirror of their problem, and in the mirror they would solve their problems themselves, ending the evening just as the doctor had hoped—by mirroring the improved dinner dynamics in bed.

In dealing with more severe problems, such as the schizophrenic's mirror fantasy world of his or her own construction, Dr. Erickson would always try to enter the mirror and work within it. He once treated a hospital inmate who believed he was Jesus Christ—draping sheets around his body, talking in vague parables, and bombarding staff and patients with endless Christian proselytizing. No therapy or drugs seemed to work, until one day Dr. Erickson went up to the young man and said, "I understand you have had experience as a carpenter." Being Christ, the patient had to say that he had had such experience, and Erickson immediately put him to work building bookcases and other useful items, allowing him to wear his Jesus garb. Over the next weeks, as the patient worked on these projects, his mind became less occupied with Jesus fantasies and more focused on his labor. As the carpentry work took precedence, a psychic shift took effect: The religious fantasies remained, but faded comfortably into the background, allowing the man to function in society.

Interpretation

Communication depends on metaphors and symbols, which are the basis of language itself. A metaphor is a kind of mirror to the concrete and real, which it often expresses more clearly and deeply than a literal description does. When you are dealing with the intractable willpower of other people, direct communication often only heightens their resistance.

This happens most clearly when you complain about people's behavior, particularly in sensitive areas such as their lovemaking. You will effect a far more lasting change if, like Dr. Erickson, you construct an analogy, a symbolic mirror of the situation, and guide the other through it. As Christ himself understood, talking in parables is often the best way to teach a lesson, for it allows people to realize the truth on their own.

When dealing with people who are lost in the reflections of fantasy worlds (including a host of people who do not live in mental hospitals), never try to push them into reality by shattering their mirrors. Instead, enter their world and operate inside it, under their rules, gently guiding them out of the hall of mirrors they have entered.

Observance VI

The great sixteenth-century Japanese tea master Takeno Sho-o once passed by a house and noticed a young man watering flowers near his front gate. Two things caught Sho-o's attention—first, the graceful way the man performed his task; and, second, the stunningly beautiful rose of Sharon blossoms that bloomed in the garden. He stopped and introduced himself to the man, whose name was Sen no Rikyu. Sho-o wanted to stay, but he had a prior engagement and had to hurry off. Before he left, however, Rikyu invited him to take tea with him the following morning. Sho-o happily accepted.

When Sho-o opened the garden gate the next day, he was horrified to see that not a single flower remained. More than anything else, he had come to see the rose of Sharon blossoms that he had not had the time to appreciate the day before; now, disappointed, he started to leave, but at the gate he stopped himself, and decided to enter Sen no Rikyu's tea room. Immediately inside, he stopped in his tracks and gazed in astonishment: Before him a vase hung from the ceiling, and in the vase stood a single rose of Sharon blossom, the most beautiful in the garden. Somehow Sen no Rikyu had read his guest's thoughts, and, with this one eloquent gesture, had demonstrated that this day guest and host would be in perfect harmony.

Sen no Rikyu went on to become the most famous tea master of all, and his trademark was this uncanny ability to harmonize himself with his guests' thoughts and to think one step ahead, enchanting them by adapting to their taste.

One day Rikyu was invited to tea by Yamashina Hechigwan, an admirer of the tea ceremony but also a man with a vivid sense of humor. When Rikyu arrived at Hechigwan's home, he found the garden gate shut, so he opened it to look for the host. On the other side of the gate he saw that someone had first dug a ditch, then carefully covered it over with canvas and earth. Realizing that Hechigwan had planned a practical joke, he obligingly walked right into the ditch, muddying his clothes in the process.

Apparently horrified, Hechigwan came running out, and hurried Rikyu to a bath that for some inexplicable reason stood already prepared. After bathing, Rikyu joined Hechigwan in the tea ceremony, which both enjoyed immensely, sharing a laugh about the accident. Later Sen no Rikyu explained to a friend that he had heard about Hechigwan's practical joke beforehand, "But since it should always be one's aim to conform to the wishes of one's host, I fell into the hole knowingly and thus assured the success of the meeting. Tea is by no means mere obsequiousness, but there is no tea where the host and guest are not in harmony with one another." Hechigwan's vision of the dignified Sen no Rikyu at the bottom of a ditch had pleased him endlessly, but Rikyu had gained a pleasure of his own in complying with his host's wish and watching him amuse himself in this way.

Interpretation

Sen no Rikyu was no magician or seer—he watched those around him acutely, plumbing the subtle gestures that revealed a hidden desire, then producing that desire's image. Although Sho-o never spoke of being enchanted by the rose of Sharon blossoms, Rikyu read it in his eyes. If mirroring a person's desires meant falling into a ditch, so be it. Rikyu's power resided in his skillful use of the Courtier's Mirror, which gave him the appearance of an unusual ability to see into other people.

Learn to manipulate the Courtier's Mirror, for it will bring you great power. Study people's eyes, follow their gestures—surer barometers of pain and pleasure than any spoken word. Notice and remember the details—the clothing, the choice of friends, the daily habits, the tossed-out remarks—that reveal hidden and rarely indulged desires. Soak it all in, find out what lies under the surface, then make yourself the mirror of their unspoken selves. That is the key to this power: The other person has not asked for your consideration, has not mentioned his pleasure in the rose of Sharon, and when you reflect it back to him his pleasure is heightened because it is unasked for. Remember: The wordless communication, the indirect compliment, contains the most power. No one can resist the enchantment of the Courtier's Mirror.

Observance VII

Yellow Kid Weil, con artist extraordinaire, used the Deceiver's Mirror in his most brilliant cons. Most audacious of all was his re-creation of a bank in Muncie, Indiana. When Weil read one day that the Merchants Bank in Muncie had moved, he saw an opportunity he could not pass up.

Weil rented out the original Merchants building, which still contained bank furniture, complete with teller windows. He bought money bags, stenciled a bank's invented name on them, filled them with steel washers, and arrayed them impressively behind the teller windows, along with bundles of boodle—real bills hiding newspaper cut to size. For his bank's staff and customers Weil hired gamblers, bookies, girls from local bawdy houses, and other assorted confederates. He even had a local thug pose as a bank dick.

Claiming to be the broker for a certificate investment the bank was offering, Weil would fish the waters and hook the proper wealthy sucker. He would bring this man to the bank and ask to see the president. An "officer" of the bank would tell them that they had to wait, which only heightened the realism of the con—one always has to wait to see the bank president. And as they waited the bank would bustle with banklike activity, as call girls and bookies in disguise floated in and out, making deposits and withdrawals and tipping their hats to the phony bank dick. Lulled by this perfect copy of reality, the sucker would deposit $50,000 into the fake bank without a worry in the world.

Over the years Weil did the same thing with a deserted yacht club, an abandoned brokerage office, a relocated real estate office, and a completely realistic gambling club.

Interpretation

The mirroring of reality offers immense deceptive powers. The right uniform, the perfect accent, the proper props—the deception cannot be deciphered because it is enmeshed in a simulation of reality. People have an intense desire and need to believe, and their first instinct is to trust a well-constructed facade, to mistake it for reality. After all, we cannot go around doubting the reality of everything we see—that would be too exhausting. We habitually accept appearances, and this is a credulity you can use.

In this particular game it is the first moment that counts the most. If your suckers' suspicions are not raised by their first glance at the mirror's reflection, they will stay suppressed. Once they enter your hall of mirrors, they will be unable to distinguish the real from the fake, and it will become easier and easier to deceive them. Remember: Study the world's surfaces and learn to mirror them in your habits, your manner, your clothes. Like a carnivorous plant, to unsuspecting insects you will look like all the other plants in the field.

Authority: The task of a military operation is to accord deceptively with the intentions of the enemy . . . get to what they want first, subtly anticipate them. Maintain discipline and adapt to the enemy. . . . Thus, at first you are like a maiden, so the enemy opens his door; then you are like a rabbit on the loose, so the enemy cannot keep you out. (Sun-tzu, fourth century B.C.)

A WARNING: BEWARE OF MIRRORED SITUATIONS

Mirrors contain great power but also dangerous reefs, including the mirrored situation—a situation that seems to reflect or closely resemble a previous one, mostly in style and surface appearance. You can often back into
such a situation without fully understanding it, while those around you understand it quite well, and compare it and you to whatever happened before. Most often you suffer by the comparison, seeming either weaker than
the previous occupant of your position or else tainted by any unpleasant
associations that person has left behind.

In 1864 the composer Richard Wagner moved to Munich at the behest
of Ludwig II, known variously as the Swan King or the Mad King of
Bavaria. Ludwig was Wagner's biggest fan and most generous patron. The
strength of his support turned Wagner's head—once established in Munich
under the king's protection, he would be able to say and do whatever he
wanted.

Wagner moved into a lavish house, which the king eventually bought
for him. This house was but a stone's throw from the former home of Lola
Montez, the notorious courtesan who had plunged Ludwig II's grandfather
into a crisis that had forced him to abdicate. Warned that he could be infected by this association, Wagner only scoffed—"I am no Lola Montez,"
he said. Soon enough, however, the citizens of Munich began to resent the
favors and money showered on Wagner, and dubbed him "the second
Lola," or "Lolotte." He unconsciously began to tread in Lola's footsteps—
spending money extravagantly, meddling in matters beyond music, even
dabbling in politics and advising the king on cabinet appointments. Meanwhile Ludwig's affection for Wagner seemed intense and undignified for a
king—just like his grandfather's love for Lola Montez.

Eventually Ludwig's ministers wrote him a letter: "Your Majesty now stands at a fateful parting of the ways: you have to choose between the love and respect of your faithful people and the 'friendship' of Richard Wagner." In December of 1865, Ludwig politely asked his friend to leave and never return. Wagner had inadvertently placed himself in Lola Montez's reflection. Once there, everything he did reminded the stolid Bavarians of that dread woman, and there was nothing he could do about it.

Avoid such association-effects like the plague. In a mirrored situation you have little or no control over the reflections and recollections that will be connected to you, and any situation beyond your control is dangerous. Even if the person or event has positive associations, you will suffer from not being able to live up to them, since the past generally appears greater than the present. If you ever notice people associating you with some past event or person, do everything you can to separate yourself from that memory and to shatter the reflection.

PREACH THE NEED

FOR CHANGE, BUT

NEVER REFORM

TOO MUCH AT ONCE

JUDGMENT

Everyone understands the need for change in the abstract, but on the day-to-day level people are creatures of habit. Too much innovation is traumatic, and will lead to revolt. If you are new to a position of power, or an outsider trying to build a power base, make a show of respecting the old way of doing things. If change is necessary, make it feel like a gentle improvement on the past.

TRANSGRESSION OF THE LAW

Sometime in the early 1520s, King Henry VIII of England decided to divorce his wife, Catherine of Aragon, because she had failed to bear him a son, and because he had fallen in love with the young and comely Anne Boleyn. The pope, Clement VII, opposed the divorce, and threatened the king with excommunication. The king's most powerful minister, Cardinal Wolsey, also saw no need for divorce—and his halfhearted support of the king cost him his position and soon his life.

One man in Henry's cabinet, Thomas Cromwell, not only supported him in his desire for a divorce but had an idea for realizing it: a complete break with the past. He convinced the king that by severing ties with Rome and making himself the head of a newly formed English church, he could divorce Catherine and marry Anne. By 1531 Henry saw this as the only solution. To reward Cromwell for his simple but brilliant idea, he elevated this son of a blacksmith to the post of royal councillor.

By 1534 Cromwell had been named the king's secretary, and as the power behind the throne he had become the most powerful man in England. But for him the break with Rome went beyond the satisfaction of the king's carnal desires: He envisioned a new Protestant order in England, with the power of the Catholic Church smashed and its vast wealth in the hands of the king and the government. In that same year he initiated a complete survey of the churches and monasteries of England. And as it turned out, the treasures and moneys that the churches had accumulated over the centuries were far more than he had imagined; his spies and agents came back with astonishing figures.

To justify his schemes, Cromwell circulated stories about the corruption in the English monasteries, their abuse of power, their exploitation of the people they supposedly served. Having won Parliament's support for breaking up the monasteries, he began to seize their holdings and to put them out of existence one by one. At the same time, he began to impose Protestantism, introducing reforms in religious ritual and punishing those who stuck to Catholicism, and who now were called heretics. Virtually overnight, England was converted to a new official religion.

A terror fell on the country. Some people had suffered under the Catholic Church, which before the reforms had been immensely powerful, but most Britons had strong ties to Catholicism and to its comforting rituals. They watched in horror as churches were demolished, images of the Madonna and saints were broken in pieces, stained-glass windows were smashed, and the churches' treasures were confiscated. With monasteries that had succored the poor suddenly gone, the poor now flooded the streets. The growing ranks of the beggar class were further swelled by former monks. On top of all this, Cromwell levied high taxes to pay for his ecclesiastical reforms.

In 1535 powerful revolts in the North of England threatened to topple Henry from his throne. By the following year he had suppressed the rebellions, but he had also begun to see the costs of Cromwell's reforms. The king himself had never wanted to go this far—he had only wanted a di-

WHERE CHRISTMAS CAME FROM
Celebrating the turn of the year is an ancient custom. The Romans celebrated the Saturnalia, the festival of Saturn, god of the harvest, between December 17 and 23. It was the most cheerful festival of the year. All work and commerce stopped, and the streets were filled with crowds and a carnival atmosphere. Slaves were temporarily freed, and the houses were decorated with laurel branches. People visited one another, bringing gifts of wax candles and little clay figurines.
Long before the birth of Christ, the Jews celebrated an eight-day Festival of Lights [at the same season], and it is believed that the Germanic peoples held a great festival not only at midsummer but also at the winter solstice, when they celebrated the rebirth of the sun and honored the great fertility gods Wotan and Freyja, Donar (Thor) and Freyr. Even after the Emperor Constantine (A.D. 306–337) declared Christianity to be Rome's official imperial religion, the evocation of light and fertility as an important component of pre-Christian midwinter celebrations could not be entirely suppressed. In the year 274 the Roman Emperor Aurelian (A.D. 214–275) had established an official

cult of the sun-god
Mithras, declaring his
birthday, December 25,
a national holiday. The
cult of Mithras, the
Aryan god of light, had
spread from Persia
through Asia Minor to
Greece, Rome, and as
far as the Germanic
lands and Britain.
Numerous ruins of his
shrines still testify to
the high regard in
which this god was
held, especially by the
Roman legions, as a
bringer of fertility,
peace, and victory.
So it was a clever move
when, in the year A.D.
354, the Christian
church under Pope
Liberius (352–366) co-
opted the birthday of
Mithras and declared
December 25 to be
the birthday
of Jesus Christ.
NEUE ZÜRCHER
ZEITUNG,
ANNE-SUSANNE
RISCHKE,
DECEMBER 25, 1983

vorce. It was now Cromwell's turn to watch uneasily as the king began slowly to undo his reforms, reinstating Catholic sacraments and other rituals that Cromwell had outlawed.

Sensing his fall from grace, in 1540 Cromwell decided to regain Henry's favor with one throw of the dice: He would find the king a new wife. Henry's third wife, Jane Seymour, had died a few years before, and he had been pining for a new young queen. It was Cromwell who found him one: Anne of Cleves, a German princess and, most important to Cromwell, a Protestant. On Cromwell's commission, the painter Holbein produced a flattering portrait of Anne; when Henry saw it, he fell in love, and agreed to marry her. Cromwell seemed back in favor.

Unfortunately, however, Holbein's painting was highly idealized, and when the king finally met the princess she did not please him in the least. His anger against Cromwell—first for the ill-conceived reforms, now for saddling him with an unattractive and Protestant wife—could no longer be contained. In June of that year, Cromwell was arrested, charged as a Protestant extremist and a heretic, and sent to the Tower. Six weeks later, before a large and enthusiastic crowd, the public executioner cut off his head.

Interpretation

Thomas Cromwell had a simple idea: He would break up the power and wealth of the Church and lay the foundation for Protestantism in England. And he would do this in a mercilessly short time. He knew his speedy reforms would cause pain and resentment, but he thought these feelings would fade in a few years. More important, by identifying himself with change, he would become the leader of the new order, making the king dependent on him. But there was a problem in his strategy: Like a billiard ball hit too hard against the cushion, his reforms had reactions and caroms he did not envision and could not control.

The man who initiates strong reforms often becomes the scapegoat for any kind of dissatisfaction. And eventually the reaction to his reforms may consume him, for change is upsetting to the human animal, even when it is for the good. Because the world is and always has been full of insecurity and threat, we latch on to familiar faces and create habits and rituals to make the world more comfortable. Change can be pleasant and even sometimes desirable in the abstract, but too much of it creates an anxiety that will stir and boil beneath the surface and then eventually erupt.

Never underestimate the hidden conservatism of those around you. It is powerful and entrenched. Never let the seductive charm of an idea cloud your reason: Just as you cannot make people see the world your way, you cannot wrench them into the future with painful changes. They will rebel. If reform is necessary, anticipate the reaction against it and find ways to disguise the change and sweeten the poison.

OBSERVANCE OF THE LAW

As a young Communist in the 1920s, Mao Tse-tung understood better than any of his colleagues the incredible odds against a Communist victory in

China. With their small numbers, limited funds, lack of military experience, and small arsenal of weapons, the Party had no hope of success unless it won over China's immense peasant population. But who in the world was more conservative, more rooted in tradition, than the Chinese peasantry? The oldest civilization on the planet had a history that would never loosen its power, no matter how violent the revolution. The ideas of Confucius remained as alive in the 1920s as they had been in the sixth century B.C., when the philosopher was alive. Despite the oppressions of the current system, would the peasantry ever give up the deep-rooted values of the past for the great unknown of Communism?

The solution, as Mao saw it, involved a simple deception: Cloak the revolution in the clothing of the past, making it comforting and legitimate in people's eyes. One of Mao's favorite books was the very popular medieval Chinese novel *The Water Margin,* which recounts the exploits of a Chinese Robin Hood and his robber band as they struggle against a corrupt and evil monarch. In China in Mao's time, family ties dominated over any other kind, for the Confucian hierarchy of father and oldest son remained firmly in place; but *The Water Margin* preached a superior value— the fraternal ties of the band of robbers, the nobility of the cause that unites people beyond blood. The novel had great emotional resonance for Chinese people, who love to root for the underdog. Time and again, then, Mao would present his revolutionary army as an extension of the robber band in *The Water Margin,* likening his struggle to the timeless conflict between the oppressed peasantry and an evil emperor. He made the past seem to envelop and legitimize the Communist cause; the peasantry could feel comfortable with and even support a group with such roots in the past.

Even once the Party came to power, Mao continued to associate it with the past. He presented himself to the masses not as a Chinese Lenin but as a modern Chuko Liang, the real-life third-century strategist who figures prominently in the popular historical novel *The Romance of the Three Kingdoms.* Liang was more than a great general—he was a poet, a philosopher, and a figure of stern moral rectitude. So Mao represented himself as a poet-warrior like Liang, a man who mixed strategy with philosophy and preached a new ethics. He made himself appear like a hero from the great Chinese tradition of warrior statesmen.

Soon, everything in Mao's speeches and writings had a reference to an earlier period in Chinese history. He recalled, for example, the great Emperor Ch'in, who had unified the country in the third century B.C. Ch'in had burned the works of Confucius, consolidated and completed the building of the Great Wall, and given his name to China. Like Ch'in, Mao also had brought the country together, and had sought bold reforms against an oppressive past. Ch'in had traditionally been seen as a violent dictator whose reign was short; the brilliance of Mao's strategy was to turn this around, simultaneously reinterpreting Ch'in, justifying his rule in the eyes of present-day Chinese, and using him to justify the violence of the new order that Mao himself was creating.

After the failed Cultural Revolution of the late 1960s, a power struggle emerged in the Communist Party in which Mao's main foe was Lin Piao, once a close friend of his. To make clear to the masses the difference between his philosophy and Lin's, Mao once again exploited the past: He cast his opponent as representing Confucius, a philosopher Lin in fact would constantly quote. And Confucius signified the conservatism of the past. Mao associated himself, on the other hand, with the ancient philosophical movement known as Legalism, exemplified by the writings of Han-fei-tzu. The Legalists disdained Confucian ethics; they believed in the need for violence to create a new order. They worshiped power. To give himself weight in the struggle, Mao unleashed a nationwide propaganda campaign against Confucius, using the issues of Confucianism versus Legalism to whip the young into a kind of frenzied revolt against the older generation. This grand context enveloped a rather banal power struggle, and Mao once again won over the masses and triumphed over his enemies.

Interpretation

No people had a more profound attachment to the past than the Chinese. In the face of this enormous obstacle to reform, Mao's strategy was simple: Instead of struggling against the past, he turned it to his advantage, associating his radical Communists with the romantic figures of Chinese history. Weaving the story of the War of the Three Kingdoms into the struggle between the United States, the Soviet Union, and China, he cast himself as Chuko Liang. As the emperors had, he welcomed the cultlike adoration of the masses, understanding that the Chinese could not function without some kind of father figure to admire. And after he made a terrible blunder with the Great Leap Forward, trying to force modernization on the country and failing miserably, he never repeated his mistake: From then on, radical change had to be cloaked in the comfortable clothes of the past.

The lesson is simple: The past is powerful. What has happened before seems greater; habit and history give any act weight. Use this to your advantage. When you destroy the familiar you create a void or vacuum; people fear the chaos that will flood in to fill it. You must avoid stirring up such fears at all cost. Borrow the weight and legitimacy from the past, however remote, to create a comforting and familiar presence. This will give your actions romantic associations, add to your presence, and cloak the nature of the changes you are attempting.

> *It must be considered that there is nothing more difficult to carry out,*
> *nor more doubtful of success, nor more dangerous to handle,*
> *than to initiate a new order of things.*
> *Niccolò Machiavelli, 1469–1527*

KEYS TO POWER

Human psychology contains many dualities, one of them being that even while people understand the need for change, knowing how important it is for institutions and individuals to be occasionally renewed, they are also irritated and upset by changes that affect them personally. They know that change is necessary, and that novelty provides relief from boredom, but deep inside they cling to the past. Change in the abstract, or superficial change, they desire, but a change that upsets core habits and routines is deeply disturbing to them.

No revolution has gone without a powerful later reaction against it, for in the long run the void it creates proves too unsettling to the human animal, who unconsciously associates such voids with death and chaos. The opportunity for change and renewal seduces people to the side of the revolution, but once their enthusiasm fades, which it will, they are left with a certain emptiness. Yearning for the past, they create an opening for it to creep back in.

For Machiavelli, the prophet who preaches and brings change can only survive by taking up arms: When the masses inevitably yearn for the past, he must be ready to use force. But the armed prophet cannot last long unless he quickly creates a new set of values and rituals to replace the old ones, and to soothe the anxieties of those who dread change. It is far easier, and less bloody, to play a kind of con game. Preach change as much as you like, and even enact your reforms, but give them the comforting appearance of older events and traditions.

Reigning from A.D. 8 to A.D. 23, the Chinese emperor Wang Mang emerged from a period of great historical turbulence in which the people yearned for order, an order represented for them by Confucius. Some two hundred years earlier, however, Emperor Ch'in had ordered the writings of Confucius burned. A few years later, word had spread that certain texts had miraculously survived, hidden under the scholar's house. These texts may not have been genuine, but they gave Wang his opportunity: He first confiscated them, then had his scribes insert passages into them that seemed to support the changes he had been imposing on the country. When he released the texts, it seemed that Confucius sanctioned Wang's reforms, and the people felt comforted and accepted them more easily.

Understand: The fact that the past is dead and buried gives you the freedom to reinterpret it. To support your cause, tinker with the facts. The past is a text in which you can safely insert your own lines.

A simple gesture like using an old title, or keeping the same number for a group, will tie you to the past and support you with the authority of history. As Machiavelli himself observed, the Romans used this device when they transformed their monarchy into a republic. They may have installed two consuls in place of the king, but since the king had been served by twelve lictors, they retained the same number to serve under the consuls. The king had personally performed an annual sacrifice, in a great spectacle that stirred the public; the republic retained this practice, only transferring it to a special "chief of the ceremony, whom they called the *King* of the sacrifice." These and similar gestures satisfied the people and kept them from clamoring for the monarchy's return.

Another strategy to disguise change is to make a loud and public display of support for the values of the past. Seem to be a zealot for tradition and few will notice how unconventional you really are. Renaissance Florence had a centuries-old republic, and was suspicious of anyone who flouted its traditions. Cosimo de' Medici made a show of enthusiastic support for the republic, while in reality he worked to bring the city under the control of his wealthy family. In form, the Medicis retained the appearance of a republic; in substance, they rendered it powerless. They quietly enacted a radical change, while appearing to safeguard tradition.

Science claims a search for truth that would seem to protect it from conservatism and the irrationality of habit: It is a culture of innovation. Yet when Charles Darwin published his ideas of evolution, he faced fiercer opposition from his fellow scientists than from religious authorities. His theories challenged too many fixed ideas. Jonas Salk ran into the same wall with his radical innovations in immunology, as did Max Planck with his revolutionizing of physics. Planck later wrote of the scientific opposition he faced, "A new scientific truth does not triumph by convincing its opponents and making them see the light, but rather because its opponents eventually die, and a new generation grows up that is familiar with it."

The answer to this innate conservatism is to play the courtier's game. Galileo did this at the beginning of his scientific career; he later became more confrontational, and paid for it. So pay lip service to tradition. Identify the elements in your revolution that can be made to seem to build on the past. Say the right things, make a show of conformity, and meanwhile let your theories do their radical work. Play with appearances and respect past protocol. This is true in every arena—science being no exception.

Finally, powerful people pay attention to the zeitgeist. If their reform is too far ahead of its time, few will understand it, and it will stir up anxiety and be hopelessly misinterpreted. The changes you make must seem less innovative than they are. England did eventually become a Protestant nation, as Cromwell wished, but it took over a century of gradual evolution.

Watch the zeitgeist. If you work in a tumultuous time, there is power to be gained by preaching a return to the past, to comfort, tradition, and ritual. During a period of stagnation, on the other hand, play the card of reform and revolution—but beware of what you stir up. Those who finish a revolution are rarely those who start it. You will not succeed at this dangerous game unless you are willing to forestall the inevitable reaction against it by playing with appearances and building on the past.

Authority: He who desires or attempts to reform the government of a state, and wishes to have it accepted, must at least retain the semblance of the old forms; so that it may seem to the people that there has been no change in the institutions, even though in fact they are entirely different from the old ones. For the great majority of mankind are satisfied with appearances, as though they were realities. (Niccolò Machiavelli, 1469–1527)

Image: The Cat.
Creature of habit, it loves the
warmth of the familiar. Upset its
routines, disrupt its space, and it will
grow unmanageable and psychotic.
Placate it by supporting its rituals. If
change is necessary, deceive the cat by
keeping the smell of the past alive;
place objects familiar to it in
strategic locations.

REVERSAL

The past is a corpse to be used as you see fit. If what happened in the recent past was painful and harsh, it is self-destructive to associate yourself with it. When Napoleon came to power, the French Revolution was fresh in everyone's minds. If the court that he established had borne any resemblance to the lavish court of Louis XVI and Marie-Antoinette, his courtiers would have spent all their time worrying about their own necks. Instead, Napoleon established a court remarkable for its sobriety and lack of ostentation. It was the court of a man who valued work and military virtues. This new form seemed appropriate and reassuring.

In other words, pay attention to the times. But understand: If you make a bold change from the past, you must avoid at all costs the appearance of a void or vacuum, or you will create terror. Even an ugly recent history will seem preferable to an empty space. Fill that space immediately with *new* rituals and forms. Soothing and growing familiar, these will secure your position among the masses.

Finally, the arts, fashion, and technology would seem to be areas in which power would come from creating a radical rupture with the past and appearing cutting edge. Indeed, such a strategy can bring great power, but it has many dangers. It is inevitable that your innovations will be outdone by someone else. You have little control—someone younger and fresher moves in a sudden new direction, making your bold innovation of yesterday seem tiresome and tame today. You are forever playing catch-up; your power is tenuous and short-lived. You want a power built on something more solid. Using the past, tinkering with tradition, playing with convention to subvert it will give your creations something more than a momentary appeal. Periods of dizzying change disguise the fact that a yearning for the past will inevitably creep back in. In the end, using the past for your own purposes will bring you more power than trying to cut it out completely—a futile and self-destructive endeavor.

NEVER APPEAR

TOO PERFECT

JUDGMENT

Appearing better than others is always dangerous, but most dangerous of all is to appear to have no faults or weaknesses. Envy creates silent enemies. It is smart to occasionally display defects, and admit to harmless vices, in order to deflect envy and appear more human and approachable. Only gods and the dead can seem perfect with impunity.

TRANSGRESSION OF THE LAW

Joe Orton met Kenneth Halliwell at the Royal Academy of Dramatic Arts, London, in 1953, where both had enrolled as acting students. They soon became lovers and moved in together. Halliwell, twenty-five at the time, was seven years older than Orton, and seemed the more confident of the two; but neither had much talent as actors, and after graduating, having settled down together in a dank London apartment, they decided to give up acting and collaborate as writers instead. Halliwell's inheritance was enough to keep them from having to find work for a few years, and in the beginning, he was also the driving force behind the stories and novels they wrote; he would dictate to Orton, who would type the manuscripts, occasionally interjecting his own lines and ideas. Their first efforts attracted some interest from literary agents, but it sputtered. The promise they had shown was leading nowhere.

Eventually the inheritance money ran out, and the pair had to look for work. Their collaborations were less enthusiastic and less frequent. The future looked bleak.

In 1957 Orton began to write on his own, but it wasn't until five years later, when the lovers were jailed for six months for defacing dozens of library books, that he began to find his voice (perhaps not by chance: This was the first time he and Halliwell had been separated in nine years). He came out of prison determined to express his contempt for English society in the form of theatrical farces. He and Halliwell moved back in together, but now the roles were reversed: Orton did the writing while Halliwell put in comments and ideas.

In 1964 Joe Orton completed his first full-length play, *Entertaining Mr. Sloane.* The play made it to London's West End, where it received brilliant reviews: A great new writer had emerged from nowhere. Now success followed success, at a dizzying pace. In 1966 Orton had a hit with his play *Loot,* and his popularity soared. Soon commissions came in from all sides, including from the Beatles, who paid Orton handsomely to write them a film script.

Everything was pointing upwards, everything except Orton's relationship with Kenneth Halliwell. The pair still lived together, but as Orton grew successful, Halliwell began to deteriorate. Watching his lover become the center of attention, he suffered the humiliation of becoming a kind of personal assistant to the playwright, his role in what had once been a collaboration growing smaller and smaller. In the 1950s he had supported Orton with his inheritance; now Orton supported him. At a party or among friends, people would naturally gravitate towards Orton—he was charming, and his mood was almost always buoyant. Unlike the handsome Orton, Halliwell was bald and awkward; his defensiveness made people want to avoid him.

With Orton's success the couple's problems only worsened. Halliwell's moods made their life together impossible. Orton claimed to want to leave him, and had numerous affairs, but would always end up returning to his

THE PARABLE OF THE GREEDY MAN AND THE ENVIOUS MAN
A greedy man and an envious man met a king. The king said to them, "One of you may ask something of me and I will give it to him, provided I give twice as much to the other." The envious person did not want to ask first for he was envious of his companion who would receive twice as much, and the greedy man did not want to ask first since he wanted everything that was to be had. Finally the greedy one pressed the envious one to be the first to make the request. So the envious person asked the king to pluck out one of his eyes.

JEWISH PARABLE, THE SEVEN DEADLY SINS, SOLOMON SCHIMMEL, 1992

An admirer who feels that he cannot be happy by surrendering himself elects to become envious of that which he admires. So he speaks another language—the thing which he really admires is called a stupid, insipid and queer sort of thing. Admiration is happy self-surrender; envy is unhappy self-assertion.

SØREN KIERKEGAARD, 1813–1855

old friend and lover. He tried to help Halliwell launch a career as an artist, even arranging for a gallery to show his work, but the show was a flop, and this only heightened Halliwell's sense of inferiority. In May of 1967, the pair went on a brief holiday together in Tangier, Morocco. During the trip, Orton wrote in his diary, "We sat talking of how happy we felt. And how it couldn't, surely, last. We'd have to pay for it. Or we'd be struck down from afar by disaster because we were, perhaps, too happy. To be young, good-looking, healthy, famous, comparatively rich *and* happy is surely going against nature."

Halliwell outwardly seemed as happy as Orton. Inwardly, though, he was seething. And two months later, in the early morning of August 10, 1967, just days after helping Orton put the finishing touches to the wicked farce *What the Butler Saw* (undoubtedly his masterpiece), Kenneth Halliwell bludgeoned Joe Orton to death with repeated blows of a hammer to the head. He then took twenty-one sleeping pills and died himself, leaving behind a note that read, "If you read Orton's diary all will be explained."

Interpretation

Kenneth Halliwell had tried to cast his deterioration as mental illness, but what Joe Orton's diaries revealed to him was the truth: It was envy, pure and simple, that lay at the heart of his sickness. The diaries, which Halliwell read on the sly, recounted the couple's days as equals and their struggle for recognition. After Orton found success, the diaries began to describe Halliwell's brooding, his rude comments at parties, his growing sense of inferiority. All of this Orton narrated with a distance that bordered on contempt.

The diaries made clear Halliwell's bitterness over Orton's success. Eventually the only thing that would have satisfied him would have been for Orton to have a failure of his own, an unsuccessful play perhaps, so that they could have commiserated in their failure, as they had done years before. When the opposite happened—as Orton grew only more successful and popular—Halliwell did the only thing that would make them equals again: He made them equals in death. With Orton's murder, he became almost as famous as his friend—posthumously.

Joe Orton only partly understood his lover's deterioration. His attempt to help Halliwell launch a career in art registered for what it was: charity and guilt. Orton basically had two possible solutions to the problem. He could have downplayed his own success, displaying some faults, deflecting Halliwell's envy; or, once he realized the nature of the problem, he could have fled as if Halliwell were a viper, as in fact he was—a viper of envy. Once envy eats away at someone, everything you do only makes it grow, and day by day it festers inside him. Eventually he will attack.

Only a minority can succeed at the game of life, and that minority inevitably arouses the envy of those around them. Once success happens your way, however, the people to fear the most are those in your own circle, the friends and acquaintances you have left behind. Feelings of inferi-

ENVY TORMENTS
AGLAUROS

The goddess Minerva made her way to the house of Envy, a house filthy with dark and noisome slime. It is hidden away in the depths of the valleys, where the sun never penetrates, where no wind blows through; a gloomy dwelling, permeated by numbing chill, ever fireless, ever shrouded in thick darkness. When Minerva reached this spot she stopped in front of the house . . . and struck the doors with the tip of her spear, and at the blow they flew open and revealed Envy within, busy at a meal of snake's flesh, the food on which she nourished her wickedness. At the sight, Minerva turned her eyes away. But the other rose heavily from the ground, leaving the half-eaten corpses, and came out with dragging steps. When she saw the goddess in all the brilliance of her beauty, in her flashing armor, she groaned. . . . Envy's face was sickly pale, her whole body lean and wasted, and

ority gnaw at them; the thought of your success only heightens their feelings of stagnation. Envy, which the philosopher Kierkegaard calls "unhappy admiration," takes hold. You may not see it but you will feel it someday—unless, that is, you learn strategies of deflection, little sacrifices to the gods of success. Either dampen your brilliance occasionally, purposefully revealing a defect, weakness, or anxiety, or attributing your success to luck; or simply find yourself new friends. Never underestimate the power of envy.

OBSERVANCE OF THE LAW

The merchant class and the craft guilds to which medieval Florence owed its prosperity had created a republic that protected them from oppression by the nobility. Since high office could only be held for a few months, no one could gain lasting dominance, and although this meant that the political factions struggled constantly for control, the system kept out tyrants and petty dictators. The Medici family lived for several centuries under this system without making much of a mark. They had modest origins as apothecaries, and were typical middle-class citizens. Not until the late fourteenth century, when Giovanni de' Medici made a modest fortune in banking, did they emerge as a force to be reckoned with.

Upon Giovanni's death, his son Cosimo took over the family business, and quickly demonstrated his talent for it. The business prospered under his control and the Medicis emerged as one of the preeminent banking families of Europe. But they had a rival in Florence: Despite the city's republican system, one family, the Albizzis, had managed over the years to monopolize control of the government, forging alliances that allowed them to constantly fill important offices with their own men. Cosimo did not fight this, and in fact gave the Albizzis his tacit support. At the same time, while the Albizzis were beginning to flaunt their power, Cosimo made a point of staying in the background.

Eventually, however, the Medici wealth could not be ignored, and in 1433, feeling threatened by the family, the Albizzis used their government muscle to have Cosimo arrested on charges of conspiring to overthrow the republic. Some in the Albizzi faction wanted Cosimo executed, others feared this would spark a civil war. In the end they exiled him from Florence. Cosimo did not fight the sentence; he left quietly. Sometimes, he knew, it is wiser to bide one's time and keep a low profile.

Over the next year, the Albizzis began to stir up fears that they were setting up a dictatorship. Meanwhile, Cosimo, using his wealth to advantage, continued to exert influence on Florentine affairs, even from exile. A civil war broke out in the city, and in September of 1434 the Albizzis were toppled from power and sent into exile. Cosimo immediately returned to Florence, his position restored. But he saw that he now faced a delicate situation: If he seemed ambitious, as the Albizzis had, he would stir up opposition and envy that would ultimately threaten his business. If he stayed on

she squinted horribly; her teeth were discolored and decayed, her poisonous breast of a greenish hue, and her tongue dripped venom. Only the sight of suffering could bring a smile to her lips. She never knew the comfort of sleep, but was kept constantly awake by care and anxiety, looked with dismay on men's good fortune, and grew thin at the sight. Gnawing at others, and being gnawed, she was herself her own torment. Minerva, in spite of her loathing, yet addressed her briefly: "Instill your poison into one of Cecrop's daughters— her name is Aglauros. This is what I require of you." Without another word she pushed against the ground with her spear, left the earth, and soared upwards. From the corner of her eye the other watched the goddess out of sight, muttering and angry that Minerva's plan should be successful. Then she took her staff, all encircled with thorny briars, wrapped herself in dark clouds, and set forth. Wherever she went she trampled down the flowery fields, withered up the grass, seared the treetops, and with her breath tainted the peoples, their cities and their homes, until at length she came to Athens, the home of wit and wealth, peaceful and prosperous. She could scarcely refrain from weeping when she saw no cause for tears.

the sidelines, on the other hand, he would leave an opening for another faction to rise up as the Albizzis had, and to punish the Medicis for their success.

Cosimo solved the problem in two ways: He secretly used his wealth to buy influence among key citizens, and he placed his own allies, all cleverly enlisted from the middle classes to disguise their allegiance to him, in top government positions. Those who complained of his growing political clout were taxed into submission, or their properties were bought out from under them by Cosimo's banker allies. The republic survived in name only. Cosimo held the strings.

While he worked behind the scenes to gain control, however, publicly Cosimo presented another picture. When he walked through the streets of Florence, he dressed modestly, was attended by no more than one servant, and bowed deferentially to magistrates and elder citizens. He rode a mule instead of a horse. He never spoke out on matters of public import, even though he controlled Florence's foreign affairs for over thirty years. He gave money to charities and maintained his ties to Florence's merchant class. He financed all kinds of public buildings that fed the Florentines' pride in their city. When he built a palace for himself and his family in nearby Fiesole, he turned down the ornate designs that Brunelleschi had drawn up for him and instead chose a modest structure designed by Michelozzo, a man of humble Florentine origins. The palace was a symbol of Cosimo's strategy—all simplicity on the outside, all elegance and opulence within.

Cosimo finally died in 1464, after ruling for thirty years. The citizens of Florence wanted to build him a great tomb, and to celebrate his memory with elaborate funeral ceremonies, but on his deathbed he had asked to be buried without "any pomp or demonstration." Some sixty years later, Machiavelli hailed Cosimo as the wisest of all princes, "for he knew how extraordinary things that are seen and appear every hour make men much more envied than those that are done in deed and are covered over with decency."

Interpretation

A close friend of Cosimo's, the bookseller Vespasiano da Bisticci, once wrote of him, "And whenever he wished to achieve something, he saw to it, in order to escape envy as much as possible, that the initiative appeared to come from others, and not from him." One of Cosimo's favorite expressions was, "Envy is a weed that should not be watered." Understanding the power envy has in a democratic environment, Cosimo avoided the appearance of greatness. This does not mean that greatness should be suffocated, or that only the mediocre should survive; only that a game of appearances must be played. The insidious envy of the masses can actually be deflected quite easily: Appear as one of them in style and values. Make alliances with those below you, and elevate them to positions of power to secure their support in times of need. Never flaunt your wealth, and carefully conceal the degree to which it has bought influence. Make a display of deferring to others, as if they were more powerful than you. Cosimo de' Medici perfected this game; he was a consummate con artist of appearances. No one could gauge the extent of his power—his modest exterior hid the truth.

Never be so foolish as to believe that you are stirring up admiration by flaunting the qualities that raise you above others. By making others aware of their inferior position, you are only stirring up "unhappy admiration," or envy, which will gnaw away at them until they undermine you in ways you cannot foresee. The fool dares the gods of envy by flaunting his victories. The master of power understands that the appearance of superiority over others is inconsequential next to the reality of it.

Of all the disorders of the soul, envy is the only one no one confesses to.
*Plutarch,*c.a.d. *46–120*

KEYS TO POWER

The human animal has a hard time dealing with feelings of inferiority. In the face of superior skill, talent, or power, we are often disturbed and ill at ease; this is because most of us have an inflated sense of ourselves, and when we meet people who surpass us they make it clear to us that we are in fact mediocre, or at least not as brilliant as we had thought. This disturbance in our self-image cannot last long without stirring up ugly emotions. At first we feel envy: If only we had the quality or skill of the superior person, we would be happy. But envy brings us neither comfort nor any closer to equality. Nor can we admit to feeling it, for it is frowned upon socially—to show envy is to admit to feeling inferior. To close friends, we may confess our secret unrealized desires, but we will never confess to feeling envy. So it goes underground. We disguise it in many ways, like finding grounds to criticize the person who makes us feel it: He may be smarter than I am, we say, but he has no morals or conscience. Or he may have more power, but that's because he cheats. If we do not slander him, perhaps we praise him excessively—another of envy's disguises.

There are several strategies for dealing with the insidious, destructive emotion of envy. First, accept the fact that there will be people who will surpass you in some way, and also the fact that you may envy them. But make that feeling a way of pushing yourself to equal or surpass *them* someday. Let envy turn inward and it poisons the soul; expel it outward and it can move you to greater heights.

Second, understand that as you gain power, those below you will feel envious of *you.* They may not show it but it is inevitable. Do not naively accept the facade they show you—read between the lines of their criticisms, their little sarcastic remarks, the signs of backstabbing, the excessive praise that is preparing you for a fall, the resentful look in the eye. Half the problem with envy comes when we do not recognize it until it is too late.

Finally, expect that when people envy you they will work against you

The envious hides as carefully as the secret, lustful sinner and becomes the endless inventor of tricks and stratagems to hide and mask himself. Thus he is able to pretend to ignore the superiority of others which eats up his heart, as if he did not see them, nor hear them, nor were aware of them, nor had ever heard of them. He is a master simulator. On the other hand he tries with all his power to connive and thus prevent any form of superiority from appearing in any situation. And if they do, he casts on them obscurity, hypercriticism, sarcasm and calumny like the toad that spits poison from its hole. On the other hand he will raise endlessly insignificant men, mediocre people, and even the inferior in the same type of activities.
Arthur
Schopenhauer,
1788–1860

For not many men, the proverb says, can love a friend who fortune prospers without feeling envy; and about the envious brain, cold poison clings and doubles all the pain life brings him. His own woundings he must nurse, and feels another's gladness like a curse.
Aeschylus,
c. 525–456 b.c.

*Now Israel loved
Joseph more than all
his children, because he
was the son of his old
age; and he made him a
coat of many colors. . . .
And his brothers
.envied him. . . . And
when they saw him afar
off, they conspired
against him to slay
him. And now they said
to one another,
"Behold, this dreamer
cometh. Come now
therefore, and let us
slay him, and cast him
into some pit, and we
shall say, some evil
beast hath devoured
him; and we shall see
what will become of his
dreams."*

OLD TESTAMENT,
GENESIS 37:3–20

THE TRAGEDY
OF THE TOMB

*[When Pope Julius first
saw Michelangelo's
design for his tomb] it
pleased him so much
that he at once sent him
to Carrara to quarry
the necessary marbles,
instructing Alamanno
Salviati, of Florence, to
pay him a thousand
ducats for this purpose.
Michelangelo stayed in
these mountains more
than eight months with
two workmen and his
horse, and without any
other provision except
food. . . . Enough
marbles quarried and
chosen, he took them to
the sea-coast, and left*

insidiously. They will put obstacles in your path that you will not foresee, or that you cannot trace to their source. It is hard to defend yourself against this kind of attack. And by the time you realize that envy is at the root of a person's feelings about you, it is often too late: Your excuses, your false humility, your defensive actions, only exacerbate the problem. Since it is far easier to avoid creating envy in the first place than to get rid of it once it is there, you should strategize to forestall it before it grows. It is often your own actions that stir up envy, your own unawareness. By becoming conscious of those actions and qualities that create envy, you can take the teeth out of it before it nibbles you to death.

Kierkegaard believed that there are types of people who create envy, and are as guilty when it arises as those who feel it. The most obvious type we all know: The moment something good happens to them, whether by luck or design, they crow about it. In fact they get pleasure out of making people feel inferior. This type is obvious and beyond hope. There are others, however, who stir up envy in more subtle and unconscious ways, and are partly to blame for their troubles. Envy is often a problem, for example, for people with great natural talent.

Sir Walter Raleigh was one of the most brilliant men at the court of Queen Elizabeth of England. He had skills as a scientist, wrote poetry still recognized as among the most beautiful writing of the time, was a proven leader of men, an enterprising entrepreneur, a great sea captain, and on top of all this was a handsome, dashing courtier who charmed his way into becoming one of the queen's favorites. Wherever he went, however, people blocked his path. Eventually he suffered a terrific fall from grace, leading even to prison and finally the executioner's axe.

Raleigh could not understand the stubborn opposition he faced from the other courtiers. He did not see that he had not only made no attempt to disguise the degree of his skills and qualities, he had imposed them on one and all, making a show of his versatility, thinking it impressed people and won him friends. In fact it made him silent enemies, people who felt inferior to him and did all they could to ruin him the moment he tripped up or made the slightest mistake. In the end, the reason he was executed was treason, but envy will use any cover it finds to mask its destructiveness.

The envy elicited by Sir Walter Raleigh is the worst kind: It was inspired by his natural talent and grace, which he felt was best displayed in its full flower. Money others can attain; power as well. But superior intelligence, good looks, charm—these are qualities no one can acquire. The naturally perfect have to work the most to disguise their brilliance, displaying a defect or two to deflect envy before it takes root. It is a common and naive mistake to think you are charming people with your natural talents when in fact they are coming to hate you.

A great danger in the realm of power is the sudden improvement in fortune—an unexpected promotion, a victory or success that seems to come out of nowhere. This is sure to stir up envy among your former peers.

When Archbishop de Retz was promoted to the rank of cardinal, in 1651, he knew full well that many of his former colleagues envied him.

Understanding the foolishness of alienating those below him, de Retz did everything he could to downplay his merit and emphasize the role of luck in his success. To put people at ease, he acted humbly and deferentially, as if nothing had changed. (In reality, of course, he now had much more power than before.) He wrote that these wise policies "produced a good effect, by lessening the envy which was conceived against me, which is the greatest of all secrets." Follow de Retz's example. Subtly emphasize how lucky you have been, to make your happiness seem more attainable to other people, and the need for envy less acute. But be careful not to affect a false modesty that people can easily see through. This will only make them more envious. The act has to be good; your humility, and your openness to those you have left behind, have to seem genuine. Any hint of insincerity will only make your new status more oppressive. Remember: Despite your elevated position, it will do you no good to alienate your former peers. Power requires a wide and solid support base, which envy can silently destroy.

Political power of any kind creates envy, and one of the best ways to deflect it before it takes root is to seem unambitious. When Ivan the Terrible died, Boris Godunov knew he was the only one on the scene who could lead Russia. But if he sought the position eagerly, he would stir up envy and suspicion among the boyars, so he refused the crown, not once but several times. He made people insist that he take the throne. George Washington used the same strategy to great effect, first in refusing to keep the position of Commander in Chief of the American army, second in resisting the presidency. In both cases he made himself more popular than ever. People cannot envy the power that they themselves have given a person who does not seem to desire it.

According to the Elizabethan statesman and writer Sir Francis Bacon, the wisest policy of the powerful is to create a kind of pity for themselves, as if their responsibilities were a burden and a sacrifice. How can one envy a man who has taken on a heavy load for the public interest? Disguise your power as a kind of self-sacrifice rather than a source of happiness and you make it seem less enviable. Emphasize your troubles and you turn a potential danger (envy) into a source of moral support (pity). A similar ploy is to hint that your good fortune will benefit those around you. To do this you may need to open your purse strings, like Cimon, a wealthy general in ancient Athens who gave lavishly in all kinds of ways to prevent people from resenting the influence he had bought in Athenian politics. He paid a high price to deflect their envy, but in the end it saved him from ostracism and banishment from the city.

The painter J. M. W. Turner devised another way of giving to deflect the envy of his fellow artists, which he recognized as his greatest obstacle to his success. Noticing that his incomparable color skills made them afraid to hang their paintings next to his in exhibitions, he realized that their fear would turn to envy, and would eventually make it harder for him to find galleries to show in. On occasion, then, Turner is known to have temporarily dampened the colors in his paintings with soot to earn him the goodwill of his colleagues.

one of his men to have them embarked. He himself returned to Rome.
... The quantity of marbles was immense, so that, spread over the piazza, they were the admiration of all and a joy to the pope, who heaped immeasurable favors upon Michelangelo; and when he began to work upon them again and again went to see him at his house, and talked to him about the tomb and other things as with his own brother. And in order that he might more easily go to him, the pope ordered that a drawbridge should be thrown across from the Corridore to the rooms of Michelangelo, by which he might visit him in private.
These many and frequent favors were the cause (as often is the case at court) of much envy, and, after the envy, of endless persecution, since Bramante, the architect, who was loved by the pope, made him change his mind as to the monument by telling him, as is said by the vulgar, that it is unlucky to build one's tomb in one's lifetime, and other tales. Fear as well as envy stimulated Bramante, for the judgment of Michelangelo had exposed many of his errors.... Now because he had no doubt that Michelangelo knew these errors of his, he always sought to remove him from Rome, or, at least, to deprive him of the

To deflect envy, Gracián recommends that the powerful display a weakness, a minor social indiscretion, a harmless vice. Give those who envy you something to feed on, distracting them from your more important sins. Remember: It is the reality that matters. You may have to play games with appearances, but in the end you will have what counts: true power. In some Arab countries, a man will avoid arousing envy by doing as Cosimo de Medici did by showing his wealth only on the inside of his house. Apply this wisdom to your own character.

Beware of some of envy's disguises. Excessive praise is an almost sure sign that the person praising you envies you; they are either setting you up for a fall—it will be impossible for you to live up to their praise—or they are sharpening their blades behind your back. At the same time, those who are hypercritical of you, or who slander you publicly, probably envy you as well. Recognize their behavior as disguised envy and you keep out of the trap of mutual mud-slinging, or of taking their criticisms to heart. Win your revenge by ignoring their measly presence.

Do not try to help or do favors for those who envy you; they will think you are condescending to them. Joe Orton's attempt to help Halliwell find a gallery for his work only intensified his lover's feelings of inferiority and envy. Once envy reveals itself for what it is, the only solution is often to flee the presence of the enviers, leaving them to stew in a hell of their own creation.

Finally, be aware that some environments are more conducive to envy than others. The effects of envy are more serious among colleagues and peers, where there is a veneer of equality. Envy is also destructive in democratic environments where overt displays of power are looked down upon. Be extrasensitive in such environments. The filmmaker Ingmar Bergman was hounded by Swedish tax authorities because he stood out in a country where standing out from the crowd is frowned on. It is almost impossible to avoid envy in such cases, and there is little you can do but accept it graciously and take none of it personally. As Thoreau once said, "Envy is the tax which all distinction must pay."

Image: A Garden of Weeds. You may not feed them but they spread as you water the garden. You may not see how, but they take over, tall and ugly, preventing anything beautiful from flourishing. Before it is too late, do not water indiscriminately. Destroy the weeds of envy by giving them

nothing to feed on.

Authority: Upon occasion, reveal a harmless defect in your character. For the envious accuse the most perfect of sinning by having no sins. They become an Argus, all eyes for finding fault with excellence—it is their only consolation. Do not let envy burst with its own venom—affect some lapse in valor or intellect, so as to disarm it beforehand. You thus wave your red cape before the Horns of Envy, in order to save your immortality. (Baltasar Gracián, 1601–1658)

REVERSAL

The reason for being careful with the envious is that they are so indirect, and will find innumerable ways to undermine you. But treading carefully around them will often only make their envy worse. They sense that you are being cautious, and it registers as yet another sign of your superiority. That is why you must act before envy takes root.

Once envy is there, however, whether through your fault or not, it is sometimes best to affect the opposite approach: Display the utmost disdain for those who envy you. Instead of hiding your perfection, make it obvious. Make every new triumph an opportunity to make the envious squirm. Your good fortune and power become their living hell. If you attain a position of unimpeachable power, their envy will have no effect on you, and you will have the best revenge of all: They are trapped in envy while you are free in your power.

This is how Michelangelo triumphed over the venomous architect Bramante, who turned Pope Julius against Michelangelo's design for his tomb. Bramante envied Michelangelo's godlike skills, and to this one triumph—the aborted tomb project—he thought to add another, by pushing the pope to commission Michelangelo to paint the murals in the Sistine Chapel. The project would take years, during which Michelangelo would accomplish no more of his brilliant sculptures. Furthermore, Bramante considered Michelangelo not nearly as skilled in painting as in sculpture. The chapel would spoil his image as the perfect artist.

Michelangelo saw the trap and wanted to turn down the commission, but he could not refuse the pope, so he accepted it without complaint. Then, however, he used Bramante's envy to spur him to greater heights, making the Sistine Chapel his most perfect work of all. Every time Bramante heard of it or saw it, he felt more oppressed by his own envy—the sweetest and most lasting revenge you can exact on the envious.

Know how to triumph over envy and malice. Here contempt, although prudent, counts, indeed, for little; magnanimity is better. A good word concerning one who speaks evil of you cannot be praised too highly: there is no revenge more heroic than that brought about by those merits and attainments which frustrate and torment the envious. Every stroke of good fortune is a further twist of the rope round the neck of the ill-disposed and the heaven of the envied is hell for the envious. To convert your good fortune into poison for your enemies is held to be the most severe punishment you can inflict on them. The envious man dies not only once but as many times as the person he envies lives to hear the voice of praise; the eternity of the latter's fame is the measure of the former's punishment: the one is immortal in his glory, the latter in his misery. The trumpet of fame which sounds immortality for the one heralds death for the other, who is sentenced to be choked to death on his own envy.

BALTASAR GRACIÁN, 1601–1658

DO NOT GO PAST THE

MARK YOU AIMED FOR;

IN VICTORY,

LEARN WHEN TO STOP

JUDGMENT

The moment of victory is often the moment of greatest peril. In the heat of victory, arrogance and overconfidence can push you past the goal you had aimed for, and by going too far, you make more enemies than you defeat. Do not allow success to go to your head. There is no substitute for strategy and careful planning. Set a goal, and when you reach it, stop.

TRANSGRESSION OF THE LAW

In 559 B.C., a young man named Cyrus gathered an immense army from the scattered tribes of Persia and marched against his grandfather Astyages, king of the Medes. He defeated Astyages with ease, had himself crowned king of Medea and Persia, and began to forge the Persian Empire. Victory followed victory in quick succession. Cyrus defeated Croesus, ruler of Lydia, then conquered the Ionian islands and other smaller kingdoms; he marched on Babylon and crushed it. Now he was known as Cyrus the Great, King of the World.

After capturing the riches of Babylon, Cyrus set his sights on the east, on the half-barbaric tribes of the Massagetai, a vast realm on the Caspian Sea. A fierce warrior race led by Queen Tomyris, the Massagetai lacked the riches of Babylon, but Cyrus decided to attack them anyway, believing himself superhuman and incapable of defeat. The Massagetai would fall easily to his vast armies, making his empire immense.

In 529 B.C., then, Cyrus marched to the wide river Araxes, gateway to the kingdom of the Massagetai. As he set up camp on the western bank, he received a message from Queen Tomyris: "King of the Medes," she told him, "I advise you to abandon this enterprise, for you cannot know if in the end it will do you any good. Rule your own people, and try to bear the sight of me ruling mine. But of course you will refuse my advice, as the last thing you wish for is to live in peace." Tomyris, confident of her army's strength and not wishing to delay the inevitable battle, offered to withdraw the troops on her side of the river, allowing Cyrus to cross its waters safely and fight her army on the eastern side, if that was his desire.

Cyrus agreed, but instead of engaging the enemy directly he decided to play a trick. The Massagetai knew few luxuries. Once Cyrus had crossed the river and made his camp on the eastern side, he set the table for an elaborate banquet, full of meat, delicacies, and strong wine. Then he left his weakest troops in the camp and withdrew the rest of the army to the river. A large Massagetai detachment soon attacked the camp and killed all of the Persian soldiers in a fierce battle. Then, overwhelmed by the fabulous feast that had been left behind, they ate and drank to their hearts' content. Later, inevitably, they fell asleep. The Persian army returned to the camp that night, killing many of the sleeping soldiers and capturing the rest. Among the prisoners was their general, a youth named Spargapises, son of Queen Tomyris.

When the queen learned what had happened, she sent a message to Cyrus, chiding him for using tricks to defeat her army. "Now listen to me," she wrote, "and I will advise you for your own good: Give me back my son and leave my country with your forces intact, and be content with your triumph over a third part of the Massagetai. If you refuse, I swear by the sun our master to give you more blood than you can drink, for all your gluttony." Cyrus scoffed at her: He would not release her son. He would crush these barbarians.

The queen's son, seeing he would not be released, could not stand the humiliation, and so he killed himself. The news of her son's death overwhelmed Tomyris. She gathered all the forces that she could muster in her kingdom, and whipping them into a vengeful frenzy, engaged Cyrus's troops in a violent and bloody battle. Finally, the Massagetai prevailed. In their anger they decimated the Persian army, killing Cyrus himself.

After the battle, Tomyris and her soldiers searched the battlefield for Cyrus's corpse. When she found it she cut off his head and shoved it into a wineskin full of human blood, crying out, "Though I have conquered you and live, yet you have ruined me by treacherously taking my son. See now—I fulfill my threat: You have your fill of blood." After Cyrus's death, the Persian Empire quickly unraveled. One act of arrogance undid all of Cyrus's good work.

Interpretation

There is nothing more intoxicating than victory, and nothing more dangerous.

Cyrus had built his great empire on the ruins of a previous one. A hundred years earlier, the powerful Assyrian Empire had been totally destroyed, its once splendid capital of Nineveh but ruins in the sand. The Assyrians had suffered this fate because they had pushed too far, destroying one city-state after another until they lost sight of the purposes of their victories, and also of the costs. They overextended themselves and made many enemies who were finally able to band together and destroy them.

Cyrus ignored the lesson of Assyria. He paid no heed to the warnings of oracles and advisers. He did not worry about offending a queen. His many victories had gone to his head, clouding his reason. Instead of consolidating his already vast empire, he pushed forward. Instead of recognizing each situation as different, he thought each new war would bring the same result as the one before as long as he used the methods he knew: ruthless force and cunning.

Understand: In the realm of power, you must be guided by reason. To let a momentary thrill or an emotional victory influence or guide your moves will prove fatal. When you attain success, step back. Be cautious. When you gain victory, understand the part played by the particular circumstances of a situation, and never simply repeat the same actions again and again. History is littered with the ruins of victorious empires and the corpses of leaders who could not learn to stop and consolidate their gains.

OBSERVANCE OF THE LAW

No single person in history has occupied a more delicate and precarious position than the king's mistress. She had no real or legitimate power base to fall back on in times of trouble; she was surrounded by packs of envious courtiers eagerly anticipating her fall from grace; and finally, since the source of her power was usually her physical beauty, for most royal mistresses that fall was inevitable and unpleasant.

King Louis XV of France began to keep official mistresses in the early days of his reign, each woman's good fortune rarely lasting more than a few years. But then came Madame de Pompadour, who, when she was a middle-class child of nine named Jeanne Poisson, had been told by a fortune-teller that she would someday be the king's favorite. This seemed an absurd dream, since the royal mistress almost always came from the aristocracy. Jeanne nevertheless believed herself destined to seduce the king, and doing so became her obsession. She applied herself to the talents the king's favorite had to have—music, dancing, acting, horseback riding—and she excelled in every one of them. As a young woman, she married a man of the lower nobility, which gave her an entrée to the best salons in Paris. Word quickly spread of her beauty, talent, charm, and intelligence.

Jeanne Poisson became close friends with Voltaire, Montesquieu, and other great minds of the time, but she never lost sight of the goal she had set herself as a girl: to capture the heart of the king. Her husband had a château in a forest where the king would often go hunting, and she began to spend a lot of time there. Studying his movements like a hawk, she would make sure he would "happen" to come upon her while she was out walking in her most alluring dress, or riding in her splendid coach. The king began to take note of her, making her gifts of the game he caught in the hunt.

In 1744 Louis's current mistress, the Duchesse de Châteauroux, died. Jeanne went on the offensive. She placed herself everywhere he would be: at masked balls at Versailles, at the opera, wherever their paths would cross, and wherever she could display her many talents: dancing, singing, riding, coquetry. The king finally succumbed to her charms, and in a ceremony at Versailles in September of 1745, this twenty-four-year-old daughter of a middle-class banking agent was officially inaugurated as the king's mistress. She was given her own room in the palace, a room the king could enter at any time via a hidden stairway and back door. And because some of the courtiers were angry that he had chosen a woman of low origins, he made her a marquise. From now on she would be known as Madame de Pompadour.

The king was a man whom the slightest feeling of boredom would oppress out of proportion. Madame de Pompadour knew that keeping him under her spell meant keeping him amused. To that end she put on constant theatrical productions at Versailles, in which she starred. She organized elaborate hunting parties, masked balls, and whatever else it would take to keep him diverted outside the bedroom. She became a patroness of the arts, and the arbiter of taste and fashion for all of France. Her enemies at the court only grew in number with each new success, but Madame de Pompadour thwarted them in a totally novel way for a king's mistress: with extreme politeness. Snobs who resented her for her low birth she won over with charm and grace. Most unusual of all, she befriended the queen, and insisted that Louis XV pay more attention to his wife, and treat her more kindly. Even the royal family begrudgingly gave her their support. To

nature of men is ambitious as well as suspicious, and puts no limits to one's good fortune, it is not impossible that the suspicion that may suddenly be aroused in the mind of the prince by the victory of the general may have been aggravated by some haughty expressions or insolent acts on his part; so that the prince will naturally be made to think of securing himself against the ambition of his general.
And to do this, the means that suggest themselves to him are either to have the general killed, or to deprive him of that reputation which he has acquired with the prince's army and the people, by using every means to prove that the general's victory was not due to his skill and courage, but to chance and the cowardice of the enemy, or to the sagacity of the other captains who were with him in that action.

NICCOLÒ MACHIAVELLI, 1469–1527

crown her glory, the king made her a duchess. Her sway was felt even in politics: Indeed she became the untitled minister of foreign affairs.

In 1751, when Madame de Pompadour was at the height of her power, she experienced her worst crisis. Physically weakened by the responsibilities of her position, she found it increasingly difficult to meet the king's demands in bed. This was usually the point at which the mistress would meet her end, struggling to maintain her position as her beauty faded. But Madame de Pompadour had a strategy: She encouraged the king to set up a kind of brothel, Parc aux Cerfs, on the grounds of Versailles. There the middle-aged king could have liaisons with the most beautiful young girls in the realm.

Madame de Pompadour knew that her charm and her political acumen had made her indispensable to the king. What did she have to fear from a sixteen-year-old who had none of her power and presence? What did it matter if she lost her position in the bedroom, as long as she remained the most powerful woman in France? To secure that position she became still closer friends with the queen, with whom she started attending church. Although her enemies at the court conspired to have her toppled from her official position as king's mistress, the king kept her on, for he needed her calming effect. It was only when her part in the disastrous Seven Years' War drew much criticism on her that she slowly withdrew from public affairs.

Madame de Pompadour's health had always been delicate, and she died at the age of forty-three, in 1764. Her reign as mistress had lasted an unprecedented twenty years. "She was regretted by all," wrote the Duc de Croy, "for she was kindly and helpful to everyone who approached her."

Interpretation

Aware of the temporariness of her power, the king's mistress would often go into a kind of frenzy after capturing the king: She would try to accumulate as much money as possible to protect her after her inevitable fall. And to extend her reign as long as possible, she would be ruthless with her enemies in the court. Her situation, in other words, seemed to demand from her a greed and vindictiveness that would often be her undoing. Madame de Pompadour succeeded where all others had failed because she never pressed her good fortune. Instead of bullying the courtiers from her powerful position as the king's mistress, she tried to win their support. She never revealed the slightest hint of greed or arrogance. When she could no longer perform her physical duties as mistress, she did not fret at the thought of someone replacing her in bed. She simply applied some strategy—she encouraged the king to take young lovers, knowing that the younger and prettier they were, the less of a threat they posed, since they could not compare to her in charm and sophistication and would soon bore the monarch.

Success plays strange tricks on the mind. It makes you feel invulnerable, while also making you more hostile and emotional when people challenge your power. It makes you less able to adapt to circumstance. You come to believe your character is more responsible for your success than your strategizing and planning. Like Madame de Pompadour, you need to realize that your moment of triumph is also a moment when you have to rely on cunning and strategy all the more, consolidating your power base, recognizing the role of luck and circumstance in your success, and remaining vigilant against changes in your good fortune. It is the moment of victory when you need to play the courtier's game and pay more attention than ever to the laws of power.

> *The greatest danger occurs at the moment of victory.*
> Napoleon Bonaparte, 1769–1821

KEYS TO POWER

Power has its own rhythms and patterns. Those who succeed at the game are the ones who control the patterns and vary them at will, keeping people off balance while they set the tempo. The essence of strategy is controlling what comes next, and the elation of victory can upset your ability to control what comes next in two ways. First, you owe your success to a pattern that you are apt to try to repeat. You will try to keep moving in the same direction without stopping to see whether this is still the direction that is best for you. Second, success tends to go to your head and make you emotional. Feeling invulnerable, you make aggressive moves that ultimately undo the victory you have gained.

The lesson is simple: The powerful vary their rhythms and patterns, change course, adapt to circumstance, and learn to improvise. Rather than letting their dancing feet impel them forward, they step back and look where they are going. It is as if their bloodstream bore a kind of antidote to the intoxication of victory, letting them control their emotions and come to a kind of mental halt when they have attained success. They steady themselves, give themselves the space to reflect on what has happened, examine the role of circumstance and luck in their success. As they say in riding school, you have to be able to control yourself before you can control the horse.

Luck and circumstance always play a role in power. This is inevitable, and actually makes the game more interesting. But despite what you may think, good luck is more dangerous than bad luck. Bad luck teaches valuable lessons about patience, timing, and the need to be prepared for the worst; good luck deludes you into the opposite lesson, making you think your brillliance will carry you through. Your fortune will inevitably turn, and when it does you will be completely unprepared.

According to Machiavelli, this is what undid Cesare Borgia. He had many triumphs, was actually a clever strategist, but had the bad luck to have good luck: He had a pope for a father. Then, when he had bad luck for real—his father's death—he was unprepared for it, and the many enemies he had made devoured him. The good luck that elevates you or seals your success brings the moment for you to open your eyes: The wheel of fortune will hurtle you down as easily as up. If you prepare for the fall, it is less likely to ruin you when it happens.

People who have a run of success can catch a kind of fever, and even when they themselves try to stay calm, the people below them often pressure them to go past their mark and into dangerous waters. You have to have a strategy for dealing with these people. Simply preaching moderation will make you look weak and small-minded; seeming to fail to follow up on a victory can lessen your power.

When the Athenian general and statesman Pericles led a series of naval campaigns around the Black Sea in 436 B.C., his easy triumphs enflamed the Athenians' desire for more. They dreamed of conquering Egypt, overrunning Persia, sailing for Sicily. On the one hand Pericles reined in these dangerous emotions by warning of the perils of hubris. On the other hand he fed them by fighting small battles that he knew he could win, creating the appearance that he was preserving the momentum of success. The skill with which Pericles played this game is revealed by what happened when he died: The demagogues took over, pushed Athens into invading Sicily, and in one rash move destroyed an empire.

The rhythm of power often requires an alternation of force and cunning. Too much force creates a counterreaction; too much cunning, no matter how cunning it is, becomes predictable. Working on behalf of his master, the shogun Oda Nobunaga, the great sixteenth-century Japanese general (and future emperor) Hideyoshi once engineered a stunning victory over the army of the formidable General Yoshimoto. The shogun wanted to go further, to take on and crush yet another powerful enemy, but Hideyoshi reminded him of the old Japanese saying: "When you have won a victory, tighten the strings of your helmet." For Hideyoshi this was the moment for the shogun to switch from force to cunning and indirection, setting his enemies against one another through a series of deceptive alliances. In this way he would avoid stirring up needless opposition by appearing overly aggressive. When you are victorious, then, lie low, and lull the enemy into inaction. These changes of rhythm are immensely powerful.

People who go past the mark are often motivated by a desire to please a master by proving their dedication. But an excess of effort exposes you to the risk of making the master suspicious of you. On several occasions, generals under Philip of Macedon were disgraced and demoted immediately after leading their troops to a great victory; one more such victory, Philip thought, and the man might become a rival instead of an underling. When you serve a master, it is often wise to measure your victories carefully, letting him get the glory and never making him uneasy. It is also wise to establish a pattern of strict obedience to earn his trust. In the fourth century B.C., a captain under the notoriously severe Chinese general Wu Ch'i charged ahead before a battle had begun and came back with several enemy heads. He thought he had shown his fiery enthusiasm, but Wu Ch'i was unimpressed. "A talented officer," the general said with a sigh as he ordered the man beheaded, "but a disobedient one."

Another moment when a small success can spoil the chances for a larger one may come if a master or superior grants you a favor: It is a dangerous mistake to ask for more. You will seem insecure—perhaps you feel you did not deserve this favor, and have to grab as much as you can when you have the chance, which may not come again. The proper response is to accept the favor graciously and withdraw. Any subsequent favors you should earn without having to ask for them.

Finally, the moment when you stop has great dramatic import. What comes last sticks in the mind as a kind of exclamation point. There is no better time to stop and walk away than after a victory. Keep going and you risk lessening the effect, even ending up defeated. As lawyers say of cross-examination, "Always stop with a victory."

Image: Icarus Falling from the Sky. His father Daedalus fashions wings of wax that allow the two men to fly out of the labyrinth and escape the Minotaur. Elated by the triumphant escape and the feeling of flight, Icarus soars higher and higher, until the sun melts the wings and he hurtles to his death.

Authority: Princes and republics should content themselves with victory, for when they aim at more, they generally lose. The use of insulting language toward an enemy arises from the insolence of victory, or from the false hope of victory, which latter misleads men as often in their actions as in their words; for when this false hope takes possession of the mind, it makes men go beyond the mark, and causes them to sacrifice a certain good for an uncertain better. (Niccolò Machiavelli, 1469–1527)

REVERSAL

As Machiavelli says, either destroy a man or leave him alone entirely. Inflicting half punishment or mild injury will only create an enemy whose bitterness will grow with time, and who will take revenge. When you beat an enemy, then, make your victory complete. Crush him into nonexistence. In the moment of victory, you do not restrain yourself from crushing the enemy you have defeated, but rather from needlessly advancing against others. Be merciless with your enemy, but do not create new enemies by overreaching.

There are some who become more cautious than ever after a victory, which they see as just giving them more possessions to worry about and protect. Your caution after victory should never make you hesitate, or lose momentum, but rather act as a safeguard against rash action. On the other hand, momentum as a phenomenon is greatly overrated. You create your own successes, and if they follow one upon the other, it is your own doing. Belief in momentum will only make you emotional, less prone to act strategically, and more apt to repeat the same methods. Leave momentum for those who have nothing better to rely upon.

48

ASSUME FORMLESSNESS

JUDGMENT

By taking a shape, by having a visible plan, you open yourself to attack. Instead of taking a form for your enemy to grasp, keep yourself adaptable and on the move. Accept the fact that nothing is certain and no law is fixed. The best way to protect yourself is to be as fluid and formless as water; never bet on stability or lasting order. Everything changes.

TRANSGRESSION OF THE LAW

By the eighth century B.C., the city-states of Greece had grown so large and prosperous that they had run out of land to support their expanding populations. So they turned to the sea, establishing colonies in Asia Minor, Sicily, the Italian peninsula, even Africa. The city-state of Sparta, however, was landlocked and surrounded by mountains. Lacking access to the Mediterranean, the Spartans never became a seafaring people; instead they turned on the cities around them, and, in a series of brutal, violent conflicts lasting more than a hundred years, managed to conquer an immense area that would provide enough land for their citizens. This solution to their problem, however, brought a new, more formidable one: How could they maintain and police their conquered territories? The subordinate peoples they ruled now outnumbered them ten to one. Surely this horde would take a horrible revenge on them.

Sparta's solution was to create a society dedicated to the art of war. Spartans would be tougher, stronger, and fiercer than their neighbors. This was the only way they could ensure their stability and survival.

When a Spartan boy reached the age of seven, he was taken from his mother and placed in a military club where he was trained to fight and underwent the strictest discipline. The boys slept on beds of reeds; they were allotted only one outer garment to wear for an entire year. They studied none of the arts; indeed, the Spartans banned music, and permitted only slaves to practice the crafts that were necessary to sustain them. The only skills the Spartans taught were those of warfare. Children seen as weaklings were left to die in a cavern in the mountains. No system of money or trading was allowed in Sparta; acquired wealth, they believed, would sow selfishness and dissension, weakening their warrior discipline. The only way a Spartan could earn a living was through agriculture, mostly on state-owned lands, which slaves, called helots, would work for him.

The Spartans' single-mindedness allowed them to forge the most powerful infantry in the world. They marched in perfect order and fought with incomparable bravery. Their tight-knit phalanxes could vanquish an army ten times their size, as they proved in defeating the Persians at Thermopylae. A Spartan column on the march would strike terror in the enemy; it seemed to have no weaknesses. Yet although the Spartans proved themselves mighty warriors, they had no interest in creating an empire. They only wanted to keep what they had already conquered and to defend it against invaders. Decades would pass without a single change in the system that had succeeded so well in preserving Sparta's status quo.

At the same time that the Spartans were evolving their warlike culture, another city-state was rising to equal prominence: Athens. Unlike Sparta, Athens had taken to the sea, not so much to create colonies as for purposes of trade. The Athenians became great merchants; their currency, the famous "owl coins," spread throughout the Mediterranean. Unlike the rigid Spartans, the Athenians responded to every problem with consummate creativity, adapting to the occasion and creating new social forms and new

---

In martial arts, it is important that strategy be unfathomable, that form be concealed, and that movements be unexpected, so that preparedness against them be impossible. What enables a good general to win without fail is always having unfathomable wisdom and a modus operandi that leaves no tracks. Only the formless cannot be affected. Sages hide in unfathomability, so their feelings cannot be observed; they operate in formlessness, so their lines cannot be crossed.

THE BOOK OF THE
HUAINAN MASTERS,
CHINA,
SECOND CENTURY B.C.

THE DOG WITH THE
CROPPED EARS

"What crime have I committed that I should be thus mutilated by my own master?" pensively exclaimed Jowler, a young mastiff. "Here's a pretty condition for a dog of my pretentions! How can I show my face among my friends? Oh! king of beasts, or rather their tyrant, who would dare to treat you thus?" His complaints were not unfounded, for that very morning, his master, despite the piercing shrieks of our young friend, had

arts at an incredible pace. Their society was in constant flux. And as their power grew, they came to pose a threat to the defense-minded Spartans.

In 431 B.C., the war that had been brewing between Athens and Sparta for so long finally erupted. It lasted twenty-seven years, but after many twists of fortune, the Spartan war machine finally emerged victorious. The Spartans now commanded an empire, and this time they could not stay in their shell. If they gave up what they had gained, the beaten Athenians would regroup and rise against them, and the long war would have been fought for naught.

After the war, Athenian money poured into Sparta. The Spartans had been trained in warfare, not politics or economics; because they were so unaccustomed to it, wealth and its accompanying ways of life seduced and overwhelmed them. Spartan governors were sent to rule what had been Athenian lands; far from home, they succumbed to the worst forms of corruption. Sparta had defeated Athens, but the fluid Athenian way of life was slowly breaking down its discipline and loosening its rigid order. And Athens, meanwhile, was adapting to losing its empire, managing to thrive as a cultural and economic center.

Confused by a change in its status quo, Sparta grew weaker and weaker. Some thirty years after defeating Athens, it lost an important battle with the city-state of Thebes. Almost overnight, this once mighty nation collapsed, never to recover.

Interpretation

In the evolution of species, protective armor has almost always spelled disaster. Although there are a few exceptions, the shell most often becomes a dead end for the animal encased in it; it slows the creature down, making it hard for it to forage for food and making it a target for fast-moving predators. Animals that take to the sea or sky, and that move swiftly and unpredictably, are infinitely more powerful and secure.

In facing a serious problem—controlling superior numbers—Sparta reacted like an animal that develops a shell to protect itself from the environment. But like a turtle, the Spartans sacrificed mobility for safety. They managed to preserve stability for three hundred years, but at what cost? They had no culture beyond warfare, no arts to relieve the tension, a constant anxiety about the status quo. While their neighbors took to the sea, learning to adapt to a world of constant motion, the Spartans entombed themselves in their own system. Victory would mean new lands to govern, which they did not want; defeat would mean the end of their military machine, which they did not want, either. Only stasis allowed them to survive. But nothing in the world can remain stable forever, and the shell or system you evolve for your protection will someday prove your undoing.

In the case of Sparta, it was not the armies of Athens that defeated it, but the Athenian money. Money flows everywhere it has the opportunity to go; it cannot be controlled, or made to fit a prescribed pattern. It is inherently chaotic. And in the long run, money made Athens the conqueror,

barbarously cut off his long pendent ears. Jowler expected nothing less than to give up the ghost. As he advanced in years, he perceived that he gained more than he had lost by his mutilation; for, being naturally inclined to fight with others, he would often have returned home with this part disfigured in a hundred places. A quarrelsome dog always has his ears lacerated. The less we leave others to lay hold of the better. When one has but one point to defend, it should be protected for fear of accident. Take for example Master Jowler, who, being armed with a spiked collar, and having about as much ear as a bird, a wolf would be puzzled to know where to tackle him.

FABLES,
JEAN DE LA FONTAINE,
1621–1695

One seductive and ulti-
mately always fatal
path has been the
development of protec-
tive armor. An organ-
ism can protect itself by
concealment, by swift-
ness in flight, by effec-
tive counterattack, by
uniting for attack and
defense with other indi-
viduals of its species
and also by encasing
itself within bony plates
and spines. . . . Almost
always the experiment
of armor failed. Crea-
tures adopting it tended
to become unwieldy.
They had to move rela-
tively slowly. Hence
they were forced to live
mainly on vegetable
food; and thus in
general they were at a
disadvantage as
compared with foes
living on more rapidly
"profitable" animal
food: The repeated fail-
ure of protective armor
shows that, even at a
somewhat low evolu-
tionary level, mind
triumphed over mere
matter. It is this sort of
triumph which has
been supremely exem-
plified in Man.
SCIENTIFIC THEORY
AND RELIGION,
E. W. BARNES,
1933

by infiltrating the Spartan system and corroding its protective armor. In the
battle between the two systems, Athens was fluid and creative enough to
take new forms, while Sparta could grow only more rigid until it cracked.

This is the way the world works, whether for animals, cultures, or individuals. In the face of the world's harshness and danger, organisms of any
kind develop protection—a coat of armor, a rigid system, a comforting ritual. For the short term it may work, but for the long term it spells disaster.
People weighed down by a system and inflexible ways of doing things cannot move fast, cannot sense or adapt to change. They lumber around more
and more slowly until they go the way of the brontosaurus. Learn to move
fast and adapt or you will be eaten.

The best way to avoid this fate is to assume formlessness. No predator
alive can attack what it cannot see.

OBSERVANCE OF THE LAW

When World War II ended and the Japanese, who had invaded China
in 1937, had finally been thrown out, the Chinese Nationalists, lead by
Chiang Kai-shek, decided the time had come to annihilate the Chinese
Communists, their hated rivals, once and for all. They had almost succeeded in 1935, forcing the Communists into the Long March, the grueling
retreat that had greatly diminished their numbers. Although the Communists had recovered somewhat during the war against Japan, it would not
be difficult to defeat them now. They controlled only isolated areas in the
countryside, had unsophisticated weaponry, lacked any military experience or training beyond mountain fighting, and controlled no important
parts of China, except areas of Manchuria, which they had managed to take
after the Japanese retreat. Chiang decided to commit his best forces in
Manchuria. He would take over its major cities and from those bases would
spread through this northern industrial region, sweeping the Communists
away. Once Manchuria had fallen the Communists would collapse.

In 1945 and '46 the plan worked perfectly: The Nationalists easily
took the major Manchurian cities. Puzzlingly, though, in the face of this
critical campaign, the Communist strategy made no sense. When the Nationalists began their push, the Communists dispersed to Manchuria's most
out-of-the-way corners. Their small units harassed the Nationalist armies,
ambushing them here, retreating unexpectedly there, but these dispersed
units never linked up, making them hard to attack. They would seize a
town only to give it up a few weeks later. Forming neither rear guards nor
vanguards, they moved like mercury, never staying in one place, elusive
and formless.

The Nationalists ascribed this to two things: cowardice in the face
of superior forces and inexperience in strategy. Mao Tse-tung, the Communist leader, was more a poet and philosopher than a general, whereas
Chiang had studied warfare in the West and was a follower of the German
military writer Carl von Clausewitz, among others.

Yet a pattern did eventually emerge in Mao's attacks. After the Nationalists had taken the cities, leaving the Communists to occupy what was generally considered Manchuria's useless space, the Communists started using that large space to surround the cities. If Chiang sent an army from one city to reinforce another, the Communists would encircle the rescuing army. Chiang's forces were slowly broken into smaller and smaller units, isolated from one another, their lines of supply and communication cut. The Nationalists still had superior firepower, but if they could not move, what good was it?

A kind of terror overcame the Nationalist soldiers. Commanders comfortably remote from the front lines might laugh at Mao, but the soldiers had fought the Communists in the mountains, and had come to fear their elusiveness. Now these soldiers sat in their cities and watched as their fast-moving enemies, as fluid as water, poured in on them from all sides. There seemed to be millions of them. The Communists also encircled the soldiers' spirits, bombarding them with propaganda to lower their morale and pressure them to desert.

The Nationalists began to surrender in their minds. Their encircled and isolated cities started collapsing even before being directly attacked; one after another fell in quick succession. In November of 1948, the Nationalists surrendered Manchuria to the Communists—a humiliating blow to the technically superior Nationalist army, and one that proved decisive in the war. By the following year the Communists controlled all of China.

Interpretation

The two board games that best approximate the strategies of war are chess and the Asian game of go. In chess the board is small. In comparison to go, the attack comes relatively quickly, forcing a decisive battle. It rarely pays to withdraw, or to sacrifice your pieces, which must be concentrated at key areas. Go is much less formal. It is played on a large grid, with 361 intersections—nearly six times as many positions as in chess. Black and white stones (one color for each side) are placed on the board's intersections, one at a time, wherever you like. Once all your stones (52 for each side) are on the board, the object is to isolate the stones of your opponent by encircling them.

A game of go—called *wei-chi* in China—can last up to three hundred moves. The strategy is more subtle and fluid than chess, developing slowly; the more complex the pattern your stones initially create on the board, the harder it is for your opponent to understand your strategy. Fighting to control a particular area is not worth the trouble: You have to think in larger terms, to be prepared to sacrifice an area in order eventually to dominate the board. What you are after is not an entrenched position but mobility. With mobility you can isolate the opponent in small areas and then encircle them. The aim is not to kill off the opponent's pieces directly, as in chess, but to induce a kind of paralysis and collapse. Chess is linear, position oriented, and aggressive; go is nonlinear and fluid. Aggression is indi-

THE HARE AND
THE TREE

The sage neither seeks to follow the ways of the ancients nor establishes any fixed standard for all times but examines the things of his age and then prepares to deal with them.
There was in Sung a man, who tilled a field in which there stood the trunk of a tree. Once a hare, while running fast, rushed against the trunk, broke its neck, and died. Thereupon the man cast his plough aside and watched that tree, hoping that he would get another hare. Yet he never caught another hare and was himself ridiculed by the people of Sung. Now supposing somebody wanted to govern the people of the present age with the policies of the early kings, he would be doing exactly the same thing as that man who watched the tree.
HAN-FEI-TZU,
CHINESE PHILOSOPHER,
THIRD CENTURY B.C.

rect until the end of the game, when the winner can surround the opponent's stones at an accelerated pace.

Chinese military strategists have been influenced by go for centuries. Its proverbs have been applied to war time and again; Mao Tse-tung was an addict of *wei-chi,* and its precepts were ingrained in his strategies. A key *wei-chi* concept, for example, is to use the size of the board to your advantage, spreading out in every direction so that your opponent cannot fathom your movements in a simple linear way.

"Every Chinese," Mao once wrote, "should consciously throw himself into this war of a jigsaw pattern" against the Nationalists. Place your men in a jigsaw pattern in go, and your opponent loses himself trying to figure out what you are up to. Either he wastes time pursuing you or, like Chiang Kai-shek, he assumes you are incompetent and fails to protect himself. And if he concentrates on single areas, as Western strategy advises, he becomes a sitting duck for encirclement. In the *wei-chi* way of war, you encircle the enemy's brain, using mind games, propaganda, and irritation tactics to confuse and dishearten. This was the strategy of the Communists—an apparent formlessness that disoriented and terrified their enemy.

Where chess is linear and direct, the ancient game of go is closer to the kind of strategy that will prove relevant in a world where battles are fought indirectly, in vast, loosely connected areas. Its strategies are abstract and multidimensional, inhabiting a plane beyond time and space: the strategist's mind. In this fluid form of warfare, you value movement over position. Your speed and mobility make it impossible to predict your moves; unable to understand you, your enemy can form no strategy to defeat you. Instead of fixing on particular spots, this indirect form of warfare spreads out, just as you can use the large and disconnected nature of the real world to your advantage. Be like a vapor. Do not give your opponents anything solid to attack; watch as they exhaust themselves pursuing you, trying to cope with your elusiveness. Only formlessness allows you to truly surprise your enemies—by the time they figure out where you are and what you are up to, it is too late.

When you want to fight us, we don't let you and you can't find us. But when we want to fight you, we make sure that you can't get away and we hit you squarely . . . and wipe you out. . . . The enemy advances, we retreat; the enemy camps, we harass; the enemy tires, we attack; the enemy retreats, we pursue.

Mao Tse-tung, 1893–1976

KEYS TO POWER

The human animal is distinguished by its constant creation of forms. Rarely expressing its emotions directly, it gives them form through language, or through socially acceptable rituals. We cannot communicate our emotions without a form.

The forms that we create, however, change constantly—in fashion, in style, in all those human phenomena representing the mood of the moment. We are constantly altering the forms we have inherited from previous generations, and these changes are signs of life and vitality. Indeed, the things that *don't* change, the forms that rigidify, come to look to us like death, and we destroy them. The young show this most clearly: Uncomfortable with the forms that society imposes upon them, having no set identity, they play with their own characters, trying on a variety of masks and poses to express themselves. This is the vitality that drives the motor of form, creating constant changes in style.

The powerful are often people who in their youth have shown immense creativity in expressing something new through a new form. Society grants them power because it hungers for and rewards this sort of newness. The problem comes later, when they often grow conservative and possessive. They no longer dream of creating new forms; their identities are set, their habits congeal, and their rigidity makes them easy targets. Everyone knows their next move. Instead of demanding respect they elicit boredom: Get off the stage! we say, let someone else, someone younger, entertain us. When locked in the past, the powerful look comical—they are overripe fruit, waiting to fall from the tree.

Power can only thrive if it is flexible in its forms. To be formless is not to be amorphous; everything has a form—it is impossible to avoid. The formlessness of power is more like that of water, or mercury, taking the form of whatever is around it. Changing constantly, it is never predictable. The powerful are constantly creating form, and their power comes from the rapidity with which they can change. Their formlessness is in the eye of the enemy who cannot see what they are up to and so has nothing solid to attack. This is the premier pose of power: ungraspable, as elusive and swift as the god Mercury, who could take any form he pleased and used this ability to wreak havoc on Mount Olympus.

Human creations evolve toward abstraction, toward being more mental and less material. This evolution is clear in art, which, in this century, made the great discovery of abstraction and conceptualism; it can also be seen in politics, which over time have become less overtly violent, more complicated, indirect and cerebral. Warfare and strategy too have followed this pattern. Strategy began in the manipulation of armies on land, positioning them in ordered formations; on land, strategy is relatively two dimensional, and controlled by topography. But all the great powers have eventually taken to the sea, for commerce and colonization. And to protect their trading lanes they have had to learn how to fight at sea. Maritime warfare requires tremendous creativity and abstract thinking, since the lines are constantly shifting. Naval captains distinguish themselves by their ability to adapt to the literal fluidity of the terrain and to confuse the enemy with an abstract, hard-to-anticipate form. They are operating in a third dimension: the mind.

Back on land, guerrilla warfare too demonstrates this evolution toward abstraction. T. E. Lawrence was perhaps the first modern strategist to de-

CHARACTER ARMOR

To carry out the instinctual inhibition demanded by the modern world and to be able to cope with the energy stasis which results from this inhibition, the ego has to undergo a change. The ego, i.e., that part of the person that is exposed to danger, becomes rigid, as we say, when it is continually subjected to the same or similar conflicts between need and a fear-inducing outer world. It acquires in this process a chronic, automatically functioning mode of reaction, i.e., its "character." It is as if the affective personality armored itself, as if the hard shell it develops were intended to deflect and weaken the blows of the outer world as well as the clamoring of the inner needs. This armoring makes the person less sensitive to unpleasure, but also restricts his libidinal and aggressive motility and thus reduces his capacity for achievement and pleasure. We say the ego has become less flexible and more rigid, and that the ability to regulate the energy economy depends on the extent of the armoring.
WILHELM REICH, 1897–1957

velop the theory behind this kind of warfare, and to put it into practice. His ideas influenced Mao, who found in his writings an uncanny Western equivalent to *wei-chi*. Lawrence was working with Arabs fighting for their territory against the Turks. His idea was to make the Arabs blend into the vast desert, never providing a target, never collecting together in one place. As the Turks scrambled to fight this vaporous army, they spread themselves thin, wasting energy in moving from place to place. They had the superior firepower but the Arabs kept the initiative by playing cat and mouse, giving the Turks nothing to hold on to, destroying their morale. "Most wars were wars of contact. . . . Ours should be a war of detachment," Lawrence wrote. "We were to contain the enemy by the silent threat of a vast unknown desert, not disclosing ourselves till we attacked."

This is the ultimate form of strategy. The war of engagement has become far too dangerous and costly; indirection and elusiveness yield far better results at a much lower cost. The main cost, in fact, is mental—the thinking it takes to align your forces in scattered patterns, and to undermine the minds and psychology of your opponents. And nothing will infuriate and disorient them more than formlessness. In a world where wars of detachment are the order of the day, formlessness is crucial.

The first psychological requirement of formlessness is to train yourself to take nothing personally. Never show any defensiveness. When you act defensive, you show your emotions, revealing a clear form. Your opponents will realize they have hit a nerve, an Achilles' heel. And they will hit it again and again. So train yourself to take nothing personally. Never let anyone get your back up. Be like a slippery ball that cannot be held: Let no one know what gets to you, or where your weaknesses lie. Make your face a formless mask and you will infuriate and disorient your scheming colleagues and opponents.

One man who used this technique was Baron James Rothschild. A German Jew in Paris, in a culture decidedly unfriendly to foreigners, Rothschild never took any attack on him personally or showed he had been hurt in any way. He furthermore adapted himself to the political climate, whatever it was—the stiffly formal Restoration monarchy of Louis XVIII, the bourgeois reign of Louis-Philippe, the democratic revolution of 1848, the upstart Louis-Napoleon crowned emperor in 1852. Rothschild accepted them one and all, and blended in. He could afford to appear hypocritical or opportunistic because he was valued for his money, not his politics; his money was the currency of power. While he adapted and thrived, outwardly never showing a form, all the other great families that had begun the century immensely wealthy were ruined in the period's complicated shifts and turns of fortune. Attaching themselves to the past, they revealed their embrace of a form.

Throughout history, the formless style of ruling has been most adeptly practiced by the queen who reigns alone. A queen is in a radically different position from a king; because she is a woman, her subjects and courtiers are likely to doubt her ability to rule, her strength of character. If she favors one side in some ideological struggle, she is said to be acting out of emotional attachment. Yet if she represses her emotions and plays the authoritarian, in the male fashion, she arouses worse criticism still. Either by nature or by experience, then, queens tend to adopt a flexible style of governing that in the end often proves more powerful than the more direct, male form.

Two female leaders exemplifying the formless style of rule are Queen Elizabeth of England and Empress Catherine the Great of Russia. In the violent wars between Catholics and Protestants, Elizabeth steered a middle course. She avoided alliances that would commit her to one side, and that over time would harm the country. She managed to keep her country at peace until it was strong enough for war. Her reign was one of the most glorious in history because of her incredible capacity to adapt and her flexible ideology.

Catherine the Great too evolved an improvisatory style of governing. After she deposed her husband, Emperor Peter II, taking sole control of Russia in 1762, no one thought she would survive. But she had no preconceived ideas, no philosophy or theory to dictate her policies. Although a foreigner (she came from Germany), she understood Russia's moods, and how it was changing over the years. "One must govern in such a way that one's people think they themselves want to do what one commands them to do," she said, and to do this she had to be always a step ahead of their desires and to adapt to their resistance. By never forcing the issue, she reformed Russia in a strikingly short period of time.

This feminine, formless style of ruling may have emerged as a way of prospering under difficult circumstances, but it has proved immensely seductive to those who have served under it. Being fluid, it is relatively easy for its subjects to obey, for they feel less coerced, less bent to their ruler's ideology. It also opens up options where an adherence to a doctrine closes them off. Without committing to one side, it allows the ruler to play one enemy off another. Rigid rulers may seem strong, but with time their inflexibility wears on the nerves, and their subjects find ways to push them from the stage. Flexible, formless rulers will be much criticized, but they will endure, and people will eventually come to identify with them, since they are as their subjects are—changing with the wind, open to circumstance.

Despite upsets and delays, the permeable style of power generally triumphs in the end, just as Athens eventually won victory over Sparta through its money and its culture. When you find yourself in conflict with someone stronger and more rigid, allow them a momentary victory. Seem to bow to their superiority. Then, by being formless and adaptable, slowly insinuate yourself into their soul. This way you will catch them off guard, for rigid people are always ready to ward off direct blows but are helpless against the subtle and insinuating. To succeed at such a strategy you must play the chameleon—conform on the surface, while breaking down your enemy from the inside.

For centuries the Japanese would accept foreigners graciously, and appeared susceptible to foreign cultures and influences. João Rodriguez, a Portuguese priest who arrived in Japan in 1577 and lived there for many years, wrote, "I am flabbergasted by the Japanese willingness to try and accept everything Portuguese." He saw Japanese in the streets wearing Portuguese clothing, with rosary beads at their necks and crosses at their hips. This might seem like a weak, mutable culture, but Japan's adaptability actually protected the country from having an alien culture imposed by military invasion. It seduced the Portuguese and other Westerners into believing the Japanese were yielding to a superior culture when actually the foreign culture's ways were merely a fashion to be donned and doffed. Under the surface, Japanese culture thrived. Had the Japanese been rigid about foreign influences and tried to fight them off, they might have suffered the injuries that the West inflicted on China. That is the power of formlessness—it gives the aggressor nothing to react against, nothing to hit.

In evolution, largeness is often the first step toward extinction. What is immense and bloated has no mobility, but must constantly feed itself. The unintelligent are often seduced into believing that size connotes power, the bigger the better.

In 483 B.C., King Xerxes of Persia invaded Greece, believing he could conquer the country in one easy campaign. After all, he had the largest army ever assembled for one invasion—the historian Herodotus estimated it at over more than five million. The Persians planned to build a bridge across the Hellespont to overrun Greece from the land, while their equally immense navy would pin the Greek ships in harbor, preventing their forces from escaping to sea. The plan seemed sure, yet as Xerxes prepared the invasion, his adviser Artabanus warned his master of grave misgivings: "The two mightiest powers in the world are against you," he said. Xerxes laughed—what powers could match his gigantic army? "I will tell you what they are," answered Artabanus. "The land and the sea." There were no safe harbors large enough to receive Xerxes' fleet. And the more land the Persians conquered, and the longer their supply lines stretched, the more ruinous the cost of feeding this immense army would prove.

Thinking his adviser a coward, Xerxes proceeded with the invasion. Yet as Artabanus predicted, bad weather at sea decimated the Persian fleet, which was too large to take shelter in any harbor. On land, meanwhile, the Persian army destroyed everything in its path, which only made it impossible to feed, since the destruction included crops and stores of food. It was also an easy and slow-moving target. The Greeks practiced all kinds of deceptive maneuvers to disorient the Persians. Xerxes' eventual defeat at the hands of the Greek allies was an immense disaster. The story is emblematic of all those who sacrifice mobility for size: The flexible and fleet of foot will almost always win, for they have more strategic options. The more gigantic the enemy, the easier it is to induce collapse.

The need for formlessness becomes greater the older we get, as we grow more likely to become set in our ways and assume too rigid a form.

We become predictable, always the first sign of decrepitude. And predictability makes us appear comical. Although ridicule and disdain might seem mild forms of attack, they are actually potent weapons, and will eventually erode a foundation of power. An enemy who does not respect you will grow bold, and boldness makes even the smallest animal dangerous.

The late-eighteenth-century court of France, as exemplified by Marie-Antoinette, had become so hopelessly tied to a rigid formality that the average Frenchman thought it a silly relic. This depreciation of a centuries-old institution was the first sign of a terminal disease, for it represented a symbolic loosening of the people's ties to monarchy. As the situation worsened, Marie-Antoinette and King Louis XVI grew only more rigid in their adherence to the past—and quickened their path to the guillotine. King Charles I of England reacted similarly to the tide of democratic change brewing in England in the 1630s: He disbanded Parliament, and his court rituals grew increasingly formal and distant. He wanted to return to an older style of ruling, with adherence to all kinds of petty protocol. His rigidity only heightened the desire for change. Soon, of course, he was swept up in a devastating civil war, and eventually he lost his head to the executioner's axe.

As you get older, you must rely even less on the past. Be vigilant lest the form your character has taken makes you seem a relic. It is not a matter of mimicking the fashions of youth—that is equally worthy of laughter. Rather your mind must constantly adapt to each circumstance, even the inevitable change that the time has come to move over and let those of younger age prepare for their ascendancy. Rigidity will only make you look uncannily like a cadaver.

Never forget, though, that formlessness is a strategic pose. It gives you room to create tactical surprises; as your enemies struggle to guess your next move, they reveal their own strategy, putting them at a decided disadvantage. It keeps the initiative on your side, putting your enemies in the position of never acting, constantly reacting. It foils their spying and intelligence. Remember: Formlessness is a tool. Never confuse it with a go-with-the-flow style, or with a religious resignation to the twists of fortune. You use formlessness, not because it creates inner harmony and peace, but because it will increase your power.

Finally, learning to adapt to each new circumstance means seeing events through your own eyes, and often ignoring the advice that people constantly peddle your way. It means that ultimately you must throw out the laws that others preach, and the books they write to tell you what to do, and the sage advice of the elder. "The laws that govern circumstances are abolished by new circumstances," Napoleon wrote, which means that it is up to you to gauge each new situation. Rely too much on other people's ideas and you end up taking a form not of your own making. Too much respect for other people's wisdom will make you depreciate your own. Be brutal with the past, especially your own, and have no respect for the philosophies that are foisted on you from outside.

Image: Mercury. The winged messenger,
god of commerce, patron saint of thieves,
gamblers, and all those who deceive through
swiftness. The day Mercury was born he invented
the lyre; by that evening he had stolen the cattle of
Apollo. He would scour the world, assuming
whatever form he desired. Like the liquid metal
named after him, he embodies the elusive,
the ungraspable—the power of formlessness.

Authority: Therefore the consummation of forming an army is to arrive at formlessness. Victory in war is not repetitious, but adapts its form endlessly. . . . A military force has no constant formation, water has no constant shape: The ability to gain victory by changing and adapting according to the opponent is called genius. (Sun-tzu, fourth century B.C.)

REVERSAL

Using space to disperse and create an abstract pattern should not mean forsaking the concentration of your power when it is valuable to you. Formlessness makes your enemies hunt all over for you, scattering their own forces, mental as well as physical. When you finally engage them, though, hit them with a powerful, concentrated blow. That is how Mao succeeded against the Nationalists: He broke their forces into small, isolated units, which he then could easily overwhelm with a strong attack. The law of concentration prevailed.

When you play with formlessness, keep on top of the process, and keep your long-term strategy in mind. When you assume a form and go on the attack, use concentration, speed, and power. As Mao said, "*When* we fight you, we make sure you can't get away."

SELECTED BIBLIOGRAPHY

Aesop. *Fables of Aesop.* Translated by S. A. Hanford. New York: Penguin Books, 1954.

Bloodworth, Dennis and Ching Ping. *The Chinese Machiavelli.* New York: Farrar, Straus and Giroux, 1976.

Bowyer, J. Barton. *Cheating: Deception in War and Magic, Games and Sports, Sex and Religion, Business and Con Games, Politics and Espionage, Art and Science.* New York: St. Martin's Press, 1982.

Castiglione, Baldesar. *The Book of the Courtier.* Translated by George Bull. New York: Penguin Books, 1976.

Clausewitz, Carl von. *On War.* Edited and translated by Michael Howard and Peter Paret. Princeton: Princeton University Press, 1976.

Elias, Norbert. *The Court Society.* Translated by Edmund Jephcott. Oxford: Basil Blackwell Publishers, 1983.

de Francesco, Grete. *The Power of the Charlatan.* Translated by Miriam Beard. New Haven: Yale University Press, 1939.

Haley, Jay. *The Power Tactics of Jesus Christ and Other Essays.* New York: W. W. Norton, 1989.

Han-fei-tzu. *The Complete Works of Han-fei-tzu.* Translated by W. K. Liao. 2 volumes. London: Arthur Probsthain, 1959.

Herodotus. *The Histories.* Translated by Aubrey de Sélincourt. New York: Penguin Books, 1987.

Isaacson, Walter. *Kissinger: A Biography.* New York: Simon & Schuster, 1992.

La Fontaine, Jean de. *Selected Fables.* Translated by James Michie. New York: Penguin Books, 1982.

Lenclos, Ninon de. *Life, Letters and Epicurean Philosophy of Ninon de Lenclos, The Celebrated Beauty of the 17th Century.* Chicago: Lion Publishing Co., 1903.

Ludwig, Emil. *Bismarck: The Story of a Fighter.* Translated by Eden and Cedar Paul. Boston: Little, Brown, 1928.

Machiavelli, Niccolò. *The Prince and The Discourses.* Translated by Luigi Ricci and Christian E. Detmold. New York: Modern Library, 1940.

Mao Tse-tung. *Selected Military Writings of Mao Tse-tung.* Beijing: Foreign Languages Press, 1963.

Millan, Betty. *Monstrous Regiment: Women Rulers in Men's Worlds.* Windsor Forest, Berks, U.K.: Kensal Press, 1983.

Montaigne, Michel de. *The Complete Essays*. Translated by M. A. Screech. New York: Penguin Books, 1987.

Mrazek, Col. James. *The Art of Winning Wars*. New York: Walker and Company, 1968.

Nash, Jay Robert. *Hustlers and Con Men*. New York: M. Evans and Co., 1976.

Nietzsche, Friedrich. *The Birth of Tragedy and The Genealogy of Morals*. Translated by Francis Golffing. Garden City: Doubleday Anchor Books, 1956.

Orieux, Jean. *Talleyrand: The Art of Survival*. Translated by Patricia Wolf. New York: Knopf, 1974.

Plutarch. *Makers of Rome*. Translated by Ian Scott-Kilvert. New York: Penguin Books, 1965.

———. *The Rise and Fall of Athens*. Translated by Ian Scott-Kilvert. New York: Penguin Books, 1960.

Rebhorn, Wayne A. *Foxes and Lions: Machiavelli's Confidence Men*. Ithaca: Cornell University Press, 1988.

de Retz, Cardinal. *Memoirs of Jean François Paul de Gondi, Cardinal de Retz*. 2 vols. London: J. M. Dent & Sons, 1917.

Sadler, A. L. *Cha-no-yu: The Japanese Tea Ceremony*. Rutland, Vermont: Charles E. Tuttle Company, 1962.

Scharfstein, Ben-Ami. *Amoral Politics*. Albany: State University of New York Press, 1995.

Scheibe, Karl E. *Mirrors, Masks, Lies and Secrets*. New York: Praeger Publishers, 1979.

Schopenhauer, Arthur. *The Wisdom of Life and Counsels and Maxims*. Translated by T. Bailey Saunders. Amherst, New York: Prometheus Books, 1995.

Senger, Harro von. *The Book of Stratagems: Tactics for Triumph and Survival*. Edited and translated by Myron B. Gubitz. New York: Penguin Books, 1991.

Siu, R. G. H. *The Craft of Power*. New York: John Wiley & Sons, 1979.

Sun-tzu. *The Art of War*. Translated by Thomas Cleary. Boston: Shambhala, 1988.

Thucydides. *The History of the Peloponnesian War*. Translated by Rex Warner. New York: Penguin Books, 1972.

Weil, "Yellow Kid." *The Con Game and "Yellow Kid" Weil: The Autobiography of the Famous Con Artist as told to W. T. Brannon*. New York: Dover Publications, 1974.

Zagorin, Perez. *Ways of Lying: Dissimulation, Persecution and Conformity in Early Modern Europe*. Cambridge: Harvard University Press, 1990.

INDEX

becoming focal point of their need to believe, 215–26

behaving like, while thinking as you like, 317–24

commitment to, 145–55

discovering thumbscrews of, 271–81

insulting, 142, 143, 159, 189

keeping them dependent on you, 82–88

keeping them in suspended terror, 123–29

making them come to you, 62–68

playing to their fantasies, 263–70

types of, 137–44

unhappy and unlucky, avoidance of, 76–81

using work of, 56–61

working on hearts and minds of, 367–75

overacting, 198

overstepping your bounds, 186

Ovid , *319, 402–4*

"Owl Who Was God, The" (Thurber), *217–19*

Pacific Ocean, discovery of, 238, 239

Panama, 237

Panchatantra, tale from, *207–8*

parables, *see* fables and folktales

Parc aux Cerfs, 348, 414

parents, stepping into shoes of, 347–57

Paris, liberation of, 315

past:
reinterpretation of, 397
support for values of, 397–98
using knowledge from, 59–60

patience, *xxi,* 291, 295, 298

patrons, 86, 175, 251, 342
Aretino and, 338–40
gifts to, 288–89

patterns, 28, 126, 128, 129, 415, 416

Pausanias, 318–19, 323

pawns, 367, 373

paying full price, 333, 334, 344, 346

paying your own way, 333, 346

pearls before swine, laying of, 321, 323

"Peasant and the Apple Tree, The" (Aesop), *96*

Pedrarias (Pedro Arias Dávila), 238, 239

Peloponnesian War, 97, 164, 241

Peloponnesian War, The (Thucydides), 98

Pentagon Papers, 306

people, *see* other people

perfection, appearance of, 400–409

Pergamus, 70

Pericles, *349–50, 354,* 359–60, 416

Perseus, 377, 390

Pershing, John J., 301, 302

Persia, 148, 318–19, 351, 359, 381, 382, 411–12, 420, 428

personality, 195

perspective:
anger and, 329–30
isolation and, 136

persuasion, 73
working on the hearts and minds of others, 367–75

Peru, 335, *359–60*

Perugino, Pietro, *350–51*

Peter II, Emperor, 427

Petit Trianon, 368

Petrucci, Pandolfo, *11*

pettiness, 338

Philip, King of Macedonia, 350–52, 416

Philip II, King of Spain, 353

Philippines, 354

philosopher's stone, 219, 220

Phoenicia, 331

Picasso, Pablo, 48–49, 127–28, 149, 355

pickpockets, 66

Pisa, 342

Pistoia, 153

Pizarro, Francisco, 59, 238, 335–36, *359–60,* 365

Pizarro, Gonzalo, 336

placating others, 188

plain, unassuming, and often unintelligent man, dealing with, 138–39

Plan all the way to the end (Law 29), 236–44

Planck, Max, 398

planning, 212, 419
to the end, 236–44
flexibility in, 244
and learning when to stop, 410–18

Play a sucker to catch a sucker—seem dumber than your mark (Law 21), 156–62

Play on people's need to believe to create a cultlike following (Law 27), 215–26

Play the perfect courtier (Law 24), 178–90

Play to people's fantasies (Law 32), 263–70

pleasure, being a source of, 182

Plutarch, *13,* 60, *278–79, 292–94, 310–11, 349–50, 362, 371–72,* 405

Pocket Mirror for Heroes, A (Gracián), *348*

Poe, Edgar Allan, 131–33, *381*

Poggio, Stefano di, 96–97

Poggio family, 96, 97

Poland, 255

polio vaccine, 322

politeness, *180*

politics, abstraction in, 425

Pompadour, Madame de (Jeanne Poisson), 348, 413–14, 415

Pompey, 192, *278–79*

pond of fish, image of, 331

Pontormo, Jacopo da, 135, 252